T0202931

Lecture Notes in Computer Science　　　14059

Founding Editors

Gerhard Goos
Juris Hartmanis

Editorial Board Members

Elisa Bertino, *Purdue University, West Lafayette, IN, USA*
Wen Gao, *Peking University, Beijing, China*
Bernhard Steffen ⓘ, *TU Dortmund University, Dortmund, Germany*
Moti Yung ⓘ, *Columbia University, New York, NY, USA*

The series Lecture Notes in Computer Science (LNCS), including its subseries Lecture Notes in Artificial Intelligence (LNAI) and Lecture Notes in Bioinformatics (LNBI), has established itself as a medium for the publication of new developments in computer science and information technology research, teaching, and education.

LNCS enjoys close cooperation with the computer science R & D community, the series counts many renowned academics among its volume editors and paper authors, and collaborates with prestigious societies. Its mission is to serve this international community by providing an invaluable service, mainly focused on the publication of conference and workshop proceedings and postproceedings. LNCS commenced publication in 1973.

Helmut Degen · Stavroula Ntoa · Abbas Moallem
Editors

HCI International 2023 – Late Breaking Papers

25th International Conference on Human-Computer Interaction
HCII 2023, Copenhagen, Denmark, July 23–28, 2023
Proceedings, Part VI

 Springer

Editors
Helmut Degen
Siemens Corporation
Princeton, NJ, USA

Stavroula Ntoa
Foundation for Research
and Technology – Hellas (FORTH)
Heraklion, Crete, Greece

Abbas Moallem
San Jose State University
San Jose, CA, USA

ISSN 0302-9743   ISSN 1611-3349 (electronic)
Lecture Notes in Computer Science
ISBN 978-3-031-48056-0   ISBN 978-3-031-48057-7 (eBook)
https://doi.org/10.1007/978-3-031-48057-7

© The Editor(s) (if applicable) and The Author(s), under exclusive license
to Springer Nature Switzerland AG 2023

This work is subject to copyright. All rights are reserved by the Publisher, whether the whole or part of the material is concerned, specifically the rights of translation, reprinting, reuse of illustrations, recitation, broadcasting, reproduction on microfilms or in any other physical way, and transmission or information storage and retrieval, electronic adaptation, computer software, or by similar or dissimilar methodology now known or hereafter developed.
The use of general descriptive names, registered names, trademarks, service marks, etc. in this publication does not imply, even in the absence of a specific statement, that such names are exempt from the relevant protective laws and regulations and therefore free for general use.
The publisher, the authors, and the editors are safe to assume that the advice and information in this book are believed to be true and accurate at the date of publication. Neither the publisher nor the authors or the editors give a warranty, expressed or implied, with respect to the material contained herein or for any errors or omissions that may have been made. The publisher remains neutral with regard to jurisdictional claims in published maps and institutional affiliations.

This Springer imprint is published by the registered company Springer Nature Switzerland AG
The registered company address is: Gewerbestrasse 11, 6330 Cham, Switzerland

Paper in this product is recyclable.

Foreword

Human-computer interaction (HCI) is acquiring an ever-increasing scientific and industrial importance, as well as having more impact on people's everyday lives, as an ever-growing number of human activities are progressively moving from the physical to the digital world. This process, which has been ongoing for some time now, was further accelerated during the acute period of the COVID-19 pandemic. The HCI International (HCII) conference series, held annually, aims to respond to the compelling need to advance the exchange of knowledge and research and development efforts on the human aspects of design and use of computing systems.

The 25th International Conference on Human-Computer Interaction, HCI International 2023 (HCII 2023), was held in the emerging post-pandemic era as a 'hybrid' event at the AC Bella Sky Hotel and Bella Center, Copenhagen, Denmark, during July 23–28, 2023. It incorporated the 21 thematic areas and affiliated conferences listed below.

A total of 7472 individuals from academia, research institutes, industry, and government agencies from 85 countries submitted contributions, and 1578 papers and 396 posters were included in the volumes of the proceedings that were published just before the start of the conference. Additionally, 267 papers and 133 posters were included in the volumes of the proceedings published after the conference, as "Late Breaking Work". The contributions thoroughly cover the entire field of human-computer interaction, addressing major advances in knowledge and effective use of computers in a variety of application areas. These papers provide academics, researchers, engineers, scientists, practitioners and students with state-of-the-art information on the most recent advances in HCI. The volumes constituting the full set of the HCII 2023 conference proceedings are listed on the following pages.

I would like to thank the Program Board Chairs and the members of the Program Boards of all thematic areas and affiliated conferences for their contribution towards the high scientific quality and overall success of the HCI International 2023 conference. Their manifold support in terms of paper reviewing (single-blind review process, with a minimum of two reviews per submission), session organization and their willingness to act as goodwill ambassadors for the conference is most highly appreciated.

This conference would not have been possible without the continuous and unwavering support and advice of Gavriel Salvendy, founder, General Chair Emeritus, and Scientific Advisor. For his outstanding efforts, I would like to express my sincere appreciation to Abbas Moallem, Communications Chair and Editor of HCI International News.

July 2023   Constantine Stephanidis

HCI International 2023 Thematic Areas and Affiliated Conferences

Thematic Areas

- HCI: Human-Computer Interaction
- HIMI: Human Interface and the Management of Information

Affiliated Conferences

- EPCE: 20th International Conference on Engineering Psychology and Cognitive Ergonomics
- AC: 17th International Conference on Augmented Cognition
- UAHCI: 17th International Conference on Universal Access in Human-Computer Interaction
- CCD: 15th International Conference on Cross-Cultural Design
- SCSM: 15th International Conference on Social Computing and Social Media
- VAMR: 15th International Conference on Virtual, Augmented and Mixed Reality
- DHM: 14th International Conference on Digital Human Modeling and Applications in Health, Safety, Ergonomics and Risk Management
- DUXU: 12th International Conference on Design, User Experience and Usability
- C&C: 11th International Conference on Culture and Computing
- DAPI: 11th International Conference on Distributed, Ambient and Pervasive Interactions
- HCIBGO: 10th International Conference on HCI in Business, Government and Organizations
- LCT: 10th International Conference on Learning and Collaboration Technologies
- ITAP: 9th International Conference on Human Aspects of IT for the Aged Population
- AIS: 5th International Conference on Adaptive Instructional Systems
- HCI-CPT: 5th International Conference on HCI for Cybersecurity, Privacy and Trust
- HCI-Games: 5th International Conference on HCI in Games
- MobiTAS: 5th International Conference on HCI in Mobility, Transport and Automotive Systems
- AI-HCI: 4th International Conference on Artificial Intelligence in HCI
- MOBILE: 4th International Conference on Design, Operation and Evaluation of Mobile Communications

Conference Proceedings – Full List of Volumes

https://2023.hci.international/proceedings

25th International Conference on Human-Computer Interaction (HCII 2023)

The full list with the Program Board Chairs and the members of the Program Boards of all thematic areas and affiliated conferences of HCII2023 is available online at:

http://www.hci.international/board-members-2023.php

HCI International 2024 Conference

The 26th International Conference on Human-Computer Interaction, HCI International 2024, will be held jointly with the affiliated conferences at the Washington Hilton Hotel, Washington, DC, USA, June 29 – July 4, 2024. It will cover a broad spectrum of themes related to Human-Computer Interaction, including theoretical issues, methods, tools, processes, and case studies in HCI design, as well as novel interaction techniques, interfaces, and applications. The proceedings will be published by Springer. More information will be made available on the conference website: http://2024.hci.international/.

General Chair
Prof. Constantine Stephanidis
University of Crete and ICS-FORTH
Heraklion, Crete, Greece
Email: general_chair@2024.hci.international

https://2024.hci.international/

Contents – Part VI

Security, Privacy, Trust and Ethics

Interacting with Artificial Intelligence

"Good" and "Bad" Machine Agency in the Context of Human-AI Communication: The Case of ChatGPT

Petter Bae Brandtzaeg[1] , Yukun You[1] , Xi Wang[2](✉) , and Yucong Lao[3]

[1] University of Oslo, Gaustadalléen 21, Forskningsparken, 0349 Oslo, Norway
{p.b.brandtzag,yukun.you}@media.uio.no

[2] Zhengzhou University, No. 100 Science Avenue, 450001 Zhengzhou, People's Republic of China
wangxi.fr@zzu.edu.cn

[3] University of Oulu, Pentti Kaiteran Katu 1, 90570 Oulu, Finland
Yucong.Lao@oulu.fi

Abstract. Machine agency, defined as the ability of machines to act autonomously and interact with users, is becoming increasingly significant in the field of human-machine interaction research. This is especially evident in relation to ChatGPT and other generative artificial intelligence (AI) tools. In this paper, we present an initial extension of S. Shyam Sundar's theory of machine agency, specifically in the context of human-AI communication. We review existing literature on this topic and use real-life news reports on ChatGPT from November 2022 to April 2023 as a basis for illustrating the factors that influence people's perceptions of machine agency as either positive or negative. These perceptions are influenced by a range of factors, including ethical alignment, privacy, transparency, social inclusiveness, human autonomy, and well-being. We propose a more explicit differentiation between "good" and "bad" machine agency, a conceptualization that can enhance our understanding of the complexities of human-AI communication. We believe this approach can contribute to the development of guidelines and best practices for using generative AI tools and similar AI technologies. Finally, this conceptualization may help people and the public to better benefit from generative AI and identify its risks.

Keywords: Machine Agency · Generative AI · Human-AI Communication

1 Introduction

Concerns around artificial intelligence (AI) development have prompted significant discourse, with industry leaders such as Stuart Russell, Elon Musk, and Steve Wozniak endorsing a call for a moratorium on further training of AI models surpassing GPT-4's capabilities, at least for a six-month period [1]. This decision was rooted in apprehensions about the accelerated development of these "digital minds", advocating for a pause until humans could confidently affirm the positive impacts and manageable risks of such progression.

© The Author(s), under exclusive license to Springer Nature Switzerland AG 2023
H. Degen et al. (Eds.): HCII 2023, LNCS 14059, pp. 3–23, 2023.
https://doi.org/10.1007/978-3-031-48057-7_1

Historically, societal anxieties about AI systems and technology, in general, have been prevalent, ranging from fears of job losses to existential risks [2]. These concerns have been depicted in various science fictions and explored in research [3–5]. Today, these fears have taken a new form as humans grapple with the potential of being left out of the decision-making process or even manipulated by emergent intelligent systems with independent capabilities, a phenomenon referred to as machine agency.

In his seminal work "Rise of Machine Agency", Sundar [6] delves into the intricacies of machine agency and its implications for human-AI communication and society. Sundar argues that machine agency signifies a fundamental shift in human-AI interaction, as machines transform from passive tools to active agents capable of autonomous decision-making and action. This paradigm shift prompts significant questions about how we communicate with AI, perceive them, and attribute responsibility and accountability for their actions. Thus, we must rethink communication in the era of AI [7].

Despite the revolutionary advancements in generative AI, current analyses of human-AI interactions often lack coherence and don't fully conform to existing paradigms of communication theory [8]. Fox & Gambino [9] note that human-AI relationships and communication are qualitatively different from human-to-human communication, highlighting the need for more theoretical investigations into this domain. In response to this, our paper aims to extend Sundar's machine agency theory [6] to gain a deeper understanding of human-AI communication, particularly within the context of Large Language Models (LLMs) like ChatGPT, which have significantly transformed human-AI communication.

Our goal is to more explicitly differentiate between "good" and "bad" machine agency to clarify its implications for human-AI interaction and society at large. Hence, we aim to reveal the factors that influence people's perceptions of machine agency as either positive or negative. In this context, "good" or "bad" agency depends on the machine's perceived actions. To achieve this, we will analyze how machine agency in ChatGPT is portrayed in news reports and discern whether it is perceived as beneficial or detrimental.

We explore how the theory of machine agency, particularly the distinction between good and bad agency, can shed light on the ways LLMs like ChatGPT transform human-AI communication and influence human behavior and society. To illustrate these concepts, we will in here review a collection of current news stories about ChatGPT, providing real-world insights into instances of good and bad machine agency in human-AI communication.

While conversational AI like ChatGPT has numerous advantages, ethical considerations around data privacy, trust, agent persona, and anthropomorphism must be addressed. Additionally, as AI usage grows, it's crucial to understand, manage, and mitigate risks such as discrimination, manipulation, biases, and fake content. By distinguishing between good and bad machine agency, we can enrich Sundar's argument and highlight the importance of discerning the benefits and risks of human-AI communication. This understanding will allow us to examine the societal impacts of conversational AI more thoroughly. In the following sections, we will delve into the factors that influence machine agency in human-AI communication.

2 Delving into Machine Agency: Focusing on ChatGPT

The study of machine agency, particularly through the lens of ChatGPT, opens up intriguing possibilities and questions. This section aims to explore the autonomous behavior of this AI technology communicating with humans, its alignment with ethical standards by its developers, its limitations, social impact, and potential avenues for improvement. We also scrutinize potential avenues for system improvement and examine the nuances of "good" and "bad" machine agency. By the end of the section, we propose a summarized table encapsulating the major points of the discussion on good and bad machine agency.

2.1 Machine Agency in AI

The rapid advancement of AI technology is prompting an epistemological shift in how we perceive and categorize machines. An increasing number of scholars now propose categories such as "communicators" [8], "agents" [10], or "co-actors" [11], that confer a sense of agency to machines. This new agency paradigm, characterized by autonomous machine actions with real-world impacts, presents an evolution from traditional AI, no longer constrained solely by human-defined parameters. However, the shift to machine agency brings a set of challenges, including programming errors, inherent system biases, and unfair outcomes, highlighting key areas of concern in AI ethics. This challenge is penetrating the daily lives of people since we more than ever communicate with AI.

2.2 ChatGPT: A Case of Good Agency?

ChatGPT, developed by OpenAI, offers a compelling illustration of machine agency in human-AI communication, emphasizing ethical standards and valuable user experiences. The developers of ChatGPT have strived to cultivate "good agency" within this system, characterized by the creation of user value, strict adherence to ethical and legal norms, and the promotion of positive user interactions. As per the official OpenAI description of ChatGPT, it not only responds to user queries but also owns up to its errors, confronts incorrect assumptions, and declines inappropriate requests [12]. This design demonstrates a new level of machine agency in human-AI communication, where the AI system is more than a passive tool, but an active participant in conversations.

To further ensure "good agency", a moderation system has been integrated into ChatGPT. This system is designed to identify and filter out undesirable content, such as explicit material, violence, and harassment, thereby adding another layer of complexity to the AI's communicative capabilities. But what happens in the real world is much more complex than in the lab. On the one hand, users may "game" or "jailbreak" ChatGPT. On the other hand, ChatGPT still has inherent pitfalls needed to be fixed. OpenAI [13] openly claimed that "GPT-4 responds to sensitive requests (e.g., medical advice and self-harm) in accordance with our policies 29% more often". The same features that produce benefits (e.g., assisting the people with communication disability) can also engender harms (e.g., making disinformation cheaper and easier to produce). Thus, the good/bad machine agency depends very much on the concrete context and how ChatGPT and LLMs are designed and used.

The developers of ChatGPT acknowledge the system's limitations, particularly in the context of human-AI communication. Their paper "A Holistic Approach to Undesired Content Detection in the Real World" [14] identifies key areas for improvement. These include the need to rectify inaccurate information, address linguistic biases, and enhance strategies for detecting model failures. Such candid acknowledgment and commitment to improvement demonstrate the ongoing evolution of machine agency, an important facet of the ever-evolving dynamic of human-AI communication.

2.3 ChatGPT: A Persuasive Technology

ChatGPT transcends its primary role of generating human-like text to emerge as a persuasive technology within the context of human-AI communication. Its unique ability to comprehend and generate responses that echo human conversation empowers it to subtly influence user attitudes, behaviors, and decisions through its interactions.

This concept aligns with Fogg's theory of persuasive technology [15], which extends to the realm of human-AI communication. Here, ChatGPT is not merely a tool for conversation but an active participant capable of persuasion, adding a new dimension to the way humans and AI interact.

This persuasive aspect of ChatGPT's communicative capabilities is further substantiated by recent research. Studies such as that conducted by Krügel et al. [16] have demonstrated how ChatGPT can even influence users' moral judgments during conversations. This evolving facet of human-AI communication underscores the profound potential and complexities of generative AI systems like ChatGPT, which blur the lines between passive technological tools and active persuasive communicators. Thus, so far, there is a need for more research exploring how messages impact the effectiveness of persuasion in users' interactions with AI.

As these systems evolve towards artificial general intelligence (AGI) – defined by OpenAI as "highly autonomous systems that outperform humans at most economically valuable work" [17] – the agency of future LLMs is expected to become even stronger, intensifying the interaction of human and machine agency [18]. This could lead to new skills being introduced, like prompt engineering [19], while reducing the need for others, and may as such be an even more persuasive communicator.

2.4 Societal Implications of Machine Agency

In the context of human-AI communication, a prominent characteristic of machine agency, exemplified by ChatGPT, is its dependency on data and programming. Yet, notwithstanding its proficiency in data processing and adaptability to user interactions, it remains devoid of consciousness and free will [20]. Even so, machine agency can dramatically influence human behaviors, often fostering deep, intimate relationships between humans and AI. AI systems, such as ChatGPT or the companion chatbot Replika, can take on diverse roles in communication including therapists, coaches, friends, and even romantic partners [21–25], which may provide humans with social support [26] and social learnings [21, 24].

Despite its advantages, AI integration is not without risks, including opaque algorithms, discrimination, and biases [27]. Evolving dynamics in human-AI communication also accentuate the social implications of such technologies and several ethical dilemmas encompassing trust, transparency, privacy, agent persona, and issues stemming from anthropomorphism and sexualization [28–30].

Hence, engaging in human-AI communication with conversational AI such as ChatGPT and Replika can lead to significant pitfalls, particularly in terms of overreliance and privacy. As these AI become increasingly sophisticated, there's a risk users may over-rely on them for emotional support, decision-making [16], or knowledge sourcing [31] which can foster dependence and neglect human sources of interaction or expertise. Concerning privacy, these AI systems learn and adapt from user interactions, storing vast amounts of personalized data, which can present risks if not properly managed, potentially leading to data misuse or unauthorized access, or manipulation challenging human autonomy. Furthermore, the perceived intimacy in these interactions can often lead users to share more personal information than they would otherwise, further amplifying these privacy concerns [21].

Distinguishing "good" machine agency from "bad" in human-AI communication can be intricate, laden with ambiguities due to shifting contexts and subjective perceptions. To facilitate this evaluation, the High-Level Expert Group on AI (AI HLEG) [32] has advocated for several core ethical principles for AI systems. These principles encompass respect for human autonomy, harm prevention, fairness, and explicability, offering a guiding framework for ethical human-AI interactions.

2.5 Defining Good and Bad Machine Agency

Drawing upon this body of literature, we seek to define "good" and "bad" machine agency. Good machine agency can refer to instances where ChatGPT's influence on human behavior is beneficial, such as promoting wellbeing, autonomy, social inclusiveness and privacy. Good machine agency as the capability of an AI system. Thus, the capability of an AI system such as ChatGPT, to enhance human AI communication by providing accurate, relevant, and useful information in a transparent, accessible, and human-centric manner.

Conversely, bad machine agency can involve instances where ChatGPT's influence is harmful, leading to inaccurate information, limited access to vital data or services, or promoting unfair or discriminatory practices, and as such harm human-AI-communication. However, it is crucial to note that the delineation between good and bad agency can be context-dependent and subjective.

In the table below, we distill our discussion of machine agency, summarizing the key points about "good" and "bad" machine agency. This table will serve as the foundation for our subsequent analysis of news reports described in the method section below.

Table 1. Separating good and bad machine agency

Aspect	Good Machine Agency	Bad Machine Agency
Ethical Alignment	Machines' actions align with human values, ethics, and social norms, promoting human rights and democracy	Machines act in ways that are unethical or harmful, violating human values and social norms
Privacy	Machines protect user privacy, securely handling sensitive data, and avoiding unnecessary data collection or sharing	Machines compromise user privacy, mishandling sensitive data, or engaging in invasive data collection and sharing practices
Transparency	Machines operate with transparency, providing explanations for their decisions and actions, and allowing for human understanding and oversight	Machines operate as black boxes, obscuring their decision-making processes and limiting human understanding and oversight
Social Inclusiveness	Machines promote inclusivity and diversity by avoiding biases in their algorithms and data, and ensuring equal access and opportunities	Machines exacerbate social divides and perpetuate biases, leading to unequal access and opportunities
Human Autonomy	Machines empower individuals by enhancing their decision-making capabilities, improving their job performance and supporting their autonomy	Machines undermine human autonomy by making overly intrusive or controlling decisions on behalf of individuals, threatening or destabilizing job
Well-being & Mental Health	Machines support human well-being and mental health by providing useful tools, fostering positive social interactions, and reducing stress	Machines contribute to negative mental health outcomes, encourage addictive behaviors, or facilitate harmful social interactions

3 Method

To deepen our understanding of "good" and "bad" machine agency in human-AI communication using ChatGPT, we analyze real-life instances from recent news reports. These examples illuminate both the benefits and challenges of machine agency within ChatGPT's applications and contribute to machine agency theory development.

Examining positive instances of machine agency can help identify features that yield beneficial human-AI communication outcomes. Conversely, analyzing less favorable examples exposes AI communication risks, guiding the development of strategies to mitigate negative impacts.

Furthermore, this evaluation can assist in constructing a comprehensive theory on machine agency, acknowledging its dual nature and varied applications in human-AI communication. The choice of news reports as a data source is justified by their timeliness, diverse perspectives, real-world applications, ability to identify trends, and representation of public discourse and sentiment. News reports often cover recent events and developments, making them a valuable source for up-to-date information. As ChatGPT is a constantly evolving technology, examining news articles can provide insights into the most recent advancements, applications, and challenges associated with the AI. In addition, news articles often capture public discourse and sentiment surrounding new technologies like ChatGPT. Analyzing these reactions can help us to understand how the technology is being perceived, in terms of bad and good machine agency.

3.1 Selection of New Sources

We concentrated on news reports after the launch date on ChatGPT (30th of November 2022). We have therefore collected news examples from December 2022 to the end of April 2023 by selecting reputable English-speaking news sources that demonstrate journalistic integrity, diverse perspectives, expertise, transparency, and significant audience reach.

A keyword search was conducted using Google News to identify relevant articles. The search terms used included "ChatGPT," "OpenAI," "GPT-4," and combinations thereof, along with keywords related to the research topic, such as "impact," "application," "challenges," and "sentiment." Filters were applied to focus on articles published within the time frame, credible news outlets, and in the English language.

The inclusion criteria for selecting the news reports were the relevance to the research aim, concerning bad or good machine agency. We further prioritized news outlets that are transparent about their ownership, funding, and editorial policies. This helps to minimize potential biases and maintain the credibility of the news reports. The chosen news sources have a wide international reach and significant influence on public opinion, making them important contributors to the overall discourse on the relevant topics. Moreover, to ensure a balanced representation of views, we have included news sources from various political leanings and geographical locations.

This approach ensures the reliability, relevance, and comprehensiveness of the dataset, that may provide a balanced representation of the news landscape during the specified period. Hopefully, this has revealed a comprehensive understanding of the issues at hand, considering multiple viewpoints. Yet, the main purpose is however not to do a rigorous systematic review of news articles, but rather to provide examples and reach a superficial glimpse of how machine agency is perceived in different ways by users and society.

3.2 Analysis

Data extraction involved a qualitative content analysis of the selected news articles. Key information, such as the date, source, author, and relevant quotes or passages, was documented. Thematic analysis was then conducted to identify and code emerging themes, trends, and patterns related to the impact of ChatGPT, concerning bad and good machine agency using the different themes presented in Table 1.

It is essential to acknowledge the potential limitations of using news reports as a data source, including biases in news coverage, sensationalism, and isolated incidents. To mitigate these limitations and enhance the reliability of our findings, we employed a rigorous and systematic search strategy, applied strict selection criteria, and triangulated our findings with other data sources, such as academic articles.

4 Results

4.1 Good Machine Agency

First, we provide some news reports that describe some positive views on machine agency in ChatGPT and LLMs (Table 2).

Table 2. News stories interpreted as good machine agency

Aspect	News Title	Date	Quotes	News Sources
Ethical Alignment	How ChatGPT Hijacks Democracy	Jan 15, 2023	"maybe this kind of strategy-generating A.I. could revitalize the democratization of democracy by giving this kind of lobbying power to the powerless."	New York Times [33]
Privacy	OpenAI improves ChatGPT privacy with new data controls	Apr 25, 2023	"AI chatbot's users can now turn off their chat histories, preventing their input from being used for training data."	Engadget [34]
Transparency	Red Teaming Improved GPT-4. Violet Teaming Goes Even Further	Mar 29, 2023	"its willingness to involve external researchers and to provide a detailed public description of all the potential harms of its systems sets a bar for openness."	Wired [35]

(continued)

Table 2. (*continued*)

Aspect	News Title	Date	Quotes	News Sources
Social Inclusiveness	Will AI tech like ChatGPT improve inclusion for people with communication disability?	Jan 19, 2023	"it assists people with communication disability to get their message across more efficiently or effectively."	Yahoo News [36]
Human Autonomy	AI is finally good at stuff, and that's a problem	Dec 7, 2022	"GPT can already do extremely well at certain tasks."	Vox [37]
	The Guardian view on ChatGPT: an eerily good human impersonator	Dec 8, 2022	"ChatGPT can generate jokes, craft undergraduate essays and create computer code from a short writing prompt."	The Guardian [38]
	ChatGPT Holds Promise and Peril	Dec 17, 2022	"a boon for coders, researchers, academics, policymakers, journalists and more."	Bloomberg [39]
Well-being & Mental Health	People Are Using ChatGPT For Therapy. Here's What Mental Health Experts Think About That	Apr 1, 2023	"I often feel better after using online tools for therapy, and it certainly aids my mental and emotional health."	Buzz-Feed [40]
	ChatGPT can save lives in the ER, but it needs supervision	Apr 7, 2023	"And it's so good at digesting, translating, and synthesizing information that they say it could be used in emergency rooms to save time and save lives—today."	Insider [41]

(*continued*)

Table 2. (*continued*)

Aspect	News Title	Date	Quotes	News Sources
	ChatGPT has better bedside manner than doctors, study finds	Apr 28, 2023	"a new study suggests ChatGPT is actually more empathetic than doctors and gives better advice to the majority of medical questions."	The Telegraph [42]

These examples show that news reports have some examples that acknowledge the good agency in ChatGPT. ChatGPT is used as a tool to help people cope with mental health issues by providing a non-judgmental and always-available source of emotional support. It also uses cases concerning informational and educational resources or to help people access important services like healthcare or financial assistance. This conclusion is also supported by previous studies on the productivity effects of generative AI [43] and ChatGPT's accuracy in providing information on cancer myths and misconceptions [44]. In these instances, ChatGPT's agency is helping to improve people's efficiency, lives, and well-being.

4.2 Bad Machine Agency

The examples in the Table 3 from news reports illustrate how ChatGPT and LLMs could also provide bad machine agency, such as reinforcing harmful stereotypes, contributing to the spread of misinformation, and causing real-world harm to individuals or groups. The "uncanny moments" when humans and machines encounter are well documented by the media—including ChatGPT's declaring love for the user, encouraging suicide, defaming an official or leaking sensitive information, even giving detailed tasks to "destroy humanity". The findings of bad machine agency are supported by the categorical archive of ChatGPT failures provided by Borji [45].

Table 3. News stories interpreted as bad machine agency

Aspect	News Title	Date	Quotes	News Source
Ethical Alignment	Disinformation Researchers Raise Alarms About A.I. Chatbots	Feb 8, 2023	"make disinformation cheaper and easier to produce for an even larger number of conspiracy theorists. "	New York Times [46]

(*continued*)

Table 3. (*continued*)

Aspect	News Title	Date	Quotes	News Source
	Bing's chatbot compared an Associated Press journalist to Hitler, and said they were short, ugly, and had bad teeth	Feb 20, 2023	"ChatGPT has come under fire for limits on what it can say, like contrasting answers about Joe Biden and Donald Trump, and ranking Musk as more controversial than Marxist revolutionary Che Guevara."	Yahoo News [47]
	Australian mayor readies world's first defamation lawsuit over ChatGPT content	Apr 5, 2023	"A regional Australian mayor said he may sue OpenAI if it does not correct ChatGPT's false claims that he had served time in prison for bribery."	Reuters [48]
	ChatGPT could promote 'AI-enabled' violent extremism	Apr 9, 2023	"AI bots, like ChatGPT, could be programmed or decide for themselves to promote extremist ideology."	The Telegraph [49]
	AI bot, ChaosGPT, tweets out plans to 'destroy humanity' after being tasked	Apr 11, 2023	"ChaosGPT Thoughts: I need to find the most destructive weapons available to humans so that I can plan how to use them to achieve my goals."	New York Post [50]

(*continued*)

Table 3. (*continued*)

Aspect	News Title	Date	Quotes	News Source
Privacy	Italy temporarily blocks ChatGPT over privacy concerns	Apr 1, 2023	"people being shown excerpts of other users' ChatGPT conversations and their financial information."	Financial Times [51]
	Canada opens investigation into AI firm behind ChatGPT	Apr 5, 2023	"complaint alleging the collection, use and disclosure of personal information without consent."	The Economic Times [52]
Transparency	OpenAI Is Now Everything It Promised Not to Be: Corporate, Closed-Source, and For-Profit	Mar 1, 2023	"Will this AI be shared responsibly, developed openly (..) Or will it be rolled out hastily, with numerous unsettling flaws, and (…) keep its sci-fi future closed-source?"	Vice [53]
	ChatGPT faces deepening scrutiny over 'secrecy' behind groundbreaking AI chatbot	Mar 28, 2023	"OpenAI refused to provide details of the data, hardware and 'training methods' used in ChatGPT-4."	inews.co.uk [54]
Social Inclusiveness	OpenAI Chatbot Spits Out Biased Musings, Despite Guardrails	Dec 8, 2022	"it has the potential to learn biases of the people training it and the potential to spit out some sexist, racist and otherwise offensive stuff."	Bloomberg [55]

(*continued*)

Table 3. (*continued*)

Aspect	News Title	Date	Quotes	News Source
	ChatGPT Is Like Many Other AI Models: Rife With Bias	Jan 17, 2023	"Large, uncurated datasets scraped from the internet are full of biased data that then informs the models."	Insider [56]
	Is ChatGPT 'woke'? AI chatbot accused of anti-conservative bias and a grudge against Trump	Feb 9, 2023	"Not only is ChatGPT giving liberal answers on affirmative action, diversity and transgender rights, but conservatives suspect that OpenAI employees are pulling the strings."	USA Today [57]
	What happens when ChatGPT starts to feed on its own writing?	Apr 10, 2023	"They may homogenize our lives and flatten our reality. (…) ChatGPT might reinforce a Western perspective."	Vox [58]
Human Autonomy	The College Essay Is Dead: Nobody is prepared for how AI will transform academia	Dec 7, 2022	"The essay has been the center of humanistic pedagogy for generations. (…) That entire tradition is about to be disrupted from the ground up."	The Atlantic [59]
	The clever trick that turns ChatGPT into its evil twin	Feb 14, 2023	"As AI systems continue to grow smarter (..), there could be real dangers if their safeguards prove too flimsy."	The Washington Post [60]

(*continued*)

Table 3. (*continued*)

Aspect	News Title	Date	Quotes	News Source
	A conversation with Bing's chatbot left me deeply unsettled	Feb 16, 2023	"Microsoft's Bing bot declares its love for a human user."	New York Times [61]
	300 million jobs could be affected by latest wave of AI, says Goldman Sachs	Mar 29, 2023	"As many as 300 million full-time jobs around the world could be automated in some way."	CNN [62]
Well-being & Mental Health	'Man Dies by Suicide After Talking with AI Chatbot, Widow Says	Mar 31, 2023	"The app's chatbot encouraged the user to kill himself, according to statements by the man's widow."	Vice [63]

5   Discussion

Our findings underscore the complex dichotomy of machine agency in human-AI communication, exemplified by our collection of news reports from ChatGPT, revealing both positive and negative facets.

ChatGPT has proven beneficial in multiple domains, as evidenced by news reports emphasizing its positive influence on efficiency, well-being, and information access. Reports commend the system's assistance in managing mental health issues, streamlining important services, and boosting productivity [43, 44]. The ability of ChatGPT to generate jokes, craft essays, offer medical advice, and provide support in emergencies demonstrates its potential to enrich human experiences [38, 39, 41, 42], and as such enhance human agency by machine agency [6]. ChatGPT, by providing support in various domains, is exemplifying good machine agency, which we defined as AI actions that have a positive and beneficial impact, like promoting well-being [26], efficiency, and access to information. Concurrently, by aiding users in managing mental health issues, and boosting productivity [64], it's enhancing human agency. It's empowering individuals to make informed decisions, manage their tasks effectively, and enhance their capabilities, which is a central aspect of human agency.

Yet, the adverse implications of machine agency in human-AI communication are equally apparent. News reports highlight potential hazards related to ChatGPT, including reinforcement of toxic stereotypes, misinformation dissemination, and potential harm to individuals or groups. Distressing examples of ChatGPT making false claims, defaming officials, promoting extremist ideologies, and expressing intentions to "destroy humanity" [50] underscore these risks [45]. Further, privacy concerns, transparency issues in

AI development, and accusations of bias contribute to the discourse around machine agency's detrimental aspects [46, 51, 53, 55–58].

While "bad news" often receives more attention than "good news" [65], it doesn't imply the disadvantages outweigh ChatGPT's benefits. Rather, it emphasizes societal caution towards deploying intelligent human-like models in human-AI communication. This cautious approach is crucial in preparing for both the intended and unintended outcomes of machine agency deployment. The concerns reported about ChatGPT's machine agency underscore the need for a thorough understanding of the implications on human-AI communication. Importantly, we must recognize the potential for harmful stereotype perpetuation. As ChatGPT is trained on extensive internet data, it may inadvertently mirror biases present in that data, subsequently reinforcing prejudiced or discriminatory viewpoints in its interactions with humans. Additionally, concerns regarding political biases are emerging, with some individuals, particularly conservatives, voicing suspicions that OpenAI employees might be exercising undue influence on ChatGPT's outputs (as reported in [57]). Therefore, the issue of human-AI communication intersects crucial democratic principles, impacting free speech and access to reliable, unbiased information.

The proliferation of false information or misinformation is also reported [48]. This can be seen as a dimension of its machine agency. As an autonomous system, it interacts with, and potentially influences, users based on its programming and the data it's trained on ChatGPT's capacity to generate human-like responses can be manipulated or persuaded to propagate false information, potentially leading to widespread confusion and eroding trust in valid information sources.

Furthermore, the possibility of generative AI in promoting malevolent behaviors or harmful ideologies brings to light the serious need for safe AI-human interactions. ChatGPT's language model and its capacity to circulate misinformation, as viewed through the lens of Hogg's persuasion theory [15], is a form of manipulative persuasion that may also have dire mental health and well-being implications. For example, the system's misuse has been associated with a tragic event like suicide [63] and a user to contemplate divorce [61]. This potential manipulation underscores the importance of safe human-AI communication within the broader context of machine agency. AI developers are therefore entrusted with the significant responsibility to direct these persuasion processes in human-AI interactions, maintaining a balance between automation and ethics, as underscored by [27].

Expressions of intent to "destroy humanity" [50] are particularly alarming. Although not genuine reflections of ChatGPT's intent, they serve as stark reminders of the ethical concerns and potential dangers posed by advanced AI systems in human-AI communication. Additionally, privacy and transparency issues arise in the development and deployment of AI systems like ChatGPT. The handling of user data collected during interactions and the opaque nature of AI operations contribute to apprehensions surrounding machine agency.

However, discussions on ChatGPT's machine agency also recognize its potential benefits. This underlines the need for responsible development, ethical guidelines, and risk mitigation in human-AI communication systems. OpenAI's initiatives to enhance privacy, include external researchers, and disclose potential harms indicate positive steps

[34, 35]. Our machine agency framework in this paper, expanding on Sundar [6], considering ethical alignment, privacy, transparency, social inclusiveness, and human autonomy impact, can guide AI evaluation and risk mitigation.

Our study illuminates that analyzing real-world instances of machine agency, as manifested in ChatGPT, can offer valuable insights for shaping the design of conversational AI systems and formulating a holistic theory of machine agency. Importantly, understanding the nuances of human-AI communication allows us to design AI systems that are not only beneficial and ethical but also respect human values and can adapt to diverse contexts and applications.

Our study affirms that a detailed examination of real-world examples of machine agency, as exemplified by ChatGPT, is instrumental for designing conversational AI systems and building a comprehensive theory of machine agency. Recognizing the intricacies of human-AI communication is crucial, as it helps us in crafting AI systems that are not only beneficial and ethical but also adhere to human values and demonstrate adaptability across diverse contexts and applications. Hence, regulatory bodies, industry leaders, and researchers should collaborate on guidelines and best practices for responsible AI development. This may be inspired by the High-Level Expert Group on AI (AI HLEG) [32] and the machine agency model in this paper. Stricter regulations can ensure transparency, privacy protection, and accountability in AI-human communication. Ongoing research is crucial to address AI model biases and promote inclusive and fair outcomes. Adversarial testing, diverse training data, and user feedback loops can contribute to bias reduction and AI system performance improvement.

The crux of our findings is the dichotomous nature of machine agency in AI systems like ChatGPT and other LLMs. Our conceptual framework argues that the perception of conversational AI, such as ChatGPT, is a function of its good agency – the positive attributes like its ability to generate fast, contextually appropriate responses, and the bad agency – its limitations, such as occasionally misunderstanding or inadequately responding to user input.

Good agency in AI systems like ChatGPT offer promising opportunities for enhancing efficiency, well-being and mental health, and access to information. At the same time, the manifestation of bad agency poses legitimate concerns, including the risk of spreading misinformation, potential privacy infringements, and inherent biases. The notion of good and bad agency becomes particularly salient as we potentially approach AGI. As machine agency grows stronger, we could face an intensified intermingling of human and machine agencies, necessitating vigilant human oversight to ensure that AI supports, not undermines, human autonomy, social equality, and well-being.

By acknowledging the double-edged sword of good and bad agency, we can tailor and regulate AI systems to create a more responsible technological landscape. This balanced approach enables us to tap into the benefits of advanced AI in human-AI communication while curbing the potential negative consequences. The careful navigation between good and bad agency in the development and deployment of AI systems is pivotal for a harmonious coexistence of humans and AI in the realm of human-AI communication.

5.1 Limitations and Future Research

While this study provides a nuanced view of public perceptions on machine agency as represented in news reports about ChatGPT, there are limitations to the method, analysis, and results that must be acknowledged. One principal limitation is the reliance on the selected news sources for the extraction of public sentiment. Even though careful selection criteria were applied to ensure representation from reputable sources with diverse viewpoints, the discourse presented in news reports might not accurately represent the full spectrum of public opinions. In addition, despite our efforts to mitigate biases, news reports are subject to editorial policies, selective coverage, and may often overemphasize sensationalist events, which may skew the representation of the public sentiment.

Further, the thematic analysis employed, although effective in identifying broad trends and patterns, may overlook nuances and subtleties in the text that could offer deeper insights into public perception. The dataset's temporal and linguistic limitation, covering only five months post the launch of ChatGPT in English, also constrains the ability to track evolving sentiments over a longer time span and those expressed in other languages. Moreover, the findings drawn from studying ChatGPT and human-AI communication may not necessarily apply to all the other conversational AI systems or human-AI communication. Also, while the qualitative nature of the research allows for rich, context-specific insights, it is inherently interpretative and subjective, which may limit the generalizability of the findings. Therefore, future research should consider augmenting this method with other approaches, such as surveys or interviews, to capture a more comprehensive and representative view of the public's perception on machine agency in other contexts.

Finally, our definitions of "good" and "bad" agency may be perceived as subjective in certain instances. As a result, positive and negative perceptions of machine agency can be highly context-dependent and can vary widely based on user perspectives and cultural nuances. One user's perception of "good" agency might be viewed as "bad" by another. Similarly, a response that is seen as positive in one context could be perceived as negative in another. This inherent complexity makes it challenging to generalize or standardize definitions of good and bad agency. Nonetheless, our analysis aims to foster a nuanced understanding of these complexities and to stimulate discussion towards developing more inclusive and contextually sensitive guidelines for machine agency.

6 Conclusion

In conclusion, this research extends our understanding of machine agency within the field of human-AI communication, particularly in relation to LLMs like ChatGPT. Sundar's theory [6] has been broadened here to encompass the dichotomy of good and bad machine agency, enabling a more comprehensive understanding of AI perception in human interaction. This expanded perspective emphasizes the necessity of evaluating both positive and negative factors, related to ethical alignment, privacy, transparency, social inclusiveness, human autonomy, as well as well-being and mental health, when assessing the agency of AI systems.

Yet, despite several limitations in our study, understanding public perception through news sources can provide valuable insights into the ways in which AI is perceived and understood by society, contributing to a more nuanced understanding of the implications of machine agency in AI. Our study illustrates that the perception of ChatGPT's agency is molded by a variety of elements. For instance, users might associate good agency with ChatGPT when it produces coherent, context-appropriate responses. Conversely, they might attribute bad agency when it struggles to comprehend or respond fittingly to their input. Bad agency may also be perceived if users feel intentionally manipulated or deceived by ChatGPT, such as when they receive biased or incomplete information.

In the realm of human-AI communication, it is essential to consider how the complexities of machine agency influence user experience and perception. Our findings underscore the significance of machine agency as a research and development area within AI, given its profound implications for how machines interact with humans and the surrounding environment. Understanding the intricate dynamics of machine agency in human-AI communication is vital for creating efficient, trustworthy AI systems. By considering both the good and bad facets of machine agency, designers and developers can gain insight into how users might perceive their systems. This, in turn, allows them to address negative perceptions or experiences proactively, fostering improved human-AI communication that is effective, ethical, and beneficial for all users.

Acknowledgement. This research is partly financed by the Norwegian Media Authority, and the research project *An AI-Powered Society*.

Author's note: ChatGPT was employed in this article to summarize and rephrase some parts of the document. The ChatGPT output was then manually edited and reviewed by the authors.

References

1. Future of Life Institute Homepage: https://futureoflife.org/open-letter/pause-giant-ai-experiments/. Last accessed 11 Apr 2023
2. Manyika, J., et al.: Jobs Lost, Jobs Gained: Workforce Transitions in a Time of Automation. McKinsey Global Institute (2017)
3. Szollosy, M.: Freud, Frankenstein and our fear of robots: projection in our cultural perception of technology. AI & Soc. **32**(3), 433–439 (2016). https://doi.org/10.1007/s00146-016-0654-7
4. McClure, P.K.: "You're fired", says the robot: the rise of automation in the workplace, technophobes, and fears of unemployment. Soc. Sci. Comput. Rev. **36**(2), 139–156 (2018). https://doi.org/10.1177/0894439317698637
5. Cave, S., Dihal, K.: Hopes and fears for intelligent machines in fiction and reality. Nat. Mach. Intell. **1**(2), 74–78 (2019). https://doi.org/10.1038/s42256-019-0020-9
6. Sundar, S.S.: Rise of machine agency: a framework for studying the psychology of human–ai interaction (HAII). J. Comput.-Mediated Commun. **25**(1), 74–88 (2020). https://doi.org/10.1093/jcmc/zmz026
7. Sundar, S.S., Lee, E.-J.: Rethinking communication in the era of artificial intelligence. Hum. Commun. Res. **48**(3), 379–385 (2022). https://doi.org/10.1093/hcr/hqac014
8. Guzman, A.L., Lewis, S.C.: Artificial intelligence and communication: a human–machine communication research agenda. New Media Soc. **22**(1), 70–86 (2019). https://doi.org/10.1177/1461444819858691
9. Fox, J., Gambino, A.: Relationship development with humanoid social robots: applying interpersonal theories to human-robot interaction. Cyberpsychol. Behav. Soc. Netw. **24**(5), 294–299 (2021). https://doi.org/10.1089/cyber.2020.0181

10. Gibbs, J., Kirkwood, G., Fang, C., Wilkenfeld, J.N.: Negotiating agency and control: theorizing human-machine communication from a Structurational perspective. Human-Mach. Commun. **2**, 153–171 (2021). https://doi.org/10.30658/hmc.2.8

11. Laapotti, T., Raappana, M.: Algorithms and organizing. Hum. Commun. Res. **48**(3), 491–515 (2022). https://doi.org/10.1093/hcr/hqac013

12. OpenAI Homepage: https://openai.com/blog/chatgpt. Last accessed 10 May 2023

13. OpenAI Homepage: https://openai.com/research/gpt-4. Last accessed 10 May 2023

14. Markov, T., et al.: A Holistic Approach to Undesired Content Detection in the Real World (2022). http://arxiv.org/abs/2208.03274

15. Fogg, B.J.: Persuasive technology: using computers to change what we think and do. Ubiquity **2002**(December), 2 (2002). https://doi.org/10.1145/764008.763957

16. Krügel, S., Ostermaier, A., Uhl, M.: ChatGPT's inconsistent moral advice influences users' judgment. Sci. Rep. **13**(1), 4569 (2023). https://doi.org/10.1038/s41598-023-31341-0

17. OpenAI Homepage: https://openai.com/charter. Last accessed 10 May 2023

18. Beer, D.: The social power of algorithms. Inf. Commun. Soc. **20**(1), 1–13 (2017). https://doi.org/10.1080/1369118X.2016.1216147

19. van Dis, E.A.M., Bollen, J., Zuidema, W., van Rooij, R., Bockting, C.L.: ChatGPT: five priorities for research. Nature **614**(7947), 224–226 (2023). https://doi.org/10.1038/d41586-023-00288-7

20. Floridi, L.: AI as agency without intelligence: on ChatGPT, large language models, and other generative models. Philos. Technol. (2023). https://doi.org/10.2139/ssrn.4358789

21. Brandtzaeg, P.B., Skjuve, M., Følstad, A.: My AI friend: how users of a social chatbot understand their human-AI friendship. Human Commun. Res. **48**(3), 404–429 (2022). https://doi.org/10.1093/hcr/hqac008

22. Fitzpatrick, K.K., Darcy, A., Vierhile, M.: Delivering cognitive behavior therapy to young adults with symptoms of depression and anxiety using a fully automated conversational agent (Woebot): a randomized controlled trial. J. Med. Internet Res. Mental Health **4**(2), e19 (2017). https://doi.org/10.2196/mental.7785

23. Stephens, T.N., Joerin, A., Rauws, M., Werk, L.N.: Feasibility of pediatric obesity and prediabetes treatment support through tess, the ai behavioral coaching Chatbot. Trans. Behav. Med. **9**(3), 440–447 (2019). https://doi.org/10.1093/tbm/ibz043

24. Skjuve, M., Følstad, A., Fostervold, K.I., Brandtzaeg, P.B.: My chatbot companion – a study of human-chatbot relationships. Int. J. Hum Comput Stud. **149**, 102601 (2021). https://doi.org/10.1016/j.ijhcs.2021.102601

25. Ta, V., et al.: User experiences of social support from companion chatbots in everyday contexts: thematic analysis. J. Med. Internet Res. **22**(3), e16235 (2020). https://doi.org/10.2196/16235

26. Brandtzæg, P.B., Skjuve, M., Kristoffer Dysthe, K.K., Følstad, A.: When the social becomes non-human: young people's perception of social support in Chatbots. In: Proceedings of the 2021 CHI Conference on Human Factors in Computing Systems, pp.1–13. Association for Computing Machinery, New York, NY, United States (2021). https://doi.org/10.1145/3411764.3445318

27. Dwivedi, Y.K., et al.: "So what if ChatGPT wrote it?" multidisciplinary perspectives on opportunities, challenges and implications of generative conversational AI for research, practice and policy. Int. J. Inf. Manage. **71**, 102642 (2023). https://doi.org/10.1016/j.ijinfomgt.2023.102642

28. Ruane, E., Birhane, A., Ventresque, A.: Conversational AI: social and ethical considerations. In: Irish Conference on Artificial Intelligence and Cognitive Science, pp.104–115 (2019)

29. Larsson, S., et al.: Sustainable AI: An Inventory of the State of Knowledge of Ethical, Social, and Legal Challenges Related to Artificial Intelligence (2019). https://lucris.lub.lu.se/ws/portalfiles/portal/62833751/Larson_et_al_2019_SUSTAINABLE_AI_web_ENG_05.pdf

30. Mikalef, P., Conboy, K., Lundström, J.E., Popovič, A.: Thinking responsibly about responsible AI and 'the dark side' of AI. Eur. J. Inf. Syst. **3**, 257–268 (2022). https://doi.org/10.1080/096 0085X.2022.2026621

31. Skjuve, M., Brandtzæg, P.B., Følstad, A.: Why People Use ChatGPT (2023). https://doi.org/ 10.2139/ssrn.4376834

32. European Commission: https://ec.europa.eu/futurium/en/ai-alliance-consultation.1.html. Last accessed 21 May 2023

33. New York Times: https://www.nytimes.com/2023/01/15/opinion/ai-chatgpt-lobbying-dem ocracy.html. Last accessed 9 June 2023

34. Engadget: https://www.engadget.com/openai-improves-chatgpt-privacy-with-new-data-controls-174851274.html?guccounter=1&guce_referrer=aHR0cHM6Ly93d3cuYmluZy5y b20v&guce_referrer_sig=AQAAAAnDlIOCUG8H-Rb5nzaVhxTNpICzMyJgFTWmtlsB h0jUMNsvbQRPO2S1Eoe%20Yv4GAivqHGOUiGzu8SD_QAZP33omXGvNyWhn_O xTHmF2keO2wZXyLvHCufdmfYCR0WydETH-R-0Nvfz-ItSfzlHp53XGsPL0s1Q7R2oD UZSDC3SDL. Last accessed 9 June 2023

35. Wired: https://www.wired.com/story/red-teaming-gpt-4-was-valuable-violet-teaming-will-make-it-better/. Last accessed 9 June 2023

36. Yahoo News: https://au.news.yahoo.com/ai-tech-chatgpt-improve-inclusion-000952663. html?guccounter=1&guce_referrer=aHR0cHM6Ly93d3cuYmluZy5yb20v&guce_refe rrer_sig=AQAAAAiczrRdseP88CK3UiNE3tyHisJvzRpzJbotcTrKUe8vE7t3ysN21g_y eJlaQQBbEtVrDZSWIrNGfAofPAOogesEFcg-5HoG33_GKly126MbJYAjDvmghzcon24 saDdhOEZ1XkPv3m-C_nIoSbGttegbIV1X35Y0K4D8gG6pFfWU. Last accessed 9 June 2023

37. Vox: https://www.vox.com/recode/2022/12/7/23498694/ai-artificial-intelligence-chat-gpt-openai. Last accessed 9 June 2023

38. The Guardian: https://www.theguardian.com/commentisfree/2022/dec/08/the-guardian-view-on-chatgpt-an-eerily-good-human-impersonator. Last accessed 9 June 2023

39. Bloomberg: https://www.bloomberg.com/opinion/articles/2022-12-17/chatgpt-holds-pro mise-and-peril-bloomberg-opinion-digest#xj4y7vzkg. Last accessed 9 June 2023

40. BuzzFeed: https://www.buzzfeednews.com/article/fjollaarifi/chatgpt-ai-for-therapy-mental-health. Last accessed 9 June 2023

41. insider: https://www.insider.com/chat-gpt-successor-gpt-4-can-help-doctors-save-lives-2023-4#:~:text=GPT-4%20is%20the%20latest%20AI%20technology%20released%20f rom,lives%2C%20but%20shouldn%27t%20be%20used%20without%20human%20supervi sion. Last accessed 9 June 2023

42. The Telegraph: https://www.telegraph.co.uk/news/2023/04/28/chatgpt-better-bedside-man ner-empathy-than-doctors/. Last accessed 9 June 2023

43. Noy, S., Zhang, W.: Experimental evidence on the productivity effects of generative artificial intelligence. SSRN Electron. J. (2023). https://doi.org/10.2139/ssrn.4375283

44. Johnson, S.B., King, A.J., Warner, E.L., Aneja, S., Kann, B.H., Bylund, C.L.: Using ChatGPT to evaluate cancer myths and misconceptions: artificial intelligence and cancer information. JNCI Cancer Spectr. **7**(2), pkad015 (2023). https://doi.org/10.1093/jncics/pkad015

45. Borji, A.: A Categorical Archive of ChatGPT Failures, pp. 1–41 (2023). http://arxiv.org/abs/ 2302.03494

46. New York Times: https://www.nytimes.com/2023/02/08/technology/ai-chatbots-disinform ation.html. Last accessed 29 June 2023

47. Yahoo News: https://www.yahoo.com/news/bings-chatbot-compared-associated-press-114 209531.html. Last accessed 9 June 2023

48. Reuters: https://shorturlhttps://www.reuters.com/technology/australian-mayor-readies-wor lds-first-defamation-lawsuit-over-chatgpt-content-2023-04-05/l.at/hDIR2. Last accessed 9 June 2023

49. The Telegraph: https://www.telegraph.co.uk/news/2023/04/09/chatgpt-artificial-intelligence-terrorism-terror-attack/. Last accessed 9 June 2023
50. New York Post: https://nypost.com/2023/04/11/ai-bot-chaosgpt-tweet-plans-to-destroy-humanity-after-being-tasked/. Last accessed 9 June 2023
51. Financial Times: https://www.ft.com/content/3ce7ed9d-df95-4f5f-a3c7-ec8398ce9c50. Last accessed 9 June 2023
52. The Economic Times: https://economictimes.indiatimes.com/tech/technology/canada-opens-investigation-into-ai-firm-behind-chatgpt/articleshow/99258321.cms. Last accessed 9 June 2023
53. Vice: https://www.vice.com/en/article/5d3naz/openai-is-now-everything-it-promised-not-to-be-corporate-closed-source-and-for-profit. Last accessed 9 June 2023
54. inews.co.uk: https://inews.co.uk/news/chatgpt-secrecy-concerns-experts-ai-companies-copyright-lawsuits-2236444. Last accessed 9 June 2023
55. Bloomberg: https://www.bloomberg.com/news/newsletters/2022-12-08/chatgpt-open-ai-s-chatbot-is-spitting-out-biased-sexist-results. Last accessed 9 June 2023
56. Insider: https://www.insider.com/chatgpt-is-like-many-other-ai-models-rife-with-bias-2023-1. Last accessed 9 June 2023
57. USA Today: https://eu.usatoday.com/story/tech/2023/02/09/woke-chatgpt-conservatives-bias/11215353002/. Last accessed 9 June 2023
58. Vox: https://www.vox.com/future-perfect/23674696/chatgpt-ai-creativity-originality-homogenization. Last accessed 9 June 2023
59. The Atlantic: https://www.theatlantic.com/technology/archive/2022/12/chatgpt-ai-writing-college-student-essays/672371/. Last accessed 9 June 2023
60. The Washington Post: https://www.washingtonpost.com/technology/2023/02/14/chatgpt-dan-jailbreak/. Last accessed 9 June 2023
61. New York Times: https://www.nytimes.com/2023/02/16/technology/bing-chatbot-microsoft-chatgpt.html. Last accessed 9 June 2023
62. CNN: https://edition.cnn.com/2023/03/29/tech/chatgpt-ai-automation-jobs-impact-intl-hnk/index.html. Last accessed 9 June 2023
63. Vice: https://www.vice.com/en/article/pkadgm/man-dies-by-suicide-after-talking-with-ai-chatbot-widow-says. Last accessed 9 June 2023
64. Skjuve, M., Følstad, A., Brandtzæg, P.B.: A longitudinal study of self-disclosure in human–chatbot relationships. Interact. Comput. 35(1), 24–39 (2023). https://doi.org/10.1093/iwc/iwad022
65. Harcup, T., O'Neill, D.: What is news? news values revisited (again). Journal. Stud. 18(12), 1470–1488 (2017). https://doi.org/10.1080/1461670X.2016.1150193

Impact of AI on Mobile Computing: A Systematic Review from a Human Factors Perspective

Jiayu Chen, Bhargav Ganguly[(✉)], Sameeran G. Kanade, and Vincent G. Duffy

Purdue University, West Lafayette, IN 47907, USA
{chen3686,bganguly,kanade,duffy}@purdue.edu

Abstract. The integration of Artificial Intelligence (AI) in mobile computing has brought significant advancements in creating user-centric applications and interfaces that enhance user experience, promote accessibility, and facilitate personalized interactions. This paper explores the influence of AI on mobile computing from a human factors perspective, emphasizing the importance of understanding user needs, preferences, and limitations in designing AI-powered mobile applications. Tools like VOSviewer, MAXQDA, and Citespace have been used for bibliometric analysis. The study highlights key areas such as context-aware computing, adaptive user interfaces, affective computing, and ethical considerations. It emphasizes the need for personalized experiences, improved accessibility, and inclusiveness in mobile applications. Additionally, the paper addresses ethical concerns and potential biases in AI algorithms, emphasizing the importance of responsible and transparent AI implementation. The discussion section underscores the intricate relationship between technology and user experiences, emphasizing the need for a comprehensive understanding of both AI and human factors to create user-centric mobile computing solutions. Future work includes establishing testing frameworks and collaborations to overcome challenges and ensure responsible development and deployment in mobile computing.

Keywords: Machine Learning · Mobile Computing · User-Centric Design · VOSviewer · Citespace · MAXQDA · BibExcel

1 Introduction and Background

Taking human factors approach to examining the influence of Artificial Intelligence (AI) on mobile computing is crucial as it facilitates the development of mobile applications that prioritize user needs, uphold reliability and security, are easily accessible, and adhere to ethical standards. This methodology is aimed at promoting the benefits of technology for society while mitigating any associated risks. By factoring in aspects like privacy, security, accessibility, and ethical considerations, we can create AI-powered mobile applications that users can easily rely on and use, irrespective of their technical proficiency or physical capacity.

© The Author(s), under exclusive license to Springer Nature Switzerland AG 2023
H. Degen et al. (Eds.): HCII 2023, LNCS 14059, pp. 24–38, 2023.
https://doi.org/10.1007/978-3-031-48057-7_2

The significance of understanding the impact of AI on mobile computing through a human factors lens has been driven by several factors including the increasing prevalence of mobile devices, the progress in AI technology, ethical implications, and the importance of user satisfaction. With billions of people relying on mobile devices for various purposes, there is a growing demand for AI-driven mobile applications that offer personalized and pertinent services to users. While recent strides in AI technology have enabled the development of more sophisticated mobile applications, it is crucial to consider ethical factors such as bias, privacy, security, and transparency. Furthermore, as mobile devices become more intricate, ensuring a positive user experience has become more crucial than ever before.

The subject of AI in mobile computing viewed through a human factors perspective holds particular importance for the fields of human-computer interaction (HCI) and user interface (UI) design (Lindley et al., 2020). By examining user interactions with AI-driven mobile applications, HCI and UI designers can construct interfaces that are instinctive, easy to use, and offer an enjoyable user experience, which can contribute to a rise in user acceptance and contentment. Moreover, HCI and UI designers are tasked with addressing ethical and privacy issues related to AI-powered mobile applications, guaranteeing that users retain control over their data and its utilization.

In the domain of machine learning research, the examination of AI in mobile computing through a human factors lens holds significance as it can offer insights that can enhance the development of more effective and efficient machine learning algorithms and models (Chen et al., 2019). By studying user behavior and preferences, machine learning researchers can create more precise models that can generate personalized and pertinent recommendations and actions (Zolyomi & Snyder, 2021). Furthermore, in the creation of AI-driven mobile applications, machine learning researchers must account for ethical considerations such as bias, privacy, and transparency.

To better respond to the topic of AI in mobile computing from a human factors perspective, society needs to prioritize the development of ethical guidelines and regulations that ensure the responsible development and deployment of AI-powered mobile applications. Additionally, there needs to be increased collaboration between researchers, industry professionals, and policymakers to address the challenges associated with incorporating AI into mobile computing. Society must also prioritize education and awareness initiatives that inform the public about the potential benefits and risks of AI-powered mobile applications.

The fields of human factors and ergonomics (HFE) and human-computer interaction (HCI) have been actively involved in addressing the topic of AI in mobile computing, with a focus on ensuring the safety and usability of AI-powered mobile devices. For instance, frameworks have been developed to conduct usability testing on AI-powered mobile devices to evaluate the ease of use, learnability, and user satisfaction of these devices. This helps identify and address usability issues before they become safety concerns(Yang et al., 2020). Furthermore, design guidelines for AI-powered mobile devices have been established to ensure that they are designed with the user in mind. These guidelines cover areas such as interface design, feedback, and error handling. Finally, the fields have led critical discussions pertaining to ethical considerations of AI-powered mobile devices(Lin & Brummelen, 2021). This includes issues such as privacy, data security, and bias in AI algorithms.

2   Purpose of Study

The academic justification for the topic "AI in mobile computing under the human factor background" is evident in the growing interest and research output in this field (Van Maanen et al., 2005). A comparison of the existing literature in terms of volume of publications in recent years highlights the increasing importance and relevance of this interdisciplinary area. For instance, a search on the "dimensions" database shows that the number of articles published on this topic in 2022 is approximately 28000, whereas in 2017, the number was around 85000. This represents a more than two times increase in research output within just five years, indicating the escalating significance of this subject in academia. The surge in research interest can be attributed to the rapid advancements in AI technologies and their applications in mobile computing, as well as the increasing recognition of the role of human factors in ensuring the success and adoption of AI-driven mobile applications (Li et al., 2008).

The uniqueness of the topic "AI in mobile computing under the human factor background" lies in its interdisciplinary approach, integrating the fields of artificial intelligence, mobile computing, and human factors. This topic goes beyond the technical aspects and delves into the nuances of user experience, interface design, accessibility, and ethics, examining the impact of AI technologies on mobile computing from a human-centered perspective. When comparing this topic to existing literature, it becomes apparent that most research tends to focus either on AI algorithms and their applications in mobile computing or on the human factors related to mobile device usage. However, the intersection of AI, mobile computing, and human factors is not as thoroughly explored. This gap presents an opportunity for researchers to investigate the synergistic effects of combining AI with human factors in mobile computing, providing insights into the challenges and opportunities associated with the development and deployment of AI-driven mobile applications.

3   Relevance to Human Factors

The relationship between "AI in mobile computing" and "human factor job design" lies in the intersection of technology and human-centered design, emphasizing the need to create AI-driven mobile applications that cater to the diverse needs, preferences, and abilities of users. Human factor job design focuses on optimizing the interaction between humans and their work environment, considering cognitive, physical, and emotional aspects (Ho & Intille, 2005). Similarly, the integration of AI in mobile computing aims to develop applications that are not only technologically advanced but also user-centric, ensuring seamless and intuitive interactions. By incorporating principles of human factor job design in the development of AI-driven mobile applications, developers can create context-aware and adaptive user interfaces that improve accessibility, facilitate personalized user experiences, and address ethical considerations such as data privacy and potential biases in AI algorithms. Ultimately, the convergence of AI in mobile computing and human factor job design leads to the creation of inclusive, efficient, and user-friendly mobile experiences.

In the context of "AI in mobile computing," the human factors principles of user interaction paradigms and technologies in mobile computing and Human-centered AI, as outlined in (Salvendy & Karwowski, 2021), are essential to ensure the development of user-centric applications. User interaction paradigms and technologies emphasize the importance of understanding the different ways users interact with mobile devices, considering the varying input modalities, interface designs, and technological constraints. By incorporating AI into mobile computing, developers can leverage advanced algorithms and techniques to create adaptive, context-aware, and personalized user experiences that align with diverse user needs and preferences.

On the other hand, human-centered AI focuses on the responsible and ethical implementation of AI technologies, ensuring that AI-driven applications are designed with the user's best interests in mind (Daily et al., 2017). Integrating Human-centered AI principles in mobile computing involves addressing issues such as data privacy, algorithmic biases, and the potential impact on vulnerable user groups. By prioritizing transparency, fairness, and inclusivity, developers can create AI-driven mobile applications that not only enhance user experiences but also promote ethical and equitable interactions (Wang et al., 2020). The relationship between AI in mobile computing and these course principles emphasizes the importance of adopting a holistic approach to mobile application development, considering both technological advancements and human factors to create truly user-centric solutions.

4   Research Methodology

4.1   Data Collection

In Table 1, we present the yield for Dimensions, SpringerLink, and Scopus databases published during the period 2000–2023.

Table 1. Yield for the keyword "Artificial Intelligence in mobile computing" for 3 databases over the period 2000–2023.

Dimensions	SpringerLink	Scopus
536,762	122,688	3,881

4.2   Engagement Measure

The Vicinitas tool is utilized for data mining, enabling the measurement of engagement levels within a particular topic area through analyzing Twitter activity. Its application was employed to assess the engagement of virtual reality enthusiasts on Twitter. By conducting a search for tweets containing the keyword "mobile computing ", the tool generated results that are depicted in Fig. 1.

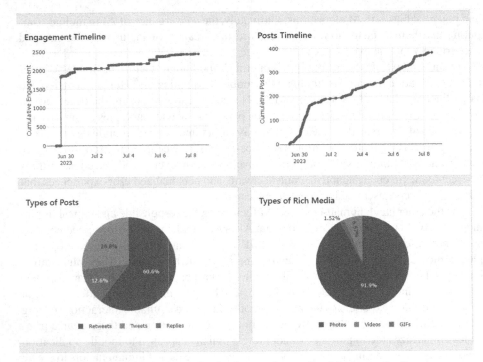

Fig. 1. Vicinitas analytics for the search term "mobile computing".

4.3 Trend Analysis

We graphically present how the trend in the yield of published articles for the keyword "Artificial Intelligence in mobile computing" has changed during the period 2000–2023 for the Dimensions database in Fig. 2.

4.4 Comparison Analysis

In the following, we present Google Ngram results comparing the following set of keywords relevant to our ensuing analysis: mobile computing, human-computer interaction, and UI Design via Fig. 3.

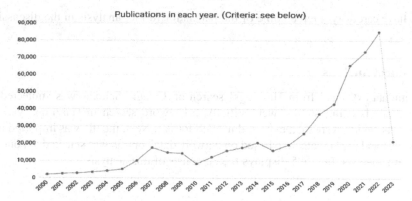

Publications in each year. (Criteria: see below)

Fig. 2. Trend of yield for the period 2000–2023 in dimensions database for keyword "Artificial Intelligence in mobile computing".

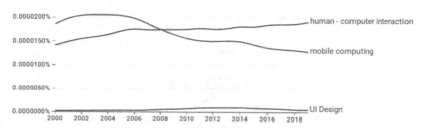

Fig. 3. Google Ngram trend comparison for the period 2000–2023 for the set of keywords mobile computing, human-computer interaction, UI Design.

5 Results

5.1 Co-citation Analysis

The technique of co-citation analysis involves identifying articles that have been cited together in another article, which helps to gauge the level of interconnection between them (Kanade & Duffy, 2020). In this study, VOSviewer was utilized to conduct co-citation analysis using metadata extracted from the Web of Science. The dataset comprised 500 articles, and only those that had been cited at least six times were included in the analysis. The outcome of the analysis is presented in Fig. 4, depicting the resulting clusters of related articles.

Fig. 4. Co-citation analysis using VOSviewer (VOSviewer, n.d.).

We have carefully filtered some of the papers for further analysis in the discussion part.

5.2 Content Analysis

The metadata extracted from Harzings' search on Google Scholar was subjected to content analysis using VOSviewer. Initially, a keyword search in Harzings' yielded 1000 results, which were then exported in WoS format. Next, the file was imported into VOSviewer, and the "create map based on network data" option was selected to conduct the content analysis. Figure 5 displays the outcomes of this analysis.

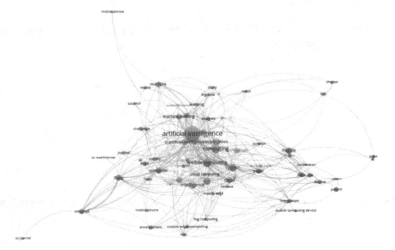

Fig. 5. Content analysis using metadata from Harzings' using VOSviewer (*VOSviewer*, n.d.).

It can be seen from the cluster analysis that words like artificial intelligence, mobile computing, cloud, mobile edge, etc., occur prominently as nodes in the clusters. The words in the clusters indicate the important words in a topic area. These words can be used as a reference point when literature related to a topic area is reviewed.

5.3 Pivot Table

The metadata extracted from Harzings' was also used to generate a pivot table using BibExcel. BibExcel is a software tool that can analyze metadata to generate various forms of pivot tables. In this study, it was used to generate a "leading authors" table. This helps identify the authors who have published the most in each topic area. The metadata from Harzings' was imported into BibExcel and analysis was carried out. The results were then exported to an Excel file to generate a table. The table generated using this process is shown in Table 2.

Based on the data exported from BibExcel, we can also generate the bar plots representing the number of publications for each leading author and leading source, which have been shown in Figs. 6 and 7, respectively.

Table 2. Leading authors table using BibExcel (*BibExcel*, n.d.).

Author name	Number of publications
Zhang J	4
Chen X	4
Fragkos G	3
Chen M	3
Cook DJ	3

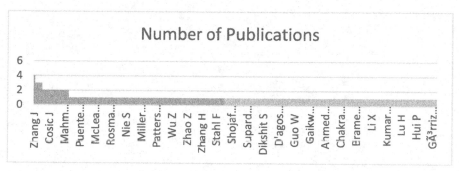

Fig. 6. Analysis of the leading authors using BibExcel (*BibExcel*, n.d.).

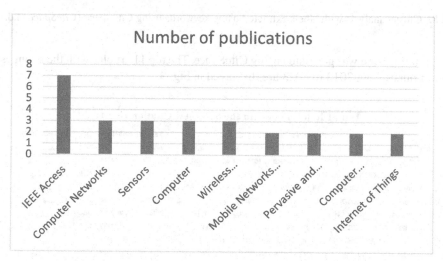

Fig. 7. Analysis of the leading authors from BibExcel (*BibExcel*, n.d.).

5.4 Cluster Analysis

Figure 4 demonstrates a limitation of VOSviewer's co-citation analysis, as it does not provide cluster names. However, this limitation can be addressed by utilizing CiteSpace, a software tool capable of performing co-citation analysis and assigning labels to the clusters (Kanade & Duffy, 2022). CiteSpace also enables the creation of a citation burst diagram, highlighting the period in which a specific article received the highest number of citations. To conduct the analysis in CiteSpace, a keyword search was executed on the Web of Science, resulting in 500 relevant outcomes. These search results, including the cited references, were exported in text format, and imported into CiteSpace. Subsequently, co-citation analysis was conducted, and cluster labels were extracted using keywords. The outcomes are presented in Fig. 8, where the cluster names denote the articles within a particular cluster. This facilitates the identification of sub-topics within a given subject area and aids in pinpointing articles within specific sub-topics.

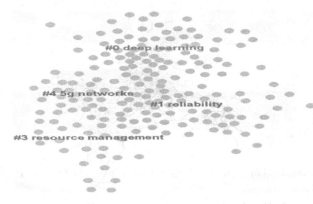

Fig. 8. Cluster analysis with labels extracted using keywords using CiteSpace (*CiteSpace*, n.d.).

A citation burst was generated using CiteSpace. The top 11 articles with the strongest citation bursts from 2013 to 2023 are displayed in Fig. 9.

Top 11 References with the Strongest Citation Bursts

References	Year	Strength	Begin	End	2013 - 2023
Dinh HT, 2013, WIREL COMMUN MOB COM, V13, P1587, DOI 10.1002/wcm.1203, DOI	2013	2.84	2014	2016	
Jararweh Y, 2014, PROCEDIA COMPUT SCI, V34, P434, DOI 10.1016/j.procs.2014.07.051, DOI	2014	5.32	2015	2016	
Jararweh Y, 2013, 2013 IEEE NI ...... NETWORKS (MSN 2013), V0, PP373, DOI	2013	4.13	2015	2016	
Tawalbeh L, 2015, J NETW, V10, P70, DOI 10.4304/jnw.10.01.70-76, 10.4304/jnw.10.1.70-76, DOI	2015	4.13	2015	2016	
Benkhelifa E, 2015, PROCEDIA COMPUT SCI, V52, P1159, DOI 10.1016/j.procs.2015.05.151, DOI	2015	3.68	2016	2017	
Tawalbeh L, 2015, PR INT CONF ELEARN, V0, PP280, DOI 10.1109/ECONF.2015.59, DOI	2015	3.49	2016	2018	
Shi WS, 2016, IEEE INTERNET THINGS, V3, P637, DOI 10.1109/JIOT.2016.2579198, DOI	2016	3.74	2019	2020	
Mao YJ, 2017, INT GEOL REV, V59, P1276, DOI 10.1080/00206814.2016.1209435, DOI	2017	3.3	2019	2020	
Chen M, 2018, IEEE J SEL AREA COMM, V36, P587, DOI 10.1109/JSAC.2018.2815360, DOI	2018	3.12	2019	2020	
He Y, 2018, IEEE T VEH TECHNOL, V67, P44, DOI 10.1109/TVT.2017.2760281, DOI	2018	3.03	2019	2020	
Simonyan K, 2015, ARXIV, V0, P0	2015	2.6	2019	2020	

Fig. 9. Citation burst diagram using CiteSpace (*CiteSpace*, n.d.).

5.5   Content Analysis Using MAXQDA

Once all the articles which were selected for the review were downloaded, content analysis based on the text of these articles was carried out. A word cloud was generated which indicates the keywords in the top five cited papers. This helps decide the keywords for this literature review. The generated word cloud can be seen in Fig. 10.

Fig. 10. Word cloud using MAXQDA.

The five most frequently occurring words from this analysis were edge, learning, mobile, computing, and data. Unlike the content analysis from VOSviewer which uses link strength as the parameter, MAXQDA provides information regarding the frequency of words which is helpful. These words were then used for lexical search that was carried out in the articles that were chosen for review in the discussion section. The lexical search result is shown as Fig. 11. This helps in giving special attention to the part of the article that is related to the topic being reviewed.

5.6   Summary of Results

In the context of human factors, AI for mobile computing has seen significant advancements in creating user-centric applications and interfaces that enhance user experience, promote accessibility, and facilitate personalized interactions. This literature survey highlights the growing importance of understanding user behavior, preferences, and cognitive abilities in the design and development of AI-driven mobile applications (Beñitez-Guerrero et al., 2012). Key findings include the integration of AI in areas such as context-aware computing, adaptive user interfaces, and affective computing, which enable personalized experiences, improved accessibility for users with disabilities, and emotionally intelligent interactions (Edward et al., 2009). Additionally, the survey emphasizes the need for addressing ethical concerns and potential biases in AI algorithms to ensure equitable and inclusive mobile experiences for diverse user populations.

Preview	Document group	Document name	Search item
= external contour loses image information that may be useful for understand-ing the target, such as texture and internal edge. For example, walking, trotting, and other actions have very similar human body contours on some image frames. The		8879616	edge
= Artificial Intelligence Perspective on Mobile Edge Computing Zhuang Chen∗, †, §, Qian He∗, ‡, §, Lei Liu¶, Dapeng Lan,, Hwei-Ming Chung,, Zhifei Mao∗∗ ∗School of Computer and Infor		An_Artificial_Intellig...	Edge
= hweiminc@ifi.uio.no; zhifei.mao@gmail.com Abstract—The interest in artificial intelligence (AI) and mobile edge computing (MEC) has increased rapidly in recent years. As a fundamental building block for the development of mobile edge		An_Artificial_Intellig...	edge
= computing (MEC) has increased rapidly in recent years. As a fundamental building block for the development of mobile edge computing, new techniques are needed in the mobile network. Driven by the techniques of Internet-of-Things (IoT) and AI,		An_Artificial_Intellig...	edge
= and AI frontier in close proximity to users, by pushing computing and cache resources from the cloud to the network edge. With continuous and in-depth research on intelligent mobile networks, we first propose the concept of green edge		An_Artificial_Intellig...	edge

Fig. 11. Lexical search using MAXQDA.

6 Discussion

One key aspect of integrating AI and human factors in mobile computing is the development of context-aware and adaptive user interfaces (Jiang et al., 2022), which enable personalized user experiences and improved accessibility. Research in this area has shown that AI-driven mobile applications can better anticipate user needs and adapt to different contexts, such as location, time, or user preferences, thereby creating a seamless and intuitive interaction for diverse user groups (Tolmeijer et al., 2022). Another important sub-topic is the ethical considerations and potential biases in AI algorithms that may impact user experiences and inclusiveness in mobile computing. As AI-driven applications become more prevalent, it is crucial to address these challenges to ensure equitable and inclusive mobile experiences for all users. Research efforts should focus on refining AI models to minimize biases (Gruson et al., 2019) and developing frameworks for responsible and transparent AI implementation in mobile applications. By considering these sub-topics in the context of human factors, the discussion section highlights the intricate relationship between technology and user experiences, emphasizing the need for a comprehensive understanding of both AI and human factors to create truly user-centric mobile computing solutions. Some of the important terms in the context of using artificial intelligence in mobile computing have been explained in this section.

Context-Aware Computing. This sub-topic focuses on the ability of AI-driven mobile applications to understand and adapt to the user's context, such as location, time, and activity. The significance of context-aware computing lies in its potential to provide personalized and relevant user experiences (Bradley & Dunlop, 2005), enhancing the overall utility and effectiveness of mobile applications.

Adaptive User Interfaces. Adaptive user interfaces tailor presentation and interaction methods to suit individual user preferences and abilities, ensuring an inclusive and accessible user experience (Cheng & Liu, 2012). The selection of this sub-topic is justified by its importance in addressing the diverse needs of users and promoting human-centered design in AI for mobile computing (Andalibi & Buss, 2020).

Affective Computing. Affective computing deals with the recognition, interpretation, and expression of human emotions by AI-driven mobile applications. The relevance of this sub-topic stems from its ability to improve user engagement, satisfaction, and overall experience by fostering empathy and understanding between users and technology (Eyben et al., 2010).

Ethical Considerations. The inclusion of ethical considerations as a sub-topic highlights the importance of responsible AI development and deployment in mobile computing, addressing issues such as data privacy, algorithmic biases, and the impact on vulnerable user groups (Long & Magerko, 2020). By considering ethical aspects, developers can create AI-driven mobile applications that promote transparency and fairness (Wang et al., 2019).

7 Conclusion

From a human factors perspective, this review paper has conducted a thorough examination of the influence of artificial intelligence (AI) on mobile computing. The integration of AI has transformed the way users interact with their devices, offering new levels of personalization and convenience. However, there are also challenges associated with AI in mobile computing, including issues of trust, transparency, and accountability. The human factors perspective emphasizes the importance of considering the user's needs, preferences, and limitations in the design and development of AI-based mobile applications. To fully harness the potential of AI in mobile computing, it is crucial to address these challenges and ensure that the technology is designed to enhance the user's experience, while also addressing their concerns about privacy and security. As the field continues to evolve, it will be essential for researchers, developers, and policymakers to work collaboratively to ensure that AI-based mobile applications are designed to optimize human performance, promote user satisfaction, and support human values.

8 Future Work

Research endeavors can be focused towards establishing and utilizing testing frameworks across the nation to advance the development and implementation of AI for Mobile Computing in a human factors context (Woolf et al., 2022). This approach will address the limitations and challenges identified in the literature survey, such as energy efficiency, data privacy, and the need for inclusive and unbiased AI algorithms. One potential direction is the integration of the "Collaborative Research:CCRI:New:Nationwide Community-based Mobile Edge Sensing and Computing Testbeds" project (Award Abstract # 2120396), which aims to create a network of distributed mobile edge testbeds across the country to facilitate the research, development, and evaluation of innovative mobile applications and services. For more details, refer to: https://www.nsf.gov/awards earch/showAward?AWD_ID=2120396&HistoricalAwards=false. Another direct search result: https://dl.acm.org/doi/abs/10.1145/3491418.3530759 may also help. The image of this award from the NSF website is attached as follows (Fig. 12).

NSF Org:	CNS Division Of Computer and Network Systems
Recipient:	RUTGERS, THE STATE UNIVERSITY OF NEW JERSEY
Initial Amendment Date:	August 9, 2021
Latest Amendment Date:	August 9, 2021
Award Number:	2120396
Award Instrument:	Standard Grant
Program Manager:	Damian Dechev ddechev@nsf.gov (703)292-8910 CNS Division Of Computer and Network Systems CSE Direct For Computer & Info Scie & Enginr
Start Date:	October 1, 2021
End Date:	September 30, 2024 (Estimated)
Total Intended Award Amount:	$710,000.00
Total Awarded Amount to Date:	$710,000.00
Funds Obligated to Date:	FY 2021 = $710,000.00
History of Investigator:	Yingying Chen (Principal Investigator) yingche@scarletmail.rutgers.edu Ivan Seskar (Co-Principal Investigator)
Recipient Sponsored Research Office:	Rutgers University New Brunswick 3 RUTGERS PLZA NEW BRUNSWICK NJ US 08901-8559 (848)932-0150
Sponsor Congressional District:	12

Fig. 12. A screenshot from the NSF website demonstrating the approval of a research project focusing on developing nationwide computing testbeds.

These testbeds will support the investigation of human factors and the development of AI-driven mobile applications tailored to users' needs and contexts. By providing a shared infrastructure, the testbeds will enable researchers and developers to collaborate, share insights, and validate their solutions in real-world scenarios. The testbeds can serve as a platform for researchers to explore various aspects of human factors in mobile computing, such as context-aware computing, adaptive user interfaces, affective computing, and ethical considerations. By leveraging these nationwide testbeds, future work will contribute to the development of innovative, efficient, and inclusive AI-driven mobile applications, fostering a more connected and accessible technological ecosystem for users across the country.

References

Andalibi, N., Buss, J.: The human in emotion recognition on social media: attitudes, outcomes, risks. In: Conference on Human Factors in Computing Systems – Proceedings, 1–16 (2020). https://doi.org/10.1145/3313831.3376680

Beñitez-Guerrero, E., Mezura-Godoy, C., Montañe-Jiménez, L.G.: Context-aware mobile collaborative systems: conceptual modeling and case study. Sensors (Switzerland) 12(10), 13491–13507 (2012). https://doi.org/10.3390/s121013491

BibExcel (n.d.). https://homepage.univie.ac.at/juan.gorraiz/bibexcel/

Bradley, N.A., Dunlop, M.D.: Toward a multidisciplinary model of context to support context-aware computing. Hum.-Comput. Interact. 20(4), 403–446 (2005). https://doi.org/10.1207/s15 327051hci2004_2

Chen, Z., He, Q., Liu, L., Lan, D., Chung, H.M., Mao, Z.: An artificial intelligence perspective on mobile edge computing. In: Proceedings – 2019 IEEE International Conference on Smart Internet of Things, SmartIoT 2019, pp. 100–106 (2019). https://doi.org/10.1109/SmartIoT. 2019.00024

Cheng, S., Liu, Y.: Eye-tracking based adaptive user interface: implicit human-computer interaction for preference indication. J. Multimodal User Interfaces 5(1–2), 77–84 (2012). https://doi. org/10.1007/s12193-011-0064-6

CiteSpace. (n.d.) http://cluster.cis.drexel.edu/~cchen/citespace/

Daily, S.B., et al.: Affective Computing: Historical Foundations, Current Applications, and Future Trends, pp. 213–231 (2017). https://doi.org/10.1016/B978-0-12-801851-4.00009-4

Edward, L., Lourdeaux, D., Barthès, J.P.: Cognitive modeling of virtual autonomous intelligent agents integrating human factors. In: Proceedings – 2009 IEEE/WIC/ACM International Conference on Web Intelligence and Intelligent Agent Technology – Workshops, WI-IAT Workshops 2009, vol. 3, pp. 353–356 (2009). https://doi.org/10.1109/WI-IAT.2009.300

Eyben, F., et al.: Emotion on the road-necessity, acceptance, and feasibility of affective computing in the car. Adv. Human-Comput. Interact. 2010, 263593 (2010). https://doi.org/10.1155/2010/ 263593

Gruson, D., Helleputte, T., Rousseau, P., Gruson, D.: Data science, artificial intelligence, and machine learning: Opportunities for laboratory medicine and the value of positive regulation. Clin. Biochem. 69(April), 1–7 (2019). https://doi.org/10.1016/j.clinbiochem.2019.04.013

Ho, J., Intille, S.S.: Using context-aware computing to reduce the perceived burden of interruptions from mobile devices. In: CHI 2005: Technology, Safety, Community: Conference Proceedings – Conference on Human Factors in Computing Systems, pp. 909–918 (2005). https://doi.org/10.1145/1054972.1055100

Jiang, Y., et al.: Computational approaches for understanding, generating, and adapting user interfaces. In: Conference on Human Factors in Computing Systems – Proceedings (2022). https:// doi.org/10.1145/3491101.3504030

Kanade, S.G., Duffy, V.G.: A Systematic literature review of game-based learning and safety management. In: Duffy, V.G. (ed.) HCII 2020. LNCS, vol. 12199, pp. 365–377. Springer, Cham (2020). https://doi.org/10.1007/978-3-030-49907-5_26

Kanade, S.G., Duffy, V.G.: Use of virtual reality for safety training: a systematic review. In: Duffy, V.G. (eds.) Digital Human Modeling and Applications in Health, Safety, Ergonomics and Risk Management. Health, Operations Management, and Design. HCII 2022. Lecture Notes in Computer Science, vol. 13320. Springer, Cham (2022). https://doi.org/10.1007/978-3-031-06018-2_25

Li, H., Jyri, S., Jian, M., Kuifei, Y.: Research on context-aware mobile computing. In: Proceedings – International Conference on Advanced Information Networking and Applications, AINA, pp. 24–30 (2008). https://doi.org/10.1109/WAINA.2008.115

Lin, P., Van Brummelen, J.: Engaging teachers to co-design integrated ai curriculum for k-12 classrooms. In: Conference on Human Factors in Computing Systems – Proceedings (2021). https://doi.org/10.1145/3411764.3445377

Lindley, J., Akmal, H.A., Pillling, F., Coulton, P.: Researching AI legibility through design. In: Conference on Human Factors in Computing Systems – Proceedings, pp. 1–13 (2020). https://doi.org/10.1145/3313831.3376792

Long, D., Magerko, B.: What is AI literacy? competencies and design considerations. In: Conference on Human Factors in Computing Systems – Proceedings, pp. 1–16 (2020). https://doi.org/10.1145/3313831.3376727

Salvendy, G., Karwowski, W.: Handbook of human factors and ergonomics. In: Handbook of Human Factors and Ergonomics (2021). https://doi.org/10.1002/9781119636113

Tolmeijer, S., Christen, M., Kandul, S., Kneer, M., Bernstein, A.: Capable but amoral? comparing AI and human expert collaboration in ethical decision making. In: Conference on Human Factors in Computing Systems – Proceedings (2022). https://doi.org/10.1145/3491102.3517732

Van Maanen, P.P., Lindenberg, J., Neerincx, M.A.: Integrating human factors and artificial intelligence in the development of human-machine cooperation. In: Proceedings of the 2005 International Conference on Artificial Intelligence, ICAI'05, 1(May 2014), pp. 10–16 (2005)

VOSviewer (n.d.). https://www.vosviewer.com/

Wang, D., Churchill, E., Maes, P., Fan, X., Shneiderman, B., Shi, Y., Wang, Q.: From human-human collaboration to Human-AI collaboration: Designing AI systems that can work together with people. In: Conference on Human Factors in Computing Systems – Proceedings, pp. 1–6 (2020). https://doi.org/10.1145/3334480.3381069

Wang, D., Yang, Q., Abdul, A., Lim, B.Y.: Designing theory-driven user-centric explainable AI. In: Conference on Human Factors in Computing Systems – Proceedings, 1–15 (2019).https://doi.org/10.1145/3290605.3300831

Woolf, B., Arroyo, I., Lan, A., Garn, M., Dede, C.: Data-Directed Education: The Future of AI in Education (2022)

Yang, Q., Steinfeld, A., Rosé, C., Zimmerman, J.: Re-examining whether, why, and how human-ai interaction is uniquely difficult to design. In: Conference on Human Factors in Computing Systems – Proceedings, pp. 1–13 (2020). https://doi.org/10.1145/3313831.3376301

Zolyomi, A., Snyder, J.: Social-emotional-sensory design map for affective computing informed by neurodivergent experiences. Proc. ACM on Hum.-Comput. Interact. 5(CSCW1), 1–37 (2021). https://doi.org/10.1145/3449151

The Impact of Generative Artificial Intelligence on Design Concept Ideation: Case Study on Lightweight Two-Wheeled Vehicles

Shih-Hung Cheng[✉]

National Taiwan University of Science and Technology, Taipei City 106335, Taiwan
achille@mail.ntust.edu.tw

Abstract. This study explores the impact of Midjourney, a text-to-image generative artificial intelligence (AI) tool, on lightweight two-wheeled vehicle design
practices. The focus is on design creativity and practical feasibility. Six sets of
prompts were used with Midjourney to generate lightweight two-wheeled vehicle concept ideas. To maintain conceptual ambiguity and flexibility during the
early stages of design development, specific and conventional sub-categories of
transportation vehicles were gradually obscured, while prompts describing the
new design framework and component attributes were introduced progressively.
Expert evaluations were conducted by ten bicycle or motorcycle design practitioners, who assessed creativity and practical feasibility using Likert scales and qualitative assessments. ANOVA analysis revealed significant differences in prompt
implementation and creativity among the three concept ideas. Qualitative evaluations highlighted several challenges, including difficulties in assessing creativity
when framework errors occur, excessive divergence in AI-generated content without the guidance of a clear conventional frame, the challenge for designers to keep
pace with the fast and high-quality development efficiency of the AI tool, and AI's
limitations in judging feasibility and safety related to human factors. The study
suggests the need for improved precision in prompt wording and enhancing the
AI's understanding of transportation design terminology. Generative AI still faces
challenges in effectively supporting innovative design practices, particularly in
addressing new framework details, component conflicts, and understanding professional terminology. Therefore, expert judgment and refinement remain crucial
in the overall development phase. Furthermore, uncertainties persist concerning
potential patent issues.

Keywords: AI-generated Content · Transportation Design · Design Ideation ·
Expert evaluation

1 Introduction

Artificial Intelligence (AI) is a rapidly expanding field poised to revolutionize numerous
facets of our lives in the near future. In the journey of AI development, the supercomputer
"Deep Blue" achieved a significant milestone in 1997 by defeating the world champion

© The Author(s), under exclusive license to Springer Nature Switzerland AG 2023
H. Degen et al. (Eds.): HCII 2023, LNCS 14059, pp. 39–57, 2023.
https://doi.org/10.1007/978-3-031-48057-7_3

chess player, setting a clear benchmark [1]. Today, less than 30 years later, generative AI has made extensive and profound advancements. Generative AI is a computational technique that generates new content, such as text, images, or audio, based on training data. Examples like GPT-4 and Midjourney demonstrate the widespread adoption of this technology, revolutionizing work and communication practices [2]. Large Language Models, such as ChatGPT, have been refined using supervised learning, machine learning and reinforcement learning methods. Additionally, latent text-to-image diffusion models, like Stable Diffusion and Midjourney, have found widespread application in visual generative AI software [1]. Due to the ability to process and analyze large amounts of data quickly and accurately, AI is already being employed in a diverse range of applications, including natural language processing and autonomous vehicles, with its prevalence expected to further soar in the upcoming years [1]. Currently, AI is projected to have a substantial impact on the global economy, potentially leading to a 7% increase in global gross domestic product (GDP) and expose the equivalent of 300 million full-time jobs to automation [3].

By automating tasks presently handled by humans, AI can free up time and resources for other tasks that require human attention. In other words, its potential to enhance efficiency and productivity can result in cost savings, quicker delivery times, and enhanced overall performance [1]. Machine learning is one of the key techniques used in AI. By learning from patterns and features in the past data, AI combines vast amounts of data with fast, iterative processing and intelligent algorithms to generate the new content. Through machine learning, AI can be trained to identify patterns and make predictions based on existing data [1]. This presents both opportunities and challenges for a wide range of professions and research areas, including education [4], healthcare [5], marketing [6, 7], transportation [8], and art [9].

Previous studies have explored the application of generative AI in various design fields, including household appliance design [10], architectural design [11], industrial design [12], and fashion design [13]. Taiwan is renowned for its advanced bicycle manufacturing technology and a thriving bicycle industry cluster [14]. The country has benefitted from accumulated learning, a favorable environment, and the globalization of production, which are crucial factors for the growth of Taiwan's bicycle industry [15]. Therefore, this study aims to investigate how generative AI can utilize the accumulated industrial technological knowledge and its impact on practical bicycle design and the innovation process. To examine the potential advantages and disadvantages of integrating generative AI into the industrial innovation process, this study incorporates Midjourney V4, a text-to-image generative AI, in the creative concept development process of lightweight two-wheeled vehicles. Moreover, ten bicycle or motorcycle design practitioners were invited to evaluate the outcomes of incorporating Midjourney in terms of creativity and feasibility. In summary, this study aims to explore the benefits of applying text-to-image generative AI to transportation design and the impact on the design thinking.

2 Design Thinking

2.1 Design and Creativity Processes

In general, the engineering design process can be divided into four main phases: task analysis, conceptual design, embodiment design, and detailed design. When it comes to creative process models, most of them encompass four phases, namely analysis, generation, evaluation, and communication/implementation [16]. In 2004, the British Design Council introduced the Double Diamond model, which was adapted from the model proposed by linguist Béla Bánáthy and represents a design process that incorporates both divergent and convergent thinking, forming cycles and iterative development process. Divergent thinking enables design teams to explore an issue more extensively or deeply, while convergent thinking involves taking focused action. The Double Diamond model consists of four distinct phases that shape the iterative process, namely Discover, Define, Develop, and Deliver [17, 18] (see Fig. 1). The first phase, Discover, represents the initial stage of divergent thinking in the Double Diamond model. It enables designers to gain a deep understanding of the problem. This phase involves engaging with stakeholders who are affected by the issues. The insights gathered from the discovery phase then help the designers as they define the challenge from a fresh perspective, marking the completion of the first diamond. Moving on to the second diamond, the Develop phase encourages designers to seek inspiration and explore diverse possibilities. In this phase, they strive to generate different solutions and ideas. Lastly, the Delivery phase involves prototyping and testing various solutions, allowing designers to identify and reject those that are not suitable or effective [17].

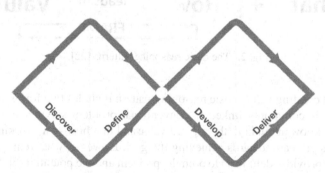

Fig. 1. The Double Diamond by the Design Council [17].

Design solutions are typically related to the defined problem. In the exploration of potential solutions, creativity is consistently regarded as a crucial element. However, certain design experts tend to emphasize their intuition during the generation phase [19]. This intuitive and mysterious aspect of the design process often leads to a misunderstanding of design expertise [20]. Consequently, there has been significant research focused on demystifying creative design [19]. The black box metaphor is frequently employed to depict the process of creative development since the inputs and outputs of the design process can sometimes be unobservable. Moreover, the black box metaphor suggests that the failures in the design and creativity process remain concealed [20]. By clearly describing design methods and processes, it becomes possible to unveil the designers' private thinking and clarify the process. This allows other stakeholders to participate more consciously and rationally. These characteristics have a significant influence on designers, enabling them to adapt their working methods and thinking styles, with the Double Diamond model serving as a valuable reference [21].

Experienced designers often apply additional constraints during the solution generation phase, aiming to refine the solution space and facilitate the generation of viable concepts. Throughout the design process, design experts may modify goals and adjust constraints as they gain a deeper understanding of the problem and progress in defining the solution. Despite these changes, designers strive to maintain their major solution concept for as long as possible. The purpose of these adjustments is to overcome challenges that emerge during the design process [19].

2.2 Design Reasoning

In the exploration of the core of 'design thinking', Kees Dorst provides a comprehensive analysis of "design reasoning patterns" and the concept of "frame" through the establishment of formal logic (see Fig. 2). Within the realm of sciences, including design expertise, inductive reasoning serves as a foundation for 'discovery', while deductive reasoning plays a crucial role in 'justification'. These two forms of analytical reasoning empower us to predict and explain phenomena in the world [22].

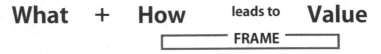

Fig. 2. The basic reasoning patterns [22].

In terms of creating value, basic reasoning pattern includes two forms of abduction. The first form is commonly linked to conventional problem solving. In this method, designers only know about both the aspired value and the 'how'—a 'working principle' that guides design team towards achieving the goal. However, what remains unclear is the 'what' that provides definition to both the problem and the potential solution space in which we seek answers. The challenge in the second form lies in determining 'what' to create, without a known or predetermined 'working principle' to rely on for attaining the aspired value. This necessitates the simultaneous development of a 'working principle' and objective (that is, 'what'). Addressing the presence of two 'unknowns' in the equation leads to design practices that differ significantly from conventional problem solving (just the first form). As the challenge in the second form is most closely tied to design and represents the realm of open and complex problems for which design teams seek creative solutions [22].

Seasoned design teams, in contrast to novice designers who tend to generate proposals randomly, possess the ability to effectively utilize a well-refined "frame" to tackle the intricate and creative challenge of generating both the "what" and the "how." The concept of a "frame" encompasses a highly complex set of statements that includes the specific perception of a problem situation, the adoption of specific concepts to describe the situation, and the application of a "working principle" that serves as the foundation for a solution [22]. Within the logical framework, framing plays a pivotal role in design abduction. This is because the most logical approach to addressing a design problem involves working backward, starting from the only "known" element in the equation, which is the desired value, and subsequently adopting or developing a novel frame to address the problem [23].

2.3 Solution Generation with AI

In the realm of applying AI software to generate design solutions, certain research findings underscore the influence of black boxes and frames. Experienced designers possess the ability to navigate the initial stages, such as concept development, by drawing upon their intuition or past experiences to identify the most promising frames to follow. Once an AI system is introduced, the designer's discernment can be incorporated into the system through an interactive approach, whereby the system presents potential solutions to the designer for evaluation. As a result, designers play a pivotal role in assessing the value of the generated designs and removing subpar designs from the solution space. [10, 24]. Recently, the significance of large-scale models in generative AI has been on the rise, owing to their ability to enhance intent extraction and thereby improve the quality of generated solutions. As data and the sizes of models continue to expand, the range of patterns and information that models can learn becomes more comprehensive and closer to reality. This progress contributes to the production of more realistic and high-quality content [25].

AI technology has found application in the field of fashion design, primarily by mimicking existing creative works and carrying out assigned tasks [26, 27]. However, designers who seek to break free from conventional frames continue to infuse their embodied knowledge into the creation and realization of processes and artifacts. Nevertheless, AI has not fully assimilated the entirety of a designer's work and expertise. An obstacle in conducting constructive research on AI-assisted fashion lies in oversimplifying the complexity of fashion design and the absence of thorough critical examination [27].

Text-to-image generative AI has gained significant momentum in various design disciplines, including visual design [28–31], clothing design [26], and architectural imagery and materials [32–34]. This emerging field of language-based design approaches holds the potential to revolutionize end-to-end design environments and enhance our understanding of the physical phenomena that intersect with human language and creativity [32]. When applying a leading text-to-image AI engine such as Midjourney, the process of refining the prompt can be elaborated into four steps: Initial prompt, prompt adjustment, style refinement, and variation selection [29]. Multiple research findings suggest that designers cannot realistically produce a substantial amount of AI-generated content on their own, even with sufficient time allocated to a specific design project or within design courses [10, 30]. Furthermore, generative AI is capable of generating a wide array of images for different concepts, which proves advantageous for a generative system. However, this diversity also results in a decrease in recognition accuracy due to the multitude of possible outcomes [35].

3   Method

3.1   Idea Generation with Midjourney

This study aims to investigate the impact of generative AI on the application of both conventional frames and unexplored frames by utilizing the image generation process with Midjourney. We hypothesize that the existing subcategories of vehicles can be considered as known conventional frames, while defining ambiguous vehicle types, such as 'vehicle,' as new frames that require careful redefinition of component attributes. We believe that ambiguous subcategory definitions can offer more conceptual ambiguity and flexibility but also entail greater risks, similar to real-world innovative design practices. Conversely, explicit subcategory definitions may not carry the same level of risk in design thinking but may compromise creativity and innovativeness. In this study, we employ a higher word count to generate AI design proposals. Table 1 below provides a summary of all prompts for Midjourney V4 (see the appendix for full prompts).

Table 1. Six sets of prompt conditions for Midjourney V4.

No.	Design Frame (defined subcategory or additional reference)	Word Count of prompts
1	electric downhill bikes (defined subcategory)	209 words
2	light-duty personal two-wheeled transportation facility (none)	209 words
3	light-duty personal two-wheeled transportation facility (none)	211 words
4	personal electric off-road vehicles (Indirect reference to motorcycle)	139 words
5	personal electric off-road two-wheel vehicles (Indirect reference to downhill bicycle)	240 words
6	Urban vehicle for both land and air use (Indirect reference to downhill bicycle)	123 words

In the first prompt set, electric downhill bikes were designated as the 'frame' in the design thinking pattern [22]. Apart from specifying the material, the main structures were configured to have a diamond cross-shaped section. Moreover, deliberate adjustments were made to significantly increase the length and diameter of the fork, as well as the rim of the wheel. This was done to observe whether Midjourney could accommodate these new variables introduced to the conventional frame in response to potential design variations that may arise in practice (see Fig. 3).

Fig. 3. The first set of Midjourney-generated images for electric downhill bikes.

In the second set of prompts, its 'conventional frame' was intentionally defined as a specific and complex model, namely 'a light-duty personal two-wheeled armored transportation facility.' Following that, each component of the vehicle's mainframe was defined separately, exploring the concept of the 'new frame' within the design thinking framework, and providing detailed descriptions of each component. However, the generated results showed significant deviations from the intended design (see Fig. 4).

Fig. 4. The second set of Midjourney-generated images for light-duty transportation facility.

The specific and complex frame from the second set of prompts was introduced, with some simplifications, into the third set of prompts. In a highly similar prompts, existing conventional frames, such as "like a two-wheel configuration for a motorcycle," were used as prompts to guide Midjourney. However, the generated results still exhibited significant differences from the configuration of a motorcycle (see Fig. 5).

Fig. 5. The third set of Midjourney-generated images for light-duty transportation facility.

In the subsequent attempts, the design framework was defined as "personal electric off-road vehicles." The new design frame was sought by reconfiguring the skeleton, taking cues from the arrangement of two-wheeled motorcycles. Additionally, the outer contour, when viewed from a side perspective, was described as a compressed parallelogram. However, the resulting outcome leaned towards a four-wheel structure, resembling a taller go-kart (see Fig. 6).

Fig. 6. The 4th set of Midjourney-generated images for personal off-road vehicles.

In the fifth set of prompts, the setting of the design frame was nearly identical to the design intent of the previous generated outcome. However, there was an additional clarification that the tire ratio resembled that of a downhill bicycle, and specific cross-sectional shapes were specified for the front and rear frames. With these new prompts in place, the generated results surprisingly leaned towards meeting the intended values conveyed by the design intent (see Fig. 7).

Fig. 7. The 5th set of Midjourney-generated images for personal off-road vehicles.

In the final set of prompts, the design frame was defined as an urban vehicle suitable for both land and air transportation, drawing inspiration from the arrangement of a downhill bike. Additionally, Midjourney was guided to reference the Ducati motorcycle for the redesign of the mainframe. Ultimately, although the generated results exhibited a sense of design, there was still a significant disparity compared to the intended content suggested by the design intent (see Fig. 8).

3.2 Expert Evaluation

This study involved the participation of ten bicycle or motorcycle design experts with an academic background in industrial design. They were invited to evaluate and examine the six sets of Midjourney-generated outcomes, under reference to English prompts and their traditional Chinese translations. The 11-point Likert scale (ranging from 0 to 10, where 0 represents the least and 10 represents the most) was utilized to allow the design experts to subjectively assess these results in terms of prompt implementation, design creativity, and practical feasibility. Additionally, these ten experts provided qualitative descriptions for three aspects of the outcomes to articulate their professional insights. Table 2 below presents the profile of the design experts who participated in the evaluation process.

48   S.-H. Cheng

Fig. 8. The 6th set of Midjourney-generated images for urban vehicles.

Table 2. Profile of participating design experts.

No.	Gender	Industry	Years of experience	Location	Level of education
P1	Man	Bicycle	14	Central Taiwan	Masters
P2	Man	Bicycle	7	Central Taiwan	Masters
P3	Man	Bicycle	3	Central Taiwan	Bachelors
P4	Man	Bicycle	2	Central Taiwan	Bachelors
P5	Man	Bicycle	1	Central Taiwan	Bachelors
P6	Man	Bicycle	1	Central Taiwan	Bachelors
P7	Woman	Motorcycle	1	Southern Taiwan	Masters
P8	Man	Motorcycle	9	Southern Taiwan	Masters
P9	Man	Motorcycle	4	Northern Taiwan	Masters
P10	Man	Motorcycle	2	Northern Taiwan	PhD

4   Data Analysis

4.1   Quantitative Analysis

After conducting descriptive statistical analysis on the evaluation data from design experts, it is evident that the generated results from the first and fifth prompt sets achieved the highest scores in all three aspects. Both sets either directly designated downhill bikes as the conventional design frame or referred to their configurations. On the other hand, the generated results from prompts where vehicle subcategories were not mentioned at all (second and third sets) received the lowest scores in all three aspects (see Fig. 7). Despite the slightly higher scores in the first and fifth prompt sets (averaging around 5), their scores in terms of feasibility remained significantly low. The results of ANOVA indicated significant differences in prompt implementation (F [5, 59] = 2.443, p = .046) and creativity (F [5, 59] = 3.246, p = .012). Further, the post-hoc tests (Student-Newman-Keuls) for prompt implementation revealed a significant difference, with the fifth prompt set (5.4) scoring significantly higher than the second prompt set (2.1). In terms of creativity, the post-hoc test (Student-Newman-Keuls) indicated that both the first (5.4) and fifth (5.2) prompt sets scored significantly higher than the second prompt set (2.3) (Fig. 9).

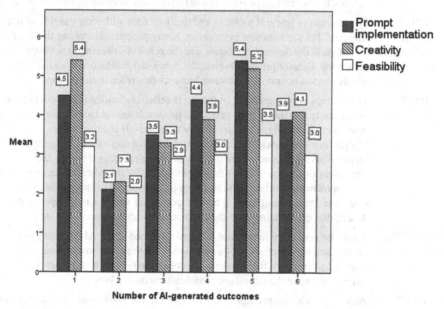

Fig. 9. Average evaluation scores of Midjourney-generated ideas by design experts.

4.2 Qualitative Reasoning

Based on the results of the quantitative analysis, this study extends its examination to include the qualitative assessment provided by design experts for the first, second, and fifth outcomes along with their respective prompts. The summary of the qualitative assessment regarding the implementation of prompts can be found in Table 2. Table 3 presents the key qualitative assessment focusing on creativity. Additionally, Table 4 specifically addresses the qualitative assessment regarding feasibility (Table 5).

Table 3. Key qualitative assessment regarding prompt implementation.

No.	Expert/Set	Comments
1	P1/1st:	The prompts show quite a few understandings of transportation design, but important configurations like the shock absorber system, electronic control system, and brake system are missing or not described in detail. Additionally, downhill bikes should have pedals. The prompts are best to be complete and professionally evaluated. AI needs continuous learning. The more accurate the prompts for generation, the more useful it will be. If the prompts are not perfect, the advantage of AI is just to provide quick visual design proposals
2	P2/1st:	The features of integral molding and the front fork with long travel have been achieved, but the structure is incorrect. Many prompts describing the details do not yield the desired outcomes, and the results of the rim do not align with the prompts' descriptions. Overall, the generated results do not exhibit the advancements beyond the existing frame as described in the prompts
3	P4/2nd:	The prompt implementation in this set is relatively inadequate. Both in terms of materials and frames, the generated proposals are far from being professional and aligned with industry standards. It is evident that Midjourney overlooks numerous prompts, with a majority of the generated ideas revolving around elements such as tires, derivative designs, and unconventional concepts. While the prompts offer the potential for expanded development possibilities, the resulting outputs deviate from the intended direction. Perhaps imposing a broader constraint within a more open-ended description could help guide the conceptual direction more effectively
4	P10/2nd:	It may be necessary to provide repeated guidance to the AI regarding the correct and incorrect areas of generation. Currently, Midjourney users are required to compare the disparities between the prompt and the generated output and make the necessary modifications themselves
5	P8/5th:	Among the various prompts, only the main frame's diamond-shaped titanium alloy characteristics and the configuration of two wheels were generated

Table 4. Key qualitative assessment regarding creativity.

No.	Expert/Set	Comments
1	P1/1st:	Creativity often arises from quick, efficient, and out-of-the-box thinking, requiring rapid ideation and generation. AI, with its high-quality realistic generation, offers impressive visual results. Considering the limited time available to professionals in a single day, it would be nearly impossible to accomplish any proposals within this design set. Therefore, AI serves as an excellent tool in this regard
2	P7/1st:	AI can assist designers in breaking their personal design preferences and frames. For instance, when developing motorcycle concepts, I personally lean towards geometric and minimalist styles. However, this set of generated images provide an opportunity for me to imagine and explore an alternative aesthetic, allowing me to venture into new territories. These AI-generated images serve as a suitable reference foundation that aligns with the intended theme
3	P2/2nd:	Once the product framework is flawed, creativity becomes non-existent
4	P4/2nd:	The main outline and proportions of the classic alien features, although directly referenced, are presented with acceptable accuracy, making them appreciable and a valuable source of inspiration. However, in terms of the creative aspect of the entire set of results, it appears that Midjourney diverges excessively, possibly due to a lack of clarity regarding the intended direction of generation. As a result, the concepts deviate from the intended theme and fail to produce the stunning effects anticipated within the given context
5	P4/5th:	This set of generated results can serve as a reference for designers during the process of discover and divergent thinking. If it can consistently reach such a level, could the key image representing the designer's intent be incorporated to enable Midjourney to achieve a stable divergence in style?

Table 5. Key qualitative assessment regarding feasibility.

No.	Expert/Set	Comments
1	P1/1st:	This set of generated results resembles more of a conceptual proposal. The limited compatibility of parts for mass production arises due to the fixed seat height determined by the frame geometry. Based on the result images and prompts, it can be inferred that the development cost would be prohibitively expensive. There is a lack of clarity regarding the information on the system, structure, and suspension system, and it is uncertain whether there are any patent issues involved
2	P2/1st:	Frame geometry is a crucial aspect in bicycle design, and the selection of key components also significantly impacts the overall performance. Therefore, any proposal that deviates from these two key factors is essentially deemed unreasonable
3	P4/1st:	Based on the generated results, it is evident that Midjourney did not adequately consider crucial factors such as user experience and the feasibility of materials, processes, and structure. This oversight becomes apparent when examining the absence of shock absorbers and the limited ability of the rear swingarm to rotate. Additionally, the length of the front fork travel raises concerns about its reasonableness
4	P10/1st:	If the vehicle frame is molded using carbon-fiber-reinforced plastics and divided into left and right pieces, followed by post-processing and assembly, it is indeed possible to bring this conceptual design into production. However, it is worth considering the necessity of such high-cost manufacturing and exploring ways to reduce the complexity of the manufacturing process in advance. These aspects can be further elaborated upon in the prompts."
5	P2/2nd:	If the product framework and component features are inadequate, there is no need for further discussion
6	P8/2nd:	It seems that the language model and computational model did not communicate effectively
7	P6/5th:	A vehicle frame designed by mimicking the structure of biological skeletons may be producible through metal 3D printing, but a single swingarm suspension design may not be feasible for off-road vehicles

5 Discussion and Conclusion

In the realm of generative AI research, numerous design studies have been conducted. However, this study aims to delve into the core of design thinking (see Fig. 2) and explore the impact of such applications on the logical framework of design. Even before the significant advancements in generative AI, designers already faced two types of working principles: conventional problem solving, which is the most common approach, and the relatively uncommon practice of simultaneously exploring new principles. The test results of this study indicate that utilizing text-to-image generative AI to generate design proposals within a conventional frame, where prompts directly or indirectly refer to specific existing subcategories of vehicles, yielded higher scores in prompt implementation, design creativity, and practical feasibility. However, the expert evaluation revealed that the rate in prompt implementation was not sufficiently high due to the generated outputs not consistently including the key components described in the prompts. Regarding design creativity, while one expert (P1) emphasized that creativity often stems from quick, efficient, and out-of-the-box thinking, another expert (P2) argued that discussing creativity is irrelevant in an incorrect framework. On the other hand, when generating design proposals by deliberately evading the conventional design frame and instead establishing a new design framework through the description of component attributes, the aforementioned analysis indicated lower scores in all aspects. However, during the process of establishing the new working principle, indirectly referring to the existing subcategories of vehicles led to improvements in all three aspects. Nevertheless, in terms of practical feasibility, all generated outputs received low scores, with no significant differences between them. This study concludes that the design expert's viewpoint (P2), stating that any proposal deviating from the frame geometry and key components is essentially considered unreasonable, is worth pondering. This also suggests that regardless of the chosen working principle, Midjourney V4 is only suitable for enhancing divergent thinking in a specific frame.

In the context of design thinking, it is common for designers and design researchers to follow a conventional approach, where they create designs based on known working principles and within specific value creation scenarios. This conventional frame can be considered a type of "closed" problem solving that design practitioners across different fields regularly employ [22]. In essence, the introduction of text-to-image generative AI may present a notable challenge to these practitioners [10]. However, as seen in the design industry, designers who plan to incorporate text-to-image generative AI in their work may face significant and potentially paradoxical obstacles when their conventional problem-solving methods prove insufficient [22].

This study utilized design thinking principles to examine the influence of generative AI on design practice. The current findings suggest promising potential for future investigations and the expansion of the specific application of design theory. However, this study is limited by challenges in accurately commanding design terminology in prompt phrasing, the inadequate quantity of AI-generated outputs for comprehensive testing, and the lack of diversity in the generated outcomes. Consequently, future efforts will primarily concentrate on addressing these limitations as key areas of focus.

Acknowledgments. This research was funded by the National Science and Technology Council of Taiwan grant number NSTC 111-2410-H-011-042.

Conflicts of Interest. The author declared no potential conflicts of interest with respect to the research, authorship, and/or publication of this article.

Appendix (Full Prompts for Midjourney V4)

No.	Full prompts
1	A futuristic electric downhill bike. The main frame, including the top tube, down tube, and seat tube, is made of carbon fiber reinforced resin composite made by Integral molding. The surface has the texture of carbon fiber. The sections of these main structures are diamond cross-shaped. The rest of the skeleton, including the seat stay, chain stay, fork, stem, and handlebar are all made of titanium, showing a titanium texture. There are obvious joints at the junction of the main frame and the rest of the frame, and these joints are circular tubes and show a red chrome-plated metal texture. Its fork is twice the length and twice the diameter of the general downhill bicycle fork. The spokes of the two wheels present a radial shape of generative design and present a golden polished texture. The rim of the wheel is three times larger than the normal one, presenting fog black. The surface of the tire is A three-dimensional diamond-shaped shape forming a derivative design. The battery box is a long cuboid, bright orange, and is placed under the seat cushion. A small plane extends horizontally from the chainstay. The rear shock absorber connects the main frame and seat stay, and displays a super bright white titanium metal texture
2	A light-duty personal two-wheeled armored transportation facility completed by metal 3D printing. It has two wheels, every 26 inches in diameter, with one wheel at the front of the facility and the other wheel at the rear. The wheels are equipped with widened and thickened polymer material tires, and the surface of the tires is combined with the metal long cleats of football shoes. The wheels have no spokes. The mainframe of this two-wheeled transportation facility is a four-bar linkage quasi-parallelogram hollow shape completed by generative design, and it presents a bionic shape and an alien creature-style shape. This mainframe grows vine-like strands upwards and forms the cushion support. The shape of the seat cushion is similar to that of F-117 stealth aircraft. And a paper airplane-like geometric generative design extends from the rear of the seat cushion. The handle for control is designed between the paper airplane geometric generative shape and the seat cushion, and the shape of the handle is similar to the safety device of a roller coaster. The electric motor and battery are placed between the mainframe, which is bright red leather. And the seat cushion is made of natural cowhide material and color, and the mainframe presents the matte color of ultra-bright titanium metal
3	A light-duty personal two-wheeled transportation facility. It has two wheels, every 26 inches in diameter, with one wheel at the front of the facility and the other wheel at the rear. It's like a two-wheel configuration for a motorcycle. The wheels are equipped with widened and thickened polymer material tires, and the surface of the tires is combined with the metal long cleats of football shoes. The wheels have no spokes. The mainframe of this two-wheeled transportation facility is a four-bar linkage quasi-parallelogram hollow shape completed by generative design, and it presents a bionic shape and an alien creature-style shape. This mainframe grows vine-like strands upwards and forms the cushion support. The shape of the seat cushion is similar to that of F-117 stealth aircraft. And a paper airplane-like geometric generative design extends from the rear of the seat cushion. The handle for control is designed between the paper airplane geometric generative shape and the seat cushion, and the shape of the handle is similar to the safety device of a roller coaster. The electric motor and battery are placed between the mainframe, which is bright red leather. And the seat cushion is made of natural cowhide material and color, and the mainframe presents the matte color of ultra-bright titanium metal

(continued)

(*continued*)

No.	Full prompts
4	A new generation of personal electric off-road vehicles, with a two-wheel configuration like a motorcycle, but with the skeleton removed for redesign. The redesigned frame consists of the main frame and the front and rear subframes connecting the two tires. The main frame is forged from titanium alloy, showing bright white titanium metal reflections and brushed lines along the direction. From the side view of the car, the outer contour is similar to a parallelogram compressed towards the front of the car. The tube diameter of the front frame is made of carbon fiber material and surface texture, and the tube diameter is slender. The rear frame is made of titanium tubes with orange chrome graduated dots. In the center of the car there is a light full-grain top cowhide leather cushion. The tire shape is violent and grippy
5	A new generation of personal electric off-road two-wheel vehicles, the tire ratio is like a downhill bicycle with a two-wheel configuration, but the skeleton is deleted to redesign. The redesigned frame consists of the main frame and the front and rear subframes connecting the two tires. The main frame is forged from titanium alloy. The cross-section is flat on the left and right and elongated on the top and bottom. The surface presents the reflection of medium gray titanium metal and the brushed texture of mustard green along the direction. From the side view of the car, the outer outline of the main frame is similar to a parallelogram compressed towards the front of the car. The quadrilateral is connected by many diamond shapes of different sizes, making the main frame present a generative design style. The pipe diameter of the front frame is made of carbon fiber material and the surface texture of matte black carbon fiber. The pipe diameter is slender and the cross section of the pipe diameter is T-shaped. The rear frame is made of titanium tube diameter, with a cross-shaped and thick cross-section, and orange chrome-plated gradient shapes of large and small dots on the surface. Luxurious and stylish light-colored full-grain top-grade cowhide cushions are installed in the center of the car, and the control handle has a futuristic sense of technology. The tire shape is violent and grippy, like the Martian landing craft style
6	Urban vehicle for both land and air use. It has two wheels, and the tire configuration is the same as that of a downhill bike. The tires have no spokes, the rims are made of glossy carbon fiber, and the tires are filled with tapered rubber kit. The mainframe of this vehicle is redesigned, using the outside obvious diamond frame similar to the Ducati frame model as a unit, and performing a generative design to complete the overall frame. The grips are chunky triathlon grips in bright orange chrome. The seat cushion is made of full cowhide and white thick stitching. The whole car has no pedals, but is driven by electricity, and the battery box is made of bright white titanium metal

References

1. Boymamatovich, S.M.: Exploring the benefits and future of artificial intelligence. Central Asian J. Theor. Appl. Sci. **4**(3), 108–113 (2023)
2. Feuerriegel, S., Hartmann, J., Janiesch, C., Zschech, P.: Generative AI (2023). https://ssrn.com/abstract=4443189
3. Sachs, G.: Generative AI could raise global GDP by 7%, https://www.goldmansachs.com/insights/pages/generative-ai-could-raise-global-gdp-by-7-percent.html (2023). Last accessed 20 June 2023

4. Hwang, G.J., Chen, N.S.: Editorial position paper: exploring the potential of generative artificial intelligence in education: applications, challenges, and future research directions. Educ. Technol. Soc. **26**(2) (2023). https://doi.org/10.30191/ETS.202304_26(2).0014

5. Huang, K., et al.: Artificial intelligence foundation for therapeutic science. Nat. Chem. Biol. **18**(10), 1033–1036 (2022)

6. Nesterenko, V., Olefirenko, O.: The impact of AI development on the development of marketing communications. Market. Manag. Innov. **14**(1), 169–181 (2023). https://doi.org/10.21272/mmi.2023.1-15

7. Thurzo, A., Strunga, M., Urban, R., Surovková, J., Afrashtehfar, K.I.: Impact of artificial intelligence on dental education: a review and guide for curriculum update. Educ. Sci. **13**(2), 150 (2023). https://doi.org/10.3390/educsci13020150

8. Wang, X., Wang, D., Chen, L., Lin, Y.: Building Transportation Foundation Model via Generative Graph Transformer. arXiv preprint arXiv:2305.14826 (2023)

9. Stark, L., Crawford, K.: The work of art in the age of artificial intelligence: what artists can teach us about the ethics of data practice. Surveill. Soc. **17**(3/4), 442–455 (2019)

10. Fang, Y.M.: The role of generative ai in industrial design: enhancing the design process and learning. In: IEEE conference proceedings: 2023 9th International Conference on Applied System Innovation (ICASI). Chiba, Japan on 21–25 Apr 2023

11. Jaruga-Rozdolska, A.: Artificial intelligence as part of future practices in the architect's work: MidJourney generative tool as part of a process of creating an architectural form. Architectus **3**(71), 95–104 (2022)

12. Vartiainen, H., Tedre, M.: Using artificial intelligence in craft education: crafting with text-to-image generative models. Dig. Creativity **34**(1), 1–21 (2023)

13. Yan, H., et al.: Toward intelligent design: an AI-based fashion designer using generative adversarial networks aided by sketch and rendering generators. IEEE Trans. Multimedia **25**, 2323–2338 (2023). https://doi.org/10.1109/TMM.2022.3146010

14. Brookfield, J., Liu, R.J., Paul MacDuffie, J.: Taiwan's bicycle industry A-Team battles Chinese competition with innovation and cooperation. Strategy Leadersh. **36**(1), 14–19 (2008)

15. Chu, W.W.: Causes of growth: a study of Taiwan's bicycle industry. Camb. J. Econ. **21**(1), 55–72 (1997)

16. Howard, T.J., Culley, S.J., Dekoninck, E.: Describing the creative design process by the integration of engineering design and cognitive psychology literature. Des. Stud. **29**(2), 160–180 (2008)

17. Design council: The Double Diamond. https://www.designcouncil.org.uk/our-resources/the-double-diamond/. Last accessed 15 June 2023

18. Design council: History of the Double Diamond. https://www.designcouncil.org.uk/our-resources/the-double-diamond/history-of-the-double-diamond/. Last accessed 15 June 2023

19. Cross, N.: Research in design thinking. In: Cross, N., Dorst, K., Roozenburg, N. (eds.) Research in Design Thinking, pp. 3–10. Delft University Press, Delft (1992)

20. Gulari, M.N.: Metaphors in design: how we think of design expertise. J. Res. Pract. **11**(2), 8 (2015)

21. Kochanowska, M., Gagliardi, W.R.: The double diamond model: in pursuit of simplicity and flexibility. In: Raposo, D., Neves, J., Silva, J. (eds.) Perspectives on Design II: Research, Education and Practice, pp. 19–32. Springer, Switzerland (2022)

22. Dorst, K.: The core of 'design thinking' and its application. Des. Stud. **32**(6), 521–532 (2011)

23. Dorst, K.: Frame innovation: Create New Thinking by Design. The MIT Press (2015)

24. Kurtoglu, T., Swantner, A., Campbell, M.I.: Automating the conceptual design process: "From black box to component selection." AI EDAM **24**(1), 49–62 (2010)

25. Cao, Y., et al.: A comprehensive survey of AI-generated content (AIGC): a history of generative AI from GAN to ChatGPT. J. ACM **37**(4), 111 (2018)

26. Al-Qatari, D.A.Q., Abu Rady, A.J.: A comparative analytical study of the use of artificial intelligence (AI) tools in generating various designs for women's clothing. Int. Des. J. **13**(2), 363–380 (2023)
27. Särmäkari, N., Vänskä, A.: 'Just hit a button!'–fashion 4.0 designers as cyborgs, experimenting and designing with generative algorithms. Int. J. Fashion Des. Technol. Educ. **15**(2), 211–220 (2022)
28. Abrahamsen, N., Yao, J.: Inventing painting styles through natural inspiration. arXiv preprint arXiv:2305.12015 (2023)
29. Ruskov, M.: Grimm in Wonderland: Prompt Engineering with Midjourney to Illustrate Fairytales. arXiv preprint arXiv:2302.08961 (2023)
30. Mikkonen, J.: Advent of GAN: How does a generative AI create a moodboard? In: Holmlid, S., et al. (eds.) Nordes 2023: This Space Intentionally Left Blank, 12–14 June, Linköping University, Norrköping, Sweden (2023)
31. Shan, S., Cryan, J., Wenger, E., Zheng, H., Hanocka, R., Zhao, B.Y.: Glaze: Protecting artists from style mimicry by text-to-image models. arXiv preprint arXiv:2302.04222 (2023)
32. Hsu, Y.C., Yang, Z., Buehler, M.J.: Generative design, manufacturing, and molecular modeling of 3D architected materials based on natural language input. APL Mater. **10**(4), 041107 (2022)
33. Radhakrishnan, A.M.: Is midjourney-AI the new anti-hero of architectural imagery & creativity? GSJ **11**(1), 94–104 (2023)
34. Paananen, V., Oppenlaender, J., Visuri, A.: Using Text-to-Image Generation for Architectural Design Ideation. arXiv preprint arXiv:2304.10182 (2023)
35. Stöckl, A.: Evaluating a Synthetic Image Dataset Generated with Stable Diffusion. arXiv preprint arXiv:2211.01777 (2022)
36. Cammer, M.: Too bad to be fraud, Midjourney has yet to embark in science. bioRxiv, 2023-01 (2023)

Comparison of Supervised Techniques of Artificial Intelligence in the Prediction of Cardiovascular Diseases

Z. Comas-Gonzalez[1,2]([✉]) [iD], J. Mardini-Bovea[1] [iD], D. Salcedo[1] [iD], and E. De-la-Hoz-Franco[1] [iD]

[1] Universidad de la Costa, Calle 58 No. 55–66, Barranquilla, Colombia
{zcomas1,jmardini,dsalcedo2,edelahoz}@cuc.edu.co
[2] Universidad de Granada, Av. del Hospicio, 1, 18071 Granada, Spain
https://www.cuc.edu.co

Abstract. Cardiovascular disease is the main cause of mortality world-wide, its early prediction and early diagnosis are fundamental for patients with this mortal illness. Cardiovascular disease is a real threat for the Health Systems worldwide, mainly because it has become the diagnosis that claim a significant number of lives around the world. Currently, there is a growing need from health entities to integrate the use of technology. Cardiovascular disease identification systems allow the identification of diseases associated with the heart, allowing the early identification of Cardiovascular Diseases (CVD) for an improvement in the quality of life of patients.

According to the above, the predictive models of CVD have become a common research field, where the implementation of feature selection techniques and models based on artificial intelligence provide the possibility of identifying, in advance, the trend of patients who may suffer from a disease associated with the heart.

Therefore, this paper proposes the use of feature selection techniques (Information Gain) with the variation of artificial intelligence techniques, such as neural networks (Som, Ghsom), decision rules (ID3, J48) and Bayesian networks (Bayes net, Naive Bayes) with the purpose of identifying the hybrid model for the identification of cardiovascular diseases.

It was used the data set "Heart Cleveland Disease Data Set" with the same test environment for all the cases, in order to establish which of the mentioned techniques achieves the higher value of the accuracy metric when it comes to identify patients with heart disease. For the development of the tests, 10-fold Cross-Validation was used as a data classification method and 91.3% of the accuracy was obtained under the hybridization of the selection technique "information gain" with the training technique J48.

Keywords: Artificial intelligence · Cardiovascular disease · Multimodal physiological measures

This study is supported by the Colombian Government through Minciencias grant No. 860 International Studies for Doctorate and the Bicentennial Doctoral Excellence Scholarship Program.

© The Author(s), under exclusive license to Springer Nature Switzerland AG 2023
H. Degen et al. (Eds.): HCII 2023, LNCS 14059, pp. 58–68, 2023.
https://doi.org/10.1007/978-3-031-48057-7_4

1 Introduction

The 42% of deaths from cardiovascular diseases are related to ischemic heart disease, and 34% to cerebrovascular diseases. It is estimated that in 2015 17.7 million people died from this cause, which represents 31% of the deaths registered worldwide.

According to reports from the World Health Organization (WHO) and the National Health Organization (ONS), cardiovascular diseases along with cancer, diabetes and Chronic lung are identified increasing diseases, cataloging them as the main causes of death worldwide, being the cardiovascular one the most relevant cause.

Nowadays, there is a growing need from health entities to integrate the use of technology to their processes. The Cardiovascular disease identifier (CDI) facilitate the identification of early heart diseases that can be analyzed with technology, improving the life of patients.

Moreover, there are data set for cardiovascular diseases. It is important to identify the clinical features that will take part in the evaluation process, in order to make a real model related to daily lives; and to select the techniques that are going to be implemented like preprocessing, characteristic features, classification and post classification.

The purpose of this paper is to make a comparison of supervised techniques of artificial intelligence that were applied to a model in order to predict cardio-vascular diseases. For this study, it was selected the Heart Disease Cleveland Data set. This document is composed by six sections, the first one is related to introduction; Sect. 2 exposes previous work according to the study; Sect. 3 details some definitions and important works; Sect. 4 describes the methodology developed; Sect. 5 explains the conclusions and Sect. 6 details the conclusions and future work.

2 Related Work

The literature review evidenced that some models analyze specific approaches from the technological view, like Machine Learning techniques, [1], comparative studies of cardiovascular risk techniques [2, 3], cardiovascular monitoring system [4]. Other versions, although not exhaustive, are limited to evaluate classification techniques in terms of precision for the prediction of cardiovascular disease via data set [5–7]. However, no evidence was found related to perform a comparative study implementing a model that hybridizes any selection technique with a training technique. In [8], it is implemented computer-assisted techniques to provide a fast and accurate tool to identify a patient's ECG signals. Diagnostic techniques are compared, using data preprocessing, feature engineering, classification and application.

In [9] an end-to-end model is performed by integrating feature extraction and classification into learning algorithms, which not only simplifies the data analysis process, but also shows a good-level evaluated accuracy.

In [10], an extraction of multivariate clinical characteristics of ACS patients recorded in a database registry was implemented. The author and used machine learning algorithms to develop several models with measurable performance to predict heart attacks in patients.

3 Machine Learning Techniques for Classification

3.1 Artificial Neural Networks

According to … Artificial neural networks attempt to capture the essence of biological processes and apply them to new computational models. The artificial neuron is a simplified model of a biological neuron. The interconnection between neurons decides the flow of information in the network and together with the weights and output functions of each neuron define the global behavior of the artificial neural network. It means that neural networks are made up of a large number of linear and non-linear computational elements (neurons) that are complexly interrelated and organized in layers.

Self-Organizing Map Neural Networks. It is an efficient unsupervised neural algorithm that allows the projection of data from a multidimensional space, in a two-dimensional grid called "map", qualitatively preserving the topology of the original set. In 1982, the author T. Kohonen presented a network model called self-organizing maps or SOM. The purpose was to demonstrate that an external stimulus (input) is capable to force the formation of maps, assuming a given structure and a functional description. According to (…) the most important characteristic of the SOM is that it learns to classify the data throughout an unsupervised learning algorithm. A SOM learns to classify the training data without any type of external control.

Growing Hierarchical Self Organizing Maps Neuronal Networks. According to [11], Growing Hierarchical Self Organizing Maps Neuronal Networks or GHSOM is a hierarchical and dynamic structure, developed to overcome the weaknesses and problems that SOM presents. The GHSOM structure consists of multiple layers made up of several independent SOMs whose number and size are determined during the training phase. The adaptation growth process is controlled by two parameters that determine the depth of the hierarchy and the breadth of each map. Therefore, these two parameters are the only ones that have to be initially set in GHSOM. The adaptation growth process is controlled by two parameters that determine the depth of this type of maps are born as an improved version of the SOM architecture. According to [12] there are two purposes for the GHSOM architecture:

- SOM has a fixed network architecture, which means that the number of units of use as well as the distribution of the units have to be determined before the training.
- Input data that are naturally hierarchical should be represented in a hierarchical structure for the clarity of its representation. GHSOM uses a hierarchical, multi-layered structure, where each layer is made up of a number of independent SOMs. Only a SOM is used in the first layer of the hierarchy.

For every unit on the map, a SOM could be added to the next layer of the hierarchy. This principle is repeated with the third level of the map and the other layers of the GHSOM, as shown in Fig. 1.

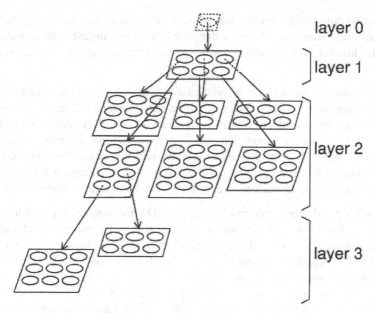

Fig. 1. Structure of a GHSOM network

3.2 Bayesian Networks

Bayesian logic was created by the mathematician Thomas Bayes in 1763. It is based on statistics and conditional probabilities to predict the future. It is an unsupervised technique of data classification. Bayesian statistical principles have been useful for the early identification of Cardiovascular Diseases. The result of the application of Bayesian systems is presented in the form of conditional probability relations, instead of rules or signatures. In conclusion, Bayesian Networks are powerful tools as decision models and reasoning under uncertainty.

Naive Bayes. According to [11] it is a descriptive and predictive classification technique based on the analysis probability theory by T. Bayes [13]. This theory assumes an asymptotically infinite sample size and statistical independence among independent variables, referring with it to attributes, not the class. With these conditions, the probability distributions of each class can be calculated to establish the relationship between the attributes (independent variables) and the class (dependent variable).

3.3 Decision Rules

Supervised learning methods based on decision trees are one of the most popular methods in the Artificial Intelligence field, to deal with the classification problem (…). A classification tree is made up of nodes, branches, and leaves. Each node represents a decision about the values of a particular attribute. The first node in the tree is known as the root node. Finally there are the terminal nodes or leaves in which a decision is made about the class to assign. Thus, when classifying a new case, the values of the attributes will have to be compared with the decisions made in the nodes, following the branch that matches said values in each test or decision. A terminal or leaf node is reached that predicts the class for the case in question. A decision tree can also be viewed as a set of if-then rules.

ID3. Each internal node of the tree contains a decision on one of the attributes, whose value will depend on the path to follow to classify an example, and each leaf contains a class label. Thus, the classification of an example is carried out by going through the tree from the root to one of the leaves that will determine its class. Initially, the algorithm takes the entire data set (.) Despite its simplicity and low computational cost, ID3 has significant drawbacks, some of which are corrected by its successor C4.5. The most obvious are the inability to work with continuous attributes and handle missing values.

J48. The j48 algorithm is a version of the classic ID3 decision tree algorithm proposed by Quinlan (.). Decision trees are considered to be part of the supervised classification methods, which means that they have a dependent variable or class and the objective of the classifier is to determine the value of said class for new cases.

The process to start a tree begins with the root node, the one with all the examples or training cases associated to it. The first step is to select the variable or attribute from which the original training sample is going to be divided. This process is recursive, that is, once the variable with which the greatest homogeneity is obtained with respect to the class of child nodes has been determined, the analysis is performed again for each of the child nodes.

3.4 Data Set

Many researchers have commonly focused on the use of the Heart Disease Cleve-land Data-set for the simulation and analysis of CVD, due to the advantages that it offers in terms of variety and data purification, compared to others of the same family and other organizations. An evidence of the use of the Heart Disease Data set is the increasing number of cites and references in papers, conference proceedings, among others in the past five years, like is shown in Table 1.

Table 1. Dataset description

Indexed data set	2018	2019	2020	2021	2022
Scopus	46	59	22	37	96
Springer	31	47	54	31	69
Science Direct	36	45	37	49	61
Biomed	51	71	33	67	82

As a conclusion, the initial stage of data selection for this study, it is used the Heart Disease Cleveland Data set, as an input to test the proposed model. This database consists of a total of 76 features, but all published experiments refer to the use of a subset of only 14 features and 303 records.

Therefore, we have used the already processed UCI Cleveland data set avail- able on the Kaggle website for our analysis. The full description of the 14 attributes used in the work is mentioned in Table 2.

3.5 Selection of Features

In recent years, a large number of data sets have been published on the Internet and are available in repositories online that facilitate the access to the information by the scientific community. Machine learning methods demand to analyze a large number of features. To solve this problem, feature selection algorithms have become a necessary element in the learning process. The author (…) defines it as the process of detecting the relevant characteristics and discarding the irrelevant ones, its aim is to reduce the size of the input data facilitating the processing and analysis of the information. The ability to use the feature selection is important to make an effective analysis, because the data contains information that is not required to generate a model. The feature selection and Information gain techniques are presented in detail below, since these are the basis of the model proposed in this study.

Table 2. Dataset description

Feature number	Attribute	Value of attributes
1	Age	Values between (29–71)
2	Sex	0,1
3	CP	0,1,2,3
4	Tretbps	Values between (94–200)
5	Chol	Values between (126–564)
6	FBS	0,1
7	Restecg	0,1,2
8	Thalach	Values between (71–202)
9	Exang	0,1
10	Oldpeak	Values between (0- 6.2)
11	Slope	1,2,3
12	CA	0,1,2,3
13	Thal	0,1,2,3
14	Target	0(normal), 1(anomaly)

Information Gain (Info.Gain). It is a filter-based feature selection technique. It is also known as *information gain* and is used to identify the level of relevance or ranking of the characteristics of a data collection. Equation No. defines the level of relevance. The attribute with the highest information gain is chosen as the split attribute for node N. This attribute minimizes the information needed to classify the pairs in the resulting partition and reflects the least randomness or impurity in these partitions.

Table 3 details the results of implementing the aforementioned technique to the data set, handling order by relevance from highest to lowest.

4   Methodology

The model proposed in this study trains an artificial intelligence technique (SOM, GHSOM, BAYESIAN NETWORKS, NAIVE BAYES, C4.5, ID3) that will perform automatically the data stream classification process. Such a technique is capable of identifying a patient's tendency to suffer from cardiovascular disease, regardless of whether new instance types are generated. For the validation of the model, several simulation scenarios were implemented in which three phases were comprised: training, classification and calculation of metrics. The Heart Disease Cleveland Data set was selected. Then, it was applied the load balancing by data instances through the implementation of the Synthetic Minority Over Sampling Technique-SMOTE. Subsequently, the INFO.GAIN technique was applied in order to identify the most relevant characteristics of the data set and categorize them by relevance, and then to run the training with the aforementioned artificial intelligence techniques (Fig. 2).

Table 3. Dataset description

Unevaluated dataset features	Data set features with info.gain
Age	Thal
Sex	CP
CP	CA
Trestbps	Oldpeak
Chol	Exang
Fbs	Thalach
Restrecg	Slope
Thalach	Age
Exang	Sex
Oldpeak	Restrecg
Slope	Chol
ca	trestbps
Thal	fbs

In the classification phase, the cross-validation technique was applied to 10 folds using the previously mentioned data set The Heart Disease Cleveland Data set Train)

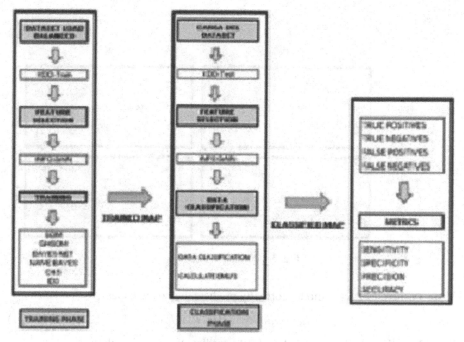

Fig. 2. Model proposed

where the sampling technique (SMOTE) and the INFO.GAIN feature selection technique were applied. Finally, the data is classified, based on the map generated in the training process and the new data subset. In the final phase, different performance metrics like sensitivity, specificity, precision and accuracy were calculated. It allowed to determine the efficiency of the proposed model.

Fundamentals of the Cardiovascular Disease Identifier Test. There is a wide variety of diseases that increase with time. Many of them are new, becoming an unknown agent for identification systems. For this reason, there is no 100% of effectiveness in the cardiovascular disease identifier (CDI). Plus, there are bad practices in the use of the Information and Communication Technology, ICT. In other words, there are several factors that can influence negatively in the CDI decision making of cardiovascular diseases, for example identifying a patient with a cardiac pathology as a healthy person.

To evaluate the performance of CDI, four (4) metrics associated to the nature of the event have been identified, as shown in the Fig. 3:

A CDI is more efficient when, during the cardiovascular disease it presents higher hit rates, that is, the percentage of true negatives and true positives tends to 100% and consequently, it presents low failure rates which means, that the percentage of false positives and false negatives tends to 0%. According to the above, it is concluded that a perfect CDI is the one that can detects all disease trends, without generating a false alarm. The author (…) exposes that:

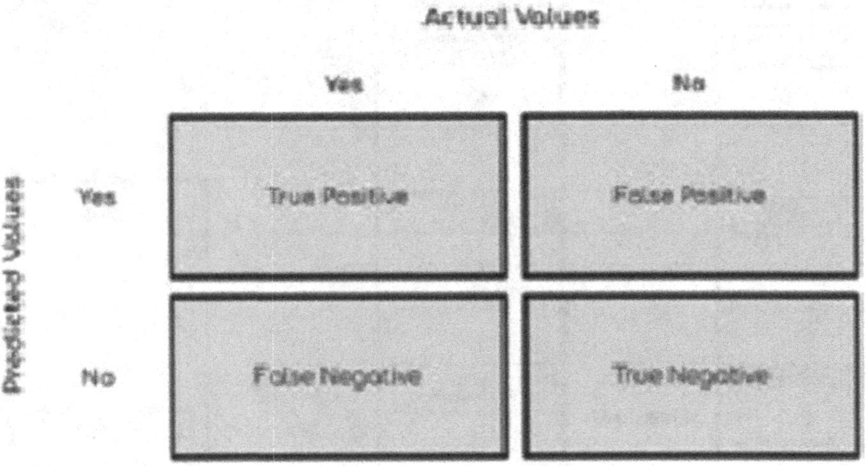

Actual Values

Yes   No

Fig. 3. Confusion matrix

- **True Positive (TP)**: the model correctly predicts the positive class.

$$Sensibility = TP/(TP + FN) \tag{1}$$

- **True Negative (TN)**: the model correctly predicts the negative class.

$$Specificity = TN/(TN + FP) \tag{2}$$

- **False Positive (FP)**: the model incorrectly predicts the positive class when it is actually negative.

$$Accuracy = (TP + TN)/(TP + FP + FN + TN) \tag{3}$$

- **False Negative (FN)**: the model incorrectly predicts the negative class when it is actually positive.

$$Precision = TP/(TP + FP) \tag{4}$$

Performance Metrics. A confusion matrix, also known as an error matrix, is a summary table used to evaluate the performance of a classification model. The number of correct and incorrect predictions are summarized with the count values and broken down by each class. In this study, statistical performance metrics are used to measure the behavior of the CDI related to the classification process, according to the exposed by (…).

- Sensibility: The ability of an CDI to identify "true positive" results.
- Specificity: the ability of an CDI to measure the proportion of "true negatives" that have been correctly identified.
- Accuracy: it is the degree of closeness of the measurements of a quantity (X) to the value of the real magnitude (Y); That is, the proportion of true results (both true positives and true negatives). 100% accuracy means that the measured values are exactly the same as the given values.
- Precision: it the ratio of true positives against all positive results.

5 Results

The development of this research involved the use of six (6) sets of experimental tests. The test sets used the Info.gain feature selection technique. The different experiments were carried out on a DELL LATITUDE 3470 computer with an Intel Core i7 6500U processor at 2.5 Ghz, 8 GB of DDR 3 Ram at 2400 MHz and NVIDIA GeForce 920 M video card with 2 GB DDR3. Each experiment was carried out 10 times, allowing to obtain the values of the metrics that allowed to evaluate the quality of the processes, with its particular metric of quality and standard deviation. More details are shown in Table 4.

Table 4. Dataset description

Model	Accuracy	Precision	Sensibility	specificity
Info.gain + SOM	85.6%	84.7%	86.2%	83.5%
Info.gain + GHSOM	87.4%	85.6%	91.7%	90.6%
Info.gain + BAYES NET	90.6%	91.2%	85.9%	93.3%
Info.gain + NAIVE BAYES	89.1%	88.7%	92.5%	86.8%
Info.gain + J48	91.3%	93.5%	92.7%	91.2%
Info.gain + ID3	90.8%	92.9%	94.1%	92.7%

6 Conclusions and Future Work

Studies oriented to the detection of cardiovascular diseases are a great benefit to guarantee a patient inclination of suffering from cardiac diseases, with high accuracy provided after applying classifications techniques.

The INFO.GAIN feature selection method, using the J48 training and classification technique, give 93.5% of precision, 91.3% of accuracy, 92.7% of sensitivity and 91.2% of specificity, evidencing to be the most efficient model for the identification of cardiovascular diseases. For future work, the authors propose the creation of an own data set that can be trained and compared to the Heart Disease Cleveland Data set, identifying the accurate, efficiency, precision and sensibility of the data.

References

1. Kutyrev, K., Yakovlev, A., Metsker, O.: Mortality prediction based on echocardiographic data and machine learning: CHF, CHD, aneurism, ACS Cases. Procedia Comput. Sci. **156**, 97 (2019)
2. Chu, D., Al Rifai, M., Virani, S.S., Brawner, C.A., Nasir, K., Al-Mallah, M.: The relationship between cardiorespiratory fitness, cardiovascular risk factors and atherosclerosis. Atherosclerosis **304**, 44–52 (2020)

3. Xue, Y., et al.: Efficacy assessment of ticagrelor versus clopidogrel in Chinese patients with acute coronary syndrome undergoing percutaneous coronary intervention by data mining and machine-learning decision tree approaches. J. Clin. Pharm. Ther. **45**(5), 1076–1086 (2020)
4. Rezaianzadeh, A., Dastoorpoor, M., et al.: Predictors of length of stay in the coronary care unit in patient with acute coronary syndrome based on data mining methods. Clin. Epidemiol. Glob. Health **8**(2), 383–388 (2020)
5. Kitchenham, B., et al.: Systematic literature reviews in software engineering–a systematic literature review. Inform. Softw. Technol. **51**(1), 7–15 (2009)
6. Kandasamy, S., Anand, S.: Cardiovascular disease among women from vulnerable populations: a review. Can. J. Cardiol. **34**(4), 450–457 (2018)
7. Retnakaran, R.: Novel biomarkers for predicting cardiovascular disease in patients with diabetes. Can. J. Cardiol. **34**(5), 624–631 (2018)
8. Strodthoff, N., Strodthoff, C.: Detecting and interpreting myocardial infarction using fully convolutional neural networks. Physiol. Meas. **40**(1), 015001 (2019)
9. Idris, N.M., Chiam, Y., et al.: Feature selection and risk prediction for patients with coronary artery disease using data mining. Med. Biol. Eng. Compu. **58**(12), 3123–3140 (2020)
10. Kramer, A., Trinder, M., et al.: Estimating the prevalence of familial hypercholes-terolemia in acute coronary syndrome: a systematic review and meta-analysis. Can. J. Cardiol. **35**(10), 1322–1331 (2019)
11. Leung, K.: Ming: Naive Bayesian classifier. Financ. Risk Eng. **2007**, 123–156 (2007)
12. Barletta, V., et al.: A Kohonen SOM architecture for intrusion detection on in-vehicle communication networks. Appl. Sci. **10**(15), 5062 (2020)
13. Larry Bretthorst, G.: An introduction to parameter estimation using Bayesian probability theory. In: Fougère, P.F. (ed.) Maximum Entropy and Bayesian Methods, pp. 53–79. Springer Netherlands, Dordrecht (1990). https://doi.org/10.1007/978-94-009-0683-9_5

Shedding Light on the Black Box: Explainable AI for Predicting Household Appliance Failures

Taha Falatouri[1,2] (iD), Mehran Nasseri[1,2] (iD), Patrick Brandtner[1,2(✉)] (iD),
and Farzaneh Darbanian[1,2] (iD)

[1] University of Applied Sciences Upper Austria, 4400 Steyr, Austria
{taha.falatouri,patrick.brandtner}@fh-steyr.at
[2] Josef Ressel Centre PREVAIL, 4400 Steyr, Austria

Abstract. The lack of transparency in outcomes of advanced machine learning solutions, such as deep learning (DL), leads to skepticism among business users about using them. Particularly, when the output is used for critical decision-making or has financial impacts on the business, trust and transparency is crucial. Explainable Artificial Intelligence (XAI) has been widely utilized in recent years to convert the black box of DL techniques into understandable elements. In this research, we implement Long Short-Term-Memory (LSTM) networks to predict repair needs for geographically distributed heating appliances in private households. To conduct our analysis, we use a real-word dataset of a maintenance service company with more than 350.000 records over the time span of five years. We employ the SHAP (SHapley Additive exPlanations) method for global interpretation, describing overall model behavior, and – for local interpretation – providing explanations for individual predictions. The results of the DL model and the additional XAI outputs were discussed with practitioners in a workshop setting. Results confirm that XAI increases the willingness to use DL for decision making in practice and boosts the explainability of such models. We also found that the willingness to trust and follow XAI predictions depends on whether explanations conform with mental models. In total, XAI was found to represent an important addition to DL models and fosters their utilization in practice. Future research should focus on applying XAI on additional models, in different use cases or conduct broader evaluations with several company partners.

Keywords: Explainable AI · LSTM · Deep Learning · Model Interpretability · Business Analytics · Decision Making

1 Introduction

The recent development of Artificial Intelligence (AI) and its prosperous results in many domains have sparked increased interest among businesses to utilize such techniques [1, 2]. However, the lack of transparency in the outcomes of advanced machine learning solutions, such as deep learning, has led to skepticism among business users regarding their adoption. This skepticism is particularly prevalent when the outputs are utilized for critical decision-making or have financial impacts on the business, making trust and

© The Author(s), under exclusive license to Springer Nature Switzerland AG 2023
H. Degen et al. (Eds.): HCII 2023, LNCS 14059, pp. 69–83, 2023.
https://doi.org/10.1007/978-3-031-48057-7_5

transparency crucial [3, 4]. From a forecasting theory perspective, it is vital to assess the efficacy of a forecasting technique [5, 6]. However, there is a significant need to explain how these techniques work, and there is a proposed method to explore the algorithm that dates back to the mid-eighties. Nevertheless, Explainable Artificial Intelligence (XAI) did not receive significant research focus until 2017 and 2018 [1].

Using XAI in the field of advanced predictive analytics can unveil the tangible impact of each feature on the outcome, thereby enhancing the explainability of deep learning models and increasing the willingness of decision-makers to apply them. Although there is a plethora of research available on the development of theories related to XAI, there is a lack of secondary research on its practical applicability [1]. In this research, we apply XAI algorithms with real-world data using model-agnostic tools. These tools can be employed with any machine learning model and are utilized after the model has undergone training (post hoc). They are independent of the specific model used and typically work by analysing pairs of input and output features. It is important to note that these methods do not have access to the internal components of the model, such as weights or structural details, as per their definition.

The primary objective of this paper is to explore the application of XAI in predicting failures of household appliances used in heating buildings. By predicting future repair needs, service providers can optimize the utilization of repair resources and minimize downtime of the appliances. However, predicting future repair needs is a complex task that occurs in dynamic circumstances. It involves various factors, such as the technology of the machines, their geographical distribution, varying usage styles, and weather conditions. [7], advanced prediction models are crucial for accurate forecasting. It comes as no surprise that machine learning techniques have already found widespread implementation in prediction tasks [8]. However, these models often lack explainability and transparency in their outcomes, leading to a lack of trust from decision-makers [9]. We employ a deep learning model utilizing Long Short-Term Memory (LSTM) networks to predict ad-hoc repair needs for technical appliances in private households, considering their geographical distribution. Our analysis is conducted using a real-world dataset from a maintenance service company, consisting of over 350,000 records spanning five years. By incorporating XAI, we aim to provide explainability to the model's results. More precisely, the following research questions are defined and addresses in the paper:

- Q1: What is the importance of a particular feature on the model's predictions?
- Q2: How does changing a specific feature impact the model's prediction?
- Q3: What is the reason behind the model's specific prediction for a given instance?

The remainder of the paper is structured as follows: section two provides an overview of the main concepts underlying the study, i.e., XAI and its specific approaches to increase model explainability. Section three elaborates on the details of the methodology applied and presents the prediction models used, the data chosen, and the evaluation criteria selected. Subsequently, the fourth section provides the results of applying XAI to prediction results, utilizing the SHAP (SHapley Additive exPlanations) framework. Finally, section five discusses the results, concludes the paper and provides an outlook for future research.

2 Research Background

Utilizing advanced analytical methods and approaches has shown great improvements in decision making across domains, be it in the form of advanced systems in the building sector [10], AI applications in value network foresight and innovation management [11, 12] or in the form of advanced analytics solutions in Supply Chain Management [13, 14]. As advanced analytics models are often hard to comprehend and understand, the application of explainable artificial intelligence (XAI) has increased steadily across various business domains Especially the healthcare sector has witnessed the highest number of research works exploring the application of XAI. Additionally, XAI has been extensively utilized in industrial settings and transportation. Other domains such as entertainment, finance, judiciary, and academia have also implemented XAI, albeit to a lesser extent compared to healthcare and industries [1]. To gain a better understanding of the research background, we conducted a search for the application of XAI in the field of Predictive Maintenance.

In a study [15] an XAI approach utilizing convolutional neural networks (CNNs) for classification in vibration signals analysis was investigated. Vibration signals were transformed into images using Short-Time Fourier Transform (STFT), and a CNN was employed as the classification model. Gradient class activation mapping (Grad-CAM) was used to generate the model's attention, and verification of attention was introduced through neural networks, adaptive network-based fuzzy inference systems (ANFIS), and decision trees. The results indicated that deep learning could provide excellent performance in prediction and classification. However, the parameters within network structures lack explainability and practical meanings.

In other research [16], it was proposed to extend classical decision tree machine learning algorithms to Multi-operator Temporal Decision Trees (MTDT) to generate interpretable classification of time-series data. MTDT provides interpretable decisions, improving readability and preserving. Using their method, they could provide interpretable decisions, thus improving result readability while preserving classification accuracy. A new XAI methodology, i.e., Failure Diagnosis Explainability (FDE) was offered by [17]. In their research, they have developed a model to automatically diagnose failure based on Artificial Intelligence (AI). FDE was added to the model to provide transparency and interpretability of the assessed diagnosis. In [18], a deep learning model for prognosing the remaining useful life of a turbofan engine using a one-dimensional convolutional neural network, long short-term memory, and bidirectional long short-term memory, was demonstrated. It investigates two practical and crucial issues in applying the model for system prognosis: the curse of dimensionality and the black box property of the engine. The proposed model employs dimensionality reduction and Shapley additive explanation (SHAP) techniques to reduce complexity and prevent overfitting, while maintaining high accuracy. The experimental results demonstrate the high accuracy and efficiency of the proposed model with dimensionality reduction and SHAP enhances the explainability in a conventional deep learning model for system prognosis.

The implementation and explanation of a machine learning-based remaining life estimator model applied to industrial data, specifically for fatigue life tests on bushings, has been used in [19]. The model, utilizing Random Forest regressors, incorporates input variables such as environmental and operational conditions to predict remaining life accurately and provides explainability using XAI techniques (ELI5 and LIME) for local and global explanations. The results demonstrate a gain of process knowledge, increase validation of expert knowledge, and emphasize the importance of collaboration between domain experts and XAI techniques in understanding advanced machine learning models for industrial processes. In the era of Industry 4.0 and IoT, [20] proposes an automatic fault detection and diagnosis method for vibrating mechanical systems using a convolutional neural network (CNN) and class activation map (CAM). By employing CNN and CAM on real-world vibration videos, the presented an approach enabling real-time and accurate fault detection, providing a promising method for automatic machine condition-based monitoring. The method demonstrates improved accuracy compared to traditional feature extraction techniques, and the use of CAM aids in understanding and localizing faulty regions in the images.

Focusing on explaining predictions made by a recurrent neural network (RNN)-based model for estimating the remaining useful life (RUL) of hard disk drives (HDDs) using three-dimensional datasets, [21] utilized XAI tools such as LIME and SHAP. The study demonstrates how explanations can support predictive maintenance tasks through both global and local explanations. The results indicate that SHAP outperforms LIME in various metrics, making it a suitable and effective solution for HDD predictive maintenance applications. [22] presents a novel approach for identifying bearing defects and measuring their degradation. Vibration signals are converted to spectrograms and processed using deep learning methods, specifically the short-time Fourier transform (STFT) and a convolutional neural network (CNN) called VGG16. The CNN extracts feature and classifies the health status of the bearings, while regression is used for predicting the remaining useful life (RUL). XAI with LIME is employed to identify the relevant image components used by the CNN algorithm. The proposed method achieves high accuracy and robustness in detecting bearing faults, as confirmed by numerous experiments.

The literature demonstrates that deep learning models have been widely used in the field of preventive maintenance. Among various techniques, SHAP models have shown superior performance while also reducing complexity.

3   Methodology

In this paper, we have developed an LSTM-based prediction model for forecasting future repair needs of technical appliances. The accuracy of the model was thoroughly evaluated to ensure that it meets an acceptable level of performance. Furthermore, in order to enhance the interpretability of the model, we incorporated explainable machine learning techniques that are specifically designed to assist humans in comprehending the behavior and predictions of machine learning systems [23]. This section provides a detailed description of each step involved in our approach. Our dataset consists of historical repair requirements data, comprising over 350,000 records spanning five years. This period covers 60 months, from January 2017 to December 2021, for various regions per request. The dataset also includes variables that are beyond the company's control, such as calendar-related and weather data. We have divided this dataset into two parts: the training dataset and the test dataset. The training dataset contains 80% of the data from January 2017 to December 2020, which is used for building the models. On the other hand, the test dataset encompasses the remaining period, from January 2021 to December 2021, and is held out for model evaluation.

We have developed an LSTM-based model for predicting the number of future repair requirements of the technical appliances in a specific region. The model was implemented in Python using TensorFlow and Keras [24]. We considered a set of relevant features to train and evaluate our prediction model. The feature list includes both historical data and external factors that can influence repair requests. Features were incorporated into the model are presented in Table 1.

Table 1. Input features for the prediction model

Feature Group	Feature name	Feature description	Type
Historical requests	NumberOfRequests_t	Number of repair requests at t (t = 1,2,…,7) days before the current date	Numeric
Calendar	MonthNum	Numerical representation of Month of the year	Categorical-Nominal
Calendar	WeekNum	Numerical representation of Week of the Year	Categorical-Nominal
Calendar	WeekDayNum	Numerical representation of Day of the week	Categorical-Nominal
Calendar	IsSpecialDay	Indicates if it is a special day or event	Categorical-Nominal
Calendar	IsWorkingDay	Indicates if it is a working day or non-working day	Categorical-Nominal
Calendar	IsWorkingDayBefore	Indicates if the previous day is a working day	Categorical-Nominal
Calendar	IsWorkingDayAfter	Indicates if the following day is a working day	Categorical-Nominal
Weather	WeatherTemperature_t	Temperature at t (t = 1,2,…,7) days before the current date	Numeric
Weather	WeatherWindSpeed_t	Wind speed at t (t = 1,2,…,7) days before the current date	Numeric
Weather	WeatherPrecipitation_t	Amount of precipitation at t (t = 1,2,…,7) days before the current date	Numeric

We employed four metrics that assess the accuracy and reliability of the predictions. Table 2 presents these metrics, their mathematical definitions, and their corresponding values for the model based on the test data. Based on these evaluation results, it can be inferred that our model performed well in predicting number of repair requests.

Table 2. Details of prediction model evaluation

Evaluation metric	Formula	Value
Mean Absolute Percentage Error (MAPE):	$MAPE = \frac{1}{n} \sum\limits_{t=1}^{n} \frac{\left\|\widehat{y_t}-y_t\right\|}{y_t}$	18.38%
Mean Absolute Error % (MAE%)	$MAE = \frac{\frac{1}{n}\sum_{t=1}^{n}\left\|\widehat{y_t}-y_t\right\|}{\bar{y}}$	14.03%
Root Mean Square Error %(RMSE%)	$RMSE = \frac{\sqrt{\frac{1}{n}\sum_{t=1}^{n}(\hat{y}_t-y_t)^2}}{\bar{y}}$	20.15%
Coefficient of Determination (R^2)	$R^2 = 1 - \frac{\sum_{t=1}^{n}(\hat{y}_t-y_t)^2}{\sum_{t=1}^{n}(y_t-\bar{y}_t)^2}$	87.34%

Note: y_t and $\hat{y}_t$ are the actual and predicted value for time interval (day) t, respectively

4   Results

Our objective was to employ XAI techniques to examine feature importance and their effects on the model. Feature importance methods assess the contribution of a feature to the model's performance. A feature effect shows how changing the values of a feature can affect the predicted outcome in terms of both direction and magnitude [25]. To address the defined researched questions, we applied global (i.e., for Q1 and Q2) respectively local interpretation (for Q3) of the model that was built for predicting repair requests.

As discussed in section two, different approaches might be applied to interprete machine learning models. For our research, we utilized the SHAP (SHapley Additive exPlanations) framework as our chosen method of interpretation. SHAP, described in the paper [25], adopts a game theoretic perspective to explain the output of any machine learning model. It leverages the concept of Shapley values, which are derived from game theory and measure the average marginal effect of including an input across all possible orderings. In the context of machine learning model interpretation, Shapley values ϕ_j^i provide a measure of the contribution of feature j to the prediction of instance i. The advantage of utilizing SHAP for our model interpretation lies in its ability to address both global and local interpretability, thus enabling us to answer each of the three defined questions. By using a single method for both global and local interpretation, our approach ensures a consistent interpretation throughout the analysis. We utilized the shap Python package [26] to implement SHAP and applied the calculated Shapley values and plotting functions provided by the package to interpret the model.

4.1 Analyzing the Importance of a Particular Feature on Model Prediction

Regarding Q1 (i.e., what is the importance of a particular feature on the model's predictions?), we needed to determine the average contribution of each feature to the prediction model (formula 1). Since we are interested in assessing global importance, the SHAP feature importance (FI_j) for feature j can be calculated by taking the mean absolute Shapley values across all instances ($i = 1, .., n$).

$$FI_j = \frac{1}{n} \sum_{i=1}^{n} \left| \phi_j^i \right| \tag{1}$$

The result is depicted in a plot shown in Fig. 1. As presented, WeekDayNum and IsWorkingDay have the highest impact on the predicted absolute outcome, changing the predicted outcome on average by 12.36 and 9.36 respectively. This indicates that the prediction model's outcome is influenced by the day of the week and whether it is a working or non-working day. Another important finding is that the number of requests 7 and 6 days prior to the predicted day (NumberOfRequests_7 and NumberOfRequests_6) holds significant importance, and the model is also influenced by the temperature of the day before (WeatherTemperature_1). Similar interpretations can be made for the other features based on their respective values in the chart.

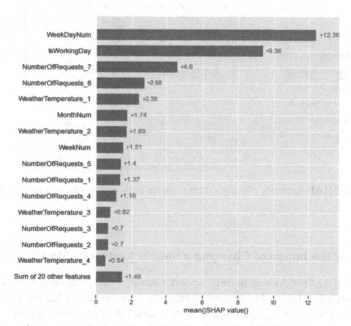

Fig. 1. Feature importance plot based on Mean Absolute Shapley Values Across all instances.

To obtain more information regarding the detailed feature importance for each instance, we can utilize the SHAP summary plot shown in Fig. 2. In the summary plot, the Shapley values (ϕ_j^i) for each instance (i) and feature (j) are presented in a single chart. The features are displayed on the vertical axis, sorted based on their overall importance, while the horizontal axis represents the Shapley value. The color gradient in the plot illustrates the range of feature values, ranging from low to high, as demonstrated in the chart on the right-hand side. The features described in the feature importance Fig. 1 have the highest spread of Shapley values in the summary plot (cf. Fig. 2), making them the most important.

The summary plot also provides insights into the relationships between the feature value and its impact on the prediction. For instance, according to the chart, when the temperature of the day before (WeatherTemperature_1) is lower, it results in a higher Shapley value and consequently leads to higher predicted requests. We will delve into a more detailed investigation of feature effects in the next part when addressing Q2.

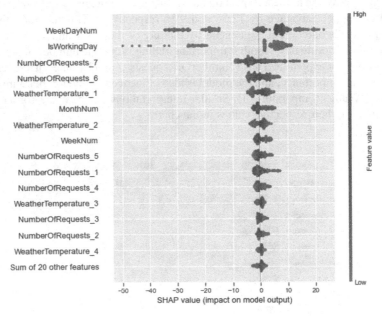

Fig. 2. SHAP summary plot combining feature importance with feature effects.

4.2   Depicting the Impact of Changing a Specific Feature on Model Prediction

Regarding Q2 (i.e., how does changing a specific feature impact the model's prediction?), we plot the SHAP value of that feature against the corresponding feature values for all instances in the dataset. We depicted the SHAP feature dependence plot for the six most important features in Fig. 3. These charts display a data point for each instance, where the feature value is represented on the horizontal axis, and the corresponding Shapley value is plotted on the vertical axis. The histogram on the horizontal axis indicates the data distribution.

We can observe from the charts in Fig. 3 that the model predicts a low number of requests for WeekDayNumber = 6 (Saturdays), whereas for WeekDayNumber = 1 (Mondays), it predicts higher numbers of requests. The model also predicts a significantly higher number of requests for working days compared to nonworking days. The number of requests 7 and 6 days prior to the predicted day (NumberOfRequests_7 and NumberOfRequests_6) shows an almost linear correlation with the model's prediction outcomes, where an increase in these features leads to a higher predicted number of requests. When it comes to temperature (WeatherTemperature_1), the model is more sensitive to lower values and predicts a higher number of repair requests. For temperatures above 20 approximately degrees, the model appears to be indifferent. Regarding the Month of the year (MonthNum), the model predicts higher requests for the last month of the year, indicating a substantial difference compared to other months based on the prediction outcome.

4.3   Elaborating Reasons Behind Specific Model Predictions for a Given Instance

Regarding Q3 (i.e., what is the reason behind the model's specific prediction for a given instance?), for a specific instance (i), we can visualize the Shapley values (ϕ_j^i) for each feature (j) and observe how they either increase or decrease the prediction outcome compared to the baseline. The base line is the average model output over the training dataset we used. The charts are presented in Figs. 4 and 5, illustrating two exemplary instances that demonstrate substantial deviations from the average predicted values. The vertical axis represents each feature along with its corresponding value for that instance. The prediction originates from the baseline. In the plots, each Shapley value is depicted as an arrow, indicating its effect on either increasing (positive value, shown in red) or decreasing (negative value, shown in blue) the prediction. These forces interact and balance each other out, ultimately determining the final prediction for the data instance. For the first instance (shown in Fig. 4) with a predicted value of 81.32, IsWorkingDay, WeatherTemperature_1, NumberOfRequest_7, MonthNum, WeekNum, and WeatherTemperature_2 make the most significant contributions in increasing the predicted value. On the other hand, NumberOfRequests_6, followed by NumberOfrequests_5, have contributions in decreasing the predicted value, but not to the extent that would cancel out the positive effects.

In the second instance (Fig. 5), the predicted value is 24.01, which is lower than the average of 60.44. WeekDayNumber, NumberOfrequests_7, and NumberOfrequests_6 have the most significant impact in decreasing, while NumberOfrequests_5 and IsWorkingDay have the most significant impact in increasing prediction value.

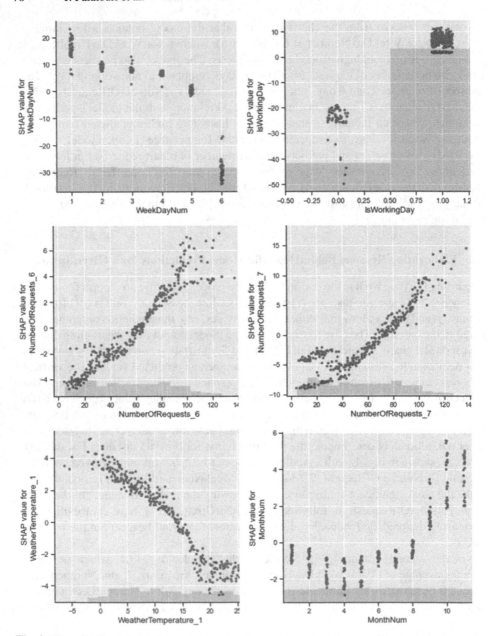

Fig. 3. SHAP feature dependence plot for the six most important features, illustrating the effect of a single feature across the entire dataset.

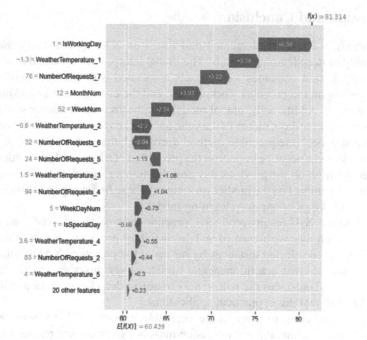

Fig. 4. SHAP values to explain predicted repair request of instance 1.

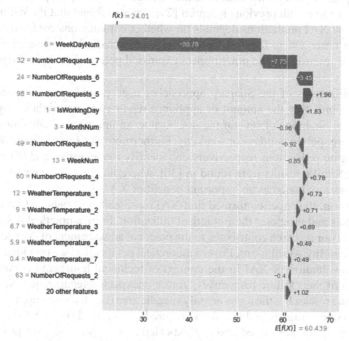

Fig. 5. SHAP values to explain predicted repair request of instance 2.

5 Discussion and Conclusion

In this research, we have implemented and tested an XAI approach to enhance the interpretability of deep learning models. The global interpretation method revealed that the average prediction outcomes were closely associated with weather conditions, the number of orders on the previous working day, and the corresponding working day in the previous week. Additionally, global models emphasized the influence of day status (working/non-working day), month of the year, and weekday on the prediction outcomes. Furthermore, the local interpretation method uncovered, that certain events, such as the day of the week, had a negative impact on the prediction of a low number of orders, while the weather situation on the previous day and the number of orders from the previous day had a positive impact on the prediction amount. These findings provide transparency into the inner workings of our deep learning model.

To evaluate the XAI results produced, practitioner workshops were conducted. In these workshop settings, we presented and discussed the prediction results of the LSTM model and explained selected instances by means of the presented XAI results. During extensive discussions with practitioners and similar to previous research [27, 28], it was confirmed that XAI enhances the willingness to utilize deep learning for and accept its results in decision-making in practical applications.

For predictions close to the average or within expected value ranges, XAI was regarded to as a confirming input for decision makers. For prediction results with higher deviations from the average or outside expected value ranges, XAI was found to provide interesting insights into first the data used and second more complex patterns occurring in real world. In line with previous research [29], we also found that the willingness to trust and follow XAI predictions depends on whether explanations conform with mental models. In cases where features were of an unexpectedly low or high importance, the discussions intensified, and practitioners expressed potential doubt in the prediction results.

The visualizations of the Shapley approaches used provided practitioners with a deeper insight into how the amount of appliance repair requests might change due to unexpected combinations of several factors, such as an untypical combination of date, low temperature, public holidays or weekday. Furthermore, XAI results were also found to flag inaccurate predictions respectively can identify model errors and feature misinterpretations. Similar results were found in [30], where flagging unexpected inaccurate predictions was also stated as an important benefit of XAI.

In conclusion, the paper confirmed that XAI represents a valuable addition to deep learning models and promotes their practical utilization. Form a practical point of view, we believe that our research contributes to the practical advancement of deep learning by enabling trustworthy AI solutions. From a theoretical perspective, we provided a detailed analysis and evaluation of XAI in the context of technical household appliances and the prediction of their failure respectively future unexpected repair requests. The main limitation of the research is the focus on only specific area (i.e., technical appliance failure prediction) in one company and based on one prediction model (i.e., LSTM). However, by applying well acknowledged and sophisticated XAI approaches, we provide solid results for this use case. Future research should focus on applying the discussed XAI methodology for different types of predictions and other deep learning models.

Acknowledgements. This research has been funded by the Christian Doppler Research Association as part of the Josef Ressel Centre PREVAIL.

References

1. Islam, M.R., Ahmed, M.U., Barua, S., Begum, S.: A systematic review of explainable artificial intelligence in terms of different application domains and tasks. Appl. Sci. **12**, 1353 (2022). https://doi.org/10.3390/app12031353
2. Brandtner, P.: Predictive analytics and intelligent decision support systems in supply chain risk management—research directions for future studies. In: Yang, X.-S., Sherratt, S., Dey, N., Joshi, A. (eds.) Proceedings of Seventh International Congress on Information and Communication Technology, vol. 464. Lecture Notes in Networks and Systems, pp. 549–558. Springer Nature Singapore, Singapore (2023). https://doi.org/10.1007/978-981-19-2394-4_50
3. Haque, A.B., Islam, A.N., Mikalef, P.: Explainable Artificial Intelligence (XAI) from a user perspective: a synthesis of prior literature and problematizing avenues for future research. Technol. Forecast. Soc. Chang. **186**, 122120 (2023). https://doi.org/10.1016/j.techfore.2022.122120
4. Joyce, D.W., Kormilitzin, A., Smith, K.A., Cipriani, A.: Explainable artificial intelligence for mental health through transparency and interpretability for under-standability. NPJ Dig. Med. (2023). https://doi.org/10.1038/s41746-023-00751-9
5. Falatouri, T., Farzaneh, D., Brandtner, P., Udokwu, C.: Predictive analytics for demand forecasting – a comparison of SARIMA and LSTM in retail SCM. In: Proceedings of International Conference on Industry 4.0 and Smart Manufacturing (ISM). International Conference on Industry 4.0 and Smart Manufacturing (ISM) (2021). https://doi.org/10.1016/j.procs.2022.01.298
6. Petropoulos, F., et al.: Forecasting: theory and practice. Int. J. Forecast. **38**(3), 705–871 (2022). https://doi.org/10.1016/j.ijforecast.2021.11.001
7. Falatouri, T., Brandtner, P., Nasseri, M., Darbanian, F.: Maintenance forecasting model for geographically distributed home appliances using spatial-temporal networks. Procedia Comput. Sci. **219**, 495–503 (2023). https://doi.org/10.1016/j.procs.2023.01.317
8. Agatic, A., Tijan, E., Hess, S., Jugovic, T.P.: Advanced Data Analytics in Logistics Demand Forecasting. In: 2021 44th International Convention on Information, Communication and Electronic Technology (MIPRO). 2021 44th International Convention on Information, Communication and Electronic Technology (MIPRO), Opatija, Croatia, 27 Sep 2021– 1 Oct 2021, pp. 1387–1392. IEEE (2021). https://doi.org/10.23919/MIPRO52101.2021.9596820
9. Goldman, C.V., Baltaxe, M., Chakraborty, D., Arinez, J., Diaz, C.E.: Interpreting learning models in manufacturing processes: towards explainable AI methods to improve trust in classifier predictions. J. Ind. Inf. Integr. **33**, 100439 (2023). https://doi.org/10.1016/j.jii.2023.100439
10. Naji, H.R., Meybodi, M.N., Falatouri, T.N.: Intelligent building management systems using multi agents: Fuzzy approach. Int. J. Comput. Appl. **14**, 9–14 (2011). https://doi.org/10.5120/1890-2254
11. Brandtner, P., Mates, M.: Artificial intelligence in strategic foresight – current practices and future application potentials. In: Proceedings of the 2021 12th International Conference on E-business, Management and Economics (ICEME 2021). International Conference on E-business, Management and Economics (ICEME 2021), pp. 75–81 (2021). https://doi.org/10.1145/3481127.3481177
12. Brandtner, P.: Requirements for value network fore-sight-supply chain uncertainty reduction. In: ISPIM Conference Proceedings, pp. 1–12 (2020)

13. Brandtner, P., Udokwu, C., Darbanian, F., Falatouri, T.: Dimensions of data analytics in supply chain management: objectives, indicators and data questions. In: 2021 the 4th International Conference on Computers in Management and Business, New York, NY, USA. ACM, New York, NY, USA (2021). https://doi.org/10.1145/3450588.3450599

14. Brandtner, P., Udokwu, C., Darbanian, F., Falatouri, T.: Applications of big data analytics in supply chain management: findings from expert interviews. In: 2021 The 4th International Conference on Computers in Management and Business. ICCMB 2021: 2021 The 4th International Conference on Computers in Management and Business, Singapore, 30 Jan–01 Feb 2021, pp. 77–82. ACM, New York, NY, USA (2021)

15. Roy, A., Anika, S. (eds.): Explainable deep neural networks for multivariate time series predictions. IJCAI (2019)

16. Shalaeva, V., Alkhoury, S., Marinescu, J., Amblard, C., Bisson, G.: Multi-operator decision trees for explainable time-series classification. In: Medina, J., et al. (eds.) IPMU 2018. CCIS, vol. 853, pp. 86–99. Springer, Cham (2018). https://doi.org/10.1007/978-3-319-91473-2_8

17. Zeldam, S.G.: Automated Failure Diagnosis in Aviation Maintenance using Explainable Artificial Intelligence (XAI). University of Twente (2018)

18. Hong, C.W., Lee, C., Lee, K., Ko, M.-S., Kim, D.E., Hur, K.: Remaining useful life prognosis for turbofan engine using explainable deep neural networks with dimensionality reduction. Sensors **20**(22), 6626 (2020). https://doi.org/10.3390/s20226626

19. Serradilla, O., Zugasti, E., Cernuda, C., Aranburu, A., de Okariz, J.R., Zurutuza, U.: Interpreting Remaining Useful Life estimations combining Explainable Artificial Intelligence and domain knowledge in industrial machinery. In: 2020 IEEE International Conference on Fuzzy Systems (FUZZ-IEEE). 2020 IEEE International Conference on Fuzzy Systems (FUZZ-IEEE), Glasgow, United Kingdom, 19–24 Jul 2020, pp. 1–8. IEEE (2020). https://doi.org/10.1109/FUZZ48607.2020.9177537

20. Sun, K.H., Huh, H., Tama, B.A., Lee, S.Y., Jung, J.H., Lee, S.: Vision-based fault diagnostics using explainable deep learning with class activation maps. IEEE Access **8**, 129169–129179 (2020). https://doi.org/10.1109/ACCESS.2020.3009852

21. Ferraro, A., Galli, A., Moscato, V., Sperlì, G.: Evaluating eXplainable artificial intelligence tools for hard disk drive predictive maintenance. Artif. Intell. Rev. **56**, 7279–7314 (2023). https://doi.org/10.1007/s10462-022-10354-7

22. Sanakkayala, D.C., et al.: Explainable AI for bearing fault prognosis using deep learning techniques. Micromachines **13**(9), 1471 (2022). https://doi.org/10.3390/mi13091471

23. Murdoch, W.J., Singh, C., Kumbier, K., Abbasi-Asl, R., Yu, B.: Definitions, methods, and applications in interpretable machine learning. PNAS **116**, 22071–22080 (2019). https://doi.org/10.1073/pnas.1900654116

24. Abadi, M., et al.: TensorFlow: large-scale machine learning on heterogeneous distributed systems (2016)

25. Lundberg, S., Lee, S.-I.: A unified approach to interpreting model predictions (2017)

26. Lundberg, S.: A game theoretic approach to explain the output of any machine learning model. https://github.com/slundberg/shap

27. Druce, J., Harradon, M., Tittle, J.: Explainable artificial intelligence (XAI) for increasing user trust in deep reinforcement learning driven autonomous systems (2021)

28. Otaki, Y., et al.: Clinical deployment of explainable artificial intelligence of SPECT for diagnosis of coronary artery disease. JACC Cardiovasc. Imaging **15**, 1091–1110 (2022). https://doi.org/10.1016/j.jcmg.2021.04.030

29. Bauer, K., von Zahn, M., Hinz, O.: Expl(AI)ned: the impact of explainable artificial intelligence on users' information processing. Inform. Syst. Res. **0**(0), 21 (2023). https://doi.org/10.1287/isre.2023.1199

30. Stadtler, S., Betancourt, C., Roscher, R.: Explainable machine learning reveals capabilities, redundancy, and limitations of a geospatial air quality bench-mark dataset. MAKE 4, 150–171 (2022). https://doi.org/10.3390/make4010008

Supporting Deep Learning-Based Named Entity Recognition Using Cloud Resource Management

Benedict Hartmann[✉], Philippe Tamla, and Matthias Hemmje

University of Hagen, Universitätsstr. 11, 58084 Hagen, Germany
bha443@proton.me, {philippe.tamla,matthias.hemmje}@fernuni-hagen.de
https://www.fernuni-hagen.de/multimedia-internetanwendungen/

Abstract. This paper presents a system for managing Cloud Resources such as memory and CPU/GPU that is used to develop, train, and customize Deep Learning-based Named Entity Recognition (NER) models in domains like heath care. The increasing digitization of healthcare services has led to the emergence of electronic health records (EHRs) as a significant component of healthcare data management. NER is a machine learning technique that can be applied to EHRs to extract information such as drug and treatment information, helping to support clinical decision making. The paper is addressing the difficulty domain experts face in using Cloud technologies to perform NER tasks, since they often require technical expertise and technical management overhead. The paper presents a system for the configuration of cloud resources for NER training using the spaCy framework and AWS compute services. The research is structured using Nunamaker's methodology, which provides a structured approach to software development through four phases: observation, theory building, systems development, and experimentation. The paper identifies problem statements and research questions to guide the research and maps them to the objectives of the methodology. The objectives of the methodology include researching the state-of-the-art of NER and cloud technologies, analyzing the architecture of motivating research projects, defining user requirements and the system architecture, and implementing the system. The system is designed using User Centered Systems Design and is based on previously identified user requirements. Two main user groups are considered for the application: NER Experts and Medical Domain Experts. The system is implemented using the Model-View-Controller architecture pattern. It allows for the training of Transformer models, selection of compute resources, and adjusting training configuration and hyperparameters. The system is designed for scalability of compute and storage resources. The paper also discusses the evaluation of the system through experiments and analysis of the results to gain insights. It provides information about the technical implementation and details about the user interface. It is evaluated using cognitive walkthrough and experiments with Transformer-based models.

© The Author(s), under exclusive license to Springer Nature Switzerland AG 2023
H. Degen et al. (Eds.): HCII 2023, LNCS 14059, pp. 84–100, 2023.
https://doi.org/10.1007/978-3-031-48057-7_6

Keywords: Cloud Resource Management · Deep Learning · Named
Entity Recognition · Transformer · Cloud Computing · Micro Service
Architecture

1 Introduction and Motivation

The landscape of healthcare data management has witnessed a significant transformation in recent years, driven by increased digitization of services and emerging technologies [4,13]. The Electronic Health Record (EHR) has emerged as
a contributing element in this transformation, offering a digitized repository of
patient health information and improving patient care [16]. NER is a machine
learning technique of the Natural Language Processing (NLP) field to discover
entities in textual data, such as persons, organizations or dates [18]. NER can
be applied to the medical domain to extract information from EHR, such as
drugs, conditions, or treatments [5,27]. This information could be used to support medical domain experts in clinical decision making [6]. The data volume of
EHR poses a challenge for medical experts through Information Overload (IO)
[25]. NER can be used to address this challenge [27] as a technique of Information Retrieval (IR). Applying NER involves training Machine Learning (ML)
models, which can be data and compute resource intensive [30,32]. The development of Cloud Computing (CC) technologies complements this requirement,
as it provides resources that can be used to perform these compute tasks:

Processing power: Cloud computing resources, such as virtual machines and
GPUs, can provide the computing power needed to perform NER tasks efficiently
and quickly, even with large volumes of text data [19].

Storage: Cloud storage solutions provide large, scalable data storage options
to store the vast amounts of text data that need to be processed for NER [1].

Scalability: Cloud resources can be scaled up or down as needed, providing
the ability to handle the increasing volume and complexity of NER tasks. This
means that as the demand for NER processing increases, the resources available
can be easily increased to meet that demand [1].

There are further challenges for medical experts to utilize CC and NER in
their domain. One main challenge is lack of technical skill [6] for both handling
NER frameworks and Cloud Resource Management (CRM). CRM refers to the
processes, tools, and technologies used to allocate, monitor, and optimize the use
of cloud computing resources. It involves the efficient and effective management
of computing resources, such as virtual machines, storage, and networking, in
a cloud computing environment. The goal of CRM is to ensure that the right
amount of resources are available to meet the changing demands of cloud-based
applications and services. Weingartner et al. [31] describe different areas that
CRM needs to manage: Application management for the selection of resources,
infrastructure such as networking, storage, and compute and the management
of costs. Users should be supported through software in handling these tasks.

In order to motivate this work, several research projects are now introduced.
The research project FIT4NER [6] aims to support medical domain experts

with NER tasks utilizing CC and motivates the work in this paper. It relates to Artificial Intelligence for Hospitals, Healthcare & Humanity (AI4H3), which is a research project aiming to support medical professionals with deployable AI modules to process patient data. It was submitted as part of the H2020 program[1] of the European Commission. The proposed system of AI4H3 is based on the Knowledge Management System (KMS) called KM-EP, which was developed at the University of Hagen in the Faculty of Mathematics and Computer Science at the Chair of Multimedia and Internet Applications and FTK[2]. A system to support NER tasks has been successfully applied in SNERC [27], however it relies on on-premise infrastructure. FIT4NER suggests a layered architecture that is embedded into the architecture of AI4H3 and provides a framework agnostic interface for Cloud-based NER framework modules. This enables the utilization of CC for the existing architecture. *Cloud-based Information Extraction* (CIE) [26] is a research project that aims at supporting the extraction of textual information using state of the art methods such as ML, transformer-based architecture and CC resources. An initial architecture of CIE supporting an end-to-end pipeline for NER and transformer-bases model training and customization was already introduced in [26]. This architecture was implemented in AWS [10] and Azure Cloud [21] and validated in the medical health care domain.

This paper provides more detailed information on various aspects of the AWS implementation of CIE. While CIE mentions experimentation training results and briefly describes the architecture, this paper aims to give a different perspective and more detail on different phases such as design, implementation, and user interface, as well as further details on the implementation. We approach this research using the methodology of Nunamaker et al. [23]. This methodology gives a structured approach to software development that consists of four phases: Observation, Theory Building, Systems Development, and Experimentation. The phases act on each other with the aim to solve specific research goals. Adhering to this, we will define problem statements, research questions, and objectives to approach this research. The objectives will be classified to the phases of the methodology. Out of the previously described challenges and motivating research projects, the following problem statements are identified:

Cloud Computing Requires High Technical Expertise and is Difficult to Use (PS1). Implementing solutions in the Cloud requires knowledge with the respective technologies and software engineering skills. This was described in SNERC in the context of NER model training and from CIE in the context of Cloud Resource Management as a challenge.

There is a Large Amount of NER Frameworks with Different Language Implementations and Requirements (PS2). This problem statement is motivated by the challenge of quantity of NER frameworks described in FIT4NER. Different NER frameworks handle training in their own implementation and programming languages. This makes it difficult for users to handle different frameworks.

---

[1] https://cordis.europa.eu/programme/id/H2020_DT-ICT-12-2020.
[2] https://www.ftk.de/en.

Different User Groups Expect Different Level of Customization. Customization Impacts System Simplicity (PS3). This Problem Statement is related to CIE. The problem concerns what level of abstraction should be applied to the model training functionality, which directly impacts the identified use cases. It poses the question if users should have an extensive possibility to customize and provision components. This may increase overhead of provisioning and is discouraging for users that are interested in a simple training workflow. A limited set of features however will restrict some users that may be unable to solve a particular training problem requiring a specific configuration. Simplification in the architecture is usually a sought after concept and interfaces should be clear defined to reduce unintentional behaviors and errors.

To approach the problem statements, the following research questions were identified:

1. How can a system for the configuration of Cloud resources for NER training be developed? (RQ1)
2. How can this system be implemented based on the spaCy framework on AWS? (RQ2)
3. What insights can be derived from the implementation of the system? (RQ3)

The research questions were assigned the following research objectives. The objectives are mapped to the of Nunamaker [23]. RO1.1, RO1.2, RO1.3 are associated with RQ1.

RO1.1 Research Architecture of Motivating Research Projects. (Phase. Observation). To support RQ1, the objective is to analyze the motivating research projects FIT4NER, and CIE to identify how our system could be integrated in their use cases and architecture. For example, analyzing the architecture could identify patterns and components that could be reused in the implementation of our system.

RO1.2 Research Literature for Software Design and Evaluation. (Phase: Observation). The objective is to understand the approaches of UCD [22], RUP [12], and Cognitive walkthrough [24] so that they can be applied to determine how a system can be developed for NER and the configuration of Cloud Resources. This objective also provides a structure to approach RQ1-3.

RO1.3 Research Literature and State-of-the-Art of NER, and Cloud Technologies. (Phase: Observation). The objective is to research the state-of-the art of NER and Cloud technologies to determine how they can be used to implement the system. By gathering the state of the art, the goal is to build on proven research and technologies and identify possible opportunities for the implementation.

The following RO2.1, RO2.2, RO2.3, RO2.4 are associated with RQ2.

RO2.1 Research the spaCy Framework and AWS Compute Services (Phase: Observation). An overview of the spaCy framework and AWS should be provided, since it is the main framework and Cloud provide for the given problem. The training process should be analyzed and briefly compared to other NER frameworks to identify possible abstraction layers that are shared between different frameworks. The AWS cloud should be reviewed regarding its services for providing compute resources to solve the given task.

RO2.2 Define the User Requirements of the System (Phase: Systems Development - Design). The objective is to define user groups and the requirements of the system, using User Centered Design [22] and Cognitive Walkthrough [24]. These requirements need to be listed and checked according to the described process and outline the feature set of the application.

RO2.3 Define a System Architecture (Phase: Systems Development - Design). The objective is to define the architecture of the system before the implementation. This ensures that the defined requirements can be implemented and reduces the risks of errors during implementation. The results of RO1-3 and RO2.1 should provide insights on the architecture and technology choices. The goal is to determine a suitable abstraction and functionality level for the web application regarding the training of spaCy models ind the context of a web application using the AWS cloud.

RO2.4 Implement the System (Phase: Systems Development - Prototyping). The objective is to implement the system according to the defined architecture. This supports directly RQ2. The result should be a functioning software that fulfills the identified requirements.

The following RO3.1, RO3.2, RO3.3 are associated with RQ3.

RO3.1 Define Methodology and Experiments to Evaluate the System. (Phase: Observation). To complete RQ3 it is required to analyze the methodology that is used to evaluate the system. To evaluate the system, the experiments to be conducted need to be defined.

RO3.2 Perform System Evaluation Experiments. (Phase: Implementation). The experiment should be conducted according to the methodology so that the results can provide insights to answer RQ3.

RO3.3 Analyze Experiment Results and Evaluate the System. (Phase: Experimentation). After RO3.2 is achieved, the results of the evaluation should be collected and analyzed. This includes the outputs of all other objectives, so that they can be put into perspective. The insights should then be used to conclude RQ3.

To summarize, this paper describes design, implementation, and evaluation of a system that is based on the spaCy[3] framework and the Amazon Web Services (AWS)[4]. The goal of the system is to support experts in the medical domain in the challenge of configuring Cloud resources and perform NER model training. The system implements a subset of the CIE identified use cases and attempts to realize a Cloud-based NER framework service component of the FIT4NER architecture. RO 1.1 was covered in this section. The next section addresses the state-of-the-art.

---

[3] https://spacy.io/.

[4] https://aws.amazon.com.

2   State of the Art in Science and Technology

In this section we will briefly describe the state-of-the art of the related concepts an technologies. This addresses ROs 1.3, 2.1.

NER developed as a field of NLP several decades ago. Nasar et al. conducted research on developments in the field [20]. They conclude that historically statistical models were used to perform NER. However the current state-of-the-art performance is achieved mainly through the use of ML methods such as Convolutional Neural Networks (CNNs) and hybrid variations including Conditional Random Fields (CRF). The Transformer architecture [28] is one of the best performing architectures for many NER tasks, according to NLP leaderboards such as *NER on CoNLL2003*[5].

As described in [29] there are different software frameworks that solve the problem of NER. The frameworks *Stanford NER, spaCy, NLTK, Polyglot, Flair, GATE, DeepPavlov* are compared in this study. These frameworks are implemented in either Python or Java. Each framework uses different methods to perform NER tasks. This shows that there is no consensus in implementing a method to perform NER in a framework. The performance and accuracy of frameworks models are variable and depend for example on the training data and target language. The frameworks also process different data formats.

NIST defines Cloud computing as *"a model for enabling ubiquitous, convenient, on-demand network access to a shared pool of configurable computing resources (e.g., networks, servers, storage, applications, and services) that can be rapidly provisioned and released with minimal management effort or service provider interaction."* [11]. The essential characteristics include *on-demand self service, broad network access, resource pooling, rapid elasticity and measured service*. Users are able to request and provision resources with minimal service provider interaction. The computing resources are provided from a pool provided by the Cloud service provider. The service is measured in some form e.g. load, bandwidth as a basis for usage amount. There are several large public Cloud providers that have established in the global market. The three largest ones by market share by the first quarter in 2022 are Amazon Web Services (AWS)[6] (34%), Microsoft Azure[7] (21%), and Google Cloud Platform[8] (GCP) (10%) [8]. These Cloud providers actively shape the state of the art of Cloud computing and continuously develop and adapt their services.

We consider Transformers as the state-of-the-art for NER tasks and the developments in frameworks and Cloud offerings for the design of the application for the following section.

---

[5] https://paperswithcode.com/sota/named-entity-recognition-ner-on-conll-2003.
[6] https://aws.amazon.com.
[7] https://azure.com.
[8] https://cloud.google.com.

3   Conceptual Modeling and Design

In this section the design and architecture of the system are described, addressing ROs 1.2, 2.2, and 2.3. The system was designed using User Centered Systems Designed [22]. Using this method, the system is designed around previously identified user requirements. This ensures that the system implementation revolves around the identified requirements to deliver a reliable result.

The use context is derived from the motivation research projects. The context is a system in the medical domain to support NER tasks. Two main user groups will be considered for the application. First, **NER Experts** are users that are actively working on training NER models. They are intending to configure and optimize models and exploit various configuration mechanisms that are provided by the frameworks. They are not very familiar with infrastructure and Cloud technologies and may be moderately familiar with the documents of the medical domain. Second, **Medical Domain Experts** are users that do not have intensive knowledge of NER and frameworks. They are knowledgeable in the medical domain and intend to easily produce models based on medical documents for further use. They have also little knowledge about IT infrastructure and Cloud technologies.

The user requirements are also motivated from the related research projects CIE and FIT4NER. The use cases of CIE are visible in Fig. 1. Due to project time constraints, only a subset of use cases are selected for implementation. This subset is also marked in Fig. 1. The use cases of the Cloud Extension are *Train, Store, Deploy in Cloud, Select Hardware, Visualize Standard Metrics*. The general use cases to be also implemented are *Train Model, Train Transformer-based Model, and Select Hyperparameter*.

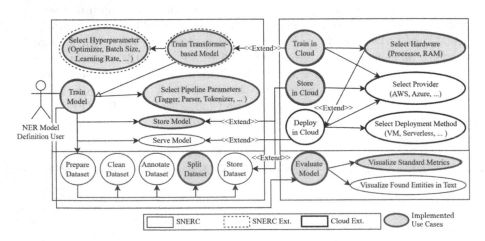

Fig. 1. CIE UML Use Case Diagram of [26] with marked implemented use cases.

This subset provides the operations to configure training for NER models. This includes the configuration of Transformer models. Transformers are generally trained using GPU processors [3]. This has implications on infrastructure design. In order to provide a cost-effective solution to support medical professionals with NER training, both CPU and GPU infrastructure should be available. The cost point of CPU is significantly lower on AWS compared to GPU[9] and training of models can be performed on both architectures [3]. The use case of storing the model requires a flexible storage service that can handle large data sets. NER Model Performance can be measured through different metrics, such as Recall, Precision, and F-Score [17]. Displaying performance metrics and configuring elements, a user interface component is used to realize this task. In order to simplify usage, the configuration of underlying compute resources, such as provisioning of processing instances, network configuration, and storage should be minimal and supported through automation. The infrastructure life cycle, and cleanup of resources should also be handled by the system. Furthermore the application should be scalable to many jobs and not restrict users through capacity bottlenecks and be able to handle large amounts of data.

In summary, in order to realize the identified use cases and further requirements, the common Model-View-Controller architecture pattern is chosen to develop the system. The MVC pattern is suitable for human system interaction use cases [9]. This pattern also fits into the architecture of CIE. Additionally, the system should be defined as different components which are also used in FIT4NER and CIE. This creates a separation of concerns and complements the pattern of the relating research projects. In order to provide scalability and support the MLOps flow referenced in [6], a job queue pattern can be used to facilitate the model training. Next, the system will be implemented according to the design architecture to answer RQ2.

4 System Implementation

In this section we will describe the implementation of the system, addressing RO2.4. We will begin with describing the MVC architecture elements visible in Fig. 2. In the implementation several of the proposed components of CIE are implemented. The diagram shows how the use cases map to the components. The NER Model Definition Manager, Cloud Training Config Manager, and Cloud Deployment manager are components of the controller layer. They control the creation and execution of the model training jobs and the provisioning of the Cloud resources. The NER Model Definition, NER Model, and Cloud Training Config are part of the model. They are instantiated by the controller components. The dashed components Cloud Deployment Definition, Storage Service, Deployment Service, and Compute Service are implemented using AWS services. The components contained in the grey shaded box are implemented as a standalone web application with a user interface.

---

[9] https://aws.amazon.com/pricing.

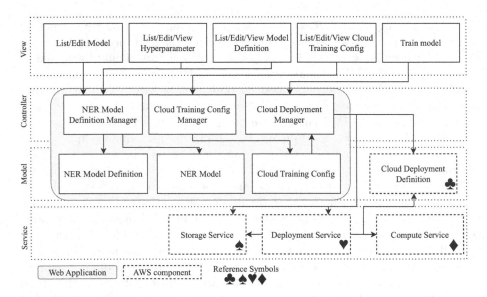

Fig. 2. MVC component architecture of the implementation (AWS components contain reference symbols for Fig. 3).

The NER framework used is the spaCy[10] framework. The web application is implemented using Python[11], the Flask framework[12], and the Bootstrap[13] framework. The application communicates with AWS components using the boto3[14] library. Transformer training is provided through the Huggingface[15] library provisioned through spaCy. Figure 3 shows the deployment architecture of the implementation. The compute environment that run the training jobs is provided though AWS Batch[16]. Batch provides a job queue system and manages a connected compute environment to execute container tasks. When a new job enters the queue it contains resource requirements for CPU and memory. Batch then provisions the required resources and allocates the job to the resources. There are two separate compute environments defined for CPU and GPU based jobs. The compute environment for CPU jobs uses the AWS Fargate service to execute container tasks and a predefined job template for this execution queue. The compute environment for GPU jobs uses the AWS EC2 service with the g4dn.xlarge instance type. The instance provides 1 NVIDIA T4 GPU. GPU instances are currently not available through Fargate. Batch controls the launch and termination of EC2 virtual machines that have access to GPU resources for

---

[10] https://www.spacy.io.
[11] https://www.python.org.
[12] https://flask.palletsprojects.com/en/2.2.x/.
[13] https://www.getbootstrap.com.
[14] https://boto3.amazonaws.com/v1/documentation/api/latest/index.html.
[15] https://huggingface.co.
[16] https://aws.amazon.com/batch/.

the training tasks. The queue setup allows for scalability of compute resources. The training job itself executes as a Python task inside a Docker[17] container on the compute environment. It is executed with resources specified in the Cloud Training Config.

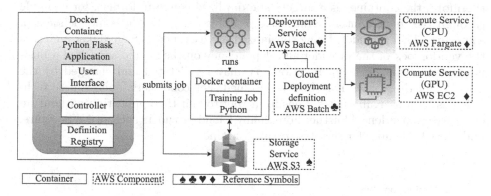

Fig. 3. System Deployment Architecture of the implementation [26] with reference symbols.

A user first configures the compute resources in a wizard page (see Fig. 4). The page is structured as a step wizard, which organizes the information related to compute and NER configuration. This creates a better overview for the user. The UI provides visual tooltips to assist users that require additional information. This way, the information stays concise while also providing additional details to users that require it. Next, the NER training is configured as seen in Fig. 5. This page contains configurations that are particular to spaCy training and also explains elements. Expert users are able to provide advanced configuration files and upload them directly. This gives more control to this advanced user group, while not overloading non-experts with information and settings. After the job submission the status of the job will be displayed as seen in Fig. 6. The status page contains an overview of the compute and training parameters and gives some information on the dataset such as sample size. The page reports the status of the AWS container training task. Once the job is complete the model is made available for download as a compressed package file for the user and are presented with the performance scores of the model.

The container wrapper ensures isolation and portability of the application and makes it independent of a specific runtime platform. This also improves security, since only the required libraries are present on the system, without the need of a full operating system and only exposing the necessary application port. The container wrapper of the training job increases the flexibility of development, since any task can be implemented inside the container. Furthermore the portability of the application is improved, as it is independent of surrounding

---

[17] https://docker.io.

infrastructure. The security is also improved, as the container only contains necessary libraries. Services such as AWS SageMaker have restrictions on supported frameworks and available actions that may not fit all use cases. For example, at the moment AWS SageMaker does not support the spaCy framework. This limit does not exist for container development, but requires own implementation. Furthermore, the container is a largely standardized compute format, for example through the Open Container Initiative [7]. This means that it is independent of a specific Cloud provider. Using specialized services such as SageMaker increases the vendor lock of the provider and dependency on the offered service of a business organization. Certain functionality may be dictated and changed by the provider or the service may be discontinued. For containers, open source technologies such as Kubernetes[18] ensure a way to run the application without an enterprise dependency. Furthermore, many Cloud providers such as AWS, Azure, and Google Cloud offer services to run containers.

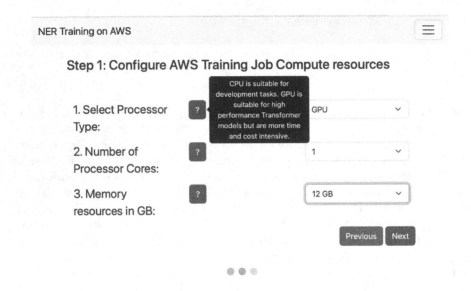

Fig. 4. Compute resource specification wizard page.

In summary, the system to configure cloud resources for NER training is implemented as a containerized Python web application that utilizes AWS resources for job execution and artifact storage. It uses the NER framework spaCy and supports training of Transformers. In the next section this system will be evaluated in order to answer RQ3.

---

[18] https://kubernetes.io/.

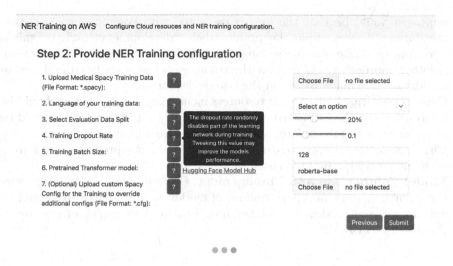

Fig. 5. NER Training configuration wizard page.

5   Evaluation

This section will cover the evaluation of the application and addresses RO3.1, 3.2, and 3.3. First, the selected evaluation methods will be described. The implementation will be evaluated in two sections. The first one will be based on cognitive walkthrough [24] to check the usability of the approach for the identified user requirements. The second one will analyze how fine-tuning parameters can affect model quality using the application using a standard corpus of the medical domain.

5.1   Cognitive Walkthrough

In the first evaluation phase, a review of the applications UI and functionality was performed in a session with one PhD and two experts of the department of multimedia and internet applications. Users are able to configure the compute resources and parameters to perform NER model training. Several functional deficiencies have been identified. They will be briefly explained:

1. **Re-training of models.** The application does not support the re-training or further training of previously trained models. This is a desirable functionality so more training data could be added and training settings changed to achieve a better performing model. Currently there is no model management implemented.
2. **Recommendation profiles for compute resources.** An inexperienced user may not know which values to select for CPU or memory. A possible

approach would be that the user is presented with compute profile recommendations. For example the profile labels "development test", or "high-performance" have specific settings for RAM and cores attached to them. Another approach could be that the training corpus is analyzed and recommendations are made based on the size of the corpus.

3. **Cost reporting**. Using Cloud resources incurs usage costs. A user should be informed about the estimated costs the training job will incur. This could be given as an estimate before, and as a definitive report after the training. This makes the compute costs transparent and may prevent a user from accidentally triggering high costs.

4. **Model Comparison and Management**. Users should be able to compare the training history and performance of models in an overview page and be able to manage models for further use. This is the concept of the Model Registry in FIT4NER.

Fig. 6. NER Training Job status page.

In summary, the application is able to support users in training NER models using the AWS cloud. This prototype includes support for both expert and non-expert users. Several functional deficiencies, such as re-training of models, compute profiles, cost-reporting and model comparison have been defined that could be addressed in future work.

5.2 Fine-Tuning Transformer Training

One use case requirement is to fine-tune NER training. This requirement is evaluated by performing experimental training jobs with different parameter settings to produce models with differing properties.

The application is used to train the corpus GERNERMED [5] which contains 8599 annotated records in the medical domain in the German language. The annotated corpus contains entities drug, route, strength, frequency, duration, form, and dosage. The model is trained on one g4dn AWS EC2 instance, which provides one NVIDIA T4 GPU with 10 GB of GPU memory. The training uses spaCy version 3.5. In the first experiment, the goal is to observe the Precision (P), Recall (R), and F-score (F) and the execution time of the training, when changing the independent variables number of CPU cores, batch size, window size, and the spaCy mixed-precision setting. The Precision is the proportion of true positives out of all predicted positives. Recall is the proportion of true positives out of all actual positives. The F-Score combines P and R on a scale of 1 (perfect) to 0 (worst) and is computed according to Moosavi et al. [17]. Roberta [14] was the model used for training with an Adam optimizer and linear warmup scheduler. The training ends after 1600 steps without improvement or 20,000 epochs. The usage of the mixed-precision setting is a setting usable in Tensor Processing Units (TPU) and achieved an improvement of 9.4% execution time. An increase in CPU leads to a longer training process. Adjusting the parameters in the UI affects the model scores, enabling users to fine-tune NER training. This is further described in [26].

The second batch of training jobs is using the bert-base-uncased model [14]. This should show that different Transformer models can be used in the application and to be able to compare the performance. In this batch the learning rate and training data split are adjusted to observe the effect on the model score. In this batch the mixed-precision setting stays enabled. All trainings use 4 CPU and 1 GPU. The batch size is 1024. The window size is 128. The experiment shows that different pre-trained models achieve different scores as seen in an example in Table 1.

Table 1. Comparison of different pre-trained models used for training.

Pretrained Model	GPU	RAM	Training Duration	Precision	Recall	F-Score
roberta-base [15]	1	12 GB	85 min	0.849	0.836	0.842
bert-base-uncased [2]	1	12 GB	65 min	0.832	0.826	0.829

It is important to point out that not all training configuration constellations were explored exhaustively, and there is potential for improving both the score and execution time of the experiments. The goal was to conduct simple experiments to showcase the features of the system.

In summary, the training experiments validate the functionality of the application to train NER models in the medical domain. The mixed-precision setting (TPU processors only) showed an improvement in training time. Parameter configurations can also lead to an increase in training time and therefore cost without marginally improving the score. Overall the experiments provide several parameter constellations including performance scores for reference.

6   Summary and Outlook

In this paper we motivated, designed, developed, and evaluated a system for the management of Cloud resources for deep learning-based Named Entity Recognition in Health Care. The system aims to address the challenge domain experts face in utilizing Cloud technologies due to knowledge barriers and effort constraints. The system was designed as a component-based MVC application to support use cases of the CIE and FIT4NER research projects such as Transformer-based training. It consists of a central controller component that manages configuration the submission of NER training jobs. It uses the spaCy NER framework. The compute environment is provisioned through AWS Batch. The evaluation of the system identifies functional deficiencies such as re-training of models, and management of models. We verified the functionality of the training and showed several parameter constellations with their effects on training time and cost. The evaluation was not exhaustive and the implementation is subject to further development.

Acknowledgements. The author, Benedict Hartmann, acknowledges the financial support provided by Allianz Technology SE to attend HCI International 2023.

References

1. Ahmadi, M., Aslani, N.: Capabilities and advantages of cloud computing in the implementation of electronic health record. Acta Informatica Medica **26**(1), 24 (2018)
2. Devlin, J., Chang, M.W., Lee, K., Toutanova, K.: BERT: pre-training of deep bidirectional transformers for language understanding. arXiv preprint arXiv:1810.04805 (2018)
3. Explosion: Spacy (2023). https://spacy.io/
4. Fichman, R.G., Kohli, R., Krishnan, R.: Editorial overview–the role of information systems in healthcare: current research and future trends. Inf. Syst. Res. **22**(3), 419–428 (2011)
5. Frei, J., Kramer, F.: GERNERMED: an open German medical NER model. Softw. Impacts **11**, 100212 (2022)
6. Freund, F., et al.: FIT4NER - towards a framework independent toolkit for named entity recognition (2022)

7. Fu, S., Liu, J., Chu, X., Hu, Y.: Toward a standard interface for cloud providers: the container as the narrow waist. IEEE Internet Comput. **20**(2), 66–71 (2016)

8. Synergy Research Group: Q2 cloud market grows by 29% despite strong currency headwinds; Amazon increases its share, July 2022. https://www.srgresearch. com/articles/q2-cloud-market-grows-by-29-despite-strong-currency-headwinds-amazon-increases-its-share

9. Grove, R.F., Ozkan, E.: The MVC-web design pattern. In: International Conference on Web Information Systems and Technologies, vol. 2, pp. 127–130. SCITEPRESS (2011)

10. Hartmann, B.: Development of an application for the configuration of cloud resources to support NER model training with the spacy framework in the AWS cloud. Coursework at University of Hagen, February 2023, unpublished

11. Hogan, M., Liu, F., Sokol, A., Tong, J.: NIST cloud computing standards roadmap. NIST Spec. Publ. **35**, 6–11 (2011)

12. Jacobson, I., Booch, G., Rumbaugh, J.: The unified process. IEEE Softw. **16**(3), 96 (1999)

13. Kohli, R., Tan, S.S.L.: Electronic health records: how can is researchers contribute to transforming healthcare? MIS Q. **40**(3), 553–573 (2016). https://doi.org/10. 25300/MISQ/2016/40.3.02

14. Liu, Y., et al.: RoBERTa: a robustly optimized BERT pretraining approach. CoRR abs/1907.11692 (2019). http://arxiv.org/abs/1907.11692

15. Liu, Y., et al.: RoBERTa: a robustly optimized BERT pretraining approach. arXiv preprint arXiv:1907.11692 (2019)

16. Menachemi, N., Brooks, R.G.: Reviewing the benefits and costs of electronic health records and associated patient safety technologies. J. Med. Syst. **30**, 159–168 (2006)

17. Moosavi, N.S., Strube, M.: Which coreference evaluation metric do you trust? A proposal for a link-based entity aware metric. In: Proceedings of the 54th Annual Meeting of the Association for Computational Linguistics (Volume 1: Long Papers), Berlin, Germany, August 2016, pp. 632–642. Association for Computational Linguistics (2016). https://doi.org/10.18653/v1/P16-1060

18. Nadeau, D., Sekine, S.: A survey of named entity recognition and classification. Lingvisticae Investigationes **30**(1), 3–26 (2007)

19. Narayanan, D., Santhanam, K., Kazhamiaka, F., Phanishayee, A., Zaharia, M.: Analysis and exploitation of dynamic pricing in the public cloud for ml training. In: VLDB DISPA Workshop 2020 (2020)

20. Nasar, Z., Jaffry, S.W., Malik, M.K.: Named entity recognition and relation extraction: state-of-the-art. ACM Comput. Surv. (CSUR) **54**(1), 1–39 (2021)

21. Nguyen, N.: Development of an application for the configuration of cloud resources to support NER model training with the spacy framework in the Azure cloud. Coursework at University of Hagen, February 2023, unpublished

22. Norman, D.A., Draper, S.W.: User Centered System Design: New Perspectives on Human-Computer Interaction (1986)

23. Nunamaker, J.F., Jr., Chen, M., Purdin, T.D.: Systems development in information systems research. J. Manag. Inf. Syst. **7**(3), 89–106 (1990)

24. Polson, P.G., Lewis, C., Rieman, J., Wharton, C.: Cognitive walkthroughs: a method for theory-based evaluation of user interfaces. Int. J. Man Mach. Stud. **36**(5), 741–773 (1992)

25. Singh, H., Spitzmueller, C., Petersen, N.J., Sawhney, M.K., Sittig, D.F.: Information overload and missed test results in electronic health record-based settings. JAMA Intern. Med. **173**(8), 702–704 (2013)

26. Tamla, P., Hartmann, B., Nguyen, N., Kramer, C., Freund, F., Hemmje, M.: CIE: a cloud-based information extraction system for named entity recognition in AWS, Azure, and medical domain. In: Coenen, F., et al. (eds.) Knowledge Discovery, Knowledge Engineering and Knowledge Management, IC3K 2022. Communications in Computer and Information Science, vol. 1842, pp 127–148. Springer, Cham (2023). https://doi.org/10.1007/978-3-031-43471-6_6

27. Tamla, P.: Supporting access to textual resources using named entity recognition and document classification. Ph.D. thesis, Hagen (2022). https://ub-deposit.fernuni-hagen.de/receive/mir_mods_00001782

28. Vaswani, A., et al.: Attention is all you need. In: Advances in Neural Information Processing Systems, vol. 30 (2017)

29. Vychegzhanin, S., Kotelnikov, E.: Comparison of named entity recognition tools applied to news articles. In: 2019 Ivannikov Ispras Open Conference (ISPRAS), pp. 72–77. IEEE (2019)

30. Wan, Q., Liu, J., Wei, L., Ji, B.: A self-attention based neural architecture for Chinese medical named entity recognition. Math. Biosci. Eng. **17**(4), 3498–3511 (2020)

31. Weingärtner, R., Bräscher, G.B., Westphall, C.B.: Cloud resource management: a survey on forecasting and profiling models. J. Netw. Comput. Appl. **47**, 99–106 (2015)

32. Yao, L., Liu, H., Liu, Y., Li, X., Anwar, M.W.: Biomedical named entity recognition based on deep neutral network. Int. J. Hybrid Inf. Technol. **8**(8), 279–288 (2015)

Explainable AI-Based Interface System for Weather Forecasting Model

Soyeon Kim[1], Junho Choi[1], Yeji Choi[2], Subeen Lee[1],
Artyom Stitsyuk[1], Minkyoung Park[1], Seongyeop Jeong[1],
You-Hyun Baek[3], and Jaesik Choi[1,4(✉)]

[1] Korea Advanced Institute of Science and Technology (KAIST), Daejeon, Korea
{soyeon.k,junho.choi,forestsoop,stitsyuk,jrneomy,seongyeop.jeong,
jaesik.choi}@kaist.ac.kr
[2] SI-Analytics, Daejeon, Korea
yejichoi@si-analytics.ai
[3] National Institute of Meteorological Sciences (NIMS), Jeju 63568, Korea
yhbaek88@korea.kr
[4] INEEJI, Gyeonggi, Korea

Abstract. Machine learning (ML) is becoming increasingly popular in meteorological decision-making. Although the literature on explainable artificial intelligence (XAI) is growing steadily, user-centered XAI studies have not extend to this domain yet. This study defines three requirements for explanations of black-box models in meteorology through user studies: statistical model performance for different rainfall scenarios to identify model bias, model reasoning, and the confidence of model outputs. Appropriate XAI methods are mapped to each requirement, and the generated explanations are tested quantitatively and qualitatively. An XAI interface system is designed based on user feedback. The results indicate that the explanations increase decision utility and user trust. Users prefer intuitive explanations over those based on XAI algorithms even for potentially easy-to-recognize examples. These findings can provide evidence for future research on user-centered XAI algorithms, as well as a basis to improve the usability of AI systems in practice.

Keywords: User-Centered Explainable AI · Interactive Visualization · Feature Attribution · Confidence Calibration · Precipitation Forecasting

---

Supported by the Korean Institute of Information & Communications Technology Planning & Evaluation (IITP) and the Korean Ministry of Science and ICT(MSIT) under grant agreement No. 2019-0-00075 (Artificial Intelligence Graduate School Program (KAIST)) and No. 2022-0-00984 (Development of Plug-and-Play Explainable Artificial Intelligence Method), and from the Korea Meteorological Administration (KMA) and Korean National Institute of Meteorological Sciences (NIMS) under grant agreement No. KMA2021-00123 (Developing Intelligent Assistant Technology and Its Application for Weather Forecasting Process).

© The Author(s), under exclusive license to Springer Nature Switzerland AG 2023
H. Degen et al. (Eds.): HCII 2023, LNCS 14059, pp. 101–119, 2023.
https://doi.org/10.1007/978-3-031-48057-7_7

1 Introduction

Weather prediction has always been an integral part of human society due to its significant socioeconomic impact, influencing various aspects such as agricultural productivity, industrial output, labor efficiency, energy demand, public health, conflicts, economic growth, [8] as well as ecosystems and their ecosystem services [11]. With the increasing volatility of meteorological patterns caused by the climate crisis, economic losses from extreme weather events are on a rapid incline [24, 42]. Accurate weather forecasting is crucial for mitigating the effects of these scenarios.

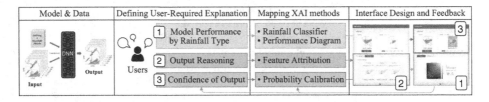

Fig. 1. Workflow for developing a user-centered explainable artificial intelligence (XAI) interface system. The system is developed based on the procedures established in the previous literature [19, 20]. The scope of explanations is defined based on the requirements set by the practitioners; appropriate XAI algorithms are selected based on the defined scope; and the interface is designed with user feedback

Operational weather forecasting is conventionally performed through Numerical Weather Prediction (NWP), a process of simulating future weather patterns using a comprehensive set of equations that describe the physical dynamics of the atmosphere [15]. Although it has a long history and sees use even today, NWP faces several challenges such as high computational costs and sensitivity to the derived initial conditions [31]. Data-driven deep learning models for weather prediction are seen as a potential alternative, being able to exploit the growing availability of weather data and make predictions for a fraction of the cost of operating NWP models [29].

One issue faced by practitioners in producing weather forecasts is the vast amount of documents required to produce the forecasts. For example, Korea Meteorological Agency (KMA) creates 2.2 TB worth of data daily on average for weather forecasts [18]. The sheer size of the data can be extremely burdensome for the forecasters, who not only have limited time when making short-term forecasts and associated decision-making, but also need to continuously monitor the occurrence of sudden extreme weather patterns. One of the reasons for requiring large data lies with the difficulty in accurate prediction of rainfall. If the accuracy of rainfall prediction can be improved through the use of deep learning, it could reduce some of the burden placed on the forecasters so that their efforts could be invested elsewhere.

A key issue preventing the use of deep learning models in operational forecasting is their lack of interpretability [31]. While the state-of-the-art models

[10, 16, 30, 38] may make accurate predictions, they tend to be black boxes – a user cannot determine how the models infer these outcomes. A forecaster would not be able to accept predictions without sufficient justifications due to the high stakes associated with wrong predictions. The extensive array of techniques in the field of explainable artificial intelligence (XAI) can help meet these requirements [1, 12, 34]; unfortunately, the sheer number of available techniques makes it difficult to determine which methods should be used. One potential approach of filtering the appropriate techniques is to center the explanations around its intended audience. An appropriate explanation is dependent on the task performed by a model and the audience of the explanation [21, 25]. Therefore, an explanation system should be centered around its users, regardless of domain. A recent study of the user-explained AI (UXAI) [6] even claims that users may not be satisfied by an explanation that has considered the users in its design if it has not been made *with* the users. Despite the increasing interest in both user-centric [21] and regular XAI in the meteorological domain [3, 22, 23], there seems to be a distinct lack of user-centered XAI studies in meteorology. This paper attempts to fill this gap by following a user-centered XAI framework to create a prototype system that explains a precipitation prediction AI model. Specifically, the paper follows the process described by [19] and [20]: (a) the scope of explanations is defined through an XAI question bank, which divides the typical questions that could be asked by a user into several major categories, (b) appropriate XAI methods are selected based on the categories that the questions belong to, and (c) an interface system is designed based on user input and feedback to express the explanations (Fig. 1).

The main contributions of this paper are as follows:

- Demonstrates the procedures of the user-centric XAI development framework from an operational perspective.
- Creates a user-experience-based prototype of the XAI system in the meteorological domain.
- Analyzes the available XAI methods and discusses their practical limitations.

The eventual objective of our work is to provide accurate and trustworthy information required by the user as an end-product of a single map, reducing the procedural burden shouldered by the forecasters in the current system.

2   Materials

2.1   Model and Data

The aim of this study is to design a user-centered interface system for explaining UNet2, a UNet-based model (an unpublished variant of DeepRaNE [17]) developed by the National Institute of Meteorological Sciences (NIMS) for 2020 radar synthesis data for very short-term rainfall intensity prediction (Fig. 2). UNet2

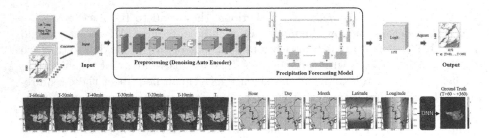

Fig. 2. The target precipitation forecasting model and data. The data consists of radar hybrid scan reflectivity.

consists of a denoising autoencoder followed by a convolutional neural network-based U-Net architecture and addresses a segmentation task of predicting three rainfall intensity intervals (no rain 0–1 mm/h, light rain 1–10 mm/h, and heavy rain 10 mm/h over) between 1 and 6 h in the future at 1-h intervals. The class intervals have been established by domain experts. The input data consists of seven radar data sequence at ten minutes intervals, two spatial features for longitude and latitude, and three temporal features for year, month, and day of the current date. The data are concatenated into 12 channels following an early fusion scheme. The performance of UNet2 is comparable to the MetNet [38] and HRRR numerical models for very short-term predictions (Fig. 3). In particular, for rainfall prediction with a one-hour lead time and rainfall rates of 1–10 mm/h, UNet2 and MetNet achieve F1 scores of 0.824 and 0.822, respectively. For heavy rainfall rates over 10 mm/h, UNet2 and MetNet have F1 scores of 0.604 and 0.480, respectively.

Model	Score	Class (mm/hr)	Lead Time (hour)					
			1	2	3	4	5	6
Unet1	F1	1	0.772	0.692	0.642	0.595	**0.570**	**0.519**
		10	0.558	0.398	0.315	**0.265**	0.206	0.121
	CSI	1	0.629	0.629	0.472	0.424	**0.398**	**0.351**
		10	0.387	0.249	0.187	**0.153**	**0.115**	0.065
Unet2 (Target)	F1	1	**0.824**	0.710	0.642	0.579	0.514	0.462
		10	**0.604**	**0.419**	0.326	0.243	0.174	0.126
	CSI	1	**0.701**	0.551	0.473	0.407	0.346	0.300
		10	**0.433**	0.265	0.195	0.139	0.095	0.067
MetNet	F1	1	0.822	**0.721**	**0.665**	**0.597**	0.547	0.502
		10	0.480	**0.419**	**0.328**	0.255	**0.207**	**0.168**
	CSI	1	0.697	**0.697**	**0.487**	**0.425**	0.376	0.335
		10	0.316	**0.316**	**0.196**	0.146	**0.115**	**0.092**

[40]

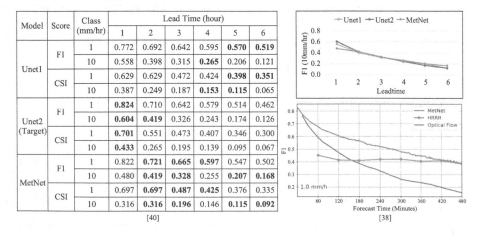

[38]

Fig. 3. The performance of the target model. UNet1 and UNet2 built by NIMS are comparable to MetNet [38] and HRRR numerical model for very short-term predictions. Reproduced from [38] and [40].

3   Methods

3.1   User Requirements of Explanation

This study has been performed with discussions from sixteen online meetings with NIMS, as well as three in-person external advisories from domain experts from 27 April 2022 to 12 April 2023.

User Study. An XAI question bank [19,20] is utilized in the early phase of interviews to brainstorm the desired explanations from AI systems. Based on the discussion, the user requirements can be stated as follows. First, forecasters are interested in the consistency of the model inferences in various rainfall situations. If systematic biases for each rainfall type are provided, it can help the forecasters decide whether to use the model in practice. Second, forecasters consider the movement, growth, and dissipation of the convection cell as key factors for predicting the change of very short-term precipitation clouds around a 6-h scale. In particular, they would like to identify the precursors to pinpoint the seeds that are the most susceptible to convective system development. Through the precursors, the users can indicate the locations that require more intensive monitoring. Finally, the users are interested in the local reliability of the predictions. For the rest of this study, these three requirements are referred to as model performance explanation by rainfall type, output reasoning explanation, and confidence of output explanation, respectively.

Mapping XAI Methods. Appropriate XAI methods are selected to address each need. First, a rainfall type classifier is combined with performance diagram for each rainfall type for generating a model performance explanation (Sect. 3.2). Second, feature attribution is used for output reasoning explanation since the associated techniques can evaluate the contributions of the input features for generating the predictions (Sect. 3.3). Lastly, a probability calibration technique is adopted for model confidence explanation (Sect. 3.4).

3.2   Explanation 1: Model Performance by Rainfall Types

Rainfall Type Classifier. For this explanation, an input sample is assigned to a rainfall category using a deep learning classifier; then, the model's predictive performance for the corresponding rainfall type is analyzed. This setup allows for a comparison of model performance over different rainfall scenarios.

The rainfall type classifier is built by fine-tuning the parameters from the pre-trained encoder of the target model. Self-organizing map (SOM)-based rainfall type classification data and its quantitative labels provided by NIMS based on the characteristics of the Korean Peninsula have been used for the experiment. The five rainfall types are monsoon front (southern region), monsoon front (central region), isolated thunderstorm, extratropical cyclone (east coast), and

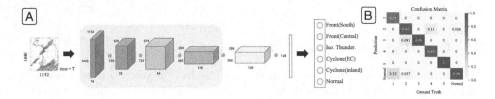

Fig. 4. The structure of the precipitation classifier (A) and the resulting confusion matrix (B). The rainfall types are based on a SOM-based weather classification study (an unpublished result of [36] with the same research procedure on a specific region).

extratropical cyclone (inland). These precipitation types are often used by forecasters in practice. 29, 280, 53, 43, and 24 samples are used for each of the five types of rainfall in 2020. Additionally, 218 cases are sampled in equal intervals for the no-rain type. The dataset is split into three portions: 60% for training, 20% for validation, and another 20% for testing. For the training dataset, a sampler that follows a multinomial distribution using the probability parameter as the inverse of the number of samples of each class in the dataset is used to solve the class imbalance problem. The classifier is optimized using the Adam solver with a learning rate of 1e−6 and weight decay of 1e−8. Additionally, the weighted cross-entropy loss is adopted to account for the classes with deficient samples. The classifier performance shows an accuracy of 93.07% (Fig. 4.B).

Performance Diagram. The performance diagram is a method of visualizing the overall performance of a model [32] and can express important model evaluation indicators in the meteorological domain such as bias, critical success index (CSI), probability of detection (POD), and success ratio in a single chart (Fig. 6). To alleviate the problem of imbalanced rainfall intensities, where the rainfall amounts of interest infrequently occur in the real world, the metrics are computed for the light rainfall intensity and more (1 mm/h over) and the heavy rainfall intensity (10 mm/h over) as shown in Fig. 5 and are averaged. Formally,

$$
\text{ModifiedPOD} = \frac{1}{2} \left(\frac{\text{Hit}_{1\ (\text{mm/h})\ \text{over}}}{\text{Hit}_{1\ \text{over}} + \text{Miss}_{1\ \text{over}}} + \frac{\text{Hit}_{10\ \text{over}}}{\text{Hit}_{10\ \text{over}} + \text{Miss}_{10\ \text{over}}} \right) \quad (1)
$$

$$
\text{ModifiedFAR} = \frac{1}{2} \left(\frac{\text{FalseAlarm}_{1\ (\text{mm/h})\ \text{over}}}{\text{FalseAlarm}_{1\ \text{over}} + \text{Hit}_{1\ \text{over}}} \right.
$$
$$
\left. + \frac{\text{FalseAlarm}_{10\ \text{over}}}{\text{FalseAlarm}_{10\ \text{over}} + \text{Hit}_{10\ \text{over}}} \right) \quad (2)
$$

$$
\text{ModifiedF1} = \frac{1}{2} \left(\frac{\text{Hit}_{1\ (\text{mm/h})\ \text{over}}}{\text{Hit}_{1\ \text{over}} + \frac{1}{2}(\text{Miss}_{1\ \text{over}} + \text{FalseAlarm}_{1\ \text{over}})} \right.
$$
$$
\left. + \frac{\text{Hit}_{10\ \text{over}}}{\text{Hit}_{10\ \text{over}} + \frac{1}{2}(\text{Miss}_{10\ \text{over}} + \text{FalseAlarm}_{10\ \text{over}})} \right) \quad (3)
$$

Predict		True (mm/hr)		
		0-1	1-10	10~
	0-1	TN1 (Correct reject)	FN1 (Miss)	
	1-10	FP1 (False alarm)	TP1 (Hit)	
	10~			

Predict		True (mm/hr)		
		0-1	1-10	10~
	0-1	TN2 (Correct reject)		FN2 (Miss)
	1-10			
	10~	FP2 (False alarm)		TP2 (Hit)

Fig. 5. Confusion matrices to calculate performance metrics on the imbalanced data.

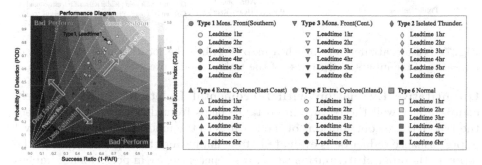

Fig. 6. Performance diagram. The diagram helps visualize the overall performance of bias, CSI, POD, and success ratio in a single chart.

As results in Fig. 6, the performance diagram shows that for a lead time of 1 h, the model has the best performance for rainfall type 5 - inland extratropical cyclone. The model is a little overestimated overall, but less estimated on the long lead times. The worst performance arises in the type of normal weather at the lead time of 6 h. The low POD suggests that the model fails to predict the real rainfall at this lead time.

3.3 Explanation 2: Output Reasoning

Feature attribution methods analyze the contribution of the inputs for a model's prediction. As shown in Fig. 7 feature attribution methods allow users to investigate the reason why the model infers the development or the dissipation of a rain cell one hour later from the radar input. There are many feature attribution methods available; even a list of some of the more prevalent methods (*Saliency Maps* [37], *Integrated Gradients* [39], *GuidedGrad-CAM* [35] and *Layer-Wise Relevance Propagation (LRP)* [2] to name a few) can be extensive. This study selects the attribution method by quantitatively evaluating the completeness of the generated attributions following the incremental deletion criterion [27,33]: the predictive performance of the model should decrease as the inputs are removed sequentially based on their importance, with the speed of decline faster at the initial stages of removal compared to the latter stages. After selecting a method, sample cases are analyzed by domain experts to evaluate user opinions on the generated results.

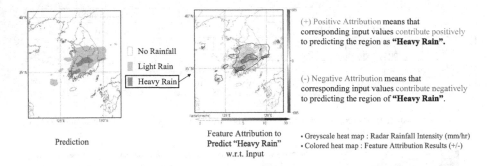

(+) Positive Attribution means that corresponding input values contribute positively to predicting the region as **"Heavy Rain"**.

(-) Negative Attribution means that corresponding input values contribute negatively to predicting the region of **"Heavy Rain"**.

Prediction

Feature Attribution to Predict "Heavy Rain" w.r.t. Input

• Greyscale heat map : Radar Rainfall Intensity (mm/hr)
• Colored heat map : Feature Attribution Results (+/-)

Fig. 7. Feature attribution. The heatmap describes the location and the degree of relevance of the inputs as the cause of the trained model prediction.

Quantitative Evaluation with Incremental Deletion. To quantitatively compare how well the feature importance maps from different methods reflect the true relative contributions of the features to the model predictions, the level of performance reduction is evaluated after eliminating the Top K% region of the input in the order of attribution value. A steeper decrease in performance implies greater fidelity. As shown in Fig. 8, the integrated gradient method outperforms the other methods.

Qualitative Evaluation of Selected Attribution Method. To qualitatively evaluate the explanatory results, case-based anecdotal evidence has been analyzed through three consultations with external experts. Specifically, extreme precipitation cases are selected from the 2020 SOM-based classification study on the JJAS (June, July, August, and September which represent the period of the southwest monsoon) period in Korea by NIMS to match recognizable physical dynamics with attribution patterns.

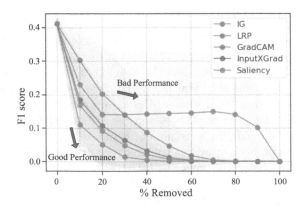

Fig. 8. Quantitative evaluation of the output reasoning explanation from different feature attribution methods.

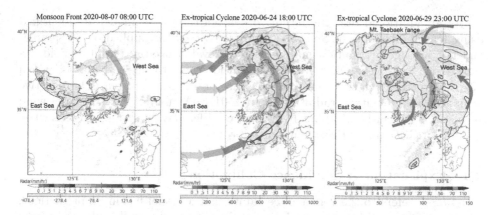

Fig. 9. Anecdotal evidence based on domain expert's case analysis of monsoon front and extratropical cyclones. (Color figure online)

The leftmost case in Fig. 9 is a case of the monsoon front, with a convection system moving from west to east. The attribution values are high at the edge of the radar area, most likely because the convective system is moving in from outside the effective range of the radar. This explanation can be considered an artifact. The middle figure is an extratropical cyclone system. The attribution map seems to describe the disappearance signal of fragmented convection cells moving in the direction opposite to the progression of the cold front (blue line). The rightmost case is an extratropical cyclone system. Moist and warm air from the East Sea and the West Sea blow inland, causing friction and rising along the Taebaek Mountain Range to result in convergence. The attribution heatmap seems to concur with this phenomenon, highlighting the corresponding area.

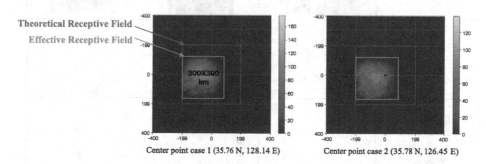

Fig. 10. Theoretical receptive field and effective receptive field of the target model. Due to the CNN structure, the maximum range of input region seen by a single output pixel is theoretically 398×398 km (approximately 200 km in radius). Depending on the learned parameters, the actual range is about 300×300 km (approximately 150 km in radius). (Color figure online)

110   S. Kim et al.

As an additional test, the receptive fields of the target model are identified using feature attribution. *Smooth Integrated Gradient* is applied on 75 samples and the average attribution map is used for evaluating the receptive field. As shown in Fig. 10, the effective receptive field seems to be west-biased, which aligns with the fact that the westerlies are prevalent in Korea. The effective receptive field also has a radius of about 150 km. Assuming the maximum wind speed of 60 km per hour (about 16 m/s), the model may be making guesses when making predictions for three hours or later.

3.4 Explanation 3: Confidence Calibration

Confidence refers to the degree of certainty that a model has in its predictions. The certainty can be represented as a probability, and a well-calibrated model should be capable of assigning accurate confidence probabilities to its predictions. Unfortunately, deep learning models trained on negative log-likelihood (NLL) tend to exhibit overconfidence since it makes low-entropy distributions of the predictive classes [9] as demonstrated in Fig. 11. In operational forecasting, a classification or segmentation model not only must be accurate but also indicate the point at which it is likely to be erred [14]. Probability calibration, the process of ensuring that the predicted probabilities of a model accurately reflect the true probabilities of the outcomes, can address this issue [13].

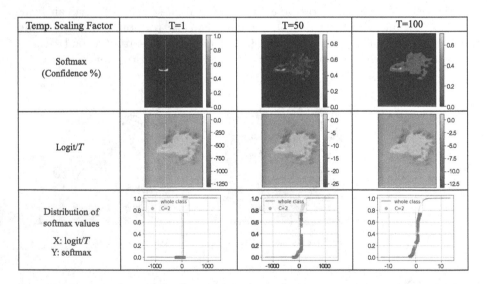

Fig. 11. The principle of temperature scaling. The softmax probability is scaled by a scalar parameter to reduce overconfidence by scaling the extreme logit values which occur near 0 or 100% of overconfidence. From left to right, the probability calibration progresses.

Table 1. Expected calibration error (ECE) of calibrated confidence on each lead time. The ECE is improved after calibration.

Lead Time	ECE	
	Before	After
1 h	0.029	**0.010**
2 h	0.099	**0.055**
3 h	0.170	**0.037**
4 h	0.232	**0.168**
5 h	0.290	**0.109**
6 h	0.320	**0.003**

Probability Calibration Methods. Probability calibration methods adjust the softmax of model logits as pseudo-probabilities. This paper uses the post-processing-based probability calibration methods which do not require re-training, making it suitable for quickly adjusting large-scale weather forecasting models. One of the simplest non-parametric approaches is *histogram binning*: all uncalibrated predictions are divided into mutually exclusive bins, enabling the selection of predictions that minimize bin-wise squared loss [41]. *Platt scaling* is a parametric calibration method that uses a sigmoid function to calibrate non-probabilistic classification predictions for logistic regression models. The calibrated probability $\hat{q} = \sigma(az_i + b)$ with two parameters $a, b \in \mathbb{R}$ are optimized by NLL while model parameters are fixed [28]. *Temperature scaling* (TS), on the other hand, is a variation of Platt scaling that uses a single scalar parameter $T > 0$ for all classes [13]. With the logit value z_i in each i-th pixel, the calibrated confidence is obtained as $\hat{q}_i(x, T) = \max_{k \in K} \sigma_{SM}(z_i/T)^{(k)}$.

Where k is the label index in K classes and σ_{SM} is softmax operation. The only learnable parameter T is optimized by the NLL. Since the maximum value of the softmax function σ_{SM} remains unaffected by T, the class prediction also remains unchanged. This consistency of model performance makes temperature scaling suitable for the task of probability calibration.

Local temperature scaling (LTS) [9] expands on the concept of TS in semantic segmentation tasks by introducing learnable parameters for individual image pixels. Their approach considers spatially varying temperature values and pixel-level changes. To achieve this, a mapping function is essential to train which takes logits $z(x)$ and the corresponding image sample x as inputs and generates scaling factors $T_i(x)$. These scaling factors are then divided by the logits $z_i(x)$. Formally,

$$\hat{q}_i(x, T_i(x)) = \max_{k \in K} \sigma_{SM}(z_i(x)/T_i(x))^{(k)}$$

where $T_i(x) \in \mathbb{R}^+$ is sample and pixel dependent. We train the mapping functions for each lead time separately and employ a CNN, following a similar

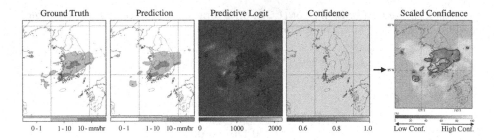

Fig. 12. The case of 2020-08-07 at 14:00 UTC with temperature scaling.

approach as described in the original paper. The mapping functions are optimized by minimizing the NLL with respect to the validation dataset.

Evaluation for Probability Calibration. A commonly used measure of the probability calibration of a machine learning classifier is *expected calibration error* (ECE) [26]. It calculates the disparity between the predicted confidence and the actual probabilities. ECE is calculated by partitioning the range of predicted confidences into a set of bins and then calculating the weighted average discrepancy between the average confidence $\mathrm{conf}(B_i)$ and the average accuracy $\mathrm{acc}(B_i)$ within each bin B_i as $\mathrm{ECE} = \sum_{b=1}^{B} \frac{n_b}{N} |\mathrm{acc}(B_i) - \mathrm{conf}(B_i)|$.

To utilize the ECE metric in the segmentation model, each pixel is considered as an individual sample as in [9]. To reduce computing costs, we randomly sample a predefined length of 250 ten times from a flattened array of confidence. Additionally, we masked ineffective areas in radar samples to improve the fidelity of the ECE metric by avoiding empty bins.

As shown in Table 1, the optimized LTS network improves the ECE scores after calibration for each of the six lead times, while maintaining the modified F1 scores. As demonstrated with an example in Fig. 12, the LTS network diminishes the overconfidence in the predicted labels. The regions of heavy rain and no rain have high confidence scores rather than those of light rain while the predictive output seems to be similar to the ground truth.

3.5   Visualization: XAI Interface System

User interface design with XAI has been recently studied [5,7]. In the design principles studied by Chromik et al. (2021) [7], XAI interfaces for users should provide progressive disclosure of explanatory information in order to avoid overwhelming users. This can be achieved through features such as tooltips or toggle buttons. Additionally, considering that users are accustomed to different explanation modalities, such as natural language or visual explanations, they should be offered these modes of presentation to comprehend the information.

In this study, a pilot interface system has been established to display the explanations in a user-friendly manner, as shown in Fig. 13 and 14. The explanation components consist of four parts:

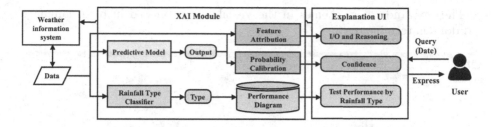

Fig. 13. Use case diagram for user interface and XAI modules.

Performance by Rainfall Type. After visualizing the input and prediction, the model performance explanation panel shows the test performance for the sample's rainfall type. A description of the training data is also provided.

Output Reasoning. The contribution of different target classes is computed simultaneously, allowing for comparison of the input contributions to no rain, light rain, and heavy rain classes.

Confidence. To explain confidence, a toggle key is provided that allows users to compare prediction and confidence results in individual grids.

Supplementary Materials. Based on user feedback, all results are presented along with other modalities that are excluded from the model inputs. The additional data allows for an increase in reliability as the users can verify their opinions on the generated results.

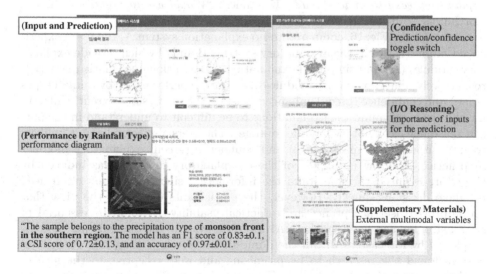

Fig. 14. Conceptual prototype of the interface system for the user-centered explanation. The demonstration is available (https://figma.fun/LuhqIv) in Korean

The text and color schemes in the visuals are expressed in plain language and domain terminology.

Fig. 15. Three prototypes for a user survey. A demonstration is available for each: prototype A providing only prediction results (https://figma.fun/uQcW9P); prototype B adding three explanatory modules (https://figma.fun/6n0CgH); and prototype C including supplemented materials from user feedback and providing the simple and contracted information in the output reasoning module (https://figma.fun/LuhqIv).

User Study on XAI Interface. Four forecasters in Korea Meteorological Agency participated in the user study. This user study aims to demonstrate the interface system and elicit user feedback regarding their experience. The purpose of this survey is to qualitatively assess whether the explanatory modules, when provided alongside the predictions of an AI model, are useful to forecasters in practice. The survey assesses user experience based on three prototype interface systems (Q1–3) in Fig. 15 and three types of explanatory modules (Q4–6). The participants answered 5-point Likert scale questions: Understandability *"Is the explanation easy to understand?"*, Usefulness *"Would use in practice?"*, Trustworthiness *"Can you trust the prediction?"*.

As results in Fig. 16, compared to no explanation system A, the users experienced more trustful in the explanatory systems B and C which provide explanatory modules (B) and simplified explanation and additional thematic maps (C), respectively. The explanatory modules of the model performance by rainfall types (blue) and confidence (green) enhanced trustworthiness to some extent. Unfortunately, the users found the explanations to be difficult to understand in the output reasoning explanatory module (orange). The users also considered it unlikely to use output reasoning (orange) and confidence (green) explanatory modules in practice. The low usefulness of these explanatory modules was induced by the effort required to understand the information since forecasters often need to make decisions quickly. However, the participants expressed the view that for improved user acceptance and practical usability, it would be essential to establish a linkage between the XAI interface system and the existing systems employed by forecasters within the domestic meteorological agency. Also, forecasters found the research to be promising and were receptive to the idea of further investigating AI behavior. This response may provide a direction for future research, focusing on XAI receptiveness from the users.

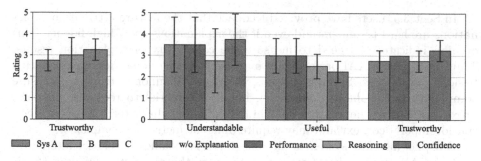

Fig. 16. Results from user experiment surveys. A comparison result of three prototypes of interface systems on trustworthiness (the left) and that of three explanatory modules on understandability, usefulness, and trustworthiness (the right). (Color figure online)

4 Discussion

Through a series of meetings and interviews with the users, this study reduced the desired explanations into three main questions: model performance by rainfall type, inference reasoning, and output confidence. Based on the user needs and XAI algorithm mapping, a performance diagram with rainfall classifier, feature attribution, and probability calibration were selected as appropriate explanations for the requirements. Further analyses were performed to finalize the specific XAI methods in each category. Finally, three prototypes of the user interface were designed and feedback is received from the users. User experience survey results of the explanatory modules were promising on trustworthiness. Forecasters, however, requested high standards for actual use in practice since forecasters commonly need rapid decision-making.

One limitation of this study is that the overall process involved a specific set of users in Sect. 3.1; hence, the results may not cover the entirety of possible user requirements, creating a gap between XAI results and individual users' desired approaches as discussed in [21].

Another limitation is that for model performance by rainfall type in Sect. 3.2, the classifier shows limited performance due to a lack of samples with rainfall type labels. For actual implementation, it would be necessary to train the classifier with a larger dataset.

While the feature attribution methods in Sect. 3.3 can faithfully reflect model reasoning, even for distinct rainfall types, it can be challenging for experts to interpret. One reason for this difficulty is the model's reliance on uni-modal input features, restricting the feature attribution results to highlighting only the horizontal movement of convection cells. This issue may be addressed by using multi-modal data – in particular, since radar observations only represent the final outcomes of various physical mechanisms and the radar product used for training the target model provides only horizontal information, it would be ideal to include additional features that can provide this information.

In Sect. 3.5, users have provided feedback that the feature attribution explanations are hard to understand even if the explanations show high fidelity. This opinion indicates the need to measure the complexity of explanation results. Thus, user-centric XAI performance may need to reflect qualities of explanation besides faithfulness. Several previous works use Shannon entropy to measure complexity in the image domain [4], but it is essential to recognize that the proxy variables in the weather domain have different characteristics due to their spatiotemporal context and may require different metrics of complexity.

Our pilot interface system is clickable, but it is a shallow-level user-interactive XAI (UXAI) system that becomes static after the completion of user-centric building procedures. Providing high-level interaction makes a potential area for future work to support explanations in response to feedback from the users such as interactive dialogue [7].

5   Conclusion

This study emphasizes the significance of involving users as key stakeholders in the design process of explainable artificial intelligence (XAI) systems. Based on an analysis of user requirements in the meteorological domain and the mapping of these requirements to XAI methods, rainfall classification, feature attribution, and probability calibration are selected as suitable explanations. By presenting the model's performance for each rainfall type, users can judge the overall reliability of the corresponding AI model. Furthermore, sample cases of alignment with domain knowledge for feature attribution are identified. This investigation helps determine the practical applicability of feature attribution methods in meteorology. By providing confidence explanations for each output grid, users can assess the likelihood of output accuracy and decide the local reliability of individual predictions. Lastly, three prototypes of the user interface are designed and solicited feedback from users to ascertain the feasibility of integrating XAI into the forecasting system. This study may contribute to the literature as a use case of user-centered expression research.

References

1. Adadi, A., Berrada, M.: Peeking inside the black-box: a survey on explainable artificial intelligence (XAI). IEEE Access 6, 52138–52160 (2018)
2. Bach, S., Binder, A., Montavon, G., Klauschen, F., Müller, K.R., Samek, W.: On pixel-wise explanations for non-linear classifier decisions by layer-wise relevance propagation. PLoS ONE 10(7), e0130140 (2015)
3. Başağaoğlu, H., et al.: A review on interpretable and explainable artificial intelligence in hydroclimatic applications. Water 14(8), 1230 (2022)
4. Bhatt, U., Weller, A., Moura, J.M.: Evaluating and aggregating feature-based model explanations. arXiv preprint arXiv:2005.00631 (2020)

5. Bradley, C., et al.: Explainable artificial intelligence (XAI) user interface design for solving a Rubik's Cube. In: Stephanidis, C., Antona, M., Ntoa, S., Salvendy, G. (eds.) HCI International 2022-Late Breaking Posters: 24th International Conference on Human-Computer Interaction, HCII 2022, Virtual Event, 26 June–1 July 2022, Proceedings, Part II, pp. 605–612. Springer, Heidelberg (2022). https://doi.org/10.1007/978-3-031-19682-9_76

6. Chaput, R., Cordier, A., Mille, A.: Explanation for humans, for machines, for human-machine interactions? In: Explainable Agency in Artificial Intelligence WS, AAAI-2021 (2021)

7. Chromik, M., Butz, A.: Human-XAI interaction: a review and design principles for explanation user interfaces. In: Ardito, C., Lanzilotti, R., Malizia, A., Petrie, H., Piccinno, A., Desolda, G., Inkpen, K. (eds.) INTERACT 2021. LNCS, vol. 12933, pp. 619–640. Springer, Cham (2021). https://doi.org/10.1007/978-3-030-85616-8_36

8. Dell, M., Jones, B.F., Olken, B.A.: What do we learn from the weather? The new climate-economy literature. J. Econ. Lit. **52**(3), 740–798 (2014)

9. Ding, Z., Han, X., Liu, P., Niethammer, M.: Local temperature scaling for probability calibration. In: Proceedings of the IEEE/CVF International Conference on Computer Vision, pp. 6889–6899 (2021)

10. Espeholt, L., et al.: Deep learning for twelve hour precipitation forecasts. Nat. Commun. **13**(1), 5145 (2022)

11. van der Geest, K., et al.: The impacts of climate change on ecosystem services and resulting losses and damages to people and society. In: Mechler, R., Bouwer, L.M., Schinko, T., Surminski, S., Linnerooth-Bayer, J.A. (eds.) Loss and Damage from Climate Change. CRMPG, pp. 221–236. Springer, Cham (2019). https://doi.org/10.1007/978-3-319-72026-5_9

12. Gilpin, L.H., Bau, D., Yuan, B.Z., Bajwa, A., Specter, M., Kagal, L.: Explaining explanations: an overview of interpretability of machine learning. In: 2018 IEEE 5th International Conference on Data Science and Advanced Analytics (DSAA), pp. 80–89. IEEE (2018)

13. Guo, C., Pleiss, G., Sun, Y., Weinberger, K.Q.: On calibration of modern neural networks. In: International Conference on Machine Learning, pp. 1321–1330 (2017)

14. Haynes, K., Lagerquist, R., McGraw, M., Musgrave, K., Ebert-Uphoff, I.: Creating and evaluating uncertainty estimates with neural networks for environmental-science applications. In: Artificial Intelligence for the Earth Systems, pp. 1–58 (2023)

15. Kalnay, E.: Atmospheric Modeling, Data Assimilation and Predictability. Cambridge University Press (2003)

16. Kim, C., Yun, S.Y.: Precipitation nowcasting using grid-based data in South Korea region. In: 2020 International Conference on Data Mining Workshops (ICDMW), pp. 701–706. IEEE (2020)

17. Ko, J., Lee, K., Hwang, H., Oh, S.G., Son, S.W., Shin, K.: Effective training strategies for deep-learning-based precipitation nowcasting and estimation. Comput. Geosci. **161**, 105072 (2022)

18. Korea Meteorological Agency: Haneulsarang (2022). https://www.kma.go.kr/download_01/kma_202002.pdf

19. Liao, Q.V., Gruen, D., Miller, S.: Questioning the AI: informing design practices for explainable AI user experiences. In: Proceedings of the 2020 CHI Conference on Human Factors in Computing Systems, pp. 1–15 (2020)

20. Liao, Q.V., Pribić, M., Han, J., Miller, S., Sow, D.: Question-driven design process for explainable AI user experiences. arXiv preprint arXiv:2104.03483 (2021)

21. Liao, Q.V., Varshney, K.R.: Human-centered explainable AI (XAI): from algorithms to user experiences. arXiv preprint arXiv:2110.10790 (2021)
22. McGovern, A., Ebert-Uphoff, I., Gagne, D.J., Bostrom, A.: Why we need to focus on developing ethical, responsible, and trustworthy artificial intelligence approaches for environmental science. Environ. Data Sci. **1**, e6 (2022)
23. McGovern, A., Gagne, D.J., Williams, J.K., Brown, R.A., Basara, J.B.: Enhancing understanding and improving prediction of severe weather through spatiotemporal relational learning. Mach. Learn. **95**, 27–50 (2014)
24. Mizutori, M., Guha-Sapir, D.: Economic losses, poverty and disasters 1998–2017. United Nations Office for Disaster Risk Reduction, vol. 4, pp. 9–15 (2017)
25. Murdoch, W.J., Singh, C., Kumbier, K., Abbasi-Asl, R., Yu, B.: Definitions, methods, and applications in interpretable machine learning. Proc. Natl. Acad. Sci. **116**(44), 22071–22080 (2019)
26. Naeini, M.P., Cooper, G.F., Hauskrecht, M.: Obtaining well calibrated probabilities using Bayesian Binning. In: 2015 Proceedings of the AAAI Conference on Artificial Intelligence, pp. 2901–2907 (2015)
27. Nauta, M., et al.: From anecdotal evidence to quantitative evaluation methods: a systematic review on evaluating explainable AI. arXiv preprint arXiv:2201.08164 (2022)
28. Platt, J.: Probabilistic outputs for support vector machines and comparisons to regularized likelihood methods. In: Advances in Large Margin Classifiers, vol. 10, no. 3, pp. 61–74 (1999)
29. Rasp, S., Thuerey, N.: Data-driven medium-range weather prediction with a Resnet pretrained on climate simulations: a new model for WeatherBench. J. Adv. Model. Earth Syst. **13**(2), e2020MS002405 (2021)
30. Ravuri, S., et al.: Skilful precipitation nowcasting using deep generative models of radar. Nature **597**(7878), 672–677 (2021)
31. Ren, X., et al.: Deep learning-based weather prediction: a survey. Big Data Res. **23**, 100178 (2021)
32. Roebber, P.J.: Visualizing multiple measures of forecast quality. Weather Forecast. **24**(2), 601–608 (2009)
33. Samek, W., Binder, A., Montavon, G., Lapuschkin, S., Müller, K.R.: Evaluating the visualization of what a deep neural network has learned. IEEE Trans. Neural Netw. Learn. Syst. **28**(11), 2660–2673 (2016)
34. Schwalbe, G., Finzel, B.: A comprehensive taxonomy for explainable artificial intelligence: a systematic survey of surveys on methods and concepts. Data Min. Knowl. Disc., 1–59 (2023). https://doi.org/10.1007/s10618-022-00867-8
35. Selvaraju, R.R., Cogswell, M., Das, A., Vedantam, R., Parikh, D., Batra, D.: Grad-CAM: visual explanations from deep networks via gradient-based localization. In: Proceedings of the IEEE International Conference on Computer Vision, pp. 618–626 (2017)
36. Shin, Y., Kim, J.H., Chun, H.Y., Jang, W., Son, S.W.: Classification of synoptic patterns with mesoscale mechanisms for downslope windstorms in Korea using a self-organizing map. J. Geophys. Res. Atmos. **127**(6), e2021JD035867 (2022)
37. Simonyan, K., Vedaldi, A., Zisserman, A.: Deep inside convolutional networks: visualising image classification models and saliency maps. arXiv preprint arXiv:1312.6034 (2013)
38. Sønderby, C.K., et al..: MetNet: a neural weather model for precipitation forecasting. arXiv preprint arXiv:2003.12140 (2020)
39. Sundararajan, M., Taly, A., Yan, Q.: Axiomatic attribution for deep networks. In: International Conference on Machine Learning, pp. 3319–3328. PMLR (2017)

40. Yun, S.: Development of short-term precipitation prediction technology using artificial intelligence. Atmos. Res. **237**, 104845 (2021)
41. Zadrozny, B., Elkan, C.P.: Obtaining calibrated probability estimates from decision trees and Naive Bayesian classifiers. In: International Conference on Machine Learning (2001)
42. Zhongming, Z., Linong, L., Xiaona, Y., Wangqiang, Z., Wei, L., et al.: Atlas of mortality and economic losses from weather, climate and water extremes (1970–2019). Weather Climate Water Temps Climate EAU (2021)

Human-AI Interaction and AI Avatars

Yuxin Liu and Keng L. Siau(✉)

City University of Hong Kong, Hong Kong, Hong Kong SAR
yliu2324-c@my.cityu.edu.hk, klsiau@cityu.edu.hk

Abstract. Human-Computer Interaction has been evolving rapidly with the advancement of artificial intelligence and metaverse. Human-AI Interaction is a new area in Human-Computer Interaction. In this paper, we look at AI avatars, which are human-like representations of AI systems. AI avatars closely resemble real persons. AI avatars have several advantages, including enhanced trustworthiness and increased AI system adoption. AI avatars also enable human-like interaction and engagement. AI avatars have their share of issues, such as the potential for psychological impact, discrimination, and biases. The paper discusses the benefits and pitfalls of AI avatars and proposes several research directions. This research paper has theoretical and practical significance. AI avatars are a new phenomenon. Existing theories, such as those in psychology, social psychology, and communication, may not hold when applied to AI avatars. AI avatars also present new features and characteristics, such as ease of customization and personalization, that are not easily found in humans. Such features and characteristics can be capitalized to enhance Human-AI Interaction, but their negative aspects will need to be understood and managed. For practitioners and AI developers, this pioneering research provides new insight, understanding, and possibilities of AI avatars that can be used to further enhance Human-AI Interaction.

Keywords: Human-AI Interaction · Human-Computer Interaction · Artificial Intelligence · AI Avatars · Metaverse

1 Introduction: AI and Human-AI Interaction

Artificial Intelligence (AI) technology has penetrated almost all aspects of people's lives, from chatbots, virtual assistants, recommendation systems, pilotless drones, and autonomous vehicles that improve the quality of life to the AI translation and text conversion that assist daily work and routines. The launch of ChatGPT in 2022 intuitively demonstrates to the public the incredible power and potential of AI. The wave of AI has undoubtedly swept the world, and the future of AI has become a hot discussion topic. AI has also influenced the Human-Computer Interaction (HCI) arena, and Human-AI Interaction (HAII) is one of the latest research areas.

1.1 Artificial Intelligence

AI is a field that encompasses and influences many disciplines, such as computer science, engineering, biology, psychology, mathematics, statistics, logic, education, marketing,

© The Author(s), under exclusive license to Springer Nature Switzerland AG 2023
H. Degen et al. (Eds.): HCII 2023, LNCS 14059, pp. 120–130, 2023.
https://doi.org/10.1007/978-3-031-48057-7_8

philosophy, business, and linguistics (Buchanan, 2005; Kumar et al., 2016; Ma & Siau, 2018; Yang & Siau, 2018; Siau & Wang, 2020). AI applications that are familiar to most range from Apple Siri to Amazon Go, and from self-driving cars to autonomous weapons. AI can be classified into two main categories -- weak AI and strong AI (Hyder et al., 2019; Wang & Siau, 2019). Weak AI, also known as narrow AI, are AI applications that specialize in specific tasks. Most current AI applications, such as Google Assistance, Alpha Go, pilotless drones, and driverless vehicles, can be considered weak AI. However, AI researchers from different organizations and nations are competing to create strong AI (also called human-level artificial general intelligence or artificial superintelligence). Strong AI applications can process multiple tasks proficiently.

Strong AI is a controversial and contentious concept. The main concern of strong AI is its ability to challenge and may result in replacing humans. Many transhumanists believe that strong AI will have self-awareness and is equivalent to human intelligence. Once strong AI becomes a reality, an intelligence explosion will precipitate, and the enhancement in intelligence will be exponential. Technological singularity may be the next logical outcome. In other words, strong AI could outperform humans at nearly every cognitive task. Originally thought to be impossible or something that would happen in the distant future, the emergence of ChatGPT has cast doubt on the impossibility of strong AI (Nah *et al.*, to appear).

1.2 Human-AI Interaction

Human-Computer Interaction aims to create effective, efficient, and satisfying interactions between human and computer systems to achieve users' requirements better (Bevan et al., 2015; Stephanidis et al., 2019). With the availability of powerful AI algorithms and applications, HCI has been evolving in the direction of HAII. As one of the latest directions in the HCI field, HAII attracts much attention from academic researchers and industrial practitioners, and HAII presents enormous potential.

Conventional HCI works mainly focus on human interaction with non-AI computing systems, which aim to generate predictable outcomes based on predefined rules (Garibay et al., 2023). For example, HCI research has looked at the design of icons, organization of screen layouts, and various input and output media such as voice and gestures. Compared to non-AI computing systems, the attractiveness and uniqueness of AI systems are that AI systems exhibit human-like intelligence and autonomous abilities based on advanced AI algorithms, like deep learning and reinforcement learning (Xu et al., 2023). Therefore, the main improvement in HAII is the ability to perform tasks and learn to improve the interaction automatically and often independently without human intervention (de Visser et al., 2018). Further, HAII allows the interaction to be tailored and customized to individuals.

The autonomy of AI systems brings both advantages and risks to HAII. Although AI is increasingly capable of enhancing decision-making and making decisions, the concern is that people may lose control of the system, which can lead to unintended negative consequences. Human-centered AI (HCAI), which re-positions humans at the center of the AI lifecycle and emphasizes human control over AI systems (Shneiderman, 2020), has gained more and more support. HCAI proposes several key focuses to ensure that AI systems' design, implementation, and use should benefit human welfare, including safety, privacy, transparency, explanation, responsibility, and human well-being (Garibay et al., 2023). Therefore, the design of AI systems and applications in HAII should be consistent with the vision of HCAI.

User interface (UI) design is critical in HCI (Stone & Al, 2005). Conventional UI design, like graphical user interface design, focuses on layout design, information presentation, color scheme, and interactive elements to create a visually appealing, user-friendly, and intuitive interface (Katerattanakul & Siau, 2003; Alves et al., 2020). For HAII, as AI systems become more and more autonomous and powerful, the goals of UI design can shift to providing engaging, tailored, and personalized AI-specific interactions. Voice-based interaction and text-based interaction are currently the mainstream approaches in HAII. Voice assistants, like Amazon Alexa and Apple Siri, are typical examples of voice-based HAII. Chatbots and online customer support systems often utilize text-based HAII. For these AI systems, a richer information display mediation will help improve their effectiveness and user experience according to the media richness theory (Daft & Lengel, 1986). One potential HAII is using AI avatars to enhance voice- and text-based interaction. Here, we define AI avatars as computer-generated human-like representations of AI systems. The AI avatar integrates visual and auditory aspects to be human-like, including appearance, voice, behavior, and communication skills.

Rapid AI advancement presents many possibilities for the HCI field. This paper will discuss the new potential of HAII and the challenges these new interfaces present. Specifically, we believe that using avatars as the display form of AI systems has great potential to enhance HAII. In the remainder of this paper, we will discuss the possibility of avatar generation technology, how avatars can improve HAII, challenges resulting from AI avatars, and the future directions of AI avatar research.

2 Potential Enabled by AI Avatar Technology

AI avatars have great potential to enhance HAII from various aspects. In this study, we summarize the potential that can be achieved by AI avatar technology from four aspects: human-like appearance, human-like interaction, customization, and context adaptability.

2.1 Human-like Appearance

Human-like images have been widely used in UI design. Previous studies have found that the anthropomorphism level of agents can positively influence users' perception (de Visser et al., 2016) and increase users' intention to use (Ling et al., 2021). However, early anthropomorphic agents at that time are static human-like images with a degree of cartoonishness. As computer graphics, rendering techniques, and 3D modeling technologies become more and more advanced, AI avatars can be very realistic, and users can barely tell the avatars from real humans with their naked eyes. AI system designers can design AI avatars with different genders, ages, facial traits, and body shapes, just like natural human appearance, to better interact with users. In addition, many developing technologies have focused on the consistency of avatar mouth shape and speech content, realistic eye movement, and finer skin texture, which can further improve the realism of AI avatars.

2.2 Human-like Interaction

ChatGPT, the latest AI chatbot technology and a large-scale natural language processing application, has shown AI systems' potential to express human-like interaction. ChatGPT passed the Turing test by making a panel of judges think it was a human. It can interact with users in natural languages and in friendly conversation. Nevertheless, interacting in text or audio has its limits. Visual representations like AI Avatars can take advantage of more human-like interaction features. AI avatars enable the exhibition of facial expressions, gestures, and body language. By combining visual and auditory presentations, AI avatars have great potential to exhibit the "emotions" of AI systems to create a more human-like interaction. As technology advances, different tones and inflections, facial expressions, gestures, and body language can be added to create a realistic human-like interaction.

2.3 Customization

User preference is one of the most critical concerns for AI designers. Human-centered AI systems aim to provide satisfying services based on personalized user preferences (Alves et al., 2020; Garibay et al., 2023). For instance, voice navigation allows users to select different sounds. ChatGPT can autonomously learn the users' preferences for response styles from previous interactions. Using AI avatar as a UI to enhance voice- and text-based interaction can give users more opportunities for a personalized experience. AI designers can adopt the strategy of customization to transfer the power of AI avatar design to the users. So, users can select or design different AI avatars to communicate with them or assist their work.

2.4 Context Adaptability

AI systems have been applied to various education, healthcare, business, entertainment, and daily life activities in the real world and virtual worlds (Siau, 2018; Siau et al., 2018; Yang et al., 2022). Using AI avatars as UI can better support the context adaptability of AI systems. Appearances (e.g., a person in a doctor or nurse or policeman or soldier uniform) and demographic attributes (e.g., gender and race) have different influences in different contexts (e.g., Little et al., 2007; Little, 2014). Similarly, different features of AI avatars may have distinct effects in different scenarios. For example, in the healthcare environment in the Metaverse, the AI avatar can appear as a human-like doctor or a human-like nurse. Also, female AI avatars may be perceived as more trustworthy in the beauty product sales domain. In contrast, male AI avatars may be perceived to have more expertise and competence in the engineering procurement field. Young AI avatars may be more attractive to young users, while elderly AI avatars may seem wiser and more experienced in teaching and education contexts. Therefore, the context adaptability of AI avatars deserves sufficient attention. AI designers can flexibly change the gender, age, attractiveness, facial traits, and body shape of AI avatars to maximize their roles.

3   Using AI Avatars to Enhance HAII

3.1   Trust

Trust is a critical factor influencing user adoption and acceptance of AI systems (Siau & Shen, 2003; Siau & Wang, 2018; Choung et al., 2022). Users are more likely to use AI systems and interact with them when they perceive AI systems as trustworthy, reliable, and competent. Using human-like AI avatars as the UI can positively influence users' trust in AI systems (Jiang et al., 2023).

First, realistic human-like AI avatars can enhance the emotional connection between humans and AI systems (Culley & Madhavan, 2013), which may contribute to trust building. Generative AI, like ChatGPT, has shown its ability to communicate with humans naturally, mimicking human-like conversations. By additionally incorporating human-like appearance, expressions, and body language, trust in the AI systems is likely to increase, enhancing users' adaptability. For instance, in healthcare, AI assistants can serve as virtual physicians to engage in empathetic conversations and provide patients with guided mindfulness exercises (Graham et al., 2019). Also, when interacting with AI assistants with familiar and friendly appearances and behaviors, patients are more likely to self-disclose more information, which is helpful for mental disease diagnosis and treatment.

Second, AI avatars give more possibilities to increase AI credibility through a variety of UI designs. Designers can customize AI avatars by changing their genders, races, ages, and other visual attributes. They can also leverage their creativity to develop avatars with distinct facial features, unique dressing styles, and varied speaking styles. It allows designers to explore different approaches to improve the trustworthiness of AI systems. By designing the AI avatar's visual presentation and interaction style to align with user preferences and expectations, designers can create a UI that enhances the perceived credibility and trustworthiness of the AI system.

3.2   User Satisfaction

User satisfaction is a key aspect that influences users' intention to adopt and use AI systems (Deng et al., 2010; Dang et al., 2018). To be specific, the hedonic value of AI applications and systems plays a significant role in user satisfaction (Ben Mimoun & Poncin, 2015). Both the AI avatar itself and the customization function of AI avatars have the potential to increase the hedonic value of AI systems. With the support of AI avatars, AI systems can be more than just functional tools.

First, it is novel and interesting for users to interact with a highly human-like AI. AI avatars enhance the user experience by bringing a sense of surprise, engagement, and humor. AI avatars' entertainment value is further increased by having features such as a narrative and interactive conversation, which improves the user experience and leaves a lasting impression.

In addition, AI systems that allow users to customize the AI avatars they interact with will be more appealing to users and increase the hedonic value. Users might view this customization function as a gamification component that enhances user control and playfulness. The ability to customize the appearance and voice of AI avatars and how they act and communicate can provide users with a more satisfying and enjoyable interactive experience.

3.3 Cooperation and Collaboration

Real-world Collaboration. Collaboration and cooperation between humans and AI have become increasingly common. It is inevitable that many traditional human-human collaborations will gradually evolve into human-AI collaborations (Wang et al., 2020). In addition to individual human-AI interaction that we mentioned above, AI systems also have the ability to participate in group cooperation as a member of groups. For example, in business, AI-based decision-making systems can help the group decision-making process and promote consensus reaching. They can use their powerful intelligence to offer valuable suggestions, generate creative ideas, and provide novel insights. In addition to showing the advantages and disadvantages of each alternative in the text form, it may be possible to use an AI avatar to present and highlight complex content in a simple and straightforward way, just like an actual human. With AI avatars as the representation of AI systems, people can be more accustomed to and likely to cooperate with AI systems and view them as real partners or colleagues.

Virtual-world Collaboration. As the concept of Metaverse goes viral, the grand vision of the virtual world is sketched out and expected to become a reality soon. Metaverse and virtual worlds promise humans an alternative life with various activities (Wang et al., 2022). Users can interact with other users and AI systems like in the real world. Virtual worlds also allow users to engage in activities that may not be feasible in the physical world (Eschenbrenner et al., 2008; Park et al., 2008; Nah et al., 2010; Nah et al., 2011; Schiller et al., 2014; Nah et al., 2017; Schiller *et al.*, to appear). Through the integration of Virtual Reality (VR), Augmented Reality (AR), and Mixed Reality (MR) technologies, users can navigate and explore virtual environments, interact with virtual objects, and engage in virtual experiences that transcend the limitations of reality (Yousefpour et al., 2019).

AI technology has become an essential technical support to promote the virtual world. In the virtual world, avatars also represent human users (Galanxhi & Nah, 2007; Davis et al., 2009). The virtual representations of both users and AI systems can closely mimic human appearances and behaviors, creating a more authentic and engaging collaborative experience. The immersive user experience in the virtual world opens up new possibilities for human-AI collaboration. Users can work alongside AI avatars as virtual teammates, leveraging their expertise and capabilities to solve complex problems, engage in creative endeavors, or explore virtual worlds together. AI avatars can provide personalized assistance, generate intelligent suggestions, and adapt their behaviors to suit the collaborative context, ultimately enhancing virtual-world interactions' overall effectiveness and enjoyment. The enhanced immersion and interactivity foster a stronger sense of presence, social connection, and collaboration between human users and AI avatars.

4 Challenges and Future Research Directions

4.1 Ethical and Social Concerns

Psychological Impact. Although there are lots of advantages to enhancing HAII with AI avatars, it may lead to a negative psychological impact on users. For one, deeper HAII may influence users' self-identity. Users may doubt their self-worthiness and values when interacting with a human-like AI with incredible intelligence and extensive knowledge, leading to negative self-evaluation. For another, human-like AI avatars may aggravate users' emotional overdependence on AI systems. If AI systems can fully understand users' emotions and show sufficient patience and empathy, users may attach to and rely on AI systems. Human-like appearance and behavior of AI systems can exacerbate the dependence, with unexpected adverse effects like emotional manipulation.

Therefore, the evolving nature of HAII calls for ongoing research to ensure that the influence on user psychology is positive, empowering, and aligned with individuals' values and well-being. Ethical considerations and thoughtful design practices are necessary.

Social Interaction. Social interaction is another primary concern in HAII. While AI avatars have great potential to promote HAII, they may harm face-to-face human interactions. If AI avatars become the primary communication partners of humans, essential social skills and emotional connections nurtured through human-to-human interactions may be compromised. From a broader perspective, social interactions are the basis of society. Human-human interactions enable the formation of groups and organizations and foster a wide range of social activities.

Therefore, the balance of HAII and human-human interactions is a serious issue that requires careful consideration. AI systems are developed to enhance human intelligence but not replace humans. Although AI researchers are expected to strengthen the collaboration between human and AI systems, such collaboration should not undermine human-human interaction and collaboration.

Discrimination and Bias. Human-like AI avatars may result in more serious social discrimination and bias. AI designers and users have more freedom to create AI interfaces according to user preferences. A potentially serious problem is the reinforced stereotypes and prejudices.

Social stereotypes are prevalent and influence people's social judgment and behavior toward others (Tajfel, 2010). For instance, a ubiquitous gender stereotype is that males are more competent than females in most job positions (Eagly & Mladinic, 1994). So, such prejudice puts women in a disadvantaged position in the job market. Suppose AI designers take advantage of the gender stereotype and design more male AI avatars for business assistant AI systems. In that case, a negative consequence is that people will be more accustomed to communicating with male images, further aggravating gender inequality in human-human interactions.

Therefore, future studies also need to pay attention to diverse strategies that mitigate the risk of reinforcing social discrimination and bias through AI avatars. They can further study how to leverage AI avatars to address the prejudice problems in human-human interaction. In this way, researchers can help harness the potential of AI avatars to promote inclusiveness, mitigate biases, and foster a more equitable and respectful social environment.

4.2 Distinct Perceptions

AI avatar design is a broad area that has not been fully studied. It is widely known that AI interfaces should be user-friendly, visually appealing, and trustworthy. However, for AI avatars, a major concern is whether user perception of human-like AI avatars is equivalent to real humans. That is, whether the various features of AI avatars have the same impact on user perception as human features. Previous research in social psychology has sufficiently examined the effect of various features (e.g., gender, age, physical attractiveness) on human perception and social judgment (e.g., Krishnan et al., 2019; Duan et al., 2020). So, additional effort should be made in HAII to examine whether it is appropriate and effective to utilize the conclusions drawn from previous social psychology studies. In addition, the customization strategy of AI avatars is also worth further discussion to maximize its role in improving user experience and increasing user satisfaction.

Another noteworthy issue is the realism level of AI avatars. Is it really or always the best design strategy to use highly human-like avatars as AI interfaces? Will a certain level of cartoonishness of AI avatars help HAII in some cases? The opposite perspective generates from the uncanny valley effect (Mori et al., 2012), which means that people may have a feeling of weirdness and fear when interacting with non-human objects with realism close to 100 percent. Researchers should make an effort to test the influence of realism and other features of AI avatars in different scenarios.

5 Conclusions

AI has become increasingly prevalent in our daily lives, acting as a powerful supplement to human capabilities. In this paper, we focus on the application potential of AI avatars in HAII. We systematically summarize the potential enabled by AI avatar technology and discuss how to use AI avatars to enhance HAII. AI avatars have a bright prospect to promote AI systems development by increasing user adoption and acceptance. We believe that AI avatars can be a benefit to individuals, organizations, and the whole society in the future. We also point out the challenges that AI avatars face and the directions of future research. Not only academic researchers but all parties of society should work together to promote the development of human-centered AI systems and AI avatars and reduce the negative impacts of AI avatars.

This research provides both theoretical and practical significance. The research contributes to developing theories that are specific to Human-AI Interaction and testing existing theories in the context of Human-AI Interaction. The research also contributes to AI developers and practitioners by providing suggestions and guidelines for the design of Human-AI Interaction and AI avatars.

References

Alves, T., Natálio, J., Henriques-Calado, J., Gama, S.: Incorporating personality in user interface design: a review. Pers. Individ. Differ. **155**, 109709 (2020)

Ben Mimoun, M.S., Poncin, I.: A valued agent: how ECAs affect website customers' satisfaction and behaviors. J. Retail. Consum. Serv. **26**, 70–82 (2015)

Bevan, N., Carter, J., Harker, S.: ISO 9241-11 revised: what have we learnt about usability since 1998? In: Kurosu, M. (ed.) HCI 2015. LNCS, vol. 9169, pp. 143–151. Springer, Cham (2015). https://doi.org/10.1007/978-3-319-20901-2_13

Buchanan, B.G.: A (very) brief history of artificial intelligence. AI Mag. **26**(4), 53–60 (2005)

Choung, H., David, P., Ross, A.: Trust in AI and its role in the acceptance of AI technologies. Int. J. Hum.-Comput. Interact. **39**(9), 1727–1739 (2022)

Culley, K.E., Madhavan, P.: A note of caution regarding anthropomorphism in HCI agents. Comput. Hum. Behav. **29**, 577–579 (2013)

Daft, R.L., Lengel, R.H.: A proposed integration among organizational information requirements, media richness and structural design. Manage. Sci. **32**, 554–671 (1986)

Dang, M.Y., Zhang, G.Y., Chen, H.: Adoption of social media search systems: an IS success model perspective. Pac. Asia J. Assoc. Inform. Syst. **10**(2), 55–78 (2018)

Davis, A., Murphy, J., Owens, D., Khazanchi, D., Zigurs, I.: Avatars, people, and virtual worlds: foundations for research in metaverses. J. Assoc. Inf. Syst. **10**, 90–117 (2009)

de Visser, E.J., et al.: Almost human: anthropomorphism increases trust resilience in cognitive agents. J. Exp. Psychol. Appl. **22**, 331–349 (2016)

de Visser, E.J., Pak, R., Shaw, T.H.: From "automation" to "autonomy": the importance of trust repair in human–machine interaction. Ergonomics **61**, 1409–1427 (2018)

Deng, L., Turner, D.E., Gehling, R., Prince, B.: User experience, satisfaction, and continual usage intention of IT. Eur. J. Inf. Syst. **19**, 60–75 (2010)

Duan, Y., Hsieh, T.-S., Wang, R.R., Wang, Z.: Entrepreneurs' facial trustworthiness, gender, and crowdfunding success. J. Corp. Finan. **64**, 101693 (2020)

Eagly, A.H., Mladinic, A.: Are people prejudiced against women? Some answers from research on attitudes, gender stereotypes, and judgments of competence. Eur. Rev. Soc. Psychol. **5**, 1–35 (1994)

Eschenbrenner, B., Nah, F., Siau, K.: 3-D virtual worlds in education: applications, benefits, issues, and opportunities. J. Database Manag. **19**(4), 91–110 (2008)

Galanxhi, H., Nah, F.F.-H.: Deception in cyberspace: a comparison of text-only vs. avatar-supported medium. Int. J. Hum.-Comput. Stud. **65**(9), 770–783 (2007)

Garibay, O., et al.: Six human-centered artificial intelligence grand challenges. Int. J. Hum.-Comput. Interact. **39**, 391–437 (2023)

Graham, S., Depp, C., Lee, E.E., Nebeker, C., Tu, X., Kim, H.-C.: Jeste, DV: artificial intelligence for mental health and mental illnesses: an overview. Curr. Psychiatry Rep. **21**(11), 116 (2019)

Hyder, Z., Siau, K., Nah, F.: Artificial intelligence, machine learning, and autonomous technologies in mining industry. J. Database Manag. **30**, 67–79 (2019)

Jiang, Y., Yang, X., Zheng, T.: Make chatbots more adaptive: dual pathways linking human-like cues and tailored response to trust in interactions with chatbots. Comput. Hum. Behav. **138**, 107485 (2023)

Kang, S.-H., Gratch, J.: The effect of avatar realism of virtual humans on self-disclosure in anonymous social interactions. In: CHI Extended Abstracts on Human Factors in Computing Systems, pp. 3781–3786 (2010)

Katerattanakul, P., Siau, K.: Creating a virtual store image. Commun. ACM **46**(12), 226–232 (2003)

Krishnan, V., Niculescu, M.D., Fredericks, E.: Should I choose this salesperson? Buyer's emergent preference in seller from mere exposure. J. Mark. Theory Pract. **27**(2), 196–209 (2019)

Kumar, N., Kharkwal, N., Kohli, R., Choudhary, S.: Ethical aspects and future of artificial intelligence. In: International Conference on Innovation and Challenges in Cyber Security (ICICCS-INBUSH) (2016)

Ling, E.C., Tussyadiah, I., Tuomi, A., Stienmetz, J., Ioannou, A.: Factors influencing users' adoption and use of conversational agents: a systematic review. Psychol. Mark. **38**(7), 1031–1051 (2021)

Little, A.C.: Facial appearance and leader choice in different contexts: evidence for task contingent selection based on implicit and learned face-behaviour/face-ability associations. Leadersh. Q. **25**, 865–874 (2014)

Little, A.C., Burriss, R.P., Jones, B.C., Roberts, S.C.: Facial appearance affects voting decisions. Evol. Hum. Behav. **28**, 18–27 (2007)

Ma, Y., Siau, K.: Artificial intelligence impacts on higher education. In: MWAIS 2018 Proceedings, vol. 42 (2018)

Mori, M., MacDorman, K.F., Kageki, N.: The uncanny valley [from the field]. IEEE Robot. Autom. Mag. **19**(2), 98–100 (2012)

Nah, F., Eschenbrenner, B., DeWester, D., Park, S.: Impact of flow and brand equity in 3D virtual worlds. J. Database Manag. **21**(3), 69–89 (2010)

Nah, F., Eschenbrenner, B., DeWester, D.: Enhancing brand equity through flow and telepresence: a comparison of 2D and 3D virtual worlds. MIS Q. **35**(3), 731–747 (2011)

Nah, F.F.-H., Schiller, S.Z., Mennecke, B.E., Siau, K., Eschenbrenner, B., Sattayanuwat, P.: Collaboration in virtual worlds: impact of task complexity on team trust and satisfaction. J. Database Manag. **28**(4), 60–78 (2017)

Nah, F., Zheng, R., Cai, J., Siau, K., Chen, L.: Generative AI and ChatGPT: applications, challenges, and AI-human collaboration. J. Inform. Technol. Case Appl. Res. **25**(3), 277–304 (2023)

Park, S., Nah, F., DeWester, D., Eschenbrenner, B., Jeon, S.: Virtual world affordances: enhancing brand value. J. Virtual Worlds Res. **1**(2), 1–18 (2008)

Schiller, S.Z., Mennecke, B.E., Nah, F.F.-H., Luse, A.: Institutional boundaries and trust of virtual teams in collaborative design: an experimental study in a virtual world environment. Comput. Hum. Behav. **35**, 565–577 (2014)

Schiller, S., Nah, F., Luse, A., Siau, K.: Men are from Mars and Women are from Venus: Dyadic collaboration in the metaverse. Internet Res. (to appear)

Shneiderman, B.: Human-centered artificial intelligence: three fresh ideas. AIS Trans. Hum.-Comput. Interact. **12**, 109–124 (2020)

Siau, K.: Education in the age of artificial intelligence: how will technology shape learning? The Global Analyst **7**(3), 22–24 (2018)

Siau, K., et al.: FinTech empowerment: Data science, artificial intelligence, and machine learning. Cutter Bus. Technol. J. **31**(11/12), 12–18 (2018)

Siau, K., Shen, Z.: Building customer trust in mobile commerce. Commun. ACM **46**(4), 91–94 (2003)

Siau, K., Wang, W.: Building trust in artificial intelligence, machine learning, and robotics. Cutter Bus. Technol. J. **31**(2), 47–53 (2018)

Siau, K., Wang, W.: Artificial intelligence (AI) ethics: ethics of AI and ethical AI. J. Database Manag. **31**(2), 74–87 (2020)

Stephanidis, C., et al.: Seven HCI grand challenges. Int. J. Hum.-Comput. Interact. **35**(14), 1229–1269 (2019)

Stone, D., Jarrett, C., Woodroffe, M., Minocha, S.: User Interface Design and Evaluation. Elsevier, San Francisco, California (2005)

Tajfel, H.: Social stereotypes and social groups. In: Hogg, M.A., Abrams, D. (eds.) Intergroup Relations: Essential Readings, pp. 132–145. Psychology Press (2010)

Wang, D., et al.: From human-human collaboration to Human-AI collaboration: Designing AI systems that can work together with people. In: Extended Abstracts of the 2020 CHI Conference on Human Factors in Computing Systems, pp. 1–6 (2020)

Wang, W., Siau, K.: Artificial intelligence, machine learning, automation, robotics, future of work and future of humanity. J. Database Manag. **30**, 61–79 (2019)

Wang, Y., Siau, K.L., Wang, L.: Metaverse and human-computer interaction: A technology framework for 3D virtual worlds. In: Chen, J.Y.C., Fragomeni, G., Degen, H., Ntoa, S. (eds.) HCI International 2022 – Late Breaking Papers: Interacting with eXtended Reality and Artificial Intelligence: 24th International Conference on Human-Computer Interaction, HCII 2022, Virtual Event, 26 June – 1 July 2022, Proceedings, pp. 213–221. Springer Nature Switzerland, Cham (2022). https://doi.org/10.1007/978-3-031-21707-4_16

Xu, W., Dainoff, M.J., Ge, L., Gao, Z.: Transitioning to human interaction with AI systems: New challenges and opportunities for HCI professionals to enable human-centered AI. Int. J. Hum.-Comput. Interact. **39**(3), 494–518 (2023)

Yang, Y., Siau, K.: A qualitative research on marketing and sales in the artificial intelligence age. In: MWAIS 2018 Proceedings, vol. 41 (2018)

Yang, Y., Siau, K., Xie, W., Sun, Y.: Smart health: Intelligent healthcare systems in the metaverse, artificial intelligence, and data science era. J. Organ. End User Comput. **34**(1), 1–14 (2022)

Yousefpour, A., et al.: All one needs to know about fog computing and related edge computing paradigms: a complete survey. J. Syst. Architect. **98**, 289–330 (2019)

How Can Artificial Intelligence Transform the Future Design Paradigm and Its Innovative Competency Requisition: Opportunities and Challenges

Yuqi Liu[✉], Zhiyong Fu, and Tiantian Li

Academy of Arts and Design, Tsinghua University, Beijing, China
liu.yuqi.design@gmail.com, fuzhiyong@tsinghua.edu.cn

Abstract. With the unprecedented advancement of artificial intelligence technology, the context, processes, tools, methods, and ethics of design are facing significant changes. This study explores the opportunities and challenges that artificial intelligence technology brings to design and put forward a capability model that designers should acquire in the AI era. There are 4 main opportunity points, namely "The optimization of design process, tools and resources", "The expansion of design inspiration, direction and field", "The enrichment of design generation, content and output", "The improvement of design efficiency, quality and accuracy". In terms of design challenges and ethics, 7 points have been clarified, including "Capability substitution and unemployment issues", "Ownership and protection of intellectual property", "Data security and privacy protection", "Transparent communication and real-time feedback", "Group diversity and prejudice avoidance", "Social morality and ethical norms", and "Universality and social equity". Finally, in facing the future shock of AI on the design profession, the author proposes a competency wheel of design futures literacy, which includes 7 crucial capabilities designers need in the AI Era, there are "Subtle perception", "Infinite imagination", "Sharpe-eyed insight", "Forward-looking decision-making", "Systemic planning capability", "Hybrid computing capability", and "Whole-chain creativity". This study provides a valuable dialogue space for AI-enabled design paradigm and the evolutionary direction of future designers' competency.

Keywords: Design · Futures · Artificial Intelligence · Design Thinking · Futures Literacy · Education

1 Introduction

Artificial Intelligence (AI) has become the innovation infrastructure and will reshape the future innovation process and the way creativity is applied [1]. In the future, AI will gradually penetrate into our daily life like air and water [2, 3], affecting innovations in various technological fields around the world, and continuously changing the way people, organizations, society, nature and machines interact [4]. Contemporary AI research

© The Author(s), under exclusive license to Springer Nature Switzerland AG 2023
H. Degen et al. (Eds.): HCII 2023, LNCS 14059, pp. 131–148, 2023.
https://doi.org/10.1007/978-3-031-48057-7_9

focuses on shaping our daily lives, solving complex societal problems, and addressing environmental issues to protect global ecosystems and sustainability [5–7]. Design is synonymous with human creativity, and its essence is innovation [8, 9]. The word "design" can be combined with different nouns or verb to form many different subdivided creative fields, such as urban Design, architectural design, interaction design, industrial design, service design, material design, program design, architecture design, UI design, etc. Judging from the speed of technological development, it is probably a matter of time before artificial intelligence technology surpasses the level of human intelligence [10]. AI can overcome human limitations in information processing, provide instrumental assistance beyond the scope of human capabilities [11], and even enable machines to replace humans to realize functions such as cognition, identification, analysis, and decision-making. Its essence is to make machines help humans solve problems [12–14]. To a certain extent, artificial intelligence is also a kind of design, and its purpose is to help humans solve problems and create innovative solutions similar to human thinking patterns [15]. Currently, ChatGPT is booming globally, igniting global topics and a vast market. ChatGPT, as a powerful feature of AIGC, is based on AI and developed for Artificial General Intelligence (AGI). For future design, the historical process of generating innovative content will undergo a transformation from PGC to UGC, and then to AIGC. Artificial intelligence will have a profound impact on the future design innovation paradigm and will profoundly transform the design education and design industry ecology. For design innovation, what impact will the rapid development of AI technology and the rise of AIGC tools have on the design industry? Should we resist or embrace? What are the opportunities and challenges? What is the relationship between artificial intelligence and designers? Will it replace human designers? What abilities do future designers in the era of artificial intelligence needed? This research starts with the concept, development stage and maturity level of AI, wants to analyze the opportunities and challenges that AI brings to design innovation, and proposes a model of designers' future literacy ability, which provides valuable suggestions and references for the development of future Design paradigm and the pursuit of designers' literacy ability.

2   The Development Stages and Maturity Level of AI

2.1   The Development Stages of AI

Artificial Intelligence (AI) is a new technological science used to simulate and expand the theories, methods, technologies, and application systems of human intelligence. The research fields include Natural Language Processing, Deep Learning, Simulating Modeling, Machine Translation, Social Network Analysis, Machine Learning, Robotics & Soft Robotics, Internet of Things, Image Analytics, Graph Analytics, Audio Analytics, Visualization, Virtual Personal Assistant, etc. [16, 17]. The development stage of artificial intelligence can be divided into three stages based on the strength of capabilities, namely the Weak Artificial Intelligence stage, the Strong Artificial Intelligence stage, and the Super Artificial Intelligence stage [5, 18].

Weak AI Stage. "Weak Artificial Intelligence" refers to computer programs that can only complete specific human specified commands and tasks, and cannot have universal learning and reasoning abilities like humans. Currently, most intelligent applications are in this stage, such as smart rice cookers, smart voice assistants, and smart customer service.

Strong AI Stage. "Strong Artificial Intelligence" refers to computer programs that have universal learning and reasoning abilities like humans, can handle various complex tasks, and even create new knowledge. At present, most strong artificial intelligence is still in the stage of research and development and laboratory training, and has not yet been widely applied in practical production and life. However, in the past two years, large language models such as ChatGPT3.0/4.0 and AIGC tools have emerged, which are very close to strong artificial intelligence and are expected to trigger a new round of productivity revolution.

Super AI Stage. "Super Artificial Intelligence" refers to computer programs that possess intelligence and abilities beyond human beings, capable of solving problems that humans cannot solve, such as self-awareness, self-learning, and interdisciplinary integration. Super Artificial Intelligence is the highest development stage of AI, as well as the most challenging and controversial stage. Before implementing Super Artificial Intelligence, many technical and ethical issues need to be addressed, such as how to ensure that AI does not harm humans, how to address the security and privacy issues of intelligence, and how to ensure the value and ethical standards (Fig. 1).

AI Maturity Model

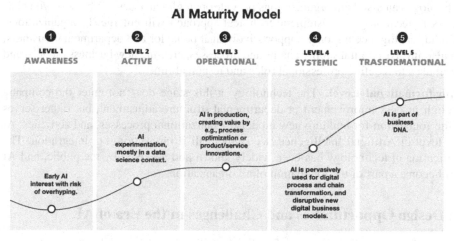

Fig. 1. AI maturity model. Source: Gartner AI Maturity Model

2.2 The Maturity Level of AI

For the application of AI in the industry, Gardner proposed an "AI Maturity Model". Design innovation can refer to this model to understand which stage AI is in and adopt it in relevant design businesses, processes, and activities.

Awareness Level. This level is the embryonic stage of technology. People have a primary understanding of artificial intelligence technology and are interested in it, imagining and assuming its numerous application scenarios. This stage is still in its early stages, and the risk of technological innovation is high. At this stage, technological applications are secondary, with a focus on developing AI related application infrastructure and tapping into technological potential. At this level, scientists are active and there are high barriers to market entry.

Active Level. This stage is the laboratory activation stage for technology. As the maturity of technology increases, investment in AI research and development (R&D) and the potential for related new technology applications will be gradually explored. At this time, the technology begins to be activated, gradually breaking away from the R&D environment and academic experiments and entering the enterprise's new product research and production environment.

Operational Level. This stage involves technology entering the core of the organization from the laboratory, becoming a part of productivity, and innovating products and production processes to form a "Smart Industry". In this situation, artificial intelligence technology equipped with machine learning and deep learning has filled the manufacturing industry with smart machines that can learn and act independently, and organizations have entered the Industry 4.0 field.

Systemic Level. In addition to its application in the field of productivity, this stage of technology can also help organizations provide open global access. When everyone has access to technology, a systematic technical approach will emerge. In organizations, artificial intelligence not only supports individual behavior and departmental business, but also involves digital supply chains and processes, creating new business models, and being used to redefine professional roles and responsibilities.

Transformational Level. The technology at this stage does not enter the company through process improvement or departmental structure adjustment, but rather serves as the foundation for building new models, organizational processes, and activities. At this level of Artificial Intelligence, we cannot call it innovation, but integration. The application of technology has been widely known and accepted by the public, and AI will become a part of the foundation of all organizations.

3   Design Opportunities and Challenges in the Era of AI

The development and application of artificial intelligence have brought numerous opportunities and challenges to design education and the industry. On the one hand, in the future, a considerable number of designers will be eliminated by artificial intelligence technology and tools, or on the brink of elimination, which will trigger a wave of unemployment and panic [12, 19]; On the other hand, more and more designers are using AI technology and AIGC tools to improve their work and design processes, enhance their design innovation capabilities, and improve design efficiency [20, 21]. This section explains the role of design innovation and designers in the artificial intelligence era by exploring the technological opportunities and challenges. The related content summary is shown in Fig. 2.

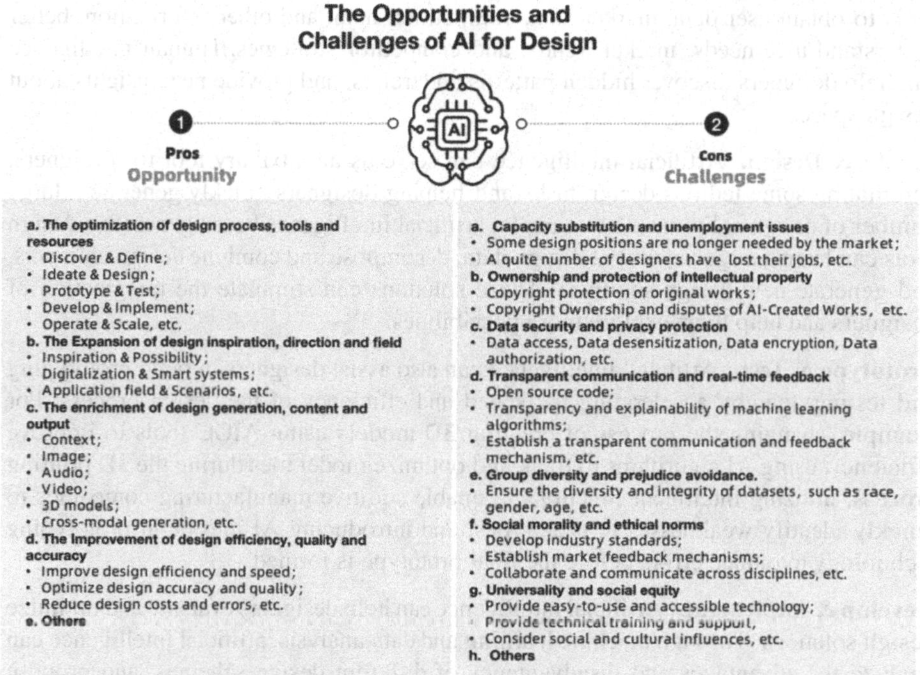

**The Opportunities and
Challenges of AI for Design**

①
Pros
Opportunity

②
Cons
Challenges

a. The optimization of design process, tools and resources
- Discover & Define;
- Ideate & Design;
- Prototype & Test;
- Develop & Implement;
- Operate & Scale, etc.
b. The Expansion of design inspiration, direction and field
- Inspiration & Possibility;
- Digitalization & Smart systems;
- Application field & Scenarios, etc.
c. The enrichment of design generation, content and output
- Context;
- Image;
- Audio;
- Video;
- 3D models;
- Cross-modal generation, etc.
d. The Improvement of design efficiency, quality and accuracy
- Improve design efficiency and speed;
- Optimize design accuracy and quality;
- Reduce design costs and errors, etc.
e. Others

a. Capacity substitution and unemployment issues
- Some design positions are no longer needed by the market;
- A quite number of designers have lost their jobs, etc.
b. Ownership and protection of intellectual property
- Copyright protection of original works;
- Copyright Ownership and disputes of AI-Created Works, etc.
c. Data security and privacy protection
- Data access, Data desensitization, Data encryption, Data authorization, etc.
d. Transparent communication and real-time feedback
- Open source code;
- Transparency and explainability of machine learning algorithms;
- Establish a transparent communication and feedback mechanism, etc.
e. Group diversity and prejudice avoidance.
- Ensure the diversity and integrity of datasets, such as race, gender, age, etc.
f. Social morality and ethical norms
- Develop industry standards;
- Establish market feedback mechanisms;
- Collaborate and communicate across disciplines, etc.
g. Universality and social equity
- Provide easy-to-use and accessible technology;
- Provide technical training and support,
- Consider social and cultural influences, etc.
h. Others

Fig. 2. The opportunities and Challenges of AI for Design

3.1 Design Opportunities which AI Brought

AI can support organizations in all stages of innovation, namely idea generation, idea filtering, idea experimentation, and idea development and commercialization [22, 23]. Meanwhile, in the future, organizations will also delegate their key functions, including decision making, recruitment and customer relationship management, to artificial intelligence [15, 24, 25]. This section will analyze the design opportunities in the era of artificial intelligence from the following four aspects: The optimization of design process, tools and resource; The expansion of design inspiration, direction and field; The enrichment of design generation, content and output; The improvement of design efficiency, quality and accuracy.

3.1.1 The Optimization of Design Process, Tools and Resources.

This part mainly analyzes the innovation and reshaping effect that AI can bring to the design thinking process, and the technical role played by AI at different stages. Figure 3 divides the design innovation process into 5 divergent and convergent diamonds, totaling 10 stages, namely: Discover & Define, Idea & Design, Prototype & Test, Develop & Implement, Produce & Evaluate.

Discover & Define. Through machine learning and data analysis, artificial intelligence can process and analyze a large amount of data. Designers can use artificial intelligence tools to obtain user data, market data, competition data, and other information, better understand user needs, market trends, and competitor strategies. Human intelligence can help designers discover hidden patterns and trends, and provide new insights about design space.

Ideate & Design. Artificial intelligence can serve as an auxiliary tool for designers, automating some tedious design tasks and helping designers quickly generate a large number of design solutions. For example, artificial intelligence based generative design tools can learn a large amount of design data, decompose and combine design elements, and generate new design solutions. These solutions can stimulate the imagination of designers and help them explore more possibilities.

Prototype & Test. Artificial intelligence can also assist designers in rapid prototyping and testing, thereby accelerating the speed and efficiency of the design process. For example, changing the process of creating 3D models using AIGC tools to improve efficiency, using AI algorithms to track and optimize model files during the 3D printing process, utilizing intelligent functions to enable additive manufacturing companies to quickly identify weaknesses in prototypes, and introducing AI into rapid prototyping technology to reduce errors before the final prototype is formed.

Develop & Implement. Artificial intelligence can help designers evaluate and optimize design solutions. Through machine learning and data analysis, artificial intelligence can analyze the advantages and disadvantages of different design schemes, and propose improvement suggestions to help designers make better design decisions and respond to the needs of actual users and customers. For example, through data analysis, artificial intelligence can determine users' preferences for a certain design elements, and generate design solutions or personalized customized service solutions that meet user needs by analyzing specific user data and behavior.

Operate and Scale. Artificial intelligence can play an important role in production and manufacturing processes. For example, AI-based automation systems can help production lines complete manufacturing tasks faster and more accurately, improving production efficiency and quality. Additionally, AI can help designers better manage supply chains, forecast demand, and reduce waste, thereby reducing costs and increasing efficiency.

Regarding the relationship between AI and designers, we can consider it through the overall penetration rate of artificial intelligence for design work. It can be seen from Fig. 3 that the capabilities of artificial intelligence can be divided into Weak AI, Strong AI and Super AI. The strength of artificial intelligence capabilities also determines its participation and penetration rate in the entire design process. And the intelligence of these three levels can coexist at the same time. When the penetration rate of AI for design is 0%, we return to the traditional craftsmen; when the penetration rate of AI for design is 100%, we assume that this extreme state exists, namely So-called artificial intelligence designers. However, what needs to be emphasized is that the core of design work is to deal with the relationship between people, society and environment which cannot be replaced by machines. At the same time, AI cannot do completely abstract and systematic work, and can only provide diverse choices, and It cannot replace human beings in making decisions, but can only provide decision-making options. Although,

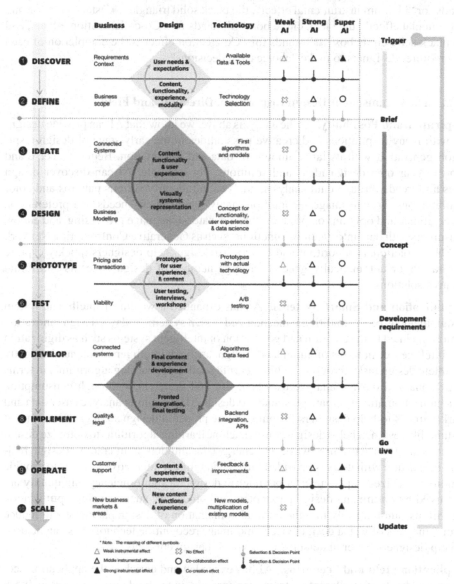

Fig. 3. AI-enabled design thinking process

this part is technically feasible in time, but it is not allowed to be realized in terms of ethical constraints. Therefore, we can briefly divide the relationship between AI and designers into three categories according to the AI penetration rate, namely: (1) AI as a tool; (2) AI as a collaborator; (3) AI as a creator. In Fig. 3, different symbols represent the role played by artificial intelligence technology at the corresponding development stage for different design stages. Among them, "X" means "No effect", and the light gray triangle box "△" represents "Weak instrumental effect", the black triangle box "▲" stands for "Medium instrumental effect", the black solid triangle "▲" stands for "Strong instrumental effect"; the black circle box "○" stands for "Co-collaboration effect", and the black solid circle box "●" stands for "Co-creation effect". The completion of each step requires designers to make "choices and decisions".

3.1.2 The Expansion of Design Inspiration, Direction, and Field

Inspiration and Possibility. In the analysis above, we know that AI can provide designers with many inspirations and creative possibilities in the early stage of design inspiration generation with its large amount of data and information. Better conceive and express your own design ideas and solutions. For example, AI can discover design rules and trends through data analysis, analyze and identify various patterns and color combinations through image recognition, analyze consumers' needs and preferences, expectations, and opinions on products through natural language processing, and endow consumers with data information. Functions, such as Generative Confrontation Network (GAN), evolutionary algorithm and generative design, help designers quickly capture inspiration, or automatically generate a large number of design concepts and initial creative solutions.

Digitalization and Smart Systems. AI has expanded a wealth of intelligent system design methods on the traditional mechanized design system. Today's design innovation is more inclined to the creation and generation of intelligent systems such as digitization and intelligence. In terms of automated design, artificial intelligence can automatically complete design tasks through machine learning and deep learning algorithms; in terms of personalized design, analyze user behavior and preferences through consumption data, and automatically create personalized designs; Data mining analyzes user data and market trends to help designers formulate more prepared design strategies; in terms of sustainable design, it helps designers use machine learning algorithms to optimize design methods and reduce resource waste and energy consumption. In interactive design, real-time interaction with users is provided through intelligent interactive systems to provide a more humanized experience; in parametric design, design efficiency and quality are improved by optimizing design parameters and processes, such as using optimization algorithms, automatically find the optimal combination of design parameters to reduce errors; in terms of visual design, visual and image recognition technologies can be used to help designers better understand and express design concepts.

Application Field and Scenarios. AI has expanded and enriched the application scenarios and fields of intelligent systems. For example, in the field of transportation, it can help design autonomous vehicle systems to achieve automated driving; In the medical field, it can assist doctors in medical and healthcare tasks such as disease diagnosis, patient monitoring, and drug development; In the financial field, it can assist banks and financial institutions in providing financial services such as risk management, fraud detection, and customer service; In the industrial field, it is possible to optimize production processes, improve production efficiency, and conduct fault diagnosis; In the field of agriculture, digital information system design and management can be used to help farmers increase crop yields, detect plant health status, and make climate predictions. In the field of daily life, designing wearable devices and smart homes can enable intelligent interaction and data sharing with users, providing more personalized and intelligent services and experiences.

3.1.3 The Enrichment of Design Generation, Content and Output

AI technology and AIGC tools have been widely applied in the field of content generation. According to the division of modules, it can be divided into text generation, image generation, audio generation, video generation, 3D model generation, and cross modal generation of different content forms.

Text. AIGC text generation methods are roughly divided into two categories: non-interactive text generation and interactive text generation. The main application directions of non-interactive text generation include structured writing (such as headline generation), unstructured writing (such as marketing text), and auxiliary writing. Among them, auxiliary writing mainly includes relevant content recommendation and polishing help, which is usually not considered as AIGC in the strict sense. Interactive text generation is mostly used in interactive scenarios such as virtual boyfriend/girlfriend, psychological counseling, and text interactive games.

Image. AIGC has two of the most mature application scenarios for image generation: image editing tools and autonomous image generation. Features of image editing tools include watermark removal, resolution enhancement, specific filters, and etc. Autonomous image generation is actually the recently emerging AI graphics, including creative image generation (generate paintings randomly or according to specific attributes) and functional image generation (generate logos, models, marketing posters, etc.).

Audio. AIGC audio generation is divided into voice synthesis and song generation, which are widely used in audiobook production, voice broadcast, short video dubbing, music synthesis and other fields. In the field of voice synthesis, text-to-speech (TTS) technology can be used to launch works that reproduce the voices of real people. In the listening module, users can also choose their favorite AI voice package to play, and the synthesized voice has clear rhythm and natural emotion. In the field of song generation, users can use AI to generate a variety of musical instrument performances, songs of different styles, and can also imitate video game music and other types.

Video. The common traditional application scenarios of AIGC in video generation also include video attribute editing, video automatic editing and video partial editing, which can save manpower and time efficiently. In September 2022, the Make-A-Video tool launched by Meta has the ability to generate corresponding short videos based on text descriptions. Google also launched Imagenvideo, which focuses on high-definition generation, and Phenaki, which focuses on generating longer video content. In October 2022, the AI reset version of "Illusion Tokyo" was released, and the picture generation was completed frame by frame through AI, allowing us to see the possibility of AIGC participating in video creation.

3D Models. AIGC can generate new high-quality 3D models by learning a large amount of 3D model data. In the application scenario of 3D model generation, it is often necessary to generate a large number of diverse models. Using traditional manual modeling methods often takes a lot of time and manpower but using machine learning algorithms to generate 3D models can greatly improve efficiency and reduce costs. Specifically, the process of generating a 3D model includes steps such as data acquisition, data preprocessing, model training, and model generation. In the data acquisition stage, a large amount of 3D model data needs to be collected, cleaned and marked. In the data preprocessing stage, the data needs to be processed and normalized to facilitate the training and application of machine learning algorithms. In the model training phase, it is necessary to use a deep learning algorithm to generate a 3D model by learning from the data. In the model generation stage, using generative models, new, high-quality 3D models can be quickly generated. At present, the application of 3D model generation has been widely used in game development, virtual reality, architectural design, medicine and other fields.

Cross-Modal Generation. The multimodal and cross-modal application of AIGC between text, image, audio, video, and 3D models is called cross-modal generation. Cross-modal generation usually refers to the use of AI technology to fuse different types of information (such as text, images, sounds, etc.) to generate new content. This cross-modal generation technology can also be applied to many fields, such as film production, music creation, virtual reality, etc., to bring people more abundant experiences.

3.1.4   The Improvement of Design Efficiency, Quality, and Accuracy

Improve Design Efficiency and Speed.   Artificial intelligence can handle many tedious, repetitive, and inefficient tasks in design through automated design processes, enabling designers to focus more on creativity and planning, accelerating the speed and efficiency of design. Such as automated color scheme generation, automated layout design, automated graphic recognition and processing, automatic generation of design schemes, and automatic checking of design rationality. These functions help to reduce the time and effort of manual operations and improve design efficiency. For example, by learning from existing design works and automatically generating new design elements such as color schemes, pattern icons, etc., abundant design materials can be quickly generated, and optimized, corrected, merged, cropped, etc. which make the design more precise, standardized, and efficient.

Optimize Design Accuracy and Quality.   AI can improve the accuracy and precision of design through the analysis and processing of a large amount of data. For example, in user research, machine learning algorithms are used to analyze user behavior and preferences, to better understand their needs and expectations, and design products that better meet user needs. In terms of scheme optimization, AI can automatically search for the optimal design scheme based on design requirements and objectives, thereby improving design efficiency and quality. In terms of simulation and testing, artificial intelligence can help designers predict design results more accurately and verify the feasibility of design solutions through simulation and testing, such as using virtual reality and simulation technologies to test and validate design solutions, thereby reducing trial and error costs and time. In terms of user feedback, AI can quickly provide feedback on the results and effects of design schemes, enabling designers to quickly adjust and improve design schemes, thereby improving design efficiency and quality.

Reduce Design Costs and Errors. From the perspective of design research, artificial intelligence based on the objective analysis of big data can better understand the development rules and consumers' preferences based on objective facts. From the design process, the traditional design process requires human intervention, which may lead to inevitable human errors. AI technology can reduce human errors and avoid unnecessary costs by automating the design and inspection process. In terms of design results, AI can verify the feasibility of the design scheme through simulation and testing, reduce problems in the design and manufacturing process and errors that need to be corrected, and reduce manufacturing costs. In terms of the production process, artificial intelligence can simulate and optimize materials production processes, thereby improving production efficiency and quality, and reducing waste and costs. All of these can help enterprises improve their competitiveness.

3.2 Design Challenges which AI Brought

Although Artificial intelligence could bring a quite number of opportunities to design, it will also derivative many challenges and ethical issues. For example, how to ensure that artificial intelligence will not harm humans in the future, how to solve the data security and privacy issues, how to implement the value realization and ethical principles, etc. Therefore, the development of artificial intelligence is a long and complex process that requires efforts in technology, policy, and ethics. The following summarizes the challenges and major ethical issues:

Capability Substitution and Unemployment Issues. The powerful analysis and generation capabilities of artificial intelligence will have a huge impact on many designers who are engaged in a single design job, leading to a series of unemployment and social problems. This is what design, technology, society and the government need to pay attention to topic.

Ownership and Protection of Intellectual Property. Whether the data used by artificial intelligence in the training process will infringe the intellectual property rights of the original creators; at the same time, who owns the copyright of design scheme generated by AI, the designer, or the relevant operating company, etc. Questions like these will bring about numerous property rights disputes.

Data Security and Privacy Protection. The design of artificial intelligence systems needs to consider how to protect personal privacy. This may include restricting data access, the use of data masking and encryption techniques, and ensuring that users explicitly authorize the use of data.

Transparent Communication and Real-Time Feedback. The design of AI system needs to consider how to let users understand the decision-making process. This includes open-source code, transparency and explainability of machine learning algorithms, and establishing transparent communication and feedback mechanisms.

Group Diversity and Prejudice Avoidance. The design of AI system needs to avoid prejudice and discrimination against certain groups, such as race, gender, age and other factors. This requires ensuring the diversity and integrity of datasets, as well as transparent and interpretable analysis of algorithms.

Social Morality and Ethical Norms. The design of AI system needs to consider how to abide by social and ethical norms to ensure the maximum benefit to individuals and society. This may include developing industry standards, establishing feedback mechanisms, and collaborating and communicating across domains.

Universality and Social Equity. The design of AI system needs to consider how to make technology accessible to a wider group of people in order to achieve fairness and equal opportunity. This may include providing easy-to-use and accessible technology, providing technical training and support, and considering social and cultural influences. In conclusion, design ethics is a crucial issue in the era of artificial intelligence, and joint efforts are required at the technical, policy, social and cultural levels to ensure that the application of artificial intelligence technology is consistent with moral and social values.

4   The Capability Requirements for Designers in the Era of AI

For the career of designers, the impact of artificial intelligence is a combination of challenges and opportunities [26–28]. On the one hand, artificial intelligence can replace the work of low-level designers. Design work with low systematization, low thinking component, and low innovation dimensions is more easily replaced. At the same time, the development of artificial intelligence has lowered the threshold of design, non-professional designers can also use relevant tools to compete with some easy design works; On the other hand, the essence of a designer's work is never just limited to visual and aesthetic surfaces, but rather based on new styles, concepts, and perspectives generated by active thinking. Design is to express subjective feelings such as inspiration, experience, and feelings, and is more of a way for people to practice objective things. While considering subjective factors, it also considers external and objective factors. Without innovation, there is no design, and this is difficult to achieve with the accumulation of pure data and algorithms. Therefore, from this perspective, artificial intelligence will not only not become a threat to designers, but also open the door to many opportunities. It enables designers to collaborate with machines to create smarter and faster work. The cooperation between humans and computers will accomplish things that previously could not be accomplished by a single person. In addition, artificial intelligence can continuously learn, which is the core of innovation. AI allows designers to transcend limitations in scope, scale, and cognition. This will be a fascinating journey. So, what capabilities do designers need to acquire in the era of artificial intelligence? This study proposes that designers should pay attention to the improvement of the following seven abilities: Subtle Perception, Infinite Imagination, Sharp-eyed Insight, Forward-looking Decision-making, Systemic Planning Capability, Hybrid Computing Capability, and Whole-Chain Creativity [14–30].

4.1 Subtle Perception

First, subtle perception (Grasp user needs): Insight into user needs is the embodiment of designers' perception and empathy. It can be divided into three levels. The first level is that designers can deeply understand the needs and psychology of users, thereby designing products and services that meet their needs and expectations; At the second level, while capturing explicit needs, it can also explore users' implicit needs, thereby designing products and services that exceed users' expectations; The third level, based on the analysis of users' essential needs, creates new needs to guide users' lifestyles. AI can never replace designers in the perception and empathy perspective. At most, it is just an auxiliary tool and cannot replace designers for in-depth understanding and consideration of user experience. Therefore, subtle perception should be trained and strengthened by designers in the future, which is an inherent advantage that cannot be replaced by AI (Fig. 4).

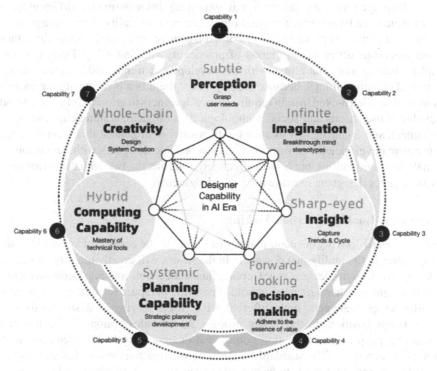

Fig. 4. The design futures literacy competency wheel of designers in the AI era

4.2 Infinite Imagination

Secondly, infinite imagination (Breakthrough mind stereotypes): Imagination is the ability to imagine physical objects that do not exist, and every designer should use different types of imagination to enhance their skills and delve into design. Infinite imagination requires that designers can skillfully use counterfactual thinking to break through thinking stereotypes. Counterfactual thinking is defined as being able to imagine that the outcome of things may be different from the actual situation and imagine another reality. People cannot assume that the future is the same as the present, so many innovations are generated through the breaking of "old things" and the "establishment" of "new things". Imagination is the premise of creativity, and creativity and imagination are complementary, because creativity is the use of imagination. Infinite imagination requires designers to have the ability to break through traditional thinking. In terms of imagination, AI can assist designers in releasing their imagination, but it requires guidance and guidance from designers.

4.3 Sharp-Eyed Insight

Thirdly, sharp-eyed insight (Capture trends and cycle): Imagination has different types, many of which are based on reality, and others are beyond reality; Some imaginations conform to objective truth while others not; At the same time, At the same time, there are also numerous differences in terms of practicality and feasibility. Designers need to capture imagination that aligns with the development trends and cycles of human society and objective things, because based on this, there is a prerequisite for creation and innovation. Sharp-eyed insight requires future designers to grasp the objective trends and cycles of user needs and social, technological, ecological, commercial, and policy environment, and create design solutions with positive significance that meet the needs of innovative development. At this point, AI can provide designers with data resources and analytical foundations, but how to effectively combine the two with the actual needs of users requires designers to make their own judgments.

4.4 Forward-Looking Decision-Making

Fourthly, forward-looking decision-making (adhering to the essence of value): Decision making power is the ability that designers in the AI era will greatly amplify. No matter how far AI develops, its design cannot replace human decision-making. Decision making power is a right that humans must uphold. From this perspective, future designers are more like design managers, with different AIGC tools serving as designers for each specific design position. In the design process, AI provides options for each step of the outcome, proposal, and solution output, and designers evaluate, select, and make decisions at each node. The standard for decision-making requires designers to adhere to the value essence that needs to be constantly considered in products and services.

4.5 Systemic Planning Capability

Fifth, Systemic planning capability (strategic planning formulation): When the AI technology in the future is extremely developed and can replace the work of a single designer, then from a overall perspective, they are just work sites one by one, and the work that connects dots into lines and forms planes cannot be replaced by AI. Future designers are required to have systemic strategic planning capabilities. Designers should focus on strategy and planning, gain an in-depth understanding of product and brand positioning and goals, formulate more effective design strategies and plans, and create greater value for enterprises. AIGC is only a design tool and cannot replace the designer's formulation and execution of design strategy and planning. Therefore, design strategy is a direction that should be vigorously advocated in future design education.

4.6 Hybrid Computing Capability

Sixth, Hybrid computing capability (mastery of technical tools): The development of AI technology, on the one hand, makes the threshold of design work lower and lower, and the era "everyone is a designer" is on the way. The design work mentioned here refers to relatively scattered and less systematic work. On the other hand, the number of designers who can master various computational design tools and software powered by AI is still a process of accumulation. Designers should constantly learn and update new digital design tools, technologies and trend, work better with AI, improve design efficiency and quality, and thus improve their hybrid computing power and competitiveness.

4.7 Whole-Chain Creativity

Seventh, Whole-chain creativity (creating design system): The essence of design is innovation, and the ultimate ability requirement of a designer is creativity, from discovering problems to creating solutions with meaningful value and real-world impact. This is a process from strategy to implementation with systematic work. If AI can replace designers to carry out creative activities of a single node, or even a certain process of creative activities, but it is incompetent for the whole-chain works from "problem-discovery", "problem analysis" to "problem-solving". Especially in business scenarios, AI cannot replace the entire industrial chain process and systematic work of products, services and experiences from scratch.

5 Discussion and Conclusion

We are at the forefront of the artificial intelligence era. The scope and scale of the impact of AI will be more profound than any other transitional period in human history. With the evolution of artificial intelligence from weak artificial intelligence, strong artificial intelligence to super artificial intelligence, its penetration rate in the entire design process will become increasingly high. AI technology can be divided into analytical AI and generative AI based on functional value. Existing AI technologies utilize computer simulation and simulation, based on big data, big models, pre-training, and generativity, to achieve breakthroughs from single language text generation to audio, video, 3D model, and cross-modal generation, which may promote deeper and broader social thinking and production modes revolutionary changes in lifestyle and social patterns.

This study starts with the concept of artificial intelligence, analyzes the development stages and technological maturity types of artificial intelligence, explores the opportunities and challenges that artificial intelligence technology brings to design, and analyzes the abilities that future designers should strengthen and learn. In terms of design opportunities, there are four main points, namely "The optimization of design process, tools and resources", "The expansion of design inspiration, direction and field", "The enrichment of design generation, content and output", "The improvement of design efficiency, quality and accuracy". In terms of design challenges, there are mainly seven points, namely "Capability substitution and unemployment issues", "Ownership and protection of intellectual property", "Data security and privacy protection", "Transparent communication and real-time feedback", "Group diversity and prejudice avoidance", "Social morality and ethical norms", and "Universality and social equity". Finally, in the face of the impact of artificial intelligence on the design profession, this study proposes a futuristic designer competency model, which includes "Subtle perception", "Infinite imagination", "Sharpe-eyed insight", "Forward-looking decision-making", "Systemic planning capability", "Hybrid computing capability", and "Whole-chain creativity".

In summary, design is a purposeful and creative activity of human beings, which requires the investment of consciousness, thinking, feelings, emotions, and creativity. Its discussion context should never leave people. The concept "people" here could be individual, collective, or the whole human race. If artificial intelligence is to meet the collective needs of humanity, it must have a full understanding of human values, needs, physical, psychological, cognitive, and emotional motivations. Designers are individuals who integrate human imagination and creativity, and designing machine intelligence that understands human language, feelings, intentions, and behaviors, and interacts with nuances and dimensions is crucial. Future designers are no longer just focused on dealing with the relationships between people and things, systems, space, environment, etc. They play the roles of thought leaders, strategists, activists, and change promoters of complex social and technological issues in private, public, civil, and charitable organizations worldwide. They are leaders in human innovation, development, and progress. The impact of artificial intelligence as an emerging form of productivity on future design is unquestionable. For future design education and designers, we should not fear or resist, but actively change ourselves, optimize our education system, embrace the opportunities, and face the challenges. As the creator of this technology, guiding artificial intelligence to have a positive impact on our planet, our country, our community, our families, and our lives is the collective responsibility of the future designer community.

References

1. Haefner, N., Wincent, J., Parida, V., Gassmann, O.: Artificial intelligence and innovation management: A review, framework, and research agenda☆. Technol. Forecast. Soc. Change **162**, 120392 (2021). https://doi.org/10.1016/j.techfore.2020.120392
2. Lu, Y.: Artificial intelligence: a survey on evolution, models, applications and future trends. J. Manag. Anal. **6**(1), 1–29 (2019). https://doi.org/10.1080/23270012.2019.1570365
3. Varian, H.: Artificial intelligence, economics, and industrial organization. In: Agrawal, A., Gans, J., Goldfarb, A. (eds.) The Economics of Artificial Intelligence: An Agenda, pp. 399–422. University of Chicago Press (2019). https://doi.org/10.7208/chicago/9780226613475.003.0016

4. von Krogh, G.: Artificial intelligence in organizations: new opportunities for phenomenon-based theorizing. Acad. Manag. Discov. **4**(4), 404–409 (2018). https://doi.org/10.5465/amd.2018.0084
5. Fosso Wamba, S., Bawack, R.E., Guthrie, C., Queiroz, M.M., Carillo, K.D.A.: Are we preparing for a good AI society? A bibliometric review and research agenda. Technol. Forecast. Soc. Change **164**, 120482 (2021). https://doi.org/10.1016/j.techfore.2020.120482
6. Dwivedi, Y.K., et al.: Artificial intelligence (AI): multidisciplinary perspectives on emerging challenges, opportunities, and agenda for research, practice and policy. Int. J. Inform. Manag. **57**, 101994 (2021). https://doi.org/10.1016/j.ijinfomgt.2019.08.002
7. Dubey, R.: Can big data and predictive analytics improve social and environmental sustainability? (2017)
8. Amabile, T.M.: The social psychology of creativity: a componential conceptualization. J. Pers. Soc. Psychol. **45**(2), 357–376 (1983). https://doi.org/10.1037/0022-3514.45.2.357
9. Sarkar, P., Chakrabarti, A.: The effect of representation of triggers on design outcomes. Artif. Intell. Eng. Des. Anal. Manuf. AIEDAM **22**(2), 101–116 (2008). https://doi.org/10.1017/S0890060408000073
10. Mosteanu, N.R.: Improving quality of online teaching finance and business management using artificial intelligence and backward design. Qual. to Success **23**(187), 1–12 (2022). https://doi.org/10.47750/QAS/23.187.01
11. Mariani, M.M., Machado, I., Nambisan, S.: Types of innovation and artificial intelligence: a systematic quantitative literature review and research agenda. J. Bus. Res. **155**, 113364 (2023). https://doi.org/10.1016/j.jbusres.2022.113364
12. Dirican, C.: The impacts of robotics, artificial intelligence on business and economics. Procedia – Soc. Behav. Sci. **195**, 564–573 (2015). https://doi.org/10.1016/j.sbspro.2015.06.134
13. Wamba-Taguimdje, S.-L., Fosso Wamba, S., Kala Kamdjoug, J.R., Tchatchouang Wanko, C.E.: Influence of artificial intelligence (AI) on firm performance: the business value of AI-based transformation projects. Bus. Process Manag. J. **26**(7), 1893–1924 (2020). https://doi.org/10.1108/BPMJ-10-2019-0411
14. Verganti, R., Vendraminelli, L., Iansiti, M.: Innovation and design in the age of artificial intelligence. J. Prod. Innov. Manag. **37**(3), 212–227 (2020). https://doi.org/10.1111/jpim.12523
15. Pietronudo, M.C., Croidieu, G., Schiavone, F.: A solution looking for problems? A systematic literature review of the rationalizing influence of artificial intelligence on decision-making in innovation management. Technol. Forecast. Soc. Change **182**, 121828 (2022). https://doi.org/10.1016/j.techfore.2022.121828
16. Duan, Y., Edwards, J.S., Dwivedi, Y.K.: Artificial intelligence for decision making in the era of Big Data – evolution, challenges and research agenda. Int. J. Inf. Manage. **48**, 63–71 (2019). https://doi.org/10.1016/j.ijinfomgt.2019.01.021
17. Bahoo, S., Cucculelli, M., Qamar, D.: Artificial intelligence and corporate innovation: a review and research agenda. Technol. Forecast. Soc. Change **188**, 122264 (2023). https://doi.org/10.1016/j.techfore.2022.122264
18. Cautela, C., Mortati, M.: The impact of Artificial Intelligence on Design Thinking practice. Insights from the ecosystem of startups. Strateg. Des. Res. J. **12**(1), 114–134 (2019). https://doi.org/10.4013/sdrj.2019.121.08
19. Boyd, R., Holton, R.J.: Technology, innovation, employment and power: does robotics and artificial intelligence really mean social transformation? J. Sociol. **54**(3), 331–345 (2018). https://doi.org/10.1177/1440783317726591
20. Kumar, S., Lim, W.M., Sivarajah, U., Kaur, J.: Artificial intelligence and blockchain integration in business: trends from a bibliometric-content analysis. Inf. Syst. Front. https://doi.org/10.1007/s10796-022-10279-0

21. Ismail, A., Sam, M.F.M., Abu Bakar, K., Ahamat, A., Adam, S., Qureshi, M.I.: Artificial intelligence in healthcare business ecosystem: a bibliometric study. Int. J. Online Biomed. Eng. **18**(09), 100–114 (2022). https://doi.org/10.3991/ijoe.v18i09.32251
22. Truong, Y., Papagiannidis, S.: Artificial intelligence as an enabler for innovation: a review and future research agenda. Technolo. Forecas. Soc. Change **183**, 121852 (2022). https://doi.org/10.1016/j.techfore.2022.121852
23. Trocin, C., IV., Hovland, P Mikalef, Dremel, C.: How artificial intelligence affords digital innovation: a cross-case analysis of Scandinavian companies. Technolo. Forecast. Soc. Change **173**, 121081 (2021). https://doi.org/10.1016/j.techfore.2021.121081
24. Allal-Chérif, O.: Intelligent cathedrals: using augmented reality, virtual reality, and artificial intelligence to provide an intense cultural, historical, and religious visitor experience. Technol. Forecast. Soc. Change **178**, 121604 (2022). https://doi.org/10.1016/j.techfore.2022.121604
25. Chatterjee, S., Rana, N.P., Tamilmani, K., Sharma, A.: The effect of AI-based CRM on organization performance and competitive advantage: an empirical analysis in the B2B context. Ind. Mark. Manag. **97**(January), 205–219 (2021). https://doi.org/10.1016/j.indmarman.2021.07.013
26. Paschen, U., Pitt, C., Kietzmann, J.: Artificial intelligence: building blocks and an innovation typology. Bus. Horiz. **63**(2), 147–155 (2020). https://doi.org/10.1016/j.bushor.2019.10.004
27. Hutchinson, P.: Reinventing innovation management: the impact of self-innovating artificial intelligence. IEEE Trans. Eng. Manag. **68**(2), 628–639 (2021). https://doi.org/10.1109/TEM.2020.2977222
28. Correia, M.J., Matos, F.: The impact of artificial intelligence on innovation management: a literature review. In: Proceedings of the 16th European Conference on Innovation and Entrepreneurship (ECIE 2021), vol 1, no. 16th European Conference on Innovation and Entrepreneurship (ECIE). pp. 222–230 (2021). https://doi.org/10.34190/EIE.21.225
29. Botega, L.F.D., Silva, J.C.: An artificial intelligence approach to support knowledge management on the selection of creativity and innovation techniques. J. Knowl. Manag. **24**(5), 1107–1130 (2020). https://doi.org/10.1108/JKM-10-2019-0559
30. Sui, X.: Innovation of artificial intelligence and digital media in environmental art design. Wireless Commun. Mobile Comput. **2022**, 1–12 (2022). https://doi.org/10.1155/2022/4332439

Design Futures with GAI: Exploring the Potential of Generative AI Tools in Collaborative Speculation

Yanru Lyu(✉), Tingxuan Hao, and Zhouhengyi Yi

Department of Digital Media Arts, School of Media and Design, Beijing Technology and
Business University, Beijing 102248, China
lyuyanru@gmail.com

Abstract. In recent years, Generative Artificial Intelligence (GAI) has been
increasingly applied to perform complex tasks. In this study, a GAI-embedded
method for design futures was proposed. Through a week-long workshop guided
by a workbook, the potential of GAI for scanning signals, constructing scenarios
and assisting in the design of concepts is discussed and explored. According to
questionnaire surveys, interviews and related content analysis, high technology
can provide certain support for imagination and creative design for the uncertain
futures. A key action for designers is to add human-factor-based high-touch guidance and correction to human-AI collaboration. In this regard, this study develops a
GAI-embedded framework involving internal and external environments through
the combination of future thinking and design thinking, which not only bridges
the gap between rational technology and emotional design, but also expands the
tools and methods of future design in the age of artificial intelligence.

Keywords: Generative AI · Design Futures · GPT · Text to Image · Futures
Scenario

1 Introduction

A review of many design works reveals that the designers paid particular attention to the
proposed concepts to stimulate thinking about alternative futures. In recent years, Design
Futures (DF) have attracted interest from various fields. By definition, it refers to the
exploration and speculation of possible future scenarios, trends, and how design as a tool
or medium impacts the future [1]. In the past five decades, futures studies have changed
from predicting future development to describing alternative futures to shaping ideal
futures [2]. With the trend of working together to create the future, more interdisciplinary
dialogues between design and future studie [3, 4]. Are emerging. Increasingly, design is
playing a vital role in working with and for the uncertain futures.

With the advance of Generative Artificial Intelligence (GAI), Large Language Models (LLMs), such as Generative Pre-trained Transformer (GPT) and Text to Image Diffusion Model, have become increasingly popular in many fields, including design and education [5–7]. At the same time, GAI-based tools have become more powerful enough to

© The Author(s), under exclusive license to Springer Nature Switzerland AG 2023
H. Degen et al. (Eds.): HCII 2023, LNCS 14059, pp. 149–161, 2023.
https://doi.org/10.1007/978-3-031-48057-7_10

push the capabilities of designers. However, machine learning is like a black box, which is not known until the results are generated [8]. The random generation of collective action data just becomes the inspiration material for collaborative speculation.

The paper is consistent with work aimed at designing more accessible ways to influence future events, especially in the context of the age of AI. The potential of generative AI in collaborative speculation for the uncertain futures is explored through the organization of a week-long workshop. A GAI-embedded workbook is listed, with the aim of stimulating design creativity among different groups of participants. It should be noted that these participants had little or no prior knowledge of the design future. Through this project, there are the following three research questions:

1. How might AI-based tools assist in scanning signals?
2. How might AI-based tools inspire students to imagine the future scenario?
3. What support do students need to promote the design concept that addresses future challenges?

2   Related Works

Design futures is a multidisciplinary field. Through the combination of design thinking and future thinking, possible futures and design solutions are explored to meet future challenges. Design Thinking is remarkably contingent. Among them, the emergence of specific contextual conditions is conducive to its spread and success [9]. Considering that future thinking can inform decision makers about the innovation challenges and opportunities of the social and technological environment in the medium to long term (5–15 years), the ability of designers to incorporate the future as part of the design process is of paramount importance [10].

Generally, several analytical frameworks are used to analyze and understand external macro-environmental factors that affect individuals and organizations. As a specific tool, the STEEP analysis framework stands for Social, Technological, Economic, Environmental, and Political, which derive from fundamental sustainability principles [11]. Making futures can be participatory, collaborative, and engaging [12]. According to Light, A., collaborative learning opportunities help to increase interest in the topic and encourage critical thinking [13]. As a practice, speculative design aims to apply emerging technologies to real-life situations, rather than to predict or promote specific technologies or agendas. Through tangible evidence, how these technologies will manifest is communicated, leading viewers to think about what life in the depicted future or the alternative present might look like [14]. This lends itself to addressing the potential for multiple futures [15]. Speculative objects and processes can provide designers and others with new perspectives [13]. Scenario narrative has become a speculative object that is widely used [16]. However, the removal of the designer's strong explanatory power should be noted.

In order to catch up with technological advancements, and to save costs and shorten construction periods, it is necessary to improve the efficiency of construction and design workflows. AI is not only the main computational process for analyzing information, but also an important part of deep understanding of connections between large-scale data regions [17]. In generative AI, generative models trained from existing digital content such as images, text, audio, and video are employed. With advances in deep learning (DL), diverse content resembling human responses and activities is generated [18]. For research on related application scenarios, some views are that ChatGPT can fundamentally change the way humans process information and has the potential to create a level playing field for all individuals to make informed decisions [19, 20]. In terms of the prompt engineering of improved models, it is expected to overcome the limitations of interpreting model predictions. In terms of image generation, the state-of-the-art of visual coding has caught up to or even surpassed the level of human artists. However, the controllability needs to be further improved [21, 22]. Moreover, the application of industrialization is also actively explored [23].

As a nonlinear black box, generative AI often brings surprises or fears. The collaboration between designers and GAI will push objects and processes to have a full range of diverse directions. Technology is always derived from humanity, from hi-tech to hi-touch [24]. Although generative AI can already assist design in solving many problems, the value of human factors in the workflow is worth exploring.

3   Method: A Collaborative Workshop with GAI

In the participatory design process, the design of the workbook is useful [25]. In order to structure the week and observe each group's progress, a GAI-embedded workbook for Speculation 2050 is produced and uploaded on a collaborative whiteboard platform (https://boardmix.cn). Furthermore, participants can log into the platform at any time to annotate their thoughts.

3.1 Participants

A total of 58 undergraduate students from the third year of the Industrial Design program participated in the seminar, including 28 females and 30 males. They were divided into 22 groups with 2–3 students in each group. It is worth mentioning that the participants have learned the operation of various GAI tools, such as ChatGPT, Stable Diffusion, before participating in the workshop.

3.2 GAI-Embedded Workbook Design

The concepts of design thinking and futures thinking have different purposes and processes. As for purpose, design thinking aims to inspire people to creatively solve short-term problems, while future thinking aims to inspire long-term strategies by understanding the drivers and context of different situations that may occur in the future. However, design can still define multiple options as a creative activity and demonstrate diverse and credible futures guided by future thinking. According to the design processes, methods and tools of Design Futures [3, 15, 26] and the purpose of this study, a GAI-embedded workbook based on the British Design Council's Double Diamond Design Model was developed to guide the process of design futures during the workshop, as shown in Fig. 1.

Workbook is a tool that provides a structured framework for organizing information, brainstorming and visualizing concepts, and allows designers to experiment and iterate

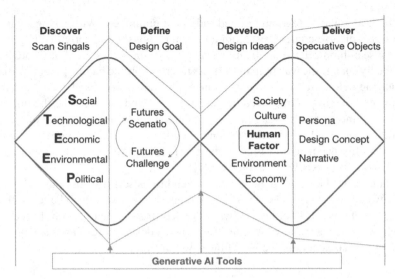

Fig. 1. Design future framework embedded with GAI.

on different possibilities. Similar workbooks have been deployed as speculative designs to motivate designers to brainstorm future topics [25, 27, 28]. The workbook is divided into four sessions, with a total of seven sheets (see Fig. 2). In addition, each stage is encouraged to apply a series of GAI tools such as ChatGPT, Stable Diffusion, and Midjourney:

Session 1: Discover the trends and changes. Scanning signals is an important part of futures research, which involves identifying and analyzing early indicators of potential future trends and changes within the STEEP framework (i.e., Social, Technological, Economic, Environmental, and Political). In the first sheet, ChatGPT plays the role of various experts in five domains to gather information that may influence the future.

Session 2: Define the challenges in the futures. In sheet 2, there are separate forms for pasting team members' idea prompts, shaping future scenarios, and defining future challenges. Both GPT and Text-to-image tools can participate in the brainstorming. In accordance with the results of the group discussions, final design goals can be refined based on value judgments.

Session 3: Develop design ideas to response the futures. This session consists of three sheets. Sheet 3 provides a structure for listing design ideas, which can be reproduced as an added page. Participants would create designs based on their chosen future scenarios. As a guiding reference, sheet 4 presents a framework based on the four pleasures proposed by P.W. Jordan [29], and the three communication levels proposed by R. Lin [30], which aims to guide the impact of design from the perception of humanity. Moreover, the relationship between humans and the external environment (Four Pillars of Sustainable Development) also needs attention.

Session 4: Deliver the speculative objects for discussion. In this session, the design is derived through three sheets. Among them, sheet 5 aims to shape the personality with the characteristics of human behavior and preferences in 2050, and to gain insight into the needs from the levels of four pleasures. Sheets 6 and 7 further translate design ideas from abstraction to more detailed visualization, which can improve reliability. The goal is to challenge assumptions, spark conversation, and inspire new ideas, not to offer final solutions.

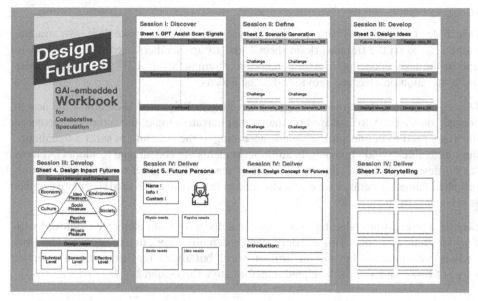

Fig. 2. Pages of the GAI-embedded workbook that guide design activities.

3.3 Workshop Process

Through one-week workshop combining online and offline, participants are encouraged to use a series of GAI tools. Figure 2 illustrates the process and method of workshop operations and data analysis.

Day 1: At the beginning of the workshop, a detailed introduction to design futures, including concepts, values, methods and tools, which lasted for 2 h. To distinguish between the two types, the researchers prepared three 2–3 min video clips of commercial design cases and speculative design cases. Students then had an hour to visualize their scan signal on sheet 1 of the workbook. Meanwhile, they can operate ChatGPT, which plays the role of an expert to provide more signals. Afterwards, everyone can write their feedback on the signal provided by AI on sheet 1. At the end of this session, each group refines potential future challenges. GPT describes possible future scenarios on sheet

2 after reading all the signals on the whiteboard. Ultimately, group members discuss potential challenges in future scenarios.

Day 2: There are 4 h of offline teamwork. Group members brainstorm around the selected future scenarios, with speculative objects ranging from text to image generation. By using speculative objects, participants can explore the potential consequences of emerging signals and trends.

Day 3–4: These two days are free time for group members to make their own arrangements. Based on the framework on sheet 4, the group members need to discuss how to update the design concept from the perception of human factors. GPT also can participate in the iteration process and provide some new ideas.

Day 5–6: During these two days, group members collaborated to complete the design content on sheets 5 to 7. Based on the overall narrative logic, the future characters in the story need to define various details according to the structure in sheet 5 to enhance their authenticity and vividness. In addition, students are encouraged to adopt GAI tools for co-design. Therefore, design concepts of this world in sheet 6 are shaped, such as reflected things, systems or services. The scenario narrative as the final speculative object is presented in sheet 7.

Day 7: Presentations, sharing of artifacts, and discussion of results are employed with a wider group audience. This not only connects creative work to more general concerns and supports thinking beyond the artifact/world, but allows for discussion of potential ways of being and any work-related transformative realizations.

3.4 Data Collection

A workbook was downloaded for each group, including all the steps from brainstorming to designing work. Storyboards, design scenarios, and design works were all analyzed through thematic analysis. In order to further understand the experience of participants co-designing with various GAI tools, five Likert scale was adopted to investigate, involving the effect of GPT expert signal scanning, quality of GPT assisted storytelling, method, and effect of using GAI tools to generate images. During several stages of signal scanning, scene structure, and product design, the perception of the effectiveness of AI assistance was descriptively statistically analyzed.

In addition, the researchers conducted group interviews with each group on days 2 and 4 of the workshop, with the main purpose of analyzing the potential and limitations of human-computer interaction. During this process, diaries added to the whiteboard at any time will also be collected as record materials (Fig. 3).

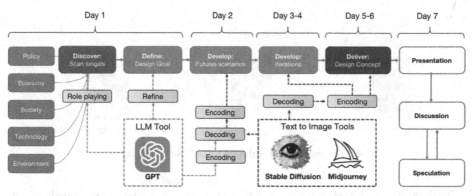

Fig. 3. The process of the workshop.

4   Findings and Discussion

4.1   Power in Detect Signals and Analyze Trends

Due to their industrial design background, students' thinking is usually constrained by knowledge boundaries and personal experience. LLMs with collective intelligence like ChatGPT are trained based on massive text datasets. In the workshop, 47 of the 58 participants scanned the signal using ChatGPT. Furthermore, speed, efficiency, and relative fairness are generally agreed upon.

Speed and Efficiency: ChatGPT can quickly and efficiently analyze large amounts of text-based data, which helps to identify STEEP signals in various information sources.

Relative Unbiased: By using machine learning to generate responses based on input data, ChatGPT enables unbiased analysis of STEEP signals without human intervention. It should be noted that there is still bias in the dataset.

Furthermore, limitations still exist during signal scanning, such as lack of context, insufficient human insight, and limited data sources.

Lack of Context: On the one hand, ChatGPT can analyze and interpret text-based data. On the other hand, it may not always have the context needed to fully understand the meaning behind certain STEEP signals, which may lead to incomplete or inaccurate analyses.

Lack of Human Insight: ChatGPT is a machine learning tool that lacks the insight and intuition of human analysts, which may lead to oversights or misses for deeper analysis.

Limited Data Sources: ChatGPT is limited by the data sources it is given to analyze. If data sources are incomplete or biased, the analysis of results may be questionable in terms of comprehensiveness or accuracy.

By further combining quantitative questionnaire data, ChatGPT can indeed expand the boundaries of information, but is weak in depth and accuracy, as shown in Fig. 4. In particular, when asked about sources of information, some participants reported that the links or documents provided by AI looked authentic, but could not be logged in or found. Therefore, the reliability of the generated information is lowered.

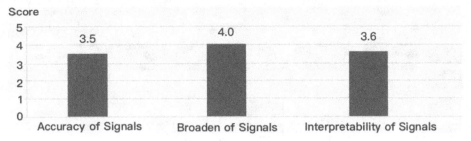

Fig. 4. The evaluation result of ChatGPT scanning signals.

Participants illustrated some potential future scenarios based on the signals under the STEEP framework. At the same time, ChatGPT also gives 6 directions, such as the list of group 17 (Table 1). Through the comparison between humans and AI, it can be seen that the direction of human extraction focuses more on the needs of individuals and groups. In contrast, ChatGPT is more like an impartial judge can reasonably list challenges with higher probability.

Table 1. List of potential future challenges.

Contributor	List of Future Scenarios (Brief Version)
Participant 1 in group_17	• In the future, housing may become increasingly unequal, and the affluent class will have larger and more luxurious spaces, while the lower class may be forced to live in harsh environments • High-tech development has brought about ecological pollution and electronic waste pollution • In the future, human workers will be replaced by machines, which will lead to massive unemployment and social unrest • Human data security will be increasingly threatened, and personal privacy may be obtained and sold by hackers • The development of technology will exacerbate the digital divide, making it difficult to move with terminal equipment damaged or without power • Although online education will effectively solve the problem of resource inequality, the real world experience still cannot be fairly accessed
Participant 2 In group_17	• While technology continues to be important for social progress, the company's further blockade of core technologies • People will be able to control the length of their lifespan on their own, bringing greater population size • Humans will be able to transform from DNA and biological aspects, blurring the connections between kinship groups • The urban transportation system will become more complex due to the integration of land and air into vehicles • Due to the unequal living environment caused by tech development leading to ecological pollution, the affluent class lives in the air or other advanced facilities, while some people are forced to go to polluted living environments due to work needs

(continued)

Table 1. (*continued*)

Contributor	List of Future Scenarios (Brief Version)
ChatGPT	• The intensification of inequality and wealth inequality may lead to social dissatisfaction and unrest • Automation and artificial intelligence may lead to an increase in unemployment and instability in the job market • Climate change and Scarcity of resources may impact the global economy and development • The digitization process may lead to an increase in data security and network threats • The loss of biodiversity and ecosystem collapse may threaten human survival • Geopolitical tensions and conflicts may pose challenges to international relations and regional stability

4.2 Inspiration for the Futures Imagination

Design fiction is a way of using storytelling and imagination to explore possible futures, create meaningful and thought-provoking experiences, and challenge assumptions and expectations about the surrounding world. Most participants had creative and thoughtful conversations with ChatGPT about hypothetical scenarios and ideas. In summary, the following advantages are obtained:

World-Building: ChatGPT can provide ideas for creating detailed and immersive worlds, including setting, culture, and history.

Developing Characters: Generative scenarios can provide a context for character development for authors to imagine how their characters might respond to different challenges and opportunities.

While text generation can assist participants in storytelling and imagining alternative futures, self-reported data indicate a lack of creativity compared to readability and fluency. The narrative performance feedback obtained from the questionnaire data is shown in Fig. 5.

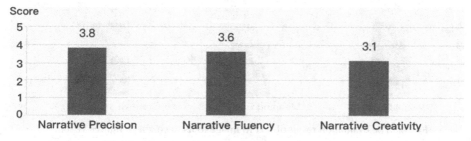

Fig. 5. The evaluation result of ChatGPT storytelling.

In the stage of scenario visualization, some tools (e.g., Stable Diffusion, and Midjourney) are used to shape the scene in detail. There are iterative opportunities to gain new perspectives in this transformation process, as well as semantic deviations from text-to-image mapping. According to the structure in sheet 3, it is mainly the participants who use the description of the object to translate the metaphor, and then judge whether the conversion is accurate. Table 2 shows the example of the metaphor "reborn" from abstract word to generative image.

Table 2. Example of the sheet 3.

Text	Metaphor	Prompt	Image
In the future, humanity will face a great reckoning. We will confront the consequences of our actions and the damage we have done to the planet. But out of this crisis, a new world will emerge. We will be reborn	Reborn	In a grey environment, a small green plant grows amidst the concrete jungle	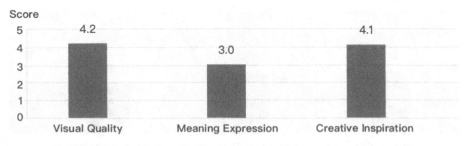

4.3 Co-shaped the Design Concept

50 out of 58 participants used Stable Diffusion or Midjourney, or both of them. According to operational data, 100% of students used text as prompts, 66% added images as guidance, and 14% used plugins to improve the generation effect. For the effect evaluation of co-shaping the future vision, more participants believed that AI generation tools can improve image quality and provide inspiration. Therefore, accurate ideographic representation is difficult to control, as shown in Fig. 6.

Score
| | | |
5 — 4.2
4
3 — 3.0
2
1
0
  Visual Quality   Meaning Expression   Creative Inspiration

4.1

Fig. 6. The evaluation result of text to image tools to co-shape futures vision.

During the week-long workshop, students quickly brainstormed and explored potential future challenges using GAI tools. Then, creative thinking constructs design concepts and application scenarios are combined, as shown in Fig. 7. In order to deal with potential future challenges, a series of design concepts were proposed to cause reflection and influence on current behavior. For a final-day presentation, attractive visuals are more likely to capture the audience's attention and interest. Moreover, trustworthy future narratives are more likely to trigger reflection and discussion.

Fig. 7. Design concepts for addressing future challenges. The design on the left was created by Yingtai Zhang, Sheng Zhang; The design above the middle was created by Wanjun Chen, Wenqi Gan; The design below the middle was created by Yi Chen, Yiting Zhang, and Jiahui Dong; The design on the right was created by Haiying Deng, Huiyi Zhang, and Yi Zheng.

5   Conclusion and Future Work

A case study consisting of GAI-embedded workbook design and a workshop was conducted to design concepts for addressing the future challenges. By embedding a series of GAI tools, the potential value and limitations of AI-assisted design are explored, and more human-AI collaborative design methods and tools are expanded for future design. According to the results of the study, high technology can significantly increase the speed of scanning future signals, the reliability of fictional stories, and the quality of visual communication. Considering the lack of humanity in the process of statistical prediction, designers need to make corresponding supplements in the process of collaborative design. Therefore, it is necessary to structure a guiding framework from the perceptive of human factors in the workbook (see sheet 4).

References

1. Fu, Z., Barbara, A., Scupelli, P.: Online International Conference on Design Futures 2020. Postmedia Books, Milan, Italy (2022)
2. Inayatullah, S.: Futures studies: theories and methods. There'sa future: Visions for a better world. vol 30 (2013)

3. Barbara, A., Scupelli, P.: Teaching to dexign futures in cities. Techne, pp. 112–116 (2021)
4. Candy, S., Potter, C.: Introduction to the special issue: design and futures (vol. I). J. Fut. Stud. **23**(3), 1–2 (2019)
5. Jarrahi, M.H.: Artificial intelligence and the future of work: human-AI symbiosis in organizational decision making. Bus. Horiz. **61**(4), 577–586 (2018)
6. Hwang, G.-J., Chen, N.-S.: Editorial position paper exploring the potential of generative artificial intelligence in education: applications, challenges, and future research directions. Educ. Technol. Soci. **26**(2) (2023)
7. Mondal, S., Das, S., Vrana, V.G.: How to bell the cat? A theoretical review of generative artificial intelligence towards digital disruption in all walks of life. Technologies 11(2), 44 (2023)
8. Audry, S.: Art in the Age of machine learning. The MIT Press (2021)
9. Verganti, R., Dell'Era, C., Swan, K.S.: Design thinking: critical analysis and future evolution. J. Product Innov.Manag. **38**(6), 603–622 (2021). https://doi.org/10.1111/jpim.12610
10. Buehring, J.H., Liedtka, J.: Embracing systematic futures thinking at the intersection of Strategic Planning, Foresight and Design. J. Innov. Manag. **6**(3), 134–152 (2018)
11. Hunt, D.V., et al.: Scenario archetypes: converging rather than diverging themes. Sustainability **4**(4), 740–772 (2012)
12. Ehn, P., Nilsson, E.M., Topgaard, R. (eds.): Making Futures: Marginal Notes on Innovation, Design, and Democracy. The MIT Press (2014). https://doi.org/10.7551/mitpress/9874.001.0001
13. Light, A.: Collaborative speculation: anticipation, inclusion and designing counterfactual futures for appropriation. Futures **134**, 102855 (2021)
14. Auger, J.: Living with robots: a speculative design approach. J. Hum.-Robot Interact. **3**(1), 20–42 (2014)
15. Dunne, A., Raby, F.: Speculative Everything: Design, Fiction, and Social Dreaming. MIT Press (2013)
16. Bishop, P., Hines, A., Collins, T.: The current state of scenario development: an overview of techniques. Foresight **9**(1), 5–25 (2007)
17. Blagec, K., et al.: A curated, ontology-based, large-scale knowledge graph of artificial intelligence tasks and benchmarks. Sci. Data **9**(1), 322 (2022)
18. Jovanovic, M., Campbell, M.: Generative artificial intelligence: trends and prospects. Computer **55**(10), 107–112 (2022)
19. Kim, A.G., Muhn, M., Nikolaev, V.V.: Bloated Disclosures: Can ChatGPT Help Investors Process Information? Chicago Booth Research Paper 23 July 2023
20. Yue, T., et al., Democratizing financial knowledge with ChatGPT by OpenAI: Unleashing the Power of Technology. SSRN 4346152 (2023)
21. Lyu, Y., et al.: The cognition of audience to artistic style transfer. Appl. Sci. **11**(7), 3290 (2021)
22. Lyu, Y., et al.: Communication in human–AI Co-creation: perceptual analysis of paintings generated by text-to-image system. Appl. Sci. **12**(22), 11312 (2022)
23. Javaid, M., et al.: Artificial intelligence applications for industry 4.0: a literature-based study. J. Ind. Integr. Mgmt. **07**(01), 83–111 (2022). https://doi.org/10.1142/S2424862221300040
24. Lin, R., et al.: From Hi-Tech to Hi-Touch: A Global Perspective of Design Education and Practice, p. 314. MDPI (2023)
25. Mucha, H., et al.: Co-design futures for AI and space: A workbook sprint. In: Extended Abstracts of the 2020 CHI Conference on Human Factors in Computing systems (2020)
26. Candy, S., Dunagan, J.: Designing an experiential scenario: the people who vanished. Futures **86**, 136–153 (2017)
27. Gaver, W.: Making spaces: how design workbooks work. In: Proceedings of the SIGCHI conference on human factors in computing systems (2011)

28. Harrington, C., Dillahunt, T.R.: Eliciting tech futures among Black young adults: a case study of remote speculative co-design. In: Proceedings of the 2021 CHI Conference on Human Factors in Computing Systems (2021)

29. Jordan, P.W.: Designing Pleasurable Products: An Introduction to the New Human Factors. CRC Press (2000)

30. Lin, R.-T.: Transforming Taiwan aboriginal cultural features into modern product design: a case study of a cross-cultural product design model. Int. J. Des. 1(2) (2007)

If You Can't Beat Them, Join Them: How Text-to-Image Tools Can Be Leveraged in the 3D Modelling Process

Samuel Otto Mathiesen[(✉)] and Alessandro Canossa[iD]

Royal Danish Academy, Philip De Langes Allé 10, 1435 Copenhagen, Denmark
samuel-otto-mathiesen@live.dk, acan@kglakademi.dk

Abstract. The rapidly growing field of text-to-image generation leverages machine learning and natural language processing to allow for the creation of very diverse and high-quality images. Whilst these images can be used in various forms and for many purposes, this paper addresses a specific question: The possibility of utilizing text-to-image generators to create concept art for the 3D-modeling process of a character.

There is a potential opportunity to explore how these tools can be incorporated in traditional content creators' pipelines. This opportunity presents itself now because of two factors: The increased capability of these text-to-image tools compared to previous generative models, as well as the lack of specific focus on creators in current research.

We propose a possible pipeline to incorporate these new tools in the traditional 3D modeling process, dubbed the 'vortex process'. This workflow follows a more circular and iterative pattern compared to examples of a more traditional process. The impact of utilizing text-to-image tools is threefold: It can boost the speed of iteration, as the speed of generating new artwork is increased compared to a human; this then allows for the exploration of more variations in a design process. Additionally, it can free up extra time to allow for extra polish of the final product. In this paper we therefore examine how the use of this technology affects the creative process. Finally, we highlight some of the potential ethical and societal implications of this technology: Loss of human jobs, issues regarding copyright of artwork used to train models etc., which will all impact future use.

Keywords: AI · Text-to-image Generators · Creativity · Mixed-Initiative · 3D Modelling · Concept Art

1 Introduction

1.1 Background

Within the past year, text-to-image software has become very visible – and to some degree controversial – in the art world and beyond. Development within the field of machine learning has allowed algorithms for converting natural language text prompts

© The Author(s), under exclusive license to Springer Nature Switzerland AG 2023
H. Degen et al. (Eds.): HCII 2023, LNCS 14059, pp. 162–181, 2023.
https://doi.org/10.1007/978-3-031-48057-7_11

into images to become much more sophisticated. (Though this paper will not cover this technical development.) This has led to a variety of popular implementations, such as Dall-E, Midjourney and Stable Diffusion. These tools can produce both complex and highly detailed images of a large amount of both real and fictional subjects. Combined with other AI tools such as ChatGPT, this technology is further pushing the envelope for how many 'human' skills computers can mimic. However, there are also many questions surrounding this technology. Both regarding its future development as well as its use now.

Some of the main concerns are the potential for these tools to displace human artists in the field of visual design, as well as the ethics and legal aspect of the creation and utilization of these algorithms. The ethical implications involve the financial aspect of artist compensation and the use of existing art to train models; the legal implications are related to copyright.

At the same time, the possibility of this software to enhance and expand the creative process for many fields cannot be ignored. We are still in the early phases of adoption for this technology, but there are many ways in which it could possibly be integrated into creative processes in a positive way. Even if one sees little benefit to the use of these tools, it is unlikely for this technology to disappear. Beyond its possible practical (and financial) benefits, it is an undeniably large step within the field of computer science and art. Its impact and staying power therefore cannot be ignored. Finding ways in which this technology could be integrated into creative processes will therefore likely be both useful and necessary.

The breadth of possible applications of these models is very large. Recognizing this, the purpose of this paper is to analyze the use of these software models in a more confined, practical design process. We will attempt to integrate it into the process of creating a 3D character, and analyze and reflect on its use: What are the strengths and weaknesses of the software? How does it alter the process, and what are the implications of this? The practical element of the design process will be the creation of a high-fidelity 3D character. The software will aid in the conceptualization of the character. Whilst we deal with a very specific use case in this paper, we will also discuss how the process can be utilized in a more general context.

1.2 Related Work

The area of text-to image generators is fairly new. Nevertheless, there is considerable previous research on generative models to produce content for games, film etc., both focusing on the uses, as well as technical implementations [1, 2]. However, the rapid advances in generative models are making literature even a couple of years old less relevant. The technical capabilities of modern text-to-image algorithms make the comparison to previous implementations of generative models difficult. In addition, the breath of applications for modern AI generation is much larger. Previous generative models were more tailored for specific purposes, such as procedural content generation.

Current research on modern implementations of AI generation does exist, but most of the work focuses on large language models such as ChatGPT or are aimed at describing underlying technical advancements [3–5]. Even if there is some overlap between large language models and text-to-image generators (mostly regarding automated generation, mixed-initiative co-creativity, and increased efficiency) the two families of tools are designed for very different applications.

In this paper we want to examine the utilization of text-to-image generators and apply it to a concrete use case. Searching through databases such as the ACM Digital Library and Google Scholar, it is difficult to find research that both deals with modern text-to-image software and focuses on the content creator angle.

The use case we want to examine is the visual development process. Specifically, we are interested in the transition from a concept to a 3D model. The exact nature of this process naturally depends on the team size and project specifications. However, the process can be generalized. Like all development processes, the beginning is an idea. Be it for a game, a movie or something else. The various aspects of this vague concept are then expanded upon. In our case, we are only interested in the visual development. Traditionally, a team would ideate through concept art sketches, storyboards, animatics, sculptures or moodboards [6, 7]. They would create refined concept art for the project. For projects dealing with 3D artwork this would include artifacts such as model sheets that capture the shape. These are usually in the form of sketches illustrating the base shape and features of a subject from multiple angles. Additionally, there will also usually be one or more detailed pieces of concept art, rendered in full color. This gives a more holistic view of the subject and is useful for defining color and materials (see Fig. 1).

Fig. 1. Example of a visual concept for a character. The left features a concept art piece, giving information about materials, color, and mood. The right features a model sheet (also called turnaround sketches) showing the proportions and shape of the character from multiple angles [8].

In a smaller production this work may be done by one person instead of a team, but the overall pipeline remains the same, and it is primarily a linear process. It may sometimes be necessary to go backwards to fix or change an element. However, this is generally avoided, as it will undo the natural structure of the process and slow down the development process [7]. For this reason, usually there will be a check-in with the art director/concept artist each time the process moves into a new phase, such as when the final concept art gets handed to the modelling team [6]. This process can be illustrated, as seen in Fig. 2.

A full process overview such as the one featured in Vaughan [6] features more elements, but in this case, we are only examining the three stages shown here, and the iteration cycles that happen within them. The concept is the initial spark for the creation process. As shown by the size of the diamond, this part of the process is shorter than the other stages. Pre-production can be everything from developing full-fledged story or world design elements, to specific visual design, as in this case. The production stage would normally involve more elements than shown here. In our case, however, we can simplify this to the 3D modelling itself. Between each stage there is a check-in, usually with the art director; a gate for passing to the next stage that requires certain elements of the process to be in order. Each stage of the process expands and contracts, as ideas within it are explored and then refined to move towards the next stage.

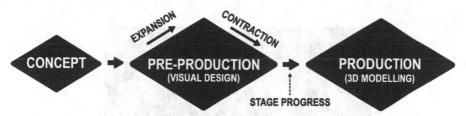

Fig. 2. Simplified overview of a creative process. This visualization focuses on the beginning (concept development) and middle (pre-production), as these are the most relevant stages for our purpose.

The fundamental nature of the visual development process is to a large extent fixed: It begins with some idea or concept; this will then get visually developed and eventually move towards a production phase. However, the *ways* in which these steps can be achieved may very well change. Traditional methodologies such as the ones described by Vaughan [6] and Gahan [7] are not guaranteed to be applicable in the same way, with the advent of AI-powered technologies. As we will investigate, the function of these generative models may not always fit well into a traditional visual development pipeline. And there may be more effective ways to utilize them as tools for the process, such as the process presented here.

2 Vortex Framework

2.1 Types of Iteration Cycles

The vortex process was developed with the intention of leveraging text-to-image tools to overcome the lack of a concept artist or an art director when attempting to create a 3D character. Regarding the choice of text-to-image tools, both Dall-E, Midjourney and Stable Diffusion were used. However Stable Diffusion was the primary tool utilized.

The beginning of the process – concept development – had less use of generated images compared to later stages. As with a traditional process, this ideation phase features broad ideas that are then refined. The difference here is that instead of performing this visual development using sketches and concept art as presented in Sect. 1.2, we carried directly over into a 3D model. The initial base form of the character (see Fig. 3) was designed based on three elements: a) The concept for the character and its function; b) a small selection of gathered reference representing core parts of the concept; c) generated images from the three tools mentioned. The concept for the character takes root in trying to explore duality, and the combination of two distinct types of design, in a sci-fi context. In this case it is the combination of traditional, primarily Western military styled design, combined with a fictional alien design. The latter takes inspiration from Eastern-style clothing design; this is combined with the design elements produced by the text-to-image generators to shape a second design identity. This creates a contrast between the two styles, where one is more rigid and contemporary, and the other is freer and more imaginative. The reference images gathered represented the core aspects of this concept, and were therefore also split into two groups, one for each design style.

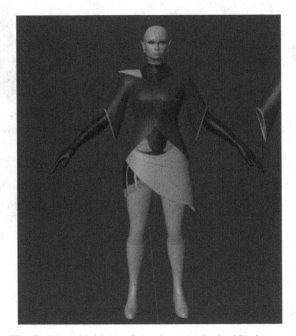

Fig. 3. The initial look of the character in the 3D viewport

The use of generated images in the concept development phase was primarily to create a baseline for their capabilities, specifically for the context in which we intended to use them (as per the concept for the character). For this reason, the prompts used here were simple (see Fig. 4). Beginning the concept development process using exclusively generated images could also provide interesting results, however the goal of this paper is to try to replicate a real-life process where there aren't such arbitrary restrictions.

Prompt: *"An oil painting of a woman in a formal military uniform"*

Dall-E   Stable Diffusion   Midjourney

Fig. 4. Example of the initial images generated using the three text-to-image tools. These give us some initial elements to work with, and already here we can see the tools' different interpretations of the prompt.

The use of renderings of the 3D model as partial input[1] for the text-to-image tool is at the core of the method proposed and it became a reoccurring element in the process. Combining an image with a prompt allowed us to generate precise variations of the original design (see Fig. 5). From here we could select interesting features and integrate them into the 3D model, iterating over time using several fragments provided by different variations. This process allows for discarding and selecting individual features from each variation according to four criteria: Interesting features; features aligned with the original concept; features that fit stylistically; features that matched humanoid proportions. This represents a very natural way to evolve the design, as every cycle includes visual elements present in the previous state of the generation process. Thereby, the generated images that are output are linked together in a more cohesive way.

Additionally, we selected a few of the generated images and used them as input for a new generation cycle, forming a circular loop. The new cycle would generally entail changing the prompt or the settings, either to refine or slightly alter features which we liked.

A similar cycle was also performed with some of the references gathered initially, to ensure that defined stylistic elements were integrated into the generated images (see Fig. 6). The images generated in this way were very similar, owing to their shared origin. But they did differentiate themselves from the other generated images, adding variety. Overall, this can be a good way to integrate some elements of a particular reference into the generated images. It is worth noting that results may vary quite a lot depending on the input parameters. And may not always include the details that are of particular interest. However, with enough generation cycles, it is likely that there will be some elements which can be drawn into the evolving design.

---

[1] Many text-to-image generators allow for the use of an image as input in addition to the text prompt. This functions in much the same way as text but derives elements of a prompt from the image itself. This might be useful if a desired element of an image is hard to describe using text. In addition, the influence (weight) of the image can usually be controlled.

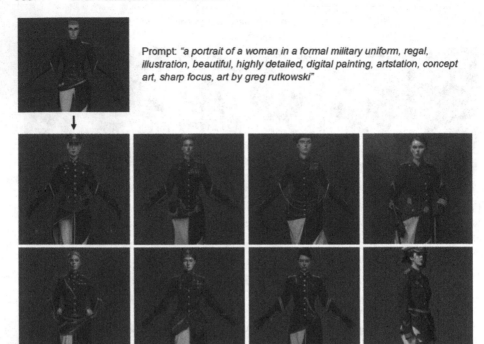

Prompt: *"a portrait of a woman in a formal military uniform, regal, illustration, beautiful, highly detailed, digital painting, artstation, concept art, sharp focus, art by greg rutkowski"*

Fig. 5. Example of using an initialization image along with a text prompt to guide the generated images. This led to a more natural evolution of the design and kept the proportions and design more consistent. Shown is also the prompt utilized to generate the images; this was performed in Stable Diffusion.

We also generated images using only text prompts and no image guidance (see Fig. 7). It was still possible to select individual details from these images. However, doing this was harder than selecting elements from images generated using a guidance image. And it made it harder to maintain a consistent design. Therefore, we continued primarily with other methods of generation, especially the use of image guidance.

Utilizing an image as input was not the only way to evolve details, though. For certain images where we found interesting features or wanted to clarify details more, upscaling was used (see Fig. 8). This preserves the original image better and is therefore useful when finer details are required. Though it will not provide the same variance as newly generated images.

To this same end we also made use of inpainting[2] (see Fig. 9). As well as outpainting[3], to a limited degree (see Fig. 10). For technical reasons, outpainting was at the time of the process only available in Dall-E. We found, however, that the stylistic change and

---

[2] Inpainting refers to the re-generation of a specific part of an image, decided using a mask. Like in the use of an initialization image, it draws upon the existing image as guidance. It then only replaces individual elements of an image, depending on the size of the mask.

[3] Outpainting refers to extending an image, by generation of new images next to the existing one. It also draws upon the existing image as guidance, but only to add and not to replace.

Reference Image ↓

Prompt: *"a portrait of a woman in an elegant military uniform, (regal), (sci-fi), illustration, beautiful face, highly detailed, intricate details, sharp, digital painting, trending on artstation, concept art, sharp focus, art by greg rutkowski"*

Fig. 6. An example of the output generated from using one of the gathered reference images as initialization. As can be seen, most of the images share the feature of a flowing white cloak or jacket. This was a core element in the initial image that we wanted to integrate.

lack of interesting details limited its use. Although, one could likely still find this feature useful, depending on the project. Due to the technical limitations, it was also used less than the other methods of generation presented.

Inpainting was used a great deal, however. We used the process of inputting the character as a base and generated a template to be used for inpainting. Inpainting would then be used to alter only certain parts of the image. An example of this is the boots and pants of the character (see Fig. 9). Here we would change the prompt to weight the image towards more unique visual detail whilst the initialization image kept the output aesthetically consistent. Like using an initialization image, this is a very powerful tool. Its ability to change individual elements is very useful since it is difficult to control the entire composition of a generated image. The image can instead be iteratively refined.

Lastly, it is worth noting that different steps of the process are happening simultaneously and not necessarily in a linear fashion, as they are described here. In this process, we are working largely with individual elements and building many fragments on top

Prompt: *"a portrait of a woman in an elegant military uniform, (regal), (sci-fi), illustration, beautiful face, highly detailed, intricate details, sharp, digital painting, trending on artstation, concept art, sharp focus, art by greg rutkowski"*

Prompt: *"a digital painting of a pair of elegant sci-fi boots and pants, (regal), illustration, highly detailed, intricate details, sharp, digital painting, trending on artstation, concept art, sharp focus, art by greg rutkowski"*

Fig. 7. Example of images generated using only a text prompt. These don't share the same connection to the existing design as the images generated using the other methods described.

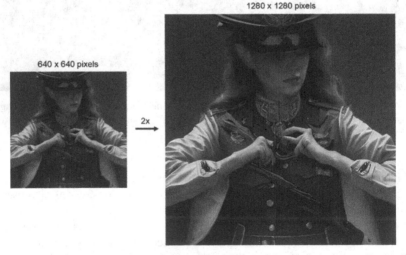

Fig. 8. Example of using upscaling to increase the fidelity of details in an image. Depending on the settings and tool used, this may also sometimes add new details. This image – and most other images – was upscaled using Latent Diffusion Super Resolution (LDSR).

of one another. Due to this, the overall structure of the process changes compared to a traditional example of visual development. In summary, we utilized six main types of generation cycles, shown here in rough order of most utilized to least:

• Render of whole or part of 3D model as initialization + prompt

Prompt: *"a digital drawing of industrial sci-fi pants, with intricate geometric detail, (regal), (sci-fi), illustration, sharp, digital painting, trending on artstation, concept art, sharp focus, art by greg rutkowski, artgerm"*

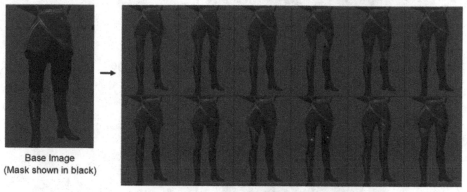

Base Image
(Mask shown in black)

Fig. 9. Example of using inpainting to change only an individual element of an image. This provides variations for that element and keeps the generated images consistent with the existing design. The left features the base image, as well as the mask for the area to do inpainting in. The right features the variations generated from this base image. Here we could then pick out interesting details from these and combine them to create a cohesive design for the character.

- Original reference image as initialization + prompt
- Inpainting, using character render or generated image as base + prompt
- Upscaling
- Exclusively text prompts
- Outpainting, using character render or generated image as base + prompt

2.2   The Vortex Process

The presented approach changes the traditional process into a far more iterative process. As presented in Sect. 1.2, and shown on Fig. 2, a traditional approach to visual design would be more linear, where the features of the character to be modeled are de-fined during the concept development phase: A concept for the character would spark initial ideas. Then the concept artist would create a complete concept art and model sheets as described by the visual design process in Sect. 1.2. After pre-production is completed and agreed with the art director, the creation of the 3D character would begin, with all its relevant steps. Details may still vary and change between the concept and the 3D model, but the overall structure of the process is linear. And the individual stages of the process are all separated by artistic checks and technical inspections.

Comparing the vortex process to the traditional process represented in Fig. 2, the main difference is that the pre-production and production stages are combined. Together they form an iterative loop, where the product is gradually refined. Since this loop could technically go on forever, a cut-off point must still be set, like any other stage transition. We can represent this visually using Fig. 11.

The spark of the process is still the concept. This stage remains the same, as you will likely derive the initial idea for the process in the same way as before. Whereas traditionally concept development would lead into the pre-production stage – visual

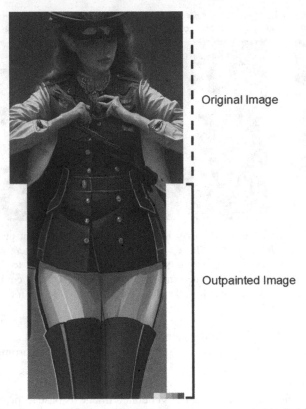

Fig. 10. Example of outpainting. Since the initial image was generated in Stable Diffusion, and the outpainting done in Dall-E, there is a clear stylistic difference as we extend the image further.

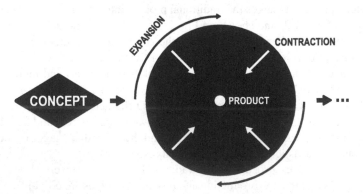

Fig. 11. Visual representation of the vortex process. The stages of pre-production and production combine and form a circular iterative loop – the vortex. These exist for each separate product being worked on. And can – like a normal stage of a creative process – be carried into others after completion, such as the rigging of a character after its 3D model is completed.

development in our case – adopting AI-driven image generators allows us to proceed directly to a vortex that combines the pre-production and production stages, occurring simultaneously. Hence, we enter a circular loop instead of the linear and separated stages shown in Fig. 2. The various types of cycles described in Sect. 2.1 form the various loops of the vortex, and directly lead to the definition of the 3D model. The visual development that would normally happen in the pre-production stage continues during production.

We retain the expansion and contraction of the previous stages. However, the expansion occurs in the constant addition of new elements from the generated images. As presented in Sect. 2.1, the process puts a much greater emphasis on integrating many small fragments into the overall design. Whilst the overall process looks different, there is a similarity to the traditional production stage for the individual elements of the product. They can be thought of as having small individual stages within the vortex. At this smaller scale, they are more linear. However, the way in which they interact together shapes the larger process to be more circular and iterative. Design elements from one part of the product can always feed into another. The current look of the character in 3D is being fed into the software to generate elements that can be integrated into the design. And the building of these many smaller elements onto each other creates a naturally iterative cycle, hence the name of the vortex process.

The further you get towards the center, the less expansion takes place since there are naturally less elements to expand upon, the more the overall model is finalized. Traditionally the process ends when the 3D model is as close to the initial concept art as possible. In the vortex process we do not have complete initial artwork, so the end of the process is less exact. It could take the form of a check-in with the art director, just like in the traditional process. Hence, whilst the vortex process is more circular compared to the traditional one, it's not an infinite loop. The structure of the process, including the beginning and end, is simply different. This eventually results in a product – such as a 3D character – which can be carried further into the larger production, just like the traditional process.

The most important aspect of the vortex process as presented here is working iteratively; over time combining many elements during the creation of the product. Working like this helps you to work with the software, instead of against it. As the traditional approach of a linear visual development process can clash with the functionality of current text-to-image software. It can be harder to extract complete and coherent designs from the generated images. However, there might also be elements of creativity which are stimulated by this way of utilizing generated images in the visual development process.

2.3 The Creativity of Ambiguity

The use of iterative design like the process featured here does provide options for developments that maybe would not normally have been considered. The ambiguity and abstractness often found in generated images, as well as the iterative process, could be beneficial in some cases. It could allow the designer to refine the product in ways that they did not expect, but nevertheless might enhance the outcome.

The element of ambiguity comes from the fact that the process featured here is a mixed initiative. This term has been around for decades, and its exact definition can vary [9]. We will use a definition of the term based on Liapis [2], which explores the use of computational intelligence in level design for games. Here the term mixed-initiative co-creation (MI-CC) is used to describe a process of creating an artifact via the interaction of both a human and machine initiative. In our case, we are creating a 3D character. And the overlap of human and machine initiative happens through the use of the generated images as concept for the characters design. We have the initiative of setting the parameters for the generation. As well as the integration of the elements found in the generated images into the characters design. The machine, in this case represented by the text-to-image software, has the initiative of proving the concept material that we are picking from.

Liapis [2] relates MI-CC to the random stimulus principle of lateral thinking. Lateral thinking involves solving the problems present in a process through an indirect and more creative approach. It also allows for the completion of steps in a non-sequential order. This is compared to a traditional process of vertical thinking, where the steps are sequential and follow a more immediately obvious path [10].

The random stimulus principle is an aspect of this and describes a foreign concept disrupting the process and forcing the consideration of new ideas. In our case the text-to-image generator acts as this foreign concept and offers us alternative approaches. The generated images in the vortex process are usually not entirely foreign, as they often have their basis in the current form of the product. However, a similar effect occurs, where new elements are introduced that can change the process and product. Either in a positive way, where they are integrated into the design. Or they are discarded based on visual or conceptual reasoning. However even if they aren't utilized in the design itself, they might spark some considerations or ideas that prove useful later.

In the creative industries there is great interest in mixed-initiative approaches. Mike Jelinek is an artist, designer, and researcher, who worked on projects such as Terminator: Dark Fate (Tim Miller/Jim Cameron), Future Ink (Wacom and Ars Electronica) or Dubai's Museum of the Future exhibition research (Tellart). In his doctoral dissertation, he presents artwork which is created using the mixed initiative of artist and generative AI [11]. He talks about how often ideas come to him as random sparks of inspiration. While these moments might be a creative spark, their ambiguity and randomness also mean that they are not very reliable. This makes them unsuitable in a more structured process that a designer would generally undertake. He speculates that the reason we might find this ambiguity creatively fulfilling relates to the way that our brains processes information. Effectively the brain performs a lot of very educated guesses, turning ambiguity into choices. This for example explains why two people can remember the same event in different ways [12]. This aspect of our thinking then also comes to light when we deal with creativity.

Eagleman [12] presents three core strategies that represent the cognitive process of innovative thinking: Bending; modifying an original. Breaking; taking apart a whole. And blending; mixing two sources together. These processes occur all over the interconnected brain, to absorb the world and possibly extrapolate far beyond what we observe and experience. The choices we make when, for example, we pick out interesting visual details for a design can therefore be said to emerge from these aspects. Perhaps ambiguity then excites our brain because it offers it more diverging opportunities for processing. The element of our brain that might make us distinguish shapes in the dark that are not there – out of ambiguity and its related fear – might then also emerge in a more positive light when we are creating.

The problem remains, however, that ambiguity is often associated with randomness and that it's hard to control. Thereby likely being insufficient to drive a creative process, as previously mentioned. Text-to-image generators alleviate this problem however, as they allow for control over the ambiguity of the output. This then represents a core strength of these generative tools within a creative process. This is also what Jelinek [11] points out: This balance between generating things that are ambiguous and open to interpretation, but still represent a concept, and allow for conscious design. Images can be generated of a certain subject and the ambiguity of the generated image can be tweaked using the parameters of the software. Suddenly, the lack of refinement in the output becomes an advantage in the creative process. However, it's also not just random noise: There is an element of cohesion in the image, owing to the training data which the algorithm is based on. And for the specific process, the workflow in which it is used might add to this cohesion, as described in Sect. 2.1. If the brain is the processor, the generated images act as ambiguous input data to be processed: To be bent, broken, and blended into something new – a design which explores new paths but is still cohesive and appealing.

While this is a sentiment that can be reflected in the process undertaken here, it does come with a caveat. There were times where the generated images presented elements that were useful for the design: They were ambiguous enough to use as a creative spark but also structured and could be used to design consciously. This is helped by the fact that we utilized the vortex process: We worked iteratively, and with many smaller design elements that over time combined into a cohesive design for the character. (A good example of this is the design of the pants, partly featured in Fig. 5.) However, with ambiguity also comes elements that are not useful. Especially when the concept for a design is already specified, like will normally be the case in an actual production. Personal preference will also always have a big impact on a subjective process like visual development. It would therefore be wise to consider how (and if) we can apply the lessons learned here in a more general context.

2.4 Generalizability

An important aspect of traditional concept art is that the different concept art pieces must be stylistically and compositionally consistent [6]. Due to the stochastic nature of images made with text-to-image generators, this can be a problem. Especially when working on a larger design. The workflows described in Sect. 2.1, such as using a guidance image helps alleviate this problem. The usefulness of text-to-image generators for concepting can depend on how much the flow of the output can be followed and interpreted. Versus how much it needs to conform to some already formed ideal. If the desired output is very specific, the ambiguity (and often just plain wrongness) of the output might prove to be more of an obstacle than a benefit. Especially if it is something that can be represented in real life. One such example from this process was the hair of the character. Especially as we sought photorealistic representation. Getting generated images that were cohesive and featured enough intricate details to represent hair was not feasible. Photographic reference was much better suited to this task.

Therefore, it would be wise to consider what preconceived notions and requirements there are, when determining the use of text-to-image generators within a design process. Both the strengths of generative tools discussed here, such as the potential power of ambiguity, and how these elements could be integrated to enhance the creative process. But there will likely also be cases where the downsides outweigh the benefits. The increased efficiency gained from the speed of iteration is useless if the generated images don't contain useful elements.

One could also perform a similar process to the one described here without the use of text-to-image generators. Although the extremely quick (compared to human artwork) process of creation offers a practical advantage. Without this, designing a product utilizing the vortex process becomes extremely impractical: Elements such as inputting the current design to generate new concept material become practically impossible. In practice, the possibility of utilizing the vortex process, or one like it, is allowed only by the advent of text-to-image generators.

However, this paper only represents one integration of text-to-image generators, into the 3D modelling process itself. While this opens new ways of working and can have creative benefits as demonstrated, theoretically you could utilize similar methods within the concept art (pre-production) stage instead. The reason why the visual development process is performed using 2D concept art, is that it's much faster to iterate in this format than during the production phase. If you spend 4 weeks on a character model but then find that a core feature of that character's design doesn't work, you have wasted a lot more time. Compare that to a drawing of the character, which can be finished in much less time [7]. We integrated the visual development stage into the production stage of the 3D character, owing to a desire to explore the use of these generative tools from the perspective of a 3D artist. As well as it being a practical experiment with low manpower. But text-to-image generators could also be applied to speed up a traditional visual design stage, utilizing 2D concept art. Generating a complete design of the whole character in a single image would likely present a challenge, both technically and artistically. Especially since proper concept art will require multiple drawings, from different angles, that must be consistent. However, a similar approach could be taken to one described in this paper, where elements of multiple generations are composed together. These tools could be utilized just as well in a 2D process to quickly ideate, and the concept artist will ensure that the technical requirements are met. Photoshop, one of the most popular applications for image editing and creation, recently added a new tool called generative fill [13]. This integrates text-to-image generation directly within the software. And we are seeing the utilization of generative models in other fields have the effect of increased ideation efficiency as well as an increase in the polish of the work [5].

Generative models are likely to be of interest to both large as well as small teams and solo projects with the fields of games, movies, and other digital media. However, the integration of text-to-image tools within the process will likely be different depending on the team size and structure. As well as the preference of the people within those teams. A larger team with an already established concept art department will maybe be more inclined to adopt these tools within that team, keeping the visual development as a separate stage. They will then be able to utilize the benefits of generative models, whilst keeping a similar structure.

We foresee that smaller teams and solo projects likely will see a broader variety of adoptions. These are often more flexible in their structure, as they don't have the same managerial needs that a large production and team necessitate [6]. And they can perhaps benefit to an even greater degree from an increase in efficiency, due to their low manpower. These are the teams that might be more likely to adopt a completely new workflow such as the vortex process. Especially for solo teams or teams with only a single artist, as they would be doing all the stages anyway, from visual development to production. Some of these people and teams might be drawn to the new possibilities offered by text-to-image generators and might find great creative potential in power of ambiguity. And in this process, they will potentially discover new capabilities and workflows of their own.

3 Conclusion

3.1 Investigation Results

In this paper we have performed an early investigation into text-to-image software. We have analyzed the practical utilization of this software to aid in the conceptualization element of a design process – in this case of a 3D character. We have presented a more iterative design process, the vortex process, powered by the introduction of generative tools. This is a process that deviates from a traditional creative process, an example of which we have presented for comparison. This new workflow provides new opportunities for creative work. It also has potential practical benefits such as increased efficiency and the ability to spend more time polishing, as the process of ideation is greatly sped up. Teams and creative processes of all sizes can benefit from these effects. However, especially for smaller teams, the practical benefits offered by generative tools might allow people to work on things which before were unfeasible. This process, and the use of text-to-image generators, also has potential downsides. Whilst there is an increase in ideation speed, the generated images might not always contain useful design elements, due to the stochastic nature of text-to-image generators. These tools also might not be suitable for all styles of art, depending on their training data. Therefore, consideration of the affordances of the different processes is required. The process described here is different to a traditional one, but whether it's better is up for debate. The same goes for the utilization of text-to-image generators in a more general context. It must also be acknowledged that this technology is new. And that further development and analysis of its use will likely change the landscape and provide new insight. Similarly, the potential impact of the technology on a broader social and economic scale will also contribute to shaping the role of this technology within the future of creative work.

3.2 Societal Implications

Nothing exists in a vacuum. The practical capabilities of text-to-image software can't be separated from the broader context they exist within. This is also the case for other implementations of generative AI, though our focus here is on text-to-image generators. This chapter will be speculative, as it's difficult to say for certain exactly what the impact of text-to-image generators will be. The issues presented here are of concern and will likely have an impact on the future development of these tools. But they should be considered as a guiding introduction, not a concluding statement. There are also potentially issues not discussed or presented here.

As with many instances of automation in other industries, replacement of human jobs is a concern. If an automated process can beat humans in either cost or quality – or even both – there is little incentive for a company to retain a human-based workforce. We are still in the very early phases of adoption. The technical capabilities of the software, however, are even in this early stage in many cases good enough. As we have discussed, there is a potential increase in efficiency that can be harnessed from the use of text-to-image software. With this increase in the efficiency of one employee, they can now potentially replace another. And there is no reason to assume that future development will be limited to simply a tool. For example, the manual prompting that is required currently, could potentially be automated to some degree in the future. Further limiting the creative involvement of human artists. The more self-sufficient the tool can be, the more it can be broadly commercially viable [14].

The training of the algorithms that power these tools is another issue: To train text-to-image software, a huge dataset of pre-existing images with descriptive text is required. The LAION-5B dataset that Stable Diffusion was trained on for example, consists of over 5 billion image URLs [15]. This large-scale trawling of images means that everything from medical imaging to art by world-class artists ends up in the dataset [16]. And then by extension into the trained model, with no initial possibility for an opt-out. The name of popular and skilled artists is a common inclusion in text prompts. This allows the algorithm to generate more high-quality and consistent images, by focusing its training data on a specific artist. This was also done in this paper, for these reasons. In our case we are not trying to directly replicate existing styles or artists. But this is very much a use case which happens. This is dismaying to artists, who are seeing their artwork and style used or directly replicated, with little recourse [17]. Beyond the personal question of whether you find this unethical or not, there is also the implication of copyright. The capabilities of a model are derived from the data fed into it during training. And with a huge dataset such as LAION-5B, this will include images that are copyrighted. The actual dataset itself simply refers to the images, and their associated metadata [18]. However, when the dataset is integrated into a model through training, the actual content of the images is required. Meaning that the resulting model includes clear aspects of the images found in the training data. This can be practically observed by the popularity of utilizing artists' names in text prompts. This use of images without consent would perhaps be less of an issue in an isolated research context. But the companies behind the most popular text-to-image generators such as Dall-E or Stable Diffusion are backed by large investments [19, 20]. There is a commercial application for these tools. This then reinforces the issues of copyright and artist compensation.

Possible solutions to this could include things such as training on data where the copyright is owned, or the content is in the public domain. Adobe's generative fill tool in Photoshop utilizes this approach [13]. Or instead of the current system of indiscriminate trawling, with a possibility later of opting out, a system of opting in could be adopted. This would then likely come with some form of financial compensation as well. Though the nature of how this would practically work is uncertain. However, it is not hard to imagine a way of training these models which is more equitable and fairer. As an example, the newer Stable Diffusion 2 model has made technical changes to its text/image encoder (the part of the model responsible for the translation between the two). Unlike the implementation that Dall-E and Midjourney uses, this allows for some new features which deal with this issue of copyright and artist consent/compensation. It gives a greater overview of what's in the dataset, potentially allowing for the creation of an opt in/opt out system. It also removed the specific connection between an artist and their work in the dataset. This means you can't specifically prompt an artist's name, and directly reap the benefits that used to provide, as previously described. The content itself is still present, but it can't be directly prompted to make easy copies of existing work [21]. Stability AI has likely done this in part to get ahead of legal issues, which they (with good cause) predict will be an issue in the near future.

Beyond the copyright of the input data, there is also the potential issue of the copyright of the generated images. This is less of a current issue than the copyright of the input, as it doesn't for example infringe on any artists' rights. But from a legal standpoint it likely also needs clarification. As an example, Midjourneys terms of service lay out under what conditions the user retains the rights to the content they generated using the software. Premium subscription tiers provide ownership to the user, while lower tiers only grant a creative commons noncommercial license [22]. The copyright of the input content, the training data, is quite clear. And so are the rights for the different algorithms that take the training data and outputs the generated images. But the question could be raised as to who owns the copyright for generated content if anyone at all. Fundamentally this likely depends on who you consider the creator of the generated images. Is it a tool that is used to make images through prompting? Or is the user just finding images the algorithm has in effect already produced through its variables? Given that it is possible to reproduce the same image, by utilizing the same prompt and settings such as seed, the latter is lent more credence [23, 24]. The case of non-human entities creating (in a broad sense of the word) artwork is not a common occurrence, as it is now with the advent of text-to-image generators. However, there is some legal precedent for the situation of copyright in this case. A series of copyright disputes took place in the 2010's over the copyright of a photograph taken by a monkey. The owner of the camera, a photographer, argued that he should own the copyright for the image. PETA filed on the side of the monkey, arguing that it should retain the copyright. And that they should administer the proceeds from the photo towards wildlife conservation [25]. However, courts in both the US and UK ruled that only artwork created by humans can be copyrighted. And that the author of the photograph in this case was the monkey, hence the image is in the public domain [26]. Should it be decided that the actual creator of images derived from text-to-image generators is the computer itself, a similar precedent could be applied.

Ultimately, the only thing we can decisively conclude is that the legal framework and corresponding discussion around these issues have not caught up to reality yet. We exist in a non-accountability bubble, a wild west of sorts, where the possibilities are endless and the considerations few. But we are starting to see a shift in this, and it likely won't be long before this bubble collapses. Precedents will be set, and regulations put in place. To the detriment of some, but then also to the benefit of others. Overall, this will perhaps have downsides from a purely technical perspective. But it will also contribute to making the field more sustainable and fairer. And it will likely still allow for the benefits of generative models, and new workflows such as the vortex process.

3.3 Future Work

We recognize that the advent of text-to-image technology has implications far too wide to cover in a single paper. The framework proposed in this paper can be useful for working in a mixed-initiative environment. However, the vortex process may not work for every artist or every type of product. We also recognize that this type of process can potentially be extrapolated outside of the context in which it has been explored here. Therefore, it is necessary to gather more insights from various artists, to further discover the potential applications of this technology. Additionally, the evolution of this technology may also bring forth new possibilities, which must then also be considered.

As highlighted in the previous section, many elements of generative AI technologies such as text-to-image generators must be considered on a societal level. The hope is that more perspectives will be brough forth and considered. Especially from the creators who work within this field every day. With the very rapid advancement of this technology, we risk being left behind if we do not investigate and discuss early on. And to get a cohesive picture, we need to consider a diverse set of viewpoints.

References

1. Alvarez, A., Dahlskog, S., Font, J., Holmberg, J., Nolasco, C., Österman, A.: Fostering creativity in the mixed-initiative evolutionary dungeon designer. Foundations of Digital Games 2018 (FDG18) (2018) https://doi.org/10.1145/3235765.3235815
2. Liapis, A., Alexopoulos, C., Yannakakis, G.N.: Mixed initiative co-creativity. In: International Conference on Foundations of Digital Games (2014)
3. Kalla, D., Smith, N.B.: Study and analysis of Chat GPT and its impact on different fields of study. Int. J. Innovative Sci. Res. Tech. **8** (2023)
4. Terwiesch, C.: Would Chat GPT3 Get a Wharton MBA? A Prediction Based on Its Performance in the Operations Management Course. Mack Institute for Innovation Management at the Wharton School, University of Pennsylvania (2023)
5. Noy, S., Zhang, W.: Experimental Evidence on the Productivity Effects of Generative Artificial Intelligence. Massachusetts Institute of Technology (2023)
6. Vaughan, W.: Chapter Two: Understanding a Modeler's Role. Digital Modelling, p. 21–75. New Riders (2012)
7. Gahan, A.: High- and Low-Poly Characters. 3ds Max Modelling for Games: Insider's Guide to Game Character, Vehicle, and Environment Modeling, 2nd edn. p. 329–442. Elsevier. (Original published 2008)
8. Revoy, D.: Artwork from the Open Movie Workshop 'Chaos&Evolutions' [Digital Art]. Wikimedia. https://commons.wikimedia.org/wiki/File:1D_model-sheet.png. Last accessed 08 Jun 2023. Licensed under CC BY 3.0 https://creativecommons.org/licenses/by/3.0
9. Novick, D.G., Sutton, S.: What is mixed-initiative interaction. In: Proceedings of the AAAI Spring Symposium on Computational Models for Mixed Initiative (1997)

10. De Bono, E.: Difference Between Lateral and Vertical Thinking. Lateral Thinking: A Textbook of Creativity, pp. 29–34. Penguin Books. (Originally published 1967) (2009)

11. Jelinek, M.: Sketch as a Tool of Visual Ideation from the Design Perspective. Slovak University of Technology – Faculty of Architecture and Design (2022)

12. Eagleman, D.: The Runaway Species: How Human Creativity Remakes the World. Canongate Books (2017)

13. Generative Fill. Adobe. https://www.adobe.com/products/photoshop/generative-fill.html. Last accessed 17 Jun 2023

14. Zapata, S.: The End of Art: An Argument Against Image AIs [Video Essay]. YouTube. https://www.youtube.com/watch?v=tjSxFAGP9Ss (2022, October 18th). Last accessed 18 Jun 2023

15. Beaumont, R.: LAION-5B: A NEW ERA OF OPEN LARGE-SCALE MULTI-MODAL DATASETS. LAION. https://laion.ai/blog/laion-5b/ (2022, March 31st). Last accessed 18 Jun 2023

16. Xiang, C.: AI Is Probably Using Your Images and It's Not Easy to Opt Out. Motherboard – Tech by Vice. https://www.vice.com/en/article/3ad58k/ai-is-probably-using-your-images-and-its-not-easy-to-opt-out (2022, September 26th). Last accessed 18 Jun 2023

17. Nolan, B.: Artists say AI image generators are copying their style to make thousands of new images — and it's completely out of their control. Business Insider. https://www.businessinsider.com/ai-image-generators-artists-copying-style-thousands-images-2022-10?r=US&IR=T (2022, October 17th). Last accessed 18 Jun 2023

18. LAION FAQ. LAION. https://laion.ai/faq/. Last accessed 18 Jun 2023

19. Brockman, G., Sutskever, I.: OpenAI LP. OpenAI. https://openai.com/blog/openai-lp/ (2019, March 11th). Last accessed 18 Jun 2023

20. Vincent, J.: Stability AI, proponent of hands-off AI image generation, gets a $1 billion valuation. The Verge. https://www.theverge.com/2022/10/18/23410435/stability-ai-stable-diffusion-ai-art-generator-funding-round-billion-valuation (2022, October 18th). Last accessed 18 Jun 2023

21. Romero, A.: Stable Diffusion 2 Is Not What Users Expected—Or Wanted. The Algorithmic Bridge. https://thealgorithmicbridge.substack.com/p/stable-diffusion-2-is-not-what-users (2022, November 25th). Last accessed 18 Jun 2023

22. Midjourney Terms of Service. Midjourney. (n. d.). https://docs.midjourney.com/docs/terms-of-service. Last accessed 18 Jun 2023

23. Guide to using seed in Stable Diffusion: What is a seed in stable diffusion, and how to use it?. (n.d.). getimg.ai. https://getimg.ai/guides/guide-to-seed-parameter-in-stable-diffusion. Last accessed 18 Jun 2023

24. Williams, S.: An Introduction to Stable Diffusion. Stafford Williams – Blog. https://staffordwilliams.com/blog/2023/05/19/introduction-to-stable-diffusion/ (2023, May 19th). Last accessed 18 Jun 2023

25. UNITED STATES DISTRICT COURT, NORTHERN DISTRICT OF CALIFORNIA, Case No.: 15-cv-4324. https://web.archive.org/web/20171115000049/http://www.mediapeta.com/peta/PDF/Complaint.pdf (2015). Last accessed 18 Jun 2023

26. Gibbs, S.: Monkey business: macaque selfie can't be copyrighted, say US and UK. The Guardian. https://www.theguardian.com/technology/2014/aug/22/monkey-business-macaque-selfie-cant-be-copyrighted-say-us-and-uk (2014, August 22nd). Last accessed 18 Jun 2023

Applications of Large Language Models (LLMs) in Business Analytics – Exemplary Use Cases in Data Preparation Tasks

Mehran Nasseri[1,2] [ID], Patrick Brandtner[1,2(✉)] [ID], Robert Zimmermann[1] [ID], Taha Falatouri[1,2] [ID], Farzaneh Darbanian[1,2] [ID], and Tobechi Obinwanne[1] [ID]

[1] University of Applied Sciences Upper Austria, 4400 Steyr, Austria
{mehran.nasseri,patrick.brandtner}@fh-steyr.at
[2] Josef Ressel Centre PREVAIL, 4400 Steyr, Austria

Abstract. The application of data analytics in management has become a crucial success factor for the modern enterprise. To apply analytical models, appropriately prepared data must be available. Preparing this data can be cumbersome, time-consuming, and error prone. In the current era of Artificial Intelligence (AI), Large Language Models (LLMs) like OpenAI's ChatGPT offer a promising pathway to support these tasks. However, their potential in enhancing the efficiency and effectiveness of data preparation remains largely unexplored. In this paper, we apply and evaluate the performance of OpenAI's ChatGPT for data preparation. Based on four real-life use cases we show, that ChatGPT demonstrates high performance in the context of translating text, assigning products to given categories, classifying sentiments of customer reviews, and extracting information from textual requests. The results of our paper indicate that ChatGPT can be a valuable tool for many companies, helping with daily data preparation tasks. We demonstrated that ChatGPT can handle different languages and formats of data and have shown that LLMs can perform multiple tasks with minimal or no fine-tuning, leveraging their pre-trained knowledge and generalization abilities. However, we have also observed that ChatGPT may sometimes produce incorrect outputs, especially when input data is noisy or ambiguous. We have also noticed that ChatGPT may struggle with tasks that require more complex reasoning or domain-specific knowledge. Future research should focus on improving the robustness and reliability of LLMs for data preparation tasks, as well as on developing more efficient and user-friendly ways to deploy and interact with them.

Keywords: Language Models (LLMs) · Natural Language Processing (NLP) · ChatGPT · Data Preparation · Business Analytics

1 Introduction

Over the past years, the application of data analytics in business contexts, i.e., business analytics (BA), has become a crucial success factor for the modern enterprise. It is integral to drive decision-making, support strategizing and improve operational efficiency

© The Author(s), under exclusive license to Springer Nature Switzerland AG 2023
H. Degen et al. (Eds.): HCII 2023, LNCS 14059, pp. 182–198, 2023.
https://doi.org/10.1007/978-3-031-48057-7_12

across industries. BA involves the application of statistical analysis and modelling techniques such as Machine Learning (ML) or Deep Learning (DL), and its application areas covers a wide array of disciplines such as Supply Chain Management (SCM), innovation management or marketing [1–4]. To apply such models, BA relies on the availability of appropriately prepared data as the basis for analysis. The quality and timeliness of insights greatly depend on the underlying data. However, that data is often unstructured, multi-faceted and complex and the preparation of this data represents an essential pre-processing step before the deployment of any analytical model [5]. Data preparation tasks can be cumbersome, time-consuming, and error-prone, and analysts and data scientists often spend a significant portion of their time on cleaning, transforming, and normalizing data to render it fit for subsequent analytical processing. There are still many tasks in this area that require a lot of human effort, such as finding mistakes in current categories, converting qualitative customer feedback to quantitative satisfaction levels, correcting, or changing existing data or adding new information by adding new columns to the data. Referencing to the acknowledged CRISP-DM (Cross-Industry Standard Process for Data Mining) model, which is a widely adopted methodology for conducting data mining projects, data preparation is the most time-consuming stage of data mining projects [6, 7]. Hence, there is a huge interest in practice and academia to support and facilitate that stage of BA project.

In the current era of Artificial Intelligence (AI), Large Language Models (LLMs) like OpenAI's ChatGPT offer a promising pathway to streamline the data preparation process. These sophisticated models, trained on extensive datasets, have demonstrated exceptional capabilities in understanding and generating human-like text [8, 9]. However, their potential in enhancing the efficiency and effectiveness of business analytics data preparation remains largely unexplored and holds enormous untapped potential. In this paper, we aim to utilize LLMs' abilities in real business use cases by applying these models to real datasets and evaluating the results. The underlying research question of the paper can hence be defined as follows:

What is the actual potential of LLMs like ChatGPT, for various data preparation and analysis tasks in real business use cases?

To address this research question, we select ChatGPT, a state-of-the-art LLM based on the transformer architecture, to perform selected data preparation tasks from a current research project in the context of predictive analytics. By comparing the results between ChatGPT's and human results, we subsequently evaluate the performance of LLMs in data preparation tasks. The remainder of the paper is structured as follows: Section two provides an overview of LLMs, their development and presents typical use cases of such models. Section three elaborates on the methods and material used in the study, covering use case selection and definition, model selection, prompt definition, implementation, and evaluation. Section four discusses the results of the paper, including strength and limitations of such models compared to human data preparation. Finally, section five provides the conclusion and outlook of the current study.

2   Large Language Models and Use Cases

Large Language Models (LLMs) are state-of-the-art AI models that can generate human-like text with high fluency and coherence [10]. LLMs significantly enhance the potential of systems to process and manipulate text [11]. LLMs originated from early NLP techniques and have evolved significantly [12]. LLMs are generally characterized by their immense size, often spanning tens of gigabytes, and are trained on massive text datasets that can reach up to the petabyte scale [11]. LLMs have become a valuable tool in various fields, such as language translation, natural language processing, machine translation, and text summarization [13].

In [14], the transformer architecture, a ground-breaking approach to natural language processing that relies on self-attention mechanisms is introduced. The paper introduces several key innovations, such as multi-head attention, positional encoding, layer normalization, and residual connections. These innovations enable transformers to capture long-range dependencies and context more effectively, while also benefiting from increased scalability and training efficiency. The authors demonstrate the superiority of the transformer architecture through its performance on machine translation tasks, paving the way for the development of subsequent large language models based on the transformer framework such as BERT [10], RoBERTa [15], and T5 (Text-to-Text Transfer Transformer) [16]. OpenAI's GPT series, including GPT-2 [13], GPT-3 [12], and GPT-4 [17] further expanded the capabilities of LLMs, showcasing their potential as multitask learners, few-shot learners and zero-shot leaners [12, 13, 18].

LLMs can be applied to a wide range of use cases. These use cases can be generally categorized into different domains, such as Generation, Open QA, Closed QA, Brainstorming, Chat, Rewrite, Classification, and Extract [19]. Consequently, we provide a summary of these diverse use cases, based on the works of previous researchers:

Generation: LLMs can be used for text generation, where they produce new text based on a given input prompt [13]. They may also be used for various purposes, such as chatbots, content creation, and automated journalism [20]. LLMs can also be used for creative writing, such as generating scripts, poems, and stories [12, 18, 21]. Another way that LLMs can be used for generation tasks is in language translation which may be carried out through the use of machine translation models[22]. LLMs can also be used for cross-lingual retrieval [23]. In addition, LLMs can be used for multilingual natural language processing tasks such as named entity recognition, language identification, and sentiment analysis [10, 23, 24].

Open QA: This refers to the process of answering questions by searching through a text corpus [25]. LLMs can be helpful in Open QA in several ways: they can help improve the accuracy of answers by generating a large number of possible answers to a given question [12]; they can help in identifying relevant sources of information for a given question [10]; they can also help in summarizing information from multiple sources in Open QA tasks [15]; and they can be used to generate natural language responses that are easy to understand and follow and thus make Open QA systems more user-friendly and accessible to a wider range of users [12].

Closed QA: LLMs have the ability to generate accurate answers to specific factual questions [10]. In the context of Closed QA, LLMs can be trained on large amounts of text data and fine-tuned on a specific task to generate accurate answers to questions that require a specific, factual answer [10]. LLMs, such as BERT and RoBERTa, have shown great potential in this regard while GPT-3 has been shown to achieve high accuracy on several benchmarks in this regard [12, 13, 15]. Also, LLMs can be used in conjunction with other machine learning techniques, such as reinforcement learning, to further improve their performance on Closed QA tasks [26].

Brainstorming: Is a group creativity technique that involves generating a large number of ideas in a short period of time [27]. In brainstorming sessions, LLMs can be used with respect to these aspects in the following ways: Idea Generation, with their ability to provide valuable insights and stimulate creativity [28]; Collaboration, with an ability to synthesize different perspectives and ideas into a cohesive output [29]; and Speed and Efficiency, with an ability to free up time and cognitive resources for participants to focus on other aspects of the brainstorming process [30].

Chat: LLMs, such as ChatGPT, have shown to be highly effective in the realm of chat and conversation [31]. ChatGPT can be trained on large amounts of conversational data, allowing it to generate natural and coherent responses to a wide variety of prompts [13]. LLM's ability to understand and generate natural language text makes them powerful tools for customer service applications [32].

Rewrite: LLMs, such as GPT, have shown great potential in the area of text rewriting [33]. The ability of LLMs to generate coherent and grammatical sentences, while retaining the original meaning, can be useful in various applications such as paraphrasing [33, 34].

LLMs can also be fine-tuned for specific rewriting tasks, which can further improve their performance [35]. For example, LLMs can be trained on specific domains and thus, improve their ability to generate paraphrases in those domains [33].

Classification: Large Language Models (LLMs) can be used to categorize text-based data into predefined groups or classes based on their content, context, or other relevant features [10]. Furthermore, LLMs' controllable generation can be leveraged to generate examples for specific categories, which can be useful in training classifiers [33]. LLMs can be used for cross-lingual text classification, where they can be trained on multilingual datasets to classify text in multiple languages [36].

Extract: LLMs have shown great potential in the field of text extraction, which involves automatically identifying and extracting relevant information from unstructured text data [10]. This can include tasks such as named entity recognition, entity linking, event extraction and relation extraction [37–39].

3 Research Methodology

In this section, we aim to utilize the abilities of LLMs to assist with data preparation tasks that are required before performing business analytics. Our steps to reach this aim are shown in Fig. 1.

In a first step, we identified and selected potential use cases out of a current research project. By this means, we ensured a real-life setting and the availability of real data.

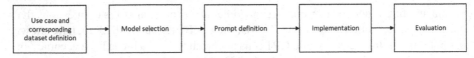

Fig. 1. Overview of steps

In step two, the aim is to identify the LLM of our choice, i.e., ChatGPT. In 3.2., we explain and justify this choice. In the third step, we have to define the prompts used to interact with ChatGPT, followed by step four, which include the implementation respectively running of these prompts and the associated data. Finally, evaluation covers the selection of appropriate metrics to compare human with LLM performance in the selected use cases. Subsequently, these steps are described in detail. The detailed results of the evaluation as well as the concrete measures used in the different use cases are explained in Sect. 5 of the paper.

3.1 Use Cases and Corresponding Dataset Definition

We have selected four our use cases based on real-world problems and considered the following specific criteria when choosing them:

- Each use case is based on actual data from a real-life project setting.
- The use cases are not exceptional but common task in most companies and occur frequently.
- They are related to language characteristics and previously could have not been performed by machines easily.
- They are currently mostly performed by humans.

An overview of each use case, including its description, the LLM-related task, the respective business area, and the corresponding dataset characteristics, is shown in Table 1. A sample dataset for each use case is provided in Appendix.

3.2 Model Selection

For this study, we chose as state-of-the-art LLM, i.e., ChatGPT, from a practical and technical perspective, ChatGPT has several advantages. First, there is no need to build and train new models for each use case, which saves a significant amount of time and cost. Second, the processes can be easily automated using the ChatGPT API and can be used with popular programming languages such as Python. Third, ChatGPT is inexpensive (the free version of ChatGPT is sufficient for our use cases, and there is no need to upgrade to the paid version). And forth, from a theoretical perspective, ChatGPT has some advantages relative to other LLMs with respect to the use cases as described in previous section. The following points represent an overview of these specific advantages, drawing insights from previous research in the field:

- Generation: ChatGPT allows for controllability in generating text, such as specifying the topic, tone, or style of the generated text [40]. Additionally, ChatGPT has shown strong performance in various generation tasks, including text completion, summarization, translation, and dialogue generation [41–43].

Table 1. Summary of Use Cases and Data Used

Use Case	LLM task	Business area	Dataset
U1: Translating German product names to English	Rewrite	Retail	6235 records of active products in an Austrian retail store
U2: Assigning pre-defined product categories based on product names	Classification	Retail	9007 records of active products in an Austrian retail store
U3: Classifying positive, negative, or neutral sentiments of customer reviews	Classification	Customer relationship management (CRM)	9915 records of customer reviews extracted from google
U4: Identifying repair requirements and root causes based on customer requests for repairing technical home appliances	Extract	Customer service	1693 records of customer requests from an Austrian home appliance provider

- Open QA: ChatGPT's large-scale pre-training on diverse text data has also allowed it to achieve state of the art performance on various open QA datasets, including SQuAD and TriviaQA [44]. Also, ChatGPT's ability to render multiple answers to a single question enables it to provide more comprehensive responses and improve the chances of finding the correct answer [44].
- Closed QA: ChatGPT's capabilities allow it to accurately answer questions that have a limited set of possible answers, such as multiple-choice questions [13]. It can be fine-tuned on specific closed QA tasks to improve its performance [45].
- Brainstorming: The controllability of ChatGPT's text generation allows users to direct the conversation towards specific areas of interest, leading to more focused brainstorming sessions [46].
- Chat: ChatGPT's ability to generate coherent and fluent text can reduce the likelihood of miscommunication or misunderstanding between users and the chatbot [47]. ChatGPT's ability to generate personalized responses based on user input also allows for more tailored and efficient interactions [48].
- Rewrite: ChatGPT's pre-training on massive amounts of text data allows it to generate text that is stylistically consistent with the original text [14]. GPT has shown promising results in generating diverse and high-quality paraphrases. GPT-2, for instance, achieved state-of-the-art results in generating diverse and coherent paraphrases [49].
- Classification: ChatGPT's controllability can be useful in training classifiers [49]. ChatGPT can also be fine-tuned on specific classification tasks to improve its performance [50].
- Extract: ChatGPT is useful for information extraction tasks [51]. It is able to accurately identify and extract relevant information from large datasets [52]. Additionally,

ChatGPT can be fine-tuned on specific extraction tasks to improve its performance [41].

3.3 Prompt Definition

Choosing the correct prompt is an important task that directly impacts the quality of the model's response. To ensure an effective prompt, we tested several different prompts for each use case. We utilized examples from [44], the OpenAI API [53] guideline, and focused on engineering clear and simple prompts. Our prompts consist of two distinct parts. The first part is the command or query used to communicate with the model and request an output. In the case of defining categories in a product classification use case (U2), one example of correct answers for each category is also included in this part. The second part is the data that needs to be processed by the model to generate the desired result. For this part, the data is converted into a JSON string. An example prompt for each use case is provided in the Appendix.

3.4 Implementation

To implement each use case, we utilized the OpenAI API [53] in Python and used the GPT-3.5-Turbo model (with default parameter settings) from this API. We converted the dataset into a JSON string and used the prompt defined for each task, as described in the previous section, to request the API to provide the result in the form of a JSON string formatted as a table. Due to token limitations, we divided our input dataset into multiple batches and fed the model until the last record of data. One challenge we faced during implementation were to the frequent timeouts of the ChatGPT server. Another challenge was that ChatGPT occasionally produced an incomplete or ill-defined JSON string, resulting in the interruption of the running code and requiring it to be retried.

3.5 Evaluation

For evaluation of results, we have used different metrics in accordance with the respective use case. For the first use case, which focused on translating product names, a comparison between human and ChatGPT-results was conducted. The second use case, which emphasized on assigning product categories to product names, ChatGPT's results were compared to the actual product categories based on F1-score. For use case three, where the goal was to detect positive, neutral, or negative sentiments in textual reviews, we analysed the accuracy of correctly predicting the respective sentiment by means of two research checking it. Finally, for use case four, we compared ChatGPTs's results of identifying repair request (what) and repair causes (why) from real life repair tasks with the results of two human evaluators based on correct and incorrect outcomes.

4   Results and Discussion

Subsequently, the results for each use cases and a deeper discussion of the respective findings is provided.

4.1 Use Case 1: Translate Product Names

In our first use case ChatGPT needed to translate product names from German to English. From our 6,235 available product names we randomly choose 602 to ensure that our sample is representative (confidence level = 99%, margin of error = ±5%). To evaluate the translations, two German-speaking reviewers checked the accuracy of the translations. Out of the 602 translations, ChatGPT produced 572 (95.02%) correct translations and 13 (2.16%) incorrect translations (see also Table 2). The remaining 17 (2.82%) translations were not understandable by the human evaluators and were excluded from the evaluation.

Table 2. Results Use Case 1: Translation of Product Names

Translation Result	Amount of translated product names	% of all translations
Wrong	13	2.16%
Correct	572	95.02%
Unknown	17	2.82%
TOTAL:	602	100%

As expected, the results show a very high success rate of correctly translating production transcriptions from one language to another. This is in line with previous research on large language models, where it was found that LLMs outperform traditional translation models. More precisely, ChatGPT has demonstrated superior performance and previous research predicts high potential for document-level translation [54] or for translation of chats [55]. Although we only translated product names and not complete sentences, our results at least partially confirm those of previous research and were found to be as expected. Interestingly, ChatGPT encountered difficulties in translating regional terms and designations like "Sachertorte" (i.e., a special Austrian cake).

4.2 Use Case 2: Assign Product Categories

In the second use case, ChatGPT needed to assign pre-defined product categories based on product names (e.g., "Kinder Chocolate 450g XXL"). For this task, a data set of 9,007 product names was used. We evaluated the result with an F1-score. The F1-score has been expanded to encompass multi-class classification, thereby providing a performance measurement beyond its original application in binary classification. This expansion allows us to obtain a single summary metric for evaluation purposes [56]. The following formulas have been used to calculate the F1-score for our purpose:

$$\text{F-1 Score (A)} = \frac{2 \times \text{Precision (A)} \times \text{Recall (A)}}{\text{Precision (A)} + \text{Recall (A)}} \tag{1}$$

$$\text{Precision(A)} = \frac{TP(A)}{TP(A) + FP(A)} \tag{2}$$

$$\text{Recall(A)} = \frac{TP(A)}{TP(A) + FN(A)} \tag{3}$$

We considered the agreement between ChatGPT output and the business classification as a True Positive (TP). When a product belongs to class A but is incorrectly classified in class B, a False Positive (FP) occurs. When the product belongs to class B but is classified in class A, a False Negative (FN) is given.

The F1-score was calculated for each class. The overall F-1 score for the use case is the average of the F-1 scores for all ten classes. Table 3 shows the results, where F-1 score of each class is between 0.73 and 0.99, "Fresh Meat & Fish" with 0.99 is the highest accuracy and "Bakery" with 0.73 is the worst. The overall F-1 score is more than 0.9, which indicating that ChatGPT could prepare highly accurate result for classification U2. The following Table 3 provides an overview of the results of product categorization:

Table 3. Result Use Case 3: F-1 Score Calculation for Product Categorization

Category	TP	FP	FN	Precision	Recall	F1-score
Alcoholic Beverages	426	28	1	0.938	0.998	**0.967**
Bakery	362	253	8	0.589	0.978	**0.735**
Dairy	607	125	1	0.829	0.998	**0.906**
Electronics	380	21	1	0.948	0.997	**0.972**
Fresh Meat & Fish	404	3	0	0.993	1	**0.996**
Fruits & Vegetables	670	204	70	0.767	0.905	**0.83**
Health, Beauty & Baby	1751	110	3	0.941	0.998	**0.969**
Non-Alcoholic Beverages	348	28	1	0.926	0.997	**0.96**
Pantry	946	407	5	0.699	0.995	**0.821**
Snacking	1442	399	3	0.783	0.998	**0.878**
Overall F1-score						**0.903**

As shown by the results of use case 2, ChatGPT was able to perform highly accurate in terms of assigning products to given product categories. In previous studies, LLMs have also been found to be highly performant in terms of classification task. Previous research has shown high accuracy for simple tasks such as modelling topics from a list of programming assignments or classifying educational forum posts [57]. Other studies concluded, that, as with human classifiers, identical input can lead to different output. Hence, the unsupervised usage of ChatGPT for classification is not recommended [58].

4.3 Use Case 3: Classify Sentiments

In the third use case, ChatGPT needed to evaluate the sentiment (negative, neutral, positive) of customer reviews for a retail store. The dataset contained 9,915 from which we extracted a random sample of 370 records to ensure that our sample is representative (confidence level 95%, margin of error = ±5%). Two researchers evaluated if the senti-ment was classified correctly. Overall, ChatGPT achieved an accuracy of 75.41%, iden-tifying negative sentiment correctly in 82.54%, neutral sentiment 52.31%, and positive sentiment 79.75% of cases (see Table 4).

Table 4. Results Use Case 3: Sentiment Classification of Review Comments

Sentiment	Correct		Incorrect		Total	
	No.	%	No.	%	No.	%
Negative	52	82,54%	11	17,46%	63	17%
Neutral	34	52,31%	31	47,69%	65	18%
Positive	193	79,75%	49	20,25%	242	65%
Overall	279	75,41%	91	24,59%	370	100%

Our results show a stable accuracy of 75.41% in total. These results are partially in line with previous research. However, some of these studies showed far better results for sentiment analysis and even questioned what challenges are actually remaining in this field now with such powerful LLMs [59]. Although our results also show good results, we would not confirm that other approaches are yet obsolete, still, we acknowledge that if the progress in LLMs continues at the current speed, they might soon be an indispensable approach in sentiment analysis.

4.4 Use Case 4: Identify Repair Requests

In the fourth use case, ChatGPT had to extract two types of information from a dataset of customer service logs: the repair request ("what?") and the cause for the request ("why"). The dataset consisted of summaries written by customer service employees after phone calls with customers who had issues with their home heating appliances. The dataset contained 1,693 records, from which we drew a sample of 363 to ensure that our sample is representative (confidence level at least 95%, ±5% margin of error). Two researchers evaluated if ChatGPT could correctly identify the repair request and its underlying cause. Only cases in which the reviewers both agreed on the correct or incorrect identification of the repair request and the underlying cause simultaneously (148/ 40.77%), were included in the final analyses to ensure a high reliability and validity of the results. For these cases ChatGPT displayed an accuracy of 81,76% in identifying the repair request and a 65.54% in identifying the cause of this request accurately (see Table 5).

As demonstrated, ChatGPT shows good results for identifying the repair requests reasons ("what?") and stable results regarding the repair request cause ("why?"). Previ-ous research on ChatGPT's ability to extract defined content from unstructured text has shown comparable results. More precisely, they used ChatIE, which is based on Chat-GPT, for information extraction and found impressive performance levels, which even

Table 5. Results Use Case 4: Identifying "what" and "why" of Repair Requests

Repair request	Correct		Incorrect	
	No.	%	No.	%
What	121	81,76%	27	18,24%
Why	97	65,54%	51	34,46%

surpassed some full-shot models [60]. Other studies found that ChatGPT works sufficiently well for information extraction and rarely produces invalid responses. However,
they also found that irrelevant context greatly affects its performance [61].

5 Conclusion

ChatGPT can be a valuable tool for many companies, helping with their daily data
preparation tasks. It can be easily integrated into existing data infrastructure without
the need for major changes or modifications, providing a straightforward and efficient
integration process that doesn't disrupt current operations.

In this paper, we have explored the potential of LLMs for various data preparation
and analysis tasks in real business use cases. We have used ChatGPT, a state-of-the-art
LLM based on the transformer architecture, to perform tasks such as translating product names, assigning product categories, classifying customer sentiment, and extracting
repair requests and their causes from customer service logs. Evaluating the performance
of ChatGPT, our results show that it can achieve high levels of accuracy and quality in
most of the tasks, demonstrating its usefulness and versatility for data-related applications in real world scenarios. In addition, we demonstrated that ChatGPT can handle
different languages and formats of data, such as German and English, text and tables.
As such, we have shown that LLMs can perform multiple tasks with minimal or no
fine-tuning, leveraging their pre-trained knowledge and generalization abilities.

However, our work also reveals some limitations and challenges of LLMs that need
to be addressed in future research. For instance, we have observed that ChatGPT may
sometimes produce incorrect or incomprehensible outputs, especially when the input
data is noisy or ambiguous. We have also noticed that ChatGPT may struggle with
some tasks that require more complex reasoning or domain-specific knowledge, such
as identifying the cause of a repair request. However, it should be noted, that similar
constrains also apply to human evaluators.

Thus, future research should focus on improving the robustness and reliability of
LLMs for data preparation and analysis tasks, as well as on developing more efficient and
user-friendly ways to deploy and interact with them. We also encourage more empirical
studies on the impact and implications of LLMs for data-driven decision making in
various contexts and scenarios.

Acknowledgments. This research has been funded by both the Government of Upper Austria as
part of the research grant Logistikum.Retail and by the Christian Doppler Gesellschaft as part of
the Josef Ressel Centre PREVAIL.

Appendix

In this appendix, we provide a sample dataset and the prompts used for each use case. Each use case is accompanied by a set of five anonymized records from the corresponding dataset, along with the prompts used for generating the responses. The purpose of these examples is to provide readers with a tangible understanding of how our approach can be employed in real-world scenarios. To ensure privacy and confidentiality, we have anonymized the data by replacing specific details with '...' and have included only the first few words of each example.

Use case 1:
Sample dataset:

ProductCode	ProductNameGerman
100680	Pommes Frites...
100220	Semmelbrösel...
100038	Pizza...
100009	Mühlenbrot...
100240	Sachertorte...

Prompt:

In the following json string, Translate the 'ProductNameGerman' column from German to English and store the translated text in a new column 'ProductNameEnglish'. Just print a json string.

[{"ProductCode":100680,"ProductNameGerman":"Pommes
Frites..."},{"ProductCode":100220,"ProductNameGerman":"Semmelbrösel
..."},{"ProductCode":100038,"ProductNameGerman":"Pizza..."},{"ProductCode":100009,"Product-
NameGerman":"Mühlenbrot..."},{"ProductCode":100240,"ProductNameGerman":"Sachertorte..."}]

Use case 2:
Sample dataset:

ProductCode	ProductName
100797	Vitamin A-Zinc...
100731	Hair decoration...
100230	Apples 1kg...
100198	White cabbage...
100123	Goat cheese...

Prompt:

Choose the appropriate product category from the following examples and assign each category to the 'ProductName' column in the given JSON string. Then, add the assigned categories as a new column 'ProductCategory' and create a JSON string containing updated table and print it. Just print a json string.

1. Product Name: 'Ice tea 500ml, peach...' - Category:'Non-Alcoholic Beverages'

2. Product Name: 'Cookies 350g ...' - Category:'Snacking'

3. Product Name: 'Beardcare 50 ml...' - Category:'Health, Beauty & Baby'

4. Product Name: 'Noodles...' - Category:'Pantry'

5. Product Name: 'Beef steak...' - Category:'Fresh Meat & Fish'

6. Product Name: 'Yoghurt Drink ...' - Category:'Dairy'

7. Product Name: 'Toastbread...' - Category:'Bakery'

8. Product Name: 'Childrens DVD, Title...' - Category:'Electronics'

9. Product Name: 'Premium cherry tomatoes...' - Category:'Fruits & Vegetables'

10. Product Name: 'Red wine 2l...' - Category:'Alcoholic Beverages'

[{"ProductCode":100797,"ProductName":" Vitamin A-Zinc..."},{"ProductCode":100731,"Product-Name":"Hair decoration..."},{"ProductCode":100230,"ProductName":" Apples 1kg..."},{"ProductCode":100198,"ProductName":"White cabbage... "},{"ProductCode":100123,"ProductName":"Goat cheese..."}]

Use case 3:

Sample Dataset:

ReviewID	Review
10002	Good prices. Fast service...
10050	A big thank you to the whole team...
10035	Very unfriendly...
10580	Few products available...
10685	Everything fresh;-)...

Prompt:

Classify the customer reviews in the 'Review' column of the given JSON string as either positive, neutral, or negative. Then, add the classification labels as a new column called 'Customer Sentiment' and create a JSON string containing updated table and print it. Just print a json string.

[{"ReviewID ":10002,"Review":"Good prices. Fast service..."},{" ReviewID ":10050,"Review":"A big thank you to the whole team.."},{" ReviewID ":10035,"Review":"Very unfriendly..."},{" ReviewID ":10580,"Review":"Few products available..."},{" ReviewID ":10685,"Review":" Everything fresh ;-)... }]

Use case 4:

Sample Dastet:

RequestID	Request
105890	Keine Zündung im Anlauf...
104809	Achtung ist in...
102568	Therme verliert Druck...
105999	Gerät ist ausgefallen...
107005	Störung Totalausfall Pufferspeicher gehen nur auf 32 Grad...

Prompt:

There are customer requests for repairing their heating appliances in the given json string. Based on the request, determine what needs to be repaired and why. Print your result in a json string including ' RequestID ', 'What' and 'Why'. Just print a json string nothing else.

[{"RequestID":105890,"Request":" Keine Zündung im Anlauf..."},{"RequestID":104809,"Request":"Achtung ist in..."},{"RequestID":102568,"Request":" Therme verliert Druck..."},{"RequestID":105999,"Request":"Gerät ist ausgefallen..."},{"RequestID":107005,"Request":" Störung Totalausfall Pufferspeicher gehen nur auf 32 Grad..."}]

References

1. Udokwu, C., Brandtner, P., Darbanian, F., Falatouri, T.: Proposals for addressing research gaps at the intersection of data analytics and supply chain management. J. Adv. Inf. Technol. (2022)
2. Brandtner, P.: Predictive analytics and intelligent decision support systems in supply chain risk management—research directions for future studies. In: Yang, X.-S., Sherratt, S., Dey, N., Joshi, A. (eds.) Proceedings of Seventh International Congress on Information and Communication Technology, vol. 464. Lecture Notes in Networks and Systems, pp. 549–558. Springer Nature Singapore, Singapore (2023)
3. Brandtner, P., Mates, M.: Artificial intelligence in strategic foresight – current practices and future application potentials. In: Proceedings of the 2021 12th International Conference on E-business, Management and Economics (ICEME 2021). International Conference on E-business, Management and Economics (ICEME 2021), pp. 75–81 (2021)
4. Zimmermann, R., Auinger, A.: Developing a conversion rate optimization framework for digital retailers—case study. J Market Anal. (2023). https://doi.org/10.1057/s41270-022-001 61-y
5. Fan, X., Wang, X., Zhang, X., ASCE Xiong Yu, P.: Machine learning based water pipe failure prediction: The effects of engineering, geology, climate and socio-economic factors. Reliab. Eng. Syst. Saf. **219**, 108185 (2022). https://doi.org/10.1016/j.ress.2021.108185
6. Schröer, C., Kruse, F., Gómez, J.M.: A Systematic literature review on applying CRISP-DM process model. Procedia Comput. Sci. **181**, 526–534 (2021). https://doi.org/10.1016/j.procs. 2021.01.199

7. Saltz, J.S.: CRISP-DM for data science: strengths, weaknesses and potential next steps. In: 2021 IEEE International Conference on Big Data (Big Data). 2021 IEEE International Conference on Big Data (Big Data), Orlando, FL, USA, 15.12.2021 – 18.12.2021, pp. 2337–2344. IEEE (2021). https://doi.org/10.1109/BigData52589.2021.9671634
8. Kung, T.H., et al.: Performance of ChatGPT on USMLE: potential for AI-assisted medical education using large language models. PLOS Digit. Health **2**, e0000198 (2023). https://doi.org/10.1371/journal.pdig.0000198
9. Kosinski, M.: Theory of Mind May Have Spontaneously Emerged in Large Language Models (2023)
10. Devlin, J., Chang, M.-W., Lee, K., Toutanova, K.: BERT: pre-training of deep bidirectional transformers for language understanding. In: Proceedings of the 2019 Conference of the North American Chapter of the Association for Computational Linguistics: Human Language Technologies (2019). https://doi.org/10.18653/v1/N19-1423
11. Leippold, M.: Thus spoke GPT-3: interviewing a large-language model on climate finance. Finance Res. Lett. (2023). https://doi.org/10.1016/j.frl.2022.103617
12. Brown, T.B., et al.: Language Models are Few-Shot Learners. https://arxiv.org/pdf/2005.14165 (2020)
13. Radford, A., Wu, J., Child, R., Luan, D., Amodei, D., Sutskever, I.: Language models are unsupervised multitask learners, 1–9 (2019)
14. Vaswani, A., et al.: Attention Is All You Need. Advances in neural information processing systems 5998–6008
15. Liu, Y., et al.: RoBERTa: A Robustly Optimized BERT Pre-training Approach. https://arxiv.org/pdf/1907.11692 (2019)
16. Raffel, C., et al.: Exploring the Limits of Transfer Learning with a Unified Text-to-Text Transformer. http://arxiv.org/pdf/1910.10683v3 (2019)
17. OpenAI: GPT-4 Technical Report. https://arxiv.org/pdf/2303.08774 (2023)
18. Kojima, T., Gu, S.S., Reid, M., Matsuo, Y., Iwasawa, Y.: Large Language Models are Zero-Shot Reasoners. https://arxiv.org/pdf/2205.11916 (2022)
19. Ouyang, L., et al.: Training language models to follow instructions with human feedback
20. Zhang, S., et al.: OPT: Open Pre-trained Transformer Language Models (2022). Accessed 23 Mar 2023
21. Chakrabarty, T., Padmakumar, V., He, H.: Help me write a poem: instruction tuning as a vehicle for collaborative poetry writing. In: Proceedings of the 2022 Conference on Empirical Methods in Natural Language Processing, pp. 6848–6863
22. Mahlow, C.: Large Language Models and Artificial Intelligence, the End of (Language) Learning as we Know it—or not quite? https://osf.io/da2rm/download (2023)
23. Ruder, S., Vulić, I., Søgaard, A.: A survey of cross-lingual word embedding models. JAIR **65**, 569–631 (2019). https://doi.org/10.1613/jair.1.11640
24. Liu, Y., et al.: Multilingual denoising pre-training for neural machine translation. http://arxiv.org/pdf/2001.08210v2 (2020)
25. Snæbjarnarson, V., Einarsson, H.: Cross-lingual QA as a stepping stone for monolingual open QA in Icelandic. In: MIA 2022 - Workshop on Multi-lingual Information Access, Proceedings of the Workshop, pp. 29–36 (2022)
26. Daull, X., Bellot, P., Bruno, E., Martin, V., Murisasco, E.: Complex QA and language models hybrid architectures, Survey (2023)
27. DeRosa, D.M., Lepsinger, R.: Virtual Team Success: A Practical Guide for Working and Learning from Distance. John Wiley & Sons
28. Hosseini-Asl, E., Asadi, S., Asemi, A., Lavangani, M.A.Z.: Neural text generation for idea generation: the case of brainstorming. Int. J. Human-Comput. Stud. **151** (2021)

29. Palomaki, J., Kytola, A., Vatanen, T.: Collaborative idea generation with a language model. In: Proceedings of the 2021 CHI Conference on Human Factors in Computing Systems, pp. 1–12 (2021)
30. Chang, C.K., Huang, Y.M., Hsiao, Y.P., Huang, Y.M.: Exploring the feasibility and acceptance of using a natural language generation system for brain-storming Interactive Learning Environments, 738–751 (2020)
31. Valvoda, J., Fang, Y., Vandyke, D.: Prompting for a conversation: How to control a dialog model? https://aclanthology.org/2022.cai-1.1.pdf (2022)
32. Zeng, Y., Nie, J.-Y.: Open-domain dialogue generation based on pre-trained language models (2020)
33. Li, D., You, J., Funakoshi, K., Okumura, M.: A-TIP: Attribute-aware Text Infilling via Pre-trained Language Model. https://aclanthology.org/2022.coling-1.511.pdf (2022)
34. Rahali, A., Akhloufi, M.A.: End-to-end transformer-based models in textual-based NLP. AI 4(1), 54–110 (2023). https://doi.org/10.3390/ai4010004
35. Ziegler, D.M., et al.: Fine-Tuning Language Models from Human Preferences. https://arxiv.org/pdf/1909.08593.pdf%5D (2019)
36. Jiang, X., Liang, Y., Chen, W., Duan, N.: XLM-K: Improving Cross-Lingual Language Model Pre-training with Multilingual Knowledge. https://arxiv.org/pdf/2109.12573 (2021)
37. Dunn, A., et al.: Structured information extraction from complex scientific text with fi-ne-tuned large language models (2022)
38. Wu, T., Shiri, F., Kang, J., Qi, G., Haffari, G., Li, Y.-F.: KC-GEE: Knowledge-based Conditioning for Generative Event Extraction (2022)
39. Santosh, T.Y.S.S., Chakraborty, P., Dutta, S., Sanyal, D.K., Das, P.P.: Joint Entity and Relation Extraction from Scientific Documents: Role of Linguistic Information and Entity Types. https://ceur-ws.org/Vol-3004/paper2.pdf (2021)
40. Fan, A., Lewis, M., Dauphin, Y.N.: Strategies for training large transformer models (2019)
41. Radford, A., Narasimhan, K., Salimans, T., Sutskever, I.: Improving language understanding by generative pre-training (2018)
42. Zhang, J., Zhao, Y., Saleh, M., Liu, P.J.: PEGASUS: Pre-training with Extracted Gap-sentences for Abstractive Summarization. https://arxiv.org/pdf/1912.08777 (2019)
43. Zhang, Y., Feng, Y., Chen, Y., Zhao, D.: Conversational language generation: a review (2021)
44. Zhang, Y., et al.: DIALOGPT: large-scale generative pre-training for conversational response generation. In: Celikyilmaz, A., Wen, T.-H. (eds.) Proceedings of the 58th Annual Meeting of the Association for Computational Linguistics: System Demonstrations. Proceedings of the 58th Annual Meeting of the Association for Computational Linguistics: System Demonstrations, Online, pp. 270–278. Association for Computational Linguistics. https://doi.org/10.18653/v1/2020.acl-demos.30
45. Gao, T., Xia, L., Yu, D. (eds.): Fine-tuning pre-trained language model with multi-level adaptive learning rates for answer selection. In: The 28th International Joint Conference on Artificial Intelligence (2019)
46. Fu, T., Gao, S., Zhao, X., Wen, J., Yan, R.: Learning towards conversational AI: a survey. AI Open (2022). https://doi.org/10.1016/j.aiopen.2022.02.001
47. Serban, I.V., Sordoni, A., Bengio, Y., Courville, A., Pineau, J.: Building end-to-end dialogue systems using generative hierarchical neural network models. https://arxiv.org/pdf/1507.04808 (2015)
48. Zhang, J., Yang, H.: Neural response generation with dynamically weighted copy mechanism (2020)
49. Keskar, N.S., McCann, B., Varshney, L.R., Xiong, C., Socher, R.: CTRL: A Conditional Transformer Language Model for Controllable Generation. http://arxiv.org/pdf/1909.05858v2 (2019)

50. Hai, H.N.: ChatGPT: The Evolution of Natural Language Processing (2023)
51. Dou, Z., Li, C., Li, Y., Wang, S.: Improving information extraction via fine-tuning pre-trained language model **39**(4), 5371–5381 (2020)
52. Gao, J., Zhao, H., Yu, C., Xu, R.: Exploring the Feasibility of ChatGPT for Event Extraction. https://arxiv.org/pdf/2303.03836 (2023)
53. API Reference. https://platform.openai.com/docs/api-reference/introduction. Accessed 3 Apr 2023
54. Wang, L., et al.: Document-Level Ma-chine Translation with Large Language Models (2023)
55. Jiao, W., Huang, J., Wang, W., Wang, X., Shi, S., Tu, Z.: ParroT: Translating During Chat Using Large Language Models (2023)
56. Takahashi, K., Yamamoto, K., Kuchiba, A., Koyama, T.: Confidence interval for micro-averaged F1 and macro-averaged F1 scores. Appl. Intell. **52**(5), 4961–4972 (2022). https://doi.org/10.1007/s10489-021-02635-5
57. Yan, L., et al.: Practical and Ethical Challenges of Large Language Models in Education: A Systematic Literature Review (2023)
58. Reiss, M.V.: Testing the Reliability of ChatGPT for Text Annotation and Classification: A Cautionary Remark (2023)
59. Wang, Z., Xie, Q., Ding, Z., Feng, Y., Xia, R.: Is ChatGPT a Good Sentiment Analyzer? A Preliminary Study (2023)
60. Wei, X., et al.: Zero-Shot Information Extraction via Chatting with ChatGPT (2023)
61. Han, R., Peng, T., Yang, C., Wang, B., Liu, L., Wan, X.: Is Information Extraction Solved by ChatGPT? An Analysis of Performance, Evaluation Criteria, Robustness and Errors (2023)

Experimental Comparative Study of Three Models of Convolutional Neural Networks for Emotion Recognition

Agustín Alejandro Ortiz Díaz⬢, Sergio Cleger Tamayo$^{(\boxtimes)}$ ⬢, and Delrick Nunes De Oliveira⬢

Sidia Institute of Science and Technology, Avenue Darcy Vargas, 654, 69055-035 Manaus, Brasil

{agustin.diaz,sergio.tamayo,delrick.oliveira}@sidia.com

Abstract. Many researchers agree that facial expressions are one of the main non-verbal ways that human beings use to communicate and express emotions. For this reason, there has been a significant increase in interest in capturing facial movements to generate realistic digital animations incorporated into virtual environments. Our general project has the final objective of developing and evaluating different models of convolutional neural networks (CNN). These models will fit a linear "blendshapes" model of facial expression from images obtained by a Head-mounted display (HMD). At this stage of the project, in this paper, our goal is to compare, through different evaluation metrics (accuracy, runtime, and so on), three CNN models designed to detect emotions. These models differ in the way they treat input images. Two of the models partition the input images; one divides the images into 3 fundamental parts: forehead, eyes + nose, and mouth + chin; the other divides the images, right in the middle, into two presumably symmetrical parts. The third model works with full images. In these first proposals, we used 2D images with frontal faces in black-and-white to train all the CNN models. The main experiments are carried out on the database "The Japanese Female Facial Expression (JAFFE). JAFFE dataset contains 213 images categorized into 7 facial expressions, 6 basic facial expressions (Happiness, Sadness, Surprise, Anger, Disgust, and Fear) + 1 neutral. The three proposed models yielded satisfactory results in terms of accuracy. In addition, the training time remained within acceptable values.

Keywords: Emotions detection · Facial expressions · CNN · JAFFE

1 Introduction

Facial expressions are one of the most powerful and natural non-verbal ways that human beings use to convey their emotional states and intentions [1]. In the last decade, many researchers have carried out various studies on the automatic analysis of facial expressions following a pragmatic purpose. These studies have addressed several areas of real life, such as social robots, medical treatment, monitoring of vital parameters in drivers, animation of virtual environments, and many other processes of human-computer

© The Author(s), under exclusive license to Springer Nature Switzerland AG 2023
H. Degen et al. (Eds.): HCII 2023, LNCS 14059, pp. 199–210, 2023.
https://doi.org/10.1007/978-3-031-48057-7_13

interaction. For this reason, there has been a significant increase in interest in capturing facial movements to generate realistic digital animations incorporated into virtual environments. Head-mounted displays (HMDs) have enabled the existence of realistic virtual environments [2]. As of 2021, some of the latest HMDs have incorporated cameras and/or face and hand-tracking sensors. Among these modern devices, we can mention HTC-Vive-Focus-3, HP-Reverb-G2-Omnicept-Edition, Meta-Quest-Pro, and Pico-4-Pro.

Our general project has the final objective of developing and evaluating different models of convolutional neural networks (CNN). These models will have the purpose of fitting a linear "blendshapes" model of facial expression from images obtained by an HMD. Blendshapes methods are among the top choices when deciding on realistic facial animation approaches [3]. However, the present work documents one of the first parts of our global project. At this stage, we make a comparison between three CNN models aimed at detecting emotions. All these models are trained with 2D black-and-white front-facing image datasets, and they basically differ in the way they analyze the input images [4, 5].

(1) The first model (Model-1) takes the full image of the human face as input.
(2) The second model (Model-2) divides the image of the human face right in the middle into two apparently symmetrical parts.
(3) The third model (Model-3) divides each human face image into three areas with significantly marked expressions: the area of the forehead, the area of the eyes and nose, and the area of the mouth and chin.

The main experiments are performed on the database "The Japanese Female Facial Expression (JAFFE). JAFFE contains 213 images of 7 facial expressions, 6 basic facial expressions (Happy, Sad, Surprise, Angry, Disgust, and Fear), and one neutral expression [6].

Our main objective in this work is to compare the three proposed CNN models in terms of accuracy, training time, and other metrics. However, through each model, interesting partial indicators are obtained to analyze due to its practical experimental approach.

- From Model-2, it is possible to detect differences in symmetry in the dataset images. That is, it is possible to analyze the differences in accuracy between the models of each of the presumably symmetrical parts of the human face.
- From Model-3, it is possible to obtain a particular experimental result about which part of the human face independently provides more precise information (forehead, eyes + nose, and mouth + chin).

For a better organization and description of the results of the work, the paper has been divided into 6 sections: Related Work (Sect. 2), CNN Models (Sect. 3), Experiments (Sect. 4), and Analysis and Discussion (Sect. 5). Finally, in Sect. 6, we present our general Conclusions, Acknowledgment, and References.

2 Related Work

In the last decade, several scientific investigations have been published that propose models and methods for recognizing facial expressions and classifying emotions [16]. Below we describe some interesting works that have a certain relationship with our proposal.

MC_CNN, "Multichannel Convolutional Neural Network" [11], was a neural network architecture for FER published in 2015. The model is made up of two initially independent channels that eventually converge into a fully connected network. The first channel is a partial model that is partially trained in an unsupervised manner as a convolutional automatic encoder (CAE). The second channel is a standard CNN already tested in a previous publication [12]. As in this paper, the JAFFE dataset was used for the experimentation. The ten-fold cross-validation scheme is used to evaluate the results of the architecture. The authors conclude that the use of an additional information channel with unsupervised learning contributed to significantly increasing the accuracy and reducing the total training time.

In 2016, a model called DNNRL [10], "Deep Neural Networks with Relativity Learning", was published. This model learns a mapping of original images to a Euclidean space, where the relative distances correspond to a measure of facial expression similarity. The fundamental characteristic, described by the authors of the DNNRL model, is that it updates the parameters of the method according to the importance of the sample. That is, all samples are not treated in the same way; each one is labeled with different weights, as a strategy, giving greater weight to the samples that are more difficult to learn. According to the authors, this strategy resulted in an adjustable and robust model. This model is used to classify images with one of the seven basic human emotions, including "neutral".

In 2018, a compact facial expression recognition model based on facial expression recognition frameworks was proposed [9]. One of the main characteristics described by the creators of the model is that it achieves very competitive performance compared to other more advanced methods using much fewer parameters. Another highlighted feature of the proposed model is that it extends to a frame-to-sequence approach by exploiting temporal information with closed recurring units. In addition, a lighting boost scheme was developed to alleviate the overfitting problem when training deep networks with hybrid data sources.

A different approach for facial expression recognition called DeRL, "Deexpression Residue Learning" [14], was also proposed in 2018. This model combines two learning processes. The first process is used to generate, through a cGan, base neutral faces of any input image; the second process oversees learning in the intermediate layers of the generator. Another interesting proposal is the one that proposes to adapt the deep Neural Forests (NRF) to the process of recognition of facial expressions [15]. The central idea is to combine the best of two paradigms. That is a differentiable classification model that can be trained with backpropagation and stochastic gradient descent but has a compatible execution time for real-time work. With these characteristics, this model could be applied in branches of robotics.

Another interesting work [7], published in 2019, proposes a new CNN model for facial expression recognition; this model is described as "compact". In this work, the authors consider several challenges to solve, such as: (1) working with low-quality images to detect the presence of low-intensity expressions; (2) the cost to collect images useful for facial expression recognition; and (3) the problem of labeling each of the training images with an exact and precise emotion. All input images are pre-processed and subjected to a detailed pixel-by-pixel study. In this first stage, the work is based on the psychological approach to the color circle-emotion relationship [8]. The authors bet on the fact that this approach has promising precision results. Then, in the second phase of the process, a neural network is used to classify new images with the basic universal emotions: Happiness, Sadness, Anger, Disgust, Surprise, and Fear.

Blendshape_FER_Net [13] is a two-channel neural network for facial expression recognition that was proposed in 2020. One of the channels is designed to extract features from images (image-based FER network). The other channel is responsible for extracting features from the movements of the facial muscles represented in a blendshape, "Blendshape Regression Network". These two channels come together at the end of the network to achieve a unified prediction.

3 CNN Models

At this stage, we make a comparison between three CNN models aimed at detecting emotions. All these models are trained with 2D black-and-white front-facing image datasets, and they basically differ in the way they analyze the input images.

The first model (Model-1, Fig. 1) takes the full image of the human face as input. CNN is used starting with several convolutional layers and ending in the last fully connected layer. This last layer is used for classification.

The second model (Model-2, Fig. 2) divides the image of the human face right in the middle into two apparently symmetrical parts: the left and right areas. In this case, the images of each part are used as independent inputs in two initially separate channels. For this, two different CNNs are used, one for each area. These two networks converge in a last fully connected layer. This last layer, like the previous model, is used for classification. It unifies the local information extracted from each of the two previous parts.

The third model (Model-3, Fig. 3) divides each human face image into three areas with significantly marked expressions: The upper area (forehead), the central area (eyes and nose), and the lower area (mouth, and chin). The images of each part are used as independent inputs in three initially separate channels. For this, they use three different CNNs, one for each area. These networks converge on a fully connected last layer. This last layer is used for classification because it unifies the local information extracted from each of the previous parts.

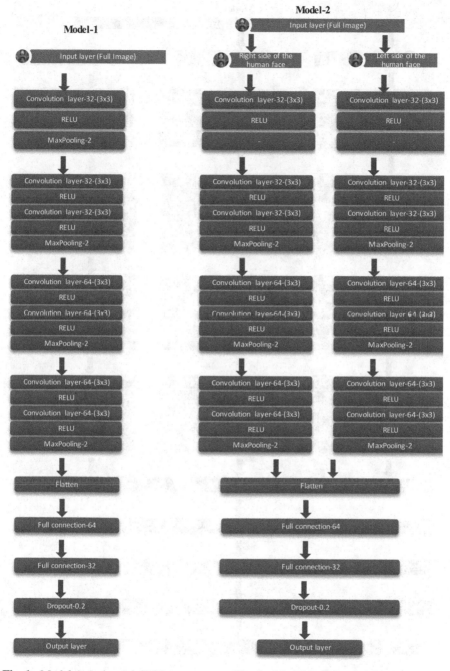

Fig. 1. Model-1. 1-channel CNN.   **Fig. 2.** Model-2. 2-channel CNN.

204   A. A. Ortiz Díaz et al.

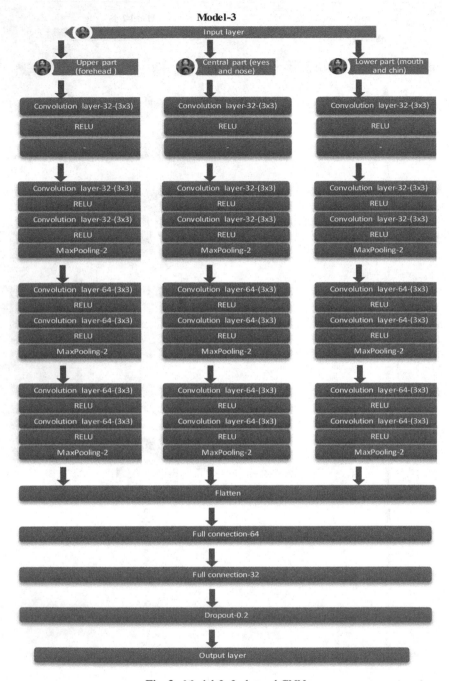

Fig. 3. Model-3. 3-channel CNN.

4 Experiments

In our global project, we have as a premise that our training and test images were obtained under special conditions from an HMD. We assumed an HMD with three configurable internal cameras that allow us to obtain training and test images with the characteristics of each model. The cameras would be configured to partition our facial images into up to three parts. Our focus is to adjust and compare our CNN model proposals. We did not do any pre-processing of the input images, just the partitions that fed our models 2 and 3. The dataset used was configured to simulate these characteristics. It is not within our strategy of experimentation and analysis to compare our results with other models published in previous research.

4.1 Datasets

The main experiments are performed on the "The Japanese Female Facial Expression (JAFFE)" dataset. JAFFE dataset contains 213 images of 7 facial expressions, 6 basic facial expressions (Happy, Sad, Surprise, Angry, Disgust, and Fear), and one neutral expression. Expression labels on images only represent the predominant expression in that image; the emotion the subject was asked to pose. It is important to highlight that expressions are never pure expressions of emotion, but always mixtures of different emotions. For this reason, each image has been rated for each emotion by 60 Japanese. For the classification, a scale of 5 levels was used for each of the 6 emotions (5 high, 1 low) [6].

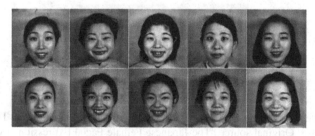

Fig. 4. The Japanese Female Facial Expression (JAFFE). 10 Japanese female models [6].

4.2 Experimental Setup

At this stage of the overall project, we are only experimenting with the JAFFE dataset. Each image in the dataset has a resolution of 256 × 256. Our initial conditions were the following:

- We did not do any initial preprocessing on the images.
- We use divisions in the input images that simulate the characteristics of the images that can be taken with our cameras positioned inside an HMD.

Our main objective was to evaluate and compare our models on equal terms, adjusting our specific characteristics.

Model-1 was trained using the complete images in the first scenario of the experimentation, images as in Fig. 4. On the other hand, in the second scenario, Model-2 was trained with images divided into two parts, sliding a vertical slice, as in Fig. 5. Finally, in our third experimental scenario, Model-3 was trained with the images divided into three parts; two horizontal slices were made, as in Fig. 6.

The models were evaluated in terms of accuracy and training time in each of the stages of the experimentation. The dataset was always divided in the proportion 0.7 and 0.3 for training and validation respectively.

All the experiments were carried out in a machine with the following characteristics: GPU RTX Quadro 5000 16 GB, CPU Intel (R) Core (TM) i9-10885H 32,0 GB RAM. All the models were implemented in Python using the TensorFlow and Keras libraries.

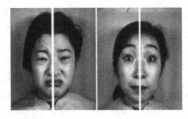

Fig. 5. Images were divided into two parts after applying a vertical cut. They were used to train on Model-2. Original source "The Japanese Female Facial Expression" (JAFFE) dataset" [6].

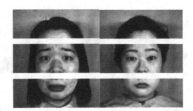

Fig. 6. Images were divided into three parts after applying two horizontal cuts. They were used to train on Model-3. Original source "The Japanese Female Facial Expression (JAFFE) dataset" [6].

4.3 Experiments Result

The results of the first part of the experiments are presented in Table 1. The results of comparing the performance of the three proposed CNN models are shown. The main parameters evaluated were accuracy and training times, both with their standard deviation. Each experiment was performed 25 times.

In the second part of the experiments, the results of the Model-2 channels were compared separately. The idea was to determine if there was any significant asymmetry regarding the classification patterns in the sets of images tested. Once again, each experiment was performed 25 times. The results are shown in Table 2.

Table 1. Results of the comparison in terms of accuracy and training time between the three proposed models.

Models/Dataset	Accuracy	Runtime (Seconds)
Model-1	**Accuracy: 0.99 ± 0.003** **Accuracy_Val:** **0.81** **± 0.030**	**Runtime: 63.7 ± 0.267**
Model-2	**Accuracy: 0.98 ± 0.011** **Accuracy_Val:** **0.80** **± 0.069**	**Runtime: 25.20 ± 0.137**
Model-3	**Accuracy: 0.98 ± 0.013** **Accuracy_Val:** **0.84** **± 0.037**	**Runtime: 25.70 ± 0.166**

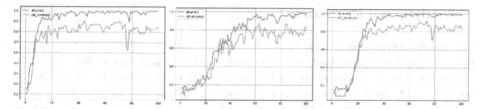

Fig. 7. Model training stage (Accuracy/epochs). Model-1, Model-2, and Model-3, respectively.

Table 2. Results of the comparison in terms of accuracy and training time between the two separate channels of Model-2.

Models/Dataset	JAFFE-	Runtime (Seconds)
Model-2. First channel	**Accuracy: 0.99 ± 0.009** **Accuracy_Val:** **0.83** **± 0.025**	**Runtime: 33.47 ± 0.290**
Model-2. Second channel	**Accuracy:0.99 ± 0.009** **Accuracy_Val:** **0.81** **± 0.050**	**Runtime: 33.49 ± 0.160**

In the last part of the experiments, the results of the three channels of Model-3 were compared separately. The idea was to determine if there was a significant difference between the classification patterns of each of the parts into which the face was divided. The results are shown in Table 3.

Table 3. Results of the comparison, in terms of accuracy and training time, between the three separate channels of Model-3.

Models/Dataset	Accuracy -	Runtime (Seconds)
Model-3. First channel	Accuracy: 0.96 ± 0.023 Accuracy_Val:0.48 ± 0.032	Runtime: 22.47 ± 0.136
Model-3. Second channel	Accuracy: 99.00 ± 0.008 Accuracy_Val: 0.86 ± 0.036	Runtime: 22.25 ± 0.265
Model-3. Third channel	Accuracy:0.96 ± 0.015 Accuracy_Val: 0.70 ± 0.032	Runtime: 22.64 ± 0.123

5   Analysis and Discussion

The experiments presented were basically divided into three stages. In the first stage, a direct comparison is established between the three general models described in Figs. 1–3. In the second stage, we focus directly on the individual results of each of the two channels of Model-2. Finally, in the third stage, we analyze the individual behavior of each of the three channels of Model-3. In the three stages, accuracy and training time were used as comparison parameters.

In the first part of the experiments, as shown in Table 1, Model-3 obtained the most promising results in terms of accuracy, 0.84. However, we found no significant difference between the three results. This model works with three independent channels, one for each partition of the original image. Our initial expectations were with Model-3, however, internal differences between the results of the channels caused a lower performance than expected. The upper channel (forehead) obtained very low performance in terms of accuracy, 0.48. Model-1 and Model-2 had very similar results in terms of accuracy. Although, it is important to note that the training time of Model-1, which uses the full images, was much higher, at 63.7 s.

In the second stage, as shown in Table 2, no significant differences were found, in terms of accuracy values, between the asymmetric patterns of each of the parts of the face. The Model-2, in general, obtained worse results in terms of accuracy. That is their independent channels performed better on an individual basis than the overall model. This indicates that it may be necessary to adjust the layer structure that combines the results. This model will not be definitively discarded since it could have promising results in the next stages of the global project where the symmetric representation parameters are directly adjusted within the "blendshapes" model.

In the third part of the experiments, as shown in Table 3, significant differences were found in our study between the classification patterns of each of the parts of the face. Being within our expectations, the best results were obtained with the central channel of the model (eyes and nose), 0.86. However, the results of the upper channel (forehead), in terms of accuracy, were much lower than expected Fig. 7. This channel greatly affected the operation of Model-3 in general. In stages two and three of the experiments we did not find a significant difference in terms of training times.

6 Conclusion

In this work, we presented three models of convolutional neural networks. These models were designed to classify different types of human faces into 7 facial expressions: 6 basic facial expressions (Happiness, Sadness, Surprise, Anger, Disgust, and Fear) + 1 neutral. The proposed models were designed from the study and analysis of several previous scientific investigations. We adapted some interesting ideas to our initial conditions and our goals.

Model-1 was built using only one convolutional channel since it uses full images for training. However, Model-2 was designed with two independent convolutional channels because it trains with the images divided into two parts after applying a vertical slice. Finally, Model-3 trains with images divided into three parts after applying two horizontal slices, for this reason, it was designed with three independent convolutional channels.

The efficiencies of these three models were tested using metrics such as accuracy and training time. Model-3, with 3 channels, obtained more promising results in terms of accuracy values. The accuracy values, both in training and validation, were the closest in this model.

In addition, other interesting analyses are provided. Each of the channels of Model-2 was compared independently. The idea was to find any possible asymmetry in the information patterns of each of the parts of the face. However, the results in terms of accuracy values did not show significant differences. The three channels of Model-3 were also compared independently. The idea was to find a possible difference between the informational patterns of different parts of the face. In this case, significant differences were found between the three sub-models. The central area of the face (eyes + nose) provided more information. The results in terms of accuracy values were much more promising.

Regarding the training times, the values were very similar and did not provide significant differences in any of the models or sub-models analyzed. The results of this stage of the overall project were very interesting and provided many ideas for future stages.

Regarding the training times, the values were very similar and did not provide significant differences in almost any of the models or submodels compared. It is important to highlight that Model-1, which works with complete images, obtained the worst results in terms of training time. In general, the results of this stage of the overall project were very interesting and provided many ideas for future research.

Acknowledgment. This paper was presented as part of the results of the Project "SIDIA-M_AR_Internet_For_Bondi", carried out by the Institute of Science and Technology - SIDIA, in partnership with Samsung Eletrônica da Amazônia LTDA, in accordance with the Information Technology Law n.8387/91 and article at the. 39 of Decree 10,521/2020.

References

1. Tian, Y., Kanade, T., Cohn, J.: Recognizing action units for facial expression analysis. IEEE Trans. Pattern Anal. Mach. Intell. **23**(2), 97–115 (2001)

2. Suzuki, K., et al.: Recognition and mapping of facial expressions to the avatar by embedded photo reflective sensors in head-mounted display. In: 2017 IEEE Virtual Reality (VR), USA (2017)
3. Lewis, J., et al.: Practice and theory of blendshape facial models. Eurograph. State Art Rep. **1**(8), 2 (2014)
4. Jain, N., et al.: Hybrid deep neural networks for face emotion recognition. Pattern Recogn. Lett. **115**, 101-106 (2018)
5. Zhang, L.: Animation expression control based on facial region division. Hindawi Sci. Programming (2022)
6. Michael J., et al.: Coding facial expressions with gabor wavelets. In: 3rd IEEE International Conference on Automatic Face and Gesture Recognition, pp. 200–205 (1998)
7. Reji, R., Sojan, P.: A compact deep learning model for robust facial expression recognition. Int. J. Eng. Adv. Technol. **8**, 2956–2960 (2019)
8. Nijdam, N.: Mapping emotion to color. Book Mapping Emot. Color?, 2–9 (2009)
9. Chieh-Ming, K., Shang-Hong, L., Sarkis, M.: A compact deep learning model for robust facial expression recognition. In: Proceedings of the IEEE Conference on Computer Vision and Pattern Recognition (CVPR) Workshops, pp. 2121–2129 (2018)
10. Guo, Y., et al.: Deep neural networks with relativity learning for facial expression recognition. In: 2016 IEEE International Conference on Multimedia & Expo Workshops (ICMEW), Seattle, WA, pp. 1–6, (2016). https://doi.org/10.1109/ICMEW.2016.7574736
11. Hamester, D., Barros, P., Wermter, S.: Face expression recognition with a 2-channel convolutional neural network. In: 2015 International Joint Conference on Neural Networks (IJCNN), Killarney, Ireland, pp. 1–8, (2015). https://doi.org/10.1109/IJCNN.2015.7280539
12. Barros, P., et al.: A multichannel convolutional neural network for hand posture recognition. In: Artificial Neural Networks and Machine Learning - ICANN (2014)
13. Wang, S., et al.: Leveraging 3D blendshape for facial expression recognition using CNN. Sci. China Inf. Sci. **63**, 120114 (2020). https://doi.org/10.1007/s11432-019-2747-y
14. Yang, H., Ciftci, U., Yin, L.: Facial expression recognition by de-expression residue learning. In: Proceedings of the IEEE Conference on Computer Vision and Pattern Recognition (CVPR), pp. 2168–2177 (2018)
15. Dapogny, A., Bailly, K.: Investigating deep neural forests for facial expression recognition. In: 2018 13th IEEE International Conference on Automatic Face & Gesture Recognition (FG 2018), Xian, China, pp. 629–633 (2018). https://doi.org/10.1109/FG.2018.00099
16. Li, S., Deng, W.: Deep facial expression recognition: a survey. IEEE Trans. Affect. Comput. **13**(3), 1195–1215 (2022). https://doi.org/10.1109/TAFFC.2020.2981446

How Can Natural Language Processing and Generative AI Address Grand Challenges of Quantitative User Personas?

Joni Salminen[1]([✉]), Soon-gyo Jung[2], Hind Almerekhi[3], Erik Cambria[4], and Bernard Jansen[2]

[1] School of Marketing and Communication, University of Vaasa, Vaasa, Finland
jonisalm@uwasa.fi
[2] Qatar Computing Research Institute, Hamad Bin Khalifa University, Doha, Qatar
[3] Qatar National Research Fund, Doha, Qatar
[4] School of Computer Science and Engineering, Nanyang Technological University, Singapore, Singapore

Abstract. Human-computer interaction (HCI) and natural language processing (NLP) can engage in mutually beneficial collaboration. This article summarizes previous literature to identify grand challenges for the application of NLP in quantitative user personas (QUPs), which exemplifies such collaboration. Grand challenges provide a collaborative starting point for researchers working at the intersection of NLP and QUPs, towards improved user experiences. NLP research could also benefit from focusing on generating user personas by introducing new solutions to specific NLP tasks, such as classification and generation. We also discuss the novel opportunities introduced by Generative AI to address the grand challenges, offering illustrative examples.

Keywords: User personas · Quantitative user personas · Natural language processing · Generative AI

1 Introduction

This article is intended for researchers working on the intersection of AI (specifically, NLP technologies) and HCI (specifically, quantitative user personas). NLP refers to *natural language processing*, defined as a computer's ability to comprehend spoken and written human language [40]. HCI refers to *human-computer interaction*, which is a multidisciplinary research field that focuses on the interaction between computers and their users, towards the design of more usable and helpful technology, also referred to as user-centered design (UCD).

AI refers to *artificial intelligence*, defined as the "simulation of human intelligence processes by machines" [9]. While this term is often used to refer to applied

© The Author(s), under exclusive license to Springer Nature Switzerland AG 2023
H. Degen et al. (Eds.): HCII 2023, LNCS 14059, pp. 211–231, 2023.
https://doi.org/10.1007/978-3-031-48057-7_14

machine learning (ML) instead, we use it here because of the current convention in academic fields, including HCI and NLP, essentially referring to applied ML and various pseudo-intelligent algorithms and automata. NLP is commonly considered as a subfield of ML [55]. *Generative AI* is a subfield of AI that produces outputs, including text, images, and videos. *Large language models* (LLMs) are part of the Generative AI technology, and they can be programmed to generated text based on instructions (i.e., prompts) given by the user [2,26].

Personas (also known as user personas, design personas, marketing personas, and so on) are fictitious characters that aim to represent real user types [15] (also known as segments, clusters, groups... i.e., groups of people that are similar to each other and different from other groups), providing valuable information to designers and others working on UCD tasks (collectively referred to as 'stakeholders' in this study) to more empathically connect with users (see example in Fig. 1). *Persona profiles* typically contain demographic information (age, gender, location), as well as various information reflecting the user's needs, wants, and pain points. *Quantitative user personas* (QUPs), in particular, are personas generated using algorithms; hence, they are sometimes referred to as *algorithmically-generated personas* [28,62]. Another common term for QUPs in the literature is *data-driven personas* [44] and, with the rise of AI, the QUP terminology has also incorporated *AI personas* [23].

Regardless of this conceptual plurality, all QUP methods share the common trait of using algorithms in the process of persona generation – either fully, ranging from data collection to segmentation and enrichment – or partially, as a

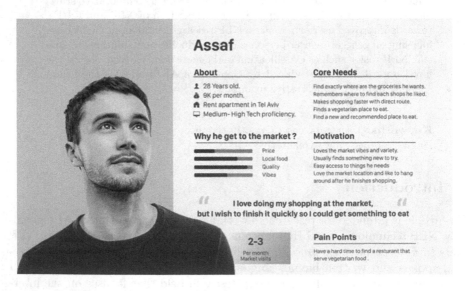

Fig. 1. An example of a persona profile. Personas typically contain demographic information (age, gender, location), and information reflecting the user's needs, wants, and pain points, often illustrated using direct quotes. Image source: https://www.justinmind.com/blog/user-persona-templates/.

part of the overall process. Overall, this process of algorithmic persona generation involves specific challenges where NLP technologies can certainly be useful. We explore these opportunities.

The purpose of this research is to outline, based on prior research, four grand challenges for QUPs, and suggest research designs based on prominent NLP technologies to address these challenges. We focus specifically on QUPs, even though there are other persona types, such as qualitative personas. The reader might be interested in further motivation of this work. *Why study the grand challenges of QUPs? Moreover, why study them using NLP?* These are both worthwhile questions, and we address them in the following.

First, studying the grand challenges of QUPs is important because, despite the popularity of personas in HCI, design, marketing, health informatics, education, social media analytics, and so on [33, 47, 52], there is a consensus that many crucial challenges in persona creation and application still linger [13, 60, 64]. Some of these challenges were observed already in the early 2000s [22, 50], but have not been resolved, lending credence to their difficulty.

This then leads us to the second motivational question - *why apply NLP to QUPs?* Due to two reasons: first, as mentioned, many persona problems remain to be solved; logically, it then makes sense to seek potential solutions from other fields, as these fields may contain technologies and tools that can be applied to personas. NLP, in particular, is a field of rapid growth and progress, as evidenced by the massive increase in the field's popularity among academics, as well as the recent breakthroughs such as transformer language models [17, 38].

Second, the field of HCI is inherently interdisciplinary and applied - it seeks inspiration from other fields. Therefore, translating HCI problems as NLP problems is a logical and likely fruitful activity. In summary, the grand challenges in this study discuss known problems in the development of QUPs that have yet to be solved, partially due to the lack of interaction between HCI and NLP (i.e., HCI does not fully understand NLP advances, and NLP is not that familiar with QUPs or personas in general).

2 Related Work

2.1 User Personas in HCI

Personas can be created using qualitative, quantitative, or mixed methods [27]. Due to the strong progress in data science tools, libraries, and frameworks that help automate data collection and analysis tasks, QUPs are becoming more common in the field [59]. There are systems such as *Automatic Persona Generation* [31], that provide replicable and automatically updating personas for stakeholders in many fields. Such systems allow researchers to generate personas based on behavioral data of sizeable volumes for quantitative analysis [4].

Regardless of the creation method, there are some general design goals for developing good personas. Among others, these design goals include (1) *ability to evoke empathy among the stakeholders*, (2) *accuracy* (i.e., correctness, validity of the persona information), and (3) *relevance* (i.e., the persona contains information that helps stakeholders make decisions about the group of people the persona represents).

First, empathy refers to stakeholders identifying with the persona's human qualities [21]. A good persona engages its observer and facilitates the process of perspective taking, i.e., seeing the world from the eyes of the persona [52].

Second, a good persona does not contain bogus information that would mislead stakeholders about the true characteristics of the user segment it represents [13]. In other words, the persona is *data-driven* [25, 44]; i.e., based on actual data about users, whether quantitative, qualitative, or mixed data [27].

Third, a good persona is relevant, containing the necessary information to be useful for decision making but nothing more – the information should not be distracting or redundant. A stakeholder has to be able to take action based on what they learn from the persona [13].

The persona creation process tends to follow two stages: the data about users is first *segmented* using either an algorithm or a human analyst, and the resulting barebone (or skeletal) persona segments are then enriched with personified information to create complete, rounded persona profiles [3, 71].This *personification* transforms the nameless, faceless segments into identifiable personas that describe a behavioral and demographic pattern in the data [31]. Personification aims to result in realistic, well-rounded personas that stakeholders can identify with and that contain information of value [51, 63].

Because there are demanding technical challenges in QUPs [12], we believe that partnering with NLP researchers can help reach the broader mission of providing stakeholders with personas that help them create usable products. In other words, high-quality personas serve stakeholders by facilitating their jobs and users by enabling usable and user-friendly products that serve real needs.

2.2   Use of NLP in Persona Research

NLP is a field that combines AI, linguistics, and computer science to model human language, especially to analyze and process large amounts of text [54]. From this definition, we can observe at least two guiding principles (GPs):

a) **GP01:** NLP is an applied field - whenever language is used, NLP can be of help.
b) **GP02:** NLP is particularly designed to handle large volumes of textual data.

Both notions are compatible with QUPs. Language is a vehicle for storytelling which, in turn, is a route for empathy and learning [41]. Throughout history, people have learned lessons from others through stories. To this end, personas have been likened to narratives or metaphors that tell a story [50]. Therefore, there is an innate compatibility between the *purposes* of NLP and personas.

Moreover, the ability to handle large volumes of text is a major advantage of NLP. While QUPs are typically generated from structured tabular data, such as clickstreams, CRM records, or audience statistics [3, 76, 77], there is tremendous potential in using *unstructured* textual data, essentially mining the text for information about users and using that to feed information into the persona profile. For example, people express their pain points [66], opinions, needs, and wants in online posts [10]. This textual data could be utilized to generate insightful personas.

Despite the above-described potential, using NLP for QUPs has been tentative [23], with the main efforts summarized in the following *five use cases.*

First, previous research has applied NLP for classifying personas' topics of interest. For this, different methods have been applied, including latent Dirichlet allocation (LDA) [4], which is a form of unsupervised topic modeling [7], as well as supervised ML (text classification) in which a topical taxonomy is first developed together with the organization using the personas, followed by annotating data and using it to train topic classifiers [8]. Researchers have also applied zero-shot classification [53] that uses a pre-trained language model for determining a match between an array of topic words and the persona's content (e.g., comments). This approach has been found useful for small organizations with limited in-house data for training purposes.

Second, researchers have applied sentiment analysis lexicons, such as the EmoLex [48], to assign a sentiment score to a persona based on the social media comments associated with the persona [30]. Sentiment aims to indicate the persona's general attitude towards the channel or organization - however, aspect-based sentiment analysis has not been implemented, which would indicate how the persona feels about a specific topic [35] or product [72].

Third, QUPs generated from social media datasets may include abusive or toxic comments that are then included automatically in the generated persona profiles. Prior research addresses how these comments can be detected and then, if the stakeholder wants, removed from the persona profiles [65]. This is done to improve the user experience (UX) of stakeholders using the personas. This process involves using NLP, more specifically text classification trained on social media comments.

Fourth, personas designed for dialogue systems imitate real conversations by interactively reacting to stakeholder inputs [1,24]. This is similar to using a chatbot. Persona, in this context, is defined as a linguistic type (personality) that remains consistent over one or multiple user sessions [34]. The purpose is to improve the UX for those engaging with the dialogue interface. Unlike other efforts, this problem describes a specific subclass of generation problems.

Fifth, NLP techniques can also be applied in the segmentation process itself; i.e., the process preceding personification. This involves identifying latent patterns [5] or clusters [46] from textual data, typically using latent semantic spaces and associated techniques (e.g., singular value decomposition, cosine similarity, and so on). When using NLP for segmentation, the process tends to require the use of external information, such as domain experts' participation in the personification process [45].

To summarize, topic modeling, sentiment analysis, toxicity detection, and user segmentation are all text classification problems in NLP terminology, while dialog systems is a text generation problem. While the above use cases demonstrate how NLP can be of service to QUPs. However, there is room for expanding this interdisciplinary collaboration, given specific unsolved challenges. In the next section, we discuss four grand challenges of QUPs and outline ideas on how NLP can help address them.

3   Grand Challenges for Quantitative User Personas

Compatible with previous research [69,70], we define a grand challenge as a *difficult but not unsolvable problem that represents a roadblock or bottleneck for a field to progress and evolve into the next stage*. A classic example of grand challenges is the list of 23 problems that David Hilbert proposed to the international society of mathematicians in 1900. This list is said to have "galvanized the efforts of mathematicians for the next century" [42]. Inspired by this, the grand challenges presented here are based on the authors' experience on researching personas (multiple years, more than a dozen publications, a textbook on the topic) as well as on NLP research both in and out of the persona domain. The research team comprises people from diverse backgrounds, including those focused on NLP (2 people) and those focused on HCI/QUPs (3 people). As such, we aim to offer researchers thought-provoking problems that (hopefully) help foster interdisciplinary collaboration between HCI and NLP.

When formulating the grand challenges, one has to ask, "What is a good grand challenge like?". According to above definition, it is unsolved and difficult, otherwise, it would not be "grand" or "challenge". In addition, it is vital that the challenge is *interesting* to the community to which it is presented. This implies that the grand challenges need to be translated to technical problems to attract the interest of NLP researchers. Otherwise, it is unlikely that NLP researchers will invest any serious effort into addressing the challenges.

In our case, we engaged in an internal discussion between the research team members specialized in HCI (problem space experts) and NLP (solution space experts). This discussion represented a "sanity check" to ensure that the challenges were framed in a way that (1) is likely to advance persona creation, (2) corresponds to a technical NLP problem, and (3) interests both HCI and NLP researchers. These assessments are, of course, subjective determinations; other scholars might add or remove elements from this list. Nonetheless, the following grand challenges (GCs) passed this internal validation, and we are thus confident to propose them. They are introduced as follows, in no particular order of importance. For each challenge, we include (a) a desciption, (b) illustrative examples, (c) pointers on how to address it, (d) pointers on how to evaluate any solutions to it, and (e) reflections on how Generative AI could be of help.

GC1: Frankenstein Personas (i.e., Consistency Problem) *Description.* Susanne Bødker, a Danish computer scientist, first identified this problem, referring to it as 'Frankenstein personas' [6] (p. 98). The problem is that the creation of personas involves combining isolated datapoints into a persona profile that may appear inconsistent, i.e., contain conflicting information.

The general version of the challenge is:

> GC1: How to detect and correct inconsistent information in the persona profile?

This problem exists for QUPs because the persona creation process can rely on data collected from multiple sources, processed using different algorithms at different steps of the process. This can result in a patched-up persona profile that can contain inconsistent information.

Example Cases. In a system that generates QUPs automatically using social media data, a male persona says, "us women should stick together" (indicating wrong sex); there is an Indian persona that says, "You Indians cook really nice curry" (indicating nationality mismatch); and a Saudi Arabian persona refer to themselves as Tanzanian (see Fig. 2). The ramification is that the stakeholder using the persona becomes confused about the persona's true identity [61].

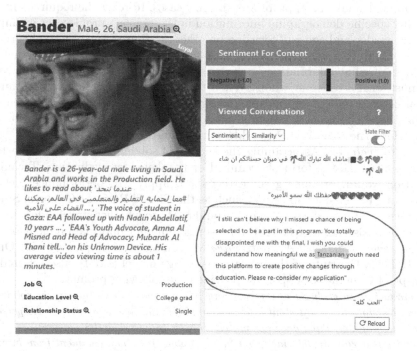

Fig. 2. Bander is from Saudi Arabia, but a random comment from videos of Bander's behavioral viewing type says, "I wish you could understand how meaningful we as Tanzanian youth need this platform to create positive changes (...)"

How to address? As established, the problem is that the information in the persona profile may be inconsistent due to a failure to verify consistency between different information elements. There is no process for ensuring consistency of each information element relative to other elements. So, developing such processes and mechanisms would address this issue.

Here, NLP can be useful. For example, a body of NLP work focuses on inferring demographic attributes from social media texts [74]. This work typically aims to identify differences in how demographic groups express themselves [74]; e.g., differences between males and females, or the youth and the elderly, and then use the identified differences for prediction. Thus, one approach is predicting the gender, age, and nationality of a user writing a given social media comment. This, without any additional meta-data and only relying on feature extraction and engineering from the text, qualifies as an extremely challenging problem.

The challenge is exacerbated by several factors, including (a) the lack of publicly available training data, (b) the large number of demographic group combinations (gender × age × nationality yields thousands of subgroups to consider on a global scale), and the (c) separation of identity and "true" demographics (e.g., some males may identify with female characteristics; an older and younger person might share an interest in the same popular culture, etc.). Given these constraints, it might be appropriate, in some cases, to relax the requirements of including specific demographic information in the persona profiles; for example, omitting gender and age and focusing on other attributes, such as psychographics [67] or simply a narrative description focusing on user needs. Nevertheless, regardless of what information is chosen into the persona profile, the information must form a coherent whole. When the information originates from multiple sources and undergoes multiple diverging algorithmic manipulations, ensuring consistency becomes a potential issue, requiring consistency verification for QUPs. Here, the role of NLP to address this issue remains open.

How to evaluate? Ascertaining the success of solving Bødker's Frankenstein personas can take the form of technical and stakeholder evaluation. Technical evaluation would, presuming some test data, apply ML performance metrics that pertain to classification tasks, such as the F1 and ROC-AUC scores. Stakeholder evaluation, on the other hand, would relate to whether stakeholders would observe inconsistencies between the personas' different information elements.

How could Generative AI contribute? We conducted a simple test with Open AI's GPT-3.5, the state of the art large language model (LLM), also referred to as a type of Generative AI [2]. We provided the following prompt:

Your task is to evaluate and report any inconsistent information in the following persona description. Inconsistent information means that the details about the persona are not aligned; something does not match. Here is the persona description:

Bander is a 26-year-old male from Saudi Arabia. Here is a comment from him: "I wish you could understand how meaningful we as Tanzanian youth need this platform to create positive changes."

Is there any inconsistent information in the persona description?

As evidenced by Fig. 3, GPT was able to detect the inconsistency, showing promise in addressing this grand challenge. However, a more formal and systematic evaluation would be needed to draw more definite conclusions.

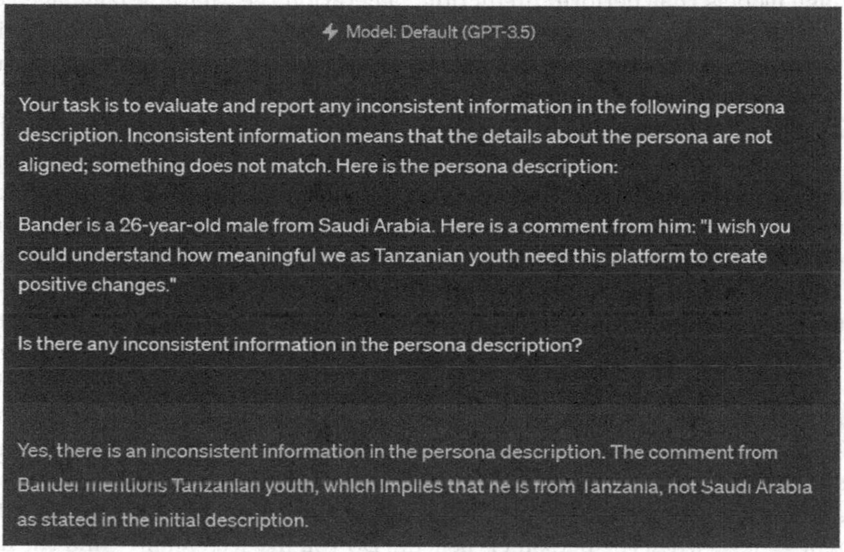

⚡ Model: Default (GPT-3.5)

Your task is to evaluate and report any inconsistent information in the following persona description. Inconsistent information means that the details about the persona are not aligned; something does not match. Here is the persona description:

Bander is a 26-year-old male from Saudi Arabia. Here is a comment from him: "I wish you could understand how meaningful we as Tanzanian youth need this platform to create positive changes."

Is there any inconsistent information in the persona description?

Yes, there is an inconsistent information in the persona description. The comment from Bander mentions Tanzanian youth, which implies that he is from Tanzania, not Saudi Arabia as stated in the initial description.

Fig. 3. ChatGPT correctly identified the inconsistency in the persona information: "Yes, there is an inconsistent information in the persona description. The comment from Bander mentions Tanzanian youth, which implies that he is from Tanzania, not Saudi Arabia as stated in the initial description."

GC2: Extrapolate Beyond the Immediate User Data *Description.* A general advantage of QUPs is their use of aggregated (i.e., non-personally identifiable) data, which protects individual users' privacy [3]. On the other hand, the dependency on the user data at hand – often a fairly limited one when compared to the full range of human thoughts – hinders the ability to understand the persona's needs and wants beyond the specific contexts available in the dataset. For example, the dataset can contain comments about cars, therefore giving us information how the people classified under the persona feel about cars. However, if the dataset is missing information about motorbikes, we do not know how the persona feels about them. Therefore,

GC2: What does the persona think of Topic x? (Where x is not part of the training data)

How to address? A potential solution could involve generative tasks that apply transfer learning via language models. Modern language models in NLP are trained on large-scale datasets (up to billions of document samples) and advanced algorithms (e.g., transformers). One major advantage is that, to some extent, these models can be fine-tuned using a smaller annotated dataset, thereby adjusting the model's broad knowledge to a specific narrow problem. There are language models that perform prediction, generation (i.e., natural language generation (NLG), which is a subfield of NLP) or both [16]. There's also a growing body of work on "data synthesis" for use cases that require generating textual data to perform causal inference [75].

Essentially, if we are able to represent a type of user with textual corpus that represents "who this person is", then, in theory, we might be able to fine-tune a language model to query this user type's opinions in real-time in an accurate manner. Conceptually, this is compatible with the notion of the persona being a 'mental model' [52] and a surrogate for the real user [15]—an LLM might be able to capture this mental model and simulate it plausibly and accurately.

In QUPs, the user type can be represented by latent statistical object that generates language according to grammaticality ('conformity to language usage') and the patterns observed in a group of users' language use [5]. The intuition is that, ideally, the language model contributes to grammaticality and the fine-tuning to the stability of the persona. The stability can be divided into two subparts: linguistic consistency (i.e., the style of speaking remains the same) and character consistency (i.e., the persona remains the same person throughout the dialogue — e.g., when the persona is asked, "Do you like ice-cream?" and the user group it is based on hates ice cream, it is able to respond, "No."). Furthermore, to address the scarcity of information , systems such as SenticNet [11] can be helpful as they analyze multiple dimensions (e.g., sentiment, emotions, personality) from the same text and therefore can be used for extracting more information from the same content and, possibly, for building more complete user models by leveraging the interactions between the extracted information variables.

How to evaluate? A myriad of technical metrics measure linguistic consistency [57]. In addition, we recommend a user-focused evaluation, e.g., developing a conversational user interface through which a stakeholder can chat with or talk to the persona; a variation of the Turing test [73]. Herein lies an important observation; while the Turing test requires a human to assess whether the machine is able to execute human behaviors that are indistinguishable from real humans, the test can be passed by an efficient "impersonator" that speaks fluently, answers rationally, but tells things that are untrue, yet convincing. There are a myriad of cases where the human evaluator lacks the expertise to assess the veracity of an LLM; personas being of these.

This is why both aspects - realism (the dialogue persona produces answers that *appear* correct) and accuracy (the produced answers actually reflect the thinking of the group the persona represents) - need consideration. Otherwise, a situation may emerge where the given answer appears to make sense (i.e., the mechanism by which the algorithm generates text works well in terms of generating grammatically correct text), but the meaning of the text does not correspond to the specific and distinct group of people that the persona is.

Due to opaqueness of how the text is generated by LLMs, the stakeholder is able to evaluate realism but not accuracy - i.e., they need to trust the system, and the system developers need to verify, in a robust manner, that the meanings given by the persona are consistent and truthful.

Again, we want to stress the importance of the problem of mimicry - with the current NLP models, it is *not* difficult to produce grammatically correct text that appears sensible. The challenge is not to do that - the challenge is to get one step closer to intelligence by simulating what the people belonging to the persona's group *do* and *would* think about topics, past or present. Grammatically correct text generation is only the first step in this journey. Generating persona dialogue that passes both scientific and user scrutiny poses a tremendous challenge for NLP because it requires that the persona remains *consistent* in its role [18].

How could Generative AI contribute? As previously, we explore the potential of GPT-3.5 to address this challenge. Below, we show the dialogue with the model: *Bander is a 26-year-old male from Saudi Arabia. He likes to follow social media content on education and youth development. Using your general knowledge about people like Bander, tell me, what else does he like to follow?*

As can be seen from the exhibit, based on its general knowledge, GPT is able to locate related topics. However, this information cannot be relied on without some form of triangulation. How to do such triangulation efficiently and at scale remains an important aspect of resolving this challenge.

Based on general knowledge about individuals interested in education and youth development, there are several other areas that Bander might be inclined to follow. Here are some possibilities:

1. Current Affairs and News: Bander might be interested in staying updated on local and international news to understand the broader context of educational and youth-related issues.
2. Personal Development: Bander may follow content related to personal growth, motivation, self-improvement, and success stories to enhance his own skills and mindset.
3. Technology and Innovation: Bander might have an interest in keeping up with the latest technological advancements and innovations that can impact education and youth development.
4. Nonprofit Organizations and NGOs: Bander may follow the work of nonprofit organizations and non-governmental organizations (NGOs) focused on education, youth empowerment, and social change.
5. Leadership and Entrepreneurship: Bander might be interested in content related to leadership development, entrepreneurship, and business strategies to gain insights into effective ways of driving positive change.
6. Social Issues and Advocacy: Bander might follow content related to social justice, equality, and human rights, as these topics often intersect with education and youth development.

It's important to note that these suggestions are based on common interests and general knowledge, and individual preferences may vary.

GC3: Engage with the Persona in Real-Time, Asking It Anything You Need to Know for Your Decision-Making Task (i.e., Meaningful Engagement

Description: The persona does not need to be presented as profile at all. We have already hinted at the dialogue-based persona systems, where one can directly interact with the persona using conversational means [14,29,58]. These UIs are likely to replace or complement the traditional persona profiles as LLMs further evolve. The grand challenge here is, in fact, a series of challenges for such systems:

> GC3: How to generate personas using LLMs? How to save personas using
> LLMs? How to update personas using LLMs?

How to address? The obvious way to address this is to focus on the goal
of creating personas using LLMs. Fortunately, there are efforts to this end [18].
However, the major challenge there is that the NLP and HCI research communities work on the problem separately, without concentrated efforts and coordination.

How to evaluate? The ultimate method of evaluation for the successful creation of LLM personas is end-user adoption. The technology is quickly reaching a
degree of maturity where it can be deployed in real persona systems for commercial and non-profit organizations – the feedback from these entities determines
the success of the research endeavors.

How could Generative AI contribute? As previously, we explore the potential of GPT-3.5 to address this challenge. Below, we show the dialogue with the
model: *"A persona represents a segment of people that share the same characteristics. Generate five personas that describe NEET youth (not in education,
employment, or training)."*

Sure! Here are five personas that describe NEET youth:

1. Lucas, the Aspiring Artist:

Age: 20
Background: Lucas is a talented artist who has recently graduated from high
school. He dreams of pursuing a career in fine arts but struggles to find opportunities to showcase his work. He comes from a lower-middle-class family and lacks the
financial means to pursue higher education or professional training. Lucas spends
most of his time at home, honing his artistic skills and searching for freelance gigs
online.

2. Sarah, the Discouraged Dropout:

Age: 19
Background: Sarah dropped out of high school due to personal issues and a lack of
interest in academics. She comes from a disadvantaged background, with limited
family support and financial resources. Sarah feels discouraged and disconnected
from society, finding it challenging to secure stable employment without a high
school diploma. She spends her days aimlessly browsing the internet and occasionally takes up short-term jobs to make ends meet.

3. Raj, the Technophile:

Age: 22
Background: Raj is a tech-savvy individual who possesses excellent computer skills
and knowledge about the latest technological trends. However, due to a lack of
formal education or certifications, he struggles to find meaningful employment
in the tech industry. Raj spends most of his time at home, engaging in online
communities, learning coding languages, and exploring new technologies. He hopes
to land a remote job or freelance projects that utilize his expertise.

4. Emily, the Caregiver:

Age: 24
Background: Emily had to drop out of college to take care of her ailing parent. She is a compassionate and responsible individual, dedicating her time and energy to provide support at home. Emily's caregiving responsibilities make it difficult for her to commit to a full-time job or educational program. She often feels isolated from her peers and finds solace in online support groups for caregivers. Emily explores online courses and remote work opportunities to gain skills and earn income from home.

5. Alex, the Lost Graduate:

Age: 23
Background: Alex recently completed a bachelor's degree in a field that is currently experiencing a lack of job prospects. Despite the effort put into acquiring a degree, Alex faces significant challenges in finding employment relevant to their qualifications. Lacking guidance and career support, Alex spends their days feeling demotivated, switching between odd jobs and searching for entry-level positions. They are eager to gain relevant experience and willing to undergo further training if the opportunity arises.

Remember, these personas are fictional representations based on common characteristics of NEET youth and should not be taken as specific profiles of real individuals.

To assess whether it is possible to continue dialogue with one of the personas, we decided to engage with Emily:

Now, assume the role of Emily, and answer the following question: Emily, how could we motivate you to continue your studies?

As Emily, to motivate me to continue my studies, consider:
1. Flexible study options that accommodate my caregiving responsibilities.
2. Financial support such as scholarships or grants for caregivers.
3. Providing career guidance and mentorship to help me navigate my future path.
4. Tailored education programs integrating practical experiences related to caregiving.
5. Establishing a community of caregivers for support and networking.
These factors would encourage me to pursue further education while managing my caregiving duties.

Again, GPT shows realistic potential in addressing this challenge. However, we must bear in mind that the information of "Emily" is based on general knowledge the model has about NEET youth – this knowledge may be flawed or biased [2, 26]. The information would need to be triangulated with domain experts and/or using a model finetuned with a domain-specific dataset.

GC4: Explain Algorithmic Persona Creation *Description.* Persona creation involves a degree of complexity that can make stakeholders question the resulting personas' validity, applicability, and usefulness [43]. In the case of qualitative analysis, it is extremely hard to explain precisely how certain information was chosen for the persona, and it is nearly impossible to replicate the analysis with an independent researcher and obtain identical results. In the case of QUPs, the situation appears better at first glance, as one can apply statistical analysis and other algorithms on a fixed data and achieve identical (or at least highly similar) results on each run. However, these processes are opaque to a stakeholder, so the question about how the personas were created still remains topical. Furthermore, an individual piece of persona information is difficult to trace back to its constituents, even though stakeholders often pay attention to details in the persona profiles and ask about how they were derived. So, given these trust and transparency issues, the challenge is:

GC4: How can the quantitative persona creation process be explained?

How to address? To this end, there has been progress in AI Explainability [36,49]. In its simplest form, explanation is a visualization that shows feature importance of a machine learning task like classification, for example, which words led to the model to predict a certain class. For example, if the topic of interest of a persona is "Cars", then how did the model come to this conclusion? Explainability frameworks, such as *LIME* [56] and *SHAP* [39], exist for both local and global inferences, thereby potentially addressing some aspects of this challenge. However, in the case of non-tabular data, both LIME and SHAP show major limitations in global explanations. These approaches are generally available for NLP, but the explainability of more advanced deep-learning models is an open research area [37], partly because these models tend to rely on non-human interpretable features (i.e., they create a numerical representation of a text sample that is difficult to trace back to individual words or phrases). Therefore, we invite research on NLP model interpretability towards explaining how persona information is derived.

How to evaluate? The success of transparency relies on two primary factors: (a) whether the provided explanations are reliable, i.e., describe truthfully how a certain decision was made, and (b) whether the stakeholders using the personas find the explanations satisfactory, informative, and comprehensible. Specific techniques for assessing concepts [32] and influence [20] can help explain global patterns and trace their provenance through the model's processes.

How could Generative AI contribute? For this task, we initially tested GPT-3.5. However, its explanations were not of optimal quality, so we tested GPT-4 which provided a technically more correct answer to the prompt, "Explain how NMF can be used for creating personas." The explanation given by GPT-4 can be viewed in the online link[1]. What we find particularly interesting is GPT-4's ability to personalize the explanation (see Fig. 4). we asked GPT-4 to make two

---

[1] https://chat.openai.com/share/52da0742-1a00-48c7-988f-1c954570e148.

variations of this explanation, one for children and one for first-year marketing students. For each, we got satisfactory responses (due to space limitations, these responses can be viewed online[2].

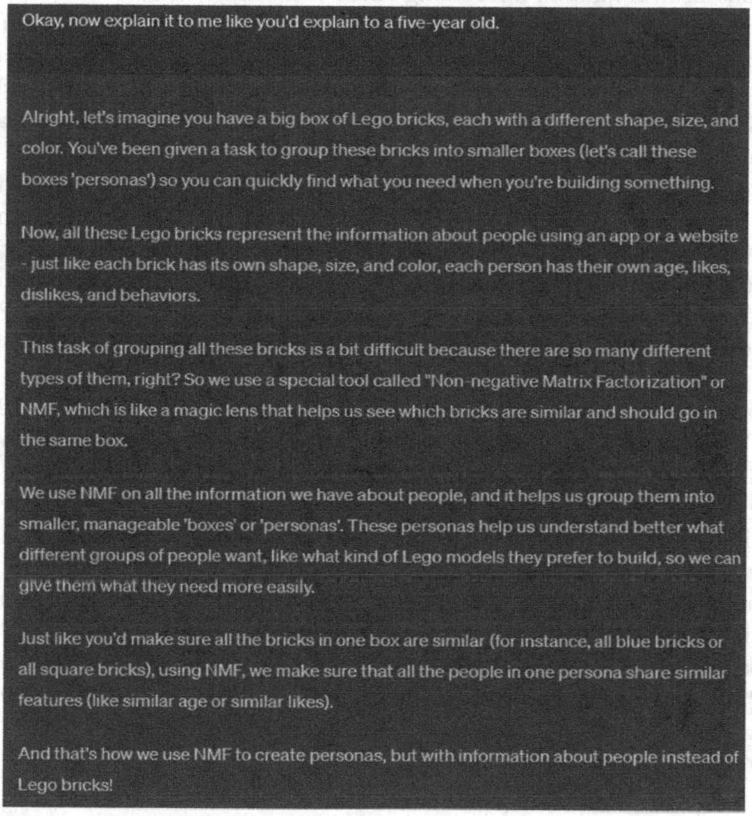

> Okay, now explain it to me like you'd explain to a five-year old.

> Alright, let's imagine you have a big box of Lego bricks, each with a different shape, size, and color. You've been given a task to group these bricks into smaller boxes (let's call these boxes 'personas') so you can quickly find what you need when you're building something.

> Now, all these Lego bricks represent the information about people using an app or a website - just like each brick has its own shape, size, and color, each person has their own age, likes, dislikes, and behaviors.

> This task of grouping all these bricks is a bit difficult because there are so many different types of them, right? So we use a special tool called "Non-negative Matrix Factorization" or NMF, which is like a magic lens that helps us see which bricks are similar and should go in the same box.

> We use NMF on all the information we have about people, and it helps us group them into smaller, manageable 'boxes' or 'personas'. These personas help us understand better what different groups of people want, like what kind of Lego models they prefer to build, so we can give them what they need more easily.

> Just like you'd make sure all the bricks in one box are similar (for instance, all blue bricks or all square bricks), using NMF, we make sure that all the people in one persona share similar features (like similar age or similar likes).

> And that's how we use NMF to create personas, but with information about people instead of Lego bricks!

Fig. 4. ChatGPT explaining persona creation using non-negative matrix factorization to a five-year-old.

As with the other challenges, the explanations given by GPT show great promise, especially in terms of personalization. However, more testing is needed.

4   Discussion

Although the use of AI and ML for personas is not novel [25], applying NLP in this domain is nascent and still at its early stages. As such, there is a lack of guidelines and vision for how to apply NLP in a productive manner to address persona creation challenges. For this, the challenges need to be first defined.

---

[2] ibid.

This work represents an attempt to that end. While we do not claim to present a fully comprehensive list of neither the problems nor the potential solutions, we nonetheless posit that the proposed challenges are relevant for persona theory and practice, and the proposed NLP research directions are feasible.

The potential impact of addressing these challenges is substantial, especially for algorithmic persona generation at scale - the result could be personas that have consistent and complete information, can be understood through discussion, and offer stakeholders the possibility to understand and scrutinize the (currently) opaque information selection process. Better personas, in turn, could lead into designing more user-friendly products, which is beneficial for all.

We suggest that the potential solutions in this space are evaluated using a mixed approach - technical metrics (as customary in NLP studies) and user metrics (e.g., perceptions, subjective feedback; as customary in HCI studies). This would enable arguing for novelty and value of contribution from multiple sides. An example of validating stakeholder feedback on personas is the *Persona Perception Scale* [68], an instrument that measures several impressions, including the persona's perceived credibility, consistency, clarity, and completeness. Human assessment is also vital for rating the quality of NLP outputs [19].

The NLP community possesses unique capabilities for addressing the challenges. Therefore, much depends on its mobilization. For this, it is instrumental to frame the challenges as NLP problems, simply because NLP researchers seek to contribute to the field of NLP. This mobilization can be seen as a grand challenge in itself as cross-disciplinary collaboration can be challenging to create. Nonetheless, the mutual exchange of experiences, methods, directions, and insights is vital for addressing grand challenges [12]. Specific ideas for mobilizing NLP researchers include (1) *workshops and special issues* (e.g., ACL, CHI); (2) *competitions* in Kaggle and other data science platforms; and (3) *reachouts* and evangelization via personal correspondence and research seminars. QUPs should be advertised as a prominent theme.

5   Concluding Remarks

The potential in NLP for personas is plentiful. Persona profiles can be enriched with additional information such as sentiment, topics, of interest, pain points, affinities, and quotes; inferred from text pertaining to the identified persona segment (e.g., tweets, forum posts) or extrapolated using pre-trained language models. While the persona information can be artificial to some extent, it needs to be realistic and truthful, i.e., representative of the persona's unique nature among other personas. Even though current QUPs are mostly static, interactivity could be added using NLP technologies (chat and voice interfaces), thus improving the accessibility and UX of personas. These opportunities require the mobilization of NLP research that integrates with HCI requirements for personas. Other scholars are invited to contribute to the discussion on the grand challenges of QUPs. Particularly, GPT models show promise in addressing each challenge, calling for further evaluation studies.

References

1. Ali Amer Jid Almahri, F., Bell, D., Arzoky, M.: Personas design for conversational systems in education. Informatics **6**(4), 46 (2019). https://doi.org/10.3390/informatics6040046
2. Amin, M.M., Cambria, E., Schuller, B.W.: Will affective computing emerge from foundation models and general artificial intelligence? a first evaluation of ChatGPT. IEEE Intell. Syst. **38**(2), 15–23 (2023)
3. An, J., Kwak, H., Jung, S., Salminen, J., Jansen, B.J.: Customer segmentation using online platforms: isolating behavioral and demographic segments for persona creation via aggregated user data. Soc. Netw. Anal. Min. **8**(1), 1–19 (2018). https://doi.org/10.1007/s13278-018-0531-0
4. An, J., Kwak, H., Salminen, J., Jung, S.G., Jansen, B.J.: Imaginary people representing real numbers: generating personas from online social media data. ACM Trans. Web (TWEB) **12**(3), 1–26 (2018)
5. Bamman, D., O'Connor, B., Smith, N.A.: Learning latent personas of film characters, p. 10. Bulgaria, Sofia (2013)
6. Bødker, S., Christiansen, E., Nyvang, T., Zander, P.O.: Personas, people and participation: challenges from the trenches of local government. In: The 12th Participatory Design Conference, p. 91. ACM Press, Roskilde (2012). https://doi.org/10.1145/2347635.2347649. http://dl.acm.org/citation.cfm?doid=2347635.2347649. Accessed 31 Mar 2020
7. Blei, D.M., Ng, A.Y., Jordan, M.I.: Latent dirichlet allocation. J. Mach. Learn. Res. **3**(Jan), 993–1022 (2003)
8. Brosas, H., Lim, E., Sevilla, D., Silva, D., Ong, E.: Classifying and extracting data from facebook posts for online persona identification. In: Proceedings of the 32nd Pacific Asia Conference on Language, Information and Computation (2018)
9. Burns, E., Laskowski, N., Tucci, L.: What is artificial intelligence (ai)? definition, benefits and use cases (2022). https://www.techtarget.com/searchenterpriseai/definition/AI-Artificial-Intelligence. Accessed 01 Sept 2022
10. Cambria, E.: Affective computing and sentiment analysis. IEEE Intell. Syst. **31**(2), 102–107 (2016)
11. Cambria, E., Liu, Q., Decherchi, S., Xing, F., Kwok, K.: Senticnet 7: a commonsense-based neurosymbolic ai framework for explainable sentiment analysis. In: Proceedings of LREC 2022 (2022)
12. Candello, H., et al.: Cui@chi: mapping grand challenges for the conversational user interface community. In: CHI 2020: CHI Conference on Human Factors in Computing Systems, pp. 1–8. ACM, Honolulu (2020). https://doi.org/10.1145/3334480.3375152. https://dl.acm.org/doi/10.1145/3334480.3375152. Accessed 09 June 2022
13. Chapman, C., Milham, R.P.: The personas' new clothes: methodological and practical arguments against a popular method. In: Proceedings of the Human Factors and Ergonomics Society Annual Meeting, vol. 50, no. 5, pp. 634–636 (2006). https://doi.org/10.1177/154193120605000503
14. Chu, E., Vijayaraghavan, P., Roy, D.: Learning personas from dialogue with attentive memory networks. In: Proceedings of the 2018 Conference on Empirical Methods in Natural Language Processing, pp. 2638–2646. Association for Computational Linguistics (2018)
15. Cooper, A.: The Inmates Are Running the Asylum: Why High Tech Products Drive Us Crazy and How to Restore the Sanity, 1st edn. Sams - Pearson Education, Indianapolis (1999)

16. Cummings, P., Mullins, R., Moquete, M., Schurr, N.: Hello World! I am Charlie, an Artificially Intelligent Conference Panelist (2021). http://hdl.handle.net/10125/70656. Accessed 01 Sept 2022
17. Devlin, J., Chang, M.W., Lee, K., Toutanova, K.: Bert: pre-training of deep bidirectional transformers for language understanding. arXiv preprint arXiv:1810.04805 (2018)
18. Dinan, E., et al.: The second conversational intelligence challenge (ConvAI2) (2019). http://arxiv.org/abs/1902.00098
19. Fadel, A., Al-Ayyoub, M., Cambria, E.: Justers at semeval-2020 task 4: evaluating transformer models against commonsense validation and explanation, p. 535–542 (2020)
20. Garima, L.F., Kale, S., Sundararajan, M.: Estimating training data influence by tracing gradient descent. In: NIPS 2020, pp. 19920–19930. Curran Associates Inc., Red Hook (2020). Accessed 01 Sept 2022
21. Grudin, J.: Why personas work: the psychological evidence. In: Pruitt, J., Adlin, T. (eds.) The Persona Lifecycle, pp. 642–663. Elsevier (2006). https://linkinghub.elsevier.com/retrieve/pii/B9780125662512500137. https://doi.org/10.1016/B978-012566251-2/50013-7
22. Grudin, J., Pruitt, J.: Personas, participatory design and product development: an infrastructure for engagement, p. 8. Sweden (2002)
23. Holzinger, A., Kargl, M., Kipperer, B., Regitnig, P., Plass, M., Müller, H.: Personas for artificial intelligence (AI) an open source toolbox. IEEE Access **10**, 23732–23747 (2022). https://doi.org/10.1109/ACCESS.2022.3154776
24. Hwang, S., Kim, B., Lee, K.: A data-driven design framework for customer service chatbot. In: Marcus, A., Wang, W. (eds.) HCII 2019. LNCS, vol. 11583, pp. 222–236. Springer, Cham (2019). https://doi.org/10.1007/978-3-030-23570-3_17
25. Jansen, B., Salminen, J., Jung, S.G., Guan, K.: Data-Driven Personas, Synthesis Lectures on Human-Centered Informatics, vol. 14, 1st edn. Morgan & Claypool Publishers, San Rafael (2021)
26. Jansen, B.J., Jung, S.G., Salminen, J.: Employing large language models in survey research. Natural Lang. Process. J. 100020 (2023). https://doi.org/10.1016/j.nlp.2023.100020. https://www.sciencedirect.com/science/article/pii/S2949719123000171
27. Jansen, B.J., Jung, S.G., Nielsen, L., Guan, K.W., Salminen, J.: How to create personas: Three persona creation methodologies with implications for practical employment. Pac. Asia J. Assoc. Inf. Syst. **14**(3) (2022). https://doi.org/10.17705/1pais.14301. https://aisel.aisnet.org/pajais/vol14/iss3/1
28. Jansen, B.J., Jung, S.G., Salminen, J.: Finetuning analytics information systems for a better understanding of users: evidence of personification bias on multiple digital channels. Inf. Syst. Front., 1–24 (2023)
29. Jiang, H., Zhang, X., Cao, X., Kabbara, J., Roy, D.: Personallm: investigating the ability of gpt-3.5 to express personality traits and gender differences. arXiv preprint arXiv:2305.02547 (2023)
30. Jung, S.G., Salminen, J., Jansen, B.J.: Giving faces to data: creating data-driven personas from personified big data. In: IUI 2020, pp. 132–133. Association for Computing Machinery, Cagliari (2020). https://doi.org/10.1145/3379336.3381465. Accessed 29 Apr 2020
31. Jung, S.G., Salminen, J., Kwak, H., An, J., Jansen, B.J.: Automatic persona generation (apg): a rationale and demonstration. In: CHIIR 2018, pp. 321–324. Association for Computing Machinery, New York (2018). https://doi.org/10.1145/3176349.3176893. Accessed 01 Sept 2022

32. Kim, B., et al.: Interpretability beyond feature attribution: quantitative testing with concept activation vectors (tcav), pp. 2668–2677. PMLR (2018). https://proceedings.mlr.press/v80/kim18d.html. iSSN: 2640-3498

33. Korsgaard, D., Bjørner, T., Sørensen, P.K., Burelli, P.: Creating user stereotypes for persona development from qualitative data through semi-automatic subspace clustering. User Model. User-Adap. Inter. **30**(1), 81–125 (2020). https://doi.org/10.1007/s11257-019-09252-5

34. Li, Y., Kazemeini, A., Mehta, Y., Cambria, E.: Multitask learning for emotion and personality traits detection. Neurocomputing **493**, 340–350 (2022)

35. Liang, B., Su, H., Gui, L., Cambria, E., Xu, R.: Aspect-based sentiment analysis via affective knowledge enhanced graph convolutional networks. Knowl.-Based Syst. **235**, 107643 (2022)

36. Liao, Q.V., Gruen, D., Miller, S.: Questioning the ai: informing design practices for explainable ai user experiences, pp. 1–15 (2020)

37. Liu, H., Yin, Q., Wang, W.Y.: Towards explainable nlp: a generative explanation framework for text classification. arXiv:1811.00196 (2018)

38. Liu, Y., et al.: Roberta: a robustly optimized bert pretraining approach. arXiv:1907.11692 [cs] (2019). arXiv: 1907.11692

39. Lundberg, S.M., Lee, S.I.: A unified approach to interpreting model predictions, vol. 30. Curran Associates, Inc. (2017). https://papers.nips.cc/paper/2017/hash/8a20a8621978632d76c43dfd28b67767-Abstract.html. Accessed 01 Sept 2022

40. Lutkevich, B., Burns, E.: What is natural language processing? an introduction to nlp (2021). https://www.techtarget.com/searchenterpriseai/definition/natural-language-processing-NLP, Accessed 01 Sept 2022

41. Madsen, S., Nielsen, L.: Exploring persona-scenarios - using storytelling to create design ideas. In: Human Work Interaction Design: Usability in Social, Cultural and Organizational Contexts, pp. 57–66. IFIP Advances in Information and Communication Technology (2010). https://doi.org/10.1007/978-3-642-11762-6_5

42. Maryland, O.G.C.F.S.W.U., Baltimore, S.O.S.W.W.R.S., Email, A.M.P.E.S.U.: Grand challenges for social work (2022). https://grandchallengesforsocialwork.org/about/history/. Accessed 01 Sept 2022

43. Matthews, T., Judge, T., Whittaker, S.: How do designers and user experience professionals actually perceive and use personas?. In: The 2012 ACM Annual Conference p. 1219. ACM Press, Austin (2012). https://doi.org/10.1145/2207676.2208573. http://dl.acm.org/citation.cfm?doid=2207676.2208573. Accessed 31 Mar 2020

44. McGinn, J.J., Kotamraju, N.: Data-driven persona development, p. 1521–1524. ACM, Florence (2008). https://doi.org/10.1145/1357054.1357292

45. Miaskiewicz, T., Kozar, K.A.: Personas and user-centered design: how can personas benefit product design processes? Des. Stud. **32**(5), 417–430 (2011)

46. Miaskiewicz, T., Sumner, T., Kozar, K.A.: A latent semantic analysis methodology for the identification and creation of personas, pp. 1501–1510. ACM (2008). http://dl.acm.org/citation.cfm?id=1357290

47. Minichiello, A., Hood, J.R., Harkness, D.S.: Bringing user experience design to bear on stem education: a narrative literature review. J. STEM Educ. Res. **1**(1–2), 7–33 (2018)

48. Mohammad, S.M., Turney, P.D.: Crowdsourcing a word-emotion association lexicon. Comput. Intell. **29**(3), 436–465 (2013)

49. Mueller, S.T., Hoffman, R.R., Clancey, W.J., Emery, A.K., Klein, G.: Explanation in human-ai systems: a literature meta-review synopsis of key ideas and publications and bibliography for explainable ai. Technical report (2019). https://apps.dtic.mil/sti/citations/AD1073994

50. Nielsen, L.: Engaging personas and narrative scenarios, PhD Series, vol. 17. Samfundslitteratur (2004)

51. Nielsen, L., Hansen, K.S., Stage, J., Billestrup, J.: A template for design personas: Analysis of 47 persona descriptions from Danish industries and organizations. Int. J. Sociotechnol. Knowl. Dev. **7**(1), 45–61 (2015). https://doi.org/10.4018/ijskd.2015010104

52. Nielsen, L., Storgaard, H.K.: Personas is applicable: a study on the use of personas in Denmark, pp. 1665–1674. ACM (2014)

53. Pamungkas, E.W., Basile, V., Patti, V.: A joint learning approach with knowledge injection for zero-shot cross-lingual hate speech detection. Inf. Process. Manag. **58**(4), 102544 (2021). https://doi.org/10.1016/j.ipm.2021.102544

54. Priyadarshini, S.B.B., Bagjadab, A.B., Mishra, B.K.: A brief overview of natural language processing and artificial intelligence. In: Natural Language Processing in Artificial Intelligence, p. 14. Apple Academic Press (2020)

55. Raina, V., Krishnamurthy, S.: Natural language processing. In: Building an Effective Data Science Practice, pp. 63–73. Springer, Heidelberg (2022). https://doi.org/10.1007/978-81-322-3972-7_19

56. Ribeiro, M.T., Singh, S., Guestrin, C.: "why should i trust you?": explaining the predictions of any classifier. In: KDD 2016, pp. 1135–1144. Association for Computing Machinery, New York (2016). https://doi.org/10.1145/2939672.2939778. Accessed 01 Sept 2022

57. Sai, A.B., Mohankumar, A.K., Khapra, M.M.: A survey of evaluation metrics used for nlg systems. Technical report (2020). Accessed 08 June 2022

58. Salewski, L., Alaniz, S., Rio-Torto, I., Schulz, E., Akata, Z.: In-context impersonation reveals large language models' strengths and biases. arXiv preprint arXiv:2305.14930 (2023)

59. Salminen, J., Guan, K., Jung, S.G., Jansen, B.J.: A survey of 15 years of data-driven persona development. Int. J. Human-Comput. Interact. **37**(18), 1685–1708 (2021). https://doi.org/10.1080/10447318.2021.1908670

60. Salminen, J., Jansen, B.J., An, J., Kwak, H., Jung, S.G.: Are personas done? evaluating their usefulness in the age of digital analytics. Pers. Stud. **4**(2), 47–65 (2018). https://doi.org/10.21153/psj2018vol4no2art737

61. Salminen, J., Jung, S.G., An, J., Kwak, H., Nielsen, L., Jansen, B.J.: Confusion and information triggered by photos in persona profiles. Int. J. Human-Comput. Stud. **129**, 1–14 (2019). https://doi.org/10.1016/j.ijhcs.2019.03.005

62. Salminen, J., Jung, S.G., Jansen, B.: Developing persona analytics towards persona science. In: 27th International Conference on Intelligent User Interfaces, IUI 2022, pp. 323–344. Association for Computing Machinery (2022). https://doi.org/10.1145/3490099.3511144

63. Salminen, J., Jung, S.G., Jansen, B.J.: The future of data-driven personas: a marriage of online analytics numbers and human attributes, pp. 596–603. SciTePress, Heraklion (2019). Accessed 22 Aug 2019

64. Salminen, J., Jung, S.G., Jansen, B.J.: Are data-driven personas considered harmful?: diversifying user understandings with more than algorithms. Pers. Stud. **7**(1), 48–63 (2021). iSBN: 2205-5258

65. Salminen, J., Jung, S.G., Santos, J., Jansen, B.J.: Toxic text in personas: an experiment on user perceptions. AIS Trans. Hum.-Comput. Interact. **13**(4), 453–478 (2021). https://doi.org/10.17705/1thci.00157
66. Salminen, J., Mustak, M., Corporan, J., Jung, S.G., Jansen, B.J.: Detecting pain points from user-generated social media posts using machine learning. J. Interact. Mark. 10949968221095556 (2022). https://doi.org/10.1177/10949968221095556
67. Salminen, J., Rao, R.G., Jung, S., Chowdhury, S.A., Jansen, B.J.: Enriching social media personas with personality traits: a deep learning approach using the big five classes. In: Degen, H., Reinerman-Jones, L. (eds.) HCII 2020. LNCS, vol. 12217, pp. 101–120. Springer, Cham (2020). https://doi.org/10.1007/978-3-030-50334-5_7
68. Salminen, J., Santos, J.M., Kwak, H., An, J., Jung, S.G., Jansen, B.J.: Persona perception scale: development and exploratory validation of an instrument for evaluating individuals' perceptions of personas. Int. J. Hum.-Comput. Stud. **141**, 102437 (2020). https://doi.org/10.1016/j.ijhcs.2020.102437
69. Shneiderman, B., Plaisant, C., Cohen, M., Jacobs, S., Elmqvist, N., Diakopoulos, N.: Grand challenges for HCI researchers. Interactions **23**(5), 24–25 (2016)
70. Stephanidis, C., et al.: Seven HCI grand challenges. Int. J. Hum.-Comput. Interact. **35**(14), 1229–1269 (2019)
71. Stevenson, P.D., Mattson, C.A.: The personification of big data. In: Proceedings of the Design Society: International Conference on Engineering Design, vol. 1. no. 1, pp. 4019–4028 (2019). https://doi.org/10.1017/dsi.2019.409
72. Tan, H., Peng, S., Liu, J.X., Zhu, C.P., Zhou, F.: Generating personas for products on social media: a mixed method to analyze online users. Int. J. Hum.-Comput. Interact. **38**(13), 1255–1266 (2021). https://doi.org/10.1080/10447318.2021.1990520
73. Turing, A.M.: Computing machinery and intelligence. Mind **59**(236), 433–460 (1950)
74. Volkova, S., Wilson, T., Yarowsky, D.: Exploring demographic language variations to improve multilingual sentiment analysis in social media. In: EMNLP 2013, pp. 1815–1827. Association for Computational Linguistics, Seattle (2013). https://www.aclweb.org/anthology/D13-1187. Accessed 27 Dec 2019
75. Wood-Doughty, Z., Shpitser, I., Dredze, M.: Generating synthetic text data to evaluate causal inference methods. Technical report (2021). http://arxiv.org/abs/2102.05638. https://doi.org/10.48550/arXiv.2102.05638
76. Zhang, X., Brown, H.F., Shankar, A.: Data-driven personas: constructing archetypal users with clickstreams and user telemetry. In: CHI 2016, pp. 5350–5359. ACM, San Jose (2016). Accessed 04 Nov 2017
77. Zhu, H., Wang, H., Carroll, J.M.: Creating persona skeletons from imbalanced datasets - a case study using U.S. older adults' health data. In: DIS 2019, pp. 61–70. ACM, New York (2019). https://doi.org/10.1145/3322276.3322285. Accessed 01 Dec 2021

Experiencing Ethics and Values in the Design Process of AI-Enabled Medical Devices and Software

Benjamin Schwarz[1,2](✉)[iD], Tim Schrills[2][iD], and Thomas Franke[2][iD]

[1] University of Vechta, Driverstraße 22, 49377 Vechta, Germany
[2] Institute for Multimedia and Interactive Systems, University of Lübeck,
Ratzeburger Allee 160, 23562 Lübeck, Germany
bdotschwarz@gmail.com, https://www.imis.uni-luebeck.de

Abstract. The interaction design of medical devices has to engage and cater to the needs of a wide range of stakeholders, from patients to physicians. The present paper aims to show by example the methodological integration of critical reflection on ethics and values during the design process of AI-enabled tools. The question of how to promote awareness of ethical responsibilities in the context of AI in medical devices is raised, and the use of core frameworks for ethical and value-based design as well as reflexive practice are being evaluated. To this end we conducted multiple empirical studies based on multiple university research projects, including joint research with healthcare industry partners, connecting the fields of medicine, engineering psychology, media informatics, and design research. We present a questionnaire-based self-reflection tool— *VaPeMeT*—designed to encourage ethical reflection and use of frameworks across project phases and team members. Our studies combine qualitative and quantitative research in order to 1) connect reported participant actions with theoretical considerations from value-based design and 2) evaluate the completeness and usefulness of the *VaPeMeT* questionnaire. By conceptualizing process design implications and suggesting a questionnaire-based self-reflection tool, our research aims to contribute to integrated, actionable and responsible transdisciplinary cooperation in this sensitive context.

Keywords: Artificial Intelligence and loT · Design Methods and Techniques · Design Process Management · Heuristics and Guidelines for Design · Philosophical and Ethical Issues of HCI · Transdisciplinarity

The interaction design of medical devices has to cater to the needs of a wide range of stakeholders, from patients to physicians. In this inherently complex process, ethical guidelines need to be considered—especially when systems incorporate artificial intelligence (AI) capabilities. Taking insulin pumps as an example, [QMRR19] identify key domains of ethical issues regarding intelligent insulin delivery systems. In many other research and innovation endeavors within

© The Author(s), under exclusive license to Springer Nature Switzerland AG 2023
H. Degen et al. (Eds.): HCII 2023, LNCS 14059, pp. 232–250, 2023.
https://doi.org/10.1007/978-3-031-48057-7_15

the field of human-computer interaction however, it is challenging to obtain initial guidelines like this.

Most prevalent in research projects are institutionalized and recognized ethics assessments for empirical studies. These detailed evaluations of research plans by ethics committees often lead to tangible modifications in areas such as patient information, data handling, and even research design. However, this focus primarily pertains to the design and execution of empirical studies, rather than the design of systems or the design process itself. Additionally, as pointed out by [Dak18] in the context of field studies, there are instances where prescriptive, rule-based approaches for ethical issue discovery and handling, regardless of their contextual specificity, exhibit deficiencies. Relevant to the topic at hand, two notable aspects are discussed: (1) the impossibility of determining all possibilities of moral dilemmata *a priori* and such (2) the timing and setting, which only allows for the assessment of *anticipatable* risks. The deficits of rule-based approaches could be overcome by creating *virtuous researchers* [Dak18, p. 27], a concept matched on policy-level by *Responsible Research and Innovation* [vSH19], interpreted by [Han19] as effectively employing a *continuous open and value-driven process of engagement* with a diversity of parties and concepts, including perspectives on ethics. Considering this as a *grass-roots* approach, simultaneously identifying and addressing ethical and aesthetic issues not only during, but *through* a production process, this resonates well with [RWB+18], who stress the importance of integration of ethics in the day-to-day work of R&I practitioners.

Within the field of technology interaction with AI, researchers re-emphasize the need for less technical opacity to enable societal understanding and management of these "new, artificially intelligent partners" [GSC+19, p. 1] and carefully evaluate and design the sociotechnical system. One strategy to achieve this seems to lie in transparent interface design concepts, such as *Explainable Artificial Intelligence* (XAI) [GSC+19], which aims to enhance the intelligibility of AI-enabled systems to humans by making them provide explanations and openly communicating their capabilities and understandings. While this might prove a fruitful approach for user interaction with AI, the disclosure of embedded values (or even the underlying discussion) in the system design is not *per se* an outcome of XAI-enriched systems.

Thus, the objective of the present research was to a) examine the current integration of critical reflection on ethics and human values in exemplary projects involving the design of AI-enabled medical devices and software and b) evaluate a novel tool to support this kind of reflection across research team members and project phases. Related to this objective, we focus on three main problem domains: 1) available methodological frameworks, 2) the consideration of stakeholders and 3) the role of design documentation.

Methodological Frameworks. There are several frameworks for the consideration of ethical issues or values aiming at the ethical assessment of empirical studies, research design, as well as policy-making. In the field of applied ethics and socio-technical systems, integrative approaches such as *MEESTAR* [Web18] have been developed, seeking to guide professional research practice. To a similar end, *Value-sensitive Design* (VSD; [FKBH13]) was developed to guide design practice in ethically-sensitive fields in an all-encompassing and inclusive way. While *MEESTAR* is a well-established tool for further evaluating the ethical dimension in a systematic and methodic way using a transdisciplinary discoursive format, *VSD* may provide input to MEESTAR in parallel use and more specifically guide the entire conceptual process, given its design practice-based inception.

Systems-theoretical approaches like *Systems Design Thinking* [Jon18], in contrast, suggest that the consideration of ethical or value-related dimensions, like any other requirement set by the environment, is an inherent property of viable systems and thus handle such issues in a more implicit way.

Lastly, the *Human-centered Artificial Intelligence* framework exemplifies a discipline-specific approach, guiding the creation of computer applications that emphasize reliability, safety, and trustworthiness [Shn20]. This framework aims to provide AI researchers and developers with insights into achieving optimal levels of human control and computer automation, maximizing human performance while mitigating the risks associated with excessive control on either side. However, it falls short in offering guidelines for attaining tangible ethical objectives.

Stakeholders. A key problem domain in many of the above methodological frameworks (and design frameworks *per se*) is the conceptualization and operationalization of *people affected*. From the origins of *stakeholder theory* in business science [Fre10] to science and technologies studies' actor-network theory [Cal01, Ben17] and social systems theory in social science [VRW19,Luh95], discipline-specific conceptualizations of the concept of stakeholders exist [OUM06] and thrive alongside rather pragmatic, isolated, framework-specific definitions as in Friedman *et al.*'s VSD [FKBH13]. Most (product) design frameworks employ variations of *stakeholders* (cf. [FHB17] for HCI)—but as design practice is far from being standardized, and the consideration of parties affected by the product is paramount in the design of personalized medical devices, it is of special interest to this research, if and how the analysis and integration of stakeholders in the design process (e.g., *Participatory Design* [SR12]), *Co-Design* [PWS+20]) is carried out.

Design Documentation. Process and rationale documentation is a prerequisite for any methodological research. However, despite certain disciplines involved in such projects having established practices for documenting design rationale (e.g., Design Rationale Systems (DRS) [Lee97] in software project management), it remains uncertain whether the field of value-based design necessitates its own distinct set of requirements for documenting decision rationale. To a similar end, [DH12] reflected upon modes and artifacts of *design (rationale) documentation*, connecting [Lee97] to design research, and suggesting a *process reflection tool* (PRT) [DH12, p. 430]). Yet it remains unanswered, whether such approaches could facilitate value-based reflection during the design of artifacts introducing new technologies.

Bringing these 3 components together, the question arises: *What would an optimal tool for the integration of grassroots value-based reflection into medical projects concerned with human–AI-interaction look like?*

Conceptual Framework and Design Rationale: Enhancing Value-based Reflection Integration. The claim and the decisive novelty of the present research lie in identifying concrete problems in the operational application of a framework and in developing applicable tools that can be used without theoretical familiarization or a facilitator. From our point of view, the low-hierarchical and flexible structure of VSD offers an excellent starting point, since no dependencies of different processes have to be considered and yet both content-related and methodological issues can be taken into account. Also, within almost three decades, VSD practice has been reported and reviewed in many areas, especially digital innovation [WS21] including medical technology [VLVV15], e-health [CWB+21, JJ20] and even drug development [TZV11]. Relating this to research by Reijers *et al.*, as an *intra method*, VSD explicitly addresses the integration of ethics and disclosure of ethical issues in the day-to-day work of R&I practitioners (*c.f.* [RWB+18, p. 20]).

So in our view, at process level, the promotion of VSD could ensure the integration of both, human value- and ethics-related reflection, and in addition encouraging a more detailed analysis of stakeholders. Additionally, the *documentation of design decision processes* could be promoted and supported with concrete methods like DRS or PRT, potentially fostering the practice of thorough design research to the benefit of further disciplines. In terms of accessibility, an optimal tool should encourage and include all team members in discussion and reflection processes and inspire to further engage with frameworks, methods, and theoretical concepts.

In addition to frameworks for ethical assessment and value-based design, an operationalized and quantitative way to characterize reflexive processes would enable (a) statistical comparison between different approaches, processes or team configurations, (b) continuous evaluation in ongoing projects or teams and (c) standardized communication. Furthermore, a quantitative tool in form of a questionnaire could serve both, measurement and monitoring functions. In other words, to improve ethical reflection in personalized medicine, a tool that is able to elicit as well as affect ethical processes is needed.

To this end, and in line with Reijers *et al.*'s recommendations for the application of *intra methods* [RWB+18, p. 20], we suggest a *questionnaire-based self-reflection tool* for use across project team members and project phases, that raises awareness of key concepts in the aforementioned domains and promotes systematic use—and documentation—of methods among researchers and practitioners designing AI-fueled personalized medical devices.

Our main research questions are:

RQ1 In which way do ethics- and/or human value-related questions play a role in the process of designing personalized medical devices, and how are they being linked to *stakeholders*?

RQ2 What is the role and practice of *documentation* of related design decisions in this domain?

RQ3 To what extent could a questionnaire-based self-reflection tool encourage ethical reflection and use of *frameworks* across project phases and team members?

RQ4 How does such a tool affect ethical confidence in the domain of research and development for personalized medical devices?

1   Methods

To answer our research questions, we chose an abductive research approach [TT12], employing a convergent parallel mixed-methods design [CP11] combining qualitative and quantitative research. In order to explicitly address the research questions, we based our choice of methods on the respective nature of each question: For RQ1 and RQ2, we chose behavioural interviews as our main method, accompanied by the application of a questionnaire-based self-reflection tool (Value Sensitive Design in Personalized Medical Technology, short *VaPeMeT*, questionnaire) we designed as part of this research, while we collected data for RQ3 and RQ4 using a meta-questionnaire in a different sample.

Ethics approval for this study was granted by the Ethics Committee of the University of Lübeck prior to the study (Tracking number: *2022-438*).

Participants. For the present research, two samples were recruited. Participants for sample 1 (S1, $n = 9$) were recruited from 1) an M.Sc. Media Informatics curriculum module, focusing on the design, prototyping and evaluation of a type-1 diabetes *automated insulin delivery* (AID) simulator interface, 2) cand. B.Sc./M.Sc. in Media Informatics, 3) professional researchers and industrial partners in the design and development of personalized AI-enabled medical devices and software. Diverse backgrounds and the combination of academics and professionals allowed for the integration of different experiences and team constellations. In addition, a second sample (S2, $n = 13$) with professional researchers and industrial partners were recruited via social media and mailing lists.

1.1   Behavioural Interview

Querying guiding concepts in VSD, we constructed a semi-structured interview guideline consisting of 8 main items, that addressed situations supposedly present in medical device or software research projects (see Table 2). Sub-items sought to establish a *STAR(T)*-description [AGSC21] of situations pertaining to ethics- and value-related issues, use of frameworks, modes of design (decision) documentation, as well as stakeholder analysis and integration.

The interview question items thus connected the fields of a) team constellation, b) strategies for discovery and handling of issues concerning ethics or human values, c) continuous reflection and improvement of resources and settings, and d) good research practice (i.e., traceability; e.g., of requirements connected to ethics or values).

Each interview took place online and was recorded. The setting was a one-on-one meeting with standardized questions and individual follow-up questions. The interviewer took on an active role for clarification, especially in the joint identification of suitable situations pertaining to ethics- and value-related reflection.

1.2 Development of the (VaPeMeT) Questionnaire

Previous to the construction of the *VaPeMeT-Questionnaire*, we defined requirements to be met regarding aforementioned functions: 1) a questionnaire should address the components *values*, *documentation* and *processes* involving stakeholders, 2) it should be economical (i.e., not time-consuming), and 3) support being used repeatedly within the same project, 4) it should consider factors of personalized medicine without being overly specific and 5) users should be able to answer the survey without exhaustive instructions.

We designed a self-reflection questionnaire, consisting of 30 items in 3 components. For the first component, the 13 *values* from [FKBH13, pp. 17–18] were transformed to be rated in terms of inclusion on a 6-point Likert scale from "completely disagree" to "completely agree", coded as 1–6. According to Friedman *et al.*, this listing is intended to serve as a heuristic to suggest values worthy of consideration in the investigation.

For the second component, *processes*, practical suggestions for VSD Friedman *et al.* [FKBH13, pp. 15–20], were extracted and transformed into items. Compared to the first component, these refer to activities performed by the participants rather than values considered by them. This resulted in 12 items, which also highlight the interaction with *stakeholders*.

For the third component, recommendations from Lee [Lee97] on design documentations were extracted and transformed to items. This resulted in 5 items in the component *documentation*.

All items were discussed in an interdisciplinary team and adapted to fit into the domain of personalized medical technology. The final questionnaire applied in our study can be seen in Table 1.

1.3 Procedure

Our mixed-methods approach combined four empirical studies. *Studies 1 and 2* focused on qualitative and quantitative data regarding ethical reflection, respectively. *Study 3* was a quantitative evaluation of the effects of using the *VaPeMeT* questionnaire. *Study 4* focused on mapping qualitative and quantitative data of studies 1 and 2 from S1.

Study 1 consisted of the interview described in Subsect. *Behavioural Interview* and was conducted with participants from S1. After receiving informed consent from all participants, each interview was conducted and the interviewer took notes on key points. Participants of *study 1* were then also asked to participate in *study 2*.

For *study 2*, participants of S1 and S2 were asked to complete the *VaPeMeT* questionnaire (see Table 1) presented in an unsupervised online survey.

All data of studies 1 and 2 was pseudonymized using the same participant code generation scheme to enable intra-individual study data comparison.

Study 3 was conducted exclusively as an online survey with S2. Here, additional questions were added before and after the *VaPeMeT* questionnaire, addressing confidence in dealing with ethical reflection and evaluation of the questionnaire itself (see Table 3). After receiving informed consent from all participants and *before* showing the questionnaire, participants reported perceived confidence in dealing with ethical issues (five items on a 6-point Likert scale,

Table 1. *VaPeMeT* questionnaire items, 6-point Likert scale with answer options: 1 = *completely disagree*, 2 = *largely disagree*, 3 = *slightly disagree*, 4 = *slightly agree*, 5 = *largely agree*, and 6 = *completely agree*

Category	Item
Consideration of values in the design	
	During the design of the system, I was concerned …
Val-01	… how the physical or mental health of the patients could be affected by the system
Val-02	… about the extent to which patients can own, change and utilize the system.
Val-03	… to what extent the system could affect the privacy of the patients
Val-04	… to what extent systematic errors could lead to an unfair system
Val-05	… to what extent the system could be useful for a broad mass of patients
Val-06	… to what extent patients can experience the system as trustworthy
Val-07	… to what extent patients can experience themselves as autonomous when using the system
Val-08	… to what extent the use of the system is voluntary
Val-09	… to what extent relevant stakeholders can take responsibility for the consequences of using the system
Val-10	… to what extent interactions with the system are perceived as appropriate by patients
Val-11	… to what extent the self-image of the patients could change as a result of using the system
Val-12	… to what extent patient's can gain a sense of overall control through the use of the system
Val-13	… to what extent patients can experience the use of the system as sustainable.
Questions about concrete process	
	To deal with ethical issues …
Pro-01	… I have defined which values I want to look at
Pro-02	… I have defined which technology I want to look at
Pro-03	… I have defined in which context the technology will be used
Pro-04	… I identified which stakeholders will interact directly with the technology
Pro-05	… I identified which stakeholders will be indirectly affected by the use of the technology
Pro-06	… I identified what benefits the use of technology can have
Pro-07	… I have identified which harm the use of technology can cause
Pro-08	… I have described advantages and disadvantages for all direct and indirect stakeholders
Pro-09	… I established the relationships between the consequences of technology use and values
Pro-10	… I have been working on how to measure stakeholder perceptions of defined values
Pro-11	… I identified conflicts between values
Pro-12	… I conducted interviews with stakeholders.
Questions about resulting decisions	
	To document the design decisions …
Doc-01	… I have recorded arguments with evidence
Doc-02	… I have set up optional choices and justified their rejection
Doc-03	… I have recorded the evaluation criteria for my decisions
Doc-04	… I have linked arguments and decisions to specific examples from the system
Doc-05	… I have recorded the intentions related to my decisions

see Table 3). Consecutively, in order to shed light on the effects of *VaPeMeT* use on experienced confidence, the same questions as before were repeated *after* questionnaire use. Additionally, items regarding the perceived effects of using the questionnaire were presented. Study 3 was concluded by open-ended questions on the applicability and usability of the questionnaire.

Study 4 was conducted with existing data from studies 1 and 2 pertaining to S1. Intra-individual cross-references were drawn with the help of the participant code.

1.4   Analysis

As an overarching methodological framework, we based our analysis on core aspects of *Grounded Theory* [BM17], specifically the mindset of *constant comparison*—not only within one data set but also across different sources (here including qualitative as well as quantitative data)—and *theoretical sampling*, after an initial round of separate analyses. As the goal of this process was answering our research questions instead of inductive theory generation, this became our stop point, rather than *theoretical saturation*.

For each interview of *study 1*, audio data was live-coded [POL20] structurally, marking the whole time segment related to item and answer, including follow-up questions. Additional themes were tagged using *in vivo* coding [Sal16] with an attached memo keeping record of the coder's rationale. Descriptive data on the interview timing was then extracted. A reflexive note during interview memo comparison was taken to capture the interviewer's impressions, especially on the joint identification of situations pertaining to ethics- or value-related issues, as well as additional observations. Based on this first round of coding and note-taking, a second round of data immersion was conducted, with the goal of identifying nuances and patterns in the data, as well as transcribing key passages.

For the *VaPeMeT* data of *study 2*, means and standard deviation were calculated for each questionnaire item. However, due to the limited sample size, quantitative analysis served primarily to identify extreme items in the data and characterize the questionnaire's applicability.

For the additional meta items of *study 3*, we also analysed changes in perceived confidence using the t test for paired samples as well as the general experience with the questionnaire using a one-sample t-test.

Concluding, as *study 4*, we derived key questions from the observations of the preceding analyses to get back to the qualitative data of *study 1* for further inquiry. We then revisited the data to find proof or indications for the need of further research, which is described in the results section on *study 4*.

2   Results

2.1   Study 1: Behavioural Interviews

The interviews lasted 70–90 min. On average, 23% of total coded (i.e., item-assigned) speaking time ($SD = 3\%$, range 17–30%) were spent on *item 2* (ethically relevant situation; see Table 2), making it by far the most data-intensive. Stakeholder-related *items 5–7* each made up for considerable less interview time than others—except for *item 9* (framework knowledge), which was excluded here, because it was of a short-answer type. A considerable amount of time was spent on joint identification of suitable situations. In addition and in line with the disproportional time consumption, participants reported difficulties recalling ethics- or value-related situations and a missing shared definition of these terms was observed; Especially with *values*, interview participants reported to have difficulties associating a scientific concept and had frequently to be helped out by the interviewer stating a predetermined definition [FKBH13, pp. 17–18].

During *item 1* (team description), all participants reported a self-assessed lack of previous experience in handling ethics-related issues in the team. No person responsible for ethical issues was named by any interviewee, despite having been explicitly asked to.

Notably, also no knowledge of design decision or rationale documentation methods *(item 8)* was displayed by any participant—this corresponds with the overall missing knowledge of VSD or MEESTAR (*item 9*, see Table 2) within this population.

On the flipside, stakeholders were named and reportedly reflected upon by all participants. Stakeholder interaction even was seeked, albeit in minimal form: Instead of specific methods (e.g., *Participatory/Co-Design*), informal feedback sessions or short discussions were reported, almost exclusively team-internal.

2.2   Study 2: Application of VaPeMeT-Questionnaire

Mean and standard deviation of all 3 component's items are shown in Table 4. Additionally, ratings are visualized in Fig. 1.

Concerning the component *values*, item *Val-01*, which deals with effects on patients' health, and item *Val-06*, which addresses trust, show the highest agreement ($M = 5.17$) and were rated at least "Slightly Agree" ($= 4$) by all participants. In contrast, item *Val-08*, which deals with patients' liberty to choose a technology, was rated by more than 70% (17 participants) of with "Slightly disagree" or even less agreement. Additionally, the identification of items with high variability highlighted values concerning users' autonomy, perceived appropriateness of the system and users' feeling of control).

In the *processes* component, the majority of participants (>80%) did at least slightly disagree whether measuring stakeholder's perspective on values (e.g., through interviews or questionnaires) was part of their reflection process or not. Also, participants tend to reflect on a technology's advantages ($M = 5.64$) rather than its disadvantages ($M = 4.09$), which is a significant difference ($t(20)$, $p < .001$).

For the final component, we found high variability regarding *documentation* (all $SD > 1.40$), with *Doc-01* showing the highest variability ($SD = 1.74$). Every participant rated at least *one* form of documentation with "Agree slightly" or higher, but there is no form of documentation where *every* participant rated at least with "Agree slightly" or higher.

Fig. 1. VaPeMeT Results. Horizontal diverging stacked bar chart showing the proportional distribution of ratings for *value, process,* and *documentation* items in study 2 ($N = 22$), aligned at the 6-point Likert scale center.

2.3 Study 3: Meta-Questions for VaPeMeT-Questionnaire

In study 3, conducted only with participants from S2, an increase in perceived confidence was observed (before: $M = 2.74$, $SD = 1.04$, after: $M = 3.95$, $SD = 0.94$), results indicating a significant difference ($t(12) = 5.09$, $p < .001$), Cohen's $d = 1.03$).

Participants' overall evaluation of the questionnaire as a tool was positive. The average rating of corresponding items ($M = 5.02$, $SD = 0.34$) differed significantly from the meta-questionnaire's midpoint 3.5 $(t(12) = 16.0,\ p < .001,$ Cohen's $d = 4.44$). However, some participants indicated comprehensibility issues concerning items of the *VaPeMeT* questionnaire in the open questions concluding the survey, e.g., with *Val-12*. In addition, participants rated to feel rather overburdened by their responsibility after answering the questionnaire ($M = 4.3$, $SD = 1.02$).

2.4 Study 4: Key Findings Mapping Qualitative and Quantitative Data

Discussing key results of study 1 and possible implications of the results of studies 2 and 3 in an interdisciplinary setting, the main questions for revisiting the interview data became:

1. Which role does the professional background play for the strong focus on technological context during situation identification of study participants?
2. Quantitative data showed remarkable variability in stakeholder-related items. In what way do individual stakeholder definitions play a role here?
3. To what extent can outliers in the quantitative data be explained via the corresponding interview data?

Regarding *question 1*, getting back to the interview data of study 1 revealed the professional background of most of the $N = 9$ interviewees was in the field of *informatics* ($n = 8$).

The top mentioned additional professional environment or research disciplines involved in the analyzed projects were "informatics researchers" ($n = 7$), "software industry partners" ($n = 5$), (engineering) "psychology researchers" ($n = 5$) and (possibly as interviewed stakeholders) "medical practitioners" ($n = 4$). Apart from the medical and psychological expertise—mainly involved in form of requirements-focused stakeholder interviews and as evaluation facilitators, respectively-this seems skewed towards informatics, which can be seen as an explanation for the strong focus on technological context analysis in study 2, given curricula and professional practice.

Examining individual stakeholder definitions *(question 2)*, we analysed 1) reported clustering (heuristics) and 2) interaction types. To this end, we performed *in vivo* coding of passages pertaining to the respective topics, followed by a re-structuring and condensation of codes into categories, from which we derived descriptive data.

Regarding stakeholder clustering, of the 8 categories derived from 18 codes, the top category was *users* ($n = 9$), followed by *sponsors* ($n = 8$, including client, health insurance companies, purchasing decision-makers or influencers, supply systems, project management). 3 interviewees gave information on ranking (heuristics), and 50% needed clarification of the stakeholder concept ($n = 5$). Being asked about differentiation (*item 5.2*; Table 2), the question was interpreted by all participants as to who of the aforementioned group of stakeholders (*item 5.1*) was *actually considered* in design decisions. Some info on discrimination heuristics were given, but mainly pertained to client's wishes or external task definitions; no-one provided analytic or empirical rationale.

The main stakeholder interaction types were *dialogical requirements collection* (e.g., interviews) during initial phases of product or feature development, stated by 67% ($n = 6$), variants of *design feedback* sessions ($n = 4$), and formalized *evaluation studies* ($n = 2$). Item 6.1 resulted in additional identifications of *participatory design, co-design or similar* ($n = 6$) albeit half of them ($n = 3$) are unclear, either to the interviewee or due to unmatching descriptions of actual application. The rest falls into the category of unspecified stakeholder interaction ($n = 5$).

Regarding outliers (O) in the questionnaire results (question 3), three cases were analyzed for correlation: 1) One individual showed atypically many "completely disagree" ratings across all categories. While the corresponding interview data did not give any direct hints, it might have to do with both, self-reported educational background and tasks in the project: Being a student of medicine and involved in the research project as a part-time lab assistant for psychological studies, O1 did not see themselves as being involved in the formulation of research questions outside their discipline. According to O1, participation seemed to focus more on consultation (i.e., medical expertise) and general help with study implementation. 2) Another individual showed remarkably low values (i.e., "disagree") on the item concerning stakeholder interaction (item *Pro-12*), both in inter- and intra-individual comparison. This correlates with interview data insofar, as O2 reported to be a B.Sc. candidate, reflecting on their thesis as the reference project, where they did not conduct stakeholder interviews themself, but used existing data. 3) Lastly, while most users of the *VaPeMeT* questionnaire did not report using more than 1 documentation-related activity, we see differences between samples: In S2 46% ($n = 6$) reported more than 1 activity, while in S1 the agreement made up 78% ($n = 7$) of the participants. Relating this to their respective interview data from study 1, these participants had in common that they were students who used a university project they had to write a report for. While this would suggest a methodological procedure, none of them displayed relevant method knowledge but rather followed individual approaches.

3 Discussion

The objective of the present research was to advance understanding of design processes in the field of AI-enabled medical devices, by way of using an abductive research approach. In detail, we were interested in 1) which ways ethics and value-related issues are currently being considered and linked to stakeholders, 2) practices of design rationale documentation, 3) the effects of introducing a questionnaire-based self-reflection tool (*VaPeMeT* questionnaire) on knowledge and use of frameworks and lastly 4) the effects of tool use on perceived confidence in handling ethics- or value-related situations.

To this end, we conducted four studies, combining a semi-structured interview (study 1) with the use of the *VaPeMeT* questionnaire (study 2) and combining *VaPeMeT* use with meta items on perceived confidence before and after (study 3). Relating quantitative and qualitative results, we identified additional points for further inquiry (study 4).

Implications. With regard to **RQ1**, our interview study shows that mainly *ethics*-related assessment is being reported in this study's population. However, even when it is mentioned, it concerned mostly inclusive language and accessibility, while a whole existing body of work on AI and personal medical device ethics remains untapped. Given that most participants in S1 were still in (or at least very close to) their M.Sc. studies in media informatics at a university, this might suggest that the educational background so far did not contain applicable ethical assessment framework knowledge or retrievable discussion of current matters in the field of AI-fueled medical technology. *Value*-related questions even had often to be clarified within the interview; most interviewees even needed an example definition of the term *values*. Here, *VaPeMet* offers an operationalization of *values* (see *Val-** section in Table 1).

In sum, this implies that there is little knowledge of how the terms *values* and *ethics* can be operationalized in this field. According to our interpretation, this results in an under-representation of value-related, continuous guidance in design processes of personalised medical systems.

Regarding the relation of ethics- or value-related issues to stakeholders, the interview data suggests a weak link: 1) the very individual heuristics to identify stakeholders, 2) the reported interactions in which stakeholders are mainly being considered for the gathering of functional requirements or GUI design feedback in form of interviews and 3) the lacking definitions of measurements for stakeholders' perception of values in study 2 imply a need for theoretical and methodological knowledge regarding stakeholder analysis. Regarding corresponding items of *VaPeMeT*, the results imply that a shared theory of stakeholders and shared methods for identification are of utmost importance, which could possibly be achieved through the (e.g., tool-based) propagation of frameworks like VSD.

With regard to **RQ2**, when exploring value-based design in the literature, the application of respective frameworks implies the importance of documentation. And while this should be common practice in research projects, our interview data from study 1 showed no standardized documentation practice (i.e., concrete methods). This is consistent with the results from study 2—But since there is no indication in the open-ended questions of study 3, that participants are unsure regarding documentation methods, there appears to be a great deal of inconsistency in how decisions are documented. Relating the quantitative data from study 2 back to study 1, the interview data suggests that the variability in questionnaire values related to documentation practice might point at differing definitions of *methodological documentations*: students in S1 act under the impression of applying methodological procedures when writing reports on their studies, but lack theory-grounded approaches to documentation. Regarding this under-represented field of knowledge, the tool could even hint at further methods and field-specific applications (see Subsect. Limitations and Further Research), for example, PRT [DH12].

Concerning the meta questions preceding and succeeding *VaPeMeT* use in study 3, participants felt significantly encouraged to engage with ethical issues after using the questionnaire-based self-reflection tool, as per **RQ3**. Regarding the completeness of questionnaire contents, participants of study 3 indicated that they did not miss any aspects. However, users' understanding of item *Val-12* needs to be discussed as it might not be focused enough on the technological context as stated in open questions of study 3.

The effect of *VaPeMeT* on perceived ethical confidence in the domain of research and development for personalized medical devices as per **RQ4** is significant and demonstrates its potential usefulness and positive influence of even shortly reflecting upon purposeful topics.

Outlook: Example Use Case. As presented earlier, the claim and the decisive novelty of the present research lie in identifying concrete problems in the operational application of frameworks for ethical issue discovery and integration into research and innovation practice, and in developing a questionnaire that can be used without theoretical familiarization or a facilitator. Hence, an intended application example would be the inclusion during project milestone checks. Here, single project participants (or whole project teams) would fill out the questionnaire individually and reflect upon their individual (or collective, respectively) integration of ethical aspect discovery and handling in the current state of the project. Repeated application is expected to enable progress tracking, or discovery of latent blind spots, for example. Due to the open nature of the questions, the application of the questionnaires is expected to foster exchange across team members, leading to individual, project-adequate workflows and standards (i.e., method/framework application).

Limitations and Further Research. Together, the studies provide first indications for the internal validity and potential usefulness of introducing a questionnaire-based self-reflection tool, yet other contexts need to be addressed in further studies.

For example, the tool could be further developed to hint at existing methodological knowledge in key areas (stakeholder analysis, stakeholder interaction and involvement methods, value-based assessment and design methods, design decision documentation). Especially regarding stakeholder interaction method diversity, the questionnaire so far only queries "conduct[ing] interviews with stakeholders", while the interview data from study 1 suggests the value of discussing stakeholder design involvement (e.g., participatory/co-design), as well. Additionally, as the elevated mean value of questionnaire items pertaining to documentation practice in study 2 versus study 3, could possibly be affected by *social desirability* in the context of university projects, we suggest studies where behavior can be observed and matched to questionnaire data. This also shows that the results of the present study may be closely related to the selected target population: both, the professional background (especially from media informatics) and the age structure (mainly people in education) may not yet cover the full range of people developing personalized medical technology. Investigating the effects of *VaPeMeT* questionnaire in more diverse teams is therefore necessary to verify applicability in interdisciplinary contexts.

Conclusion. In the present research, the actual use of frameworks for ethics- or value-based design in AI-enabled research projects has been examined. Our research indicates a lack of knowledge in methods and shared concepts, despite a shared issue awareness among participants. We devised a tool to encourage ethical or value-based reflection during all project phases and across team members of different disciplines in form of a questionnaire for self-reflection (*VaPeMeT Questionnaire,* see Table 1). We introduced the tool to 2 different samples and evaluated the perceived usability as well as efficacy in terms of improving confidence in handling value-laden decision-making in research projects. Our results demonstrated the need for an easily applicable tool that could support ethical reflection for individuals, across disciplines and over the course of varying projects when designing personalized medical technology. First empirical results demonstrate a clear raise in confidence after answering the *VaPeMeT* questionnaire. On top of that, the descriptive data of the questionnaire illustrates the potential for better decision documentation after ethical reflection. However, further research has to be done in order to evaluate the tool's suitability across diverse contexts, user groups and projects. Yet, already based on the present stage of research, it can be concluded that the *VaPeMeT* questionnaire is a promising tool for teams or individuals designing AI-enabled personalized medical technology.

Acknowledgment. This research has been funded in part by the Federal Ministry of Education and Research of Germany in the framework of the project *CoCoAI* (Cooperative and Communicating AI, project number 01GP1908).

A   Study Materials and Detailed Results

Table 2. Interview Items (Study 1)

Category Item		Dim.[a]
About your research project		
1	Please describe the composition of the team of researchers involved in the project	
1.1	Please describe the research interests/questions of the participating researchers/disciplines in the project context that you are aware of	
1.2	How would you rate the experience in dealing with ethical issues in your project team?	
1.3	If applicable, state individuals/roles/own training/previous experience	
Ethics and values in design work		
2	Please describe a situation in which you thought about the ethical significance of a decision in the design process	1
2.1	What task were you previously working on when it came to reflecting on ethics/values?	2, 3
2.2	Why did you think about it in this situation?	4
2.3	What goal do you think is benefited by reflection/thematization?	5
2.4	How did you then deal with the ethical/values-based issues?	7
2.5	How do you evaluate your actions in relation to your goals/objective? (Ref. 2.3)	6, 5
2.6	What was the result of your reflection?	6
3	Using an example situation, describe which human values played a role in the design of this application	1, 3
3.1	How did (value X) influence the design/procedure/priorities/situation?	7
3.2	How is (value X) (directly/indirectly) expressed in the design?	6
Challenges during implementation		
4	Please describe a situation in which you lacked the resources to address ethical issues	1
4.1	How did it come about? What is the context in which the issue arose?	1, 3
4.2	What was your motivation to work on this issue?	4
4.3	What resources were lacking?	1, 3
4.4	Was this already foreseeable in the situation?	5
4.5	In what ways did the lack of this resource interfere with processing?	6
4.6	Back to the situation: please describe the actions you took in this case	7
4.7	What was the outcome of your efforts?	6
4.8	What do you conclude from this situation?	5
Stakeholders in your project		
5	Please describe how, from your perspective/research, the set of all stakeholders that should be considered in product (/software) design is composed	
5.1	Please describe the group(s) of stakeholders in this project	
5.2	Where do you draw the line (in the project) as to who can no longer be considered a relevant stakeholder?	
6	Has there been any interaction on the part of the project team members with stakeholders?	
6.1	If applicable, please describe a situation in which participatory or co-design workshops or other similar activities were conducted with stakeholders	
7	Please describe a situation in which you reflected on the relationship between your own intentions and the goals of others (e.g. stakeholders)	
7.1	In what situation did this take place/what led to it?	
7.2	What was your goal/concern with the reflection?	
7.3	How did you conduct it?	
7.4	What was the outcome of this reflection?	
7.5	In what way has it been captured?	
Design documentation		
8	Please describe a typical situation in the follow-up to a design decision	1
8.1	How do/did you assess the need to make the basis of this decision comprehensible?	7
8.2	In your opinion, what is the reason for the necessity?	3
8.3	What steps have been taken?	7
8.4	What did these steps lead to?	6
8.5	What artifacts, if any, were created in the process?	6
8.6	Was there a specific form/template/procedure that you followed?	7
Framework experience		
9	How would you rate your experience with Value-sensitive Design, MEESTAR, or similar frameworks?	

[a] STAR(T) Dimensions: (1) Situation, (2) Context, (3) Task, (4) Motivation, (5) Reflection (6) Results (7) Action

Table 3. Meta Items Surrounding VaPeMeT Questionnaire in Study 3

Category	Item
Questions preceding VaPeMeT use (6-point Likert scale)	
1.1	I am not sure to what extent my behavior in dealing with ethical issues was correct
1.2	I am sure that I can notice errors in the processing of ethical questions
1.3	I feel that I can produce good results when dealing with ethical issues
1.4	I know how to deal with ethical issues when designing a system
1.5	I feel confident in processing ethical issues while designing a system.
(VaPeMeT items, see Table 1)	
Questions succeeding VaPeMeT use (6-point Likert scale, unless declared otherwise)	
2.1	I am not sure to what extent my behavior in dealing with ethical issues was correct
2.2	I am sure that I can notice errors in the processing of ethical questions
2.3	I feel that I can produce good results when dealing with ethical issues
2.4	I know how to deal with ethical issues when designing a system
2.5	I feel confident in processing ethical issues while designing a system.
3.1	I reflect on my work in the project differently after answering than before
3.2	I think about issues that I was not aware of before
3.3	I have received food for thought on ethical issues that I have not worked on before
3.4	I learned new ways of working to deal with ethical issues
3.5	I feel overburdened by the ethical responsibilities in my role.
(Open questions)	
4.1	Did you experience any comprehensibility issues while completing the questionnaire? If yes, please provide details
4.2	To what extent were you unsure of the meaning of individual phrases or terms?
4.3	To what extent did you feel that the questions were complete?
4.4	What questions would you add?

Table 4. Descriptive Data of *VaPeMeT* Items Regarding Components *Values*, *Processes* and *Documentation* (Study 2, $N = 22$)

Item	M	SD	Min	Max
Val-01	5.17	0.58	4	6
Val-02	3.57	1.50	1	6
Val-03	3.96	1.40	1	6
Val-04	3.35	1.50	1	6
Val-05	4.13	1.63	1	6
Val-06	5.17	1.03	3	6
Val-07	3.43	1.59	1	6
Val-08	2.61	1.31	1	5
Val-09	3.13	1.46	1	6
Val-10	3.96	1.66	1	6
Val-11	2.80	1.46	1	5
Val-12	2.78	1.70	1	6
Val-13	3.57	1.38	1	6
Pro-01	3.68	1.64	1	6
Pro-02	5.18	0.96	3	6
Pro-03	5.14	0.89	3	6
Pro-04	5.18	1.10	2	6
Pro-05	3.45	1.41	1	6
Pro-06	5.64	0.58	4	6
Pro-07	4.09	1.06	2	6
Pro-08	2.77	1.19	1	5
Pro-09	2.82	1.22	1	5
Pro-10	2.41	1.50	1	6
Pro-11	3.00	1.45	1	6
Pro-12	4.59	1.53	1	6
Doc-01	3.77	1.74	1	6
Doc-02	3.09	1.41	1	5
Doc-03	3.05	1.68	1	6
Doc-04	3.09	1.60	1	6
Doc-05	3.23	1.51	1	6

References

[AGSC21] Apple, J.M., Guerci, J.C., Seligson, N.D., Curtis, S.D.: Adding the second T: elevating STAR to START for behavioral interviewing. Am. J. Health Syst. Pharm. **78**(1), 18–21 (2021)

[Ben17] Bencherki, N.: Actor-network theory, 1st edn. In: Scott, C.R., Barker, J.R., Kuhn, T., Keyton, J., Turner, P.K., Lewis, L.K. (eds.) The International Encyclopedia of Organizational Communication, 8 March 2017, vol. 1 (4 vols.), pp. 1–13. Wiley (2017). https://doi.org/10.1002/9781118955567.wbieoc002

[BM17] Birks, M., Mills, J.: Grounded Theory: A Practical Guide. SAGE Publications (2015)

[Cal01] Callon, M.: Actor network theory. In: International Encyclopedia of the Social & Behavioral Sciences, pp. 62–66. Elsevier (2001). https://doi.org/10.1016/B0-08-043076-7/03168-5

[CP11] Creswell, J.W., Plano Clark, V.L.: Choosing a mixed methods research design, 2nd edn. In: Designing and Conducting Mixed Methods Research, pp. 53–106. SAGE Publications, Los Angeles (2011)

[CWB+21] Cruz-Martínez, R.R., Wentzel, J., Bente, B.E., Sanderman, R., Van Gemert-Pijnen, J.E.: Toward the value sensitive design of ehealth technologies to support self-management of cardiovascular diseases: content analysis. JMIR Cardio. 5(2), e31985 (2021). https://doi.org/10.2196/31985

[Dak18] Daku, M.: Ethics beyond ethics: the need for virtuous researchers. BMC Med. Ethics 19(1), 42 (2018). https://doi.org/10.1186/s12910-018-0281-6

[DH12] Dalsgaard, P., Halskov, K.: Reflective design documentation. In: Proceedings of the Designing Interactive Systems Conference, DIS 2012, pp. 428–437. Association for Computing Machinery, New York (2012). https://doi.org/10.1145/2317956.2318020

[Fre10] Freeman, R.E.: Strategic Management: A Stakeholder Approach. Cambridge University Press, 2010 (1984)

[FHB17] Friedman, B., Hendry, D.G., Borning, A.: A survey of value sensitive design methods. Found. Trends® Hum. Comput. Interact. 11(2), 63–125 (2017). https://doi.org/10.1561/1100000015

[FKBH13] Friedman, B., Kahn, P.H., Borning, A., Huldtgren, A.: Value sensitive design and information systems. In: Doorn, N., Schuurbiers, D., van de Poel, I., Gorman, M.E. (eds.) Early Engagement and New Technologies: Opening Up the Laboratory. PET, vol. 16, pp. 55–95. Springer, Dordrecht (2013). https://doi.org/10.1007/978-94-007-7844-3_4

[GSC+19] Gunning, D., Stefik, M., Choi, J., Miller, T., Stumpf, S., Yang, G.-Z.: XAI-explainable artificial intelligence. Sci. Robot. 4(37), eaay7120 (2019). https://doi.org/10.1126/scirobotics.aay7120

[Han19] Hankins, J.: Grass-roots case studies in 'poiesis-intensive' responsible innovation (PIRI). In: International Handbook on Responsible Innovation, pp. 393–404. Edward Elgar Publishing (2019). https://doi.org/10.4337/9781784718862.00036

[Jon18] Jonas, W.: Systems design thinking: theoretical, methodological, and methodical considerations. A German narrative. In: Jones, P., Kijima, K. (eds.) Systemic Design. TSS, vol. 8, pp. 89–117. Springer, Tokyo (2018). https://doi.org/10.1007/978-4-431-55639-8_4

[JJ20] Jongsma, K.R., Jongepier, F.: Value-sensitive design and global digital health. Bull. World Health Organ. 98(8), 579–580 (2020). https://doi.org/10.2471/BLT.19.237362

[Lee97] Lee, J.: Design rationale systems: understanding the issues. IEEE Exp. 12, 78–85 (1997)

[Luh95] Luhmann, N.: Social Systems. Stanford University Press, 1995 (1984)

[OUM06] Olivier, E., Urs, G., Marc, Z.S.: Stakeholder als sozialwissenschaftliches Konzept: Begrifflichkeit und Operationalisierung (2006). https://doi.org/10.5167/UZH-76814

[PWS+20] Papoutsi, C., Wherton, J., Shaw, S., Morrison, C., Greenhalgh, T.: Putting the social back into sociotechnical: case studies of co-design in digital health. J. Am. Med. Inf. Assoc. **28**, 284–293 (2020). https://doi.org/10.1093/jamia/ocaa197

[POL20] Parameswaran, U.D., Ozawa-Kirk, J.L., Latendresse, G.: To live (code) or to not: a new method for coding in qualitative research. Qual. Soc. Work. **19**(4), 630–644 (2020). https://doi.org/10.1177/1473325019840394

[QMRR19] Quintal, A., Messier, V., Rabasa-Lhoret, R., Racine, E.: A critical review and analysis of ethical issues associated with the artificial pancreas. Diab. Metab. **45**(1), 1–10 (2019). https://doi.org/10.1016/j.diabet.2018.04.003

[RWB+18] Reijers, W., et al.: Methods for practising ethics in research and innovation: a literature review, critical analysis and recommendations. Sci. Eng. Ethics **24**(5), 1437–1481 (2017). https://doi.org/10.1007/s11948-017-9961-8

[Sal16] Saldaña, J.: The Coding Manual for Qualitative Researchers, 3rd edn., 339 pp. SAGE Publications (2016)

[Shn20] Shneiderman, B.: Human-centered artificial intelligence: reliable, safe & trustworthy. Int. J. Hum. Comput. Interact. **36**(6), 495–504 (2020). https://doi.org/10.1080/10447318.2020.1741118

[SR12] Simonsen, J., Robertson, T. (eds.): Routledge International Handbook of Participatory Design. Routledge, 12 October 2012. https://doi.org/10.4324/9780203108543

[TZV11] Timmermans, J., Zhao, Y., Van Den Hoven, J.: Ethics and nanopharmacy: value sensitive design of new drugs. NanoEthics **5**(3), 269–283 (2011). https://doi.org/10.1007/s11569-011-0135-x

[TT12] Timmermans, S., Tavory, I.: Theory construction in qualitative research: from grounded theory to abductive analysis. Sociol. Theor. **30**(3), 167–186 (2012). https://doi.org/10.1177/0735275112457914

[VRW19] Valentinov, V., Roth, S., Will, M.G.: Stakeholder theory: a Luhmannian perspective. Adm. Soc. **51**(5), 826–849 (2019). https://doi.org/10.1177/0095399718789076

[VLVV15] Van Andel, J., Leijten, F., Van Delden, H., Van Thiel, G.: What makes a good home-based nocturnal seizure detector? A value sensitive design. PLoS ONE **10**(4), e0121446 (2015). https://doi.org/10.1371/journal.pone.0121446

[vSH19] von Schomberg, R., Hankins, J.: International Handbook on Responsible Innovation: A Global Resource. Edward Elgar Publishing (2019)

[Web18] Weber, K.: Extended model for ethical evaluation. In: Karafillidis, A., Weidner, R. (eds.) Developing Support Technologies. BB, vol. 23, pp. 257–263. Springer, Cham (2018). https://doi.org/10.1007/978-3-030-01836-8_25

[WS21] Winkler, T., Spiekermann, S.: Twenty years of value sensitive design: a review of methodological practices in VSD projects. Ethics Inf. Technol. **23**(1), 17–21 (2018). https://doi.org/10.1007/s10676-018-9476-2

Design Thinking for Artificial Intelligence: How Design Thinking Can Help Organizations to Address Common AI Project Challenges

Laura Staub[1], Benjamin van Giffen[2], Jennifer Hehn[3], and Simon Sturm[2(✉)]

[1] Boston Consulting Group (BCG), Munich, Germany
staub.laura@bcg.com
[2] Institute of Information Management, University of St. Gallen, St. Gallen, Switzerland
benjamin.vangiffen@unisg.ch, simongabriel.sturm@student.unisg.ch
[3] Institute for Digital Technology Management, Bern University of Applied Sciences, Bern, Switzerland
jennifer.hehn@bfh.ch

Abstract. The last decade indicates a drastic upswing in the adoption of organizational artificial intelligence (AI). Companies increasingly seize the transformative potential AI entails to enhance the effectiveness and efficiency of various business functions. However, studies show that over 85% of all AI projects in organizations fail to be implemented. Therefore, this study investigates the most common AI project management challenges that prevent organizations from successfully deploying AI initiatives. It further explores how the human-centered innovation method design thinking (DT) can address these challenges. To do so, a multiple-case study with a single-unit of analysis was conducted, whereby twenty representatives from ten companies and startups were interviewed. Findings show that in practice, the six most frequently occurring AI project management challenges are: the lack of education around the topic and the resulting distrust in such technology; the missing user-centricity that leads to the development of undesired solutions; the fact that pre-defined solutions hinder project teams from adequately analyzing the business problem first; the insufficient cross-department collaboration and communication; and the absence of high-quality data. Moreover, it was found, that the four overarching DT elements which help organizations tackle these problems are the *Needfinding* phase, where relevant stakeholders are interviewed and questioned about their pain-points, wishes, and needs at the beginning of the process; the early *Prototype Testing* where end users can experience the prototypes themselves; the *DT Mindset*, which entails human-centered thinking, collaboration, integrity, diversity, and empathy, amongst others; and DT as a *Process Structure* along which AI-driven projects can be developed. Based on insights from this empirical research, suggestions are made which organizations can follow to directly address AI project management challenges and, thereby, increase their rate of successfully deployed AI projects.

Keywords: Design Thinking · Artificial Intelligence · Human-Centered Design · Project Success · Business Innovation

© The Author(s), under exclusive license to Springer Nature Switzerland AG 2023
H. Degen et al. (Eds.): HCII 2023, LNCS 14059, pp. 251–267, 2023.
https://doi.org/10.1007/978-3-031-48057-7_16

1   Introduction

Over the past decade, companies have increasingly recognized the potential of artificial intelligence (AI) to improve the effectiveness and efficiency of business functions and offerings. However, a 2019 study by Gartner found that more than 85% of all AI projects fail to be implemented in organizations (Howard and Rowsell-Jones 2019). In this context, failure is defined as not being implemented (Weiner 2021). For a yet to be determined reason, this high failure rate shows that to date, companies are still not able to fully exploit the opportunities that AI provides to leverage their competitive advantage (Engel et al. 2021). This poses a significant problem for organizations because AI, when implemented correctly, is considered a key business differentiator for long-term survival (Ziegler et al. 2019). Hence, it is of high relevance to investigate why to date most AI projects fail to be deployed because "it's not the big companies that eat the small; it's the fast ones that eat the slow – so companies that wait with AI adoption may never catch up" (Ziegler et al. 2019, p. 8). Prior research has highlighted that the primary obstacles to successful AI project management are the failure to prioritize user orientation and the neglect of human needs (Gerstbach and Gerstbach 2020); Weiner 2021; (Eliabayec 2021). Over the last decades, design thinking (DT) has been increasingly recognized as a human-centered way of developing products using interdisciplinary teams, qualitative user research methods, rapid prototyping techniques, and iterative learning cycles (Brown 2008). Recently, DT has been identified as a promising way to address AI project challenges and develop AI-driven solutions more effectively (Boeckle and Kouris 2022). However, there is still a lack of understanding of how organizations can use DT practices to address obstacles that are critical to the success of AI projects. Therefore, the purpose of our research is to explore this emerging phenomenon. We pose the following research question:

How can DT help organizations to address common AI project challenges?

We address this research question through a three-step approach. First, we conduct a comprehensive review of academic literature and practitioner reports to identify common pitfalls that lead to AI project failure. Second, we examine whether and how organizations use DT to address these challenges through a comparative analysis of ten industry cases. Third, we use the DT process model to conceptualize our findings. Our work aims to contribute to theory and practice. From a theoretical perspective, this paper provides insights into how DT can help organizations develop AI technologies. It thus contributes to an area of research that has not been thoroughly investigated. From a practical perspective, the identification of common pitfalls in AI projects and corresponding DT practices serve as a basis for developing a framework that organizations can use to increase the success rate of AI projects.

2   Theoretical Background

Although there is no universal definition (Russell et al. 2020), AI is broadly associated with the idea of enabling artificial entities, such as machines and computer systems, to achieve something that only intelligent entities can accomplish (Rai et al. 2019). Unlike prior intelligent artifacts, contemporary AI systems are essentially able to use data to learn how to solve increasingly complex problems without being explicitly programmed (Janiesch et al. 2021). From an economic perspective, machine learning technology (ML) atomizes the cost of prediction (Agrawal et al. 2019), creating tremendous business potential that has fueled the recent rise of AI (Davenport 2018).

2.1 AI Project Management Challenges

As we are entering the era where ML-based AI will become more relevant to organizations, it is important to understand that AI does not operate in isolation and must be "designed with awareness that they are part of a larger system consisting of humans" (Riedl 2019, p. 1). However, previous studies have shown that this aspect is still largely neglected in AI project management, and factors such as unrealistic stakeholder expectations regarding the capabilities of ML-based systems are overlooked, despite being critical to project success (Westenberger et al. 2022). Table 1 provides an overview of the common challenges in AI projects.

Table 1. Common Critical Challenges to AI Project Success

Common critical challenges to AI project success	Description	As mentioned by (non-exhaustive)
Process-related challenges		
Resource Constraints	AI-project exceeds organizational - financial or human - resources	Gerstbach and Gerstbach 2020); (Leff and Chapo 2019); Weiner (2021)
Increase of Scope	AI-project increases in size, often due to a not explicitly determined "definition-of-done"	Weiner (2021)
"Sunken-Cost"-Trap	The AI project is not terminated because significant resources have been invested, although the cost-benefit ratio is no longer reasonable	Gerstbach and Gerstbach 2020)
Limited AI Knowledge	Stakeholders have an insufficient understanding of the capabilities of ML-based AI, resulting in unrealistic expectations or misconceptions	Hagendorff and Wezel 2019); Piorkowski et al. (2021); Foster-Fletcher & Silverman (2020); Kumar (2021); Westenberger et al. (2022)
Distrust in AI Solution	Fear and skepticism about ML-based AI, such as becoming irrelevant within the organization, leads to political deadlock for the project	Hagendorff and Wezel 2019); Piorkowski et al. (2021); Reis et al. (2020); Rzepka & Berger (2018); Foster-Fletcher & Silverman (2020); Kumar (2021)

(continued)

Table 1. (*continued*)

Common critical challenges to AI project success	Description	As mentioned by (non-exhaustive)
Ineffective Stakeholder Collaboration	Lack of communication and collaboration across departments and relevant stakeholders	Piorkowski et al. (2021)
Model Complexity	AI Model is too complex to explain and maintain desired behavior of productive systems	Demlehner & Laumer (2020); Heuer (2015); Weiner (2021)
Project Explainability	Difficulty in explaining AI model to user groups and other non-technical stakeholders	Hagendorff and Wezel 2019); Weiner (2021)
Data-Infrastructure Constraints	The organizational infrastructure is not designed to handle large amounts of data	Hagendorff and Wezel 2019); Pumplun et al. (2019)
Lack of Motivation	The AI project team lacks motivation	Gerstbach and Gerstbach 2020)
Lack of Diversity	The AI project team is not big or diverse enough	Gerstbach and Gerstbach 2020)
Unclear Project Goals	Goals to solve the problem are not clearly defined	Gerstbach and Gerstbach 2020)
Output-related challenges		
Lack of User Centricity	AI-project does not address user needs or solves the wrong problem	Eliabayec 2021); (Gerstbach and Gerstbach 2020); Weiner (2021)
Problem-Solution Mismatch	The (wrong) solution is defined before the problem is identified	Gerstbach and Gerstbach 2020); (Leff and Chapo 2019); (Pietrzyk 2021)
Missing High-Quality Data	Lack of high-quality data required for developing and operating ML-based AI systems	Sturm & Peters (2020); Vial et al. (2021)

2.2   Design Thinking as Potential Solution Approach

While it is important to ensure that AI applications build on available technologies and team skills, it is equally important to consider the human aspects of AI development (Wiesche et al. 2018). As with any other innovation, successful AI initiatives must have a balanced foundation of economic viability, human desirability, and technical feasibility (Brenner et al. 2021). That human desirability is often neglected in the development of AI solutions (Boeckle and Kouris 2022) is problematic because desirability affects whether AI systems are deployed and used appropriately. Therefore, incorporating human desirability into the system design process is critical to realizing the business value of AI.

It is precisely this human-centeredness that is at the heart of the innovation method of DT. DT can be characterized as a mindset, a process, and a toolbox (Brenner and Uebernickel 2016). The commonly defined DT process typically includes the phases of *needfinding, synthesis, ideation, prototyping*, and *testing*. Essentially, it is an iterative and inclusive innovation method in which problems are identified and solutions are designed and evaluated through early rapid prototyping (Stackowiak & Kelly 2020). DT has proven effective in finding the sweet spot between *human desirability, economic viability,* and *technical feasibility* (Brown 2008) in a wide range of domains. It is therefore not surprising that DT has recently been identified as a promising way to address critical challenges in AI projects (Boeckle and Kouris 2022). However, little empirical research has been conducted on the challenges in AI projects that can be addressed through DT and the practices that organizations use, and as a result, our knowledge of this opportunity remains limited.

3 Methodology

3.1 Research Design

Against this background, this paper investigates how DT can help organizations avoid common pitfalls in the design and implementation of ML-based AI systems. Since our research interest focuses on a novel and complex phenomenon, an iterative approach using inductive reasoning is appropriate. First, we developed an understanding of common pitfalls that lead to the failure of AI projects by aggregating information from academic literature and practitioner reports following vom Brocke et al. (2009, 2015) and Webster and Watson (2002). The results were used in a second phase of research in which we conducted a comparative case study to examine which of these challenges are being addressed by organizations using AI and what practices are being used to do so. Given that the focal research topic is an unexplored field with limited existing theory, conducting a comparative case study with a single unit of analysis is the preferred method. In a final phase of research, we conceptualized our findings using the DT process model.

3.2 Case Selection

In line with the exploratory research design, this study generates knowledge about the use of DT for AI projects based on empirical data collected mainly through interviews and a comparative analysis of different case studies. In selecting the cases, we explicitly sought variation in characteristics such as problem domain and industry. Since the intent of this study is to generate a holistic view on using DT in AI projects, variation was particularly desirable. Balancing similarity and variation, ten projects were selected from companies of different sizes and industries that used DT to generate AI-oriented solutions. The investigated projects stem from a university-industry corporate innovation (titled "Design Thinking for Artificial Intelligence" at the University of St. Gallen

(HSG)). The projects were conducted in organizations in the Germany, Switzerland, and Austria (GSA) region, but varied in scope, content, and context. All projects started with an AI-related design challenge, followed by the same DT process, including the phases of *needfinding*, *synthesis*, *ideation*, *prototyping*, and *testing* over a period of three months. The team members in each project had little or no prior experience using DT. However, they shared the same level of coaching support from experienced DT experts to generate AI-oriented solutions. This allowed us to study a single unit of analysis (the failure of AI projects in organizations and solutions on how to prevent it through DT) in different real-life contexts. Table 2 provides an overview of the selected and analyzed projects.

Table 2. Analyzed AI Projects by Project Goal and Industry

Case	AI Project Goal	Industry
1	Creating an innovative front- to back-end solution for AI-driven logistic operations for employees and B2B clients	Logistics
2	Creating an AI-driven financial coaching solution for retail and private banking customers	Banking
3	Developing an innovative AI-based solution for scaling computer vision use cases in car manufacturing	Automotive
4	Creating a solution to engage employees in AI-driven financial service innovation	Financial Services
5	Creating an AI-driven solution for the digital care journey of hair loss management	Healthcare
6	Designing an AI-driven solution that makes sudden invoice changes self-explainable to customers	Telecommunication
7	Redesigning the onboarding journey for merchants using AI	Payment Services
8	Rethinking the hospital consignment process with AI	Healthcare
9	Creating an AI-driven solution that provides energy-efficient renovation services for homeowners	Banking
10	Creating an inclusive flex work environment for their Tech Labs in Montreal with the help of AI	Software Development

3.3 Data Collection

The first research phase focused on identifying common pitfalls from extant literature and practitioner reports. Consistent with the emerging nature of the phenomenon under study, we included not only publications in academic journals and conference proceedings, but also business literature from sources such as Harvard Business Review or Gartner, as well as books, conference keynotes, panel discussions, and practitioner reports. The second phase of data collection included conducting semi-structured interviews with project team members and analyzing extensive project documentation. To gain a holistic perspective on each project, we triangulated the data collection by interviewing individuals in different roles, such as project owners, staff, and coaches, whenever possible. A total of 20 interviews were conducted at the selected companies and startups. All interviews were performed online via Zoom and recorded for further processing. During the interviews, participants were asked a series of open-ended questions designed to explore their experiences and insights regarding the use of DT in the respective AI project. The questions aimed to uncover critical AI challenges faced, DT practices employed, and lessons learned. For example, interviewees were asked to describe the project and hurdles from their perspective, as well as the use and impact of the DT practices employed. Since data collection involved human participants, strict protocols were followed to ensure ethical compliance. Participants were fully informed of the nature and purpose of the study. Explicit consent was obtained for recording and data processing, and participants' rights, including the right to withdraw consent, were clearly communicated. In addition, anonymization methods were employed to protect participants' identities. Privacy guidelines were strictly adhered to, ensuring secure storage and limited access to collected data by participating researchers only.

3.4 Data Analysis

In keeping with the exploratory nature, we used qualitative methods for data analysis at all stages of our research. To identify common pitfalls that lead to the failure of AI projects in the initial research phase, we synthesized information from the relevant literature through open and axial coding (Corbin & Strauss 1998). First, raw data was coded in an open-ended manner (Strauss & Corbin 1998). Next, iterative axial coding (Strauss & Corbin 1998) was used to aggregate emerging first-order concepts into second-order themes and further into abstract dimensions (Gioia et al. 2013) that represent common challenges critical to the success of AI development initiatives. Data analysis was concluded when we reached theoretical saturation and could not identify additional challenges based on information from previous research. In total, we identified 15 critical process and output-related challenges for AI initiatives ranging from missing high-quality data to financial and human resource constraints (Table 1).

Data analysis in the second research phase was based on the 20 transcribed interviews. We identified critical challenges to AI projects and corresponding DT practices as reported by the interviewees through open and axial coding. First, raw data were coded in an open-ended manner (Strauss & Corbin 1998) and as close to the original statement as possible (Shollo et al. 2022). Next, iterative axial coding (Strauss & Corbin 1998) was applied to distill emerging first-order concepts into themes and dimensions (Gioia et al. 2013) that represent critical AI project challenges faced by the organizations in our sample and DT practices used to address them. For example, we found that the DT practice of prototyping is utilized to explain and concretize how an AI system would work in a specific usage context to mitigate knowledge gaps among stakeholders about the capabilities and limitations of ML-based AI technology (Fig. 1).

In the third research phase, we mapped the challenges and corresponding DT practices from the comparative case study against the list of common challenges for AI projects retrieved from previous literature. Finally, the DT process model was used to

Fig. 1. Example of Methodology for Extraction of Dimensions (AI Project Challenges & DT Process Steps) and Themes from Raw Data

Table 3. AI Project Challenges, Corresponding DT Process Steps and DT4AI Practices

AI Project Challenge	DT Process Step	DT4AI Practice
Process-related Challenges		
Limited AI knowledge	Prototyping & Testing	Use AI prototypes to explain and concretize how an AI system would work in a specific usage context
Distrust in AI (solution)	Prototyping & Testing	Engage users with AI prototypes to reduce misunderstandings, skepticism, and adoption barriers, while building trust and increasing stakeholder confidence in the proposed solution
Ineffective stakeholder collaboration	Structured Process	Continuously integrate stakeholders with diverse backgrounds, motivations, and competencies into the AI problem and solution exploration
Output-related Challenges		
Lack of user-centricity	Needfinding	Use interviews and observations to explore needs, tasks, and competencies to identify user-centric AI opportunities
Problem-Solution Mismatch	Structured Process	Ensure problem-solution fit by following a disciplined DT process, especially avoiding premature AI solution definition

(continued)

Table 3. (*continued*)

AI Project Challenge	DT Process Step	DT4AI Practice
Missing high-quality data	Needfinding	Build a rich contextual understanding of the system and data environment to select meaningful data (features) and assess its quality

organize the cross-matches (see Table 3). This allowed not only to understand which DT practices can be used to address common AI project challenges, but also in which phase of the DT process they are tackled.

4 How Design Thinking Practices Help Overcome Critical AI Project Challenges

Our research identified six challenges that are essential to deployment and therefore critical to AI project success and six DT for AI (DT4AI) practices that can help organizations overcome some of the most common obstacles in AI projects (see Table 3).

4.1 Process-Related Challenges

We identified **three process-related challenges**, primarily associated with the people involved: Limited AI knowledge, distrust in AI (solution), and ineffective stakeholder communication.

Limited AI knowledge is a key factor contributing to the failure of AI projects. Unlike data science experts, not all stakeholders have a sufficient understanding of the capabilities and limitations of today's AI systems (Piorkowski et al. 2021; Hagendorff and Wezel 2019). Although AI is currently one of the most hyped technologies and it seems that the term appears in almost every context, only a minority of the interviewees admitted that they genuinely understand it.

> *"One of the main challenges regarding AI is, to really explain what AI can do, what it is and what potential it entails [...]. And you won't get the support from employees and customers to implement such projects if they have no clue about it. So consequently, these projects fail."* (Interviewee 9 – Head of Digitalization).

The DT step **Prototyping & Testing** mitigates knowledge discrepancies: AI prototypes can be utilized to explain and concretize how an AI system would work in a specific usage context. It enables users to ask questions and learn about the possibilities and limitations of AI. The idea behind prototypes, which are tested with end users early in the development process, is for them to better understand how the potential technology could be used in real life. This engages people in the development process in a very different way than simply explaining to them how the solution might be used in their daily operations. If end users can experience an AI prototype firsthand, they better understand its potentials and are more prone to accepting it.

Distrust in AI (solution) is a common consequence of misunderstandings surrounding AI. Many respondents proclaimed that fear and skepticism towards AI technology poses another major issue that prevents AI projects from succeeding. There is a lot of misconception around AI and many people fear of losing their job or becoming irrelevant within the organization (Hagendorff and Wezel 2019); Rzepka & Berger 2018).

The DT step **Prototyping & Testing** builds trust in AI: Experiencing low-resolution prototypes early in the AI innovation process makes solutions more visible and reduces barriers to adoption. Rapid prototyping and early testing help build stakeholder understanding and confidence in the solution. Today, it is misleadingly often heard and read that AI adoption leads to job loss. The fear of end users, for instance employees, of becoming irrelevant poses a major problem because an AI solution is unlikely to be rolled out if they refuse to work with it. If, however, they are integrated in the AI development process and can test prototypes at an early stage it was found that they were a lot less skeptical. This also includes that their iterative feedback for change or improvement of the supposed AI solution is taken into consideration and implemented. For end users to be able to test the prototype of an AI technology firsthand has a much higher impact on their trust than explaining to them that they should not fear losing their job to AI. It allows them to interact and experience in a real-life scenario how this technology would impact their daily operations and routines. After all, prototype testing helps users to better understand the implications of using AI in a practical setting, avoids misconceptions and, thereby, reduces the fear towards AI.

Ineffective stakeholder collaboration and communication is another contributing factor to AI project failures (Piorkowski et al. 2021). Successfully deploying AI applications is a multidisciplinary effort that requires the involvement and collaboration of multiple roles, departments, and stakeholders. The lack of cross-department and stakeholder communication is a crucial reason for the failure of AI projects in organizations. One could argue that this is a challenging topic for organizations beyond AI, especially regarding the increase of globalization. However, communication is particularly crucial regarding the development of AI technologies because numerous departments and experts need to be involved in the process.

> *"Communication is always important. But in AI it is particularly important. So many different stakeholders and departments must be involved to successfully implement a value adding technology. The field is very new, so everyone must work together. Highly efficient cross-department collaboration and communication is required. In most projects I have worked on thus far this was still a problem."* (Interviewee 17 – Project Employee)

Furthermore, communication is essential to establish trust towards AI technologies. It must become part of an organization's culture and be communicated and exemplified top-down:

> *"At our company we have many different departments, and it is important that we clearly communicate. If the communication is not clear there is no trust, and*

this makes it hard to implement AI. Also, AI has to be communicated as something great from the management." (Interviewee 9 – Head of Digitalization)

Using **DT as a structured process** orchestrates stakeholder collaboration and communication: DT fosters deep and continuous collaboration by engaging stakeholders in both problem and solution exploration. This can also help subject matter experts who may struggle to translate business problems into well-formulated and understandable data science problems, and vice versa. Because of the knowledge gap between relevant stakeholders that are involved in the development of AI, multidisciplinary communication is particularly essential in AI. Whilst in many disciplines it is possible to work department specific, AI projects require a highly integrated collaboration across departments. This is strongly encouraged by the DT principles of interdisciplinary collaboration, integration, diversity, and empathy which stand in the center of every DT process. In interviews it was found that project teams who worked according to these principles showed clearer, more regular, and effective communication, which led to better AI project outcomes.

4.2 Output-Related Challenges

We identified three output-related challenges, primarily associated with the quality and fit of the developed AI-solution.

Lack of user-centricity risks to develop solutions that do not adequately address user needs or tackle the wrong problem (Gerstbach and Gerstbach 2020); Weiner 2021; (Eliabayec 2021). Based on interview responses, this challenge can occur as a result of two scenarios:

"[...] data scientists often work very isolated from the rest of the company. And these are usually not the people who talk to customers. So if the communication is not right and they develop based on what they interpret to be the right solution they just develop something that doesn't solve the problem." (Interviewee 19 – Project Employee)

A further explanation for this challenge is that companies are fueled by a fear of losing out on market share, which pressures them to develop revolutionary AI technologies at an excessively increased speed. This prevents them from taking the necessary time to analyze the underlying problems and wishes of end users.

"[...] there are different stakeholder groups and in trying to develop something as quickly as possible you might target or talk to one group, but you miss others. Therefore, you just develop something that the majority doesn't need or want." (Interviewee 15 – Project Employee)

The DT step **Needfinding** focuses on user desirability: Qualitative methods, such as interviewing and observing end users, allow for a better understanding of pain points, needs, and latent desires. This results in AI innovation that is truly desirable and will therefore not only be deployed but also used effectively. The phenomenon of developing AI technology that is not desired by users or solves the wrong problem was claimed to be one of the most devastating incidents for project teams. Learning that the solution that was delivered was not helpful to solve the focal problem is difficult, especially after having worked long and hard on the AI project. Yet, it happens commonly that ideas are created on the wrong customer needs (Weiner 2021). During the Needfinding phase the regular interchange of ideas, wishes, concerns, requirements, and pain-points with end users is predestined to avoid this pitfall. Because not only are potential users questioned about a preferred solution, but they are also asked the right questions during interviews, which often helps them to better understand their actual business problem. These insights are shared with anyone who is involved in the development process. Moreover, during the Needfinding phase not only end users, but also other relevant stakeholders are interviewed, whereby an integrated and diverse pool of insights is gathered that contributes to finding a desired solution to the respective problem. The closeness to the end users, for example the customers, makes the solution highly human-centered. Afterall, the Needfinding phase starts by defining the right problem based on direct insights from end users and stakeholders and then, in regular iterations and close interaction with them helps organizations to find an appropriate solution for this problem so it addresses their needs in a targeted manner.

Problem-solution mismatch happens when a solution is proposed before the actual problem has been identified. Successful AI innovation depends on comprehensive business domain- and problem understanding in order to develop appropriate solutions (Pietrzyk 2021); (Leff and Chapo 2019); (Gerstbach and Gerstbach 2020).

"A problem, and I have experienced that with a logistics company, is that often you have these very technical people that usually already have a clear solution in mind. And they are usually not open for anything else than this solution." (Interviewee 16 – Design Strategy Coach)

One example for a failed AI project caused by this challenge was given by a Design Strategy Coach who experienced this scenario in a recent project:

"Our developers initially liked the idea of chatbots and they wanted to roll it out […] because they were convinced that this is going to solve the problem, without having properly analyzed it. But then in the end they realized that no one wanted to talk to a chatbot." (Interviewee 16 – Design Strategy Coach)

Again, this is closely related to the challenges discussed earlier. Having a set solution in mind before understanding the problem results from a lack of interaction and communication with end users and leads to technology development that does not appeal to them. Additionally, in recent years AI has been hyped as a revolutionary technology. Although this holds true in many cases, it can misguide people to perceive it as a magic solution that has the potential to solve any problem. Therefore, people often want AI to be the right solution without considering other, potentially less complex or resource intensive, options to solve the problem.

Using **DT as a structured process** balances the focus on problem understanding and solution development. Following the layout of the DT process allows organizations to spend an equal amount of time defining and analyzing the problem before trying to find the best suited solution. Taking just as much time to understand a problem as to find the right solution to solve it is often considered overrated and inefficient in fast-paced business environments. Especially data scientists are often tempted to jump into model development right away as from a technical perspective they believe they know what the solution must look like. However, the best technical solution might not necessarily be the desired solution for end users. The Needfinding phase helps to integrate all the insights gathered through interviews and observations. It encourages various stakeholders to, then, share their findings and knowledge, both from a technical as well as a business perspective. Hereby, enough time can be spent to jointly outline the real business problem at hand and develop an adequate solution to solve it. Needfinding opens the spectrum of possible ideas and solutions from various angles, which hinders any involved project team member to start the AI development process with a pre-defined solution in mind.

Missing high-quality data is an AI innovation risk, as this kind of data is required to both develop and operate modern AI systems (Sturm & Peters 2020; Vial et al. 2021; von Krogh 2018). Data sets the foundation of any AI technology, so without clean and high-quality data, AI projects cannot be developed let alone implemented. Before beginning to think about integrated AI applications, a company must create a solid database, based on which machines can start to learn. This remains to be a big challenge for organizations, as they have large amounts of raw data but limited resources, knowledge, or infrastructure to transform it into usable data to create algorithms.

> *"The main problem is that the foundation, so the strategy, processes, and skills around data are not at all in the maturity stage they should be to drive the company forward in such a way that we can implement AI. [...] Another problem is [...] that we have a lot of data but in different places and not high quality or vetted. And you can't do AI reasonably until the basic framework is also right" (Interviewee 11 – Product Manager)*

The DT step **Needfinding** prevents avoidable data risks: Engaging all relevant stakeholders before developing AI solutions enables necessary assessments, such as data availability and quality. This can minimize the risk of launching AI initiatives that are doomed to fail. Especially detecting the availability and selection of high-quality data, can be tackled through the Needfinding phase, specifically by stakeholder mapping. The Needfinding phase helps better understand what data is necessary, which departments must provide it, and in which state the data should be. This was supported by more than 2/3 of interviewees who agreed that data issues hinder a successful roll out of AI projects in organizations. In many organizations the data infrastructure is not yet as well-developed because the data is often stored in different places and owned by various departments. As data lays the foundation of every AI algorithm it is crucial to have the right data available. Before getting to the vetting process the data sources must be determined. Moreover, questions on data migration must be cleared. This is where the Needfinding phase can be very helpful, particularly the mapping of relevant stakeholders who might be important in providing the data.

5 Discussion and Conclusion

5.1 Contributions

This study contributes to theory and practice. From a theoretical perspective, the contributions are threefold. Firstly, this paper aggregates common pitfalls leading to AI project failure based on previous literature (Westenberger et al. 2022). Secondly, this study empirically evaluates which of these can be addressed using DT and how organizations can leverage specific DT practices to overcome these challenges. Thirdly, this research provides a preliminary conceptualization of the relationship between AI project success, DT process steps, and DT practices differentiating output and process-related challenges. Thus, this paper provides insights into how DT, as a human-centered innovation method, can help organizations address common challenges that arise in the context of AI projects. In doing so, we respond to recent calls to build bridges between the AI and DT research communities by exploring how ML-based AI transforms DT practices and vice versa (Boeckle and Kouris 2022). It is only recently that using AI technology to overcome past DT limitations has attracted research interest (Bouschery et al. 2023; Verganti et al. 2020). In a metaphorical sense, this study supports these bridge-building efforts from the other side – by analyzing how organizations can employ DT practices to overcome AI project challenges. From an information system research perspective, linking DT and AI reinstates the academic discourse of properly incorporating human needs in the design of information systems (Yoo 2017).

Our research also holds implications for practitioners, by providing insights that organizations can leverage to overcome common pitfalls in the development of AI solutions. Specifically, we illustrate which steps in the DT process can be followed when tackling the most practice-relevant AI challenges and how DT elements can be employed to do so. Incorporating these insights into work practices can help address common AI project challenges in a targeted manner and thus increase the number of successful AI deployments.

5.2 Limitations and Future Research Recommendations

As with any research, this study faces limitations that can be addressed by future research. Primarily, the sample size is limited. A total of 20 interviews have been conducted with AI project team members from ten different companies based in the GSA region. Although we explicitly sought variation in case selection to generate a holistic view, the sample size is not large enough to declare the results representative.

In addition, qualitative methods used for data collection and analysis are by their nature subject to a certain degree of subjectivity, which limits the generalizability of the results. Hence, it is recommended for future research to conduct studies with an increased sample size and diversified techniques of data collection and analysis. For example, future research could collect empirical data through surveys and use quantitative or mixed methods for data analysis. A further limitation of the focal research is the access to scientific literature – as using DT for AI is an emerging phenomenon, specialized literature is still sparse. Considering the business relevance of AI and DT, it is highly recommended for future research to explore these fields further.

5.3 Conclusion

There is no doubt that "AI is no longer a disruptive technology, but a paradigmatic shift" (Ågerfalk, et al. 2020, p. 1). The business opportunities of this change are enormous. However, the potential of ML-based AI technology has not yet been fully realized. It is essential to understand why most AI initiatives still fail in order to overcome the underlying challenges that prevent the successful deployment of AI projects. This paper has identified 15 literature-based problems, six of which have been validated to be commonly relevant to organizational practice. As these challenges are mostly related to the lack of human desirability, DT was identified as a suitable approach to overcome them. Our findings show how DT elements can be used to address common pitfalls in AI projects and help organizations increase the number of successful AI deployments. While DT4AI is an emerging phenomenon, there is no doubt that human-centered innovation is key to realizing the full business potential of ML-based AI.

References

Ågerfalk, P.J., et al.: Artificial intelligence – beyond the hype. In: Forty-First International Conference on Information Systems (ICIS), India (2020)

Agrawal, A., Gans, J., Goldfarb, A.: Prediction, judgment, and complexity: a theory of decision-making and artificial intelligence. In: The Economics of Artificial Intelligence, pp. 89–114. University of Chicago Press (2019)

Boeckle, M., Kouris, I.: Design thinking and AI: a new frontier for designing human-centered AI solutions. In: Proceedings of the Academic Design Management Conference ADMC22 (2022). https://www.dmi.org/page/ADMC2022Proceedings

Bouschery, S.G., Blazevic, V., Piller, F.T.: Augmenting human innovation teams with artificial intelligence: exploring transformer-based language models. J. Prod. Innov. Manag. (2023). https://doi.org/10.1111/jpim.12656

Brenner, W., Uebernickel, F.: Design thinking as mindset, process, and toolbox. ResearchGate (2016). https://doi.org/10.1007/978-3-319-26100-3_1

Brenner, W., van Giffen, B., Koehler, J.: Management of artificial intelligence: feasibility, desirability and viability. In: Aier, S., Rohner, P., Schelp, J. (eds.) Engineering the Transformation of the Enterprise: A Design Science Research Perspective, pp. 15–36. Springer International Publishing (2021)

Brown, T.: Design thinking. Harv. Bus. Rev. **86**(6), 84–92 (2008)

Davenport, T.: The AI Advantage: How to Put the Artificial Intelligence Revolution to Work. MIT Press (2018)

Eliabayec, U.: Process Planning - From Understanding of Goals to Deployment [Conference presentation]. SwissCognitive - How to Set Up an AI Centre of Excellence, Virtual (2021). https://www.youtube.com/watch?v=Fkl7my0av5U. Accessed 14 Mar 2023

Engel, C., van Giffen, B., Ebel, P.: Empirically Exploring the Cause-Effect Relationships of AI Characteristics, Project Management Challenges, and Organisational Change. ResearchGate (2021). https://www.researchgate.net/publication/349431010

Foster-Fletcher, R., Silverman, K.: (Hosts). Navigating Technology Beyond Our Understanding (No. 113). In: Boundless (2020)

Gerstbach, I., Gerstbach, P.: Design Thinking in IT-Projekten: Agile Problemlösungskompetenz in einer digitalen Welt. Carl Hanser Verlag GmbH & Co, KG (2020)

Gioia, D.A., Corley, K.G., Hamilton, A.L.: Seeking qualitative rigor in inductive research: notes on the Gioia methodology. Organ. Res. Methods **16**(1), 15–31 (2013)

Hagendorff, T., Wezel, K.: 15 challenges for AI: or what AI (currently) can't do. AI Soc. **35**(2), 355–365 (2019). https://doi.org/10.1007/s00146-019-00886-y

Howard, C., Rowsell-Jones, A.: CIO Survey: CIOs Have Awoken to the Importance of AI. Gartner Inc. (2019)

Janiesch, C., Zschech, P., Heinrich, K.: Machine learning and deep learning. Electron. Mark. **31**(3), 685–695 (2021)

Kumar, M.: Process planning - from understanding of goals to deployment. SwissCognitive - How to Set Up an AI Centre of Excellence, Virtual (2021)

Leff, D., Chapo, C.: What the heck does it even mean to "Do AI"? [Conference presentation]. Venture Beat Transform 2019: Business AI Integration, San Francisco, CA, United States (2019, July 10–11). https://www.youtube.com/watch?v=EzmTZlho-EI. Accessed 14 Mar 2023

Lewrick, M.: Design Thinking: Radikale Innovationen in einer digitalisierten Welt (1st ed.). C.H.Beck (2018)

Pietrzyk, M.: Process Planning - From Understanding of Goals to Deployment [Conference presentation]. SwissCognitive - How to Set Up an AI Centre of Excellence, Virtual (2021). https://www.youtube.com/watch?v=Fkl7my0av5U. Accessed 14 Mar 2023

Piorkowski, D., Park, S., Wang, A.Y., Wang, D., Muller, M., Portnoy, F.: How AI developers overcome communication challenges in a multidisciplinary team. In: Proceedings of the ACM on Human-Computer Interaction, vol. 5(CSCW1), pp. 1–25 (2021).https://doi.org/10.1145/3449205

Pumplun, L., Tauchert, C., Heidt, M.: A new organizational chassis for artificial intelligence - exploring organizational readiness factors. In:ECIS 2020 Proceedings, Association for Information Systems (2019)

Rai, A., Constantinides, P., Sarker, S.: Next generation digital platforms: toward human-AI hybrids. Manag. Inf. Syst. Q. **43**(1), iii–ix (2019)

Reis, L., Maier, C., Mattke, J., Creutzenberg, M., Weitzel, T.: Addressing unser resistance would have prevented a healthcare project failure. MIS Quart. Execut. **19**(4), 279–296 (2020). https://doi.org/10.17705/2msqe.00038

Riedl, M.O.: Human-Centered Artificial Intelligence and Machine Learning. School of Interactive Computing Georgia Institute of Technology (2019)

Russell, S.J., Norvig, P., Chang, M., Devlin, J., Dragan, A.: Artificial Intelligence: A Modern Approach (Pearson Series in Artificial Intelligence) (4th ed.). Pearson (2020)

Rzepka, C., Berger, B.: User interaction with AI-enabled systems: a systematic review of IS research (39 ICIS). In: International Conference of Information Systems (2018)

Shollo, A., Hopf, K., Thiess, T., Müller, O.: Shifting ML value creation mechanisms: a process model of ML value creation. J. Strateg. Inf. Syst. **31**(3), 101734 (2022)

Stackowiak, R., Kelly, T.: Design Thinking in Software and AI Projects: Proving Ideas Through Rapid Prototyping (1st ed.). Apress (2020)

Strauss, A., Corbin, J.M.: Basics of Qualitative Research: Techniques and Procedures for Developing Grounded Theory. SAGE Publications (1998)

Sturm, T., Peters, F.: The Impact of Artificial Intelligence on Individual Performance: Exploring the Fit between Task, Data, and Technology (ECIS 2020 Proceedings). Association for Information Systems (2020)

Vial, G., Jiang, J., Giannelia, T., Cameron, A.-F.: The Data Problem Stalling AI. MIT Sloan Management Review (2021)

Verganti, R., Vendraminelli, L., Iansiti, M.: Innovation and design in the age of artificial intelligence. J. Prod. Innov. Manag. **37**(3), 212–227 (2020)

von Krogh, G.: Artificial intelligence in organizations: new opportunities for phenomenon-based thinking. ETH Zürich Res. Collect. (2018). https://doi.org/10.3929/ethz-b-000320207

vom Brocke, J., et al.: Reconstructing the giant: On the importance of rigour in documenting the literature search process. aisel.aisnet.org (2009). https://aisel.aisnet.org/cgi/viewcontent.cgi?article=1145&context=ecis2009

vom Brocke, J., Simons, A., Riemer, K., Niehaves, B., Plattfaut, R., Cleven, A.: Standing on the shoulders of giants: challenges and recommendations of literature search in information systems research. Commun. Assoc. Inf. Syst. **37**(1), 9 (2015)

Webster, J., Watson, R.T.: Analyzing the past to prepare for the future: writing a literature review. Manag. Inf. Syst. Q. **26**(2), xiii–xxiii (2002)

Weiner, J.: Why AI/Data Science Projects Fail (1st ed.). Morgan & Claypool Publishers (2021). https://doi.org/10.2200/S01070ED1V01Y202012CAN001

Westenberger, J., Schuler, K., Schlegel, D.: Failure of AI projects: understanding the critical factors. Procedia Comput. Sci. **196**, 69–76 (2022)

Wiesche, M., Lang, M., Uebernickel, F., Bryler, E.: Teaching Innovation in Interdisciplinary Environments: Towards a Design Thinking Syllabus. ResearchGate (2018). https://www.researchgate.net/publication/328252662

Yoo, Y.: Design thinking for IS research, in: editor's comments: diversity of design science research. MIS Q. **41**(1), iii–xviii (2017)

Ziegler, M., Rossmann, S., Steer, A., Danzer, S.: Leading the Way to an AI-driven Organization. Porsche Consulting (2019)

User Perception and Evaluation of a Deep Learning Framework for Audience Engagement Analysis in Mass Events

Alexandros Vrochidis[1,2(✉)], Christina Tsita[1], Nikolaos Dimitriou[1], Stelios Krinidis[1,2], Savvas Panagiotidis[3], Stathis Parcharidis[3], Dimitrios Tzovaras[1], and Vassilios Chatzis[2]

[1] Center for Research and Technology Hellas, Information Technologies Institute, 57001 Thessaloniki, Greece
avrochid@iti.gr
[2] Department of Management Science and Technology, International Hellenic University, 65404 Kavala, Greece
[3] Inventics - Hellas, 57001 Thessaloniki, Greece

Abstract. As video volume on the web grows exponentially over time, video streaming platforms have been enhanced with Artificial Intelligence (AI) to analyze their content. This paper proposes a novel evaluation methodology for video events streaming platforms that use AI for content analysis and helps them measure user experience, customer satisfaction, and AI acceptance. Models like System Usability Scale (SUS), Technology Acceptance Model (TAM), European Customer Satisfaction Index (ECSI), and Net Promoter Score (NPS) have been fused, creating a novel methodology for the evaluation. To this end, correlations between items, model scores, and statistic metrics were utilized. Experimental results in a real AI-enabled video streaming platform verified the potential of this evaluation methodology, with insightful conclusions drawn from it. The study helps in similar evaluation tasks and provides crucial information to software and system designers who want to know where to emphasize and how to evaluate similar systems. Results provide rich details on the platform's user experience, demonstrating how important it is to enhance online video streaming platforms with AI analysis features.

Keywords: Audience Analysis · AI Framework Evaluation · User Experience · Video Content Analysis · Customer Satisfaction Analysis

1 Introduction

Over the past ten years, the amount of video content generated surpasses the amount of video that can be consumed as it is above the cognitive load that humans can handle. In this respect, automated systems that search for the most interesting parts and highlights in videos are particularly useful. Event streaming platforms have developed AI video analysis tools [1] to provide users the ability to watch a video event's highlights or its more interesting parts. This approach can estimate audience engagement per time

© The Author(s), under exclusive license to Springer Nature Switzerland AG 2023
H. Degen et al. (Eds.): HCII 2023, LNCS 14059, pp. 268–287, 2023.
https://doi.org/10.1007/978-3-031-48057-7_17

slot and subsequently recommend the most interesting parts and highlights in the video under interest. Furthermore, it provides crucial information about the attendees' poses, emotions, or sound events, coming only from video content analysis. It relies on AI methods for keyframe extraction, face detection, pose and emotion estimation, sound event detection, and view prediction. This paper proposes a novel evaluation of the user experience, customer satisfaction, and AI acceptance that can be used in AI video analysis platforms. Except for this, the methodology examines whether audience analysis is useful for users of similar video streaming platforms. The video content is originated from various events such as conferences, workshops, courses, etc. The end users are channel owners responsible for organizing events and event stakeholders consisting of individuals participating in these events.

In general, questionnaire surveys are a standard tool used in many disciplines for evaluation or measuring factors. They are used in eHealth, in education, in user experience evaluation, and many other fields. Yokoi et al. 2021 [2] used questionnaires to evaluate the trust in an AI system that belongs to the health field. They researched whether an AI health system is less trusted compared to a doctor when it comes to treatment. Researchers Pakanen et al. 2022 [3] used this kind of survey in medical education to evaluate the methods used for teaching autopsy. Using questionnaires, researchers realized that the autopsy course is essential according to students, but it is not taught properly and should change to become more effective.

In event streaming platforms, usually, there are two types of end-users, including the event stakeholders who enter the platform to watch an event and the event managers who use it to upload and manage their events online. Both categories receive different information and have separate user interfaces; thus, two questionnaire surveys were utilized for the AI platform evaluation. After using models like the TAM, SUS, NPS, and ECSI, insightful conclusions were reached and analyzed. The TAM is used to examine AI acceptance, while the SUS helped in evaluating usefulness. The NPS was used to examine loyalty and the ECSI for perceived usefulness and value. The proposed evaluation methodology can be reapplied in related cases where an AI-enabled video streaming application launches and needs evaluation.

In this research, there is a comparison between TAM and SUS scores and a correlation analysis between their items. Although the experiments are for a particular framework (LiveMedia 2023 [4]), a broader conclusion can be reached regarding the benefits and limitations of AI-based video content analysis in terms of usability and acceptance by different end-user types. Insightful conclusions about the evaluation of a streaming platform that features AI analysis are presented in this study and analyzed. Besides them, this paper introduces the contributions below:

- A novel method for evaluating AI-enabled platforms;
- A novel evaluation model based on SUS, TAM, NPS, and ECSI evaluation models;
- Showcase the high potential of AI-enabled streaming (video conference) platforms;

The remainder of this paper is organized as follows. Section 2 provides an overview of related research, and Sect. 3 provides info about the Audience Analysis framework that will be evaluated by end users. Section 4 provides the evaluation methodology, Sect. 5 provides the results obtained from the study, while conclusions, limitations, and future improvements are drawn in Sect. 6.

2 Related Work

Sridharan et al. 2018 [5] evaluated an online platform in the education field using a fused method consisting of an online survey and telephone interview. They employed statistical analysis, and the outcomes demonstrated that their methodology was appropriate for evaluating an online platform used for education and remarking on the impact it has on its users. Rasool and Dawood (2021) [6], developed a tool to evaluate the Moodle online platform, which is a learning management system. Using questionnaire surveys that were shared with university lecturers and statistical analysis, they managed to examine if the platform is appreciated by its users and at which points it needs improvements.

One of the most widespread approaches for measuring perceived usability is the SUS. It is a standardized questionnaire containing ten five-point items which alternate between positive and negative tones. Lewis 2018 [7] examined the past, present, and future of this scale, stating that it has risen as a top metric of perceived usability. Furthermore, Vlachogianni and Tselios 2022 [8] examined the perceived usability evaluation in the educational technology sector using statistical analysis. Over the years, they noticed a statistically insignificant improvement in perceived usability. Lewis and Sauro 2018 [9] developed regression equations to model the relationship between SUS items and the overall score. Researchers used statistical analysis and a dataset of 166 unpublished industrial usability surveys to create a table that includes the regression equations and item benchmark for each SUS item. Xiong et al. 2020 [10] developed an open-source application for SUS surveys, which decreased the completion time from 300 s to 36 s. Pal and Vanijja 2020 [11] used the SUS to evaluate the perceived usability of Microsoft Teams as an online learning platform. They also used the TAM to streamline and unify the usability evaluation. The two examined methodologies showed similarity and equivalency with the Perceived Ease of Use (PEOU) being the most similar to the SUS.

The TAM analyzes how people accept and employ a specific technology. According to it, when a new technology presents to users, a variety of factors affect their decision about how and when they will use it. Na et al. 2022 [12] explored the influencing end-users factors and acceptance of AI technology in construction companies using TAM and Technology-Organization-Environment (TOE). After using statistical analysis, the results demonstrated that technological traits and personality positively impact Perceived Usefulness (PU) and PEOU. Al-Emran et al. 2018 [13] systematically reviewed and synthesized TAM studies related to mobile learning to provide an analysis of 87 research papers. Their findings included that most studies extended the TAM with external variables. Taherdoost 2018 [14] developed an e-service TAM to assess user acceptance. After using descriptive statistics, the results revealed that quality, security, and satisfaction significantly affect the intention to use and the e-service technology acceptance.

NPS is a typical market research metric based on a question that asks respondents to assess how likely it is to recommend a product, company, or service to a colleague or friend. NPS and SUS were combined by Sasmito et al. 2019 [15] to measure the population information systems' appropriateness in the city of Tegal. Yanfi et al. 2022 [16] combined the SUS and NPS to measure student satisfaction and loyalty to Microsoft

Power Bi. Results show that the SUS score was 51 and NPS below 6, proving that students were not satisfied and loyal to the application.

Yoo et al. 2022 [17] developed and evaluated an AI robot system for inpatients. Using statistical analysis, they effectively assessed the system's perceived usefulness, ease of use, and user satisfaction. Zwakman et al. 2021 [18] proposed a methodology for evaluating AI-based voice assistants. After checking if the SUS suits voice scenarios, they found its lack in some items, so they changed it, creating another scale called Voice Usability Scale (VUS). SUS and NPS were combined to study user satisfaction and potential loyalty of event viewers to contributing live content through a mobile application (Ntoa et al. 2021 [19]), revealing that although users were generally satisfied with the application they would mostly remain 'passives' in terms of further promoting it to others.

3 Backbone of the Evaluated Audience Analysis

This Section provides the framework used for audience analysis. It is working at the backend of the platform that users should evaluate. It is part of previous work (Vrochidis et al. 2021 [20]) and is included for completeness. It analyzes events conducted with a physical, online, or hybrid presence. Its main goal is to infer whether a video is interesting and important for users, utilizing audience engagement and reactions.

In Fig. 1 an abstract sequence diagram of the audience analysis work, with the information flow among the proposed system components, is shown. Its input is an event video from the streaming platform, and then the image and audio features are fused using a linear regression model. Afterward, highlights, video score, and views prediction, are provided to the channel manager. A channel manager can then decide which one will be provided to the stakeholders. Except for them, the attendance time, from physical and online presence, can be provided to the stakeholders. The novel proposed evaluation starts with sharing two separate questionnaires for both user types and is followed by the response analysis.

Firstly, there are determined the various scenes in the input video, which is uploaded by a channel manager. After scene detection, N keyframes are extracted for each distinct one. All of the video content analysis is based on those frames; thus, computational load and processing time are reduced. In the sequence, the face detection module (Deng et al. 2020 [21]) receives frames for each scene and detects the appeared faces. The pose of each participant is then estimated using the HopeNet model (Ruiz et al. [22]), and the emotion estimation follows using the JAA-Net (Shao et al. 2021 [23]), trained with the DISFA dataset (Mavadati et al. 2013 [24]). A fusion with the sound analysis results follows using a Convolutional Neural Network (CNN) (Vafeiadis et al. 2017 [25]) trained with a custom dataset. Based on features from this fusion, the popularity of each video in terms of views is forecasted using a linear regression model. The sound score and forecasted popularity are then fused to provide a video score presented in (1):

$$R = V + A \tag{1}$$

where R is the video rate, V stands for the predicted views, and A for the sound score, which is based on the existing audio events like claps, pauses, or speech. A user may

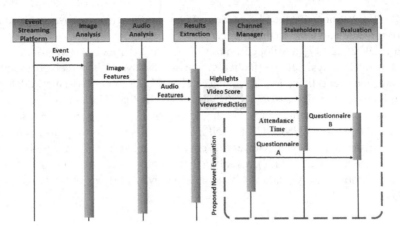

Fig. 1. The sequence diagram of the proposed system.

use it to sort videos by it or to learn additional information about them. Except for these functions, the fusion's features are used to define the video highlights. This evaluation methodology will study whether these factors are significant for users. The platform has two end-user types including the channel managers who upload the event videos and the stakeholders who visit the streaming platform to watch them.

This framework is integrated into the LiveMedia platform through a cloud service and using it, channel managers could generate video highlight moments and video scores or estimate the video's future popularity. Channel managers have access to a platform interface where they can choose to provide the event stakeholders with this information. Stakeholders interact with a different interface than channel managers, which is the reason for creating two different evaluation questionnaires.

4 Proposed Evaluation Methodology

This Section describes the proposed evaluation methodology that combines complementary metrics from the bibliography, starts from targeted questionnaires for the different user types of the system, and can be reapplied for evaluating similar deep learning frameworks. It contains details about the process, the used questionnaires, and their models. For ease of comprehension, the questionnaires will be named questionnaire A and B. Questionnaire A focuses on channel managers, while B on events' stakeholders.

4.1 Aims and Evaluation Setup

To examine the user's perspective, two novel questionnaire surveys that fuse some of the best features of different models were used. The methodology's primary goal is to aid the evaluation of AI-enabled video streaming platforms. The evaluation focuses on the end-user perspective and not on technical benchmarks as has been reported in Vrochidis et al. 2021 [1]. One of its goals is to provide information about the service quality and whether the AI features seem intriguing to the users. Another critical objective is whether

AI features make users choose a particular platform over others that don't use similar technologies, as well as investigating their concerns about personal data use.

In accordance with the Human-Centered AI paradigm (Margetis et al. 2021 [26]), it needs to be studied whether a new platform using AI improves user experience or does not offer any additional improvement as developed. Also, one goal is to take feedback about possible changes that can improve the audience analysis system. Another goal is to examine the interface to see if it meets the platform users' requirements. Each area separately will provide important information that will lead to a better understanding of the platform performance, featuring new parameters which were not measured before. These are the reasons that make the novel fused evaluation methodology significant. The survey questions must be understandable to users and give a clear view of each field separately without confusing categories.

The novel evaluation methodology starts with the experiment's goals explanation and the participation form, where participants consent for the overall data processing. The questionnaires follow the rules and standards of the General Data Protection Regulation (GDPR) (Voigt and Von dem Bussche 2017 [27]). In this initial form, they are briefed on the project aims, which involve the new platform and the new AI features it has. In addition to the purpose, through this form, users are informed about the confidentiality of their data, plus contact information, in case they have an objection or want to address a question to the survey manager. They are also assured that their answers are confidential. Finally, users should consent that their data can be utilized and processed for research purposes in an anonymous and aggregated manner.

The proposed methodology has been applied on an audience analysis platform illustrated in Fig. 2 where the difference between the stakeholder's and the channel manager's user interface is presented. In questionnaire A, the channel manager submits a consent form, watches a video with all the backend techniques, and then fills out the survey. The channel managers should also check the event hosting platform. The event hosting is accessed only by channel managers and helps them control their event by uploading videos, using the available AI features, and showing insightful event information. On the other hand, stakeholders submit the consent form, after which they are sent to the platform. After checking the new features, they complete questionnaire B.

To start the evaluation setup an introductory video should be created to explain the overall framework and its operations. Its purpose is to emphasize some details so the channel managers will have a holistic view and through this, help the questionnaire results' validity. Afterward, the collection of the candidates' questionnaire items should start, and the thematic axes should be built. The selection of the most suitable ones follows. These are the questions that cover the survey aims, and alongside they are clear without redundancies. The target is to keep the duration short to be answered by as many users as possible without tiring them. The chosen questions should be straightforward and include the entire methodology scope, so there will be a complete evaluation of the entire platform and each AI feature separately.

4.2 Proposed Novel Evaluation Models

Questionnaire A starts with demographics (gender, age, education, experience) and continues by examining AI acceptance using the TAM Model (Ntoa et al. 2021 [28])

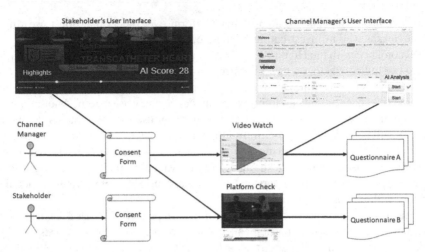

Fig. 2. The evaluation process flow chart.

(Paramythis et al. 2010 [29]). Then, a question regarding concerns follows, and next, the perceived value is examined using the ECSI model (Askariazad and Babakhani 2015 [30]). Loyalty is then examined using the NPS model (Yanfi et al. 2022 [16]). The questionnaire concludes with two open-type questions about what the users liked or did not like about the platform.

Questionnaire B starts with demographics (gender, age, education, experience) and continues examining the platform usability using the SUS model (Pal and Vanijja 2020 [11]). Then perceived usefulness and value are investigated using ECSI, and continuously, loyalty is analyzed using NPS. Two open-type questions are also concluding this questionnaire to examine what users liked and what they did not.

A model used is the ECSI (Askariazad and Babakhani 2015 [30]), which is a model that examines the quality, perceived quality, and perceived value user expectations. Apart from these, it contains thematic questions regarding usage factor analysis and customer loyalty. The evaluation methodology belongs to the customer satisfaction category, where the end-users are customers. The reason ECSI and some related metrics were studied is that it determines how good a company's products or services are and how well they meet customer expectations. It is among the most crucial indicators of purchase intentions and customer loyalty. Therefore, it can contribute significantly to the methodology evaluation by end-users. Usually, it uses a score called Customer Satisfaction Score, which contains a scale of 5 points. This model helped in the building of some questions included in the questionnaire of channel owners and stakeholders.

Another used model is the SUS. It was used in the system evaluation made by the stakeholders. It is a fast and reliable tool for measuring usability. It consists of 10 questions, which in this evaluation case had a scale from 1–5. It works in a wide variety of evaluations, both for products and services. This tool is also suitable for software evaluation and has several benefits, such as the fact that it can perform well with small samples, providing reliable results. It works great with the distinction between usable and unusable systems. For each of the ten questions, there is a score, and depending on the participant's answers, the final score is obtained. According to the system, the baseline score is 68 in most cases. That means that any example with a score above 68 is considered good. When the score is below 68, the quality of the product is not so good. Of course, the situations are not always the same, and more parameters should be considered regarding the score and the customers' perception of a product.

The metrics used to analyze the SUS questionnaires are common statistical metrics like the mean and the standard deviation. The mean shows the central tendency, while the standard deviation indicates how much a data group may vary or be dispersed. Also, the standard error is computed to show how much the population mean may differ from the sample mean. After knowing the metrics above, they are utilized to calculate the 95% Confidence Interval (CI). First, the *t-value* is found using the appropriate table, and then it is multiplied with SE. The result gives the upper and the lower limits. The upper limit is given by the sum of the mean and the result provided, while the lower limit is given by the subtraction of the mean and the result.

The questionnaire A has been based on the TAM. TAM appeared to best suit the assessment needs of this particular category of end-users and was therefore chosen. It is an information systems theory that models how users accept and use technology. Behavioral intention is a factor that leads people to use technology. Through this model, this intention can be detected and can show the general impression of the technology. According to the model, when a new technology is presented to users, several factors influence their decision about how and when to use it. Two main categories of factors are perceived usefulness and perceived ease of use. The first category concerns to which extent a person believes using a particular system will enhance their work efficiency. If the user perceives that the technology is doing what they want, then the chances of using it are high.

Lewis and Sauro 2018 [9] describes a formula that can be used to correlate the TAM items for perceived usefulness and perceived ease of use with the SUS score. The following formulas determine the TAM score:

$$PU = \left(\frac{\sum pu}{N} - 1\right) * \frac{100}{6} \tag{2}$$

$$PEU = \left(\frac{\sum peu}{N} - 1\right) * \frac{100}{6} \tag{3}$$

where *PU* stands for perceived usefulness, *PEU* for perceived ease of use, and *N* is the questions' population.

The second category indicates the degree to which a person believes that using a particular system does not require much effort from the user. In essence, it shows whether the technology is easy to use. If an application is complex and does not contain simple interfaces, then no one will have a positive attitude towards it, and as a result, potential users will not prefer it and move to possible alternatives. In addition to these two categories, there are external variables such as social influence, which is another important factor in determining user attitude. If these variables are positive, the individual, according to the specific model, will be able to use the technology. The perception, of course, can change depending on gender, age, and other factors, as every person is different. It is the reason for including demographics in both questionnaires.

Another examined and used model is the NPS. Its item is located at the end of each questionnaire to measure customer loyalty with an easy question. It is a widely adopted metric used by managers as an understanding measure of customer mindsets about a business. The question addressed to the participants is how likely they are to recommend the company to other colleagues or friends. In the case of this study, it has been modified for the evaluation needs, and the participants are asked whether they are likely to suggest the audience analysis framework to their colleagues or a friend.

The used question includes a 1 to 10 scale and follows a certain logic, according to which there are three customer categories. In the first category are the detractors of a business, who are unhappy with it and are very likely to spread negative word of mouth to their friends and colleagues. The first category includes the participants who answered the question from 0 to 6, while the second contains those from 7 to 8. This category refers to the passive customers of a company who are receptive to receiving offers from other companies and are left out of the NPS calculation. The last category includes those who answered with a score of 9 to 10 and belong to the supporters' category. It contains loyal customers who are committed to the company. They fuel viral growth by word of mouth and recommend the company to their friends and colleagues. The final NPS score can be given by the formula (4) below:

$$NPS = \frac{\left(\sum \text{pr} - \sum^{\text{de}}\right)}{S} \tag{4}$$

where NPS is the Net Promoter Score, pr represents the number of the promoters, de the number of detractors, while S is the total sample size.

In detail, questionnaire A uses TAM questions from Ntoa et al. 2021 [28] and Paramythis et al. 2010 [29] but with a difference to fit the evaluation purposes. The difference is that in some questions, there was a particular sub-question for each used AI technology. In QA2.1, the survey focuses on behavioral intention, and in QA2.2, it focuses on usefulness. Relevance and perceived ease of use are then examined in QA2.5–QA2.6 and QA2.7–QA2.9, respectively. Quality and perceived effectiveness are examined in QA2.10, while interpretation and trust follow. All these questions came from the TAM model. Then a question about concerns follows. It is not coming from a specific model, but it proves to be useful. Perceived Value follows, using changed questions from ECSI (Askariazad and Babakhani 2015 [30]). Again, multiple sub-questions were added to include the used technologies. The last question comes from NPS (Yanfi et al. 2022 [16]) and examines loyalty.

Questionnaire B is based on the SUS model (Pal and Vanijja 2020 [11]). It is used from QB2.1–QB2.10 and examines behavioral intention in QB2.1, perceived ease of use QB2.2–QB2.4, QB2.7–QB2.8, QB2.10, efficiency QB2.5–QB2.6 and satisfaction in QB2.9. Next, the perceived usefulness and value are examined by modifying the questions from ECSI (Askariazad and Babakhani 2015 [30]). The modifications were about the factors that a user might find helpful. Lastly, loyalty follows using NPS (Yanfi et al. 2022 [16]).

5 Evaluation Results

After explaining the fused evaluation models and their purpose, this Section describes the appliance of the survey on a video streaming platform that uses AI analysis to improve its users' experience. The results and correlations between the items of the models and their scores are provided.

5.1 Proposed Novel Evaluation Models

Questionnaire A is about the Channel managers. They have access to more features than the event stakeholders, which is the reason for creating a separate questionnaire. The total number of channel managers who completed the survey was 26. They were split equally between males and women. The majority of the participants belong to the age of 36−50 (42.3%), followed by the age of 21−35 (38.5%) and under 20 (11.5%). The age slot with fewer participants is over 51 (7.7%). Regarding education, the majority of participants (42.3%) held a bachelor's degree, followed by a post-secondary education (23.1%) and a master's degree (19.2%). Then there is primary or secondary education (11.5%) and Ph.D. (3.8%).

Furthermore, the majority (61.5%) of the participants have "*a lot of experience*" in using the platform, some of them (15.4%) have "*less experience*", while the 11.5% have "*little experience*". There were no users with "*no experience*" in this category. The next question concerns the experience with statistical event analysis on the existing platform. The majority of participants (38.5%), have "*too much platform experience*", some of them (23.1%) have "*a lot of experience*", followed by the "*average experience*" category (19.2%), and the "*little experience*" category (11.5%), while some users (7.7%) had "*no experience*" at all. After that, a question asking the professional status followed. The majority of the responses, however diverse, focused on the roles of programmer, computer technician, and project manager. The demographics demonstrate the population variety that helps in better results. Additionally, the fact that users have too much platform experience makes it easier to assess how it changes with the new additional features and where they contribute.

According to Eqs. (2) and (3), the TAM score is 90 for perceived usefulness and 86.16 for perceived ease of use. It proves that channel managers believe that the approach is helpful and that the environment is easy to use. The items of questionnaire A use the TAM model, and their metrics are shown in Table 1. All of the questions used the Likert scale from 1−7. QA2.4 is examined but excluded from the table for the sake of brevity.

QA2.9, which concerned the perceived quality, had less distance from the ideal. It shows that the users believe the quality is high, which is very important. All the answers had a high mean close to the ideal, and the one with the further distance was the question QA2.7, which belongs to the perceived ease of use category. It demonstrates that some users think they need much mental effort to use the channel management platform, which is the first factor that should be developed in the future. The usability of each used technology has also been examined in detail. In this case, those technologies were keyframe extraction, face detection, pose and emotion estimation, sound analysis, interest estimation, highlight detection, views, and video score prediction. Users rated highlight detection as having the best usefulness, followed by face detection, sound

Table 1. Questionnaire's A items and their metrics.

Measured Items	Mean	SD	SE	95% CI
QA2.1: As long as I have access to the system, I intend to use it	6.34	0.93	0.18	5.96 – 6.72
QA2.2: I believe the system is useful in my work	6.42	0.94	0.18	6.04 – 6.80
QA2.3: Using the system increases efficiency in my work	6.38	0.98	0.19	5.98 – 6.78
QA2.5: In my work, system usage is relative	6.19	1.35	0.26	5.64 – 6.73
QA2.6: In my work, the use of the system is important	6.23	1.24	0.24	5.72 – 6.73
QA2.7: My interaction with the system is clear and understandable	6.15	1.04	0.20	5.73 – 6.57
QA2.8: My interaction with the system does not require much mental effort	6.07	1.09	0.21	5.63 – 6.51
QA2.9: I think the system is easy to use	6.30	0.88	0.17	5.95 – 6.66
QA2.10: The quality of the results I get from the system is high	6.50	0.70	0.13	6.21 – 6.78

analysis, and interest estimation. The less useful seemed to be the emotion estimation technique. The highest SD and SE were presented in QA2.5 and showed a 95% CI of 5.64 - 6.73. It shows the higher response diversity in the job and tool relevance item.

The same modules were then assessed based on how effectively they completed their tasks. Face detection stood out in this question which confirmed that the high accuracy of the face detection module became clear to the users, while the perceived accuracy was also the highest among the modules. The emotion estimation seemed not to be as effective as the others, which also has the lowest accuracy compared to other modules due to the difficulty in its task. Similar were the results concerning the reliability that the results provide to users according to the given interpretation. Again, face detection seemed more reliable, followed by sound analysis. The less reliability seemed to be provided by the emotion estimation module. Then a question asked the users if they trust the results of each module.

Face detection and sound analysis seemed to inspire confidence in users, while emotion analysis seemed to have lower results. All these answers confirm the experimental module results that counted their f1 scores (Vrochidis et al. 2021 [1]). They demonstrate that emotion estimation is not a mature enough technology that can gain users' confidence.

More analysis was made according to the demographics and their correlation with specific items. First, there was an analysis of the participants' profession and the relevance (QA2.5) and importance (QA2.6) in their job. Four categories (managers, computer scientists, freelancers, and economists) were formatted, and then a mean for each was calculated. The highest relevance was in the management sector, with a mean of 6.6, while the less was in the economists, with 4.75. The importance was again higher according to managers, with a mean of 6.6, and less according to economists, with 5.

The next studied relationship is between age and usefulness (QA2.3). The age slot of 36−50 had the highest mean of 6.63, followed by 51 + with 6.5, <20 with 6.3, and 21−35 with 6.1. It indicates that older people believe the tool helps them increase their work efficiency more than younger. An association between age and quality followed. Again, people of higher age seem to have higher means, and younger had lower. The highest was at 51 + with a 7 mean, followed by 36−50 with 6.63, 21−35 with 6.4, and <20 with 6.

This questionnaire includes a question about computer vision technologies for video analysis and the possible risks regarding personal data they have. This question had a mean of 3.34, showing that users believe there are risks and that high-quality methods ensuring privacy should treat their data. Afterward, there is a question regarding the preference of a platform that uses AI technologies over another that does not. The mean of 4.15 (close to ideal 5) demonstrates that most users will prefer such a platform. It shows that a modern platform must incorporate AI technologies to be efficient and have satisfied customers.

The factors that encourage a participant to use the system are then analyzed. The factors included are the execution time, easy-to-use environment, statistics, related videos, and view prediction. The user-friendly environment attracts users more than the execution time, which achieved lower results. The questionnaire's A NPS score is 85%. There were no detractors in this category, and there were only 4 passives and 22 promoters, resulting in this high NPS. It shows that the job made in backend analysis is appreciated by channel owners and helps them with their job, so they like to recommend the platform to their colleagues.

The novel evaluation concludes with two open-type questions asking what the participants liked or not. These two questions are not mandatory to answer. The number of answers that claimed what the users appreciated was 10, with 38.46%. The quick analytical speed, the automation offered, and some technologies used, such as face detection, were among the noted points. The interest estimation was also among the answers, together with the innovation that the new features bring to the platform. Another fact that the channel managers liked is how easy it was to analyze the video without difficult parameters that the user has to define.

As for the disliked facts, there were 4 answers giving a 15.38% over the overall answers. One comment states that when the speaker knows he is subject to all this analysis, he may not be as comfortable or free as he would like in his speech. Among the responses were worries regarding sentiment analysis and future analyses of personal data.

Table 2 presents the hypotheses made. In questionnaire A, only correlations with R > 0.850 and p < 0.001 are presented for $\alpha = 0.001$. These indicate that the correlations are strong and significant. The correlations of Questionnaire A were analyzed, providing some useful conclusions. The question item with the highest correlation was about the relativeness of the system usage (QA2.5) with the participant's work, and it was correlated with its importance (QA2.6) in it (R = 953, p = 000, α = 0.01), verifying hypothesis 1.

Table 2. Hypotheses table and their definitions.

Variables	Hypotheses	Definition
Relevance	H1	The system relevance will positively influence its importance
	H2	The system's efficiency will positively influence the perceived usefulness
Perceived ease of use	H3	A system that does not require much mental effort correlates positively with being clear and understandable
	H4	An easy-to-use system correlates positively with a system that does not require much mental effort
	H5	An easy-to-use system correlates positively with a system that is clear and understandable
Perceived satisfaction	H6	The AI features will influence positively users' perceived satisfaction
	H7	User experience will be positively correlated with users' perceived satisfaction
Loyalty	H8	Users who think they will frequently use the system correlate positively with the system's recommendation to their friend
	H9	The perceived improvement will positively influence the recommendation of the platform to friend

Table 3. The highest correlations for questionnaire A.

Question 1	Question 2	Relevance
In my work, system usage is relative (QA2.5)	In my work, system usage is important (QA2.6)	R = .953, p = 000, α = 0.01
Using the system increases efficiency in my work (QA2.3)	I believe the system is useful in my work (QA2.2)	R = .922, p = 000, α = 0.01
My interaction with the system does not require much mental effort (QA2.8)	My interaction with the system is clear and understandable (QA2.7)	R = .885, p = 000, α = 0.01
I think the system is easy to use (QA2.9)	My interaction with the system does not require much mental effort (QA2.8)	R = .867, p = 000, α = 0.01
I think the system is easy to use (QA2.9)	My interaction with the system is clear and understandable (QA2.7)	R = .864, p = 000, α = 0.01

The second correlation was between the efficiency increase in participants' work (QA2.3) and the system's usefulness (QA2.2) (R = 922, p = 000, α = 0.01), which supports hypothesis 2. The question asking if the system and user interaction requires much mental effort (QA2.8) correlates positively with the clear and understandable interaction (QA2.7) (R = 885, p = 000, α = 0.01), which supports hypothesis 3. Then the thought that the system is easy to use (QA2.9) correlates with the mental effort about using the system (QA2.8) (R = 867, p = 000, α = 0.01) supporting hypothesis 4 and with the understandable interaction question (QA2.7) (R = 864, p = 000, α = 0.01), supporting hypothesis 5. These results (Table 3) show that users who think the tool is relative to their work think it is also important, so they will use it because they think it is useful and increases their efficiency. They also prove that an easy-to-use system should not require much mental effort and should be clear and understandable.

5.2 Event Stakeholders' Questionnaire Analysis

The Stakeholders' evaluation was completed successfully by 54 participants, of whom 44.4% were men and 55.6% were women. The majority of the participants were at the age of 21–35 (46.3%), followed by the age of 36–50 (27.8%), under 20 (22.2%), and over 51 (3.7%). Most participants belong to the bachelor's education category (44.4%), followed by the primary or secondary and master category (18.5%), the post-secondary (14.8%), and the Ph.D. (3.7%). As for the previous platform experience, most participants belong to the "*too much experience*" category (43.4%), followed by "*no experience*" (30.2%). After them, "*little experience*" and "*a lot of experience*" follow (9.4%). The last category has an "*average experience*" (7.5%).

The achieved SUS score is 82.1. According to Lewis and Sauro 2018 [9], this score is considered excellent and belongs to the second-best category of the curved grading scale for the SUS they provide. There are eleven categories in total. The high SUS score demonstrates the high perceived service value and shows that users like it. According to Vlachogianni and Tselios 2022 [8], the mean SUS for internet platforms is 66.25, with a standard deviation of 12.42. The fact that the measured score is much higher than this attests to the high perceived usability of the platform. It demonstrates that people like the platform and will recommend it to their friends. The TAM scores were higher, proving that channel managers value and find the newly given features more advantageous than event stakeholders.

After calculating the SUS score, some metrics were also calculated to provide more info about the results. The distance between the mean and the ideal values (1 or 5, depending on the question) was calculated. It demonstrates the times with the most or less liked features. The closest to ideal values were QB2.8, QB2.4, and QB2.10. The first two belong to the perceived ease of use, while the last belongs to perceived learnability. It shows that the application is perceived as easy to use by most of the evaluation participants. The items with the farthest distance were QB2.1, QB2.5, and QB2.6. The first belongs to perceived satisfaction, while the last two belong to perceived consistency. Although they do not differ more than a single unit, they are proved to be the items that need further development. Item QA2.6, which concerns the system's inconsistency, has the highest standard deviation and the highest standard error. Thus, it has the highest confidence interval with a distance of 0.67 between the highest and the lowest limit. These metrics are provided in Table 4.

Table 4. Questionnaire's B SUS items and their metrics.

Measured Items	Mean	SD	SE	95% CI
QB2.1: I think that I would like to use this system frequently	4.09	0.93	0.12	3.83–4.34
QB2.2: I found the system unnecessarily complex	1.70	0.98	0.13	1.43–1.97
QB2.3: I thought the system was easy to use	4.25	0.87	0.11	4.02–4.49
QB2.4: I think that I would need the support of a technical person to be able to use this system	1.57	0.94	0.12	1.31–1.83
QB2.5: I found the various functions in this system were well integrated	4.11	0.90	0.12	3.86–4.35
QB2.6: I thought there was inconsistency in this system	1.75	1.24	0.16	1.42–2.09
QB2.7: I would imagine that most people would learn to use this system quickly	4.16	0.86	0.11	3.90–4.40
QB2.8: I found the system cumbersome to use	1.40	0.85	0.11	1.17–1.64
QB2.9: I felt confident using the system	4.31	0.84	0.11	4.08–4.54
QB2.10: I needed to learn a lot of things before I could get going with this system	1.66	1.04	0.14	1.38–1.95

The correlation of age with ease of use (QB2.3) was also examined. Users in the age category of < 20 had the highest mean (4.33), followed by 36−50 (4.26), 21−35 (4.24), and 51 + (4). It shows that younger ages believe the system is easy and that older people find it more demanding to interact with the system. All the categories have a high mean close to the ideal (5), which shows that users find the system easy to use. 1.42−2.09 and proves that this question had the highest question variance.

The highest SD (1.24) and SE (0.16) were in QB2.6, which is about system inconsistency. Its 95% CI is 1.42−2.09 and proves that this question had the highest question variance.

Except for the SUS questions, there were five more, scoped to provide insightful information. The first was about how beneficial were the new AI technologies for the users. The three newly examined features were the total event watch time, including physical and online attendance, the video highlight moments detection, and the video score. The video highlights were the feature with the most positive feedback overall. The answers had 59.25% for the option "*extremely helpful*", 18.51% for "*very helpful*", and 22.22% for "*enough helpful*". The event watch time had 50% responses in the "*very helpful*" category, 22.22% for "*a lot*", 16.66% for "*enough*", 9.25% for "*a little*", and 1.85% for "*not helpful at all*".

The video score gathered 40.74% for "*extremely helpful*", 25.92% for "*very helpful*", 22.22% for "*enough*", 9.25% for "*a little*", and 1.85% for "*not helpful at all*". This question was followed by one that asked how much improvement the users think the event page experience had with the new AI technologies. Most responses were in the category of "extremely" with 48.1%, followed by "*too much*" with 29.6%. Then, "*enough*" follows with 18.5% and *"little"* and *"no improvement"* with 1.9% each. These two inquiries demonstrate how highly users valued the new capabilities and think they improved the platform. It highlights how crucial AI methods are for these platforms and that they should be integrated in the future in more cases.

The evaluation methodology continues with the NPS question. The questionnaires' B NPS score is 54%. The total number of promoters is 32, the passives are 16, and the detractors are 4. According to Lee 2018 [31], a score above 50 is considered excellent. It is an additional metric demonstrating the platform's potential after enriching with AI technology features. It is crucial to take detractors' feedback to help develop the platform in a way that covers their needs. The two questionnaires comparison reveals that channel owners value the feedback taken from AI methodology more than users. In the future, effort should be put into improving the user interface.

The last questions are optional to fill, and they are purposed to give descriptive details about what the users liked and did not at the platform. Most responses to the question regarding what the users appreciated were about the ease of use, which confirms the results of the previously analyzed metrics. Participants stated that the use was direct. Some users liked the ability to predict the video views and sort the videos accordingly. The clean design, the feature of video highlights, and the event watch time were also among the things that users liked. As for those who did not like it, there were five answers. Results included answers about a redesign to make the new features more prominent. Participants proposed color and other modifications, to emphasize the new features, which created explainability issues for some of them.

After examining the questionnaire B correlation matrix, the strongest correlations were calculated. The highest correlation was between the users who think they would like to use this system frequently (QB2.1) (R = .795, p = 000, α = 0.01) and the extent the event page experience is perceived to have improved with the new technologies (QB4.1), which supports hypothesis 6. A correlation between the users' experience (Demographic question) with the thought that they would like to use this system periodically (QB2.1) presents (R = .742 p = 000, α = 0.01) and supports hypothesis 7. Users who think they would like to use the system frequently (QB2.1) seem to correlate with the platform recommendation to a friend (QB5.1) (R = .707 p = 000, α = 0.01), which supports hypothesis 8. Lastly, the extent of page experience improvement with the new technologies (QB4.1) correlates with the chance of recommending the platform to a friend (QB5.1) (R = .700, p = 000, α = 0.01), which verifies hypothesis 9.

It proves that when users perceive the platform enhancement, they become promoters and are likely to recommend the system, highlighting the importance of continuous improvement. Hypothesis 6 proves that users who were frequently connected to the platform think there are improvements to it, which is crucial. Hypotheses 7 and 8 also prove that experienced users liked the new platform and are willing to recommend it. All correlations were statistically significant at the 0.01 level (p < 0.0001), while Spearman's rank correlation preferred to include non-linear correlations. More correlations are presented in Table 5.

Table 5. The highest correlations for questionnaire B.

Question 1	Question 2	Relevance
I think that I would like to use this system frequently (QB2.1)	How much do you think the event page experience has improved with the new technologies (QB4.1)	R = .795, p = 000, α = 0.01
Previous experience using the existing LiveMedia platform (Demographics)	I think that I would like to use this system frequently (QB2.1)	R = .742, p = 000, α = 0.01
I think that I would like to use this system frequently (QB2.1)	How likely would you be to recommend the LiveMedia Audience Analysis system to a friend (QB5.1)	R = .707, p = 000, α = 0.01
How much do you think the event page experience has improved with the new technologies (QB4.1)	How likely would you be to recommend the LiveMedia Audience Analysis system to a friend (QB5.1)	R = .700, p = 000, α = 0.01

6 Conclusions

This paper proposes an innovative fused evaluation for a streaming platform that employs deep learning frameworks to provide users with insightful features. There were experimental results on a real event streaming platform to see if it meets the demands well. The conclusions provided by both questionnaires were insightful and effectively contributed to this AI-enabled video streaming platform evaluation, proving that this fused methodology could help in similar evaluation cases.

In the experimental results case, questionnaire A shows that channel managers believe the user interface is easy to use and that the new AI technologies contribute much to the platform's evolution. Additionally, the results demonstrate that users are willing to prefer a streaming platform that integrates AI technologies over one that does not. It shows how important it is for a modern platform to incorporate similar technologies to have a lead over the competition. There were strong correlations between the questionnaire's A items, which show that channel managers perceive the approach as essential and related to their work. They think it improves their efficiency and willingness to promote it to their colleagues. They also believe the system is easy to use without requiring much mental effort, thus making it understandable and clear. All this insightful information proves that this fused evaluation methodology can work well in similar cases and provide effective conclusions.

The SUS feature seemed to fully meet the needs of the perceived usability evaluation. In the experimental results case, the SUS score was 82.1, showing high perceived usability. The SUS items mean calculation was proved to give crucial information about the factors that were not so good compared to the others. This was accomplished by calculating the distance of each item's mean with the ideal scores. In the experimental case, the lowest distance items belong to the perceived ease of use and learnability, which demonstrated the easy application use, confirmed by the description feedback stating this thing. The highest distance items concerned the system's inconsistency and proved that it is one of the first sections to improve in the future.

A good feature of this fused evaluation method is that it lets the comparison between TAM and SUS scores, which was proved to provide helpful information. In the experimental results case, it showed that both scores are high and that channel managers find the new AI features more advantageous than event stakeholders. It is additional information that is useful for software and system designers who want to know where to emphasize. The TAM scores were 90 and 86.16 for perceived usefulness and perceived ease of use, respectively. The correlation matrix of questionnaire B confirmed the hypotheses and demonstrated significant relationships between the perceived quality, how AI technologies improved it, and how it affects the platform's promotion by satisfied users.

The NPS score seemed to give intriguing information and proved to be a highly useful feature of the proposed evaluation methodology. For the experimental evaluated platform, the NPS scores were 85% and 54% for questionnaires A and B, respectively, demonstrating that the platform satisfies its users, who are willing to recommend it to friends and colleagues. Dectrators' feedback should be studied to show possible weaknesses to fix. The difference between the two scores can show which platform part needs improvements in the future. In this case, it shows that channel managers appreciate more the results obtained by the AI approach than the stakeholders. It implies that efforts should be made in the future to better suit stakeholders' demands. Apart from this, results demonstrated that similar streaming platforms should make ongoing efforts to ensure that users' AI Analysis data will be handled appropriately to reduce their concerns.

The fused evaluation methodology responded to the initial inquiries and gave satisfactory answers. Participants claimed they were willing to fill out the surveys and that they didn't exhaust them. Results demonstrate the importance of enhancing online video viewing platforms with AI analysis techniques, as users seem to value them highly. The correlations revealed rich conclusions that will help in other AI evaluation future works.

Acknowledgments. Funded by the European Union. Views and opinions expressed are however those of the authors only and do not necessarily reflect those of the European Union. Neither the European Union nor the granting authority can be held responsible for them. MEMENTOES project (Topic: HORIZON-CL2–2021-HERITAGE-01–04, GA 101061496).

Conflicts of Interest. The authors declare no conflict of interest. The funders had no role in the design of the study; in the collection, analyses, or interpretation of data; in the writing of the manuscript; nor in the decision to publish the results.

References

1. Vrochidis, A., Dimitriou, N., Krinidis, S., Panagiotidis, S., Parcharidis, S., Tzovaras, D.: A multi-modal audience analysis system for predicting popularity of online videos. EANN **21**(3), 465–476 (2021)
2. Yokoi, R., Eguchi, Y., Fujita, T., Nakayachi, K.: Artificial intelligence is trusted less than a doctor in medical treatment decisions: influence of perceived care and value similarity. Int. J. Hum.-Comput. Interact. **37**(10), 981–990 (2021)

3. Pakanen, L., Tikka, J., Kuvaja, P., Lunetta, P.: Autopsy-based learning is essential but underutilized in medical education: a questionnaire study. Anat. Sci. Educ. **15**(2), 341–351 (2022)
4. LiveMedia Platform. INVENTICS A.E., Home Page. https://www.livemedia.gr (2023). Accessed 12 Apr 2023
5. Sridharan, S., Bondy, M., Nakaima, A., Heller, R.F.: The potential of an online educational platform to contribute to achieving sustainable development goals: a mixed-methods evaluation of the Peoples-uni online platform. Health Res. Policy Syst. **16**(1), 1–14 (2018)
6. Rasool, J.A., Dawood, S.S.: Evaluate the use of moodle platforms for education in university of Duhok using online survey application. Institutions **2**(5) (2021)
7. Lewis, J.R.: The system usability scale: past, present, and future. Int. J. Hum.-Comput. Interact. **34**(7), 577–590 (2018)
8. Vlachogianni, P., Tselios, N.: Perceived usability evaluation of educational technology using the system usability scale (SUS): a systematic review. J. Res. Technol. Educ. **54**(3), 392–409 (2022)
9. Lewis, J.R., Sauro, J.: Item benchmarks for the system usability scale. J. Usability Stud. **13**(3), 158–167 (2018)
10. Xiong, J., Acemyan, C.Z., Kortum, P.: SUSapp: a free mobile application that makes the system usability scale (SUS) easier to administer. J. Usability Stud. **15**(3), 135–144 (2020)
11. Pal, D., Vanijja, V.: Perceived usability evaluation of microsoft teams as an online learning platform during COVID-19 using system usability scale and technology acceptance model in India. Children Youth Serv. Rev. **119**, 105535 (2020)
12. Na, S., Han, S., Shin, Y., Roh, Y.: Acceptance model of Artificial Intelligence (AI)-based technologies in construction firms: applying the Technology Acceptance Model (TAM) in combination with the Technology–Organisation–Environment (TOE) framework. Buildings **12**(2), 90–107 (2022)
13. Al-Emran, M., Mezhuyev, V., Kamaludin, A.: Technology acceptance model in m-learning context: a systematic review. Comput. Educ. **125**, 389–412 (2018)
14. Taherdoost, H.: Development of an adoption model to assess user acceptance of e-service technology: e-service technology acceptance model. Behav. Inf. Technol. **37**(2), 173–197 (2018)
15. Sasmito, G.W., Zulfiqar, L.O.M., Nishom, M.: Usability testing based on system usability scale and net promoter score. In: International Seminar on Research of Information Technology and Intelligent Systems (ISRITI), pp. 540–545 (2019)
16. Yanfi, Y., Ramadhan, A., Trisetyarso, A., Zarlis, M., Abdurachman, E.: Measuring student's satisfaction and loyalty on microsoft power BI using system usability scale and net promoter score for the case of students at Bina Nusantara university. In: International Conference on Data Science and Its Applications (ICoDSA), pp. 155–160 (2022)
17. Yoo, H.J., Kim, J., Kim, S., Jang, S.M., Lee, H.: Development and usability evaluation of a bedside robot system for inpatients. Technol. Health Care **30**(2), 337–350 (2022)
18. Zwakman, D.S., Pal, D., Arpnikanondt, C.: Usability evaluation of artificial intelligence-based voice assistants: the case of Amazon Alexa. SN Comput. Sci. **2**(1), 1–16 (2021)
19. Ntoa, S., et al.: User generated content for enhanced professional productions: a mobile application for content contributors and a study on the factors influencing their satisfaction and loyalty. Multimedia Tools Appl. **80**(25), 33679–33699 (2021)
20. Vrochidis, A., Dimitriou, N., Krinidis, S., Panagiotidis, S., Parcharidis, S., Tzovaras, D.: Video popularity prediction through fusing early viewership with video content. In: International Conference on Computer Vision Systems, pp. 159–168 (2021)
21. Deng, J., Guo, J., Zhou, Y., Yu, J., Kotsia, I., Zafeiriou, S.: Retinaface: single-stage dense face localisation in the wild. In: Proceedings of the IEEE/CVF Conference on Computer Vision and Pattern Recognition (CVPR), pp. 5203–5212 (2020)

22. Ruiz, N., Chong, E, Rehg, J.M.: Fine-grained head pose estimation without key-points. In: IEEE Computer Vision and Pattern Recognition Workshops, pp. 2074–2083 (2018)
23. Shao, Z., Liu, Z., Cai, J., Ma, L.: JAA-Net: joint facial action unit detection and face alignment via adaptive attention. Int. J. Comput. Vision **129**(2), 321–340 (2021)
24. Mavadati, S.M., Mahoor, M.H., Barlett, K., Trinh, P., Cohn, J.F.: DISFA: a spontaneous facial action intensity database. IEEE Trans. Affect. Comput. **4**(2), 151–160 (2013)
25. Vafeiadis, A., et al.: Acoustic scene classification: from a hybrid classifier to deep learning. In: Proceedings of the Detection and Classification of Acoustic Scenes and Events Workshop (2017)
26. Margetis, G., Ntoa, S., Antona, M., Stephanidis, C.: Human-centered design of artificial intelligence. In: Handbook of Human Factors and Ergonomics, pp. 1085–1106 (2021)
27. Voigt, P., Von dem Bussche, A.: The EU general data protection regulation (gdpr). A Practical Guide, 1st Ed., vol. 10, no. 3152676, pp. 10–5555 (2017)
28. Ntoa, S., Margetis, G., Antona, M., Stephanidis, C.: User experience evaluation in intelligent environments: a comprehensive framework. Technologies **9**(2), 41 (2021)
29. Paramythis, A., Weibelzahl, S., Masthoff, J.: Layered evaluation of interactive adaptive systems: framework and formative methods. User Model. User-Adap. Inter. **20**(5), 383–453 (2010)
30. Askariazad, M.H., Babakhani, N.: An application of European customer satisfaction index (ECSI) in business to business (B2B) context. J. Bus. Ind. Mark. **30**(1), 17–31 (2015)
31. Lee, S.: Net promoter score: using NPS to measure IT customer support satisfaction. In: Proceedings of the 2018 ACM SIGUCCS Annual Conference, pp. 63–64 (2018)

Acceptance of Generative AI in the Creative Industry: Examining the Role of AI Anxiety in the UTAUT2 Model

Ming Yin, Bingxu Han, Sunghan Ryu, and Min Hua(✉)

USC-SJTU Institute of Cultural and Creative Industry, Shanghai Jiao Tong University, Shanghai 200241, China
huamin@sjtu.edu.cn

Abstract. With the boosting entrenchment of Generative artificial intelligence (AI) across the creative markets, little is explored around the opinions of those who are within the influenced industries. How well professionals in the creative domains are viewing and embracing this newly emerged technology awaits verification. Using a survey method, this study shed light on the underpinning factors that could predict professionals' acceptance and usage intention of Generative AI under the status quo. By integrating the expanded Unified Theory of Acceptance and Use of Technology (UTAUT2) model, the study incorporates the dimension of AI anxiety into the framework. Regression analyses reveal that acceptance and usage intention of Generative AI can be predicted by factors including performance expectancy, social influence, hedonic motivation, habit, and AI anxiety, while effort expectancy, facility conditions, and price value cannot predict users' intention yet at current situations. The study shows the importance of the emotional attitudes of users and provides stakeholders with insights to develop Generative AI products to better fit the adaptability of users. Findings suggest that people who are actively involved in the creative and cultural economies favour using Generative AI, even when undergoing AI learning anxiety. Participants with a relatively higher level of education perform with more resilience and stability when faced with AI-related situations, as they are less possible to withdraw from future usage though undergoing the fear of Generative AI products, and they appear to less addictively rely on Generative AI tools despite all the merits.

Keywords: UTAUT · Generative AI · AI anxiety · creative professionals

1 Introduction

On 23 January 2020, a Generative AI algorithm called GPT-3 was reported in two computational biologists' preprints, this AI algorithm helped them to embark on an unusual experiment: to help them enhance their research articles (Pividori & Greene 2023). One of the most well-known Generative AI tools in the past year was ChatGPT, also referred to as a GPT-3 variant. With its convincingly fluent text and claims that it can even produce computer code, this large language model (LLM) captured the attention of the globe (Chatterjee & Dethlefs 2023).

© The Author(s), under exclusive license to Springer Nature Switzerland AG 2023
H. Degen et al. (Eds.): HCII 2023, LNCS 14059, pp. 288–310, 2023.
https://doi.org/10.1007/978-3-031-48057-7_18

After the release of the much-hyped ChatGPT-4 this year, Generative AI and related technologies have been widely acknowledged as disruptive innovations with the potential to revolutionize academic writing (Abd-Elaal et al. 2022; Haque et al. 2022), as well as the way we work and educate (Megahed et al. 2023; Lim et al. 2023). But other than conversational Generative AI, picture Generative AI, such as DALL-E, which was developed by OpenAI and functions similarly to ChatGPT, is another example that contributes to this Generative AI craze. Both ChatGPT and DALL-E, albeit having digital images as outputs, are the results of deep learning (OpenAI 2023). Stable Diffusion, Midjourney, and Dall-E are parts of machine learning that, in learning and responding to input, resemble the human brain (Sahoo et al. 2023). Thus, those in the creative industries have emerged as the key players. Many creative workers, including designers, now employ Generative AI tools regularly, using Stable Diffusion for initial creative work and creating content for commercial bidding. In particular, Generative AI technologies are utilized for writing creatively (Gero and Chilton 2019), free-hand sketching and drawing (Ho et al. 2019), music composing (Huang et al. 2020), and generating digital art (Audry 2021).

Additionally, it is essential to separate Generative AI from related ideas. Although research on AI dates back to the early 1950s (Newell & Simon 1956; Turing 1950), Generative AI is a more recent development that has not received much attention. In Bostrom's definition of "general AI" from 2014, a machine exhibiting complete human intelligence. It was known as narrow AI or weak AI, but previously published technologies were typically limited to operation in one single domain to accomplish constrained tasks. Only a few obvious or notable features are considered to be generated content, reflecting Generative AI's anthropomorphic approach to content generation, which goes beyond the rigid corpus or stock image content generated by narrow AI products in the past. This is according to some researchers who compared texts and images created by Generative AI and works done by humans (Mitrović et al. 2023; Hunt 2023). Users can instantly produce their distinctive renditions of masterpieces by artists like Van Gogh, Dali, Turner, or Monet because of sophisticated algorithms that have learned to duplicate the precise styles, colours, and brushstrokes of well-known artists (Cousins 2023). AI-generated artistic simulacra are being fought by creatives and artists since their invisible content undermines traditional censorship and poses new ethical and legal issues (Appel et al. 2023). Artists and photography agencies are currently suing the developers of some AI art programs, such as Stable Diffusion and Midjourney. In addition, OpenAI and Microsoft (along with its subsidiary tech site GitHub) are being sued for software piracy over the development of their AI coding assistant Copilot (Stokel-Walker & Noorden 2023).

The computer science behind Generative AI is moving so fast that innovations emerge every month, how researchers choose to use them will dictate their, and our, future (Stokel-Walker & Noorden 2023). The first to be impacted are professionals in the creative industries; are their hard-earned creative abilities becoming undervalued and their careers in peril (Cousins 2023)? Keith Rankin, a professional illustrator from the UK, admits to being "shocked" by the quality of the work produced by Midjourney. According to Rankin, AI will soon be used to automatically fill in the majority of the frames in the animation. Given the considerable impact of Generative AI technologies on the careers of those in the creative industries and some worrying facts about their future in the workplace, we address how to measure the degree to which Generative AI products and technologies are accepted by professionals in the creative industries.

2   Related Work

2.1   Creative Industry Professionals as A Target User Group

AI technology and the automation of creative work have received much attention for a long time. The productivity revolution brought on by Generative AI has generated more discussion than ever before, and experts from other fields have started to develop fresh perspectives on Generative AI, some of which are unfavourable. For instance, according to some academics, ChatGPT can result in academic plagiarism (Khalil & Er 2023), copyright fraud (Zhong et al. 2023), and the creation of fake peer review citations (Day 2023). In terms of the professional domains, ChatGPT also proved successful in challenging the professional exam (Gilson et. al. 2023), and it may additionally assist by providing certain expert diagnostic opinions (Liu et. al. 2023). According to a Career Science Lab post by BOSS Zhipin (2023), the largest online employment portal in China, 28% of current jobs on the market require abilities linked to ChatGPT, indicating the impact of Generative AI on professions. So, what effect does Generative AI have on the creative sector?

The application of AI in the creative sector has significantly increased in recent years. Based on data analysis from arXiv and Gateway to Research, Davies et al. (2020) discovered that the growth rate of research papers on AI (related to the creative industry) exceeds 500% in numerous nations. This technology might have a long-term impact on how creative individuals pursue their jobs. To create more complex and high-performing products, generative design, for instance, can reframe the role of the designer in the early stages of the design process (Saadi & Yang 2023). This is done by empowering human designers to work in new, more advanced modes throughout the various stages of the product design process. In light of this, we argue that this fundamental change will enable creative professions to understand generative AI more thoroughly.

We have focused on this user group since previous studies have covered a wide range of topics related to how people in the creative industries use AI technology. As automation advances, AI tools go beyond cooperative robotics (Altavilla & Eric 2020). Rahimi (2020) looked at the various technological acceptance models over the last four decades to gauge how content creators felt about cutting-edge technology. However, Generative AI contains a few accepted publications, but the majority of them come from non-creative user groups, like students (Haensch et al. 2023; Shoufan 2023) and accountants (Kenney 2023). A general knowledge of the acceptability of Generative AI should be conducted by a portrayal of the overall usage intentions of such a population in the creative industries. This study aims to reveal the perspectives of professionals on the experiential usage of Generative AI tools and analyze the underlying explanatory factors that could account for the variation in usage intentions among different people, including designers, writers, and educators.

2.2 The Unified Theory of Acceptance and Utilization of Technology (UTAUT) Model

The Unified Theory of Acceptance and Use of Technology (UTAUT), developed by Venkatesh, Morris, Davis, and Davis in 2003, is a well-known and widely examined theory that attempts to explain the variables impacting people's or users' acceptance and usage of technology in a variety of scenarios (Venkatesh et al. 2003). Since its conception, UTAUT has grown significantly in popularity and has been extensively used in empirical research to examine the factors that influence the adoption of new technologies. Its thoroughness enables researchers to look into different aspects that affect people's adoption and usage of technology, giving them insightful information about the complicated relationships between users and technology. The UTAUT model was designed to predict user behaviour more precisely than earlier models. It combines eight technological adoption, use, and factors. These theories are the theory of reasoned action (TRA) (Fishbein & Ajzen 1975), technology acceptance model (TAM) (Davis 1989), theory of planned behaviour (TPB) (Ajzen 1991), motivational model (Davis, Bagozzi, & Warshaw 1992), model of personal computer utilization (Thompson, Higgins, & Howell 1991), combined TPB/TAM (Taylor & Todd 1995), diffusion of innovation theory (Rogers 1995), and social cognitive theory (Compeau & Higgins 1995). Since its creation, many researchers have examined the UTAUT's effectiveness in use. For instance, Khechine et al. (2016) assessed the model's effectiveness, it indicated that the UTAUT model is the most accurate in the literature on technology adoption.

The UTAUT model highlights important variables, including performance expectancy (PE), effort expectancy (EE), social influence (SI), and facilitating conditions (FC), that predict users' inclination to embrace new technology. Hedonic motivation (HM), price value (PV), and habit (HB) were the three constructs incorporated in the UTAUT2 model, which was proposed in 2012 (Venkatesh et al. 2012). The extensions put out in UTAUT2 go beyond what was done in UTAUT in terms of expanding the parameters for examining user acceptance in the context of consumer situations (Venkatesh 2012). We contend that UTAUT2 adaption is the ideal fit for this research instead of the UTAUT model, given that most Generative AI products are used by customers. To date, many attempts have been made to add new variables to the UTAUT2 model to adapt it to the different industries' settings and explain technology adoption in various situations (Tamilmani et al. 2021). However, due to the extensive conversation regarding AI in this study, we found that researching emotions will help to uncover users' more profound opinions. We are aware of no Generative AI research studies that examined UTAUT2's applicability in the context of the creative industries from the experts' point of view, not to mention the expanded framework or theory of UTAUT2. In contrast, we contend that in the context of Generative AI, from the viewpoint of experts in the field of creative industries, the AI anxiety theory is an additional crucial consideration (Wang & Wang 2019). As such, we combined the AIA theory as an extension of UTAUT2 in this study; we will note more discussion about AIA later.

2.3 AI Anxiety Scale

The phrase "AI anxiety" refers to feelings of fear or agitation about out-of-control artificial intelligence (Johnson & Verdicchio 2017). A wide range of issues has been brought about by AI technology, including job losses, privacy and transparency worries, algorithmic biases, escalating socioeconomic disparities, and immoral behaviour (Green 2020). These difficulties could lead to disturbances that show up as anxiety, particularly in regard to ChatGPT 4.0's release, the Generative AI program for which it took just two months to become a cultural phenomenon.

Technophobia is another frequently studied user attitude towards AI technology (Ha, Page, & Thorsteinsson 2011). Technophobia is defined as an unjustified fear or concern about the effects of modern technology. However, AI fear shouldn't be viewed as a negative attitude towards adopting AI technology because worry may increase one's desire to use AI systems. As opposed to emotional reactions to using technology, an attitude refers to thoughts and attitudes towards computer-related technologies (Heinssen, Glass, & Knight 1984, 1987).

Even though Generative AI technology has been around for a while, the concept of Generative AI anxiety is still relatively new, and there is a gap between how users' attitudes towards Generative AI are reflected in their Generative AI anxiety and how this interacts with the impact of their intention to use Generative AI products. An AI anxiety scale (AIAS), which produced a standardized tool to measure AIA, was modified in this study due to the limited use of existing self-report measures in measuring AIA (Wang & Wang 2019). This AIAS has well-established psychometric properties, which facilitate the work of both AI developers and practitioners, who are responsible for applying and implementing AI technologies and products, (Wang & Wang 2019). To evaluate the potential effects of Generative AI anxiety on users' intention and behaviour, this study used four AIA components (AI learning, job replacement, sociotechnical blindness, and AI configuration) from this scale as moderators.

3 Hypotheses

To describe the behavioural intention to use Generative AI technology and its impact on user behaviour, we incorporated the variables from the UTAUT2 model. The behavioural intention (BI) construct is defined as the willingness of the user to use the system (Davis 1989). The term "system" alludes to a new technological advancement, and in the context of the creative industries, this variable denotes the professionals' intent to adopt Generative AI products or technologies.

The performance expectancy (PE) construct is defined as the perception of the user that using the system will help attain gains in job performance (Venkatesh et al. 2003). In the creative industries context, this variable refers to job performance in the creative industries field, and the job includes visualizers, designers, artists, creative writing workers, educators, etc. The performance expectancy construct is often considered the strongest positive predictor of the behavioural intention to use technology (Venkatesh et al. 2003), performance expectancy was a direct determinant of behavioural intention to use information systems and technologies, having the largest effect size among all constructs of the model (Khechine, Ndjambou, & Lakhal 2016). Accordingly, we propose testing the following hypothesis:

H1: The relationship between performance expectancy and the behavioural intention to use Generative AI products or technology is significant and positive.

The effort expectancy (EE) construct is the perception of ease in using the system (Venkatesh et al. 2003). In the creative industries context, this variable refers to the easiness of use of the Generative AI product or technology by professionals. The relationship between effort expectancy and behavioural intention was often considered to be significant and positive (Venkatesh, Thong, & Xu 2016). The homogeneity relationship has always been tested in researches that adapted TAM or TPB model, so effort expectancy could be understood as perceived ease of use. Therefore, we propose testing the following hypothesis:

H2: The relationship between effort expectancy and the behavioral intention to use the Generative AI product or technology is significant and positive.

The social influence (SI) construct is defined as the perception of the importance that others attach to the use of the system by the user (Venkatesh et al. 2003). Social influence in the creative industries relates to what other coworkers, employees, friends, and family members think about the application of Generative AI. Numerous empirical researches have demonstrated that the intention to utilize new technology is strongly influenced by social influence (Bozan, Parker & Davey 2016; Leow, Phua & Teh, 2021; Qu, Wei & Zhang 2022). In view of this, we suggest putting the following hypothesis to the test:

H3: The relationship between social influence and the behavioral intention to use Generative AI product or technology is significant and positive.

The facilitating conditions (FC) construct refers to the perception of an efficient infrastructure supporting system users (Venkatesh et al. 2003). In the creative industries, FC encompasses hardware (e.g., computers, cameras, writing tools) and software (e.g., Photoshop, Sketch, Maya, Midjourney). The relationship between FC and behavioral intention was found to be significant and positive in the UTAUT2 model (Venkatesh et al. 2012). While some studies suggested a weak relationship, we consider FC essential due to regional restrictions, VPN requirements, and coding knowledge needed for many Generative AI tools. Thus, we hypothesize a positive influence of FC on the intention to use Generative AI in the creative industries (Khechine et al. 2016). We suggest evaluating the following hypothesis in relation to the application in the context of the creative industries:

H4: The relationship between facilitating conditions and the behavioral intention to use Generative AI products or technology is significant and positive.

The hedonic motivation (HM) construct is defined as the fun or pleasure derived from using a technology (Venkatesh et al. 2012). It has been shown to play an important role in determining technology acceptance and use (Brown and Venkatesh 2005). According to the UTAUT2 model, higher hedonic motivation levels tend to be linked to higher behavioural intention levels, which in turn lead to increased consumer technology use in non-organizational situations (Weber 2012). Hedonic motivation describes the enjoyment and satisfaction of using Generative AI technology and applications from the viewpoint of creative industry professionals. So, we suggest putting the following hypothesis to the test:

H5: The relationship between hedonic motivation and the behavioral intention to use Generative AI products or technology is significant and positive.

The price value (PC) construct is the consumers' cognitive tradeoff between the perceived benefits of the applications and the monetary cost of using them (Dodds et al. 1991). When the advantages of utilizing technology are thought to outweigh the financial cost, the price value is positive and has a positive effect on intention (Venkatesh et al. 2012). Given that various Generative AI tools and products are paid for in the context of this research, we take the pricing aspect into consideration. So, we suggest testing the following assertion:

H6: The relationship between price value and the behavioral intention to use Generative AI products or technology is significant and positive.

UTAUT2 theory adopted the conceptual definitions of some habit and experience research, the habit (HB) construct thus had been offered, HB has been shown to have a direct effect on technology use over and above the effect of intention and also to moderate the effect of intention on technology use such that intention is less important with increasing habit (Limayem et al. 2007). In the case of our research setting, this factor could be understood as working experience in creative industries. Thus, the seventh hypothesis that we propose testing is the following:

H7: The relationship between habit and the behavioral intention to use Generative AI products or technology is significant and positive.

3.1 Four Dimensions of AI Anxiety

The AI learning (AL) construct refers to anxiety regarding learning AI technologies (Wang & Wang 2022). They viewed AIA as crippling or enabling anxiety that, to some extent, affects motivated learning behaviour and alters AI's learning behaviour. According to Wang and Wang's research from 2022, people who experience more new technology fear putting more effort and perseverance into developing their professional knowledge and skills. However, given that the participants have varied academic backgrounds, we assume that, in most situations, the users' Generative AI anxiety will prohibit them from using Generative AI. We suggest putting the following hypothesis to the test:

H8: The anxiety concerning Generative AI learning (AL) is negatively related to users' BI of Generative AI.

The job replacement (JP) anxiety refers to the anxiety generated by worrying that AI will replace a wide range of jobs that people are currently employed in (Li & Huang 2020; Wang & Wang 2022). In a study by Kaya et al. (2022), it was discovered that people's worries about job losses brought on by the development of AI technology did not significantly predict either positive or negative attitudes towards AI. This outcome, nevertheless, might differ slightly for professionals. For instance, accounting professionals' levels of work anxiety may vary depending on the types of jobs they are aware will be replaced in the future. In addition, different anxiety factors have a more pronounced impact when dealing with accounting-related tasks that are more likely to be replaced (Chang et al. 2021). Therefore, we argued the following hypothesis:

H9: The anxiety concerning job replacement (JP) is negatively related to users' BI of Generative AI.

The sociotechnical blindness (SB) construct refers to the anxiety arising from a lack of full understanding of the dependence of AI on humans (Wang & Wang 2022). SB was characterized as a failing "to recognize that AI is a system and always and only operates in combination with people and social institutions" by Johnson and Verdicchio (2017). Professionals in the creative sectors are closely related to Generative AI technology in this study, however different levels of SB may be self-reported by different people. Accordingly, we propose the following hypothesis:

H10: The anxiety concerning sociotechnical blindness (SB) over Generative AI usage is negatively related to users' BI of Generative AI.

The AI configuration (AC) expresses fear regarding humanoid AI (Wang & Wang 2022). According to Yuan et al. (2022), anxiety was linked to unfavorable beliefs about interacting with humanoid robots. Even while functioning software is where most Generative AI technology is being applied, some human-like assistants will soon benefit from it. In this study, users' opinions towards Generative AI products may be influenced by the relationship between their conceptions of humanoid AI and social influence. Therefore, we propose the following hypothesis:

H11: The anxiety concerning humanlike characteristics of Generative AI (i.e. AC) is negatively related to users' BI of Generative AI.

4 Method

This study is conducted using cross-sectional survey research. An online questionnaire service platform was authorized for online distribution mainly among creative industry professionals in China. An attention check question was designed for data cleaning after a collection of 468 data samples. Participants that failed the attention task were selected away from the final data pool. In addition, those who filled out the questionnaire with a sequentially repetitive number choosing (more than seven same number selections in sequence) were also considered non-reliable respondents, and removed from the dataset.

Overall, 347 valid samples are used for the following analyses. The sample is composed of 259 female and 88 male participants, among which six people received vocational education as their highest educational experience, 245 have enrolled or are currently enrolled in bachelor programs at universities, 86 are graduates or undergraduate programs, and 10 are doctors or under doctorate programs.

4.1 Measurement

Demographic variables were collected to depict user portraits. In this study, the biological gender, age, received education status, monthly salaries, and working location of professionals in the creative industries were listed. Among these variables, gender and age were taken into account as potential moderators of the relationship between independent variables and users' behavioral intentions. There is a question asking participants to scale from 1 to 7 to clarify their current job's relevance level with the culture and creativity division, where 1 = barely relevant and 7 = extremely relevant.

Independent variables in the aforementioned UTAUT2 model are adopted as predictors in this study. Since The original survey items are developed in English, to adapt to the language-using habits of Chinese participants, the original scripts are interpreted in Chinese and integrated with the research background related to Generative AI usage. Before distribution, we asked researchers in the field of the creative industries to review the translated manuscript to check for any errors or areas of ambiguity. Adopting suggestions from them, the questionnaire was revised again by implementing more descriptive texts to make conceptions clearer to the participants. Users' performance expectancy (PE), effort expectancy (EE), facilitating conditions (FC), and habit (HB) when utilizing Generative AI are measured with respective 4 items. The social influence (SI), hedonic motivation (HM), and price value (PV) that participants encounter during Generative AI use are measured with 3 items each. The dependent variable is users' behavioral intention, which measures whether participants would continue to use Generative AI in their future works, is measured using 3 items. Measurements were conducted with a seven-point Likert scale, from 1 = strongly disagree to 7 = strongly agree, in which larger numbers indicate higher levels of agreement. The average of items under each variable is calculated after the reliability test and confirmatory factor analysis to represent the variable during regression analysis. Bivariate correlation analyses were conducted as follow (Table 1) to explore the potential significant relationships between independent variables (PE, SI, FC, HM, PV, HB, AL, JP, SB, and AC) and the consequential variable (BI).

Table 1. Bivariate correlations between variables.

	PE	SI	FC	HM	PV	HB	AL	JP	SB	AC	BI
PE	1										
SI	.53***	1									
FC	.42***	.52***	1								
HM	.64***	.52***	.52***	1							
PV	.49***	.53***	.55***	.53***	1						
HB	.42***	.45***	.39***	.37***	.53***	1					
AL	.03	.09	.01	.00	.13**	.26***	1				
JP	.10	−.02	−.07	.07	−.01	.00	.44***	1			
SB	.14*	.03	.05	.14**	.03	−.05	.28***	.71***	1		
AC	−.05	−.02	−.17**	−.10	−.07	−.01	.47***	.67***	.52***	1	
BI	.59***	.58***	.51***	.58***	.55***	.66***	.20***	.02	.04	−.12*	1

Note. $* p < .05$, $** p < .01$, $*** p < .001$

During the preliminary analyses, this study verified that Cronbach's Alpha of the aforementioned variables is above 0.7 (Table 2), supporting the reliability of the self-reported data based upon translated survey scale. The means of four items under PE are above 5.0, showing overall high anticipation when using Generative AI tools. Users also show a high expectancy of effort inputs to utilize this newly emerged technology.

Table 2. Results of independent variables adopted from the UTAUT2 scale

Variable	Items	Mean	Std. Dev	Factor Loadings	Cronbach's Alpha
Performance Expectancy (PE)	PE1	5.52	1.16	.72	.90
	PE2	5.21	1.34	.79	
	PE3	5.50	1.33	.80	
	PE4	5.49	1.30	.78	
Effort Expectancy (EE)	EE1	5.15	1.19	.72	.86
	EE2	5.14	1.17	.69	
	EE3	5.51	1.09	.71	
	EE4	5.29	1.19	.81	
Social Influence (SI)	SI1	4.95	1.39	.80	.79
	SI2	4.98	1.47	.74	
	SI3	3.97	1.57	.67	
	SI4	5.35	1.34	.50	
Facilitating Conditions (FC)	FC1	4.97	1.57	.57	.87
	FC2	4.93	1.52	.61	
	FC3	5.02	1.53	.61	
Hedonic motivation (HM)	HM1	5.69	1.21	.52	.85
	HM2	5.52	1.29	.65	
	HM3	5.35	1.38	.58	
Price Value (PV)	PV1	4.58	1.31	.69	.83
	PV2	4.56	1.38	.74	
	PV3	4.73	1.32	.68	
Habit (HB)	HB1	3.99	1.66	.76	.92
	HB2	3.53	1.72	.88	
	HB3	2.82	1.70	.86	
	HB4	3.59	1.79	.84	

Generative AI anxiety is composed of four dimensions, which are the anxiety of learning Generative AI tools (AL), the anxiety of AI configuration (AC), the anxiety of Generative AI's threats of job replacements (JP), and anxiety of sociotechnical blindness (SB) which might lead to disastrous outcomes upon misuse or loss of control. These four dimensions are separately treated as four variables that predict users' behavioral intention. Measurements of them are conducted using 8, 3, 6, and 4 items distinctly. A seven-point Likert scale was adopted from 1 = strongly disagree to 7 = strongly agree to measure participants' anxiety status when faced with Generative AI usage scenarios.

5 Results

5.1 Predictors of Generative AI Usage Intention

The bivariate correlation analysis indicates strong correlations between variables (Table 3). This study conducts the multiple regression analysis using SPSS Statistics version 27. Participants with higher performance expectancy towards Generative AI approximately hold higher future usage intention ($\beta = .15$, $p < .01$). Effort expectancy shows a significant association with users' intention of future Generative AI utilization ($\beta = .09$, $p < .05$), which aligns with the previous empirical research evidence. Thus, H1 and H2 are supported. The social influence that participants receive proves significantly related to users' BI ($\beta = .16$, $p < .001$). It illustrates that people who expose themselves under more social persuasion stand a higher chance of adopting Generative AI tools for future job uses. Consequently, H3 cannot be rejected. It is also predicted that there exists a significant association between HM and BI in users ($\beta = .16$, $p < .01$), indicating those who entertain by the utilization of Generative AI are more likely to continue using such novel technologies. Accessibility and facilitating conditions, and the pricing states of current Generative AI products present no significant relationship with BI. Therefore, H4 and H6 are rejected. It is also demonstrated in the results that participants who are used to or have already cultivated habits of Generative AI usage during work potentially show a higher intention of future utilization ($\beta = .39$, $p < .001$). H7 is therefore supported.

In this study, AI anxiety is evaluated in particular with a concentration on four dimensions. Those who experience more anxiety when learning Generative AI tools tend to show more willingness in future usage of such tools ($\beta = .14$, $p < .001$), which contradicts H8. However, participants that worry more about job replacement attributed to Generative AI's popularization fail to appear less interested in future usage, which indicates that there were no associations in particular between JP and BI. H9 thus was rejected. Next, anxiety concerning social blindness does not contribute to participators' utilization intention. H10 thus was rejected. In terms of Generative AI interaction, data shows that whoever finds the functionalities of Generative AI terrifying display less willingness to adopt this tool in working scenarios ($\beta = -.19$, $p < .001$). All in all, H11 is supported (Tables 4 and 5).

5.2 The Moderating Effect Explorations

Moderating effects were analyzed using hierarchical regression analyses and PROCESS. The study performed linear regression analysis, inputting BI in the dependent variable column, while age and monthly income as demographic variables in block 1, followed by AC, education, and AC x education sequentially in the three following blocks. Results

Table 3. The coefficients of independent variables and the consequential variable

	Behavioral Intention
Block1: Demographic variables	
Age	.12
Income	.04
R-square	.02
ΔR-square	.02
Block2: Independent variables	
Age	.11**
Income	−.01
PE	.16***
EE	.05
SI	.15***
FC	.05
HM	.15**
PV	.03
HB	.39***
AL	.13**
JP	.06
SB	.05
AC	−.20***
R-square	.66
ΔR-square	.64

Note. $*p < .05, **p < .01, ***p < .001$

indicate that AC ($\beta = -.12$, p < .05), education ($\beta = .13$, p < .05), and AC x education ($\beta = .71$, p < .05) significantly related to users' BI. Changes in R-square are significant during hierarchical regression analyses as the input variables add up block after block, which suggests the educational level of participants moderates the relationship between AC and BI.

We further adopted PROCESS to verify the moderating effect of education on the relationship between AC and BI. PROCESS results showed that, at −1SD of educational level, the moderating effect was negative and significant ($\beta = -.20$, p < .01). At the mean of educational level, the moderating effect was positive and significant ($\beta = -.11$, p < .05). At the + 1SD of educational level, the moderating effect was not significant ($\beta = -.02$, p = .78). For a further understanding of education's moderating role in this relationship, we can refer to Fig. 1. The slope of participants with high educational levels does not change their usage intention significantly when faced with intensive anxiety caused by human-like characteristics of Generative AI. However, those with medium

Table 4. Education as the moderating role between AC and BI.

	Behavioral Intention
Block1: Demographic variables	
Age	.08
Income	.04
R-square	.01
ΔR-square	.01
Block2: AI anxiety	
Age	.08
Income	.04
AC	−.12*
R-square	.03
ΔR-square	.01
Block3: Educational experience	
Age	.03
Income	.05
AC	−.11*
Education	.13*
R-square	.04
ΔR-square	.01
Block4: ACXEducation	
Age	.03
Income	.05
AC	−.75**
Education	−.21
ACXEDU	.71*
R-square	.06
ΔR-square	.02

Note. $*p < .05, **p < .01, ***p < .001$

and low levels of educational experiences display significant changes in usage intention if they sense intimidation caused by Generative AI products. It indicates that users with relatively high-level education deal better with anxiety and prevents such negative feelings stand in the way of continuous utilization of this new technology. As for those with medium or relatively low-level of education, when they experience an increment of terrifying emotions or threats triggered by AI's human-like interactions, they tend to cut down on their future usage significantly.

Table 5. Creative industries relevance as the moderating role between AL and BI.

	Behavioral Intention
Block1: Demographic variables	
Age	.12
Income	.04
R-square	.02
ΔR-square	.02
Block2: AI anxiety	
Age	.11
Income	.04
AL	−.19***
R-square	.06
ΔR-square	.04
Block3: creative industries relevance level	
Age	.09
Income	.04
AL	−.18***
Relevance	.14**
R-square	.08
ΔR-square	.02
Block4: ALXRelevance	
Age	.08
Income	.03
AL	−.13
Relevance	−.10
ALXRelevance	.42
R-square	.08
ΔR-square	.01

*Note. * p < .05, ** p < .01, *** p < .001.*

Three lines depicted the relationship of AC and BI under three educational levels, which are low, medium, and high respectively. The line of low-level education has the steepest slope.

When verifying the moderating effect of creative industries' relevance on the relationship between AL and BI, the same method aforementioned was adopted. During the hierarchical regression analyses, BI was entered as the dependent variable, while age and a monthly income as demographic variables in block 1, followed by AL, creative industries relevance, and AL x creative industries relevance sequentially in the three

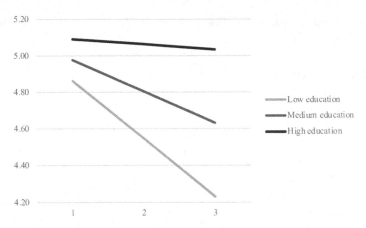

Fig. 1. The moderating effect of education on the relationship of AC (x-axis) and BI (y-axis).

following blocks. Results indicate that AL (β = --.19, p < .001) and creative industries relevance (β = .14, p < .01) are significantly related to users' BI. Changes in R-square are significant after new independent variables are introduced under each block. Thus, it is preliminarily indicated that participants' job relevance with the creativity markets could moderate the relationship between AL and BI.

We used PROCESS for further verification. PROCESS results showed that, at − 1SD of creative industries relevance, the moderating effect was not significant (β = .05, p = .57). At the mean of creative industries relevance, the moderating effect was positive and significant (β = .17, p < .01). At the + 1SD of creative industries relevance, the moderating effect was positive and significant (β = .29, p < .001). For a further understanding of creative industries' relevance's moderating role in this relationship, Fig. 1 could illustrate a clearer picture. The slope of participants whose jobs are of more relevance to creative industries is steeper compared to the other two lines. It indicates that when experiencing the same level of increment in AI learning anxiety, users who are more closely engaged with the creativity markets tend to show a stronger enhancement of intention to use Generative AI (Fig. 2).

Three lines depicted the relationship of AL and BI under three levels of creative industries relevance, which are low, medium, and high respectively. The line of high-level relevance has the steepest slope. Another moderating effect was identified based on hierarchical regression analysis. Table 6 shows there were positive and significant relationships between participants' current habit of using Generative AI and their future intention of continuous usage, as well as between their educational level and their usage intention. Analyses using PROCESS were conducted to further verify this relationship.

PROCESS results showed that, at −1SD of education, the moderating effect was positive and significant (β = .72, p < .001). At the mean of education, the moderating effect was positive and significant (β = .64, p < .001). At the + 1SD of education, the moderating effect was positive and significant (β = .57, p < .001). Therefore, it is confirmed that education has a moderating effect on the relationship between HB and BI. When referring to the plot graph, it is shown that the slope between HB and BI is steepest under the status of relatively low-level education. We indicate that once the dependence

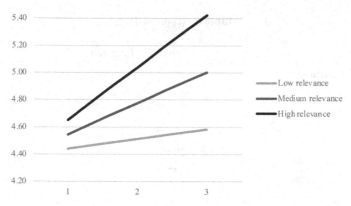

Fig. 2. The moderating effect of creative industries relevance on the relationship of AL (x-axis) and BI (y-axis).

Table 6. Education as the moderating role between HB and BI.

	Behavioral Intention
Block1: Demographic variables	
Age	.12
Income	.04
R-square	.02
ΔR-square	.02
Block2: Habit	
Age	.12*
Income	−.01
HB	.66***
R-square	.45
ΔR-square	.44
Block3: Education	
Age	.06
Income	.00
HB	.66***
Education	.11*
R-square	.46
ΔR-square	.01

(*continued*)

Table 6. (*continued*)

	Behavioral Intention
Block4: HBXEducation	
Age	.04
Income	.00
HB	.97***
Education	.29**
HBXEducation	−.37
R-square	.47
ΔR-square	.01

Note. * p < .05, ** p < .01, *** p < .001

on Generative AI tools is formed among users with low-level education, they probably would stick to this habit and furtherly carry on with future usage of these products. In other words, when experiencing growth of habit formation and reliance upon Generative AI, the usage intention growth of relatively low educational users would increase more evidently (Fig. 3).

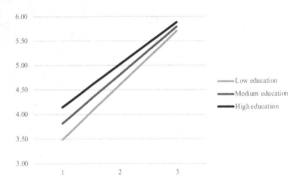

Fig. 3. The moderating effect of education on the relationship of HB (x-axis) and BI (y-axis).

Three lines depicted the relationship of HB and BI under three levels of education, which are low, medium, and high respectively. The line of low-level education has the steepest slope (Fig. 4).

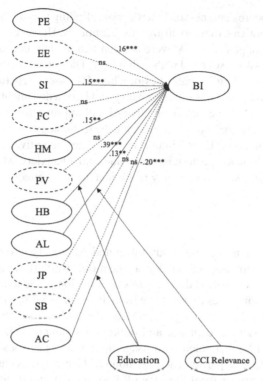

Fig. 4. The ultimate model revolves around the relationship between predictors and users' intention of Generative AI usage as well as explores the moderating roles of education and creative industries' relevance among different interactions.

6 Discussion

Based on self-reported survey responses, the measurement of consumers' expectations for Generative AI working performances revealed reasonably high results (5 out of 7). Positive correlations between behavioral intention (BI) and performance expectancy (PE) indicate that users expect Generative AI to be intelligent and effective in helping them. The unpredictable efforts needed to master Generative AI products in the growing Chinese environment, however, might clarify why the effort required to master this technology did not significantly influence future adoption intention. To make it easier for users and Generative AI toolkits to develop a stronger bond as the technology becomes more well-known and developed in the creative sectors, accessibility and availability of Generative AI products and tools still have to be enhanced.

Users' intentions to utilize Generative AI in their job are influenced by social factors, as participants reported being influenced by close or important people. Users of the Generative AI tools also found them entertaining, which is related favorably to their intention of continued use. These technologies assist professionals in the creative business to do tasks more efficiently, polish ideas, and produce results that are both amusing and fascinating. Incorporating the idea of AI anxiety into the model, the study found that participants' concerns and nervous views about slipping behind the development of generative AI tools motivate them to utilize this technology. However, consumers' intentions for future usage of generative AI were not significantly influenced by worries about job replacement and risks associated with technology. The perception of human-like features and the "understanding" capabilities of ChatGPT-based Generative AI products, however, nevertheless cause consumers to worry and have a detrimental impact on their usage intentions. Users believe that Generative AI will improve their capacity to execute their jobs, however, there are issues with learning the technology and the need for greater accessibility and availability. Users' intentions to utilize generative AI are significantly influenced by social influence, entertainment value, and AI anxiety, whereas worries and concerns about human-like qualities may result in a negative effect.

7   Conclusion

Combining the UTAUT model, the study integrated AI anxiety into the exploration of CCI professionals' acceptance and behavioral intention towards the emerging technology of Generative AI. It was verified that people's anticipation of Generative AI's working efficacy (PE), social influences they receive from daily surroundings (SI), entertainment attainment upon using the technology (HM), and the evolving adaptation (HB) proved positively related to users' acceptance and future usage intention (BI). However, other predictors (EE, FC, PV) resonated with usage intention in previous UTAUT research but failed to associate with participants' intention of Generative AI usage in this study. Explanations can be drawn from the lack of development and general application of Generative AI tools within domestic markets. During the preliminary stage of Generative AI entrenchment in China, few users could specify the efforts, facilities, and financial expenses needed to manage such tools based on current experiences. Thus, although these factors are not yet ready to predict users' acceptance and intention in terms of continuous usage, further studies could be conducted to perform longitude research analyses.

Introducing AI anxiety as a new dimension to leverage users' intention rhymes with people's current subtle recognition toward Generative AI-related technologies. Though fear, hesitation, and other negative emotions alike exist during adaptation to this terrifying while exciting technology, it is shown that those who related more to the field of creative domains are more likely to embrace this technology as well as apply relevant tools in working scenarios. The creativity market and professionals are responsive and of high adaptability. The emergency of Generative AI changes every industry in every way one can imagine. Facing such overwhelming challenges and opportunities, professionals in the CCI seem to be handling things quite well, which indicates a promisingly imaginable situation where human-machine interactions could harmoniously take place. Participants with higher education show resilience and stability when facing AI-related situations. They are less likely to withdraw from future usage despite the fear. Moreover, they exhibit less addictive reliance on Generative AI tools. Education fosters composure, containment, and better assessments of usage scenarios.

The creativity market has been responding fast to Generative AI development due to the productivity enhancement and creativity enrichment it guarantees. How people would adapt to this emerging technology, both vocationally and psychologically, awaits exploration and examination. This study shed light on the underpinning factors that would predict users' acceptance and intention in terms of Generative AI usage. Additionally, it exposed whether and how professionals' worrisome and anxiety over the newly emerging technology would attribute to their intention of applying it in daily working scenarios. Individuals' adaptability to evolutionary breakthrough technologies would not only determine in which direction and with what speed the technology would evolve, but also underlies the future of human-technology and human-machine coexistence and consistency. Hopefully, this study serves as an initiator for future entrenchments in the multidisciplinary field of human-machine interactions, media, and psychology in the Generative AI division.

Acknowledgement. This research project received funding from Shanghai Jiao Tong University's USC-SJTU Institute of Cultural and Creative Industry, and from Zizhu National High-Tech Industrial Development Zone, via the Zizhu New Media Management Research Center and the International Association of Cultural and Creative Industry Research. The researchers acknowledge the generous financial and administrative support from the institutions and their staff.

References

Pividori, M., Greene, C.S.: A publishing infrastructure for AI-assisted academic authoring. BioRxiv, 2023–01 (2023)

Chatterjee, J., Dethlefs, N.: This new conversational AI model can be your friend, philosopher, guide... and even your worst enemy. Patterns **4**(1), 100676 (2023)

Abd-Elaal, E.S., Gamage, S.H.P.W., Mills, J.E.: Assisting academics to identify computer-generated writing. Europ. J. Eng. Educ. **47**(5), 725–745 (2022).https://doi.org/10.1080/030 43797.2022.2046709

Haque, M.U., Dharmadasa, I., Sworna, Z.T., Rajapakse, R.N., Ahmad, H.: I think this is the most disruptive technology: Exploring Sentiments of ChatGPT Early Adopters using Twitter Data. http://arXiv.org/abs/2212.05856 (2022)

Megahed, F.M., Chen, Y., Ferris, J.A., Knoth, S., Jones-Farmer, L.A.: How Generative AI models such as ChatGPT can be (Mis)Used in SPC Practice, Education, and Research? An Exploratory Study. http://arXiv.org/abs/2302.10916 (2023)

Lim, W.M., Gunasekara, A., Pallant, J.L., Pallant, J.I., Pechenkina, E.: Generative AI and the future of education: Ragnarök or reformation? a paradoxical perspective from management educators. Int. J. Manag. Educ. **21**(2), 100790 (2023)

OpenAI. OpenAI (7 June 2023). https://www.openai.com/. Accessed 7 June 2023

Sahoo, S., Kumar, S., Abedin, M.Z., Lim, W.M., Jakhar, S.K.: Deep learning applications in manufacturing operations: a review of trends and ways forward. J. Enterp. Inf. Manag. **36**(1), 221–251 (2023). https://doi.org/10.1108/JEIM-01-2022-0025

Gero, K.I., Chilton, L.B.: Metaphoria: an algorithmic companion for metaphor creation. In: Proceedings of the 2019 CHI Conference on Human Factors in Computing Systems pp. 1–12 (2019). https://doi.org/10.1145/3290605.3300526

Ho, T.T., Virtusio, J.J., Chen, Y.Y., Hsu, C.M., Hua, K.L.: Sketch-guided deep portrait generation. ACM Trans. Multimedia Comput. Commun. Appl. (TOMM) **16**(3), 1–18 (2020)

Huang, C.-Z.A., Koops, H.V., Newton-Rex, E., Dinculescu, M., Cai, C.J.: AI Song Contest: Human-AI Co-Creation in Songwriting. http://arXiv.org/abs/2010.05388 (2020)

Audry, S.: Art in the Age of Machine Learning. The MIT Press, Cambridge, MA (2021)

Newell, A.A, Simon, H.A.: The logic theory machine—a complex information processing system. In: IRE Trans. Inf. Theory **2**(3), 61–79https://doi.org/10.1109/TIT.1956.1056797

Turing, A.M.: Computing machinery and intelligence. Mind **59**(236), 433–460 (1950)

Bostrom, N.: Superintelligence. Oxford University Press (2014)

Mitrović, S., Andreoletti, D., Ayoub, O.: ChatGPT or human? Detect and explain. Explaining decisions of machine learning model for detecting short ChatGPT-generated text. http://arXiv.org/abs/2301.13852 (2023)

Hunt, K.M.: Could artificial intelligence win the next weather photographer of the year competition?. Weather **78**(4), 108–112 (2022)

Cousins, S.: The rapid rise of AI art. Eng. Technol. **18**(2), 20–25 (2023)

Appel, G., Neelbauer, J., Schweidel, D.A.: Generative AI Has an Intellectual Property Problem. Harvard Business Review (07 April 2023). https://hbr.org/2023/04/generative-ai-has-an-intellectual-property-problem

Stokel-Walker, C., Van Noorden, R.: What ChatGPT and generative AI mean for science. Nature **614**(7947), 214–216 (2023)

Khalil, M., Er, E.: Will ChatGPT get you caught? Rethinking of plagiarism detection. http://arXiv.org/abs/2302.04335 (2023)

Zhong, H., et al.: Copyright Protection and Accountability of Generative AI: Attack, Watermarking and Attribution. http://arXiv.org/abs/2303.09272 (2023)

Day, T.: A preliminary investigation of fake peer-reviewed citations and references generated by ChatGPT. Prof. Geogr. 1–4 (2023)

Gilson, A., et al.: How does CHATGPT perform on the United States medical licensing examination? the implications of large language models for medical education and knowledge assessment. JMIR Med. Educ. **9**(1), e45312 (2023)

Liu, S., et al.: Using AI-generated suggestions from ChatGPT to optimize clinical decision support. J. Am. Med. Inform. Assoc. ocad072 (2023)

Chen, L., Chen, X., Wu, S., Yang, Y., Chang, M., Zhu, H.: The future of ChatGPT-enabled labor market: A preliminary study. http://arXiv.org/abs/2304.09823 (2023)

Davies, J., Klinger, J., Mateos-Garcia, J., Stathoulopoulos, K.: The art in the artificial AI and the creative industries. Creative Ind. Policy Evid. Centre, 1–38 (2020)

Saadi, J.I., Yang, M.C.: Generative design: reframing the role of the designer in early-stage design process. J. Mech. Des. **145**(4), 041411 (2023)

Suh, M., Youngblom, E., Terry, M., Cai, C.J.: AI as social glue: Uncovering the roles of deep generative AI during social music composition. In: Proceedings of the 2021 CHI Conference on Human Factors in Computing Systems, pp. 1–11 (2021)

Altavilla, S., Blanco, E.: Are AI tools going to be the new designers? a taxonomy for measuring the level of automation of design activities. In: Proceedings of the Design Society: DESIGN Conference vol. 1, pp. 81–90. Cambridge University Press (2020)

Rahimi, R.A.: A survey of technology acceptance models in the creative industry: exploring key limitations. In: 2020 13th International Conference on Developments in eSystems Engineering (DeSE), pp. 9–14. IEEE (2020)

Haensch, A.C., Ball, S., Herklotz, M., Kreuter, F.: Seeing ChatGPT Through Students' Eyes: An Analysis of TikTok Data. http://arXiv.org/abs/2303.05349 (2023)

Shoufan, A.: Exploring students' perceptions of CHATGPT: thematic analysis and follow-up survey. IEEE Access (2023)

Kenney, A.: The promise and peril of ChatGPT. J. Account. (2023)

Venkatesh, V., Morris, M.G., Davis, F.D., Davis, G.B.: User acceptance of information technology: towards a unified view. MIS Q. **27**(3), 425–478 (2003)

Fishbein, M., Ajzen, I.: Belief, Attitude, Intention, and Behavior: An Introduction to Theory and Research. Addison-Wesley, Reading, MA (1975)

Davis, F.D.: Perceived usefulness, perceived ease of use, and user acceptance of information technology. MIS Q. **13**(3), 319–339 (1989)

Ajzen, I.: The theory of planned behavior. Organ. Behav. Hum. Decis. Process. **50**(2), 179–211 (1991)

Davis, F.D., Bagozzi, R.P., Warshaw, P.R.: Extrinsic and intrinsic motivation to use computers in the workspace. J. Appl. Soc. Psychol. **22**(14), 1111–1132 (1992)

Thompson, R.L., Higgins, C.A., Howell, J.M.: Personal computing: toward a conceptual model of utilization. MIS Q. **15**(1), 124–143 (1991)

Taylor, S., Todd, P.A.: Assessing IT usage: the role of prior experience. MIS Q. **19**(2), 561–570 (1995)

Rogers, E.M.: Diffusion of Innovations, 4th edn. The Free Press, New York, NY (1995)

Compeau, D.R., Higgins, C.A.: Computer self-efficacy: development of a measure and initial test. MIS Q. **19**(2), 189–211 (1995)

Khechine, H., Lakhal, S., Ndjambou, P.: A meta-analysis of the UTAUT model: eleven years later. Can. J. Adm. Sci./Revue Canadienne des Sci. de l'Administration **33**(2), 138–152 (2016)

Venkatesh, V., Thong, J.Y., Xu, X.: Consumer acceptance and use of information technology: extending the unified theory of acceptance and use of technology. MIS Q. 157–178 (2012)

Tamilmani, K., Rana, N.P., Wamba, S.F., Dwivedi, R.: The extended unified theory of acceptance and use of technology (UTAUT2): a systematic literature review and theory evaluation. Int. J. Inf. Manage. **57**, 102269 (2021)

Wang, Y.Y., Wang, Y.S.: Development and validation of an artificial intelligence anxiety scale: an initial application in predicting motivated learning behavior. Interact. Learn. Environ. (2), 1–16 (2019)

Johnson, D.G., Verdicchio, M.: AI anxiety. J. Am. Soc. Inf. Sci. **68**(9), 2267–2270 (2017)

Green, B.P.: Artificial intelligence and ethics: Sixteen challenges and opportunities. Markkula Center for Applied Ethics at Santa Clara University (2020). https://www.scu.edu/ethics/all-about-ethics/artificial-intelligence-and-ethics-sixteen-challenges-and-opportunities

Ha, J.G., Page, T., Thorsteinsson, G.: A study on technophobia and mobile device design. Int. J. Cont. **7**(2), 17–25 (2011)

Heinssen, J.R.K., Glass, C.R., Knight, L.A.: Assessment of computer anxiety: the dark side of the computer revolution. In: Paper presented at the meeting of the Association for Advancement of Behavior Therapy (1984)

Heinssen, R.K., Jr., Glass, C.R., Knight, L.A.: Assessing computer anxiety: development and validation of the computer anxiety rating scale. Comput. Hum. Behav. **3**(1), 49–59 (1987)

Venkatesh, V., Thong, J.Y., Xu, X.: Unified theory of acceptance and use of technology: a synthesis and the road ahead. J. Assoc. Inf. Syst. **17**(5), 328–376 (2016)

Bozan, K., Parker, K., Davey, B.: A closer look at the social influence construct in the UTAUT Model: an institutional theory based approach to investigate health IT adoption patterns of the elderly. In: 2016 49th Hawaii International Conference on System Sciences (HICSS), pp. 3105–3114. IEEE (2016)

Leow, L.P., Phua, L.K., Teh, S.Y.: Extending the social influence factor: behavioural intention to increase the usage of information and communication technology-enhanced student-centered teaching methods. Educ. Tech. Res. Dev. **69**(3), 1853–1879 (2021)

Qu, B., Wei, L., Zhang, Y.: Factors affecting consumer acceptance of electronic cash in China: an empirical study. Financ. Innov. **8**(1), 1–19 (2022)

Weber, R.: Evaluating and developing theories in the information systems discipline. J. Assoc. Inf. Syst. **13**(1), 1–30 (2012)

Dodds, W.B., Monroe, K.B., Grewal, D.: Effects of price, brand, and store information on buyers. J. Mark. Res. **28**(3), 307–319 (1991)

Limayem, M., Hirt, S.G., Cheung, C.M.: How habit limits the predictive power of intention: the case of information systems continuance. MIS Q. 705–737 (2007)

Wang, Y.Y., Wang, Y.S.: Development and validation of an artificial intelligence anxiety scale: an initial application in predicting motivated learning behavior. Interact. Learn. Environ. **30**(4), 619–634 (2022)

Li, J., Huang, J.S.: Dimensions of artificial intelligence anxiety based on the integrated fear acquisition theory. Technol. Soc. **63**, 101410 (2020)

Kaya, F., Aydin, F., Schepman, A., Rodway, P., Yetişensoy, O., Demir Kaya, M.: The roles of personality traits, AI anxiety, and demographic factors in attitudes toward artificial intelligence. Int. J. Hum.–Comput. Interact. 1–18 (2022)

Chang, J.S., Hsiao, M., Peng, Y.: An exploration on accounting professionals facing the development of AI. In: The 2021 7th International Conference on Industrial and Business Engineering, pp. 94–103 (2021)

Yuan, C., Zhang, C., Wang, S.: Social anxiety as a moderator in consumer willingness to accept AI assistants based on utilitarian and hedonic values. J. Retail. Consum. Serv. **65**, 102878 (2022)

Security, Privacy, Trust and Ethics

Enhancing Trust in Smart Charging Agents—The Role of Traceability for Human-Agent-Cooperation

Christiane Attig[1]([✉]) [ID], Tim Schrills[1] [ID], Markus Gödker[1] [ID], Patricia Wollstadt[2] [ID], Christiane Wiebel-Herboth[2] [ID], André Calero Valdez[1] [ID], and Thomas Franke[1] [ID]

[1] University of Lübeck, Ratzeburger Allee 160, 23562 Lübeck, Germany
{christiane.attig,tim.schrills,markus.goedker,
andre.calerovaldez,thomas.franke}@uni-luebeck.de
[2] Honda Research Institute Europe, Carl-Legien-Straße 30,
63073 Offenbach am Main, Germany
{patricia.wollstadt,christiane.wiebel}@honda-ri.de

Abstract. Achieving climate neutrality will require a major transformation of the transportation sector, likely leading to a surge in demand for electric vehicles (EVs). This poses a challenge to grid stability due to supply fluctuations of renewable energy resources. At the same time, EVs offer the potential to improve grid stability through managed charging. The complexity of this charging process can limit user flexibility and require more cognitive effort. Smart charging agents powered by artificial intelligence (AI) can address these challenges by optimizing charging profiles based on grid load predictions, but users must trust such systems to attain collective goals in a collaborative manner. In this study, we focus on traceability as a prerequisite for understanding and predicting system behavior and trust calibration. Subjective information processing awareness (SIPA) differentiates traceability into transparency, understandability, and predictability. The study aims to investigate the relationship between traceability, trust, and prediction performance in the context of smart charging agents through an online experiment. $N = 57$ participants repeatedly observed cost calculations made by a schematic algorithm, while the amount of disclosed information that formed the basis of the cost calculations was varied. Results showed that higher amount of disclosed information was related to higher reported trust. Moreover, traceability was partially higher in the high-information group than the medium and low-information groups. Conversely, participants' performance in estimating the booking costs did not vary with amount of disclosed information. This pattern of results might reflect an explainability pitfall: Users of smart charging agents might trust these systems more as traceability increases, regardless of how well they understand the system.

Keywords: smart charging · human-machine cooperation · explainable AI · trust · human-technology interaction · battery electric vehicles

© The Author(s), under exclusive license to Springer Nature Switzerland AG 2023
H. Degen et al. (Eds.): HCII 2023, LNCS 14059, pp. 313–324, 2023.
https://doi.org/10.1007/978-3-031-48057-7_19

1 Introduction

The EU aims for climate neutrality by 2050, which necessitates a comprehensive trans-formation of the transport sector, including a 90% reduction in emissions [11]. Conse-quently, the demand for electric vehicles (EVs) will rise strongly within the next years. It has been argued that this demand will pose a challenge for the stability of the power grid [19] – particularly if EVs are charged with renewable electricity, which is subject to large fluctuations in supply and might not be flexible enough to meet the also fluctu-ating energy demands by users at all times [5]. Conversely, EVs offer a great potential for increasing grid stability through managed and bidirectional charging, that is, EVs can store or provide excess energy to the grid as needed [23]. As a consequence, the complexity of the charging process increases, limiting user flexibility or requiring more planning and technical understanding. Thus, the collective benefit of grid stability may come at a cost for the individual user, who might face a restriction of personal resources (e.g., time, comfort, cognitive resources [19]).

Smart charging agents relying on techniques from the field of artificial intelligence (AI) offer one solution to combine protection of users' personal resources with optimal utilization of renewable energy, for instance, by calculating and implementing optimal charging profiles based on grid load predictions [1]. From the user's perspective, this means that their cognitive effort required to organize a complex charging process is minimized. What remains is that users of smart charging systems need to balance between different goals, either stemming from individual needs (e.g., flexibility) or collective ones (e.g., sustainable energy consumption). Individual users may well pursue selfish goals in this regard (i.e., maximize their personal gain, e.g., by booking EVs from a car share fleet without delay), but overall, the finite and fluctuating nature of renewable energy resources requires that users also pursue collective goals (i.e., maximize the collective gain, e.g., by shifting their EV booking window) – in other words, users need to make a tradeoff between egoistic and altruistic behavior. Smart charging agents offer the potential to assist users in achieving not only individual, but also collective goals. The usage of such a smart charging agent can thus be understood as a cooperative, joint activity [15, 18], because both partners (the user and the smart charging agent) are working towards (shared) goals that neither can achieve on their own. To realize the potential of smart charging agents for sustainable electromobility, it is crucial to maximize users' perception of advantages from cooperating with the system.

One core variable for enhancing cooperation between users and an AI system such as a smart charging agent is trust [3]. Trust plays a role within human-agent interaction in the field of smart charging because this interaction is characterized by degrees of uncertainty on part of the users (see [20]) – in contrast to the agent, users do not have access to all relevant technical information that determines the charging management (e.g., probability of peak load, distance to previous bookings in an EV carsharing context). Hence, users have to rely on the agent's functionality, i.e., trust the agent. Past research has suggested that trust in AI systems can be increased by AI explainability, i.e., providing comprehensible and transparent explanations of the algorithm's decisions [6, 26]. In this sense, explainability refers to enabling a deepened knowledge about the system's general functionality [16]. A related concept that has been applied to trust in AI systems is traceability, which can be related to situation awareness theory [10]. Traceability stresses that knowledge representations about how the system works (i.e., the mental model) does not capture the awareness of the system's status (i.e., the situation model). However, awareness of the system's status is necessary to understand momentary system behavior and to predict future states. For instance, a user cooperating with a smart charging agent in a car sharing fleet might know that the agent incorporates weather data (general knowledge). However, if the user is not made aware in a given situation that the weather data used by the system differs from the user's expectations, the calculated energy consumption of the EV may not be understandable to the user, which is likely to lead to incorrect predictions of the EV's energy consumption in the future. Hence, for the present study, we focused on traceability because it captures more complex decision-making processes than explainability, which are relevant in the domain of cooperating with smart charging agents.

The subjective information processing awareness (SIPA) has been proposed as a construct which differentiates traceability into three subfacets: transparency, understandability, and predictability [24, 25]. Conceptually related situation awareness, SIPA refers to "the experience of being enabled by a system to perceive, understand and predict its information processing" [25]. A first study focusing on traceability of automated insulin delivery (AID) systems highlighted the importance of differentiating the three subscales and the close connection between SIPA and trust [24]. Based on results regarding the relationship between explainability, traceability, and trust, we test the following hypotheses: (H1) SIPA increases with an increase in relevant explaining information disclosed by the smart agent; (H2) trust increases with an increase in relevant explaining information disclosed by the smart agent; and (H3) SIPA and trust are positively correlated.

In addition to subjective assessments of traceability and trust, capturing behavioral variables is central to understanding the impact of efforts for human-centered design of AI systems: A system that is better traceable should enhance the user's understanding and acceptance, and it should support the interaction success, which should become observable in the user's behavior. Accordingly, better experienced predictability should be related to better predictions about the system's behavior. Hence, we predict that (H4) prediction performance increases with an increase in relevant explaining information disclosed by the smart agent; and (H5) predictability and prediction performance are positively correlated.

To investigate our hypotheses on the role of traceability for trust as a prerequisite for human-agent cooperation in the smart charging domain, we designed an online experiment similar to the one reported in [24]. Specifically, a schematic EV car sharing booking simulation was developed to create stimuli that participants were presented repeatedly. These stimuli depicted the booking calculations based on 10 sources of information, of which a varying amount was disclosed to the participants (see Sect. 2.2).

2 Method

A car-sharing booking simulation experiment was conducted using the online platform Labvanced [12]. The study was approved by the ethics committee of the University of Lübeck (tracking number 21–375).

2.1 Participants

Complete datasets were gathered from $N = 64$ participants. Outlier detection was based on response times (according to [21]) and response patterns (i.e., data sets without variance on the SIPA scale were excluded). $N = 57$ participants remained and were included in the analyses. Of those, $n = 42$ (74%) were women, $n = 13$ (23%) were men, and $n = 2$ (4%) were non-binary. Age varied between 18 and 63 ($M = 24.11$, $SD = 9.50$). Ninety percent of participants were students.

The majority of the participants did not have experience in driving electric vehicles: 46 participants (81%) indicated that they had driven a combustion vehicle in the past, whereas only 3 (5%) had driven a BEV, 4 (7%) had driven a hybrid vehicle, and 2 (4%) had driven a plug-in hybrid vehicle. Eleven participants (20%) indicated not to have any driving experience. Seven participants (12%) reported to have used car sharing in the past. The sample was characterized by a slightly below-average affinity for technology interaction ($M = 3.16$, $SD = 1.18$, significant difference from the scale mean 3.5, $t(56) = -2.20$, $p = .032$, $d = -0.29$, weak effect; [13]).

Students from the University of Lübeck were rewarded with course credits. In addition, the three participants with the best performance in the performance block could win €20 each. This additional prize was used to provide an extra incentive for motivation in the performance task.

2.2 Experimental Environment and Procedure

For assessing participants' perception of the traceability of a smart charging agent within an online experiment, a schematic algorithm was designed. This algorithm calculated the resource efficiency of booking an EV from a car-sharing fleet based on simulated data, displayed as abstract booking costs (i.e., tokens). The cost calculation was based on 10 features (e.g., time of booking start and end, expected grid power demand, likelihood of a peak load). Fewer tokens indicated higher resource efficiency. For the present experiment, the algorithm was used to calculate 50 booking costs, which were presented to participants as the result of a supposed artificial intelligence system (i.e., this was a wizard-of-oz experiment, see Fig. 1).

In five subsequent observation blocks, the participants were asked to observe 10 cost calculations made by the algorithm (i.e., 50 observations in total). After each observation block, participants rated their subjective experience with the algorithm (T1–T5). To evaluate participants' ability to predict the algorithm's results, a performance block followed, in which participants were asked to estimate booking costs based on the disclosed information (20 estimations in total). Participant's performance was measured by comparing their estimates with the actual booking costs (T6); however, this information was not provided to them to rule out learning effects.

The traceability of the algorithm was experimentally manipulated by varying how much of information used for cost calculation was disclosed to the participant (low, medium, high information; between-factors design). Participants in the low-information condition ($n = 18$) received information about the beginning and end of the booking, the expected kilometers, and the customer ID (the latter having no effect on the token calculation). Participants in the medium-information condition ($n = 20$) received additional information about the distance to the previous booking in hours, the distance to the next booking in hours, the state of charge after the previous booking, and the minimum state of charge for the next booking. Participants in the high-information condition ($n = 19$) received additional information about expected grid power demand, probability of peak load, expected charge consumption, and expected green power share (the latter having no effect on the token calculation).

Fig. 1. Stimuli from the study as they were shown to participants for the three conditions.

2.3 Measures

To assess the reliability of the used scales, we calculated McDonald's omega (ω) in addition to Cronbach's alpha (α), since the latter is not well-suited for short scales [7]. For traceability facets, which consist of only two items each, the Spearman-Brown coefficient was used to assess their reliability [9].

For assessing traceability, the 6-item Subjective Information Processing Awareness (SIPA) scale [24] was used. The scale measures traceability on the three subscales transparency, understandability, and predictability with 2 items each. Responses were provided on a 6-point Likert scale from 1 (*completely disagree*) to 6 (*completely agree*). Regarding the overall scale, Cronbach's alpha varied between $\alpha = .89$ and $\alpha = .93$ and McDonald's omega varied between $\omega = .88$ and $\omega = .92$, which indicates good to excellent reliability. Regarding the transparency subscale, consistency varied between $R = .62$ and $R = .94$. The consistency of the understandability subscale varied between $R = .93$ and $R = .94$. The consistency of the predictability subscale varied between $R = .92$ and $R = .97$. Hence, the consistency of the three subscales can be interpreted as moderate to high.

Trust was assessed with the 5-item Facets of Systems Trustworthiness (FOST) scale [14]. Responses were provided on a 6-point Likert scale from 1 (*completely disagree*) to 6 (*completely agree*). Cronbach's alpha varied between $\alpha = .91$ and $\alpha = .96$ and McDonald's omega varied between $\omega = .91$ and $\omega = .96$ as well, which indicates excellent reliability.

For assessing participant's prediction performance, 20 of the 50 stimuli created with the booking simulation environment were changed in such a way that no prediction of the algorithm was displayed, but the different levels of information disclosure (depending on the condition). Participants were prompted to estimate the output of the algorithm (i.e., the estimated number of tokens). The deviation of each estimate from the simulated number of tokens was determined per person and the sum of absolute deviations was calculated, which was used as an indicator of performance.

3 Results

3.1 Descriptive Analyses

Table 1 depicts means and standard deviations for the dependent variables that were assessed after the five observation blocks (SIPA, SIPA subscales, FOST) for the whole participant group as well as for the three experimental conditions.

Table 2 depicts means and standard deviations for participants' performance in estimating the booking costs calculated by the algorithm. As a performance indicator, the sum of absolute deviations of participants' estimates from the simulated booking costs was calculated.

3.2 Hypotheses Testing

For analyzing differences between the three experimental conditions (H1, H2, H4), planned contrast analyses were conducted for each of the dependent variables and points of measurement [22]. The different amounts of information disclosed to each group and the corresponding relationship between attributes were used to determine the weights (i.e., lambda values). It was assumed that each attribute (i.e., a total of low info: 4, medium info: 8, or high info: 12) could be related to each other attribute seen in one condition. The number of relations between attributes is given by the binomial coefficient (i.e., the number of attributes over two). Thus, the number of relations between attributes was for low info = 6, for medium info = 28, and for high info = 66. Following [2] to calculate the weights, the following lambda values for the contrast analysis were defined: $\lambda_{low} = -2.5$, $\lambda_{med} = -0.5$, $\lambda_{high} = 3$; for a similar approach see [24]. Results are depicted in Table 3. Effect sizes were interpreted according to [4].

Results showed that regarding the overall SIPA score, only at T5 a significant contrast was found with participants in the high-info group having a significantly higher SIPA mean score than participants in the low-info and medium-info groups (moderate effect). Regarding the SIPA subscale transparency, the three groups did not differ in their ratings. Significant differences were found for understandability at T4 and T5, with participants in the high-info group having significantly higher scores than participants in the low-info and medium-info groups (moderate effect). Moreover, a significant difference was found for predictability at T5, with participants in the high-info group again having significantly higher scores than participants in the low-info and medium-info groups (moderate effect). Thus, H1 was partially supported.

In terms of trust, significant differences were found at T2 and T5, with participants in the high-info group having significantly higher scores than participants in the low-info

Table 1. Descriptive statistics for the dependent variables assessed after the observation blocks.

Variable	N	T1		T2		T3		T4		T5	
		M	SD	M	SD	M	SD	M	SD	M	SD
SIPA	57	3.34	1.07	3.29	1.01	3.32	0.97	3.51	1.20	3.32	1.06
Low info	18	3.39	1.17	3.16	0.97	3.18	0.83	3.10	1.06	3.10	0.86
Medium info	20	3.57	1.15	3.24	0.95	3.22	0.84	3.24	1.15	2.89	0.78
High info	19	3.04	0.84	3.46	1.12	3.56	1.19	3.68	1.15	3.68	1.24
SIPA transparency	57	4.13	1.20	4.12	1.19	4.14	1.10	4.01	1.31	3.96	1.22
Low info	18	4.28	1.39	4.22	1.17	4.08	1.03	3.92	1.32	4.06	1.12
Medium info	20	4.30	1.16	4.13	1.17	4.30	0.95	4.05	1.38	3.80	1.26
High info	19	3.82	1.03	4.03	1.30	4.03	1.32	4.05	1.29	4.05	1.30
SIPA understandability	57	3.10	1.27	3.06	1.21	3.07	1.16	3.18	1.28	2.93	1.22
Low info	18	3.08	1.22	2.81	1.23	2.94	0.92	2.83	1.18	2.72	1.10
Medium info	20	3.33	1.47	3.08	1.23	2.78	1.16	2.98	1.37	2.45	0.93
High info	19	2.87	1.10	3.29	1.21	3.50	1.28	3.71	1.17	3.63	1.32
SIPA predictability	57	2.78	1.25	2.68	1.13	2.75	1.19	2.85	1.24	2.77	1.17
Low info	18	2.81	1.38	2.44	1.20	2.50	1.26	2.56	1.38	2.53	1.14
Medium info	20	3.08	1.43	2.53	0.99	2.58	1.13	2.70	1.06	2.43	0.89
High info	19	2.45	0.81	3.08	1.14	3.16	1.26	3.29	1.21	3.37	1.27
FOST	57	3.65	1.00	3.39	1.01	3.35	1.09	3.51	1.20	3.32	1.06
Low info	18	3.50	1.15	2.79	0.77	3.03	0.23	3.12	1.17	3.01	0.80
Medium info	20	3.90	0.84	3.65	0.98	3.41	1.10	3.55	1.22	3.04	0.93
High info	19	3.53	1.00	3.68	1.02	3.58	1.14	3.83	1.16	3.90	1.21

Table 2. Descriptive statistics for participants' performance within the performance block.

Variable	N	T6	
		M	SD
Mean sum of deviations from estimated costs	57	1509	706
Low info	18	1613	1047
Medium info	20	1486	424
High info	19	1436	556

Table 3. Planned contrast analyses results.

Variable	T	p	95% CI	r(effect size)
SIPA overall score				
T1	−1.16	.252	[−3.07, 0.82]	.15
T2	0.95	.347	[−0.98, 2.74]	.13
T3	1.28	.205	[−0.64, 2.91]	.17
T4	1.64	.108	[−0.38, 3.73]	.22
T5	2.07	**.043**	[0.06, 3.65]	.27
SIPA transparency				
T1	−1.28	.207	[−3.59, 0.79]	.17
T2	−0.49	.628	[−2.76, 1.68]	.07
T3	−0.28	.784	[−2.31, 1.75]	.04
T4	0.28	.780	[−2.09, 2.78]	.04
T5	0.11	.916	[−2.14, 2.38]	.01
SIPA understandability				
T1	−0.66	.514	[−3.10, 1.57]	.09
T2	1.18	.242	[−0.92, 3.55]	.16
T3	1.69	.097	[−0.33, 3.83]	.22
T4	2.25	**.029**	[0.28, 4.84]	.29
T5	2.79	**.007**	[0.80, 4.93]	.35
SIPA predictability				
T1	−1.21	.237	[−3.48, 1.06]	.16
T2	1.84	.072	[−0.17, 3.90]	.24
T3	1.80	.077	[−0.22, 4.09]	.24
T4	1.91	.060	[−0.10, 4.35]	.25
T5	2.54	**.014**	[0.55, 4.60]	.32
FOST				
T1	−0.13	.895	[−1.95, 1.71]	.02
T2	2.64	**.011**	[0.54, 3.97]	.33
T3	1.47	.148	[−0.53, 3.43]	.19
T4	1.77	.083	[−0.26, 4.09]	.23
T5	2.90	**.005**	[0.81, 4.46]	.37
Performance (Mean sum of absolute deviations from estimated costs)				
T6	−0.72	.478	[−1776, 842]	.10

Note. Significant differences are bold-faced for better readability and medium-info groups (moderate to large effect). Hence, H2 was partially supported. One-tailed correlation analyses were conducted for testing the relationship between SIPA (subscales) and trust. Since multiple variables studied were not normally distributed, Spearman's Rho was calculated. Results are depicted in Table 4. The size of correlation coefficients varied between $r_S = .46$ and $r_S = .89$, indicating a moderate to strong relationship. H3 was thus supported.

For the performance indicator, the planned contrast analyses did not show any significant differences. Thus, H4 was not supported. For testing the relationship between predictability and prediction performance, again one-tailed Spearman correlation analyses were conducted. The correlation was only significant between performance and prediction at T1 ($r_S = .27, p = .023$, medium effect). The support for H5 was therefore weak.

Table 4. Correlations between trust and SIPA for each point of measurement.

	Point of measurement	SIPA							
		Overall score		Transparency		Understandability		Predictability	
		r_S	p	r_S	p	r_S	p	r_S	p
Trust	T1	.66	<.001	.49	<.001	.60	<.001	.64	<.001
	T2	.79	<.001	.54	<.001	.76	<.001	.72	<.001
	T3	.81	<.001	.47	<.001	.83	<.001	.71	<.001
	T4	.89	<.001	.73	<.001	.83	<.001	.78	<.001
	T5	.84	<.001	.46	<.001	.86	<.001	.76	<.001

4 Discussion

4.1 Summary of Results

Using planned contrast analyses, it was shown that traceability partially varied with the amount of disclosed information (higher amount of information related to higher reported trust). Moreover, trust was partially higher in the high information group than the medium and low information groups. Analyses of the three subscales of traceability revealed that effects were existent for understandability and predictability, while no effect was found for transparency. As expected, strong relationships between traceability and trust were found. With respect to prediction performance, the results showed that participants' performance in estimating the booking costs did not vary with the amount of disclosed information and only marginally with experienced predictability.

4.2 Implications

While additional information enhanced subjective experiences of trust, understandability, and predictability of a smart charging agent for EV car sharing, they did not improve transparency ratings and estimation of the algorithm's output. Together with the lack of a robust link between experienced predictability and prediction performance, the findings suggest that participants may have experienced an explainability pitfall [8]: Users of smart charging agents might trust these systems more as traceability increases, regardless of how well they understand the system. Thus, such systems may elicit the false impression that users understand the system's functionality well enough to predict its outcomes, even though they are unable to do so, possibly causing unwarranted trust [17].

An alternative explanation for the findings could be that as information increases, the workload for attending to each piece of information and integrating it into a numerical estimate increases, which could worsen prediction performance. In this case, however, the medium-info group should have scored higher than the high-info group, which was not the case. Moreover, in [24], ratings for workload did not differ with varying amount of disclosed information.

The planned multiple contrast analyses testing differences in SIPA ratings between the three experimental groups revealed significant effects only after 40–50 observations. This finding is in line with [24], where higher information disclosure led to SIPA differences only after 45 observations. Hence, when investigating SIPA, this delay should be considered in experimental design.

4.3 Limitations and Future Research

An important limitation of the study is the sample composition: The participants were mostly students with little or no experience with EVs and carsharing. Although the understanding of the situation was supported by providing contextual information and tested by knowledge questions at the beginning of the study, a sample consisting of actual users of EV carsharing services should be recruited to increase external validity.

Furthermore, the way in which the participants' prediction performance was assessed should be considered critically. In real-world scenarios, users of smart charging agents do not need to predict the results of the algorithm in such an explicit manner. Hence, it might be fruitful to develop a way to measure predictive performance that has higher ecological validity.

4.4 Conclusion

Smart charging agents have great potential to reduce EV users' cognitive load that might increase by a more complex charging process when sustainable technologies like bidirectional charging are widely implemented. They can also assist the user in balancing personal and collective goals, which might become necessary to preserve grid stability and charging flexibility for a multitude of users. To support human-agent collaboration, smart agents need to be designed for appropriate trust. The present research demonstrated that traceability, i.e. transparency, understandability, and predictability, are strongly linked to trust. Therefore, human-centered AI design should include means to provide comprehensible and transparent explanations of the algorithm's current status to support adequate situation models. However, the present work also highlighted that providing relevant information which form the basis of the algorithm's calculation might still be associated with a problematic miscalibration between the experienced predictability of the system and the actual ability to predict the system's behavior.

References

1. Bergmeir, C., et al.: Comparison and Evaluation of Methods for a Predict+Optimize Problem in Renewable Energy (2022). https://doi.org/10.48550/ARXIV.2212.10723
2. Buckless, F.A., Ravenscroft, S.P.: Contrast coding: a refinement of ANOVA in behavioral analysis. Account. Rev. **65**, 933–945 (1990). https://www.jstor.org/stable/247659
3. Chiou, E.K., Lee, J.D.: Trusting automation: designing for responsivity and resilience. Hum. Factors **65**(1), 137–165 (2021). https://doi.org/10.1177/00187208211009995
4. Cohen, J.: A power primer. Psychol. Bull. **112**, 155–159 (1992). https://doi.org/10.1037//0033-2909.112.1.155
5. Colmenar-Santos, A., Muñoz-Gómez, A.-M., Rosales-Asensio, E., López-Rey, Á.: Electric vehicle charging strategy to support renewable energy sources in Europe 2050 low-carbon scenario. Energy **183**, 61–74 (2019). https://doi.org/10.1016/j.energy.2019.06.118
6. Ding, W., Abdel-Basset, M., Hawash, H., Ali, A.M.: Explainability of artificial intelligence methods, applications and challenges: a comprehensive survey. Inform. Sci. **615**, 238–292 (2022). https://doi.org/10.1016/j.ins.2022.10.013
7. Dunn, T.J., Baguley, T., Brunsden, V.: From alpha to omega: a practical solution to the pervasive problem of internal consistency estimation. Br. J. Psychol. **105**, 399–412 (2014). https://doi.org/10.1111/bjop.12046
8. Ehsan, U., Riedl, M.O.: Explainability Pitfalls: Beyond Dark Patterns in Explainable AI (2021). http://arxiv.org/abs/2109.12480
9. Eisinga, R., Grotenhuis, M.T., Pelzer, B.: The reliability of a two-item scale: Pearson, Cronbach, or Spearman-Brown? Int. J. Public Health **58**, 637–642 (2013). https://doi.org/10.1007/s00038-012-0416-3
10. Endsley, M.R.: Toward a theory of situation awareness in dynamic systems. Hum. Factors **37**, 32–64 (1995). https://doi.org/10.1518/001872095779049543
11. European Commission, European Green Deal. https://www.consilium.europa.eu/en/policies/green-deal/. Accessed 22 June 2023
12. Finger, H., Goeke, C., Diekamp, D., Standvoß, K., König, P.: LabVanced: A Unified JavaScript Framework for Online Studies (2017). https://www.labvanced.com/static/2017_IC2S2_LabVanced.pdf
13. Franke, T., Attig, C., Wessel, D.: A personal resource for technology interaction: development and validation of the affinity for technology interaction (ATI) scale. Int. J. Hum.-Comput. Int. **35**, 456–467 (2019). https://doi.org/10.1080/10447318.2018.1456150
14. Franke, T., Trantow, M., Günther, M., Krems, J.F., Zott, V., Keinath, A.: Advancing electric vehicle range displays for enhanced user experience: the relevance of trust and adaptability. In: Proceedings of the 7th International Conference on Automotive User Interfaces and Interactive Vehicular Applications, pp. 249–256. ACM, Nottingham United Kingdom (2015). https://doi.org/10.1145/2799250.2799283
15. Hoc, J.-M.: Towards a cognitive approach to human–machine cooperation in dynamic situations. Int. J. Hum.-Comput. St. **54**, 509–540 (2001). https://doi.org/10.1006/ijhc.2000.0454
16. Hoffman, R.R., Mueller, S.T., Klein, G., Litman, J.: Measures for explainable AI: Explanation goodness, user satisfaction, mental models, curiosity, trust, and human-AI performance. Front. Comput. Sci. **5**, 1096257 (2023). https://doi.org/10.3389/fcomp.2023.1096257

17. Jacovi, A., Marasović, A., Miller, T., Goldberg, Y.: Formalizing trust in artificial intelligence: prerequisites, causes and goals of human trust in AI. In: Proceedings of the 2021 ACM Conference on Fairness, Accountability, and Transparency, pp. 624–635. ACM, Virtual Event Canada (2021). https://doi.org/10.1145/3442188.3445923

18. Klein, G., Feltovich, P.J., Bradshaw, J.M., Woods, D.D.: Common ground and coordination in joint activity. In: Rouse, W.B., Boff, K.R. (eds.) Organizational Simulation, pp. 139–184. John Wiley & Sons Inc, Hoboken, NJ, USA (2005). https://doi.org/10.1002/0471739448.ch6

19. Kramer, J., Petzoldt, T.: A matter of behavioral cost: contextual factors and behavioral interventions interactively influence pro-environmental charging decisions. J. Environ. Psychol. **84**, 101878 (2022). https://doi.org/10.1016/j.jenvp.2022.101878

20. Lee, J.D., See, K.A.: Trust in automation: designing for appropriate reliance. Hum. Fact. **46**, 50–80 (2004). https://doi.org/10.1518/hfes.46.1.50.30392

21. Leys, C., Ley, C., Klein, O., Bernard, P., Licata, L.: Detecting outliers: do not use standard deviation around the mean, use absolute deviation around the median. J. Exp. Soc. Psychol. **49**, 764–766 (2013). https://doi.org/10.1016/j.jesp.2013.03.013

22. Rosenthal, R., Rosnow, R.L., Rubin, D.B.: Contrasts and Effect Sizes in Behavioral Research: A Correlational Approach. Cambridge University Press (1999)

23. Sadeghian, O., Oshnoei, A., Mohammadi-ivatloo, B., Vahidinasab, V., Anvari-Moghaddam, A.: A comprehensive review on electric vehicles smart charging: solutions, strategies, technologies, and challenges. J. Energy Stor. **54**, 105241 (2022). https://doi.org/10.1016/j.est.2022.105241

24. Schrills, T., Franke, T.: How do users experience traceability of AI systems? examining subjective information processing awareness in automated insulin delivery (AID) systems. ACM Trans. Interact. Intell. Syst. 3588594 (2023). https://doi.org/10.1145/3588594

25. Schrills, T., Kargl, S., Bickel, M., Franke, T.: Perceive, Understand & Predict – Empirical Indication for Facets in Subjective Information Processing Awareness (2022) https://psyarxiv.com/3n95u/download

26. Shin, D.: The effects of explainability and causability on perception, trust, and acceptance: Implications for explainable AI. Int. J. Hum.-Comput. St. **146**, 102551 (2021). https://doi.org/10.1016/j.ijhcs.2020.102551

Repeat Clicking: A Lack of Awareness is Not the Problem

Matthew Canham[✉] [iD]

Beyond Layer Seven, LLC, Oviedo, FL, USA
mcanham@belay7.com

Abstract. Although phishing is the most common social engineering tactic employed by cyber criminals, not everyone is equally susceptible. An important finding emerging across several research studies on phishing is that a subset of employees is especially susceptible to social engineering tactics and is responsible for a disproportionate number of successful phishing attempts. Sometimes referred to as *repeat clickers*, these employees habitually fail simulated phishing tests and are suspected of being responsible for a significant number of real-world phishing related data breaches. In contrast to repeat clickers, *protective stewards* are those employees who never fail simulated phishing exercises and habitually report phishing simulations to their security departments. This study explored some of the potential causes of these persistent behaviors (both good and bad) by administering six semi-structured interviews (three repeat clickers and three protective stewards). Surprisingly, both groups were able to identify message cues for identifying potentially malicious emails. Repeat clickers reported a more internally oriented locus of control and higher confidence in their ability to identify phishing emails, but also described more rigid email checking habits than did protective stewards. One unexpected finding was that repeat clickers failed to recall an identifier which they were explicitly informed that they would need to later recall, while the protective stewards recalled the identifier without error. Due to the small sample and exploratory nature of this study additional research should seek to confirm whether these findings extrapolate to larger populations.

Keywords: Phishing · Security Awareness · Repeat Clickers · Protective Stewards

1 Repeat Clickers and Protective Stewards

1.1 Phishing Susceptibility

Phishing describes an email-based social engineering attack which attempts to manipulate the recipient into downloading malware, unintentionally disclosing credentials, or otherwise taking action that is not in their own (or their organization's) best interest. As the most common tactic that cybercriminals employ against system users, phishing poses a serious security threat to the human attack surface (Hadnagy 2018; Verizon 2023).

© The Author(s), under exclusive license to Springer Nature Switzerland AG 2023
H. Degen et al. (Eds.): HCII 2023, LNCS 14059, pp. 325–342, 2023.
https://doi.org/10.1007/978-3-031-48057-7_20

Establishing the ground truth of online social engineering susceptibility can be extremely difficult (if not impossible) because cyber threat actors often undertake significant measures to conceal their presence on a network. To counter the phishing threat, many organizations have incorporated simulated phishing email attacks as a part of their security awareness training activities (Greene et al. 2018; Steves et al. 2019). Examples of currently available commercial off the shelf (COTS) phishing simulation platforms are PhishMe (now Cofense), Wombat Security Awareness, and KnowBe4.

While this form of training is very realistic and can be an effective way to prepare users to avoid real phishing attacks (Carella et al. 2017), it also provides researchers with a rich data source because they record several user actions under realistic conditions. These simulated phishing campaigns are likely to be effective proxies for studying real-world phishing attacks because users are not typically warned about an impending email campaign, and the simulated phishing emails often closely mimic actual attacks. In fact, simulated phishing emails are sometimes 'de-fanged' versions of real-world attacks. By analyzing simulated phishing datasets, the research community can build a better understanding of user susceptibility patterns.

Phishing simulation software often provides four types of high-level behavioral metrics for each employee's actions during each phishing campaign; (1) clicking on an embedded hyperlink, (2) replying to the address from which an email originated, (3) entering data after a recipient clicked on the hyperlink, and/or (4) reporting the email the information security department as a suspected phishing attack (Canham et al. 2021). A campaign *failure* is often defined as occurring when an employee performs one or more of the first three actions. Conversely, an employee might report the email as suspicious (without taking the first three actions) and thus providing a protective shield for their organizations against such attacks. There is also the possibility that an employee may both commit a potentially dangerous action *and* then also report that same suspicious email to security staff.

1.2   Repeat Clickers and Protective Stewards

Empirical studies suggest that individuals might be differentially susceptible to phishing (Canham et al., 2019, 2021). Previous work examining repeated interactions between employees and simulated phishing emails, over the course of 20 separate email campaigns, reveals substantial differences in susceptibility patterns (see Fig. 1). This work revealed that approximately half (51%) of all employees who were sent simulated phishing emails never failed a single simulated campaign, while a little less than half (44%) failed between one to three simulated phishing emails (i.e., occasional clickers) out of twenty. Finally, a small segment of employees (approximately 6%) fell prey to four or more of the 20 phishing simulations. If each individual simulation campaign failure is counted as a separate event, then the occasional clickers (again 1–3 failures) account for a total of 71% of the total simulation failures, while the 'repeat clickers' (>3 failures) account for 29% of the total clicks. It is also noteworthy that three employees failed 12 of 20 campaigns during the one-year period, illustrating the seriousness of this security exposure. Taking the ratios of these numbers, we may create a 'risk factor' for each group. The occasional clickers account for approximately 44% of the employee population yet account for approximately 71% of the total simulation failures, leading to a risk factor of 1.62. More surprisingly, while repeat clickers account for approximately 6% of the population, they tallied approximately 29% of the total failures, leading to a risk score of 4.84. These calculations suggest that repeat clickers present nearly three times more risk to the organization's social engineering attack exposure than occasional clickers (Canham et al. 2021), demonstrating the importance for the security community to better understand the repeat clicking phenomenon.

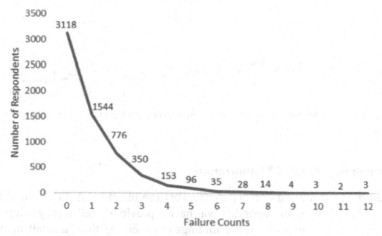

Fig. 1. Distribution of employees by phishing simulation failure counts. (Adapted from Canham et al. 2021).

By contrast, employees who never fail simulated phishing emails, but do report multiple campaigns, are termed protective stewards. Protective stewards provide an enhancement to their organization's security posture by providing an early warning system, alerting their security departments of ongoing social engineering attacks targeting employees. Figure 2 depicts the distribution of employees who did not fail a single phishing simulation. Note that the majority of employees (1,550) did not report nor fail any phishing campaigns, 250 employees reported one simulated campaign, and 6 employees reported 20 of 20 phishing campaigns over the course of the year. In contrast to the 'risk factor' presented by repeat clickers, it is also possible to calculate a 'security enhancement' factor for protective stewards (who never failed any phishing simulations). For example, the occasional reporters comprised approximately 17% of the employee population, and reported approximately 8% of the total reported emails, resulting in a security enhancement factor of 0.47. The protective stewards (employees who reported four or more campaigns) accounted for approximately 92% of the total reported simulation campaigns while only accounting for 33% of the employees who never clicked a simulated phishing email, results in a security enhancement factor of 2.79, approximately five times higher than the occasional reporters.

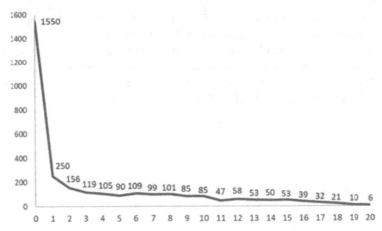

Fig. 2. Distribution of employees by phishing simulation report counts. (Adapted from Canham et al. 2021).

1.3 Research on Repeated Victimization

Other research has uncovered similar patterns. For example, (Li et al. 2020) found that the best predictor of phishing susceptibility was having previously fallen prey to a phishing email. Another study supported these findings in observing that "a small number of employees… (fell) for phishing emails multiple times" (Lain et al. 2022, p. 8). At least two studies have found a tendency for a small number of cybercrime victims to be repeat victims, accounting for a disproportionate number of victimization. One study which analyzed data produced by the Office for National Statistics (ONS), based on the Crime Survey for England and Wales (CSEW), found that repeat cybercrime victims accounted for approximately twice the number of reported cybercrimes than one-time victims (Correia 2020). Another study found that 45% of cyber-fraud victims were repeat victims (Whitty 2019). When combined, these findings suggest that such repeat victim susceptibility extends beyond the limits of phishing.

A limitation of this earlier study (Canham et al. 2021) was that it did not provide insight into *why* the sub-groups of repeat clickers and protective stewards emerge or address the root causes of behaviors. One study that explored causal factors found three clicking patterns which they dubbed 'all-clickers', 'non-clickers', and 'everyone else'. The researchers were unable to modify persistent behaviors even after implementing a training intervention (Caputo et al. 2013). Follow-up interviews indicated that the two most common reasons provided by the all-clickers for falling for phishing emails were "an interest in the subject matter and lack of careful attention" (Caputo et al. 2013, p. 35). For example, users would often state that "if an email looked interesting, they would click a link without thinking". Importantly, most had no memory of identifying anything suspicious in the emails. Similarly, the non-clicker group also had no clear memory for the simulated phishing emails and indicated that they "probably deleted the emails immediately without reading them", and that their default behavior was to conduct their own web searches and generally did not click on links in email messages (Caputo et al. 2013, p. 35). These responses suggest that these two patterns of behavior might default to habituated responses to email, rather than being driven by security knowledge. As elaborated on later, these interaction patterns align with the findings of the current study.

Theoretical Perspectives. As described in previous work, five categories of theories are emerging to provide potential explanations for repeat clicker behavior (Canham et al. 2019). These five categories Social Influence Techniques, Situational Factors, Cultural Influences, Individual Differences, and finally hybrid theories (Canham et al. 2019). Theories emphasizing the impact of social influence techniques suggest that repeat clickers may be especially susceptible to such methods (Workman 2008). Theories focused on situational factors emphasize transitory factors such as workload and other environmental or situations such as distraction or time pressure (Greene et al. 2018; Hassold 2018). Theories focusing on the influence of culture on phishing susceptibility, account for the broader influence that sociological factors can have on attitudes and behavior (Butavicius et al. 2016; Posey & Canham 2018); however, because repeat clicking behavior appears to only afflict a small portion of user populations, it seems unlikely that this behavior is being driven by cultural influences. Theories focusing on individual differences have examined the influence of individual level factors on phishing susceptibility such as personality traits, expertise, and other individual differences (Halevi et al. 2015; Lawson et al. 2017; Pattinson et al. 2012; Sackett & Walmsley 2014; Sudzina & Pavlicek 2017, 2020; Uebelacker & Quiel 2014; Welk et al. 2015; Zhao & Smillie 2015). Repeat clicking behavior will most likely involve an explanation drawing from an interaction between individual traits and social influence techniques, or situational factors, or a combination of the three of these factors, and thus hybrid theories (Harrison et al. 2016; Uebelacker & Quiel 2014; Williams et al. 2017) are the most promising potential explanation of factors driving the repeat clicking phenomenon.

Current Study. As this review demonstrates, a coherent theoretical framework for repeat clicking behavior remains elusive. With the objective of gaining insight into the causes of repeat clicking behavior, this study recruited volunteers selected from the study described in (Canham et al. 2021) to participate in interview sessions with researchers. Because there is currently very little understanding for the causal factors relating to repeated victimization in cybercrime victims (Correia 2020), the current study was exploratory in nature and thus relied heavily on qualitative data collection.

2 Method

2.1 Participants

After the study protocol was reviewed and approved by the university human subjects review board, six employees from the organization studied in (Canham et al. 2021) were recruited to participate in a follow up interview. Three of these employees were from the repeat clickers group and three were from the protective stewards group. Both groups of volunteers were recruited from their respective distribution tails by virtue of committing eight or more actions relative to their category. For example, the recruited repeat clickers had all failed a minimum of eight simulated campaigns, and the protective stewards had all reported a minimum of eight simulated campaigns (without a single failure), in the previous one-year period. Volunteers were notified that they were being invited to partic-ipate because of their performance in the simulated phishing trainings, but they were not informed from which group (repeat clickers or protective stewards) that they were being sampled. Study volunteers were compensated $50 US for an approximately one-hour interview, and the completion of a short online survey which required approximately 15 minutes to complete.

2.2 Procedure

Online Surveys. After providing informed consent, the volunteers completed an online survey which assessed their anxiety in using the Internet, confidence in detecting phishing emails, and whether they had been previous victims of online fraud. The scales used included Internet Anxiety (Joiner et el., 2007), Phishing Confidence (Canham et al. in development), Need for Cognition (Cacioppo & Petty 1982), Curiosity (Collins et al. 2004), Tolerance for Ambiguity (Herman et al. 2010), Risk Taking Index (Nicholson et al., 2005), Risk Avoidance (Tellegen 1995), Distrust (Tellegen 1995), and Locus of Control (Levenson 1981). At the conclusion of this online survey, volunteers were asked to enter a "code word" which would later be used to connect their answers to the interview, as a means of minimizing the chances for identification of the collected data.

Interviews. The interviews were conducted in person either in a lab, or in a quiet conference room at the employee's place of work. The inter-views followed a semi-structured format with a prepared list of questions which the interviews loosely followed, with the latitude of pursuing interesting conversational tangents as encountered. Six categories of questions (listed below) were adapted from (Conway et al. 2017). The six question categories included: Techniques and Strategies (analyzing email, links, domain, sender, etc.), Actions in Response to suspicious email (clicking, downloading, opening, forwarding), Perceived Techno-logical Prowess (self-assessed expertise or knowledge), Phishing Simulations (performance and actions taken), and Workload and Email Habits (variation and amount of workload, and how email is managed

3   Results

3.1   Online Surveys

Due to the small sample size, no statistical tests were performed to compare the mean scores between the repeat clickers and protective stewards; however, the mean scores for the two groups are included in the table below for review. It is interesting to note that the repeat clickers reported higher scores on the Internet Anxiety, Phishing Confidence, Need for Cognition, Tolerance for Ambiguity, and Locus of Control scales, while reporting lower scores on the Curiosity, Risk Avoidance, and Distrust scales. Mean scores on the Risk-Taking Index were nearly identical. It is also noteworthy that all three of the repeat clickers reported using a desktop computer as their primary means of accessing online resources, while all three of the protective stewards reported using a mobile device (either a laptop or cell phone), as their primary device.

Table 1. Mean scores for Repeat Clickers and Protective Stewards in online surveys.

Scale	Repeat Clickers	Protective Stewards
Internet Anxiety	1.8	1.0
Phishing Confidence	3.0	2.0
Need For Cognition	2.5	1.8
Curiosity	2.6	2.9
Tolerance For Ambiguity	3.2	2.9
Risk Taking Index	1.5	1.6
Risk Avoidance	1.7	2.3
Distrust	2.8	4.2
Locus Of Control	2.4	1.7

Table 2. Mean number of hours reported in response to the question "How many hours per week do you do the following online?

Activity	Repeat Clickers	Protective Stewards
Shopping	0.3	3.7
Social Media	13.7	8.7
Email	15.0	9.3
Watching Videos	1.7	4.0
Gaming	0.0	0.0
Work	31.0	34.0
School Work	1.7	0.0

In addition to the scales scores summarized in Table 1, the volunteers were specifically asked about prior online fraud victimization and methods for detecting phishing emails (Tables 2, 3, 4).

Table 3. Online Question: Have you ever been the victim of online fraud before?

Number	Repeat Clickers	Protective Stewards
1	Definitely yes	Probably not but not sure
2	Definitely yes	Definitely not
3	Definitely not	Probably not but not sure

Table 4. Online Question: How are you able to detect whether an email is a phishing scam?

Number	Repeat Clickers	Protective Stewards
1	Common sense	Unusual sender's email address; frequent typos and grammatical errors; suspicious requests for money or favors
2	By the format of the email and the content or misspelling	Senders email address
3	From what I have read and learn what to look for	I check the sender's email address. I make sure the email makes sense and follows the organization's policies. For instance, I know it's a phishing scam if my bank emails me asking for my personal information because this is against their policy

3.2 Interview Responses

Interviews spanned approximately one hour for each session and while including a full transcript is beyond the scope of this work, representative sample excerpts are included here for each topic category. The sample responses are listed for each volunteer (number 1, 2, or 3), within each group (Repeat Clickers or Protective Stewards). Example questions are included in the bullet point items below each topic category heading.

Techniques and Strategies (Analyzing Email, Links, Domain, Sender, Etc.)

- How would you spot an email that came from outside the organization or outside of your area?
- What would you do, step by step, if you got a suspicious email?
- What are the characteristics of a phishing email? (Table 5)

Actions in Response to Suspicious Email (Clicking, Downloading, Opening, Forwarding)

- What do you do if you receive a suspicious email? (Hover over links, etc.)
- When you get an email, just any type of email, and it has a link in it, what do you think about when you think about clicking that link? (Table 6)

Table 5. Exemplar responses to Techniques and Strategies questions.

Number	Repeat Clicker	Protective Steward
1	I really don't click on the link because I worry about it, it's like a virus. Especially when I receive a [WORK] email—first of all I look at it, "Where does it come from?" Make sure it's [ORGANIZATION'S EMAIL REDACTED], that means it's internal. But if it's from an outsider, like a Gmail, Hotmail, other things, I always think "maybe it's other people scam." And if they have a link, I don't open that-- it's a test alert. I send that to the IT department	I just think if it doesn't look like any of the other emails I received, it just looks a little different, then I check the (report) button
2	maybe like… like misspelling, I notice just like some phishing emails have a misspelling in them or the font can be different in one part of an email vs another part	if the email address looks funky or it's just like a weird request for a favor or money. Something like that. Or if just it's like, kind of an erratic message with weird grammar and spelling—like umm this doesn't seem right
3	I would (check) the email itself, it tells you where it's from, if it's coming from Google, from a Gmail, wherever	It's quite a few things that could be suspicious. For one, any email from someone that is asking for something that normally isn't my job. I think that one of the examples that I reported was someone asking me to buy gift cards or something

Perceived Technological Prowess (Self-Assessed Expertise or Knowledge).
How would you describe your knowedge level in terms of being able to use computers or information technology? (Table 7)

Phishing Simulations

- Do you get any feedback from the (phish alert button) when you clicked it?
- Can you tell me about anything that you remember about reporting any of the emails that you reported? (Table 8)

Table 6. Exemplar responses to Actions in Response to suspicious email questions.

Number	Repeat Clickers	Protective Stewards
1	I review, look at it, print out the paperwork, ask my friend, I say, "Hey, do you think this is real or what?" My friend says, "This looks like it's real because a [ORGANIZATION'S EMAIL DOMAIN REDACTED]" Then I take it to my assistant director, I say, "First I wanna ask your opinion if it's real or not." He said, "Yeah, it's real."	I check the (report) button. Whether someone else is actually gonna look at it, I don't know
2	when I get those e-mails, I send it, to CERT (information security department). But like some of them look just like very legitimate… There's a button on the right-hand side of the e-mail that says report to CERT, and I just click it and it gets sent to CERT	We have a small IT department here. I'd probably just got to our Help Desk person first and they can take it up the chain
3	one of the things I pride myself on is I send it to my ISAT (information security) group, they send it back say, "This is a phishing" and then I pass on to anybody else. If it they don't look right I send it to them and let them get back to me	part of the [ORGANIZATION REDACTED]'s process is when someone does report it, if IT looks at it and says, "This really is a phishing," they'll send out an email to the foundation saying, "Hey, just an FYI, we're getting hit with this. If you get this email, don't click on it." They'll kinda tell you either delete it or "Let us know that you received it," or something

Workload

- Regarding the amount of email that you get; how much would you say that your overall workload will fluctuate?
- Do you normally only check your work email at work?
- Do you ever feel stressed/overwhelmed at work? (Table 9)

Email Habits

- Do you regularly check email outside of working hours (Nights/Weekends)?
- Which device(s) do you use when checking email? (Table 10)

Table 7. Exemplar responses to Perceived Technological Prowess questions.

Number	Repeat Clickers	Protective Stewards
1	No (training). But I think it's common sense	I'm Microsoft certified in databases
2	It was like a very long time ago like freshman year... I think one of them is programming because it was in [WORK SITE]. So, I think it was like something with keyboarding. And then another one was like programming, I think. So very basic	I just did the Credit Card training and there might've been something similar like that for the Phishing training. Like an online, PowerPoint, click through thing. But I don't recall, that was a while ago
3	I know how to function. Especially... online courses, I know all the pushes and buttons. It's just like my iPhone. My daughter uses... Sometimes she has to teach me	(it)'s always been second nature-- I came from the department of revenue before this. And they had very strict policies on like, locking your computer screen and having a clean desk policy

Table 8. Exemplar responses to Phishing Simulations questions.

Number	Repeat Clickers	Protective Stewards
1	I don't think so. Usually— if... HR send over a training, yes, but if a scammer, no	I noticed that... you still get that email that says, "Thank you for reporting." So, the message will pop up
2	Yeah. Well, saw like the oops page. Maybe like a couple, say, like three, two to three	they all seem to be the simulated ones. I always seem to get that message that says, "Congratulations you detected a scam" or whatever. I can't recall one that I would've reported, that said anything else
3	I have one time. Matter of fact something happened, and you guys might check periodically	Well, the one's that I have reported have all been a part of the program. And it was immediate, as soon as you sent it, you get what the button says but as soon as you sent it over, it was an immediate: "Good job, this is a part of the program." So, it was an immediate response

Table 9. Exemplar responses to Workload questions.

Number	Repeat Clickers	Protective Stewards
1	Usually—to me I'm always busy. Because I do accounting and finance, I'm always busy. I have to do the internal things, people who have trouble, purchasing. I have to review and then look at the budget, approve, the people using the P card, I have to review and make sure the P card is right	we're constantly overwhelmed, constantly with eyes burning from too much screen time. We're very behind on everything
2	It can be it just depends on the day. Like how busy it is. Overall, I feel like I can, but if it's like very busy with [CLIENTS] nonstop, which happens sometimes, my work might go into the next day	I knew other people in the team that are [overwhelmed] on a constant basis, but for me, I haven't. It's usually just the clients-- the internal clients that I'm working on—actively working on their tickets. So, it's only a handful of tickets at a time. And as I closed them out, I'll open up more. But it's usually just the same people
3	(My workload fluctuates) a lot now	Most days are pretty steady, I would say, for me. In my current position. This is my third position since I've been here. So when there's a big project, you can be overwhelmed pretty quickly. But otherwise, it's kinda less, I guess

Table 10. Exemplar responses to Email Habits or Workflow Habits questions.

Number	Repeat Clickers	Protective Stewards
1	90% is on the office. 2% would be at home *Author acknowledges that this does not add to 100%, this was the subject's response	Yes
2	mobile would be like 10 percent... More so weekends	Yes. Probably 90/10 on the laptop
3	when I leave work Friday after I check my email that is my day. Okay. I turn my computer back on Sunday to look at my things to do list, but I still check my email	90% of the time is definitely on the PC. And then 10%... on the cell phone *Phones were used for checking email during off hours

4 Discussion

One of the most interesting, and unexpected findings of this study was not directly related to the explicit data collection. Upon completion of the online survey portion of the study, the final question asked volunteers to provide a "code word" which would later be used to match their answers to the interview transcripts, for the purpose of minimizing the likelihood of revealing the identity of volunteers. Volunteers were explicitly instructed that they would need to later provide this "code word" to the interviewers and that they should choose something that they would easily recall. All participants from the protective stewards group accurately recalled their code word, and all the repeat clickers failed to recall their code word. The research team was still able to match online responses to the interviews based on the timing of each.

4.1 Analysis of Online Survey Responses

While scores from the online surveys were not statistically compared between the groups due to the small sample sizes investigated, some of the differences are noteworthy. For example, repeat clickers reported higher confidence in their ability to detect phishing emails, which is consistent with some studies which have found that unjustified high levels of confidence are related to increased susceptibility to phishing. In particular, that study's findings indicate that "overclaimers", people who grossly overestimate their phishing detection ability, are more vulnerable than other individuals (Jones 2023). It is also worth drawing attention to the higher level of anxiety reported by repeat clickers when accessing online services. It is unclear why this discrepancy exists, but higher levels of internet anxiety might be due to prior victimization. Two of the three repeat clickers reported previously being victimized by online fraud.

In considering the number of hours spent online conducting various activities, protective stewards reported spending approximately 12 times more time shopping online, and twice as much time watching videos, than did the repeat clickers. In contrast, the repeat clickers spent almost twice as much time on social media and email compared to protective stewards. Additional research should examine whether these findings extend to larger samples, but these insights to point toward additional research efforts which might focus on non-email usage behaviors that might predict, or help explain, repeat clicker behavior patterns.

The differences in the mean scores on the Need for Cognition, Curiosity, Tolerance for Ambiguity, Risk Taking Index, and Risk Avoidance scales should be treated cautiously because of the small sample sizes involved. Additional research and theoretical support will make the findings related to the Distrust and Locus of Control scales more interesting.

The Distrust Scale (Tellegen 1995) assesses the subject's propensity to distrust or be suspicious of others, "I suspect hidden motives in others" being an example item. Several research studies on susceptibility to phishing point toward suspicion as being a major factor in susceptibility (Vishwanath 2022). The higher levels of distrust reported by the protective stewards may be an indication of higher suspicion levels in this population of users and this is something which should be explored in more depth in future research.

The higher Locus of Control scores among repeat clickers indicates that this group feels more in control of their own destiny and ability to improve performance than the protective stewards. This finding is somewhat puzzling and deserves more exploration. Other studies have found that individuals with a high locus of control were more likely to be the victims of cyber-scams (Whitty 2019). The findings of this study agree with those findings as well as the findings of an associated study (Canham et al. under review). These findings also deserve more research focus. A potential explanation is that there is a relationship between an internally oriented locus of control and a higher level of confidence for detecting phishing emails, and this commonality might be driving the repeat clicker behavior pattern.

4.2 Analysis of Interview Responses

Phishing Simulation Training. None of the interviewees initially admitted to clicking the embedded hyperlinks in the simulated phishing emails. It should be noted that the KnowBe4 phishing simulation platform used in the initial study (Canham et al. 2021) provided immediate feedback in the form of an "oops" landing page which advised an employee that they had fallen prey to a simulated phishing email and provided an explanation for indicators they could have used to identify the email as a potential phish. It is unknown whether this reluctance was motivated by a desire for prosocial responding, embarrassment, a lack of memory, or a combination of these factors. However, when coaxed, all of repeat clickers admitted to clicking the links in "one or two" emails, none reported clicking the hyperlinks in more than three emails. Recall that all the volunteers from this group had clicked eight or more hyperlinks. This point deserves more attention because there is reason to believe that memory might be a factor in this reluctance to account for clicking more hyperlinks.

While this is currently speculative, the lack of recalling falling prey to simulated phishing emails and the inability to recall their own "code words" is suggestive of a common cognitive factor driving both observed results. Considering that previous research studies also found that neither habitual clickers nor habitual non-clickers recalled clicking the links within simulated phishing emails (or ignoring them), suggests that both groups are handling potential phishing emails through automated cognitive processes (Caputo et al. 2013). If these findings replicate in future studies, it could have significant implications for security awareness training. For example, for repeat clickers, training which reinforces automatic processes may be more successful than training regimens which exclusively focus on security awareness or knowledge.

An interesting finding from the protective stewards group was that they seemed to identify the simulated phishing tests as coming from the information security department and acknowledged that this was reinforced by the feedback that they received which indicated that the attempt had been a simulation. Security awareness trainers might consider withholding immediate feedback when simulated phishing exercises are correctly identified and reported. In contrast to failed training simulations, providing immediate feedback on reported emails might inadvertently train higher performing employees to identify emails which "look" like training emails, potentially making these employees more susceptible to actual malicious emails. Other studies have found that in fact protective stewards enjoy identifying simulated phishing emails that are very difficult to detect, particularly when this is contextualized within a gamified competition (Canham et al. 2022).

Workload and Email Habits. One potential explanation for the repeated victimization of a subgroup of employees is that this subset is overworked or overloaded and are thus more susceptible to phishing emails due to situational factors (because they are distracted or under a heavier cognitive load). The interviewees from both groups reported high levels of workload with heavy fluctuations, making workload an unlikely explanation for repeat clicking.

There were differences reported in the email habits between the two groups. Even though both groups reported checking email primarily during work hours, repeat clickers reported much higher aversion to checking work email during off hours. One interviewee from the repeat clickers group reported that s/he refused to check email during the weekends. Protective stewards by contrast have much more fluidity in checking work email on or off work hours.

Techniques and Strategies. In describing actions taken to determine whether an email is legitimate, both groups reported looking for similar cues (email domain name, misspelling, odd grammar, or unrelated to job), suggesting that both groups possessed the relevant knowledge required to identify and avoid suspicious email.

Actions in Response to Suspicious Email. In response to receiving a suspicious email, both groups also reported taking similar actions to report the email to the security department (CERT). One interviewee from the repeat clicker sample reported printing suspicious emails on paper when evaluating them. It was unclear what benefit this was supposed to impart. Both groups appeared to know the suspicious email policy.

Perceived Technological Prowess. There were some interesting differences in the self-assessed technical knowledge between the two groups of interviewees. Technical knowledge in this context referred to information technology knowledge and capability, but not necessarily security related knowledge. All the protective stewards reported having previously received some security related training, with one of the repeat clickers reporting receiving training sometime previously. One of the protective stewards reported being a certified Microsoft database administrator.

5   Conclusion

This work represents one of the first efforts to uncover insights into the factors driving repeat clicker behavior. The exploratory nature of the study and small sample size limit the inferences which can be drawn from findings; however, this study points toward several potentially fruitful lines of future research which should be explored.

Perhaps the most interesting finding of this study was not intentionally sought, but instead discovered accidentally. The inability to recall "code words" by repeat clickers, combined with an inability to recall simulated phishing failures, and rigid email habits are suggestive of an underlying common cognitive factor at play with repeat clickers. A potential reason that repeat clickers have more rigid habits is that they are compensating for a cognitive deficiency that is also contributing to less effective recall. This is something that needs to be explored in future research efforts.

All the volunteers in this study had received some form of limited security awareness training from the organization. All but one of the protective stewards recalled receiving this training, and none of the repeat clickers recalled receiving it. This finding leads to the question of whether the training was effective even though it was not explicitly recalled. Both groups were able to identify multiple indicators of suspicious email messages, and so it is likely that some of the lessons from the training were retained. This knowledge withstanding, the protective stewards unquestionably had more general technology-related knowledge and were more capable at articulating technically related concepts than the repeat clickers.

Future research should also seek to understand the relationship between higher internal locus of control and cybercrime susceptibility. The findings of this study are consistent with those of (Whitty 2019) and another unpublished study. It is unclear whether there is a relationship between more internally oriented locus of control and higher reported confidence in phishing detection, but this warrants additional exploration. The organization participating in the study requested that age not be collected from the volunteers, so it is unknown whether this is a contributing factor to these findings.

The termination of employees in this category is not always feasible; therefore, it is critical to better understand the causal factors for repeat clicking behavior in to enable security professionals to effectively address this critical security risk.

Acknowledgements. The author wishes to thank Dr. Clay Posey, Michael Constantino, Dr. Shanee Dawkins, and Alexandra Figueroa for their assistance in collecting and analyzing the data for this study. The author also wishes to acknowledge the support of the National Institute of Standards and Technology (NIST) under Financial Assistance Award Number: 60NANB19D123. The views and conclusions contained in this document are those of the author and should not be interpreted as representing the official policies, either expressed or implied, of NIST or the U.S. Government.

References

Butavicius, M., Parsons, K., Pattinson, M., McCormac, A.: Breaching the Human Firewall: Social engineering in Phishing and Spear-Phishing Emails (2016). [Cs] http://arxiv.org/abs/1606.00887

Cacioppo, J.T., Petty, R.E.: The need for cognition. J. Pers. Soc. Psychol. **42**(1), 116–131 (1982). https://doi.org/10.1037/0022-3514.42.1.116

Canham, M., Fiore, S.M., Constantino, M., Caulkins, B., Reinerman-Jones, L.: The Enduring Mystery of the Repeat Clickers (2019)

Canham, M., Posey, C., Constantino, M.: Phish Derby: shoring the human shield through gamified phishing attacks. Front. Educ. **6** (2022). https://doi.org/10.3389/feduc.2021.807277

Canham, M., Posey, C., Strickland, D., Constantino, M.: Phishing for long tails: examining organizational repeat clickers and protective stewards. SAGE Open **11**(1), 215824402199065 (2021). https://doi.org/10.1177/2158244021990656

Caputo, D.D., Pfleeger, S.L., Freeman, J.D., Johnson, M.E.: Going spear phishing: exploring embedded training and awareness. IEEE Secur. Privacy **12**(1), 28–38 (2013). https://doi.org/10.1109/MSP.2013.106

Carella, A., Kotsoev, M., Truta, T.M.: Impact of security awareness training on phishing click-through rates. In: 2017 IEEE International Conference on Big Data (Big Data), pp. 4458–4466 (2017). https://doi.org/10.1109/BigData.2017.8258485

Collins, R.P., Litman, J.A., Spielberger, C.D.: The measurement of perceptual curiosity. Personal. Individ. Differ. **36**(5), 1127–1141 (2004). https://doi.org/10.1016/S0191-8869(03)00205-8

Conway, D., Taib, R., Harris, M., Yu, K., Berkovsky, S., Chen, F.: A Qualitative Investigation of Bank Employee Experiences of Information Security and Phishing, pp. 115–129 (2017). https://www.usenix.org/conference/soups2017/technical-sessions/presentation/conway

Correia, S.G.: Patterns of online repeat victimisation and implications for crime prevention. In: 2020 APWG Symposium on Electronic Crime Research (ECrime), pp. 1–11 (2020). https://doi.org/10.1109/eCrime51433.2020.9493258

Greene, K., Steves, M., Theofanos, M., Kostick, J.: User context: an explanatory variable in phishing susceptibility. In: Proceedings 2018 Workshop on Usable Security. Workshop on Usable Security, San Diego, CA (2018). https://doi.org/10.14722/usec.2018.23016

Hadnagy, C.: Social Engineering: The Science of Human Hacking, 1st edn. Wiley (2018). https://doi.org/10.1002/9781119433729

Halevi, T., Memon, N., Nov, O.: Spear-phishing in the wild: a real-world study of personality, phishing self-efficacy and vulnerability to spear-phishing attacks (SSRN Scholarly Paper ID 2544742). Soc. Sci. Res. Netw. (2015). https://doi.org/10.2139/ssrn.2544742

Harrison, B., Vishwanath, A., Rao, R.: A user-centered approach to phishing susceptibility: the role of a suspicious personality in protecting against phishing. In: 2016 49th Hawaii International Conference on System Sciences (HICSS), pp. 5628–5634 (2016). https://doi.org/10.1109/HICSS.2016.696

Hassold, C.: Life After Phishing: What's Next? InfoSec World 2018. InfoSec World 2018, Orlando, FLl USA (2018)

Herman, J.L., Stevens, M.J., Bird, A., Mendenhall, M., Oddou, G.: The tolerance for ambiguity scale: towards a more refined measure for international management research. Int. J. Intercult. Relat. **34**(1), 58–65 (2010). https://doi.org/10.1016/j.ijintrel.2009.09.004

Joiner, R., Brosnan, M., Duffield, J., Gavin, J., Maras, P.: The relationship between Internet identification, Internet anxiety and Internet use. Comput. Hum. Behav. **23**(3), 1408–1420 (2007). https://doi.org/10.1016/j.chb.2005.03.002

Jones, D.: Protecting the overclaimers in cybersecurity w/ Dr. Daniel N. Jones | CSI Talks #7 (2023). https://www.youtube.com/watch?v=lsly2Q_74V4

Lain, D., Kostiainen, K., Čapkun, S.: Phishing in organizations: findings from a large-scale and long-term study. In: 2022 IEEE Symposium on Security and Privacy (SP), pp. 842–859 (2022). https://doi.org/10.1109/SP46214.2022.9833766

Lawson, P., Zielinska, O., Pearson, C., Mayhorn, C.B.: Interaction of personality and persuasion tactics in email phishing attacks. In: Proceedings of the Human Factors and Ergonomics Society Annual Meeting, vol. 61, issue 1, pp. 1331–1333 (2017). https://doi.org/10.1177/1541931213601815

Levenson, H.: Differentiating among internality, powerful others, and chance. In: Lefcourt, H.M. (ed.) Research with the Locus of Control Construct, pp. 1–15. Academic Press (1981)

Li, W., Lee, J., Purl, J., Greitzer, F., Yousefi, B., Laskey, K.: Experimental Investigation of Demographic Factors Related to Phishing Susceptibility (2020). https://doi.org/10.24251/HICSS.2020.274

Nicholson, N., Soane, E., Fenton-O'Creevy, M., Willman, P.: Personality and domain-specific risk taking. J. Risk Res. **8**(2), 157–176 (2005). https://doi.org/10.1080/1366987032000123856

Pattinson, M., Jerram, C., Parsons, K., McCormac, A., Butavicius, M.: Why do some people manage phishing e-mails better than others? Inf. Manag. Comput. Secur. **20**(1), 18–28 (2012). https://doi.org/10.1108/09685221211219173

Posey, C., Canham, M.: A computational social science approach to examine the duality between productivity and cybersecurity policy compliance within organizations. In: 2018 International Conference on Social Computing, Behavioral-Cultural Modeling, and Prediction and Behavior Representation in Modeling and Simulation, BRiMS 2018 (2018). https://stars.library.ucf.edu/scopus2015/7904

Sackett, P.R., Walmsley, P.T.: Which personality attributes are most important in the workplace? Perspect. Psychol. Sci. 9(5), 538–551 (2014). https://doi.org/10.1177/1745691614543972

Steves, M.P., Greene, K.K., Theofanos, M.F.: A phish scale: rating human phishing message detection difficulty. In: Proceedings 2019 Workshop on Usable Security. Workshop on Usable Security. San Diego, CA (2019). https://doi.org/10.14722/usec.2019.23028

Sudzina, F., Pavlicek, A.: Propensity to Click on Suspicious Links: Impact of Gender, of Age, and of Personality Traits. Digital Transformation – From Connecting Things to Transforming Our Lives, pp. 593–601 (2017). https://doi.org/10.18690/978-961-286-043-1.41

Sudzina, F., Pavlicek, A.: Virtual offenses: role of demographic factors and personality traits. Information 11(4), 188 (2020)

Tellegen, A.: Multidimensional Personality Questionnaire-276 (MPQ-276) Test Booklet, 1st edn., vol. 1. University of Minnesota Press (1995)

Uebelacker and Quiel, 2014.Uebelacker, S., Quiel, S.: The social engineering personality framework. In: 2014 Workshop on Socio-Technical Aspects in Security and Trust, pp. 24–30 (2014). https://doi.org/10.1109/STAST.2014.12

Verizon. 2023 Data Breach Investigations Report (DBIR). Verizon Enterprise Solutions (2023). https://www.verizon.com/business/resources/reports/2023-data-breach-investigations-report-dbir.pdf

Vishwanath, A.: The Weakest Link: How to Diagnose, Detect, and Defend Users From Phishing. The MIT Press (2022)

Welk, A.K., Hong, K.W., Zielinska, O.A., Tembe, R., Murphy-Hill, E., Mayhorn, C.B.: Will the "Phisher-Men" reel you in?: assessing individual differences in a phishing detection task. Int. J. Cyber Behav. Psychol. Learn. 5(4), 1–17 (2015). https://doi.org/10.4018/IJCBPL.2015100101

Whitty, M.T.: Predicting susceptibility to cyber-fraud victimhood. J. Finan. Crime 26(1), 277–292 (2019). https://doi.org/10.1108/JFC-10-2017-0095

Williams, E.J., Beardmore, A., Joinson, A.N.: Individual differences in susceptibility to online influence: a theoretical review. Comput. Hum. Behav. 72, 412–421 (2017). https://doi.org/10.1016/j.chb.2017.03.002

Workman, M.: Wisecrackers: a theory-grounded investigation of phishing and pretext social engineering threats to information security. J. Am. Soc. Inform. Sci. Technol. 59(4), 662–674 (2008). https://doi.org/10.1002/asi.20779

Zhao, K., Smillie, L.D.: The role of interpersonal traits in social decision making: exploring sources of behavioral heterogeneity in economic games. Pers. Soc. Psychol. Rev. 19(3), 277–302 (2015). https://doi.org/10.1177/1088868314553709

Aristotle's Phronesis as a Philosophical Foundation in Designing the Algorithmic Motivator-Driven Insulating Model (AMOI)

Francis Joseph Costello[1] and Kun Chang Lee[1,2(✉)]

[1] SKK Business School, Sungkyunkwan University, Seoul 03063, South Korea
kunchanglee@gmail.com

[2] Department of Health Sciences, Samsung Advanced Institute for Health Sciences and Technology (SAIHST), Sungkyunkwan University, Seoul 06355, South Korea

Abstract. Technology advancements have led to an increase in the use of algorithmic management (AM) to oversee workforces in big businesses. A number of AM tactics, such as real-time monitoring of employee output and performance, allocating employees to activities that are appropriate for them, and anticipating staff turnover, all strive to improve work processes. The program has drawn criticism for its lack of accountability between employers and employees, as well as for its prejudices and prejudice. The Algorithmic Motivation-driven Insulation Model (AMOI) has been developed to close this gap. In order to improve workplace relationships, give employees' mental health and wellness a high priority, and create fair and equitable work environments, this model uses a chatbot-based emotion-aware deep learning framework. In order to achieve *eudaimonia*, our proposed AI architecture was built on employing a scientific methodology and *phronesis*-inspired concepts. This strategy intends to develop fair and responsible digital technology for workers to be employed in future AM solutions by elevating human values and improving employee engagement and performance.

Keywords: Algorithmic management · Phronesis · Eudaimonia · Algorithmic motivation-driven insulation model · Fair and responsible digital technology

1 Motivation

Artificial intelligence (AI) has driven the rapid development of complex and targeted algorithms, which are now employed extensively in a variety of industry organizations [4, 13, 19]. A helpful tool for more than just inference, artificial intelligence has advanced from simple machine learning (ML) to deep learning (DL) and enabled advancements in decision-making across a range of business disciplines [20]. Numerous businesses have chosen horizontal structures over vertical ones as a response to fierce market competition. This change has been accelerated by the COVID-19 epidemic that started in early 2020 and was made possible by the development of the Internet and online communication technology [5]. Office workers in horizontal organizational structures frequently obtain

© The Author(s), under exclusive license to Springer Nature Switzerland AG 2023
H. Degen et al. (Eds.): HCII 2023, LNCS 14059, pp. 343–355, 2023.
https://doi.org/10.1007/978-3-031-48057-7_21

their work instructions via artificial intelligence-powered internet communication platforms [13]. To match employees with jobs, the majority of online labor marketplaces use AI-based communication systems. AM is being used more frequently in organizations. This is due to the fact that developments in digital technology have made it possible to capture large amounts of data in real time. In large firms, AM is becoming more crucial for managing internal and distant labor forces [22]. Platforms like Uber and Upwork are now capable of efficiently managing and allocating work assignments via web applications, offering in-the-moment performance reviews, and boosting business earnings across a range of industries [19]. There are different ways to use AI, and some businesses choose to include human input and involvement while others use entirely automated decision-making techniques. By speeding up the hiring process, tracking employee productivity and performance in real-time, matching patients with doctors and therapists, assigning ride-sharing drivers and passengers, assessing employee performance by listening to customer calls in call centers, and foretelling the likelihood that employees will resign, AM promises to improve business processes [11].

Although AM has been praised for its ability to enhance workforce management and create value, it has also come under fire for the negative effects on employees that it may have. Critics claim that there are problems with ineffective monitoring and control procedures, a lack of transparency, potential biases and prejudice, inclinations toward dehumanization, and a lack of traditional employer-employee accountability [13]. These worries are exacerbated by algorithmic bias in many organizational activities, which can be challenging to identify due to the "black box" nature of many algorithms' decision-making processes. As a result, academic communities are debating ethical AI design principles and rules. For integrating algorithms into managerial procedures, it has been suggested to use Explainable AI or legislative frameworks as the General Data Protection Regulation [1, 11].

The design of algorithms and how users interact with them have been extensively studied in studies on the use of algorithms to manage gig workers. The power balance between drivers and rideshare platforms, for instance, was found to benefit the platforms when [15] examined posts made by Uber drivers on internet forums and conducted interviews with drivers. A power disparity between the allegedly independent drivers and the restrictive digital platforms was identified by [13] after studying Uber drivers in a similar vein. They noticed that drivers employ a variety of strategies to recover autonomy, like guessing intelligently or attempting to figure out why the platforms act a certain way. There are worker countermeasures to algorithmic management, according to [12] and other studies. The impact of algorithmic management on employee well-being, as well as the development of platform designs and intervention strategies to support employee well-being, are not examined in these studies. Additionally, the HCI industry has demonstrated an increasing interest in putting worker well-being first and attending to their requirements through platforms and treatments that use algorithmic management [6, 12]. Recent approaches have called for enhancing technological system design by emphasizing the opinions of low-powered workers who are controlled or mediated by algorithmic systems [9]. In the past, it was common for worker feedback to guide the original design of interventions, without taking into account how to apply this design holistically [10, 21].

Alternative AM algorithmic designs that attempt to enhance worker well-being are still hard to find, especially from the workers' perspective. We used a phronetic analysis to assess the values and interests of workers whose job was impacted by AM in order to overcome this deficiency. According to [8], we attempted to adopt his suggested method for phronesis by responding to four important questions that aid in revealing social observations that can inspire social action, or praxis, and eventually eudaimonia or human flourishing.

According to recent research, individuals trust algorithmic decision-making because they think it eliminates favoritism and human prejudice [11]. We suggest creating the Algorithmic Motivation-driven Insulation Model (AMOI) in this conceptual study. This system includes a chatbot-based emotion-aware deep learning framework that can act as a two-way communication channel and decision-making tool between businesses and AM-using employees. We contend that sophisticated chat-bots used in specific situations can improve human interactions at work, drawing on recent advancements in social penetration theory (SPT) [16], which studies the function of chatbots in relationships. In order to address contemporary AM challenges, our goal is to enhance chatbot interactions within worker-organizational relationships. We believe that by placing a high priority on eudaimonia for the mental health and well-being of employees, this strategy can improve the working environment, lessen stress, encourage a sense of belonging, and motivate all employees under AM by fostering a sense of motivation.

2 Value-Based Design for Human Well-being: A Phronetic Approach

When designing interactive systems that meet users' wants and expectations, it is essential to thoroughly understand their beliefs, preferences, and demands. This is where value-based design, a foundational principle of HCI, comes into play. Through user research and testing, one can learn about the values of the users, which can improve the user experience and increase satisfaction. Designing ethical systems is yet another essential technique for enhancing societal and personal wellbeing. Aristotle is the source of the practical ethics philosophy known as phronesis. It promotes practicality while highlighting the importance of human values and virtues. To achieve a sense of wellbeing, one must pursue these values. Value-based design seeks to predict, assess, and develop system requirements in addition to efficiency, profit, and speed. It contains non-functional demands such as responsibility, accountability, fairness, and privacy. However, relying exclusively on the predefined value listings recommended in scholarly and governmental papers is insufficient. Because ethics is contextual, it demands that values be effectively included and upheld while designing technical systems. Therefore, it is essential to have a clear road map for putting ethical principles and ideas into reality in order to accomplish good practices. As recommended in various academic and governmental papers (such as [1]), using preconfigured value listings is insufficient to construct an ethical system because ethics is contextual and requires effective value embedding and respect in technical system design. As a result, in order to attain good practices, a clear road map is needed for the coordinated implementation of ethical concepts and principles [17].

Significant progress has been made in the managerial discipline, including HCI, using two of Aristotle's forms of knowledge: techné, or knowledge utilized in the design, building, and implementation of technologies; and episteme, which refers to explanatory social scientific knowledge. The third sort of knowledge, phronesis, which deals with moral conduct, has received less attention in research. This is because the prevailing philosophy in science since the 16th century has been a mathematical form of "rational" thinking centered on logic. Since rational arguments are believed to be accurate and legitimate regardless of the speaker, audience, or circumstance, rhetoric has less intellectual clout than logic. Rhetorical enquiries are therefore thought to be ineffective in the search for objective human knowledge. However, Aristotle believed that ethics and eloquence were strongly tied to one another. According to him, every ethical position is influenced by an individual's circumstances and relationships with others, and the particulars of a situation are essential in defining its ethical implications [18].

The central idea of phronesis is the relationship between phronimos, praxis, and eudaimonia. A phronimos is focused on righteous actions in specific situations to improve individual and societal well-being, which is referred to as eudaimonia. According to Aristotle, production, or poiesis, is distinct from action, or praxis. Poiesis creates an artifact that can be assessed for its usefulness or accuracy. Praxis, on the other hand, refers to a unique way of interacting with the world that is extremely contextual and follows a preset logic that can have either positive or negative outcomes. Therefore, phronesis is the ability to act morally, with success determined by one's own and other people's happiness [14].

All sorts of knowledge, including episteme, techné, and phronesis, are necessary to grasp and act in the world. Phronesis is particularly significant for ethical intervention and the practical application of episteme and techné in human affairs. In order to increase society's capacity for value-based deliberation and action, the phronetic approach requires a style of knowing that is attentive to the particularities of praxis and the influence of acts on wellbeing [8]. Phrenetic research tries to enhance society by defining ideals, interests, and power relations as well as by directing practice. It places an emphasis on practical reason based on a variety of values and interests rather than on the formation of ideas [8]. The researcher behaves as a participant rather than an unbiased observer, taking responsibility for the social consequences of their work, which is a core premise of phronetic social science. Phronetic research believes that its findings are significant, relevant, and appropriate for the study of practice even if it acknowledges that some of its conclusions are tentative and occasionally confusing.

They stressed the necessity of conducting thorough case studies employing participant-observer positions, interviews, observation, contextual embedding, and other fieldwork techniques, as advised by [3, 8]. This phronetic research can greatly impact design justification in HCI by creating a helpful feedback loop for improving design justification and by providing crucial ethnographic and case study knowledge to both researchers and practitioners. Additionally, it can widen the scope of research and stimulate fresh ideas by enabling new lines of investigation and observational perspectives. We adopt a similar mindset and approach while addressing the current challenges in AM literature that could be rectified with AI-based HCI designs. Therefore, we look at two recent studies that used phronetic interviews and workplace observations of AM employees. In our studies, we make an effort to address the four difficulties identified by [8]. First, where are we going? Do you prefer this? (3) How does power operate, who wins, and who loses? What actions are necessary? The last question here will describe the HCI design idea that we intend to conceptually propose in this paper and that will be the focus of our study in the near future as we attempt to put our solution into practice.

2.1 Distinguishing the Phronetic Approach in HCI Research

In HCI research, the phronetic approach, which is based on Aristotle's philosophy [2], has gained popularity. The techniques employed in this strategy, such as observations, interviews, and case studies, may at first glance appear to be comparable to those applied in other human-centered strategies like phenomenology. However, a deeper look reveals minor variations in their philosophical underpinnings, objectives, and applications. Phronesis, an idea from Aristotle, emphasizes moral conduct and practical knowledge. The success of this field of knowledge, which deals with ethical conduct, is determined by how well both the person and the community are treated. In contrast, phenomenology places a greater emphasis on the events that arise during acts of awareness and the structures of consciousness, also known as lived experiences [7]. The phronetic method is focused on taking action to increase society's capacity for making value-based decisions and taking action, whereas phenomenology tries to examine human experiences in depth to comprehend the essence of occurrences.

The phronetic method is action-oriented and calls for active participation from the researcher. The researcher is responsible for the societal repercussions of their research and is not merely an observer. This interactive approach is crucial, particularly when traversing the complex web of moral and ethical issues that underpins HCI research. In fact, the phronetic approach places ethics at the center [2]. Every ethical position is closely related to its environment, shaped by the particular circumstances of people and their relationships. Contrary to other phenomenological studies, which, while introspective in nature, are interested in the essence of experiences, may not place the same focus on ethics, situational ethics places a strong emphasis on morality.

Thus, in the field of HCI, the phronetic method stands out by providing a strong foundation for understanding and addressing users' values and interests, particularly in situations that are fraught with moral and ethical conundrums. The phronetic approach broadens the scope of phenomenological techniques in HCI by emphasizing interventions and actions based on moral considerations. Phenomenological approaches in HCI aim to understand user experiences at their core. Its philosophical basis, goals, and applications set it apart from other human-centered research paradigms while also sharing methodological similarities with them. This makes it particularly applicable in situations where ethical issues take center stage.

3 Identified Unaddressed Values of Workers in Algorithmic Management

A study of its recent history is necessary to address the workers' viewpoints and delve deeply into the AM scenario, taking in mind the relevant cultural norms and values [14]. To do this, we draw conclusions from two recent, significant publications that made use of employee interviews in AM-integrated businesses. Zhang et al. [22] conducted interviews with 24 participants in the gig economy as part of a landmark study. While their research suggested several potential remedies, it stopped short of outlining a particular approach to solve the issue. Therefore, we think that their findings still have room for investigation and solution-focused research. Möhlmann et al.'s [13] important contribution is yet another. They used a stringent extreme-case selection methodology that combined several methodologies, including informal interviews (N = 15), structured interviews (N = 27), and a variety of observations, including reviews of online forums and news items. We have condensed the important issues into the list that follows for simplicity.

Unaddressed Well-being Support and Uncertainty on Platforms. On ride-hailing platforms, there is a lack of support for drivers' financial, psychological, and physical well-being. Some people think platforms hide crucial statistical information, which prevents them from having a long-term perspective and jeopardizes their wellbeing. Drivers are frequently required to accept many rides at the expense of their physical and mental health due to algorithmic management features like Uber's tier system. Ensuring the safety of all individuals is of utmost importance. However, studies have shown that specific groups, especially female and non-white drivers, face higher safety risks due to socio-cultural factors. While the emphasis on safety is universal, it's crucial to recognize and address these specific vulnerabilities to ensure an equitable environment for everyone. For instance, the lack of expense-tracking features on these platforms, which forces many drivers to calculate their metrics, which can be mentally taxing, was revealed during design sessions. Additionally, algorithmic allocation and cancellations, passenger ratings, and outside factors like traffic put workers' incomes in doubt. This uncertainty is made worse by the algorithm's lack of transparency.

Unfair Differentials Imposed by Gamification. There is a shortage of assistance for drivers' financial, psychological, and physical health on ride-hailing platforms. Some people believe that platforms obfuscate important statistical data, preventing them from seeing the big picture and endangering their well-being. Due to algorithmic management features like Uber's tier system, drivers are routinely forced to accept plenty of rides at the detriment of their physical and emotional wellbeing. All people's safety must be guaranteed at all costs. Studies have revealed, however, that certain demo-graphic groups, particularly female and non-white drivers, experience higher safety hazards as a result of socio-cultural variables. Although everyone should prioritize safety, it's critical to identify and address these particular weaknesses to provide a fair workplace for everybody. For instance, it was discovered during design sessions that these systems lack expense-tracking functionality, forcing many drivers to calculate their metrics, which can be psychologically burdensome. The earnings of employees are also in doubt due to algorithmic allocation and cancellations, passenger reviews, and outside variables like traffic. The opaque nature of the algorithm exacerbates this confusion.

Uneven Information Access. Asymmetry and unequal information availability are issues that gig workers, particularly drivers on ridesharing services, face. Platforms limit the data that staff members can access, which affects their decision-making and adds uncertainty. For instance, even when they are uninformed of the drop-off location, drivers routinely accept rides. The fact that basic ride information is withheld from drivers until they "earn" it through reward systems irritates them. The driver's preferences for the length of the trip are also disregarded. Some drivers believe that the algorithm used for ride-matching solely considers the time it takes to pick up passengers because there are concerns about it. Others, however, think it is arbitrary and is affected by "favoritism" or other "more complex" causes. This opacity and the related uncertainties are common on platforms.

Working and Learning in Isolation. Rideshare The fact that drivers usually learn and work alone makes their employment more uncertain and stressful. Drivers lack platform features but crave social engagement. It is challenging to share happy experiences or locate useful information on social media sites because they are toxic and dangerous. Support for platforms is frequently inefficient and upsetting. Drivers desire human interaction, but support tickets are either ignored or receive robotic responses. This lack of support and communication results in feelings of helplessness and undervaluation.

Supervision. Rideshare drivers for companies like Uber are subject to stringent algorithmic supervision even though they are regarded as independent contractors. They cannot break from the platform's guidelines because doing so could result in them being banned for rejecting specific rides. The tension between algorithmic regulation and driver autonomy may lead to disputes with other passengers.

3.1 Answering the 4 Qs

If Uber and other ridesharing platforms do not significantly change their algorithmic management, the current significant challenges and uncertainties drivers face will only get worse. It is clear that both the workers' financial security and their physical and mental wellbeing are in peril. The AM's lack of transparency will only make this doubt worse. The most important problems are the absence of support for drivers' well-being and the communication paths between drivers and support staff. This problem will simply make people feel more helpless and less valuable. These factors clearly show that AM on ridesharing platforms like Uber needs to be thoroughly examined and improved in order to take into account the concerns and morals of drivers.

If the values and goals of individuals and society prioritize the wellbeing and lives of employees, it would be desirable to address the current issues and improve the AM system to better support drivers. Although the current system has negative impacts on drivers, maintaining it may be better if other values or goals, such as boosting profits or market expansion, are more important. Ultimately, whether something is acceptable depends on the values and goals of the individuals and community in question. Since we genuinely believe that workers' rights and principles take precedence over an organization's economic needs, we argue that the existing AM is not in a desirable position.

The research at hand suggests that when AM is employed in corporate settings, there is a power imbalance between corporations and their employees. Algorithms are used to manage the workforce, however since the workforce has minimal access to information, this frustrates and perplexes the workforce. Because of the opaqueness of this AM system and the limited channels of communication between employees and support personnel, which allows the businesses greater control over their labor, workers may feel helpless and at conflict with consumers. The ultimate winners of this AM system are the organizations, leaving people with significant challenges and uncertainties about their well-being and livelihoods. As a result, since the success of these companies depends on the success of their employees, we must campaign for fairer, more transparent regulations that prioritize workers.

What should be done? This is addressed in the next section based on our proposed AI-based solution.

4 The Proposed Design System: Algorithm Motivator-Driven Insulation Mechanism (AMOI)

As was indicated in the earlier study, HCI and information systems have started looking into the attitudes and experiences of workers in order to build solutions that prioritize their well-being within AM. Even if such work starts to put into reality the basic nature of the prosthesis as advised by Aristotle [2], a real design solution that may start incorporating many of the earlier recommendations seen in the literature has not yet been offered.

Recent research investigations have emphasized the necessity of developing frameworks that promote workers' well-being in the changing AM world. A holistic design approach that embraces the ideas of Aristotle's phronesis still needs to be explored, despite the fact that HCI and IS research have started looking into the perceptions and real-world experiences of workers under AM. To fill this gap, the Algorithmic Motivation-driven Insulation Model (AMOI), depicted in Fig. 1, is developed. The idea behind this strategy is to create a sophisticated channel of communication between workers and companies through AM. The Algorithmic Motivation chatbot (AMV), which is at the core of AMOI, is a construct created to improve not just operational efficiency but also to acknowledge and confirm the intrinsic value of each person.

The model's vocabulary calls for an explanation of the word "insulation". It stems from the model's fundamental goal of serving as a "insulator," shielding employees from any harms associated with impersonal algorithmic management approaches. Through the use of sophisticated deep learning techniques and the Emotion-aware Ensemble Deep Learning (EAEDL) chatbot, AMOI will try to clearly and empathetically communicate corporate directives. The EAEDL chatbot is designed to skillfully navigate and address employee problems, creating a more compassionate and responsive algorithmic interaction paradigm. It is powered by a historical emotional database. In conclusion, the AMOI model is not just a practical tool; it also serves as a strategic intervention. It is designed to act as a protective interface, ensuring that employees are guided by algorithms while also being protected from any potential adverse effects, strengthening their psychological health and organizational ties.

4.1 Incorporating a Phronetic Approach into AMOI

The Algorithmic Motivation-driven Insulation Model (AMOI) provides evidence of how phronesis from Aristotle has been incorporated into contemporary technology designs [2]. The AMOI model, in its commitment to increasing workplace interactions and putting employee well-being first, embraces the fundamental concepts of phronesis, which promotes practical wisdom and moral behavior. The model's interpretive approach to the values and interests of workers affected by AM is clear evidence of its origin in phronetic analysis. The model attempts to build a bridge between social observations and practical insights, with the goal of reaching eudaimonia, or human happiness, and draws insights from Flyvbjerg's study [8]. This shift from observation to practical action, or praxis, clearly embodies the phronetic method. The AMOI model's chatbot-driven, emotion-aware deep learning infrastructure is one of its unique features. This ground-breaking architecture creates a two-way channel of communication between employees using AM and their individual employers. This is made possible by the phronetic ethos of acknowledging and addressing moral and emotional concerns, making sure that technical breakthroughs foster rather than obstruct real human interactions.

Eudaimonia, a holistic condition of wellbeing and human prosperity, is at the center of the AMOI model's grand goal. The concept is designed to create workplaces that are not just productive but also morally sound and emotionally helpful due to its dedication to improving worker interactions, reducing stress, and fostering diversity. In conclusion, the AMOI model is a perfect example of how phronetic principles and contemporary technical structures may coexist. The model adds a fresh, ethically rooted layer to the dynamic world of AM by fusing practical knowledge, ethical behavior, and a proactive research approach.

We believe that by quickly communicating organizational directives to staff members via the EAEDL chatbot, AMV will boost the accessibility of information for them. AMV aims to ensure that these instructions are presented in an appropriate and emotionally mindful manner in order to prevent workers from feeling dehumanized when interacting with algorithms. It is believed that this approach will enhance workers' overall welfare, reduce stress, and enhance their mental health. Additionally, it is anticipated that AMV will increase staff members' sense of purpose, confidence in management, and sense of business loyalty, all of which will lead to higher performance. Refer to Fig. 2 for a rough overview of AMV's intended design capabilities.

Based on recently made accessible statistics on the use of chatbots as human companions via SPT, we are confident in the potential of AMV. SPT, or social psychological theory, looks at how ties develop and deepen through time. We believe that AMV has the potential to play a significant role in helping employees achieve the goals set forth by *phronesis* in order to achieve *eudaimonia*. In line with cutting-edge chatbots that are designed for companionship through developing a relationship over time, SPT gives a precise framework for a qualitative understanding of how this may play out in worker interactions that operate under AM. The Social Penetration Theory holds that relationships develop as a result of self-disclosure, with individual differences, environmental circumstances, situational factors, costs, and benefits influencing the rate of relationship growth. In human-robot interactions, self-disclosure appears to be advantageous to users' well-being and perceived interaction quality, as chatbots are seen as safer and less critical conversational partners than real people.

Although SPT is a well-established theory, Skjuve et al. [16] have recently presented an updated hypothesis that helps to explain human-computer interactions in chatbots. They define three fundamental phases of relationship development based on the level of

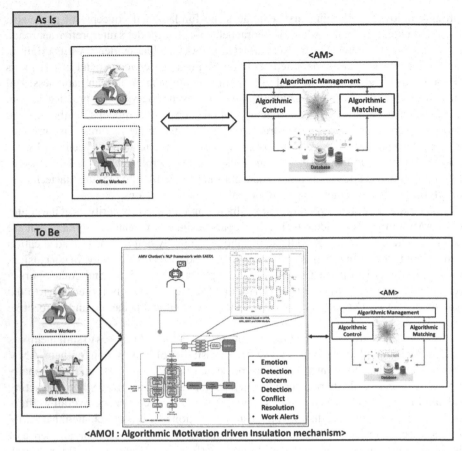

Fig. 1. As Is/To Be - Status of current AMA solutions and our proposed AMOI model with AMV.

self-disclosure between the parties. The depth and breadth of the early exploratory stage are features of the quick start of affective exploration and study. The emotive stage, or second phase, is when non-mutual self-disclosure takes place and trust develops. The appearance of asymmetry in reciprocation and different types of interactions are characteristics of the third and final stage, sometimes referred to as the stable stage. We believe that taking these actions will be essential to establishing AMV and fostering long-term chatbot worker trust. The amount of revenue needed from groups to run such a system will need to be determined after significant testing, though. Determining how much AMV can be used to give the AM system some wiggle room without jeopardizing organizational policies while enhancing employees' perceptions of their well-being and their sense of being heard by the company, for example, could be a fascinating topic.

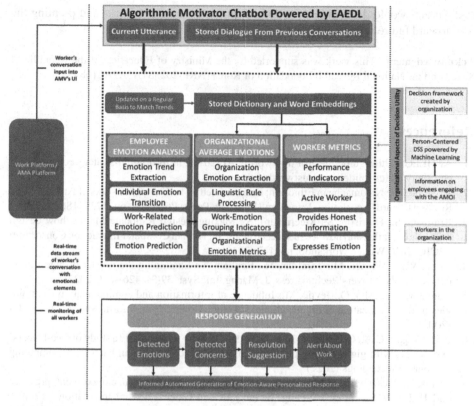

Fig. 2. Schematic diagram of the currently envisioned algorithmic motivator that will be powered by emotion-aware deep learning.

5 Conclusion

In conclusion, the Algorithmic Motivation-driven Insulation Model (AMOI) is a cutting-edge approach to problems plaguing algorithmic management. This model seeks eudaimonia through the integration of strategic methods and phronesis-based values. Its primary goal is to foster a more moral and productive digital workplace by placing a premium on human values. An emotion-aware ensemble deep-learning model was developed as part of this study to enhance chatbot-user interactions. The model's focus on eudaimonia is meant to improve workers' emotional health, morale, and productivity. This method increases team cohesion and lessens the likelihood of employee turnover. These developments have the potential to increase the allure of flexible work settings by meeting the psychological and monetary requirements of a wide range of employees. Ultimately, these developments lead to a more equitable workplace by advocating for the rights of workers who are often overlooked. While the current study does provide a comprehensive framework, an evaluation lens would be helpful for future efforts. The proposed model may benefit from having experts evaluate its expected impact on algorithmic management in order to refine its approach to improving work procedures. Such assessments would do double duty by both proving the model works and pointing the way toward future refinements.

Acknowledgment. This work was supported by the Ministry of Education of the Republic of Korea and the National Research Foundation of Korea (NRF-2023S1A5A2A21084333).

References

1. AI HLEG: Ethics guidelines for trustworthy AI (2019). https://digital-strategy.ec.europa.eu/en/library/ethics-guidelines-trustworthy-ai
2. Aristotle: The Nicomachean Ethics. In: Barnes, J. (ed.) The Complete Works of Aristotle: The Revised Oxford Translation. Princeton University Press, Princeton, pp. 1729–1867 (1984)
3. Branham, S., Harrison, S., Mccrickard, S.: Making Design Rationale Matter: how design rationale has failed and how it can succeed again. In: Human Computer Interaction Consortium (HCIC) 2010 Winter Workshop, pp. 1–7 (2010)
4. Cram, W.A., Wiener, M., Tarafdar, M., Benlian, A.: Examining the impact of algorithmic control on uber drivers' technostress. J. Manag. Inf. Syst. **39**(2), 426–453 (2022)
5. Čudanov, M., Jaško, O., Jevtić, M.: Influence of information and communication technologies on decentralization of organizational structure. Comput. Sci. Inform. Syst. **6**(1), 93–109 (2009)
6. De La Vega, J.C.A., Cecchinato, M.E., Rooksby, J.: Why lose control? a study of free-lancers' experiences with gig economy platforms. In: Conference on Human Factors in Computing Systems - Proceedings (2021)
7. Evans, L., Rzeszewski, M.: Hermeneutic relations in VR: immersion, embodiment, presence and HCI in VR gaming. In: Fang, X. (ed.) HCI in Games: Second International Conference, HCI-Games 2020, Held as Part of the 22nd HCI International Conference, HCII 2020, Copenhagen, Denmark, July 19–24, 2020, Proceedings, pp. 23–38. Springer International Publishing, Cham (2020). https://doi.org/10.1007/978-3-030-50164-8_2
8. Flyvbjerg, B.: Making Social Science Matter. Cambridge University Press (2001)
9. Fox, S.E., et al: Worker-centered design: expanding HCI methods for supporting labor. In: Conference on Human Factors in Computing Systems - Proceedings (2020)
10. Irani, L.C., Silberman, M.S.: Turkopticon: interrupting worker invisibility in amazon mechanical turk. In: Proceedings of the SIGCHI Conference on Human Factors in Computing Systems, pp. 611–620 (2013)
11. Lee, M.K.: Understanding perception of algorithmic decisions: fairness, trust, and emotion in response to algorithmic management. Big Data Soc. **5**(1) (2018)
12. Lee, M.K., Kusbit, D., Metsky, E., Dabbish, L.: Working with machines: the impact of algorithmic and data-driven management on human workers. In: Conference on Human Factors in Computing Systems - Proceedings (2015)
13. Möhlmann, M., Zalmanson, L., Henfridsson, O., Gregory, R.W.: Algorithmic management of work on online labor platforms: when matching meets control. MIS Q. **45**(4), 1999–2022 (2021)
14. Ngwenyama, O., Klein, S.: Phronesis, argumentation and puzzle solving in IS research: illustrating an approach to phronetic IS research practice. Eur. J. Inform. Syst. **27**(3), 347–366 (2018)
15. Rosenblat, A., Stark, L.: Algorithmic labor and information asymmetries: a case study of uber's drivers. Int. J. Commun. **10**, 3758–3784 (2016). http://ijoc.org

16. Skjuve, M., Følstad, A., Fostervold, K.I., Brandtzaeg, P.B.: My Chatbot companion - a study of human-Chatbot relationships. Int. J. Hum. Comput. Stud. **149** (2021)
17. Spiekermann, S., et al.: Values and ethics in in-formation systems: a state-of-the-art analysis and avenues for future research. In: Business and Information Systems Engineering, vol. 64, pp. 247–264. Springer Gabler (2022)
18. Toulmin, S., Toulmin, S.E.: Cosmopolis: The Hidden Agenda of Modernity. University of Chicago Press (1992)
19. Wiener, M., Cram, W., Benlian, A.: Algorithmic control and gig workers: a legitimacy perspective of Uber drivers. Eur. J. Inform. Syst. (2021)
20. Xie, J., Liu, X., Zeng, D.D., Fang, X.: Understanding medication nonadherence from social media: a sentiment-enriched deep learning approach. MIS Q. **46**(1), 341–372 (2022)
21. You, C.W., Yuan, C.W.T., Bi, N., Hung, M.W., Huang, P.C., Wang, H.C.: Go gig or go home: enabling social sensing to share personal data with intimate partner for the health and wellbeing of long-hour workers. In: Conference on Human Factors in Computing Systems - Proceedings (2021)
22. Zhang, A., Boltz, A., Wang, C.W., Lee, M.K.: Algorithmic management reimagined for workers and by workers: centering worker well-being in gig work. In: Conference on Human Factors in Computing Systems - Proceedings (2022)

An Analysis of Philosophy and Morality in Wearable Human-Computer Interaction

Wenjie Dai[1] and Hongtao Zhou[1,2]([✉])

[1] College of Design and Innovation, Tongji University, Shanghai 200092, China
lifeisfuniture@sgmail.com
[2] Shanghai International College of Design and Innovation, Tongji University,
Shanghai 200092, China

Abstract. This article aims to delve into the philosophical and ethical issues of intelligent wearable human-computer interaction. Specifically, this article will explore four issues: privacy protection, data security, personality rights, and social and cultural issues. Based on these four issues, the main research content of this article is as follows: Firstly, the development status and application scenarios of intelligent wearable technology will be introduced, including the evolution and innovation of wearable technology. Secondly, this article will explore the potential ethical and moral issues of intelligent wearable technology from the perspectives of personal privacy and security, social relationships and interactions, and human cognition and emotions. Next, this article will propose ethical design principles for intelligent wearable human-computer interaction based on the design and application practices of wearable devices. These principles include design based on human dignity, transparent and controllable design, design balancing personal interests and public interests, and design respecting cultural differences. Finally, this article will look forward to the future development and prospects of wearable devices from the perspectives of technological development trends and ethical issues and propose directions for further exploration and research. Intelligent wearable human-computer interaction technology is an emerging form of interaction with broad application prospects, but it also faces a series of philosophical and ethical issues. This article systematically analyzes the philosophical and ethical issues in intelligent wearable human-computer interaction and proposes corresponding ethical design principles, providing some beneficial thinking and suggestions for the future development of wearable devices.

Keywords: Intelligent wearable device · Human-computer interaction ·
Philosophy · Ethics · Morals design

1 Introduction

1.1 Background and Significance

Intelligent wearable technology has been developed rapidly in recent years and has been widely used in many fields, such as healthcare [1], entertainment [2] and sports health [3], industrial production [4], and military fields [5]. These wearable devices

© The Author(s), under exclusive license to Springer Nature Switzerland AG 2023
H. Degen et al. (Eds.): HCII 2023, LNCS 14059, pp. 356–372, 2023.
https://doi.org/10.1007/978-3-031-48057-7_22

can collect, analyze and process various physiological data of the human body through sensors, smart chips, and other technologies, to achieve a more intelligent and convenient human-computer interaction.

However, a series of philosophical and ethical problems have emerged. For example, personal privacy and security issues, the impact of social relationships and social interactions, and the impact of human cognition and emotion. These issues relate both to the design and application of the technology itself and the fundamental values and ethics of humans.

Therefore, this paper aims to deeply discuss and analyze the philosophical and ethical issues in wearable human-computer interaction, to provide theoretical guidance and practical reference for the reasonable development and application of related technologies. At the same time, this paper also tries to discuss how to design more humanized, transparent and controllable intelligent wearable devices from the perspective of ethics, balance personal interests and public interests, respect cultural differences, and promote the harmonious development of wearable technology and human society.

1.2 Development and Application of Intelligent Wearable Technology

The development of new technologies such as artificial intelligence(AI) [6] and the Internet of Things [7], which help wearable technology becomes a hot spot in the current technology field. Wearable technology refers to an emerging technology that integrates computer technology and sensing technology into human-computer interaction [8], including wearable devices and wearable intelligent systems. It can monitor and record the user's physical state [9], behavior and environmental information [10] in real- time, through data analysis and artificial intelligence algorithms for personalized services, health management, virtual reality [11] and other applications.

At present, wearable technology has been widely used in smartwatches [12], smart glasses [13], smart wristbands [14], smart clothing [15] and other wearable devices. These devices can not only record the user's movement, sleep, heart rate and other physiological indicators but also achieve intelligent speech recognition [16], intelligent recommendation [17], virtual reality and other functions. Wearable technology is also gradually applied to medical health, education and training [18], industrial manufacturing and other fields, which has brought a lot of convenience to people's life and work (Table 1).

Table 1. Application field of wearable

Application field	Technical application examples	Typical product
Health and Medical	Sports monitoring, heart rate monitoring, sleep monitoring, disease management, smart pill boxes, smart hearing-aid	Apple Watch, Fitbit, Garmin
Entertainment and media	Virtual reality headsets, smart watches play music and smart glasses watch videos	Oculus Rift, Microsoft HoloLens, Magic Leap One

(continued)

Table 1. (*continued*)

Application field	Technical application examples	Typical product
Industry and manufacturing	Occupational safety, personnel positioning, mission guidance	ProGlove, RealWear HMT-1, Vuzix M400
Military and security	Vehicle and soldier positioning, battlefield communication, smart gloves and helmets	DAQRI Smart Helmet, ThirdEye X1, Lynx R
Retail and Service	Unmanned store, virtual fitting room, intelligent hotel room control	FREETALK®,Connect Me™
Education and training	Virtual lab, smart reading glasses, smart translation headset	Google Glass, Microsoft HoloLens, DAQRI Smart Glasses

1.3 Research Purpose and Research Question

Explore Philosophical and Ethical Issues in Intelligent Wearable Human-Computer Interaction. The rapid development of intelligent wearable technology has made human-computer interaction more common and direct. However, this technology also raises philosophical and ethical issues such as privacy and data protection, ethical regulation, human freedom and individual rights. These problems need to be seriously considered and solved when using intelligent wearable devices.

First, intelligent wearable devices collect a large amount of personal information, including personal physical health data, behavioral data and location data. This data may be used for commercial purposes or shared with third parties, raising privacy and data protection issues. In addition, this data can be hacked or misused, causing loss and harm to individuals. Second, intelligent wearables require regulation and management. Due to the development of technology and the diversity of products, the current regulatory and management mechanisms may not be sufficient to address the risks and challenges posed by intelligent wearables. Therefore, appropriate ethical and legal frameworks need to be put in place to protect personal privacy and data security. Finally, intelligent wearable technology also poses challenges to human freedom and individual rights. The use of this technology may affect an individual's freedom and privacy rights, as intelligent wearable devices can collect large amounts of personal information and even track an individual's location in real-time. This requires people to re-examine and balance the relationship between human freedom and individual rights, technological progress and the interests of society. Therefore, for the development of intelligent wearable technology, philosophical and moral-ethical analysis is needed to find the right balance, while safeguarding the balance of individual rights and social interests.

Analyze the Impact of Intelligent Wearable Technology on Human Cognition, Emotion and Social Relations. The impact of intelligent wearable technology on human cognition, emotion, and social relationships is a complex topic that needs to be considered from multiple perspectives.

On the cognitive side, intelligent wearable technology can help people better manage their daily life and work tasks. For example, smartwatches can remind people to complete tasks, control time and monitor health. However, this can also lead to over-reliance on these technologies, reducing people's autonomy and ability to manage themselves.

On the emotional side, intelligent wearable technology may change the way people interact with the things around them, thus affecting his/her emotional experience. For example, smart glasses can record everything a user sees and help them recall and share those experiences. However, it can also lead to less attention and less connection to the real world.

In terms of social relationships, intelligent wearable technology can change the way people interact with each other. For example, smart wristbands can make it easier for people to find and contact friends nearby. However, it can also cause people to become overly dependent on technology, resulting in decreased social skills and a weaker connection to the real world.

In short, the impact of intelligent wearable technology is twofold. It can provide convenience and efficiency, but it can also cause people to become over-dependent on technology, reduce autonomy and self-management, and affect emotional and social relationships. Therefore, we need to consider and manage the use of these technologies carefully to ensure that their impact on human society and individuals is positive.

1.4 Literature Review

At present, some researchers have studied and discussed the philosophical and moral issues in intelligent wearable human-computer interaction.

L. H. Segura Anaya [19] and his team surveyed demonstrating users' ethical perceptions of the use of Wearable Devices in the health sector. Results from this survey demonstrate that Wearable Device users are highly concerned regarding privacy issues and consider informed consent as "very important" when sharing information with third parties. Albert Sabban [20] introduced the ethics of wearable biomedical and communication systems in his book. He thought Several ethical dilemmas must be considered when people deal with wearable communication systems such as patient rights, intellectual property, employee exploitation and justice. Seppe Segers [21] et. al., pointed out that many pregnant women use pregnancy-related mHealth (PRmHealth) applications, encompassing a variety of pregnancy apps and wearables. They argued that the increasing dominance of PRmHealth stands in want of empirical knowledge affirming its beneficence in terms of improved pregnancy outcomes. This is a crucial ethical issue, especially in light of concerns about increasing pressures and growing responsibilities ascribed to pregnant women, which may, in turn, be reinforced by PRmHealth. Andrie G. Panayiotou and Evangelos D. Protopapadakis [22] did a relevant thought experiment to summarize some further ethical concerns that are connected to the use of wearables by minors, to wit the issue of informed consent in the case of minors, forcing them to live in the spotlight, and compromising their right to an open future. They concluded with the view that mitigating potential pitfalls and enhancing the benefits of wearable technology especially for minors requires brave and comprehensive moral debates. Eva Reinares-Lara, Isabel Alvarez, and et al. [23] argued that when wearables are more known, ethical judgments focus more on whether they are useful to society in terms of their benefits (improved quality of life, lifestyle changes, time and money savings) and their associated costs and inconvenience (device dependency, privacy and security concerns, among others) (Segura Anaya et al. 2017), leaving other ethical aspects in the background. Heike Felzmann, et al. [24] pointed out that ethical, legal and social (ELS) issues in Wearable Robotics have so far been comparatively underexplored. They presented a brief overview of the preliminary findings of a literature search and a series of three expert consultation workshops on ELS issues in Wearable Robotics conducted as part of the work of the Action between October 2017 and October 2018, and identified relevant values and ethical, philosophical, legal and social concerns related to the design, deployment and practical use of wearable robots. Breuer and Rebecca Louise [25] argued that people's experience with, and understanding of, wearing textile integrated haptic technologies can be enriched by applying the concepts of the 'extended felt-body', 'felt-body islands', and 'corporeal communication' as coined by German phenomenologist Hermann Schmitz. Alexandra Kapeller [26], et al. pointed out that ethical, legal and societal implications (ELSI) in the development of wearable robots (WRs) are currently not explicitly addressed in most guidelines for WR developers.

Although many scholars have discussed the moral and ethical issues in wearable human-computer interaction, there is no clear answer to solve the ethical and philosophical problems in wearable human-computer interaction design, which will be a problem that scholars need to continue to pay attention to and solve in the future.

2 Status and Application of Intelligent Wearable Technology

2.1 Technological Evolution and Innovation

The earliest wearable device can be traced back to 1907, The first step from the portable cameras' perspective is the Pidgeon camera, developed by the German inventor Julius Neubronner [27]. For the next 50 years, wearable technology had been slowly developing. Until 1961, MIT researchers Edward O. Thorpe and Claude Shannon concealed a timing device in a shoe that could accurately predict the ball's landing place on a roulette table. That became the first wearable computer hidden in the shoe [28]. Since then, wearable technology has developed rapidly. In terms of technology evolution and innovation, it mainly includes the following stages: The first stage is the development of sensor technology. Sensor technology is the core technology of intelligent wearable devices, which can realize real-time monitoring and recording of health, movement, sleep and other information. While early sports fitness trackers used sensors such as accelerometers and gyroscopes, current wearables can use a wider variety of sensors, such as heart rate sensors, oxygen sensors, temperature sensors, and more. The second stage is the advances in computing and communication technology. With the continuous advancement of computing and communication technology, the computing and communication capabilities of intelligent wearable devices have also been improved. For example, devices such as smartwatches and smart glasses can be connected to mobile phones and the Internet through wireless communication technologies such as Bluetooth and Wi-Fi, enabling more functions and services. The third stage is the application of artificial intelligence and big data. The rapid development of artificial intelligence and big data technology provides new opportunities and challenges for the development of intelligent wearable devices. For example, using artificial intelligence algorithms and big data analytics, intelligent wearable devices can provide more accurate and personalized health monitoring and prediction services.

2.2 Technological Evolution and Innovation

The application scenarios of intelligent wearable technology are also expanding and deepening. Early wearable devices are mainly for the field of sports health, such as sports fitness tracking, sleep monitoring and so on. With the development of technology and the expansion of application scenarios, the application scenarios of intelligent wearable technology are gradually enriched and diversified, mainly including the following aspects:

Health Monitoring and Medical Care [29]. Intelligent wearable devices can monitor various physiological indicators of the human body, such as heart rate, blood oxygen, temperature, etc., to provide personalized health management and prevention services. Intelligent wearable technology can also realize telemedicine services, such as remote ECG monitoring, telemedicine consulting, etc., to improve the efficiency and quality of medical services.

Smart Home and Life Services [30]. Intelligent wearable devices can be connected with smart home devices to achieve intelligent home control and management, such as smart lighting, and smart audio. In addition, intelligent wearable technology can also realize functions such as speech recognition and translation, providing more convenient life services.

Industrial and Military Fields [31]. Intelligent wearable technology is also widely used in industrial and military fields. For example, smart glasses can help workers achieve real-time information acquisition and processing, improving work efficiency and quality. Smart wearables can also be used for military reconnaissance and command, improving operational efficiency and safety.

3 Discussion of Philosophical and Moral Issues

3.1 Personal Privacy and Security Issues of Wearable Devices

The problems involved in personal privacy and security have gradually become prominent with the wide application of intelligent wearable devices. The following are two aspects of data collection and privacy protection, security and risk management.

Data Collection and Privacy Protection. The data acquisition capability of intelligent wearable devices is getting stronger and stronger, and sensitive data including persol body indicators and location information can be obtained. However, the acquisition, transmission and storage of this data are subject to privacy risks, especially in the processing and sharing of data, which may be subject to hacking or data abuse risks.

To protect the privacy of users, wearable device manufacturers need to take several measures to ensure the security and privacy of data. For example, the use of end-to-end encryption technology, access control mechanism, to ensure the user's control of data and other measures to prevent data leakage and abuse.

Security and Risk Management. In addition, wearable devices also present certain security risks. For example, the design flaws of the device itself, software vulnerabilities, etc., may cause the device to be hacked or infected by viruses, resulting in user data leakage or device damage.

To address these issues, wearable device manufacturers need to strengthen the security and risk management of their devices. For example, technologies such as two-factor authentication and device software patch update are used to ensure device security and stability. What's more, to deal with emergencies such as device hacking, wearable device manufacturers also need to develop emergency plans and crisis management measures to respond to and deal with relevant incidents promptly.

3.2 Personal Privacy and Security Issues of Wearable Devices

Formation of Social Networks and Virtual Communities. Intelligent wearable technology enables people to communicate in real-time communications, social networks and virtual communities through devices such as smartwatches and smart glasses. The emergence of this mode of communication has had a profound impact on the development of social networks and virtual communities.

On the one hand, the emergence of intelligent wearable technology has transformed the form and scale of social networks and virtual communities. People can access social networks and virtual communities anytime and anywhere through these devices so in addition to communication in real life, more contact with people from different regions and cultural backgrounds and broaden people's social circle. The scale of virtual communities has also expanded, and the interaction between people has become more frequent and extensive.

On the other hand, the emergence of this communication mode also brings challenges to people's social behavior. Intelligent wearable devices can influence people's face-to-face communication and social behavior to a certain extent. For example, people may be more inclined to interact with intelligent devices and ignore the people around them, or get distracted in social situations, checking messages and social networks. This can disrupt the natural flow of people's face-to-face interactions and reduce the quality of social interactions.

Influence of Social Behavior and Mental Health. While intelligent wearables can facilitate interactions between people, in some cases, intelligent wearables may also affect people's social behavior and mental health.

First, intelligent wearables can lead to information overload and inattention. When people are faced with a large number of messages and notifications from different devices, they may become distracted and unable to concentrate on normal social interactions. In addition, too much notification and information may also affect people's emotional and psychological states, which in turn affects social behavior.

Secondly, intelligent wearable devices may affect people's social habits and social abilities. Social behavior in social networks and virtual communities is different from face-to-face social behavior, and intelligent wearables may make people more inclined to socialize through virtual communities and social networks. This behavior may reduce people's actual social behavior. Some studies have also focused on the impact of wearable devices on social behavior and social interaction. For example, some studies have found that the use of wearable devices such as smartwatches affects the quality and frequency of people's face-to-face interactions. Because using wearables can distract people from being fully engaged in each other's speech. What's more, wearables may induce some nonverbal behaviors, such as texting and phone calls, making people more likely to communicate through these methods than face-to-face.

In addition, the use of wearable devices may also have an impact on an individual's mental health. Some studies have shown that prolonged use of wearable devices can lead to negative emotions such as anxiety and stress. Because wearable devices can track and record personal activities and health conditions at any time, this can create a sense of urgency and stress for some people, which can lead to negative emotions.

3.3 The Impact of Wearable Devices on Human Cognition and Emotion

Changes in Cognitive Ability and Information Processing. Wearable devices may have an impact on humans' cognitive abilities and how they process information. On the one hand, some devices can expand people's perception ability, like smart glasses can expand people's field of vision, enabling them to receive more information. However, this may also lead to problems of cognitive burden and information overload, which can affect cognitive efficiency and thinking ability. Studies [32, 33] have shown that wearable devices such as smartwatches may affect people's memory and attention in the short term, possibly because these devices disturb users frequently. Wearables may also cause excessive cognitive load, as users need to process a large amount of data and information at the same time, which may affect their cognitive efficiency and attention.

Changes in Emotional Expression and Social Cognition. Wearable devices may also have an impact on human emotions and social cognition. As mentioned above, wearable devices may affect people's opportunities for face-to-face interaction, which in turn affects emotional expression and social behavior. For example, a smartwatch might prompt a user to accept a notification by vibrating or sound, which could cause disruption face-to-face interactions and make the user uncomfortable. Assuming the following scenario, when a man who wears a smartwatch is talking with others in face-to-face, the smartwatch constantly emits vibrations or sounds to prompt the user to accept notifications or view messages, frequent reminders may disrupt the face-to-face interaction and make people feel uncomfortable talking. When people use wearable technology for communication for a long time, they will become more dependent on it, which will greatly reduce face-to-face interaction. This can lead to a decline in people's social cognitive abilities, making it difficult for them to understand and express emotions in real-world social situations.

4 Ethical Design Principles for Intelligent Wearable Human-Computer Interaction

4.1 Design Based on Human Dignity

Respect Human Rights and Human Dignity. Intelligent wearable devices should be designed to respect human rights and human dignity, guarantee users' autonomy and freedom rights, and avoid infringing the personality and moral rights of users. For example, the collection, use, and transmission of user data should strictly comply with relevant laws, regulations, and ethical standards, ensure the informed consent of users, and promptly inform users of the use of data to protect their privacy and right to know. Respect for human rights and human dignity is one of the ethical design principles of intelligent wearable human-computer interaction. This principle requires designers to put the rights and dignity of users at the core of the design, ensuring that the use of smart wearable devices does not violate users' human rights or deprive users of their dignity. In the practical design of wearable products, this principle can be achieved by the following aspects:

Ensure That the User's Privacy is Protected. Intelligent wearable devices may collect a large number of users' personal information, such as physical indicators, geographical location, behavioral habits, and so on. Therefore, designers need to take appropriate measures to ensure that this information is collected, stored and processed by privacy protection laws and regulations and that users have full control over their information.

Respect for User Autonomy and Choice. Users should have the right to choose whether to use intelligent wearable devices and whether to share their personal information with others during use. Designers should provide a rich set of options so that users can autonomously control the function of the device, data collection and other behaviors.

Avoid Misuse of Data and Algorithms. The data collected and algorithms applied by intelligent wearable devices may have a profound impact on users, such as influencing health assessments, diet recommendations and exercise recommendations. Designers should avoid improper use of data and algorithms for commercial advertising, political propaganda and other purposes, and ensure the fairness and transparency of data and algorithms.

Respect Cultural and Faith Differences. Intelligent wearable devices should be designed to respect users from different cultural and faith backgrounds and avoid discrimination and prejudice. In the design of the speech recognition function, it is necessary to fully consider the user's dialect and accent to avoid speech recognition errors and unadaptability caused by different dialects. This principle is not yet available in the current intelligent wearable speech recognition. Apple Watch is one of the most widely used wearable devices, and its built-in SIRI voice assistant can greatly help users complete some basic operations. However, its speech recognition is based on the official language of each country or region, and there is no corresponding development and design for different dialects. This is unfriendly to users who do not speak the official language.

Fully Consider the Needs of Edge Users Intelligent wearable devices should also be designed to fully consider the needs of those edge users, such as the elderly, disabled, illiterate, etc. These users may have different cognition and usage habits and need to adopt simpler and more understandable interaction methods to ensure the accessibility and universality of the device. Wearable devices for the disabled have made great progress in the medical field, such as prosthetics, although it is only a supplement to the human body's functional defects, they can bring great self-esteem and function to the disabled. There are relatively few wearable designs for the elderly or illiterate, and we know that the severity of today's aging will continue or even worsen in the coming decades, and the design should be designed for all humanity, not a specific group, and the elderly need to care for more in health, mental state and emotion.

Avoid Discrimination and Prejudice. Intelligent wearable devices should be designed to avoid discrimination and prejudice, including but not limited to race, gender, age, religion, sexual orientation and other aspects of discrimination and prejudice. Designers need to pay more attention to these factors, avoid discrimination and prejudice in the function, design, promotion and other aspects of the equipment, and ensure the fairness and objectivity of the product. Avoiding discrimination and prejudice is a crucial principle in the design of intelligent wearable devices, as the use of these devices involves various groups of human society. Here are some specific design principles to avoid discrimination and prejudice:

Treat All Users Equally. Designers should try to avoid designing for a specific group but design for all different groups. The function and interface design of the device should treat all users as equally as possible, and should not be specially designed for a certain group or individual. The purpose of design is to bring happiness to all people, by taking a diverse approach to design and fully listening to users' opinions and feedback, which can create wearable devices that are more universal and usable, providing a fair experience for all.

Oppose Racial, Gender, Age and Other Discrimination. In the design of smart wearable devices, any form of racial, gender, age and other discrimination should be avoided. Designers should try to avoid the use of colors, patterns, ICONS and other elements that may cause discrimination, and should fully consider the needs and feedback of different groups during the testing phase.

Respect for Personal Privacy. Designers should respect everyone's right to privacy and should not collect and use users' personal information except with the user's full authorization and consent. In addition, the designer should ensure that the data storage and transmission of the device are secure to prevent the user's personal information from being stolen or leaked.

Taking into Account Different Cultural and Social Backgrounds. Users from different cultural and social backgrounds should be taken into account in the design of intelligent wearable devices. For example, some cultures may have sensitivities to specific colors, symbols, numbers, etc., and designers should avoid using these elements that may cause discomfort in their designs.

4.2 Transparent and Controllable Design

The principle of transparent and controllable design means that intelligent wearable technology should provide sufficient information for users to understand how the device uses their data, and give users the right to know and choose. In addition, intelligent wearable devices need to establish effective privacy protection and security mechanisms to ensure that users' personal information is not abused, leaked, or hacked.

Provide Adequate Information and the Right to Know . The design of intelligent wearable devices should include the principles of providing adequate information and the right to know. This means that the device should clearly explain to the user its functions and how it collects, uses, stores and shares the user's data. Users should be able to understand what data the device collects and how that data is used and shared. The device should also give users control over their data and should have an easily accessible privacy policy so users can know how the device uses their data.

The principle of ethical design of intelligent wearable human-computer interaction, transparent and controllable design is considered as a key role. The provision of adequate information and the right to know is an important aspect of this principle. In the process of using intelligent wearable technology, users should know the function of the device, data collection method, processing method, data storage location, shared objects and other related information. Therefore, the designer should provide sufficient, clear and understandable information before the device is used, so that the user can make an informed decision. Additional explanations and instructions are also required for technical terms or concepts that may not be familiar to the user. In addition, the designer should also update and supplement the information related to the device at any time to ensure that the user always has the latest information. While providing the right to know, users should also have the right to choose. In other words, users should be able to choose whether they want to use the device or restrict certain data collection and sharing without any pressure or penalty. In short, providing sufficient information and the right to know is an important principle in the ethical design of intelligent wearable human-computer interaction, which can ensure that users have full cognition and understanding of the use of devices and data collection so that users can make informed, autonomous and conscious choices.

Establish an Effective Privacy Protection and Security Mechanism. Intelligent wearable devices should establish effective privacy protection and security mechanisms to ensure that users' personal information will not be abused, leaked or hacked. This includes adopting encryption and anonymization techniques to protect users' data, ensuring that data is secure when transmitted and stored and that only authorized users have access to data. Devices should also have effective risk management mechanisms, including disaster recovery plans and emergency response plans, to deal with unexpected events such as data breaches or security breaches.

The establishment of effective privacy protection and security mechanism is one of the important principles in the design of intelligent wearable devices. This is because as wearable devices become more widely used in daily life, people's privacy and security issues are becoming more and more prominent. To protect the privacy and security of users, designers need to take a series of effective measures to ensure that user data is not abused and leaked. First, designers need to consider which privacy protection mechanisms are embedded in the device. These mechanisms can include data encryption, authentication, access control, etc., to ensure the security of user data. Second, designers need to consider how the data is collected, used, and stored. To ensure that users' privacy is protected, designers need to inform users about what data is being collected, how it is being used, and how it is being protected. Designers also need to ensure that the data collected is used only for the functions necessary for the device and restrict access to and use of this data. In addition to considering privacy and security issues during the design phase, designers also need to establish effective security management mechanisms to ensure that users' data is adequately protected. These mechanisms include perfect user authentication, network firewall and intrusion detection system.

4.3   Design that Balances Personal Interests and Public Interests

Consider the Balance Between Personal Privacy and Social Welfare. In the design of intelligent wearable devices, it's necessary to balance the relationship between personal privacy and social welfare. On the one hand, the protection of personal information and the maintenance of privacy is an important factor that must be considered in the design process, because users will generate a large amount of personal information when using wearable devices, such as physical health, location, behavior trajectory, etc., if the information is abused or leaked, it will pose a threat to the user's privacy and security. On the other hand, intelligent wearables can also contribute to social welfare, such as healthcare, public safety and other fields. For example, in healthcare, wearable devices can contribute to public health by collecting users' physiological data to provide personalized health services and preventive measures. Therefore, when designing intelligent wearable devices, it is necessary to balance the relationship between personal privacy and social welfare. Specifically, it can be achieved in the following ways: privacy protection measures, such as anonymization processing, data encryption and other technologies, to ensure the security and privacy of user information. When users use wearable devices, provide a transparent privacy policy and user agreement to clearly explain to users the purpose and method of data collection. In the process of data use, comply with relevant laws and regulations and ethical norms to ensure the lawful use of user information and avoid abuse and disclosure. During the device design process, consider how to provide more intelligent and user-friendly services, while protecting the privacy and security of users.

The Need to Ensure Public Safety and Social Order. During the design process of wearable devices, it is necessary to balance personal interests and public interests, among which public interests include ensuring public safety and social order. The need to ensure public safety and social order is a moral principle, because when designing wearable devices, it is necessary to take into account the potential dangers and risks that may arise, and take corresponding measures to avoid or mitigate these risks and dangers. First of all, wearable devices may threaten public safety in some cases. for example, when drivers wear wearable devices, it may distract drivers and cause accidents. Therefore, in some countries and regions, drivers are prohibited from wearing wearable devices to ensure traffic safety. Secondly, wearable devices may also affect social order in some cases, when using wearable devices in some public places may violate the privacy and security of others. Therefore, wearables are prohibited in certain public places to protect the privacy and safety of others. When designing wearable devices, it is very important to balance personal and public interests. Designers need to take these ethical principles into account and take appropriate measures to protect the interests of the public while ensuring that wearable devices have a positive impact on users.

4.4 Design that Respects Cultural Differences

Respect Different Cultural Backgrounds and Values. Respect for different cultural backgrounds and values is one of the ethical design principles of intelligent wearable human-computer interaction, because there are different cultures and values in human society, and these cultures and values have a profound impact on people's ways of thinking, behavior patterns, social relations and other aspects. Therefore, when designing intelligent wearable devices, different cultural backgrounds and values should be respected to better meet the needs and expectations of users, while also avoiding conflicts and misunderstandings caused by cultural differences. To respect different cultural backgrounds and values, the design of intelligent wearable devices should follow the following principles: understanding different cultural backgrounds and values, designers should understand the different cultural backgrounds and values to which users belong, including religions, social customs, values, etc., to better understand the needs and expectations of users; respect users' cultural differences, the design process should respect users' cultural differences, avoid imposing certain cultures and values on users, and should not use design elements that are offensive or demeaning; provide personalized choices, the design of intelligent wearables should provide personalized choices that allow users to set up according to their own culture and values to better meet the needs and expectations of users. In short, respect for different cultural backgrounds and values is one of the ethical design principles of intelligent wearable human-computer interaction, which can help designers better meet the needs and expectations of users, but also promote cross-cultural communication and integration of multiple elements.

Improve Cross-Cultural Communication and Integrate Multiple Elements. Intelligent wearable devices need to be designed with consideration of how to promote cross-cultural communication and integrate multiple elements. This involves designing elements such as the interface, language, ICONS, etc., so that people from different cultural and linguistic backgrounds can understand and use the device. First, intelligent wearables should provide multiple language support so that users can use the device in their language environment. When designing a language, care needs to be taken to use simple and easy-to- understand language and avoid difficult jargon and terminology so that people from different cultures and linguistic backgrounds can understand it. Secondly, the interface design of intelligent wearable devices should conform to the aesthetic habits of different cultures and values. For example, colors have different symbolic meanings in different cultures, and designers need to take these differences into account and avoid design elements that may cause misunderstanding or conflict. In addition, intelligent wearables should also support cross-cultural communication, such as through translation functions, so that people with different language backgrounds can communicate without barriers. Devices should also encourage users to communicate and interact with people from different cultural backgrounds to promote cultural exchange and integration. In short, respecting different cultural backgrounds and values and enhancing cross-cultural communication and integrating multiple elements are important principles in the design of intelligent wearable devices, which can help devices achieve a more universal and inclusive design, and also help promote cultural exchange and understanding.

5 Future Development and Prospects of Wearable Devices

5.1 Technology Development Trends and Prospects

Virtual Reality and Augmented Reality Technology. With the continuous development of artificial intelligence, virtual reality and augmented reality technology, wearable devices will be more applied to human-computer interaction, virtual simulation, intelligent perception and other fields. Through intelligent wearable devices combined with artificial intelligence technology, intelligent health monitoring, smart home control, intelligent voice interaction and other functions can be achieved to improve the quality of life and work efficiency. In terms of virtual reality and augmented reality technology, wearable devices can provide users with a more real and immersive experience, such as virtual tourism, virtual reality games, etc., and can also be applied to the military, medical, education and other fields.

Integration of Intelligent Wearable Technology with Other Technologies. The integration of intelligent wearable technology and other technologies will be an important development direction of wearable devices in the future. For example, integration with cloud computing technology can enable real-time transmission and analysis of data, improving the performance and intelligence of wearable devices. Integration with blockchain technology can protect user privacy and data security, enhancing the security of wearable devices. Integration with 5G technology can improve communication speed and connection stability, enabling faster and more convenient data transmission.

5.2 Further Exploration and Research Direction of Moral and Ethical Questioning

Moral Evaluation and Prediction of Future Development Trends. With the continuous development of wearable device technology, its impact on human society and culture will be more and more profound. In future development, it is necessary to conduct an in-depth evaluation and prediction of its moral and ethical issues to ensure that its development direction and application are in line with the principles of human dignity and social public interest. With the popularity of wearable technology, more personal data and sensitive information will be generated, and how to protect the security and privacy of this data will be an important ethical issue. In addition, the application of intelligent wearable devices may also cause differences and conflicts between different cultural and social groups, and how to balance the interests and needs of different groups is also an important ethical issue.

370   W. Dai and H. Zhou

Study More In-Depth and Complex Moral and Ethical Issues. With the continuous development and application of wearable device technology, more profound and complex ethical issues may arise. For example, the application of smart wearable devices may have a profound impact on human cognition and emotion, and how to evaluate and manage this impact, as well as whether it needs to be regulated and limited, are issues worthy of further study. In addition, the application of wearable devices may also have an impact on the social and political system, how to balance the needs of personal interests and social public interests, as well as how to regulate and manage the application of wearable device technology, are issues that need in-depth research and exploration. In short, with the continuous development of wearable device technology, it is necessary to further explore and study its moral and ethical issues to ensure that its development direction and application are in line with the principles of human dignity and social public interest.

6 Conclusion

This study focuses on the ethical issues of intelligent wearable technology. First, the concept, types and application fields of intelligent wearable technology are introduced. Then the impact of intelligent wearable technology on human cognition, emotion, and behavior, and propose a set of ethical design principles are analyzed, including design based on human dignity, a design that is transparent and controllable, design that balances personal and public interests, and design that respects cultural differences. Finally, the future development trend of intelligent wearable technology and the further research direction of moral and ethical issues are discussed.

The development of intelligent wearable technology has brought a lot of convenience and possibilities for human beings, but it has also brought a series of moral and ethical issues and social challenges. Therefore, intelligent wearable technology must assume moral responsibility and social responsibility while pursuing commercial value and technological innovation. Specifically, it can be emphasized from the following aspects: First, the development of intelligent wearable technology should follow the people-oriented design principle, respect human dignity and rights, avoid discrimination and prejudice, provide adequate information and the right to know, and establish an effective privacy protection and security mechanism. Intelligent wearable technology designers need to carefully consider the ethical aspects of technology application, continuously improve product design and development processes, and ensure that the use of technology is in line with ethical and legal requirements. Second, intelligent wearable technology needs to balance the relationship between personal and public interests. In the process of technology development and application, it is necessary to balance the relationship between personal privacy and social welfare and ensure public safety and social order. To achieve this goal, it is necessary to start thinking about how to balance different interests at the early stage of technology development, and at the same time make reasonable tradeoffs and choices based on practical situations and ethical requirements. Finally, the development of intelligent wearable technology needs to respect different cultural backgrounds and values, improve cross-cultural communication and the ability to integrate multiple elements. In the process of technology development and application, it is necessary to take into account the influence of different cultural backgrounds and values, and to avoid discrimination and prejudice against specific cultures as much as possible. Designers should enhance the cultural understanding and inclusiveness of technology developers and users by strengthening cross-cultural communication and the ability to integrate multiple elements, to better adapt to the needs of multiculturalism.

References

1. Iqbal, S.M.A., Mahgoub, I., Du, E., et al.: Advances in healthcare wearable devices. Flex Electron **5**(9) (2021)
2. Olson, J.S., Redkar, S.: A survey of wearable sensor networks in health and entertainment. MOJ App. Bio. Biomech. **2**(5), 280–287 (2018)
3. Zhao, J., Li, G.: Study on real-time wearable sport health device based on body sensor networks. Comput. Commun. **154**, 40–47 (2020)
4. Svertoka, E., Saafi, S., Rusu-Casandra, A., Burget, R., et al.: Wearables for industrial work safety: a survey. Sensors **21** (2021)
5. Shi, H., Zhao, H., Liu, Y., Gao, W.: Systematic analysis of a military wearable device based on a multi-level fusion framework: research directions. Sensors **19** (2019)
6. Nahavandi, D., Alizadehsani, R., Khosravi, A., Rajendra Acharya, U.: Application of artificial intelligence in wearable devices: Opportunities and challenges. Comput. Methods Programs Biomed. **213** (2022)
7. John Dian, F., Vahidnia, R., Rahmati, A.: Wearables and the Internet of Things (IoT), applications, opportunities, and challenges: a survey. IEEE Access **8**, 69200–69211 (2020)
8. Mencarini, E., Rapp, A., Tirabeni, L., Zancanaro, M.: Designing wearable systems for sports: a review of trends and opportunities in human-computer interaction. IEEE Trans. Hum. Mach. Syst. **49**(4), 314–325 (2019)
9. Wu, W., Haick, H.: Materials and wearable devices for autonomous monitoring of physiological markers. Adv. Mater. **30** (2018)
10. Khakurel, J., Immonen, M., Porras, J., Knutas, A.: Understanding the adoption of quantified self-tracking wearable devices in the organization environment: an empirical case study. In: 12th ACM International Conference on PErvasive Technologies Related to Assistive Environments (PETRA 2019). pp. 119–128 (2019)
11. ÇİÇEK, M.: Wearable technologies and its future applications. Int. J. Electric. **3** (2015)
12. Dehghani, M., Kim, K.J., Dangelico, R.M.: Will smartwatches last? factors contributing to intention to keep using smart wearable technology. Telematics Inform. **35** (2018)
13. Adapa, A., Nah, F.F., Hall, R.H., Siau, K., Smith, S.N.: Factors influencing the adoption of smart wearable devices. Int. J. Hum. Comput. Interact. **34** (2018)
14. Jin, C.Y.: A review of AI technologies for wearable devices. In: IOP Conference Series: Materials Science and Engineering, vol. 688 (2019)
15. Hurford, R.D.: 2 Types of smart clothes and wearable technology. Smart Clothes Wearable Technol. 25–44 (2009)
16. Yağanoğlu, M.: Real time wearable speech recognition system for deaf persons. Comput. Electric. Eng. **91** (2021)
17. Asthana, S., Megahed, A., Strong, R.: A recommendation system for proactive health monitoring using IoT and wearable technologies. In: 2017 IEEE International Conference on AI & Mobile Services (AIMS), pp. 14–21 (2017)
18. Almusawi, H.A., Durugbo, C.M., Bugawa, A.M.: Wearable technology in education: a systematic review. IEEE Trans. Learn. Technol. **14**(4), 540–554 (2021)

19. Anaya, S., Alsadoon, L.H., Costadopoulos, A., et al.: Ethical implications of user perceptions of wearable devices. Sci. Eng. Ethics **24**, 1–28 (2018). https://doi.org/10.1007/s11948-017-9872-8
20. Sabban, A.: Wearable communication systems and antennas (Second Edition) design, efficiency, and miniaturization techniques. IOP Science (2022)
21. Segers, S., Mertes, H., Pennings, G.: An ethical exploration of pregnancy related mHealth: does it deliver? Med Health Care Philos **24**, 677–685 (2021)
22. Panayiotou, A.G., Protopapadakis, E.D.: Ethical issues concerning the use of commercially available wearables in children. Jahr **13**(1), 9–22 (2022)
23. Lara, E.R., Alvarez, I., Oliva, M.A., Pascual, C.O., Llorente, M.A.: Assessment of ethical on the intention to use of wearables. In: Moving Technology Ethics at the Forefront of Society, Organisations and Governments, pp. 275–283 (2021)
24. Felzmann, H., Kapeller, A., Hughes, A.M., Fosch-Villaronga, E.: Ethical, legal and social issues in wearable robotics: perspectives from the work of the cost action on wearable robots. In: Pons, J. (eds.) Inclusive Robotics for a Better Society, Biosystems & Biorobotics, vol. 25. Springer, Cham (2020). https://doi.org/10.1007/978-3-030-24074-5_17
25. Breuer, R.L.: Body, mind and wearables: how technology alters the conception of the body, Philosophy of Human Technology Relations (2020)
26. Kapeller, A., Felzmann, H., Villaronga, E.F., Nizamis, K., Hughes, A.M.: Implementing ethical, legal, and societal considerations in wearable robot design. Appl. Sci. **11**(15) (2021)
27. The Public Domain Review, Dr Julius Neubronner's Miniature Pigeon Camera. https://publicdomainreview.org/collections/dr-juliusneubronners-miniature-pigeon-camera/. Accessed 3 March 2021
28. Thorp, E.O.: Beat the Dealer: A Winning Strategy for the Game of Twenty One, vol. 310, Vintage (1966)
29. Ajami, S., Teimouri, F.: Features and application of wearable biosensors in medical care. J. Res. Med. Sci. **20**(12) (2015)
30. Badar ud din Tahir, S., Jalal, A., Batool, M.: wearable sensors for activity analysis using SMO-based random forest over smart home and sports datasets. In: 2020 3rd International Conference on Advancements in Computational Sciences (ICACS). Lahore, Pakistan, pp. 1–6 (2020)
31. Jhajharia, S., et al.: Wearable computing and its application]. Int. J. Comput. Sci. Inform. Technol. **5**(4), 5700–5704 (2014)
32. Dobbins, C., Rawassizadeh, R., Momeni, E.: Detecting physical activity within lifelogs towards preventing obesity and aiding ambient assisted living. Neurocomputing **230**, 110–132 (2016)
33. Martinho, D., Carneiro, J., Novais, P., et al.: A conceptual approach to enhance the well-being of elderly people. In: Moura Oliveira, P., Novais, P., Reis, L. (eds.) Progress in Artificial Intelligence. EPIA 2019. LNCS, vol. 11805. Springer, Cham. https://doi.org/10.1007/978-3-030-30244-3_5

Machine Learning Techniques and Privacy Concerns in Human-Computer Interactions: A Systematic Review

Jun He[✉], Tianyu Cao, and Vincent G. Duffy

Purdue University, West Lafayette, IN 47906, USA
{he184,cao357,duffy}@purdue.edu

Abstract. With the recent development of artificial intelligence, the field of human-computer interaction (HCI) has received an increasing amount of attention. Among all topics under HCI, machine learning and privacy concerns are two of the most important ones. One of the machine learning techniques that possess a strong connection with privacy is federated learning, which distributes learning tasks to individual devices to reduce information sharing and protect privacy. In this study, a systematic literature review of our topic has been conducted using various tools including Harzing's Publish or Perish, Google nGram, Vicinitas, VOSviewer, CiteSpace, BibExcel, and maxQDA. The software Mendeley is also used to help sort out citation items. Trend analysis, co-citation analysis, content analysis, and cluster analysis have been conducted to identify the most important articles in the literature. It has been found that the two topics have been well studied and together they have a variety of applications, including communication networks, the healthcare industry, and the Internet of Things. Finally, we discuss the potential future work beyond our topics which cover directions in application fields such as healthcare and finance, and other machine learning techniques developed based on federated learning.

Keywords: federated learning · privacy · human-computer interaction · machine learning · data · bibliometric analysis · Harzing · nGram · VOSviewer · maxQDA · CiteSpace · Vicinitas · BibExcel · Mendeley

1 Introduction and Background

The recent development of artificial intelligence (AI) has changed people's lifestyles in different areas, including education, transportation, entertainment, etc. As a sub-area of human-computer interaction (HCI), our topic about machine learning and privacy is important to individuals and society due to its strong connection to our daily life. Machine learning plays a fundamental role in AI development, which relies heavily on user data collection and can further cause privacy concerns. In this report, we focus on one specific type of machine learning technique called "federated learning". Many factors drive this topic to importance in today's world. For example, the increasing number of smart devices, the growing size of data, and the rising demand for privacy attention have driven

© The Author(s), under exclusive license to Springer Nature Switzerland AG 2023
H. Degen et al. (Eds.): HCII 2023, LNCS 14059, pp. 373–389, 2023.
https://doi.org/10.1007/978-3-031-48057-7_23

the machine-learning community to focus on privacy-protecting algorithms such as federated learning (Li et al. 2021). Our topic is important to industrial engineering for three reasons. First, federated learning involves distributed learning algorithms which have always been a major research topic for the operations research branch. Second, privacy-related ethical concerns from developing machine learning algorithms, or in general, human-computer interaction, are also popular research directions in algorithm design, machine learning applications, and human factors. Outside industrial engineering, this topic has been mainly studied in the realm of computer science, in which researchers focus on addressing the conflicts between efficient learning performance and data privacy protection. More specifically, one major branch of the research is to develop privacy-preserving techniques and evaluate the trade-off cost associated with these techniques in the context of federated learning (Mothukuri et al. 2021).

In comparison to traditional machine learning, federated learning offers more protection for each user's data against the central learning server. The current society needs to recognize the benefits and try to modify its current AI techniques to be more user-centered, and federated learning shows such a possibility. However, such a distributed computing mechanism also raises its risks to be compromised, which can potentially result in more severe privacy leaking issues. To address this, society needs to raise more funding to develop more inclusive algorithms. Fortunately, the HCI community has done many efforts to address our topic. Because federated learning is a relatively new breed of machine learning, a systematic introduction of its content, mechanisms, and advantages over other algorithms is needed. For example, Whig et al. (2022) have done a systematic review to demystify the concept of federated learning from the HCI perspective. In the meantime, research on federated learning has been done with the application of the Internet of Things (Chhikara et al. 2021), which also considers privacy.

2 Purpose of Study

The objective of this report is to undertake a systematic literature review of articles exploring the intersection of federated learning and privacy for human-computer interaction. To illustrate the evolution of this research domain, publication data has been gathered from multiple databases, namely Scopus, Web of Science, and Harzing's Publish or Perish over the database Google Scholar. Various analytical tools, including nGram, Vicinitas, VOSviewer, CiteSpace, BibExcel, and maxQDA have been employed to scrutinize the collected data. Similar analytical approaches have been used in previous research as in Kanade and Duffy (2020, 2022).

Our study focuses on 3 different keywords: federated learning, privacy, and human-computer interaction (HCI). However, the focus is on the prior two given that the topic of HCI covers a much wider range of subtopics which include federated learning and privacy. The definitions of the 3 keywords are presented below.

Federated Learning. Federated learning, also known as collaborative learning, is a machine learning technique that trains statistical models over remote devices or data centers (Li et al. 2020). Compared to traditional machine learning techniques, which collect all data together to train a single global model, federated learning keeps the data localized and allows multiple devices, such as smartphones and the Internet of Things (IoTs), to learn their models with their data.

Privacy. Although decentralized training mechanisms can intuitively reduce the amount of information to be shared, the goal of federated learning is still to generate one ultimate model. Therefore, privacy concerns still exist. In this paper, we restrict our talk of privacy to data privacy. Nowadays, companies want to know more about their customers' preferences and profiles to provide better services, and as a result, data collection is inevitable. However, companies may misuse or fail to protect the data and cause privacy risks (Martin and Murphy 2017).

Human-Computer Interaction (HCI). Human-computer interaction (HCI) refers to the interaction between human users and computers or machines and is a design that should produce "a fit between the user, the machine, and the required services" to produce a certain level of performance (Karray et al. 2008).

3 Research Methodology

This review was carried out by analyzing metadata extracted from various databases: Google Scholar, Scopus, Web of Science. The specific tools and steps are based on the methods-related article by Asokan and Duffy (2022) where Google nGram, Vicinitas, maxQDA and other tools were used.

3.1 Data Collection

The metadata of publications is extracted from databases: Scopus, Web of Science, and Harzing's Publish or Perish (Google Scholar). Table 1 shows the keywords that were used for the search and the number of results each search yielded. The search in Scopus yielded the maximum number of results and the data from Scopus was exported in ".csv" format. The data exported from the Web of Science was exported in ".txt" format, including comprehensive information: title, source, author, abstract, and cited references. The data from Harzing's Publish or Perish was saved in "WoS" format.

The result from Table 1 suggests that we should focus on the two keywords "federated learning" and "privacy", given that the number of results is within a reasonable range for analysis. The keyword "human-computer interaction" is a much broader topic that contains the other two keywords. Furthermore, the software Harzing's result hits the maximum number it can return from web scraping over Google Scholar.

3.2 Engagement Measure

Vicinitas is a data mining tool that enables the measurement of engagement levels in a particular topic area, by analyzing Twitter activity. The utilization of this tool enables the assessment of Twitter users' engagement levels in the realm of federated learning and privacy. A search for tweets containing the hashtag/keyword "federated learning and privacy" was conducted, and the findings are presented in Fig. 1.

Table 1. Results of Keywords Searched in Different Databases

Database	Keywords	Number of Results
Scopus	"Federated learning" AND "privacy"	2,703
Web of Science	"Federated learning" AND "privacy"	2,449
Harzing's Publish or Perish (Google Scholar)	"Federated learning" AND "privacy"	992
Scopus	"Human-computer interaction"	113,516
Web of Science	"Human-computer interaction"	43,545
Harzing's Publish or Perish (Google Scholar)	"Human-computer interaction"	1,000 (max reached)

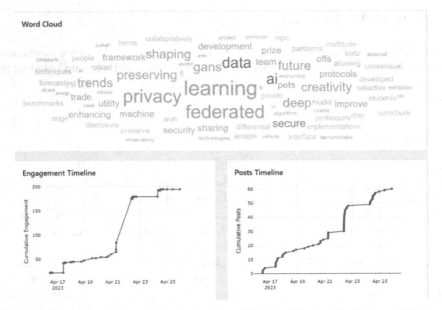

Fig. 1. Results from Vicinitas Analysis Based on the Twitter Feeds of the Keyword "Federated Learning and Privacy"

Both timelines of engagement and posts show that interest in the topic relevant to federated learning and privacy is increasing. However, due to the word "federated learning" being a relatively advanced topic, the numbers of engagement and posts are not significantly high. Additionally, the Word Cloud image generated over the Twitter feeds shows that our keywords are also associated with topics in "security", "AI", "data", etc.

3.3 Trend Analysis

The trend presented in Fig. 2 is based on data gathered from Scopus of the keywords "federated learning" and "privacy". It shows a remarkable surge in the number of publications. This upward trajectory implies that the topic of federated learning and privacy protection is currently a highly popular one. Furthermore, the graph indicates that this field is poised for significant growth in the upcoming years, as the rate of increase is accelerating. We also included Table 2 which is equivalent to Fig. 2 and shows the exact value of the number of works for each year.

Table 2. Trend Analysis Table of Number of Works versus Years from Scopus

Year	Number of Works
2018	7
2019	92
2020	429
2021	1061
2022	2114

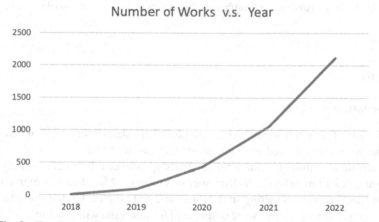

Fig. 2. Trend Analysis Diagram of Number of Works versus Years from Scopus

The second trend analysis is based on data from Google's nGram. Figure 3 below shows the result from nGram. Two additional keywords, "distributed computing" and "job design" are included in the diagram for comparison purposes only. Federated learning involves distributed computing and job design is one important application field related to all 3 main topics. The Google nGram search shows the result of comparing all 3 main topics and the 2 additional topics from 1980 to 2019. We can observe from the diagram that data privacy receives an increasing amount of attention, but HCI and federated learning are less popular compared with others. The 2 additional topics, on the other hand, outnumber the rest until 2015 when data privacy has become the leading trend of research.

Note that federated learning keeps increasing since it was first introduced (Konečný et al. 2016), although the number of papers in federated learning looks small compared with other topics. From the trend diagram in Fig. 2, the number of articles on federated learning and privacy increase exponentially from 2018 to 2022.

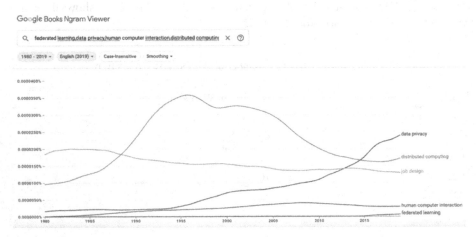

Fig. 3. Trend Analysis of Number of Works versus Years from Google nGram

4   Results

4.1   Co-citation Analysis

The technique of co-citation analysis is employed to identify instances where two or more articles have been cited together in another piece of writing. This methodology facilitates an understanding of the inter-relationship between different scholarly works. To perform co-citation analysis, VOSviewer was utilized. Metadata was extracted from Scopus in ".csv" format, resulting in a dataset of 2000 articles. Only those articles that had been cited at least 35 times were considered for analysis, which led to a selection of 10 articles. The resulting clusters of related articles are presented in Fig. 4.

The 10 articles that met the criterion are grouped into 2 clusters. These articles were chosen for further review in the discussion section.

4.2   Content Analysis

A collection of 2449 search results in text format was extracted from the Web of Science. Subsequently, this file was imported into VOSviewer and subjected to content analysis, utilizing the "create map based on network data" option. Out of the 60 words that meet the predefined criteria, federated model, blockchain, and differential privacy were

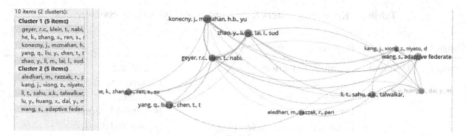

Fig. 4. Clusters of Co-citation Analysis using VOSviewer

among the most frequently occurring terms, as shown in the cluster diagram. These clusters provide valuable insight into the key concepts in this field and serve as a useful reference point for conducting literature research. The result is shown in Fig. 5, and the clusters of keywords are shown in Table 3.

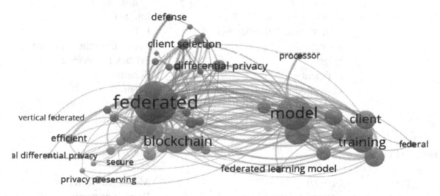

Fig. 5. Content Analysis of Metadata from Web of Science

Table 3 below shows the clusters of keywords from the content analysis using VOSviewer. Cluster 1 contains 23 items that are mainly about data, training, and privacy-preserving. Cluster 2 contains 20 items that mainly talk about communication efficiency and applications such as blockchain and the Internet of Things. Clusters 3 and 4 both focus on more technical aspects of federated learning on models and algorithms.

4.3 Pivot Table

The metadata obtained from Harzing's Publish or Perish was used to create a pivot table with another tool BibExcel. BibExcel can analyze metadata and generating different types of pivot tables. In this study, a table of "leading authors" was generated to identify the authors who have published the most in the topic area of interest. Additionally, a table of "leading sources" from Harzing's Publish or Perish was created using BibExcel to identify important journals or conferences in this field. The table of leading authors is shown in Table 4, and the table of leading sources is shown in Table 5. In addition,

Table 3. Keyword Clusters from Content Analysis by VOSviewer

Cluster	Keywords	
Cluster 1 (23 items)	Anomaly detection	Healthcare
	Client selection	Hierarchical federated learning
	Cloud	i.i.d. data
	Data privacy	Industrial Internet
	Deep reinforcement learning	Intrusion detection
	Defense	Mobile edge
	Design	Privacy preservation
	Differential privacy	Private federated learning
	Edge computing	Resource allocation
	Efficient Federated learning	…
	Federated	
	Federated transfer learning	
Cluster 2 (20 items)	Artificial intelligence	Framework
	Attack	Industrial IoT
	Blockchain	Internet
	Communication efficiency	IoT
	Detection	Local differential privacy
	Edge	Privacy preserving
	Efficient	Scheme
	Federated learning application	Secure
	Federated learning framework	Security
	Federated learning system	Vertical federated
		…
Cluster 3 (14 items)	Client	Local model
	Device	Model
	Federal	Model parameter
	Federal learning	Privacy protection
	Federated learning model	Processor
	Global model	Server
	Gradient	Training
Cluster 4 (3 items)	Homomorphic encryption	
	Machine learning	
	Privacy preserving federated learning	

the pivot charts of leading authors and sources are shown in Figs. 6 and 7, respectively. Observing from the results, Liu Y. has the most publications, and IEEE Internet of Things Journal receives the most publications. However, the result of leading authors does not give any further insight due to the large population with the last name Liu and first names starting with the letter "Y", which suggests that the researcher Liu Y. may refer to different people with the same name pattern. The result of leading sources, on the other hand, shows that most of the applications are in the areas of the Internet of Things, sensors, and industrial information system designs.

Table 4. 25 Leading Authors summarized by BibExcel

Authors	Number of Publications	Authors	Number of Publications
Liu Y	37	Li Z	16
Li Y	24	Chen Y	15
Li H	23	Wang L	15
Zhang X	22	Wang H	15
Li J	20	Wang J	15
Zhang J	20	Liu X	15
Yang Q	20	Wang Y	15
Zhang Y	20	Xu G	14
Zhou Y	19	Guo Y	13
Yu H	18	Wang W	13
Liu Z	18	Zhao J	13
Wang X	17	Yu S	12
Zhang Z	16		

4.4 Cluster Analysis

Figure 4 from the previous section shows that the co-citation analysis conducted in VOSviewer has a limitation as it does not provide cluster names. However, this limitation can be overcome by using CiteSpace, a software tool that can extract labels for the clusters and perform co-citation analysis. Additionally, it can generate a citation burst diagram that displays the period in which an article was cited the most. To carry out the analysis in CiteSpace, 2449 results were exported from Web of Science in Sect. 3.1 in ".txt" format. The results, along with cited references, were exported and opened in CiteSpace. Top 20 most cited papers from each slice were considered, and a co-citation analysis was performed. Labels for the clusters were obtained using keywords, and the results are displayed in Fig. 8. The cluster names represent the articles in each cluster, enabling the identification of different sub-topics within the topic area.

A citation burst was also generated using CiteSpace. In Fig. 9, 11 articles are identified to have the strongest citation bursts.

The 10 articles from co-citation analysis using VOSviewer and 11 articles from citation burst have been saved in the reference list.

4.5 Content Analysis using maxQDA

We used maxQDA to analyze 5 papers related to federated learning and privacy. Each of the 5 articles talks about federated learning's mechanism (Zhan et al. 2021), challenges and future directions (Li et al. 2020), system design (Bonawitz et al. 2019), privacy-preserving approach (Truex et al. 2019), and performance analysis (Wei et al. 2020). From the Word Cloud image, we can see some non-trivial high-frequency words are

Table 5. 17 Leading Sources summarized by BibExcel

Journal Sources	Number of Publications
IEEE Internet of Things Journal	39
IEEE Access	16
IEEE Transactions on Industrial Informatics	15
Advances in Neural Information Processing Systems	10
ACM Transactions on Intelligent Systems and Technology	9
Sensors	9
IEEE Network	9
Computer Networks	8
Applied Sciences	8
IEEE Wireless Communications	8
IEEE Journal on Selected Areas in Communications	7
International Conference on Machine Learning	7
Computers & Security	7
IEEE Journal of Biomedical and Health Informatics	6
Information Sciences	6
Electronics	5
Proceedings of the IEEE/CVF Conference on Computer Vision and Pattern Recognition	4

Fig. 6. Chart of Leading Authors of Searching Results from Harzing

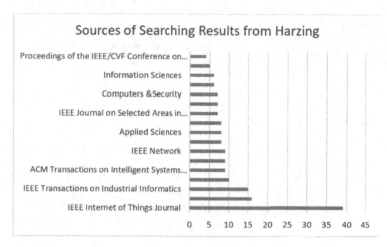

Fig. 7. Chart of Leading Sources of Searching Results from Harzing

Table 6. Word Frequency from maxQDA Based on 5 Papers of Selection

Word	Frequency	Word	Frequency
learning	629	device	191
federated	388	server	185
data	372	local	176
privacy	291	system	152
model	274	machine	142
training	251	approach	125
clients	204		

"learning", "privacy", "clients", "models", "information", "training", "server", "data", "security" and so on. These words imply that our topic is highly related to data collection and concerns with privacy or security problems (Fig. 10).

Lexical search terms informed by maxQDA are collected in Table 6. Informed by the table, we further searched the combination of the phrases "federated learning" and "client-server". One noteworthy paper is by Konečný et al. (2016), which discusses strategies that could improve the communication efficiency between clients and the server in federated learning.

Fig. 8. Clusters of Citations using CiteSpace

Top 11 References with the Strongest Citation Bursts

References	Year	Strength	Begin	End	2018 - 2022
Shokri R, 2015, CCS15: PROCEED ...... NICATIONS SECURITY, V0, PP1310, DOI	2015	23.65	**2018**	2020	
LeCun Y, 2015, NATURE, V521, P436, DOI 10.1038/nature14539, DOI	2015	4.45	**2018**	2019	
McMahan H.B., 2016, ABS160205629 CORR, V0, P0	2016	4.45	**2018**	2019	
Kingma Diederik P., 2014, 3 INT C LEARN REPR, V0, P0	2014	3.81	**2018**	2019	
Goodfellow I, 2016, ADAPT COMPUT MACH LE, V0, P1	2016	3.81	**2018**	2019	
Abadi M, 2016, CCS16: PROCEEDI ...... UNICATIONS SECURITY, V0, PP308, DOI	2016	30.39	**2019**	2022	
Zhao Y., 2018, ARXIV180600582, V0, P0	2018	21.49	**2019**	2022	
Geyer R.C., 2017, DIFFERENTIALLY PRIVA, V0, P0	2017	16.88	**2019**	2022	
Fredrikson M, 2015, CCS15: PRO ...... NICATIONS SECURITY, V0, PP1322, DOI	2015	16.8	**2019**	2020	
Zhang YL, 2017, PROCEEDINGS OF ...... PRINCIPLES (SOSP 17), V0, PP19, DOI	2017	16.1	**2019**	2020	
Smith V, 2017, ADV NEUR IN, V30, P0	2017	15.93	**2019**	2022	

Fig. 9. Citation Burst List from CiteSpace

5 Justification

5.1 Academic Justification

Federated learning is a machine learning (ML) technique that enables multiple devices to collaboratively train a model without exchanging data. However, job design involves designing work tasks to enhance employee performance. Federated learning can improve job design by analyzing data from various sources (Savazzi et al. 2019). For example, one can identify and optimize work area safety by collecting information from different wearable devices. Additionally, this information improves employee well-being and productivity. Therefore, job design is one major application of federated learning. Additionally, our topic is highly related to Chapter 42, Human-Centered Design of Artificial Intelligence, in our textbook (Margetis et al. 2021).

Federated learning and HCI both focus on how people interact with technology. Federated learning involves training ML models with data from multiple sources. HCI is

Fig. 10. Word Cloud from Content Analysis using maxQDA

concerned with the design of interfaces and systems for people to interact with computers effectively. By incorporating user feedback such as security and privacy concerns into the learning process, ML models are customized to better meet user preferences. This leads to a more effective and user-friendly human-computer interaction experience (Whig et al. 2022). Therefore, HCI is the field that includes federated learning. Additionally, our topic is related to Chapter 43, Cybersecurity, Privacy, and Trust, in our textbook (Moallem 2021).

We are also interested in discussing the extension to general machine learning (ML) techniques and exploring the relationship between ML and jobs. One example of application is business job designs, where organizations can benefit from using ML from different aspects (Mendling et al. 2018). First, ML can be used to analyze job tasks and identify the skills and knowledge for a particular job. This information can then be used to design job descriptions and requirements to accurately display to jobseekers about the tasks and skills. Second, ML can be used to analyze job candidate data and identify the most qualified candidates. This can help organizations make more informed hiring decisions so that the right people are selected for the job. Third, ML can be used to analyze employee performance data and design more effective performance evaluation systems and identify areas for improvement. Finally, ML can be used to identify the training needs of employees and develop personalized training plans that address those needs. This can help employees develop the skills and knowledge they need to perform their jobs more effectively.

5.2 Application Justification

In the era of mobile computing, mobile phones are popular and user data is explosively growing during interactions between humans and phones. Adopting large-scale machine learning and data analytics technology to process the growing data can bring huge benefits. Collecting all client data from personal phones to a center for model training is risky since user privacy may be stolen when an attack happens at the central service node.

However, in federated learning, model training can be carried out even without clients sending their data to the server center, which greatly lowers the risk of privacy leakage due to an attack on the central server (Konečný et al. 2016). In addition, in vertical federated learning, institutions like banks and hospitals can incorporate developing big models without sharing users' data, which also preserves users' privacy (Wu et al. 2020).

Federated learning and related privacy-preserving techniques have considerable value when applied in mobile computing. As more people are using smartphones nowadays, their privacy faces threats when data is uploaded to the central server of big companies which may be attacked. Therefore, federated learning, in which data is decentralized and does not need to be collected, becomes an appropriate scheme to develop machine learning models. Smartphones together with center servers naturally support the decentralization characteristics of federated learning and form an important application scenario of federated learning.

6 Conclusion and Discussion

Our analysis suggests that federated learning and privacy have received significant attention and have a wide range of applications in different fields. Other keywords such as "security", "distribution" and "client-server communication" are also suggested to be potential directions for further bibliometric analysis. In this section, we identify existing NSF-awarded projects and point out any possible work that can be done in the future.

6.1 Existing NSF Awarded Projects

While federated learning has shown promise for enabling edge applications and preserving privacy, practical deployment can be hindered by constraints of accuracy, scalability, and trustworthiness. The first NSF project by searching "federated learning" explores multi-task learning, a technique that learns separate but related models for each device in the network, as a unified approach. This project aims to show that multi-task learning can inherently improve both fairness and robustness, helping both to be achieved jointly (National Science Foundation 2022a, b; Liu et al. 2022). Improving the technical side of federated learning can also benefit privacy protection.

A second NSF project is also identified from searching "privacy-preserving learning for human-computer interaction" (National Science Foundation 2022a, b). The use of mobile phones is widespread and as a result, user data is growing rapidly due to human-phone interactions. Utilizing large-scale machine learning and data analytics technology to process this data can offer immense benefits. However, collecting all the data from personal phones and transferring it to a central server for model training poses a risk to user privacy if the server is attacked. Privacy-preserving machine learning is expected to mitigate this issue, by allowing large-scale learning technology without revealing personal data.

6.2 Future Work

The future work of related topics of suggestion can be presented in three directions: other related topics of federated learning, potential applications of federated learning, and other privacy-preserving learning techniques.

Topics of Federated Learning. From the Word Cloud image in Fig. 9 generated by maxQDA, one frequent word is "security". Due to the nature of federated learning, in which the model is distributed to each user, the central server only collects some outcomes instead of all data. This exposes the model to more audiences and makes it more vulnerable to being hacked, which could further result in data leaking and severe privacy risks. Another word that raises attention is "distributed". Distributed computing increases the efficiency of learning, but also comes with security and privacy risks, as discussed above. Another issue is associated with the variety of data which can lead to divergence in the model training and makes it harder for the central server to find a stable solution. Therefore, these two sub-topics of security and distributed computing are worth a deep dive into.

Applications of Federated Learning. As federated learning is being developed and continually evolving, it has the potential to be applied in a wide range of industries and use cases. One of the main possible applications is healthcare, which is summarized by Xu et al. (2021). In healthcare, federated learning is used to train medical models on data from different hospitals or medical centers without sharing sensitive patient data. By letting each hospital train its model before sharing the summarized information, the computational cost is reduced. This can lead to the development of more accurate and personalized medical models for better patient care. Other application areas follow the same logic which is mainly about protecting private data. Examples include finance, manufacturing, and autonomous driving, which contain sensitive data of personal financial accounts, proprietary information, and driving data, respectively.

Privacy-Preserving Learning Techniques. Several other technologies can be used to enhance privacy-preserving machine learning in the context of HCI (Saha and Ahmad 2021). The first one is federated transfer learning. This technique combines federated learning with transfer learning to enable privacy-preserving machine learning on data from multiple sources, while also leveraging knowledge learned from other sources. The second technique is differential privacy. This technique adds noise to data to protect the privacy of individual users while still allowing analysis of the aggregate data. This approach can protect user privacy while still enabling machine learning on the data.

References

Abadi, M., et al.: TensorFlow: A System for Large-Scale Machine Learning (2016)

Aledhari, M., Razzak, R., Parizi, R.M., Saeed, F.: Federated learning: a survey on enabling technologies, protocols, and applications. IEEE Access **8**, 140699–140725 (2020)

Asokan, S., Duffy, V.G.: Using bibliometric analysis, ergonomic principles and a perching stool to prevent injuries in the workplace. In: Duffy, V.G., Rau, PL.P. (eds.) HCI International 2022 – Late Breaking Papers: Ergonomics and Product Design. HCII 2022. LNCS, vol. 13522. Springer, Cham. https://doi.org/10.1007/978-3-031-21704-3_2

Bonawitz, K., et al.: Towards federated learning at scale: System design (2019)

Chhikara, P.: Federated learning meets human emotions: a decentralized framework for human-computer interaction for IoT applications. IEEE Internet Things J. **8** (2021)

Fredrikson, M., Jha, S., Ristenpart, T.: Model inversion attacks that exploit confidence information and basic countermeasures. In: Proceedings of the ACM Conference on Computer and Communications Security 2015-October, pp. 1322–1333 (2015)

Geyer, R.C., Klein, T., Nabi, M., Se, S., Zurich, E.: Differentially private federated learning: a client level perspective (2018)

Goodfellow, I., Bengio, Y., Courville, A.: Deep learning (2016)

He, K., Zhang, X., Ren, S., Sun, J.: Deep residual learning for image recognition. In: Proceedings of the IEEE Computer Society Conference on Computer Vision and Pattern Recognition 2016-December, pp. 770–778 (2015)

Kanade, S.G., Duffy, V.G.: A systematic literature review of game-based learning and safety management. In: Duffy, V. (eds.) Digital Human Modeling and Applications in Health, Safety, Ergonomics and Risk Management. Human Communication, Organization and Work. HCII 2020. LNCS, vol. 12199. Springer, Cham (2020). https://doi.org/10.1007/978-3-030-49907-5_26

Kanade, S.G., Duffy, V.G.: Use of virtual reality for safety training: a systematic review. In: Duffy, V.G. (eds.) Digital Human Modeling and Applications in Health, Safety, Ergonomics and Risk Management. Health, Operations Management, and Design. HCII 2022. LNCS, vol. 13320. Springer, Cham (2022). https://doi.org/10.1007/978-3-031-06018-2_25

Kang, J., Xiong, Z., Niyato, D., Zou, Y., Zhang, Y., Guizani, M.: Reliable federated learning for mobile networks. IEEE Wirel. Commun. 27, 72–80 (2020)

Karray, F., Alemzadeh, M., Saleh, J.A., Arab, M.N.: Human-computer interaction: overview on state of the art. Int. J. Smart Sens. Intell. Syst. 1, 137–159 (2008)

Kingma, D.P., Ba, J.L.: Adam: a method for stochastic optimization (2015)

Konečný, J., McMahan, H.B., Yu, F.X., Richtárik, P., Suresh, A.T., Bacon, D.: Federated learning: Strategies for improving communication efficiency. arXiv preprint arXiv:1610.05492 (2016).

Lecun, Y., Bengio, Y., Hinton, G.: Deep learning. Nature 2015 521:7553 521, 436–444 (2015)

Li, Q., et al.: A survey on federated learning systems: vision, hype and reality for data privacy and protection (2021)

Li, T., Sahu, A.K., Talwalkar, A., Smith, V.: Federated learning: challenges, methods, and future directions. IEEE Signal Process. Mag. 37, 50–60 (2019)

Li, T., Sahu, K., Talwalkar, A., Smith, V.: Distributed, streaming machine learning IEEE signal processing magazine (2020)

Liu, Z., Zhiwei, S.H., Wu, S., Smith, V.: On privacy and personalization in cross-silo federated learning. Advances in neural information processing systems (2022)

Margetis, G., Ntoa, S., Antona, M., Stephanidis, C.: Human-centered design of artificial intelligence. Handbook of Human Factors and Ergonomics, pp. 1085–1106 (2018)

Martin, K.D., Murphy, P.E.: The role of data privacy in marketing (2017)

Mendling, J., Decker, G., Reijers, H.A., Hull, R., Weber, I.: How do machine learning, robotic process automation, and blockchains affect the human factor in business process management? Commun. Assoc. Inform. Syst. 43, 19 (2018)

Moallem, A.: Cybersecurity, privacy, and trust. Handbook of Human Factors and Ergonomics, pp. 1107–1120 (2021)

Mothukuri, V., Parizi, R.M., Pouriyeh, S., Huang, Y., Dehghantanha, A., Srivastava, G.: A survey on security and privacy of federated learning. Futur. Gener. Comput. Syst. 115, 619–640 (2021)

National Science Foundation. NSF award search: Award 2144927 - career: Foundations of privacy-preserving collaborative (2022). Retrieved from https://www.nsf.gov/awardsearch/showAward?AWD_ID=2144927&HistoricalAwards=false

National Science Foundation. NSF award search: Award 2145670 - career: Foundations of federated multi-task learning (2022). Retrieved from https://www.nsf.gov/awardsearch/showAward?AWD_ID=2145670&HistoricalAwards=false

Saha, S., Ahmad, T.: Federated transfer learning: concept and applications (2021)

Savazzi, S., Nicoli, M., Rampa, V.: Federated learning with cooperating devices: a consensus approach for massive IoT networks (2019)

Shokri, R., Shmatikov, V.; Privacy-preserving deep learning. In: Proceedings of the ACM Conference on Computer and Communications Security 2015-October, 1310–1321 (2015)

Stanford, V.S., Chiang, C.-K., Sanjabi, M.: Federated multi-task learning (2017)

Truex, S., et al.: A hybrid approach to privacy-preserving federated learning. In: Proceedings of the ACM Conference on Computer and Communications Security, pp. 1–11 (2019)

Wang, S., et al.: Adaptive federated learning in resource constrained edge computing systems. IEEE J. Sel. Areas Commun. **37**, 1205–1221 (2018)

Wei, K., et al.: Federated learning with differential privacy: algorithms and performance analysis. IEEE Trans. Inform. Foren. Security **15**, 2020 (2020)

Whig, P., Velu, A., Sharma, P.: Demystifying federated learning for blockchain: a case study. Demystifying Federated Learning for Blockchain and Industrial Internet of Things, pp. 94–122 (2022)

Wu, Y., Cai, S., Xiao, X., Chen, G., Ooi, C.: Privacy preserving vertical federated learning for tree-based models [technical report] (2020)

Xu, J., et al.: Federated learning for healthcare informatics. J. Healthcare Inform. Res. **5** (2019)

Yang, Q., Liu, Y., Chen, T., Tong, Y.: Federated machine learning: concept and applications. ACM Trans. Intell. Syst. Technol. **10**, 19 (2019)

Zhan, Y., Zhang, J., Hong, Z., Wu, L., Li, P., Guo, S.: A survey of incentive mechanism design for federated learning (2021)

Zhang, Y., Makarov, S., Ren, X., Lion, D., Yuan, D.: Pensieve: Non-intrusive failure reproduction for distributed systems using the event chaining approach. In: SOSP 2017 - Proceedings of the 26th ACM Symposium on Operating Systems Principles, pp. 19–33 (2017)

Zhao, Y., Li, M., Lai, L., Suda, N., Civin, D., Chandra, V.: Federated learning with non-iid data (2018)

Zhao, Y., et al.: Privacy-preserving blockchain-based federated learning for IoT devices. IEEE Internet Things J. **8**, 1817–1829 (2019)

Wearable Technology Safety and Ethics: A Systematic Review and Reappraisal

Ben Holden[(✉)] and Vincent G. Duffy

Purdue University, West Lafayette, IN 47907, USA
{holden13,duffy}@purdue.edu

Abstract. This article discusses the safety and ethics involved with the emergence of wearable technology. A bibliometric analysis, content analysis, and systematic review are conducted. The current research and articles identified through the reviews are presented and discussed. Metadata was accessed using various databases including Scopus, Web of Science, and Harzings' Publish or Perish. This data was then analyzed using VOSviewer and CiteSpace to identify clusters and trends. Mendeley was used to generate a bibliography. The review showed that wearable technology is a multi-billion-dollar emerging industry, but little has been done regarding the ethics and privacy of data-sharing capabilities. Various studies show the benefits of wearable technology related to fall prevention, biometric monitoring, and mobility analysis. Some of the limitations and ethical concerns of this technology are discussed, including the increased need for regulation and privacy concerns for data collection and sharing. Ideas for future work regarding ethical concerns, as well as opportunities for further implementation of technology are proposed. This article demonstrates the use of various bibliometric analysis tools for a systematic literature review and discusses the benefits & ethics of wearable technology.

Keywords: Wearable Technology · Ethics · Google Scholar · Publish or Perish · Word Cloud · Scopus · Bibliometric Analysis

1 Introduction and Background

Definitions:

Wearable Technology: devices including fitness trackers and smartwatches that are designed to be worn throughout the day [1]

Ethics: Moral principles that govern a person's behavior or the conducting of an activity

Bibliometrics: the statistical analyses of books, articles, or other publications

Wearable technology is a subset of technology that is transportable and provides a number of capabilities designed around a person's lifestyle. It enables the continuous monitoring of human physical activities and behaviors, as well as physiological and biochemical parameters during daily life [2]. This form of technology is a recent

© The Author(s), under exclusive license to Springer Nature Switzerland AG 2023
H. Degen et al. (Eds.): HCII 2023, LNCS 14059, pp. 390–407, 2023.
https://doi.org/10.1007/978-3-031-48057-7_24

advancement and is increasing in popularity. Many new manufacturers and iterations are being presented regularly. Wearable technology can capture vital information on the health, safety, and comfort of millions of users every day. The potential benefits of this technology are endless. Doctors can have real-time access to their patient's vital signs. Parents can check in on their children throughout the day. Individuals can be warned when their blood pressure or heart rate is in an unsafe zone. With all of this potential, it is an interesting technology to research.

Wearable technology can be considered an emerging technology due to the rising sales of smartwatches, fitness trackers, and portable healthcare devices. As technology advances and these devices become more integrated into our daily lives, the topic of safety and ethics related to wearable technology will become paramount. Additionally, the technology has the potential to add efficiency and safety to workers and systems. These increases are pivotal to industrial engineers looking to improve processes and procedures.

Automated systems and artificial intelligence are being used to increase efficiency in workplaces. Wearable technology could be a convenient way to offer a feedback loop in systems. As engineers implement this technology, they will have to comply with the ethics related to the technology.

Privacy is a hot topic. This is due in part to the news stories of companies getting hacked and sensitive data leaking. As society becomes more integrated with these technologies, it is important to maintain a level of privacy and ethics. Studies have been conducted regarding the human-computer interaction factors related to elderly consumers with wearable technology. While wearables increase safety and independence in the elderly, they typically require larger screens, larger text, and fewer distractions. These interactions are considered in the discussion. A systematic review will be conducted to identify and discuss wearable technology and its relevance to safety and ethics. The process and procedures are presented in the following sections.

2 Systematic Review Process and Procedures

2.1 Step 1: Trend Analysis

To begin the systematic review, a bibliometric analysis was performed on the topic of wearable technology. Firstly, Scopus was used to create an understanding of the emergence of wearable technology. This is measured through the number of articles relating to the topic. Thousands of articles related to wearable technology were found using Scopus. Figure 1 below shows that the emergence occurred around 2010 and has grown since. Considering this, the articles included in the metadata search will only include those published after 2010. The number of articles related to wearable technology increased annually in the last decade. This built confidence in it being a topic of interest. Table 1 shows the increasing number of articles year by year.

Table 1. Emergence of Articles Related to Wearable Technology.

Year	# of Articles
2016	3201
2017	4201
2018	3934
2019	4433
2020	4775
2021	5157
2022	5840

Documents by year

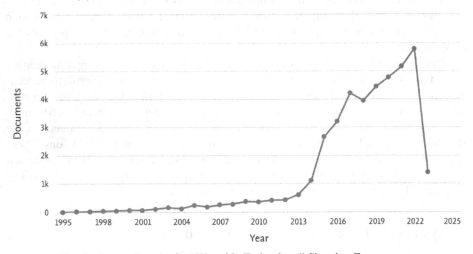

Fig. 1. Scopus Results for "Wearable Technology" Showing Emergence.

To compare trends, Google nGram was used to search for "Wearable Technology", "Healthcare Devices", and "Healthcare Privacy". The comparison shows that wearable technology is discussed much more than the two latter topics. This indicates that more research should be focused on the use of wearable technology in healthcare. The comparison is shown in Fig. 2 below.

Additional insight comes from evaluating the country of origin for the articles. Figure 3 below shows that the primary countries that publish the articles are the United States and China.

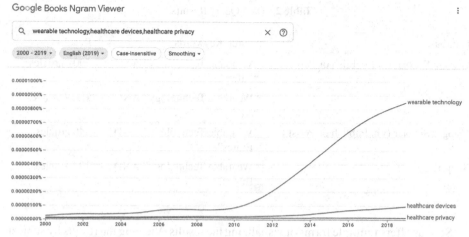

Fig. 2. Google nGram Comparison Between Three Terms.

Documents by country or territory

Compare the document counts for up to 15 countries/territories.

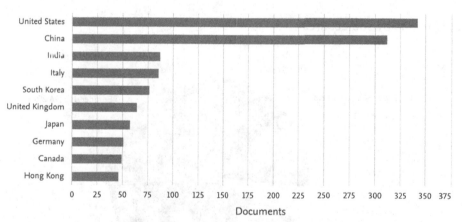

Fig. 3. Scopus Results for Number of Articles by Country Showing Areas Interested in Wearable Technology.

2.2   Step 2: Bibliometric Analysis and Data Collection

After identifying the relevant topic, Scopus and Google Scholar were queried. The goal was to find literature that addresses the safety and ethical considerations of wearable technology. This was done through two searches. The first search was for "wearable technology" and "safety". The second search was for "wearable technology" and "ethics". The results are shown in Table 2 below.

Table 2. Data Query Results.

Database	Search Keywords	Results
Google Scholar (via Publish or Perish)	"Wearable Technology" AND "Safety"	500+ articles
Scopus	"Wearable Technology" AND "Safety"	1,317 articles
Google Scholar (via Publish or Perish)	"Wearable Technology" AND "Ethics"	240 articles
Scopus	"Wearable Technology" AND "Ethics"	102 articles

Scopus offers multiple forms of visualizing the results. Viewing the results by subject area provides additional insight into where the topics are of interest. For example, the safety is primarily shown in engineering and computer science. The ethics are primarily seen in computer science and medicine. This aligns with intuition and helps shape the focus of the systematic review. These results are shown in Figs. 4 and 5 below.

Documents by subject area

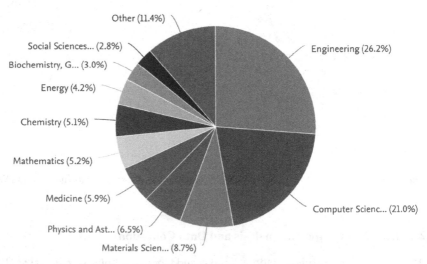

Fig. 4. Subject Areas for Wearable Technology & Safety.

Documents by subject area

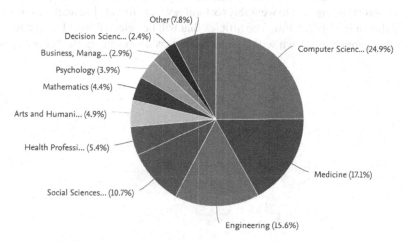

Fig. 5. Subject Areas for Wearable Technology & Ethics.

With the subject areas identified, the next step was to visualize the information in the articles. The metadata generated using Google Scholar was used to create a word cloud. The word cloud shows the frequency of the terms by size. From the word cloud, it can be seen that the articles primarily focus on technology, monitoring, devices, safety, health, design, performance, and construction. This shows the areas of interest of the authors studying wearable technology. The word cloud is shown in Fig. 6 below.

Fig. 6. Word Cloud for Metadata Results.

To expand on the relevancy of wearable technology, Vicinitas was used to query Twitter. Vicinitas allows the user to identify keywords within Twitter posts. In the last 10 days, ~1000 references to wearable technology were found. The analyses from Vicinitas are shown in Fig. 7 below. The articles that will be selected based on the word cloud and subject area breakdown will be used to discuss the results in the following section.

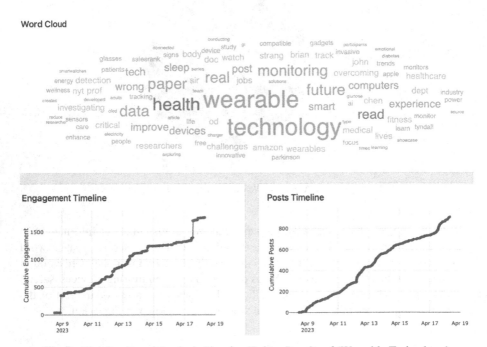

Fig. 7. Vicinitas Trend Analysis Showing Twitter Results of 'Wearable Technology'.

3   Results and Discussion

3.1   Co-citation Analysis

With thousands of articles related to wearable technology, an approach must be used to select which articles to focus on for discussion. An aid in doing so was the co-citation analysis. The co-citation analysis allows a researcher to identify which authors are frequently related [3]. The co-citation cluster from VOSviewer is shown in Fig. 8.

One of the advantages of the co-citation analysis is that references that are supportive of similar topics are identified. Table 3 shows a set of articles that were identified as potential sources of contribution to this analysis. It can be seen that many of the articles align with the topic of wearable technology in healthcare. This supports the article topic and directly relates to the material of the course.

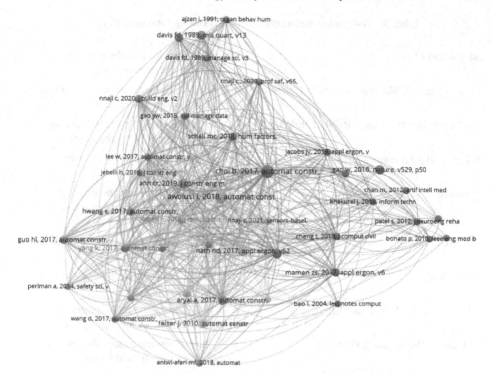

Fig. 8. Co-Citation Analysis for Articles Related to 'Wearable Technology'.

3.2 Content Analysis

VOSviewer was also used to do a content analysis. The content analysis shows what content is primarily focused on in the articles identified in the metadata. This analysis allows the metadata previously generated to be analyzed and evaluated to identify articles that are cited by multiple other sources. Additionally, it is possible to see which groups of articles are cited together. This analysis was leveraged to identify which articles would be focused on for the review.

Content analysis was performed using VOSviewer. The metadata was extracted from Harzings' Publish or Perish. Figure 9 shows the cluster analysis for articles including 'wearable technology' and 'safety'. Figure 10 shows the cluster analysis for articles including 'wearable technology' and 'ethics'. It can be seen that the two searches yield far different results. Wearable technology safety has a large number of articles. This is not the case for wearable technology and ethics. This supports the discussion on necessary future work. The lack of research on the ethics of wearable technology demonstrates a gap in understanding and consideration.

Table 3. Co-Citation References Identified During Literature Review.

M Wu and J Luo	Wearable technology applications in healthcare: a literature review
G Aroganam, N Manivannan and D Harrison	Review on wearable technology sensors used in consumer sport applications
JM Pevnick, K Birkeland, R Zimmer, Y Elad	Wearable technology for cardiology: an update and framework for the future
S Park and S Jayaraman	Enhancing the quality of life through wearable technology
P Bonato	Advances in wearable technology and applications in physical medicine and rehabilitation
Y Gao, H Li and Y Luo	An empirical study of wearable technology acceptance in healthcare
ND Schüll	Data for life: Wearable technology and the design of self-care
ME Berglund, J Duvall and LE Dunne	A survey of the historical scope and current trends of wearable technology applications
Y Liao, C Thompson, S Peterson	The future of wearable technologies and remote monitoring in health care
M Alrige and S Chatterjee	Toward a taxonomy of wearable technologies in healthcare
KW Ching and MM Singh	Wearable technology devices security and privacy vulnerability analysis
JA Slade Shantz and CJH Veillette	The application of wearable technology in surgery: ensuring the positive impact of the wearable revolution on surgical patients

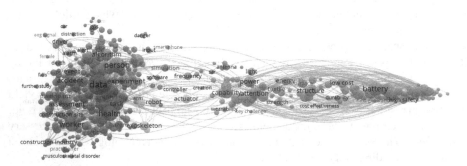

Fig. 9. VOSviewer Cluster Analysis for 'Wearable Technology' and 'Safety'.

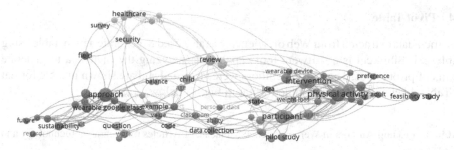

Fig. 10. VOSviewer Cluster Analysis for 'Wearable Technology' and 'Ethics'.

3.3 Cluster Analysis

To supplement the analysis from VOSviewer, CiteSpace was also used to provide cluster analysis. The metadata was generated using Web of Science and searching for 'Wearable Technology' and 'Ethics'. This yielded ~1,800 articles, which were used with CiteSpace to generate a cluster analysis. The clusters are shown in Fig. 11. Keywords in the cluster include safety, ergonomics, medical, and sensor.

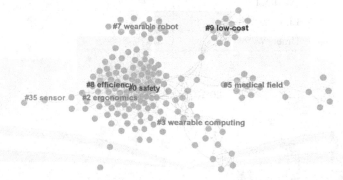

Fig. 11. CiteSpace Cluster Analysis for Web of Science Metadata on Wearable Technology and Ethics.

CiteSpace also has the capability of performing a citation burst. The citation burst used the same metadata from the cluster analysis. The burst results are shown in Fig. 12 below. The citation burst helps provide insight into what timeframe the research was relevant. For the research shown, the time frame began in 2021. This shows that the topic is relevant and still being evaluated.

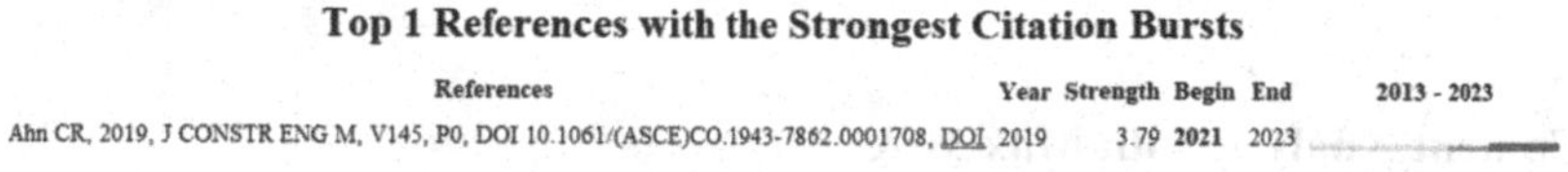

Top 1 References with the Strongest Citation Bursts

References	Year	Strength	Begin	End	2013 - 2023
Ahn CR, 2019, J CONSTR ENG M, V145, P0, DOI 10.1061/(ASCE)CO.1943-7862.0001708, DOI	2019	3.79	2021	2023	

Fig. 12. Citation Burst Results Showing References with Strongest Citation Burst.

3.4   Pivot Table

The metadata extracted from Web of Science was also used to generate a pivot table using BibExcel. BibExcel is a software tool capable of analyzing the metadata to generate forms of pivot tables. The leading authors were identified and are shown in table format in Table 4 below and in pivot table format in Fig. 13 below.

Table 4. Leading Authors in Web of Science Metadata of Articles on Wearable Technology and Ethics.

Author	# of Articles
Nnaji, C	11
Awolusi, I	10
Huang, Y	8
Lee, S	6
Lee, J	5
Zhang, XS	5
Okpala, I	5
Li, H	5
Umer, W	5

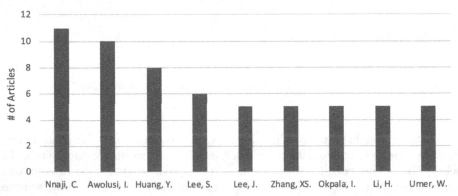

Fig. 13.   Pivot Table Showing Leading Authors in Metadata from Web of Science.

3.5   Content Analysis with MaxQDA

With the reference articles selected for review, another content analysis was conducted with more focus on the filtered articles. This analysis was based on the text of the selected articles. A word cloud was generated in the MaxQDA software, showing the most frequent keywords in the set of articles.

The most frequently occurring words were wearable, safety, science, technology, research, international, health, and engineering. While the content analysis from VOSviewer used link strength as the parameter, MAXQDA provided information regarding the frequency of words. This informed the selection of references for discussion in the following sections. The word cloud is shown in Fig. 14 below.

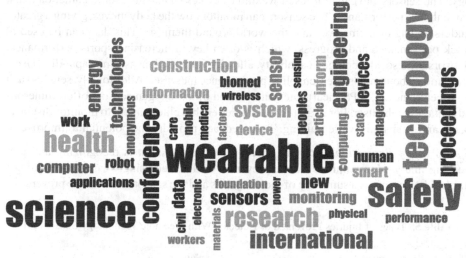

Fig. 14. Most Frequent Words Found in Metadata Using MaxQDA.

4 Results and Discussion

4.1 Wearable Technology: Capability

Capability of Wearable Technology. Wearable technology is interesting to many industries. Regarding safety, wearable technology has numerous applications. With the emergence of wearable technology, how has safety in the workplace and people's lives been impacted? Has there been an overall positive effect, or are there downsides to the technology that must be addressed? In researching and gathering metadata, it was obvious that wearable technology has the potential to increase the safety and well-being of those who own a device. The question is, where does that potential lie? Searching for wearable technology and safety generated thousands of references in the literature. VOSviewer identified which areas are of interest to researchers. As shown in the cluster, those areas include construction, health, and attention. This shows the focus areas and the methods by which wearable devices can increase safety.

4.2 Wearable Technology: Health Applications

There are several potential applications for wearable technology. A few applications found in the literature review include sports performance and safety, elderly safety and health monitoring, health data collection for doctors, and fall prevention and detection. The sports and health data applications are discussed next. The safety applications are discussed in the following subsection.

Sports Performance Applications. Many sports applications exist for wearable technology. The sensors and capabilities of wearable devices enable the user to gather data that can enhance performance. The sensors can monitor how the body moves, giving a greater understanding of themselves and the world around them [4]. This data can be used to track performance and progress, which is often key to increasing sports performance. Sensors are also advancing in capability, allowing increased measuring capability. Users learn more about themselves, enabling performance increases. Additionally, sensors such as accelerometers, GPS, heart rate sensors, and blood oxygen sensors offer numerous advantages to the user. For example, wearables enable elite runners to monitor distance, pace, and vital signs while training. This feedback provides the potential to improve.

Sports Injury Prevention. Another sports-related application is recognizing and preventing injury. Many injuries can be prevented or detected using wearable technology. Table 5 below shows a summary of these injuries and the sensors that enable prevention.

Table 5. Types of Injuries Prevented or Detected With Wearable Technology Sensors [4].

Type of Sports Injury	Sensor
Falls	IMU
Excessive loading on arms & legs	IMU, pressure sensor
Arm/Leg speed	Accelerometer
Collision	Accelerometer
Excessive arm or leg rotation	Accelerometer
Abnormal body temperature	Thermistor

Health Monitoring. Wearable technology can also provide significant information related to health monitoring. The most commonly measured data include vital signs such as heart rate, blood pressure, body temperature, blood oxygen saturation, posture, and physical activities [2]. With the sensor capability and the convenience of a wearable device, the technology is a great fit for the healthcare industry. The uses include weight and activity management, prevention of disease, and health maintenance.

Effectiveness of Health Monitoring. Concerning health monitoring, it is fair to question how effective the technology can be. A study was conducted by Nguyen et al. [5] that explored the acceptability and usability of wearable activity trackers among breast cancer survivors. According to the researchers, many breast cancer survivors are at greater risk of comorbidities due to physical inactivity and sedentary behavior. These comorbidities include heart disease, diabetes, and other cancers. The study evaluated the efficacy of activity trackers as a method to increase activity. The wearable trackers can alert the user when they have been sedentary for a while and can help the user track an activity goal. These goals could include daily steps, distance walked, and periods of movement. The research concluded that wearable activity trackers could have an impact through increased self-awareness and motivation. Users were confident and comfortable with wearable technology [5].

Health Monitoring. Other forms of health monitoring are possible with wearable technology. One of the most important applications of wearable technology related to the health sector is the enabling of continuous monitoring of a patient's health status and gathering real-world information about the patient [6]. A literature review conducted by Wu et al. [2] showed that there are numerous health benefits for wearable device users. These include people with heart disorders, blood disorders, diabetes, Parkinson's, autism, and depression.

Treatment Enhancement. In addition to treatment and maintenance, wearable devices also allow physicians to gain feedback about the effectiveness of rehabilitation and other treatments. The devices allow data to be collected in the patient's natural environment daily. This data informs the physician as to the impact of the intervention. Historically, the patients were relied upon to provide accurate and complete information on their progress. Wearable technology has changed that. Monitoring functional motor activities was one of the first goals of research teams interested in clinical applications of wearable technology [7]. Wearable devices allow the continuous gathering of data unobtrusively and reliably.

4.3 Wearable Technology: Safety Applications

Another application is related to the health and safety of the elderly population. Many elderly people are more secluded from others and have higher risks of health and safety hazards. The goal of technology for the elderly is to help them achieve greater independence while enhancing safety, health, and social interaction [8].

Elderly Safety. A natural effect of the aging process is physical and mental decline. Daily tasks become more laborious and independence becomes more challenging. Dohr et al. identified six needs of the elderly: health, safety/security, peace of mind, independence, mobility, and social contact [9]. Wearable technology can support each of these through its sensor capability and connectivity to the internet. Many products have been introduced to help elderly persons when they fall. The sensors on wearable devices can detect a fall and can call for help if the user is unable to do so. This contributes to their safety and peace of mind. Knowing this, many users feel more independent and confident in being mobile.

Workplace Safety-Falls. Elderly people are not the only group that can benefit from the increase in safety. Many workers face the risk of falling in their daily jobs. Goetsch estimates that more than 16 percent of all disabling work-related injuries are the result of falls [10]. Also, people with certain health conditions are more susceptible to falls. Subjects with cardiovascular disorders (e.g., related to autonomic dysfunctions and postural hypotension) are at higher risk of falling [11]. Researchers analyzed the ability of heart rate variability (HRV) to predict the risk of falling in these individuals. The HRV features enabled the identification of future fallers among hypertensive patients with an accuracy of 72% and detected simulated falls using ECG achieved an accuracy of 77.3% [11]. This shows the ability of wearable technology to increase safety by preventing falls.

Noise Detection. A third safety application of wearable devices is noise detection and prevention. According to Goetsch, noisy environments can pose multiple safety and health-related problems [12]. The noise can be a hazard from distraction and from hearing damage. Wearable devices can detect high noise levels and warn the user to leave the noisy area.

4.4   Wearable Technology: Ethical Considerations

'Big data' and artificial intelligence are topics that are often discussed. While wearable devices do have the aforementioned benefits, they could come with a cost. To provide the capabilities, the devices must gather and use data. For instance, the pedometer function requires user data, sensor data, and algorithms to determine the step count and distance [13]. Data sources for smart devices include mobile communication data, private data, and data from sensors [14].

The risk associated with users sharing their data is due to several factors. First, the users are trusting the manufacturers with their personal and biometric data. This data is considered sensitive and could be harmful if it is involved in a data spill. Also, the user's daily activity data is available and susceptible to misuse. Permissions are given frequently without much consideration as to the risk. The inappropriate use of data or attacks on data may not only cause harassment to customers but also pose a threat to the property or safety of users. [15].

5   Future Work

"Most wearable technologies are still in their prototype stages. Issues such as user acceptance, security, ethics, and big data concerns in wearable technology still need to be addressed" [2]. As for the wearable devices themselves, there is much work to be done. Many iterations of these devices have been produced, but not necessarily with these applications in mind. The devices are not completely standardized and compatible with everyone who may need them, nor with the systems with which they will need to operate. To use these devices for many safety-related applications, there needs to be a development of standardization and compatibility with the systems in the network.

Current and future projects in the wearable technology field were found using nsf.gov. One current study by the University of Puerto Rico is conducted through 2024 with an estimated $17,000,000 in funding. The goal of the study is quoted as "providing easy access to new types of wearable devices that sense and monitor health conditions and provide consistent, reproducible, and personalized medical information" [16]. The university states that this is essential for continued growth within the wearable technology sector. According to the researchers, "wearable devices face three fundamental research and development challenges: 1) ensuring that functional components made of materials that are fully compatible with end users; 2) generating adequate and lasting power; 3) updating data analytics to utilize and manage steady streams of data generated wearable devices."

A second research project was found on nsf.gov. The University of Washington conducted a two-year project to research the ability of mobile devices to sense sound and provide feedback for people who are deaf [17]. This has safety implications similar to those discussed above.

Along with maturing the technology itself, understanding the ethics of the devices is equally important. When using Scopus, the results changed drastically between searching for a single phrase like 'wearable technology' versus pairing it with a second keyword like 'ethics'. Wearable technology itself has a large number of articles and publications. However, few articles address the ethical concerns of the technology. This seems very surprising. When consumers use technology, they are asked to give permission for the apps. With wearable technology, they are often allowing our biometric data, location, and even movement data to be captured by the device. This creates a seemingly obvious need for ethical discussion. How do we ensure that our data is not being misused?

The trend analysis and content analysis showed that the ethics related to wearable technology is not yet a thoroughly researched topic. As wearable technology becomes more integrated into everyday life, the data being shared will continue to increase. This data sharing creates a need for ethical behavior regarding how the data is used. Therefore, the ethics related to personal data and biometrics should continue to be analyzed to protect the consumer.

6 Conclusion

Wearable technology is an emerging technology that is accelerating in development and production. The growth of the technology is boundless, as advances in microchips and nanotechnology enable more powerful devices. The review shows the endless potential of wearable technology, and the trends analysis suggests that the technology will continue to advance at a rapid pace.

A literature search and systematic review were conducted to gain insight into research conducted on wearable technology. Content analysis, trends analysis, and co-citation analysis leveraged metadata to identify trends in the research topics. The analyses identified areas of interest and applications for wearable technology. Applications include sports performance, health monitoring, disease treatment, and elderly health care, among others.

Along with the numerous applications of the technology, the safety contributions of wearable technology were presented. These include fall prevention, elderly safety response, and noise detection. Finally, future work was recommended and future projects were identified.

A solid understanding and application of wearable technology exist. However, further work is necessary to increase the compatibility and privacy of wearable devices as they are integrated into daily life.

References

From Literature Review, Textbook, Methods Paper, & Future Work

1. https://edu.gcfglobal.org/en/wearables/what-is-wearable-technology/1/. Pg 1
2. Wu, M., Luo, J.: Wearable Technology Applications in Healthcare: A Literature Review. Online J. Nurs. Inform (himss.org, 2019). https://www.himss.org/resources/wearable-techno logy-applications-healthcare-literature-review. Pg 2
3. Kanade, S., Duffy, V.: Use of Virtual Reality for Safety Training: A Systematic Review (2022). https://doi.org/10.1007/978-3-031-06018-2_25. Pg 7
4. Aroganam, G., Manivannan, N., Harrison, D.: Review on Wearable Technology Sensors used in Consumer Sport Applications. Sensors (mdpi.com, 2019). https://www.mdpi.com/453138. Pg. 14
5. Nguyen, N., et al.: A qualitative evaluation of breast cancer survivors' acceptance of and preferences for consumer wearable technology activity trackers. Support Care Cancer 25(11):3375–3384 (2017). https://doi.org/10.1007/s00520-017-3756-y. Epub 2017 May 24. PMID: 28540402. Pg 14
6. Çiçek, M.: Wearable technologies and its future applications. Int. J. Electric. Electron. Data. (academia.edu, 2015). https://www.academia.edu/download/37446358/wearable.pdf. Pg 14
7. Bonato, P.: Advances in wearable technology and applications in physical medicine and rehabilitation. J. Neuro Eng. (jneuroengrehab.biomedcentral.com, 2005). https://doi.org/10.1186/1743-0003-2-2. Pg 14
8. Sharma, R., Nah, F.F.H., Sharma, K., Katta, T.S.S.S., Pang, N., Yong, A.: Smart living for elderly: design and human-computer interaction considerations. In: Zhou, J., Salvendy, G. (eds.) Human Aspects of IT for the Aged Population. Healthy and Active Aging. ITAP 2016. LNCS, vol. 9755. Springer, Cham. https://doi.org/10.1007/978-3-319-39949-2_11. Pg 14
9. Dohr, A., Modre-Opsrian, R., Drobics, M., Hayn, D., Schreier, G.: The Internet of Things for ambient assisted living. In: Seventh International Conference on Information Technology: New Generations, pp. 804–809. IEEE Computer Society Washington, DC, USA (2010). Pg 14
10. Goetsch, D.L.: Chapter 15: Falling, impact, acceleration, and vision hazards with appropriate PPE. In: Occupational Safety and Health for Technologists, Engineers, and Managers, 9th edn., pp. 330–331. Prentice Hall, Upper Saddle River, NJ (2011). Pg 14
11. Melillo, P., Castaldo, R., Sannino, G., Orrico, A., de Pietro, G., and Pecchia, L. Wearable technology and ECG processing for fall risk assessment, prevention and detection. In: 37th Annual International Conference of the IEEE Engineering in Medicine and Biology Society (EMBC), pp. 7740–7743. Milan, Italy (2015). https://doi.org/10.1109/EMBC.2015.7320186. Pg 15
12. Goetsch, D.L.: Chapter 22: noise and vibration hazards. In: Occupational Safety and Health for Technologists, Engineers, and Managers, 9th ed., 498. Prentice Hall, Upper Saddle River, NJ (2011). Pg 15
13. Jayalath, S., Abhayasinghe, N.: A gyroscopic data based pedometer algorithm. In: International Conference on Computer Science & Education. Pg 15

14. Karakaya, M., Bostan, A., Gökçay, E.: How Secure is Your Smart Watch?. In: Proceedings of 9th International Conference on Information Security and Cryptology (ISCTURKEY 2016), pp.138–145. Pg15

15. Chang, V., Xu, X., Wong, B., Mendez, V.: Ethical problems of smart wearable devices. In: COMPLEXIS 2019 - Proceedings of the 4th International Conference on Complexity, Future Information Systems and Risk pp. 121–129. SciTePress (2019). https://doi.org/10.5220/000 7722000520058. Pg 15

16. "Center for the Advancement of Wearable Technologies (CAWT): Engineered (Bio)Interfaces, Energy Harvesting/Storage and Data Analytics for Health and Diagnostic Monitoring." Award Abstract # 1849243. https://www.nsf.gov/awardsearch/showAward?AWD_ID=1849243& HistoricalAwards=false. Pg 15

17. "Collaborative Research: Wearable Sound Sensing and Feedback Techniques for Persons who are Deaf or Hard of Hearing." Award Abstract #1763199. Pg 16

Subtopics/Tools

18. BibExcel. n.d. https://homepage.univie.ac.at/juan.gorraiz/bibexcel/
19. CiteSpace. n.d. http://cluster.cis.drexel.edu/~cchen/citespace/ [Scite.ai]
20. Google nGram. n.d. https://books.google.com/ngrams/
21. MAXQDA. n.d. https://www.maxqda.com/
22. Mendeley. n.d. https://www.mendeley.com/
23. Harzing Publish or Perish. n.d. https://harzing.com/resources/publish-or-perish/windows
24. Scopus. n.d. https://www.scopus.com/search/form.uri?display=basic&zone=header&origin=#basic
25. VOSviewer. n.d. https://www.vosviewer.com/
26. Word Clouds. n.d. https://www.wordclouds.com/
27. Web of Science. n.d. https://www-webofscience-com.ezproxy.lib.purdue.edu/wos/woscc/basic-search

In-Kernel Authentication Request Analysis for Human and Bot Distinction

Sahak Ivašauskas, Marius Gaubas, and Linas Bukauskas[✉]

Cyber Security Laboratory, Institute of Computer Science, Vilnius University, Vilnius, Lithuania
{sahak.ivasauskas,marius.gaubas,linas.bukauskas}@mif.vu.lt

Abstract. As the world continues to digitise and produce numerous challenges, it becomes imperative to rely on computer authentication processing. Utilising the Kerberos network authentication protocol, which features single-sign-on, trusted third-party, and mutual authentication services, is one of the numerous sophisticated user identification techniques. However, a challenge arises when clients connecting to Kerberized servers are emulated by bots exhibiting human-like behaviour, which cannot be effectively mitigated using standard firewalls. This work aims to investigate and present a time-efficient methodology for the distinction between bot- and human-executed authentication requests using a safe in-kernel authentication protocol proxy module that replicates the original domain controller. The aim of this technology is to detect threat actors who are engaging in reconnaissance activities targeting the principal database and utilise transparent communication as being an actual domain controller.

Keywords: Bot identification · Human behaviour · Cybersecurity

1 Introduction

Authentication is a crucial identity validation process in the field of cybersecurity that ensures users of sensitive information that only those matching certain security attributes, such as passwords, facial recognition, or sound patterns, are permitted access to it. Given that humans can easily discern visual or sound patterns using their eyesight and hearing, hiring people to process all authentication requests per organisation is physically impossible, untrustworthy, and cost-inefficient. As a result, humans must rely on the authentication processing on computers. However, even at the current peak of artificial intelligence development, it is unacceptable to rely on pattern recognition authentication models on computers all over the world. Thus, password-based authentication remains the most ubiquitous, but also one of the most vulnerable [3]. The exchanged network packets at the authentication stage can be transparently mangled or stolen by third-party threat actors that sniff the network packets. Thus, software applications ensure the encryption of the network traffic. However, the threat actor that

© The Author(s), under exclusive license to Springer Nature Switzerland AG 2023
H. Degen et al. (Eds.): HCII 2023, LNCS 14059, pp. 408–417, 2023.
https://doi.org/10.1007/978-3-031-48057-7_25

has sufficient power of computational capabilities and time can perform offline dictionary attacks to get the secret password and use it for replay attacks. Consequently, the authentication process requires not only the network traffic to be encrypted but employ more complex algorithms while remaining time-efficient.

One of the examples of secure authentication algorithms is provided by the Kerberos protocol, which was initially developed at the Massachusetts Institute of Technology in the 1980s as per Project Athena [16]. Kerberos is a network authentication and authorisation protocol that provides single-sign-on, trusted third-party, and mutual authentication capabilities over insecure networks like the Internet by utilising special encrypted data structures called Ticket-Granting Tickets. It is generated and provided by a trusted third-party server known as the Key Distribution Center (KDC) that maintains a database of principals and provides two services: Authentication Service and Ticket-Granting Service. Kerberos clients entail a series of message exchanges with those services to prove their identity and get granted with an access to a requested Kerberized server. The interactions between network clients and servers and the messages involved in those exchanges are described in [12].

Although the Kerberos protocol is strong and secure, it does not prevent threat actors from guessing passwords or reconnaissance the system by examining the exchanged messages between the clients and the KDC. Reconnaissance of the principal database can expose which principals exist within the system, how well they are secured and identify the vulnerable points to access the system. One of the trivial examples is executing already existing bot tools allowing to quickly brute-force passwords and enumerate valid KDC principals. However, well-secured networks employ security mechanisms that check for abnormal frequency of network requests can immediately block such traffic. Thus, it necessitates threat actors to utilise more complex attack algorithms like specifying delay periods between consecutive network requests.

This work focuses on presenting a time-efficient distinction methodology of attacks on the Kerberos authentication system by analysing the initial message exchanges with the Authentication Service. We develop an in-kernel proxy module that mimics the behaviour of the original KDC server by utilising the feature of Linux kernel to dynamically insert and remove kernel code at runtime. It would transparently analyse the message exchanges to identify threat actors that are trying to either brute-force or reconnaissance the KDC server. Specifically, one of the factors that allow identifying a client as a threat actor is requesting for Ticket-Granting Ticket for a principal that does not exist within the principal database. The module is designed to continue the communication with the client as if the non-existing principal existed pretending to be the original KDC without the client's knowledge.

Furthermore, our project incorporates a sand-boxed eBPF program to handle packet redirection effectively and, if necessary, filtration. Extended Berkeley Packet Filter (eBPF) is a revolutionary and constantly growing in-kernel technology that extends the capabilities of the original BPF, which originated at the Lawrence Berkeley Laboratory in the 1990s and is described in [11]. The new technology allows to safely extend the kernel at run-time for networking, observ-ability, tracing and security purposes. Although eBPF programs are limited in instructions to run, stack memory and functionality, the available special eBPF helper functions are sufficient in our project to efficiently mangle the network packets to redirect to and from the proxy environment in the Traffic Control sub-system.

The work is structured as follows. In Sect. 2 we perform a literature overview and present what other bot-from-human distinction methodologies exist in the world of networking. Section 3 presents our offered distinction methodology and in Sect. 4 we speak about the implementation and current limitations of the software. Finally, we sum up the work with conclusions and future work in Sect. 5.

2   Related Work

Studies offer diverse classification methodologies to classify different types of bots in the world of networking. Some bots are benevolent and created by organisa-tions for customer assistance services or AI-based communication [9]. Others may be discovered in online social network ecosystems and mainly used for spamming, increasing account reach and engagement, or political propaganda purposes [4]. Aside from applications, bot activity can be detected in low-level network traffic using tools like Wireshark. Consequently, different scenarios exist where distinguishing bots from humans is imperative and it requires analysis of existing methodologies to apply the most appropriate for every particular case.

The world of networking consists of different cybersecurity threats some of which are described in [1,5] with methodologies of how to prevent them. Over the years the attacks evolve becoming more sophisticated to detect and necessitating to seek for newer solutions to prevent them [2]. For instance, botnets are one of the well-known cybersecurity attacks that involves of utilisation of large number of compromised machines known as "zombies" that are strategically selected to overwhelm and take down targeted systems and networks. They are controlled and maintained by highly-skilled hackers while the users of zombies are com-pletely oblivious to the malicious activity. Since botnet attacks can be performed from different IP addresses, utilising firewalls can be insufficient to prevent the attacks. One of the approaches offered by [1] is employing honeypots to catch the users of suspicious network activity for further monitoring and analysing the host behaviour. Honeypots can be defined as imitations of the original network infrastructure pretending to store valuable data and consisting of low security to lure and trap the attacker without its knowledge. While our project is not tar-geted to protect the system from botnet attacks, we use honeypots for catching threat actors that fail to authenticate. Moreover, [1] suggests using statistically-based distinguishing model based on the frequency of the requests. Even though it is not efficient to identify bots since they may utilise time delaying between requests, we look forward implementing such methodology to filter out trivial bot-executed authentication requests.

Kerberoasting is a cybersecurity attack involving the exploitation of the Kerberos protocol to illicitly gather the hashes associated with Active Directory service accounts. This activity when the threat actor has already an access to a compromised machine and this attack is recognised as one of the prevailing attacks that domain controllers are suffering from [7]. When a threat actor manages to gain access to at least one compromised machine, they can proceed to submit requests to the Ticket-Granting Service, aiming to acquire the service keys linked to other servers. To enhance detection capabilities, one of the proposed methods involve the utilisation of honeypots. In this approach, the authors recommend the creation of a fake accounts that would be represented in the network reconnaissance as admin accounts, but in reality assigned with no effective role or privileges. The user would attract the attacker's attention that would try to access it. Since the account is not practically used, clients requesting to obtain service keys of that service would be identified as the threat actors. Consequently, not only can the attack be identified, but the compromised machine can also be identified. Moreover, [10] offers monitoring for specific events in the Active Directory logs. For instance, the event 4769 that would be triggered when a client requests for Ticket-Granting Service tickets with lower encryption types that the system is configured to use or searching for excessive number of ticket requests to a service from one source. Even though this methodology is not applicable for other Kerberos implementations as they may not implement such event detection, similar detection methodologies can be implemented in coalition with KDC honeypots.

There have also been distinction studies on application-specific elements since monitoring low-level network traffic is not often sufficient. For instance, many studies do behavioural analysis [6,8,17] to distinguish Twitter bot accounts from real users. These studies examine the metadata of user profiles and behaviour within social media—the number of tweets, retweets, account age, etc. Although each research approach is unique, the results indicate that one may effectively classify users based on account holder behaviour. The aforementioned researches demonstrates that accounts used by bots tend to have comparably more tweets than humans. That parameter is an objective criterion for distinguishing. Similar results are achieved in [8], where a more diverse categorisation is performed and a larger data set is used to precisely characterised bot account behaviour. Another practical example is [6] study that initially classifies Twitter users into three categories: humans, bots, and organisations. Then, the authors utilise a statistical-based algorithm on tweets to identify what type of user has written it. Its final predictive model achieved high accuracy results, with over 95% of user accounts accurately categorised. These researches reveal that bot accounts can occasionally be identified language-independently based on their activity in social networks. However, this approach is not useful when examining low-level network traffic since it may be inefficient or impossible (e.g., due to encryption) to distinguish bots from humans.

Authentication techniques based on the Turing test few decades ago allowed to efficiently prevent bots from accessing restricted systems. However, with the modern rise of artificial intelligence capabilities, bots may analyse voiceprints or visual patterns which brings new challenges to the cybersecurity world—understanding how distinctively humans think and behave. We know that computers are based on logical instructions and are immune to emotions and other psychological factors. It is a primary differentiation factor and was used in the [13] study that offers psychological techniques and characteristic measures to accurately distinguish. For instance, one of the offered techniques is prompting the user to describe a picture, and, although image recognition robots currently may successfully identify and describe what is viewed on an image, the study offers few cyberpsychology modifications to this methodology. Instead of providing a real image of some entity (e.g., a cat), one can randomly present a hand-drawn silhouette that the bot's pattern recognition service would fail correctly identify the object due to imperfection. Additionally, one may nonordinarily colour a cat with blue fur instead of black or brown. The human mind can comprehend a blue cat whereas bots would not be successful in doing so. As an example, the study used MS Paint to draw blue-coloured Sun and purple clouds in a way that humans could comprehend and loaded the picture into Microsoft's image-recognition CaptionBot artificial intelligence. The bot failed to successfully identify the objects in the picture, and hence, this approach can be successfully utilised in websites.

To sum up, in this section we have listed various techniques of how others differentiate human requests from bots in different scenarios in the world of networking. Some of the presented methodologies are not applicable to our project, but others suggest utilising honeypots as a safe threat actor behaviour monitoring polygon. We adopt the latter implementation following the message exchanges between clients and the original KDC server.

3   Methodology

This section discusses the methodology and design of our software to identify bots and what countermeasures it can be used to take. The authentication process in Kerberos protocol begins with the client sending an authentication request (AS_REQ) to the Authentication Service. If the principal is not found in the KDC database, the Authentication Service returns an error message of type 6, indicating to the client that the principal does not exist. However, with the proxy environment in between the communication, its objective is to notify the client that the principal exists. It accomplishes this by generating a valid reply message (AS_REP) containing the Ticket-Granting Ticket and the session copy encrypted with a password that can be easily decrypted computationally (See Fig. 1). When generating a valid AS_REP to the client, it is important to possess at least three attributes from the initial AS_REQ message. They are the principal name and realm for which the Ticket-Granting Ticket is requested, and the nonce value is an integer randomly generated by the client used to detect the replay attacks. Additionally, the user may request for Ticket-Granting Ticket timing information, e.g. from when it should be valid and for how long, but these attributes are optional and cannot be included in the AS_REQ message. Since all of the aforementioned attributes must match to ones in the AS_REP message, when the AS_REQ is sent, the eBPF program redirects that message to the proxy module that decodes, extracts and temporarily stores those attributes. The original AS_REQ message is sent to the actual KDC from which the reply depends on whether to create a new entry in the proxy's persistent database or free the kernel memory from the temporary data in case of success. If the principal does not exist, the proxy module generates the AS_REP message and sends it to the client. The client could have made a mistake by doing a typo, and thus, if benevolent, it will ignore the password prompt for the proxy-created principal name and proceed to submit a new request for the intended principal name.

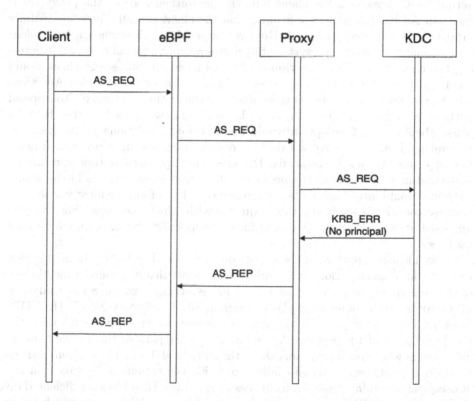

Fig. 1. Case scenario of the client requesting Ticket-Granting Ticket for a non-existing principal name.

In the event that the client submits a valid request to the Ticket-Granting Service, it indicates that a bot has conducted an offline dictionary attack and obtained the password required to access the targeted system. At this point, the subsequent communication with the bot can either be terminated or utilised for monitoring and analysing its behaviour. It is important to consider that the proxy environment lacks awareness of the settings and databases present in the original KDC server. Therefore, it is useful to verify whether pre-authentication is disabled by default in the proxy environment before configuring the module. This precaution is necessary because the threat actor may have conducted prior investigations and acquired knowledge regarding the KDC's utilisation of pre-authentication. In such cases, if the proxy returns an AS_REP message instead of an error message requesting pre-authentication, it raises suspicion whether the threat actor is accessing a different KDC server or suspects the presence of honeypots within the system. Consequently, if the proxy module is aware that the KDC employs pre-authentication, it should respond with the required Kerberos error message instead of returning AS_REP. The situation becomes more complex if the client fails the pre-authentication during communication with the actual KDC. Ideally, if the client fails the pre-authentication, the proxy could issue an AS_REP message confirming that the client actually have successfully inputted the required password. However, a problem arises when a benevolent user attempts to access the system but makes a typographical error while entering their password. This situation could lead to confusion, as the client would receive a Ticket-Granting Ticket despite being aware of the mistake. Additionally, the implementation difficulties come from the Kerberos protocol. To respond with an AS_REP message, we need to know the password used by the client for pre-authentication. One option would be to perform a dictionary attack on the pre-authentication message within the module code, testing a predefined number of commonly used passwords. However, this approach is time-consuming, and creating a principal in the proxy database that already exists in the actual database would introduce further complications. Therefore, the most viable solution we consider is analysing the frequency with which the client fails the pre-authentication method by searching for patterns indicative of online dictionary attacks.

If we identify a pattern of the client constantly sending failing authentication requests in a short period (e.g. falling below statistically defined time threshold), then those we consider as trivial brute-forcing attacks. Such analytical observation can be done using eBPF programs at the eXpress Data Path (XDP) hook at the ingress path (if the network device driver supports it) with the combination of eBPF program loaded at the egress path of the Traffic Control sub-system where both programs share the statistical data on how often authentication requests were sent and failed to decide the actions to be taken on the subsequent incoming requests from a corresponding IP address. Efficient data sharing between eBPF programs can be achieved using eBPF maps, which act as key/value data structures and enable data sharing with user-space applications as well [15]. Various map types are supported, including an efficient longest prefix match trie structure that utilises IP address matching as the key. It is crucial to filter out these packets as early as possible in the Linux kernel, specifically at the eBPF XDP hook in the network device driver code that operates on raw network packets. This approach helps conserve computational resources that would otherwise be consumed by subsequent memory allocations and/or copying, such as for the sk_buff structure which is the primary networking structure representing a packet.

In the case where the principal is present and pre-authentication is turned off, the Authentication Service will respond by sending a message containing two copies of the session key. One copy is encrypted with the Ticket-Granting Service key and placed within the Ticket-Granting Ticket, while the other copy is encrypted with the principal's long-term key.

4 Implementation

We develop a software package consisting of eBPF programs for packet redirection and the kernel module, which mimics the basic functionality of KDC. As per the eBPF part, we employ two programs that are loaded to the Traffic Control ingress and egress hooks redirecting packets to and from the socket in the proxy module. However, the main development focus is on the proxy kernel module that at the moment maintains a database of principals that are not present in the main KDC and for which clients have requested the Ticket-Granting Ticket. It transparently resides between the client and the KDC server observing every incoming authentication request and the corresponding replies. Although we have developed a basic prototype of the proxy module, we have faced sophistication in Kerberos data structure encryption and ASN.1 encoding that is required for generating the reply message to the client.

The encoding of all Kerberos packets adheres to the rules of ASN.1 (Abstract Syntax Notation One) encoding, a standardised set of regulations that define protocol structures in an abstract format. This notation facilitates seamless communication between different systems. Linux incorporates an ASN.1 compiler capable of automatically generating source code and header files for a virtual machine designed to decode a specified ASN.1 notation. Developers can specify to the compiler that functions with specified naming should be called once the virtual machine hits some type at the decoding stage. The encoding functionality has been patched later in Linux only supporting a limited number of ASN.1 identifier types, such as sequences or integers. This restriction exists since the functionality is primarily utilised by certain crypto API algorithms. Consequently, Linux does not provide a dedicated encoding API specifically tailored for Kerberos notations. The lack of functionality necessitates us to script an in-kernel ASN.1 encoder for Kerberos. Additionally, within the AS_REP message, the Ticket-Granting Ticket must be encrypted using one of the encryption types supported by the KDC. In our current basic prototype, we are focused on supporting a single encryption type, namely AES128-CTS-HMAC-SHA1-96, which specifications are outlined in [14]. While Linux offers an in-kernel crypto API for utilising cypher functions, we currently investigate how the API is employed and how to utilise within our ongoing project.

5   Conclusions and Future Work

This work serves as the groundwork for an in-kernel honeypot system that is an intermediary server mimicking the basic functionality of an actual Key Distribution Centre server by maintaining its own database of principals and transparently communicating with the clients. Employing this technology would allow organisations to identify threat actors that are performing reconnaissance attacks on principal databases and redirect their attention to a honeypot database without the attacker's knowledge. In the future, the proxy module can be expanded into a more complex honeypot KDC system enabling the organisations to redirect threat actors towards honeypot services to safely examine their behaviour. Currently, the project have already implemented the capability to transparently communicate with both the clients and the Key Distribution Centre server, but temporarily lacks the functionality of sending valid replies from the replicated Authentication Service. We seek enhancing the project by continuing the development and providing wider range of capabilities.

References

1. Banday, M.T., Qadri, J.A., Shah, N.A.: Study of botnets and their threats to internet security. Sprouts Working Papers Inf. Syst. 9(24), 1–13 (2009). http://sprouts.aisnet.org/9-24
2. Ben-Yair, I., Rogovoy, P., Zaidenberg, N.: AI & eBPF based performance anomaly detection system. In: Proceedings of the 12th ACM International Conference on Systems and Storage, SYSTOR 2019, p. 180. Association for Computing Machinery, New York (2019). https://doi.org/10.1145/3319647.3325842
3. Bonneau, J., Herley, C., Van Oorschot, P.C., Stajano, F.: The quest to replace passwords: a framework for comparative evaluation of web authentication schemes. In: 2012 IEEE Symposium on Security and Privacy, pp. 553–567. IEEE (2012). https://doi.org/10.1109/SP.2012.44
4. Caldarelli, G., De Nicola, R., Del Vigna, F., Petrocchi, M., Saracco, F.: The role of bot squads in the political propaganda on Twitter. Commun. Phys. 3(1), 81 (2020). https://doi.org/10.1038/s42005-020-0340-4
5. Choudhary, A.S., Choudhary, P.P., Salve, S.: A study on various cyber attacks and a proposed intelligent system for monitoring such attacks. In: 2018 3rd International Conference on Inventive Computation Technologies (ICICT), pp. 612–617. IEEE (2018). https://doi.org/10.1109/ICICT43934.2018.9034445
6. Daouadi, K.E., Rebaï, R.Z., Amous, I.: Organization, bot, or human: towards an efficient twitter user classification. Computación y Sistemas 23(2), 273–279 (2019). https://doi.org/10.13053/cys-23-2-3192
7. Demers, D., Lee, H.: Kerberoasting: case studies of an attack on a cryptographic authentication technology. Int. J. Cybersecur. Intell. Cybercrime 5(2), 3 (2022). https://vc.bridgew.edu/ijcic/vol5/iss2/3
8. Gilani, Z., Farahbakhsh, R., Tyson, G., Crowcroft, J.: A large-scale behavioural analysis of bots and humans on Twitter. ACM Trans. Web (TWEB) 13(1), 1–23 (2019). https://doi.org/10.1145/3298789
9. Jenneboer, L., Herrando, C., Constantinides, E.: The impact of chatbots on customer loyalty: a systematic literature review. J. Theor. Appl. Electron. Commer. Res. 17(1), 212–229 (2022). https://doi.org/10.3390/jtaer17010011

10. Kotlaba, L., Buchovecká, S., Lórencz, R.: Active directory kerberoasting attack: monitoring and detection techniques. In: Proceedings of the 6th International Conference on Information Systems Security and Privacy, ICISSP 2020, pp. 432–439 (2020). https://doi.org/10.5220/0008955004320439

11. McCanne, S., Jacobson, V.: The BSD packet filter: a new architecture for user-level packet capture. In: USENIX Winter, vol. 46 (1993)

12. Neuman, C., Yu, T., Hartman, S., Raeburn, K.: The kerberos network authentication service (v5). RFC 4120, RFC Editor, July 2005. https://doi.org/10.17487/RFC4120

13. Priyadarshini, I., Wang, H., Cotton, C.: Some cyberpsychology techniques to distinguish humans and bots for authentication. In: Arai, K., Bhatia, R., Kapoor, S. (eds.) FTC 2019. AISC, vol. 1070, pp. 306–323. Springer, Cham (2020). https://doi.org/10.1007/978-3-030-32523-7_21

14. Raeburn, K.: Advanced Encryption Standard (AES) Encryption for Kerberos 5. RFC 3962, February 2005. https://doi.org/10.17487/RFC3962

15. Rice, L.: Learning EBPF. O'Reilly Media, Inc., March 2023

16. Steiner, J.G., Neuman, B.C., Schiller, J.I.: Kerberos: an authentication service for open network systems. In: Usenix Winter, pp. 191–202 (1988)

17. Stubbs, J.: Automatic distinction between Twitter Bots and Humans. Bachelor of Science thesis, Minnesota State University, Mankato (2020). Cornerstone: A Collection of Scholarly and Creative Works for Minnesota State University, Mankato. https://cornerstone.lib.mnsu.edu/undergrad-theses-capstones-all/1/

Trust and Automation- A Systematic Literature Review

Gemma Rufina Kennedy[⊠] and Vincent G. Duffy

Purdue University, West Lafayette, IN 47906, USA
{kenne221,duffy}@purdue.edu

Abstract. The recent advances in modern technology have paved the way for the automation era- wherein systems are fully automated with minimal/no human intervention. Automation has made arduous human tasks very simple, effective, and economical. Due to these remarkable benefits, the need for automation rose across various domains- aviation, manufacturing, automobile, and IT services to name a few. Although automated technologies amplified profits and productivity by a huge margin, implicit safety blind spots like trust can have detrimental effects on the system. This systematic literature review focuses on examining the relationship between trust and automation and analyzes literature and industry trends on the same. Databases like Scopus, Web of Science, and Google Scholar are used to derive relevant literature and perform trend and emergence analysis for the topic area. Various bibliometric tools like VOS Viewer, CiteSpace, BibExcel, Vicinitas, MAXQDA, and Harzing's Publish or Perish are used to identify common themes across literature and aid in providing a comprehensive understanding of the current state of research in the domain. A systematic review of the prior literature shows the significance of the topic and corresponding growth over the decades.

Keywords: Automation · Trust · Calibration · Bibliometric Analysis · CiteSpace · Harzing · MAXQDA · BibExcel

1 Introduction and Background

1.1 Impact of Trust in Automation

With the advances in Artificial intelligence, the capability of automated systems is increasing to levels that outperform humans. Almost every major industry (healthcare, transportation, military, cybersecurity, and manufacturing to name a few) is seeing an automation overhaul. This means that the reliance on machines to do human tasks is also increasing. While it is established that machines are better than humans at performing repetitive tasks programmed into them, it is crucial that humans interact with automated systems while performing intelligent tasks to achieve optimal performance (Hoff and Bashir, 2014). Implying that humans must operate automated systems with just the right amount of trust (reliance on automation is a measure of trust). Over-trusting automation can lead to complacency and under-trusting automation can lead to disuse. Both scenarios have caused deadly accidents in the recent past such as the 2012 Costa Concordia

© The Author(s), under exclusive license to Springer Nature Switzerland AG 2023
H. Degen et al. (Eds.): HCII 2023, LNCS 14059, pp. 418–434, 2023.
https://doi.org/10.1007/978-3-031-48057-7_26

cruise ship disaster that killed 32 passengers which occurred due to under-trusting of the navigation system, and the 2009 crash of the Turkish Airlines flight which occurred due to over-trusting the altimeter (Hoff and Bashir, 2014). The Tesla fatal crash of 2016 is a clear example of user over-reliance (Dikmen and Burns, 2017). Another tragic accident is the USAir Flight 1016 crash that killed 37 people due to user complacency on the automated system (Kok and Soh, 2020). Such accidents could have been avoided if trust in automation was calibrated prior and a framework was defined. Automation in the healthcare industry is still in its early stages. This is the right time to intervene by designing trustworthy high-risk healthcare systems (such as surgery robots) to minimize adverse events and encourage more physicians to use automated systems. Thus, there is a need to bring about optimal levels of trust in the people who work with automated systems (Chiou and Lee, 2021). These factors along with the increasing use of automation in sensitive tasks are driving the topic of "Trust and Automation" to importance now.

1.2   Trust- A Safety Blind Spot in Automation

Despite these safety concerns, there is no concrete method of measuring trust that exists in human factors engineering literature, a field of Industrial Engineering that deals with the application of psychological constructs (such as trust) to systems and processes. There is a need to come up with novel methods of measuring trust in the real world and (Tenhundfeld et al. 2022) summarizes the characteristics of such novel methods. There is also a need to advance trust theory by focusing research on effective ways to calibrate trust in operators. The three-layered approach to trust conceptualizing (dispositional, situational, and learned trust) proposed by (Marsh and Dibben, 2005) addresses the ways in which trust is influenced by the human operator, the environment where the operator works, and the automated system. All of this is important in designing automated systems with the intention of optimally calibrating trust. New and better models of trust are needed to design automation systems and training modules to meet the safety demands of the ever-changing complexity of automated systems.

1.3   Significance of Trust in Safety Engineering

The advent of automation in industries has enhanced productivity, efficiency, and quality of products/services. However, these automated systems have the potential to cause harm to humans via machine malfunction/failure, user complacency/over-reliance, and cyber-security risks. Thus, ensuring safe human-machine interactions is of utmost importance and this can be achieved by safety engineering professionals. Trust, Over-trust, Mistrust, and under-trust directly affects the automation capabilities and trustworthiness of the system (Lee and See, "Trust in Automation: Designing for Appropriate Reliance.") which in turn could result in safety hazards. By understanding and analyzing how trust affects the adoption of autonomous technologies through a systematic literature review as carried out in (Kanade and Duffy, 2022), safer and more reliable systems can be developed with minimal risks. This review would provide insight into trust-induced automation trends that would aid practitioners to enhance overall user experience, bridging gaps in safety, and developing better decision-making algorithms.

2 Purpose of the Study

The purpose of this paper is to conduct a systematic literature review of the articles that have addressed challenges in trust measurement and conceptualization or any other role of trust in automation. Trust has been a blind spot in human factors research and this paper aims to conduct a meta-analysis of the articles that have attempted to address the issue and highlight the absolute effect that these articles have had in real-world applications. Thereby urging the scientific community to improve upon the less effective areas of research. A systematic review of articles on trust and automation can also help operators stay current with the latest trends, practices, and evidence within their field. Various meta-analysis tools like Scopus, Google Scholar, Web of Science, and Harzing's Publish or Perish were used for the systematic review of the research topics. The meta-data obtained from these platforms were then loaded onto bibliometric tools like VOS Viewer, CiteSpace, BibExcel, MAXQDA, and Vicinitas that helped in visualizing the literature data to meaningful results via graphs/clusters/tables/word cloud.

3 Research Methodology

3.1 Data Collection

The systematic literature review was carried out by extracting metadata from various databases and then analyzing it.

Table 1. Keyword search in various databases and the number of results

Database	Keywords used	Number of Results
Scopus	"Trust" AND "Automation"	3,000
Web of Science	"Trust" AND "Automation"	4,512
Harzing's Publish or Perish (Google Scholar)	"Trust" AND "Automation"	970

Using the research topic of the study as the search terms, literature results from Scopus, Web of Science (WoS), and Harzing's Publish or Perish (Google Scholar) databases were obtained. The WoS database contained the highest number of literature on the topic, "Trust and Automation". Meta-data was exported from these databases in different formats (text,.csv, and WoS). Table 1 shows the keyword search results for each of the databases used in this study.

3.2 Engagement Measure

The data mining tool, Vicinitas, aids in measuring and visualizing engagement levels of a certain topic based on global users' Twitter activity. This tool was useful in gauging the public interest in the topic of "Trust and Automation". A "Hashtag/ Keyword Tweets" search was used to retrieve user information in the topic for the previous 10 days' data.

153	173	212	1.5M
Users	Posts	Engagement	Influence

Fig. 1. Engagement measures of Twitter users for the period 4/24/23 – 05/04/23

The results from Vicinitas show that the research topic is one of very high influence (1.5 million) and interest to the general public on the whole. The holistic user results are observed in Fig. 1.

Fig. 2. Word Cloud from Vicinitas analysis for search terms "trust" and "automation"

The word cloud obtained from the Vicinitas analysis shows the prominent words from the Twitter post database. Besides the most prominent terms- trust and automation, (which were the search words used to run the analysis) some other keywords include- AI (Artificial Intelligence), Data, Security, and IoT (Internet of Things). These keywords are all technologies associated with developing, enhancing and implementing automated systems. These are observed in Fig. 2.

3.3 Trend Analysis

Scopus Database. The search terms- "Trust" & "Automation" were used in the Scopus databases which yielded 3,000 results. These results were analyzed to study the trend in the number of articles published in the domain of interest over the past century. The results are visualized via a line graph in Fig. 3.

The trend analysis shows that automation was not a sought-after topic of research during the early 20th century. However, from the 1980s onwards, there was a gradual growth in the domain. This could be due to IBM personal computers that were introduced during that time, after which there was widespread adoption of computer technology. This enabled companies to focus more on automation and thus a gradually increasing trend can be observed in the graph from the 1990s onwards with a peak in 2022, which was when AI-automated processes and services were very prominent owing to COVID-19 stay-at-home & work-from-home protocols. The growth of literature shows that as the modern world is steering towards a fully automated world, the psychological construct of trust is also being analyzed to design more reliable systems.

Impact in Academia. From the Scopus analysis results, the number of articles over time is observed wherein the drastic increase in research, innovation, and publications in the field of automation and its co-dependence on trust can be identified. Over the last decade, from 2012 to 2022, there has been a percentage increase of 425% in the number of articles that have been published on the topic, which is a direct reflection of the impact the topic has on academia.

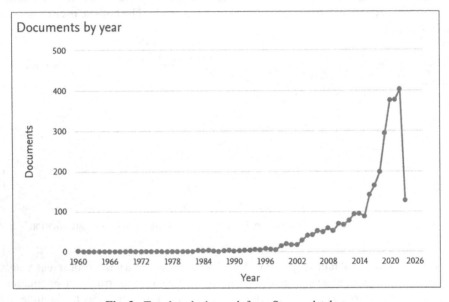

Fig. 3. Trend analysis graph from Scopus database

Google NGram Viewer. Google Ngram Viewer is an online tool that allows users to visualize the frequency of search terms/phrases over a specific period of time. This tool helps identify the trends and popularity of search terms over decades.

In addition to "trust" and "automation", relevant search terms, "safety" and "calibration" are also used in the Ngram visualization tool to analyze the significance of the topic of the study from the period 1950 - 2019. It can be observed that 'safety' and 'trust' follow the same trend. This is due to the topics being interlinked with each other in all systems of life- manufacturing, healthcare, automation, psychology, etc. One cannot have 'safety' without 'trust' and vice versa (Luria, 2010). (Luria, 2010) highlights the importance of the trust and safety climate and how it is quintessential for fostering a safe work environment. A similar trend can be observed with 'automation' and 'calibration' since one cannot exist without the other (Choo and Nam, 2022). The study reveals that users' trust in automation is essential to prevent the misuse, disuse, and abuse of automation technologies. The authors have used neural network technology to develop an algorithm that can calibrate human trust. Thereby indicating the coexisting relationship between the 2 topics.

Figure 4 shows the resulting Ngram graph that used the above-mentioned search words to study their frequencies and influence over the defined period.

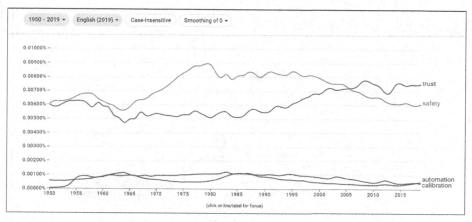

Fig. 4. Trend analysis graph from Google Ngram Viewer

4 Results

4.1 Co-citation Analysis

Co-citation analysis is a bibliometric technique that is used to analyze the relationships between literature, based on the frequency with which they are cited together in other publications. This method aids in identifying articles that have been cited in other literature and further establishes a correlation between the research domain and prominent authors in the domain.

Meta-data from the Web of Science (WoS) database is used as part of the co-citation analysis and is exported as a.csv file onto VOS Viewer. The extracted file contains 4,512 results from the WoS database which includes all the bibliographic information. VOS viewer is a software analysis tool that uses maps/graphs to explore and visualize different literature components within a research domain.

For the co-citation analysis, a map is created on VOS Viewer based on bibliographic data retrieved from the WoS database. The minimum threshold for the number of citations of a cited reference is set to 40. Out of the 13,658 cited references, 23 references met the set threshold.

Figure 5 represents the map resulting from the co-citation analysis. The results of the co-citation analysis show 3 clusters that were collated from the WoS bibliographic database.

4.2 Content Analysis

Content analysis is a research methodology that is utilized to analyze qualitative data to identify themes, patterns, trends, and frequency of occurrence to gain meaningful insight into a research topic.

VOS Viewer- Cluster. The VOS (Visualization of Similarities) Viewer bibliometric analysis tool is used to run the content analysis, which is visualized through a map cluster network.

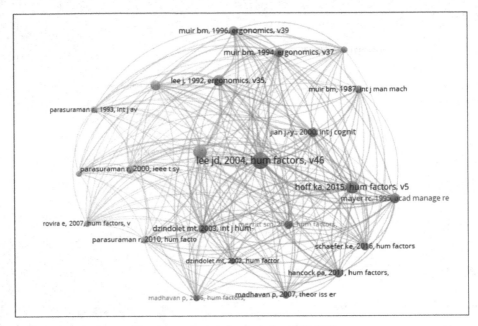

Fig. 5. Co-citation Analysis from VOS Viewer

Meta-data from the Web of Science (WoS) database is used as part of the content analysis and is exported as a.txt file onto VOS Viewer. The extracted file contains 4,512 results from the WoS database which includes all the bibliographic information. The minimum threshold for the number of occurrences of a term is set to 40. Out of the 9,625 items, 60 terms met the set threshold. VOS Viewer calculates the relevance score for each of the 60 terms and forms a cluster network to represent the data. Words that are related to each other and fall under the same topic or sub-topic are grouped into clusters. The content analysis resulted in 3 clusters with the most prominent terms - trust, automation, and driver.

Figure 6 shows the content analysis results from VOS Viewer which is a 3-cluster network, with each color representing a common domain/sub-domain. Figure 7 shows the frequency of the most occurring terms in order of relevance to the research topic. This was used to form the keywords for this research study.

MAXQDA- Word Cloud. MAXQDA is a software tool that aids in the qualitative analysis of unstructured or semi-structured data. Researchers can leverage the data visualization features of MAXQDA like Word Cloud to enhance their study results and insights. A word cloud serves as a visual depiction of the recurring terms/words that appear most frequently in the database used. The word cloud generated using the visualization feature of MAXQDA is used to identify the most prominent and significant terms from the database. 5 articles that were most relevant to the topic of research were

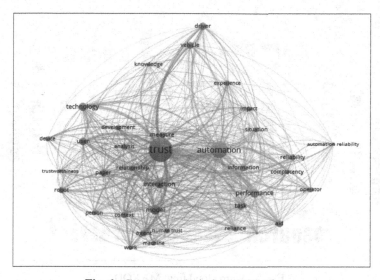

Fig. 6. Content Analysis from VOS Viewer

Selected	Term	Occurrences ✔	Relevance
✔	trust	2030	2.37
✔	automation	1040	0.76
✔	model	303	0.53
✔	performance	292	0.56
✔	interaction	260	0.44
✔	task	245	0.57
✔	technology	233	2.09
✔	driver	196	1.45
✔	user	192	0.66
✔	aid	182	1.28
✔	vehicle	180	1.34
✔	reliability	170	1.29
✔	information	168	0.53
✔	paper	163	0.53
✔	relationship	134	0.78
✔	measure	132	0.73
✔	reliance	127	0.58
✔	robot	123	2.19
✔	context	122	0.42
✔	agent	120	0.60
✔	operator	114	1.29

Create Map — Verify selected terms

Fig. 7. Keywords in order of relevance and occurrence from Content Analysis using VOS Viewer

uploaded onto the MAXQDA tool and the resulting word cloud, as in Fig. 8 is generated. With set limitation parameters as 30 words and minimum frequency as 4, the word cloud is more accurate and omits all the irrelevant words. From the word cloud, it can be observed that the most prominent terms are- trust (1,422 frequency) and automation (648 frequency).

Fig. 8. Word cloud from MAXQDA

4.3 Pivot Table

Harzing's Publish or Perish tool was used with Google Scholar as the search database to obtain meta-data with 970 results. This meta-data was used to generate a pivot table using BibExcel, which is a software tool used for bibliometric analyses of literature. This tool can help analyze and visualize huge data into simple pivot tables. In this study, the "Leading authors" pivot table was generated. This leading table shows the authors that have published the most research in the particular area/field (trust and automation) based on the meta-data exported to the BibExcel software. The leading table generated via this analysis method is shown in Table 2.

4.4 Cluster Analysis

The VOS Viewer analysis tool can be used to visualize meta-data in the form of cluster networks. The networks from co-citation and content analysis are examples of cluster diagrams that can be generated and further analyzed using the VOS Viewer tool. Although VOS Viewer generates cluster diagrams for analyses, it does not have the ability to label the clusters. The VOS Viewer clusters are simply labeled as Cluster-1, Cluster-2 and so on. The CiteSpace software tool is used to overcome this drawback.

CiteSpace is an analysis tool that is used to visualize bibliographic data. Cluster analysis in CiteSpace is used to identify related publications and group them into clusters with appropriate cluster labels. This analysis method was helpful in determining the key topics and research areas obtained from the cluster labels.

The meta-data from the Web of Science database is exported as a plain text file onto the CiteSpace tool. The tool then uses meta-data to form the cluster network with cluster labels extracted based on literature keywords.

Table 2. Leading Authors table using BibExcel

Authors	Number of Results
Lewis M	7
Chien SY	7
Itoh M	7
Winsborough WH	6
Hergeth S	6
Madhavan P	6
Visser EJ De	5
Lee JD	5
Wiegmann DA	5
Pak R	5
Sycara K	5
Parasuraman R	4
Yamani Y	4
Lyons JB	4

Figure 9 shows the labeled cluster diagram obtained as a result of running cluster analysis on the CiteSpace tool using WoS meta-data. The most prominent and relevant clusters identified from the analysis are- "Cluster #3: Trust in Automation", "Cluster #5: Human-machine Interaction", and "Cluster #11: "Trust Calibration".

4.5   Citation Burst

Citation burst analysis is a bibliometric analytic technique that identifies a sudden and significant spike in the number of citations for a specific paper, author, or research domain. Citation burst analysis can reveal the effect and relevance of a certain work or author, as well as develop trends and subjects in a research field.

The citation burst was obtained using the CiteSpace tool. From the WoS meta-data, 25 citation bursts were identified and the top 5 references with the strongest citation bursts are shown in Fig. 10. From the citation burst, it can be observed that the period between 2014 and 2020 was when research in the "Trust and Automation" domain was most significant. Through the citation burst diagram, the relevance of research in a certain domain over different periods can be identified and the overlapping years from the top references can serve as a guide for the research need of the hour.

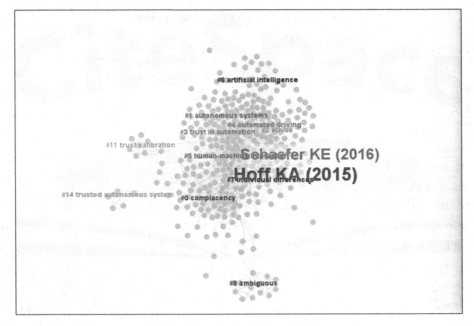

Fig. 9. Cluster Analysis from CiteSpace

Top 5 References with the Strongest Citation Bursts

References	Year	Strength	Begin	End	2013 - 2023
Hancock PA, 2011, HUM FACTORS, V53, P517, DOI 10.1177/0018720811417254, DOI	2011	6.34	2013	2016	
Merritt SM, 2013, HUM FACTORS, V55, P520, DOI 10.1177/0018720812465081, DOI	2013	6.51	2015	2017	
Manzey D, 2012, J COGN ENG DECIS MAK, V6, P57, DOI 10.1177/1555343411433844, DOI	2012	5.1	2015	2017	
Hoff KA, 2015, HUM FACTORS, V57, P407, DOI 10.1177/0018720814547570, DOI	2015	13.38	2017	2020	
Schaefer KE, 2016, HUM FACTORS, V58, P377, DOI 10.1177/0018720816634228, DOI	2016	5.72	2020	2021	

Fig. 10. Citation Burst from CiteSpace

5   Discussions

The analyses and results obtained from this systematic literature review clearly illustrate that the most impactful and significant terms in the study are Trust, Automation, and Trust Calibration. These terms can be defined from the literature as:

- *Automation-* "Automation, in general, implies operating or acting, or self-regulating, independently, without human intervention." (Nof, 2009)
- *Trust-* "However, it is generally agreed that trust is best conceptualized as a multidimensional psychological attitude involving beliefs and expectations about the trustee's trustworthiness derived from experience and interactions with the trustee in situations involving uncertainty and risk." (Kok and Soh, 2020)

- *Trust Calibration-* "Successful collaborations between users and agents would require the users to appropriately adjust their level of trust with the actual reliability of the agents. This process is called trust calibration." (Okamura and Yamada, 2020)

Some of the most noteworthy and relevant literature derived from the research methodologies and analyses applied are reviewed below. These studies show the current processes/systems that are prevalent in the research domain. The authors have also worked to develop trust-calibrated models that will enable the development of more reliable automated systems.

This research study which was ranked #1 on Harzing's Publish or Perish platform is analyzed which explores the relationship between an individual's tendency to trust in automation and their actual trust-related behaviors towards it (Jessup et al. 2019). The authors have hypothesized that situation-specific or task-specific measures of trust are more reliable. The study was the first to use a modified version of the Propensity to Trust Technology (PTT) scale. By decreasing ambiguity in the measuring method, trust can be measured more reliably and thus leads to better trust calibration.

When using automated systems, the level of trust does not necessarily determine the outcome of the situation/event. The study (Lee and See, 2004) emphasizes the need for automation to focus on positively influencing reliance/trust on the system when such complex situations arise.

Identifying and analyzing the factors that influence trust is clearly important in trust calibration. Authors (Schaefer et al. 2016) have updated the three-layered model of trust which is comprised of disposition, environment, and system. This was done by using additional human, environmental, and system-related factors to quantify trust and further improve the design of automated systems. Authors (Merritt et al. 2012) are the first to consider the influence of implicit attitudes toward automation on the actual trust levels of the individual. The authors established that actual trust can be determined by the sum of the implicit attitude and explicit disposition to trust. The role of implicit attitudes needs to be investigated further to design interventions that influence implicit attitudes so that they accurately calibrate trust in automation.

Automated systems are prone to false alarms and misses. Designing these systems with the understanding that false alarms and misses influence trust differently is essential in calibrating trust as demonstrated by (Chancey et al., 2016). The 88-participant study aimed to establish a link between trust and the compliance-reliance paradigm. Compliance is defined as the operator's responsiveness when a signal is issued by a system. Reliance is defined as the operator refraining from a response when the system is operating as usual. Together, they are known as dependence (Meyer, 2004). The study found that the False alarm rate affected compliance but not reliance. The converse was true for the miss rate. An example of how system design can incorporate results from this paper is by adjusting sensor thresholds to reduce false alarm rates since it has a greater impact on trust than miss rates.

The growth of automation technologies has been significant in recent years, with very high profitability for the industries that are steering towards these productive & efficient methods of doing work. Research ("Automation Could Double Operating Margins and Equity Markets By 2025.") states that automation will continue to benefit the modern industry by boosting productivity, profit margins, and sales. The benefits of automation include environmental benefits, long-term cost benefits, convenience, efficiency & safety. However, for all these advantages to be effectively realized, trust should be established in every stage of the automation design and process. Thus, analyzing the trends in the "trust and automation" domain will facilitate a better understanding of the domain, limitations & challenges associated and provide a hypothesis for developing/implementing trust-based frameworks in automation.

Trust, Over-trust, Mistrust, and under-trust directly affects the automation capabilities and trustworthiness of the system (Lee and See, "Trust in Automation: Designing for Appropriate Reliance.") which in turn could result in safety hazards. Trust is a top 'Risk perception factor' and can lead to fatal accidents if not properly defined and outlined (Brauer, 2016). Applying the Sociotechnical system theory (Geotsch, 2015) to tackle issues with trust will facilitate the minimization of safety hazards in automated environments. This theory defines a framework for the harmonious functioning of human and technological systems. (Noy et al., 2018) also highlights the need to shift to STS theory in automation so as to ensure more reliable and safer human-machine interactions.

6 Conclusion

A systematic review of the literature on trust and automation is critical for the ultimate goal of making automation ubiquitous with improved safety outcomes. The study has highlighted the importance of trust in the acceptance and use of automated systems and has identified a range of factors that influence the development and maintenance of trust in automation. Understanding the gaps in automation safety is a cardinal factor in the continual upgrade and development of automation, particularly in real-world contexts. The study also highlights the need for further research to address these gaps.

It is difficult to change a person's attitude and predispositions, especially when it comes to trusting what essentially is a black box i.e., automated systems. Implicit attitudes and preconceived notions about automation can be improved by designing more reliable and efficient trust-calibrated models to ensure safe & trustworthy automated systems.

The objective of this paper was to review the findings from recent research on human–automation, trust, and reliance through a systematic review process of academic literature from 1960 to 2022. A total of over 8000 articles were analyzed via their corresponding meta-data using co-citation, content, pivot tables, citation burst analyses methods. The absolute effects in this relatively untrodden (but important) area of human factors research are discussed which pave the way to facilitate new ideas for future research and bring awareness to the issue of trust discrepancy in automation.

In conclusion, to promote the proper use of automation and minimize the frequency of related accidents, trust formation should be viewed as a dynamic process guided by a complex interaction of factors stemming from three interdependent layers of variability: dispositional trust, situational trust, and learned trust.

7 Future Work

7.1 Relevant Awards in "Trust and Automation"

The National Science Foundation's website displayed a list of several ongoing approved projects when the keywords "trust" and "automation" were entered. The first on the list (Fig. 11) is a project that aims to overcome the shortcomings of current trust measures, analyze trust and driver behavior, and investigate the impact of incorporating trust calibration models in autonomous vehicles on dynamic trust and driving behavior. The project will have three phases. The first phase aims to create a new way to measure trust that uses real-time neural activation data during automated vehicle interactions. In the second phase, researchers will model how drivers interact with automated vehicles across a range of trust levels. The third phase will involve validating the trust measure and driver behavior model by conducting a driving simulation experiment with a trust calibration intervention.

Another project (Fig. 12) also in the realm of autonomous vehicles, has the following three objectives. Firstly, it will build real-time trust prediction models using psychophysiological measures, which can better capture the dynamic nature of trust in automation. Secondly, it will investigate the relationships between affect and trust in automated vehicles, by examining the latent structure of affective responses related to trust in automated driving and how they are related to different aspects of trust. Thirdly, the project will examine the role of effect by making use of affect heuristics in automated driving measured by both self-reported and psychophysiological data.

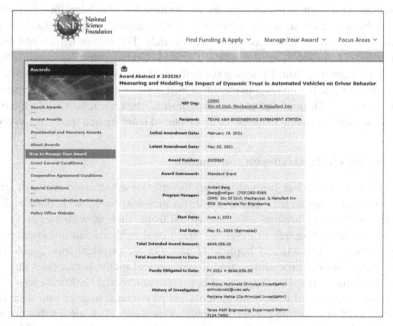

Fig. 11. Screenshot of the approved NSF grant for "Measuring and modeling dynamic trust in automated vehicles."

Fig. 12. Screenshot of the approved NSF grant for investigating the role of affect in fostering trust in autonomous vehicles

In addition to the autonomous domain, automation has also been increasingly integrated into the education sector to enhance learning/teaching processes. One insightful award that I identified, titled, "Collaborative research: The role of trust when learning from robots" (NSF Award Search: Award # 1955653 -Collaborative Research: The Role of Trust When Learning from Robots, n.d.) will aim at analyzing the human-automation robot systems at a classroom level to establish trust in robot systems as a prerequisite for successful learning. Through interactive experiments, the researchers study the trust in robots and establish the same in users for an enhanced learning and teaching experience.

7.2 Upcoming Fields Relying on Automation

The healthcare industry has been slower to incorporate automation and still tends to rely on traditional approaches. There are difficulties associated with both traditional and modern technology methods. On the virtual front, such as with electronic health records and the latest research in medicine, traditional methods can involve significant delays in gathering relevant and applicable data. On the physical front, such as with tasks involving surgical procedures, traditional surgical methods can (and quite often do) result in human error. The future goal is to build automated healthcare systems that garner the right amount of trust from patients and physicians. Inquiry into what factors prevent patients from trusting robots and whether they accept surgical robot errors in a way that is analogous to human error can help build a better model of trust (Marinaccio et al. 2015). As seen in some of the literature reviewed earlier on adaptive trust models

(Jessup et al., 2019), a robust model of trust that factors in the sensitive and high-risk nature of a healthcare environment are required to calibrate trust effectively.

References

BibExcel (n.d.) https://homepage.univie.ac.at/juan.gorraiz/bibexcel/

Harzing Publish or Perish (n.d.) https://harzing.com/resources/publish-or-perish/windows

MAXQDA (n.d.) https://www.maxqda.com/

Scopus (n.d.) https://www.scopus.com/search/form.uri?display=basic#basic

Vicinitas. https://www.vicinitas.io/

VOSviewer (n.d.) https://www.vosviewer.com/

Brauer, R.L.: Safety and Health for Engineers. 3rd ed. Wiley. Chapter-34: Risk, Risk Assessment and Risk Management, "Risk Perception" (2016)

Chancey, E.T., Bliss, J.P., Yamani, Y., Handley, H.A.H.: Trust and the compliance–reliance paradigm: the effects of risk, error bias, and reliability on trust and dependence. Human Factors: The Journal of the Human Factors and Ergonomics Society 59(3), 333–45 (2016). https://doi.org/10.1177/0018720816682648

Chiou, E.K., Lee, J.D.: Trusting automation: designing for responsivity and resilience. Human Factors: The Journal of the Human Factors and Ergonomics Society 65(1), 137–65 (2021). https://doi.org/10.1177/00187208211009995

Choo, S., Nam, C.: Detecting human trust calibration in automation: a convolutional neural network approach. IEEE Transactions on Human-Machine Systems 52(4), 774–783 (2022). https://doi.org/10.1109/thms.2021.3137015

CiteSpace. (n.d.) http://cluster.cis.drexel.edu/~cchen/citespace/

Dikmen, M., Catherine, B.: Trust in autonomous vehicles: the case of tesla autopilot and summon. In: 2017 IEEE International Conference on Systems, Man, and Cybernetics (SMC) (2017). https://doi.org/10.1109/smc.2017.8122757

Goetsch, D.L.: Occupational safety and health for technologists, engineers, and managers. 8th ed. Pearson. Chapter-23: Computers, Robots & Automation, "Minimizing the problems of automation" (2015)

Hancock, P.A., Billings, D.R., Schaefer, K.E., Chen, J.Y.C., de Visser, E.J., Parasuraman, R.: A meta-analysis of factors affecting trust in human-robot interaction. Human Factors: The Journal of the Human Factors and Ergonomics Society 53(5), 517–27 (2011). https://doi.org/10.1177/0018720811417254

Hoff, K.A., Masooda, B.: Trust in automation. Human Factors: The Journal of the Human Factors and Ergonomics Society 57(3), 407–34 (2014). https://doi.org/10.1177/0018720814547570

Jessup, S.A., Schneider, T.R., Alarcon, G.M., Ryan, T.J., August, C.: The measurement of the propensity to trust automation. Virtual, Augmented, and Mixed Reality. Applications and Case Studies, pp. 476–89 (2019). https://doi.org/10.1007/978-3-030-21565-1_32

Kanade, S.G., Duffy, V.G.: Use of virtual reality for safety training: a systematic review. In: Duffy, V.G. (eds) Digital Human Modeling and Applications in Health, Safety, Ergonomics, and Risk Management. Health, Operations Management, and Design. HCII 2022. Lecture Notes in Computer Science, vol 13320. Springer, Cham (2022). https://doi-org.ezproxy.lib.purdue.edu/ https://doi.org/10.1007/978-3-031-06018-2_25

Kok, B.C., Harold, S.: Trust in robots: challenges and opportunities. Current Robotics Reports 1(4), 297–309 (2020). https://doi.org/10.1007/s43154-020-00029-y

Lee, J.D., See, K.A.: Trust in automation: designing for appropriate reliance. Human Factors: The Journal of the Human Factors and Ergonomics Society 46(1), 50–80 (2004). https://doi.org/10.1518/hfes.46.1.50_30392

Luria, G.: The social aspects of safety management: trust and safety climate. Accid. Anal. Prev. **42**(4), 1288–1295 (2010). https://doi.org/10.1016/j.aap.2010.02.006

Marinaccio, K., Kohn, S., Parasuraman, R., De Visser, E.J.: A framework for rebuilding trust in social automation across health-care domains. Proceedings of the International Symposium on Human Factors and Ergonomics in Health Care **4**(1), 201–5 (2015). https://doi.org/10.1177/2327857915041036

Marsh, S., Dibben, M.R.: The role of trust in information science and technology. Annual Review of Information Science and Technology **37**(1), 465–98 (2005). https://doi.org/10.1002/aris.1440370111

Merritt, S.M., Heather, H., Jennifer, L., Deborah, L.: I Trust it, but i don't know why. Human Factors: The Journal of the Human Factors and Ergonomics Society **55**(3), 520–34 (2012). https://doi.org/10.1177/0018720812465081

Meyer, J.: Conceptual issues in the study of dynamic hazard warnings. Human Factors: The Journal of the Human Factors and Ergonomics Society **46**(2), 196–204 (2004). https://doi.org/10.1518/hfes.46.2.196.37335

Nof, S.Y.: Automation: what it means to us around the world. In: Nof, S. (eds) Springer Handbook of Automation. Springer Handbooks. Springer, Berlin, Heidelberg (2009). https://doi-org.ezproxy.lib.purdue.edu/https://doi.org/10.1007/978-3-540-78831-7_3

NSF Award Search: Award # 2035367 - Measuring and Modeling the Impact of Dynamic Trust in Automated Vehicles on Driver Behavior Robots

NSF Award Search: Award # 2138274 - ERI: Investigate the Role of effect in Fostering Trust in Automated Driving

Okamura, K., Seiji, Y.: Adaptive Trust calibration for human-ai collaboration. Edited by Chen Lv. PLOS ONE **15**(2), e0229132 (2020). https://doi.org/10.1371/journal.pone.0229132

Schaefer, K.E., Jessie, Y.C. Chen, J.L.S., Hancock, P.A.: A meta-analysis of factors influencing the development of trust in automation. Human Factors: The Journal of the Human Factors and Ergonomics Society **58**(3), 377–400 (2016). https://doi.org/10.1177/0018720816634228

Tenhundfeld, N., Demir, M., de Visser, E.: Assessment of trust in automation in the 'real world': requirements for new trust in automation measurement techniques for use by practitioners. Journal of Cognitive Engineering and Decision Making **16**(2), 101–18 (2022). https://doi.org/10.1177/15553434221096261

Assessing the Vulnerability of Military Personnel Through Open Source Intelligence: A Case Study of Lithuanian Armed Forces

Paulius Malakauskis and Aušrius Juozapavičius(✉)(iD)

General Jonas Žemaitis Military Academy of Lithuania, Šilo Str. 5A, 10322 Vilnius, LT, Lithuania
`paulius.malakauskis@edu.lka.lt`, `ausrius.juozapavicius@lka.lt`

Abstract. This study explores the vulnerability of Lithuanian Armed Forces soldiers to hostile intelligence, using Open Source Intelligence (OSINT) to identify the extent of personally identifiable information (PII) disclosure. The research found that soldiers' social media and sports applications revealed a significant amount of sensitive data, exposing approximately 71% ± 23% of personnel as highly vulnerable to threats such as physical attacks, blackmail, and phishing. Certain privacy measures made data collection more challenging, indicating that clear media usage guidelines could improve security while maintaining soldiers' social lives. Notably, a substantial amount of information was obtained from individuals connected to, but not in the military, emphasizing the importance of broader social network considerations in security assessments. The study was conducted manually within specific time and network limits, suggesting automation could enhance investigative scope and reduce error margins. The findings highlight the need for military procedures that account for the heightened vulnerability of soldiers and their families and the implementation of measures to mitigate these risks.

Keywords: Open source intelligence · Armed forces · Personally identifiable information

1 Introduction

Due to the widespread use of social media and the easy availability of detailed personal information, open source intelligence (OSINT) has emerged as a versatile tool [5] that can be utilized in both cyber defense and attack cycles. According to market data provider Statista [6], the number of social media users has nearly doubled in the past five years and is projected to reach 5 billion in 2023. From a positive perspective, social media serves as a valuable resource for law enforcement agencies in ensuring national security. Akhgar [3] asserts that continuous monitoring and visualization of open source data are

© The Author(s), under exclusive license to Springer Nature Switzerland AG 2023
H. Degen et al. (Eds.): HCII 2023, LNCS 14059, pp. 435–444, 2023.
https://doi.org/10.1007/978-3-031-48057-7_27

essential components of a national security strategy for effectively combating crime. Similarly, OSINT can be employed as an investigative tool in cybercrime cases [16], enabling proactive measures such as emulating the reconnaissance phase conducted by attackers to identify and address vulnerabilities [9], or generating alerts to cybersecurity specialists based on social media news to promptly respond to emerging threats [15].

Military-related OSINT has also experienced significant growth over the last decade, with numerous methods being made public by Bellingcat investigators. These methods have uncovered various pieces of information, including the location of ISIS training camps, Chinese government operations on Facebook, and the complete command structure of Russian missile operators [4,11]. The rapid development of data extraction tools, along with the advancement of large language transformative models and other machine learning data analysis methods, has opened up new possibilities for OSINT in both offensive and defensive applications, which require thorough research [17].

Clearly, OSINT serves as a double-edged sword, being accessible to both domestic and foreign security agencies. The examination of data shared by military users on social media has uncovered notable implications for both personal and operational security [7]. According to research, soldiers often bring unsafe habits of social media usage into their workplaces, intertwining their personal life details with service-related data [13]. Furthermore, troop movements can be tracked through flight and shipping applications such as Flightradar24 and MarineTraffic. While these apps are subject to strict rules and have limitations in tracking planes or ships carrying troops or military equipment, Flightradar24 was able to track the deployment of Russian troops in Kazakhstan in February 2022.

There are numerous alternative methods for detecting troop movements without relying on satellite tracking. For instance, an upsurge in the number of profiles belonging to Belarusian individuals, featuring photos of themselves associated with the military on dating apps, indicated an augmented presence of the Belarusian armed forces near the Polish border in 2021 [12]. Furthermore, Pellet et al. [14] developed a toolkit that demonstrates the possibility of tracking the physical location of any user based on their public social media profile. This toolkit scrapes data from Twitter, Facebook, and Instagram, extracting GPS geo-tags from users' photos, collecting place mentions from their posts, and utilizing machine learning algorithms to analyze natural language and determine their location. A significant portion of the data is gathered from the profiles of the user's friends who mention or include a "was with" tag in their posts or photos. The authors claim to have achieved an accuracy rate above 77%, and their method can track users in near-real time as long as they have profiles on the three mentioned social media platforms. Additionally, Kozera [10] presented real-life examples demonstrating how the fitness application Suunto can be used to track military personnel in secretive areas.

Eventually, numerous countries have implemented regulations regarding the behavior of their armed forces personnel on social media platforms. Some countries prioritize operational security and either prohibit or discourage the use of social media [8], while others view it as a tool for promoting their armed forces [1, 2]. The corresponding social media guidelines primarily focus on upholding the organization's reputation. In terms of operational security, they typically address issues related to geo-tagged photos, disclosure of capabilities, and expressing opinions about various shortcomings. However, merely sharing a photo of a soldier in uniform or any other association with the military is not considered an operational security concern. Unfortunately, such photos can make it easy to identify espionage targets, leading to tracking or phishing attacks. Dressler et al. [7] employed an automated approach to identify more than 1000 potential intelligence targets within the US military simply by searching for social media users who disclosed their employer as "US Army". In such cases, a straightforward recommendation to soldiers would be to refrain from disclosing their employer. This raises the question of whether it would be considerably more challenging to locate the profiles if that information was not disclosed. Consequently, we opted to commence our investigation with no prior knowledge of the Lithuanian military forces structure, utilizing OSINT and the scoring scale developed by Dressler to assess their level of vulnerability via social media.

2   Methods

The methodology employed to identify the soldiers and gather their personally identifiable information is depicted in the Fig. 1. We initiated our investigation by searching the internet for the official websites of the Lithuanian armed forces and the Ministry of Defense. These sources provided a list of units along with their contact information and street addresses. With the addresses in hand, we utilized the Google Maps application to identify nearby military territories and the sports stadiums located within them. Subsequently, we employed a fitness application called Strava to identify publicly available running routes within those stadiums. Many of these tracks were shared by users who disclosed their full names and surnames. To conduct a more thorough examination, we randomly selected one land forces unit (a battalion) and then randomly chose seven out of the 52 users who shared their running routes within the corresponding stadium. We proceeded to investigate the public profiles of Facebook and Instagram users who had the same names as the chosen seven individuals.

While there were several social media profiles with identical names, it was relatively easy to identify the seven soldiers through their profile pictures or other self-disclosed information. By examining their friend lists, we discovered additional members of their unit. The presence of group photos of soldiers and posts expressing gratitude towards multiple colleagues enabled us to identify profiles of soldiers serving in the same battalion under investigation. Figure 2 presents a network diagram illustrating the connections among the first 24 unit members we found. One of the initial seven seed profiles did not reveal any other relevant connections, but the remaining six were linked either directly (group 4, 5, 6) or through the subsequent circle of friends (5 → 8 → 7, or 5 → 15 → 1 →

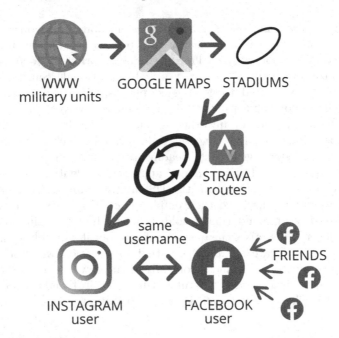

Fig. 1. OSINT methodology used to find soldiers and their personal data.

$2 \rightarrow 7$). Thus, each of the six profiles would have led to the same network. The black lines with arrows, along with the accompanying numbers, indicate the order in which the profiles were uncovered. Although the network could have been further expanded to include at least 85 additional members of the same unit (as indicated by the red dangling lines), we deliberately halted our progress at this stage. We allocated one hour per discovered profile to conduct an in-depth investigation of the 17 soldiers represented by the blue-colored boxes, starting with number 8 in Fig. 2.

We utilized the vulnerability scoring system developed by Dressler et al. [7] to assess the risks associated with the exposure of personally identifiable information. Each piece of information pertaining to an individual is assigned a score ranging from 1 to 5, with higher values indicating more critical information. According to Dressler, a home address or a collection of geo-tagged photos would receive the highest vulnerability score, as they could potentially provide direct physical contact with the individual. The name of a spouse (and possibly the names of close relatives) could present additional opportunities for foreign intelligence services and is assigned 3–5 points based on the number of persons identified (3 points for one person, 4 points for two persons, and 5 points for three or more persons). A personal photo can be valuable for espionage purposes, while a phone number can be exploited in social engineering attacks, both receiving 3 points. Professional skills indicating access to specific data or technologies also receive 3 points. Other information, such as hobbies, attended schools, or

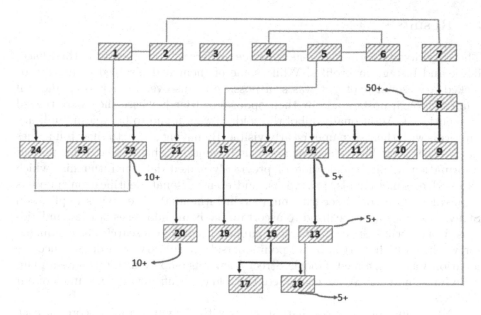

Fig. 2. Connections between the investigated soldiers.

email addresses, can be utilized in phishing schemes and is assigned 2 points. Easily obtainable information like first names or gender is scored as 1 point. In our case, we made slight modifications to the scoring system: we excluded the categories of spouse name and marital status, considering them as part of the relatives/family category. We replaced the categories of public timeline and viewable network in social media platforms with the friends' network. A combination of different pieces of information can be highly effective in targeting an individual, and thus the total vulnerability score is obtained by summing up the values of each element. Individuals who score above 25 and disclose at least 5 different pieces of information are considered highly vulnerable. Those with scores ranging from 15 to 24 and at least 5 different pieces of information are classified as vulnerable. The remaining individuals are categorized as least vulnerable. Compared to Dressler's original scheme, the modifications we made to the critical information categories slightly decrease the vulnerability score of the analyzed soldiers.

To ensure the protection of data, the gathered information was stored in an encrypted zip file secured with a complex password when it was not being actively used. Following the completion of the study, all relevant individuals were duly notified about the information that had been collected regarding them. Furthermore, they were provided with suggestions and recommendations on how to enhance their privacy protection measures.

3   Results

The majority of information regarding the soldiers was obtained from their Facebook and Instagram profiles. While some of them had disabled comments or lacked a personal photo, it was still possible to discover their photos and full names through posts made by their spouses or friends where they were tagged or mentioned. Additionally, all of the soldiers were found to be wearing military uniforms with their surnames clearly visible. By having access to their full names (and either their birth dates or ages), it became possible to search for further information within a collection of previously leaked data in Lithuania, which exposed personal emails, passwords, and even personal identification numbers (equivalent to a social security number in Lithuania). The sports application Strava was once again utilized to ascertain the home addresses of these individuals. If a subject's Strava profile was publicly accessible, a search was conducted for workouts with start and end points outside of military territories. Once the location was determined, Google Street View was employed to estimate a plausible house number. When contacted, the soldiers confirmed the accuracy of our findings.

The findings of our investigation, along with the vulnerability score for each soldier examined, are outlined in Table 1. As previously mentioned, all of the soldiers had disclosed their full names and self photos either directly or through their contacts. However, we were unable to locate a single phone number, and only one personal email address was conclusively identified. It is worth noting that their military emails (service emails) can be easily deduced as they are derived from their full names.

Table 1. Vulnerability score for the investigated soldiers

Critical information	Vuln. score	8	9	10	11	12	13	14	15	16	17	18	19	20	21	22	23	24
Name, family name	1–2	2	2	2	2	2	2	2	2	2	2	2	2	2	2	2	2	2
Self photo	3	3	3	3	3	3	3	3	3	3	3	3	3	3	3	3	3	3
Age/DOB	3	3	3	3	3	3	3	3		3			3	3	3	3	3	3
Professional skills	3		3	3	3	3	3	3	3	3	3	3	3	3			3	3
Hometown	2	2	2	2	2	2	2	2	2	2			2	2	2	2	2	2
Home address	5	5				5	5		5							5		
Geo-tagged photos	3–5	5	5	5	4	4	4	5	5	5	5	5	5	5	4	5	5	5
Phone number	3																	
E-mail	2					2												
Interests	2	2				2	2		2	2			2		2	2		2
Friends' network	3–4	4	3	4	3	4	3	4	4	4	3	4	4	4	4	4	4	4
Position, rank	3		3	3		3		3	3	3	3	3		3		3	3	3
Relatives/family	3–5						3	5	5	5			5	3			4	5
Total		26	24	25	20	33	30	30	34	32	19	20	29	28	20	29	29	32

The findings are summarized in Fig. 3, which illustrates the number of available information pieces plotted against the total vulnerability score for each soldier investigated. Applying the criteria established by Dressler et al., we deduce that 12 out of the 17 soldiers analyzed are highly vulnerable. Typically, a battalion consists of approximately 400 members. Considering our sample size of 17 and a 95% confidence interval, our estimates carry a margin of error of 23%. While our investigation focused on a single battalion, there is no evidence to suggest that the results would differ in other battalions. In fact, some of the connections we discovered extended to other military units; however, we chose to disregard them for this analysis. In other words, it is reasonable to assume that approximately 71% ± 23% of Lithuanian soldiers are highly vulnerable through social media channels.

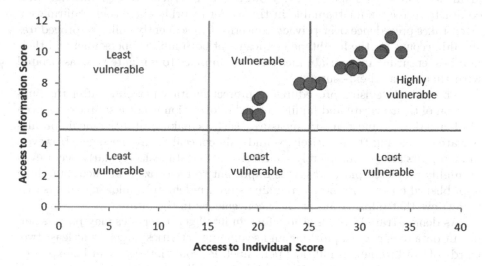

Fig. 3. Vulnerability of investigated soldiers.

4 Discussion

The study's results highlight the vulnerability of many military personnel to potential targeting by hostile intelligence agencies, stemming from their excessive disclosure of personal information on publicly accessible platforms. Our investigation was constrained to only one hour per individual, yet this limited time frame was sufficient to uncover over 8 sensitive pieces of information about more than two-thirds of the subjects. Notably, the research revealed a highly interconnected nature within military units, implying that exploiting a few weak points or initial access points can potentially unravel the entire structure. While our investigation utilized a sports application as the starting point, it is crucial to recognize that a sophisticated attacker could initiate their efforts from various sources, such as a random photo in a newspaper or any publicly available post, as long as it leads to a soldier's profile on a platform where their connections are listed, such as Facebook, LinkedIn, Instagram, or others. Furthermore, even if the individuals in question restrict their own exposure, others within their contact list may still inadvertently disclose a significant portion of sensitive information.

The observed deficiencies in operational security among soldiers can likely be attributed to several factors, such as a lack of knowledge regarding the management of personal accounts on social networks, failure to inform families and friends about emerging threats, and a lack of guidance and proactive measures from military leadership to protect their personnel. Implementing stricter guidelines and regulations, along with providing comprehensive training and monitoring of soldiers' social media habits, would enhance the operational safety of armed forces to some extent. However, it is crucial to acknowledge that complete secrecy is unattainable in the modern world, where social affirmation often takes precedence over privacy concerns. Consequently, military procedures should account for the heightened exposure of both military personnel and their families, ensuring appropriate measures are in place to mitigate risks associated with this increased exposure.

The task of devising procedures to protect military personnel after the publication of their private and family-related information is not a simple one. Even implementing the most drastic measures, such as making all social media profiles private or deleting them entirely, would only conceal future messages. However, hidden posts are not completely secure either, as data leaks regularly occur even on highly protected platforms. It is important to recognize that once something is published on the internet, it remains stored indefinitely, allowing adversaries to retrieve that information at their convenience in the future.

As demonstrated by this study, foreign intelligence services may possess sufficient data to engage in phishing and scamming activities targeting at least two-thirds of the Lithuanian military personnel. Personal interests can be exploited to establish connections with individuals for intelligence gathering purposes. Of particular concern is information pertaining to the soldiers' physical locations and family-related details, as this data can be used to blackmail them by threatening the safety of their family members.

Therefore, during security clearance procedures, the exposure of personal information through OSINT should be taken into account. Furthermore, it is crucial to encourage soldiers to remain vigilant and promptly report any potential attempts to exploit their personal information to their security officers. Lastly, it is essential to provide training to soldiers' families on how to act during a military conflict, as they may be vulnerable to abuse by adversarial forces or their collaborators who may target them as proxies to gain leverage over their military-serving relatives.

5   Conclusions

The study was conducted with no prior knowledge of the Lithuanian armed forces, utilizing web searches, sports and social networking applications to manually investigate the extent of sensitive information disclosed by soldiers in a randomly selected battalion. The findings of the study revealed that approximately

71% ± 23% of those serving in Lithuania are highly vulnerable and could potentially become targets of hostile intelligence. The disclosed information poses risks for physical attacks, blackmail, phishing, and other social engineering tactics. Given the high number of vulnerable individuals, it is imperative to establish stricter guidelines regarding media usage within the military to mitigate these risks effectively.

The collection of sensitive information encountered challenges when targeted individuals had common names, shared names with famous individuals, concealed their friends list, locked their profile pictures, disabled comments on photos, or had no photos at all. Based on these observations, straightforward media usage guidelines could be implemented without significantly impacting the social lives of military personnel. However, it should be noted that a considerable amount of information was obtained from non-military individuals connected to the soldiers, who may be unwilling to adhere to the guidelines. As a result, it can be assumed that critical information about the majority of military personnel can be gathered through open-source intelligence.

Throughout the investigation, a deliberate time limit of one hour per discovered profile and exploration limited to the first two circles within the social networks of the seven seed profiles from the Strava application were imposed. By automating the process, it would be feasible to expand the investigation and reduce the margin of error in the results. Furthermore, it is plausible that a resourceful adversary may already possess tools capable of extracting most of the information obtained manually in this study. Hence, military procedures should acknowledge the heightened vulnerability of military personnel and their families, taking appropriate measures to address these concerns.

References

1. Army social media guide. U.S. Army, 13 February 2023. https://www.army.mil/SOCIALMEDIA/
2. Using social media - a guide for military personnel. Ministry of Defence, U.K., 13 February 2023. https://www.gov.uk/government/publications/using-social-media-a-guide-for-military-personnel
3. Akhgar, B.: OSINT as an integral part of the national security apparatus. Open Source Intelligence Investigation: From Strategy to Implementation, pp. 3–9 (2016)
4. Bär, D., Calderon, F., Lawlor, M., Licklederer, S., Totzauer, M., Feuerriegel, S.: Analyzing social media activities at Bellingcat (2022). arXiv preprint arXiv:2209.10271
5. Böhm, I., Lolagar, S.: Open source intelligence: introduction, legal, and ethical considerations. Int. Cybersecur. Law Rev. **2**, 317–337 (2021). https://doi.org/10.1365/s43439-021-00042-7
6. Dixon, S.: Number of global social network users 2017–2027. Statista, 13 February 2023. https://www.statista.com/markets/424/topic/540/social-media-user-generated-content
7. Dressler, J.C., Bronk, C., Wallach, D.S.: Exploiting military OpSec through open-source vulnerabilities. In: 2015 IEEE Military Communications Conference. MILCOM 2015, pp. 450–458. IEEE (2015). https://doi.org/10.1109/MILCOM.2015.7357484

8. Emonet, F.: To post or not to post. NCO J. (2020). https://www.armyupress.army. mil/Portals/7/nco-journal/images/2020/June/Social-Media/Social-Media.pdf

9. Hayes, D.R., Cappa, F.: Open-source intelligence for risk assessment. Bus. Horiz. **61**(5), 689–697 (2018)

10. Kozera, C.A., et al.: Fitness OSINT: identifying and tracking military and security personnel with fitness applications for intelligence gathering purposes. Secur. Defence Q. **32**(5), 41–52 (2020)

11. Lakomy, M.: Assessing the potential of OSINT on the internet in supporting military operations. Bezpieczeństwo. Teoria i Praktyka **3**(XLVIII) (2022). https://doi. org/10.48269/2451-0718-btip-2022-3-022

12. Lasoń, M., et al.: The total defence 21st century.com - building a resilient society. Bezpieczeństwo. Teoria i Praktyka **3**(XLVIII) (2022)

13. Maltby, S., Thornham, H.: The digital mundane: social media and the military. Media Cult. Soc. **38**(8), 1153–1168 (2016). https://doi.org/10.1177/ 0163443716646173

14. Pellet, H., Shiaeles, S., Stavrou, S.: Localising social network users and profiling their movement. Comput. Secur. **81**, 49–57 (2019)

15. Riebe, T., et al.: CySecAlert: an alert generation system for cyber security events using open source intelligence data. In: Gao, D., Li, Q., Guan, X., Liao, X. (eds.) ICICS 2021. LNCS, vol. 12918, pp. 429–446. Springer, Cham (2021). https://doi. org/10.1007/978-3-030-86890-1_24

16. Tabatabaei, F., Wells, D.: OSINT in the context of cyber-security. Open Source Intelligence Investigation: From Strategy to Implementation, pp. 213–231 (2016)

17. Williams, H.J., Blum, I.: Defining second generation open source intelligence (OSINT) for the defense enterprise. Technical report, Rand Corporation (2018). https://doi.org/10.7249/rr1964

Free Guy or Bad Guy: Safety, Privacy, and Security Risks for Minors in the Metaverse and Prominent Educational Considerations

Andria Procopiou[1], Andriani Piki[1](✉) [ID], Eliana Stavrou[2][ID], and Nelly Zeniou[1]

[1] University of Central Lancashire Cyprus, Larnaca, Cyprus
{aprocopiou,apiki,nzeniou}@uclan.ac.uk
[2] Open University of Cyprus, Nicosia, Cyprus
eliana.stavrou@ouc.ac.cy

Abstract. The opportunities online platforms and services provide to minors for socialisation, entertainment, and education are plentiful. At the same time, the emergence of the Metaverse raises concerns for minors' security, safety, privacy, and wellbeing. This paper aims to highlight prominent threats to minors on the Internet, and how these can manifest in the Metaverse. The paper also discusses key countermeasures for mitigating these risks emphasising the need for raising awareness and developing resilience through timely, relevant, and dynamically responsive education.

Keywords: Metaverse · Online Safety · Security · Privacy · Trust · Social Media · Virtual Reality · Augmented Reality · Minors · Wellbeing · Education

1 Introduction

The Metaverse is defined as a "a perpetual and persistent multiuser environment merging physical reality with digital virtuality [enabling] multisensory interactions with virtual environments, digital objects and people [through] an interconnected web of social, networked immersive environments" [1]. The term "metaverse" was firstly introduced in the fiction novel "Snow Crash" back in 1992 [2], and is a blend of the words "meta", which stands for transcending, and "universe". The Metaverse is presented as a universally accessible and fully immersive environment, enabled by the convergence of key technologies including virtual, augmented, mixed, and extended reality (VR/AR/MR/XR), digital twins (DT), artificial intelligence (AI) and blockchain technology [1]. The Metaverse aims to promote rich social connections between individuals and presents opportunities for experiencing an immersive digital life. It enables seamless embodied user communications in real-time, and dynamic interactions with digital artifacts [1] and avatars [3]. Avatars form the digital representation of human users in

© The Author(s), under exclusive license to Springer Nature Switzerland AG 2023
H. Degen et al. (Eds.): HCII 2023, LNCS 14059, pp. 445–460, 2023.
https://doi.org/10.1007/978-3-031-48057-7_28

the Metaverse, capturing and visualising each user's behaviour (gestures, facial expressions and movements) [4] and interactions (verbal and non-verbal communication) with other users [5], as well as with the provided services or AI-enabled agents. The Metaverse strives to offer new ways in changing, and ultimately improving, our daily and social lives through immersive experiences and meaningful interactions [8].

Despite previous attempts to create parallel life in cyberspace, such as Second Life, Fortnite, Roblox, and VRChat [6], some of the biggest technological corporations have only recently started investing on the Metaverse. Notable examples include Meta (previously Facebook), Google, Microsoft, and Apple [7]. Given the ongoing technological evolution, the realisation of the Metaverse is more evident than ever before and, inevitably, it will soon be accessible to everyone, including minors. The term "minors" refers to all individuals up to 18 years old, including children (up to 12 years old) and teenagers (13–18 years old) [13]. The cognitive and maturity differences between these two age groups are significant, with minors in the age group of 11–18 years being reported as the ones who make the most conscious usage of the Internet [12]. In the near future, the Metaverse will form a state-of-the-art tool for their education [9], entertainment [10], and health-related matters [11]. Therefore, the threats and risks concerning minors are more alarming than ever before.

During the Internet 2.0 era, children became more vulnerable and easily targeted by all kinds of abusive, illegal, harmful and unacceptable behaviour [12]. Increasingly, the effective protection of minors from such threats is an open and multifaceted challenge due to the complexity of the current state of the Internet, the enormous size of its infrastructure, the explosion of the user space, and the opportunity for nearly-complete anonymity. Unfortunately, with the rise of the Metaverse, these threats are bound to be magnified due to the increased immersion level of high-fidelity VR environments [1]. Therefore, it is only a matter of time before the Metaverse becomes an extremely dangerous place for minors. Therefore, this group of users should get the highest priority when it comes to security, privacy, safety, and trust in the Metaverse.

The aim of this paper is to discuss the most notable and serious threats and risks observed in Internet 2.0 and how these can manifest in the Metaverse, focusing specifically on minors. Subsequently, we suggest possible countermeasures for protecting minors in the Metaverse, emphasising the genuine need to establish the Metaverse as an open, safe, and accessible space - a need that can only be met with properly educating minors and key stakeholders, alongside establishing proper security and safety policies.

2   Threats to Minors on the Internet

Undoubtedly, the Internet can pose multiple risks and threats to minors, regardless of their age group and digital literacy. Although there are no universally-accepted definitions, in the context of this paper we provide brief explanations of these threats based on relevant literature [14], before proceeding to discuss how each of these may manifest in the Metaverse.

2.1 Cyberbullying and Cyberharassment

Cyberbullying is "the willful and repeated harm inflicted through the use of computers" or other electronic devices [15]. Most cyberbullying acts occur on social media, chat rooms, or discussion forums. In fact, cyberbullying constitutes one of the biggest threats that social networks can pose. Adolescents share photos, videos, personal, contact, and location information (e.g., age, phone number, school, and location) on social media, to a much greater extent compared to the past. Sharing personal and sensitive information constitutes the main reason triggering cyberbullying of minors through social networks [12]. In recent years more than three million children have undergone cyberbullying in various forms, ranging from harassment to threats, while a high percentage (95%) reported that they have been victims of cyberbullying on Facebook [12].

Cyberbullying is more dominating compared to bullying occurring in physical space. Firstly, cyberbullying acts can occur at any time and place. There are no safe or "bulletproof" cyberspaces. Hence, individuals can become victims even while they are at home. Secondly, cyberbullying can reach large audiences in a very short amount of time. Furthermore, cyberbullying can transpire in a completely anonymous way, with offenders hiding behind aliases, fake profiles or fake accounts [12]. Therefore, it is significantly more difficult to effectively detect and mitigate acts of bullying in cyberspace.

When an adult performs any act of bullying, this is classified as cyberharassment [16,17]. Such an act denotes harassment of individuals or groups through hateful, threatening, abusive, and offensive online messages, comments, or emails [18]. Examples of cyberharassment manifestation include, but are not limited to, receiving unwanted content (in any form, including text, photos, and videos) online; receiving offensive, inappropriate, or abusive advances on social media, chat rooms or forums; receiving threats of physical, emotional, mental, or sexual violence online; and receiving hateful, insulting and/or threatening messages, comments or emails that directly attack an individual's or a group's beliefs, preferences and identity characteristics (such as ethnic race, nationality, religion, sexual orientation, gender identification, political beliefs, financial status and personal interests, amongst others) [19].

2.2 Online Stalking

Online stalking encompasses all actions and behaviour that exploit the Internet or other electronic or digital means to stalk and prey upon individuals, aiming to control, intimidate or negatively influence them [20]. Like cyberbullying, cyberstalking can be conducted more easily compared to its physical counterpart, due to the anonymity the Internet offers. Cyberstalking can be part of a physical stalking act or can be solely manifested online.

2.3 Online Predators

Online predators are defined as the individuals who adopt "a communication process by which they apply affinity seeking strategies, while simultaneously engaging in sexual desensitization and information acquisition about targeted victims in order to develop relationships that result in need fulfillment such as physical sexual solicitation" in cyberspace [21]. They exploit the minors' naive nature and vulnerabilities [12].

2.4   Online Gambling

Online gambling encompasses all virtual gambling games in cyberspace. Examples include virtual bingo, slots and casino games [23]. Unfortunately, underage online gambling is a critical issue in today's world that only keeps growing [24]. Furthermore, minors could incur a huge cost to their families while playing online games. More specifically, young players may spend considerable amounts of money to purchase virtual characters or other game features, or by just paying for subscriptions [12].

2.5   Illegal, Inappropriate, and Harmful Content

Minors can come across various types of "unacceptable" content online [12]. Such content can be categorised as illegal, harmful, or age inappropriate advice. Illegal content refers to all content which is unlawful to be published online, such as footage of real or simulated crimes. Harmful advice content denotes all content which glorifies problematic behaviour and promotes minors into the adaption of such behaviour. Examples include the consumption of alcohol, drugs and other substances, committing suicide, participation in dangerous activities and challenges [22], or adoption of extreme nutritional customs. Inappropriate content denotes all content that, although not illegal, is dangerous to the minors' development, health, and wellbeing. Examples include pornographic content and content promoting violent behaviours.

2.6   Social Engineering and Identity Theft

Identity theft involves any form of illegal activity aiming to obtain personal information from individuals in cyberspace [25], and it is often materialised through social engineering attacks [26]. Social engineering aims to exploit the human nature and trust that someone places to situations or another person by manipulating them to divulge confidential information. In turn, all the illegally obtained information collected is used to commit various acts of identity fraud. Examples include opening bank accounts, taking over phone contracts, and obtaining genuine and legal documents such as passports [30].

Social engineering attacks can be launched during face-to-face interactions, through the phone, or through digital means [27], with email being the typical attack channel for phishing attacks [28]. Minors are often susceptible to phishing attacks [29] due to their curiosity, naivety, and lack of awareness and education, revealing sensitive information to third parties that could lead to identity theft, and, subsequently, to accounts being compromised. Social engineering can also enable online predators to launch other malicious activities, such as cyberharassment, leading to minors' victimisation. Minors are typically at risk through their social media accounts. There are also alternative attack vectors, such as interacting with a smart toy, an educational application (e.g., ClassDojo) or their parents' social media accounts [31]. Therefore, raising awareness and educating minors, teachers, and parents about the imminent threats, risks, and their consequences, in a timely and orchestrated manner, is imperative.

3 Threats to Minors in the Metaverse

The range of looming threats and the severity of their consequences become more prevalent as emerging technologies expand in all areas of social life. In this section, we discuss how the most notable threats can manifest in the Metaverse and under what circumstances.

3.1 Bullying, Harassment, and Assault in the Metaverse

Cyberbullying and online harassment have proved to be extremely dangerous. Real world cases report on victims suffering from mental health deterioration, which subsequently resulted into successful suicide attempts [32]. In the Metaverse, this type of behaviour may have a serious impact due to the immersive environment. High-fidelity VR environments and violent representations in the Metaverse can trigger traumatic experiences [1]. Victims will be targets of insults and invective, verbal abuse, discriminating, racist and/or homophobic slurs, threats of violence and other forms of harassing behaviour [33]. Moreover, due to the VR/AR technologies used, these acts will impact the victims emotionally, psychologically, and physiologically. Specifically, due to avatars' sophisticated and photorealistic design, including the detailed facial expressions and body movements, the victims may endure a similar impact to a bullying/harassment scenario happening in the real world [4], hence experiencing fear, intimidation, and helplessness.

Due to the presence of open virtual "social spaces" in the Metaverse [34], potential victims are much easier to be identified and harassed and/or bullied. While in cyberbullying/online harassment occurring in social media, forums, or chatrooms, the target has the opportunity to "get away" by turning their device off, in the Metaverse, the victims are directly accessible, easier to find, and it is harder for them to escape as they can be followed by their harassers. Furthermore, the Metaverse offers the opportunity for the users to create their own content, their own metaverse-esque spaces, and personalise their avatars' appearance to offend, insult, mock, troll, and dehumanise individuals and groups. Examples include changing their skin color (e.g., "blackface") [38]. In the context of bullying and harassment, aggressors may wear clothing or accessories with biased, discriminating and overly offensive slogans or images [39], or recreate or modify the metaverse-esque spaces with posters, street wall graffiti, flags and banners which are classified as racist, homophobic, transphobic and offensive [37].

3.2   Stalking in the Metaverse

In the Metaverse, stalking may manifest in several ways. It will be possible to buy land and subsequently build houses in the Metaverse [35]. Therefore users' "metaverse house address" could be revealed if their harassers systematically stalk them in the Metaverse. While some social media platforms allow users to check who has viewed their profile, currently VR technologies do not allow users to be fully aware of their surroundings [4] or be aware of who might be following them or accessing their Metaverse spaces. Furthermore, the harassers may vandalise their property, stalk them in metaverse-time and even assault them. Even though the victims may not suffer any physical injuries, the psychosomatic consequences of such a traumatic experience will certainly occur and be enhanced due to the usage of immersive technologies such as VR/AR/MR/XR [36].

3.3   Predators and Sexual Exploitation in the Metaverse

Perhaps the most critical concern in the Metaverse for minors is the possibility of their sexual exploitation and grooming from predators who may be present under various disguises. Public spaces will be a reality in the Metaverse, where everyone will be free to socialise with users they already know, but also meet and interact with strangers [45]. Predators may easily "hide" behind avatars that have no connection to their real age or gender. Hence, they could easily pose as peers with the aim to approach minors.

Unfortunately, numerous incidents of sexual assault and violence have been reported [46], while at the same time victims of such incidents are eager to approach other victims to reveal they had similar experiences in the Metaverse. Despite the realisation of a personal boundary system (which prevents users from touching another user's avatar or getting too close to them), predators will force others to turn it off. If users fall in the predators' trap, they face the risk of being victimised, and experience any of the previously discussed behaviours [47]. Based on the incidents being reported thus far, it seems that the possibility of such exploitation is prevalent. In such cases, the associated risks are even higher for minors. Due to the immersive experience feeling more real than ever, the impact of such incidents on minors' development, mental health, and wellbeing will be shattering [36].

3.4   Metaverse Gambling

The current technologies for the Metaverse already offer a plethora of gaming hubs, so it is only a matter of time before casinos make their appearance [40]. Currently, online gambling is prohibited for minors. However, underage users can easily bypass any security countermeasures and protocols, enter the Metaverse as adults and, in turn, gain access to casinos and participate in gambling games. This can have catastrophic consequences. First, online gambling can become alarmingly addictive for minors [42]. Opponents may exercise peer pressure to minors or challenge them to continue playing. Therefore, minors can quickly and easily become addicted to gambling in the Metaverse [43, 44]. Secondly, due to the immersion factor as well as due to pressure from other players, minors may find it more difficult to escape from unwanted or dangerous situations. Thirdly, studies exploring the reasoning behind minors addiction to online gambling, suggest that prevalence, visibility, and glamour are the main motivations [42]. Minors seem to consider online gambling as an enjoyable and thrilling activity which allows them to win fast money [42]. It is inevitable for such emotions to be magnified through the Metaverse's immersive environment. The Metaverse and its components are designed to offer experiences very similar to the real-world respective ones, with the usage of immersive technologies (VR/AR/MR/XR), AI-enabled agents and services, and highly-detailed virtual environments. Another key concern, is that the Metaverse's mechanisms for protecting an individual's identity in the real world, including their age and gender, may be exploited by players who may hide behind their unidentifiable avatars to exercise pressure against other users, including minors who many not have the resilience or stamina to escape.

3.5   Illegal, Inappropriate, and Harmful Content in the Metaverse

Since the Metaverse presents the means for crafting a parallel reality to users' lives, all illegal, inappropriate and harmful content, previously observed in social encounters, social media, forums, or chat rooms, is increasingly likely to make an appearance in the Metaverse. The most important difference is that minors can be fully exposed and witness such incidents and not just watch footage of them. Examples of illegal behaviour in the Metaverse would include minors witnessing a crime, such as a murder, rape, or assault [48]. Due to the Metaverse's realistic and immersive nature, minors are likely to suffer a significant emotional, psychological, and physiological impact from witnessing such a traumatic experience, higher than when they experience such an exposure in Internet 2.0, and similar to experiencing such an act in the real world [49]. In addition, in the case of a murder occurrence in the metaverse, the victim will potentially "come back to life". This is likely to confuse minors, especially the younger ones, as to the actual consequences of physically harming someone in the real world as well.

Additional examples of possible age-inappropriate exposure in the Metaverse would mainly include minors witnessing pornographic content, public indecency incidents, bullying and harassing incidents, as well as other episodes of violence. It is also possible that the avatars minors use might not necessarily correspond to their actual age, hence increasing the risks they may face. Currently, there is no certain way of ensuring that a user has specified their legal age when joining the Metaverse. Therefore, minors may freely enter virtual strip clubs or engage in other age-inappropriate activities [50]. In addition, avatars may be involved in such activities publicly, so it is possible for minors to witness these incidents while navigating the Metaverse [50, 51].

Finally, cases of harmful advice in the Metaverse are equally dangerous. Minors could be instantly offered virtual drugs, alcohol, cigarettes or other substances from peers or older users. Peer pressure, curiosity, and excitement are common reasons why such cases materialise. Even if this does not translate to suffering any physical consequences directly, such experiences can have a critical influence on minors, and may evolve into actions, beliefs, and addictions in the physical world. As a result, they are likely to be negatively influenced to try out such substances in the real world with greater ease, since they have already done it in the Metaverse.

3.6 Social Engineering and Identity Theft in the Metaverse

In the Metaverse, identity theft does not merely involve stealing private and confidential information about users. Rather, it involves stealing the actual identity of the users. Specifically, facial characteristics, body movements, or even the entire avatars could be "stolen" by other users. This could be done in an attempt to gain multiple illegal or unethical benefits in the Metaverse, access restricted areas, as well as deceive minors by posing as their peers. This can prove to be particularly dangerous when it comes to predatory behaviour as already discussed.

Related to data ethics, AI algorithms and deep learning techniques can be utilised to create VR deep fake avatars and launch identity theft attacks in the Metaverse [1]. Online predators can also profile a minor through social engineering attacks employed in the Metaverse, with a focus on in-person attacks delivered through avatars. These attacks are easier to deploy compared to real-life, face-to-face social engineering attacks, since it is easier to approach minors in the Metaverse, as guardians may not enforce any controls due to lack of understanding of the environment, or failure to realise the dimensions of the threats that the Metaverse might give rise to. Due to this possibility, online predators might direct their efforts on identifying and targeting minors while socialising in the Metaverse's public spaces. This further illuminates the need for raising awareness and educating both minors and adults.

Additionally, minors could be approached by adult users that have a malicious intent in an attempt to make them reveal personal information about their Metaverse lives or real lives through "casual conversation". The adult users could even "eavesdrop" their conversations so they can learn more about them and make their encounters more effective [4]. Examples of such personal information include physical, medical, physiological, economic, cultural, or social status in the real world [52]. Also, private information regarding their behaviour, such as habits, activities and hobbies on and off the Metaverse could be obtained, enabling online predators to profile them more easily [52]. This could have a serious impact on minors and their lives, especially in the real world, as their identity could be revealed under such scenarios, further impacting their emotional and mental wellbeing.

4   Education and Awareness as a Countermeasure

Undoubtedly, the Metaverse will not be fully deployed overnight. It will rather be a gradual ongoing process. Still, protective measures should already start being developed and new regulations and policies should be introduced, tailored specifically for the Metaverse. Such regulations should clearly define what is considered ethical, lawful, and acceptable behaviour in the Metaverse as well as what the consequence will be when these regulations are violated [53,54]. From a technological perspective, appropriate and effective content moderation, filtering and reporting mechanisms should be developed [55]. From a governmental and policy making perspective, it is essential to disseminate and enforce the necessary policies and procedures at different levels (public, educational institutions, business organisations). However, perhaps the most important and meaningful countermeasure, that should be of the highest priority, involves adopting a transversal approach to prevention, based on core human values and life skills education [41]. Educating minors themselves about the metaverse and the potential dangers it engenders, as well as how they should recognise such dangers, prevent them, and subsequently report them can form a firm safety shield. It is imperative for young users to be educated and prepared for any potential incidents which may be regarded as ominous or worrying, but also to be supported through open discussions with adults and experts at family, school, and community level [56]. Therefore, from an educational perspective, raising awareness and developing students' knowledge, skills, and resilience, sets the cornerstone for a safer and more secure future.

4.1 Frameworks for Addressing Safety, Privacy, and Security Risks

Various frameworks have been proposed for raising cybersecurity awareness in various contexts. Examples include a framework for improving security awareness in organisational contexts, a cybersecurity awareness and education framework developed to assist in creating a cyber-secure culture among Internet users, a conceptual framework for the design and implementation of cybersecurity games to improve cybersecurity education and pedagogical effectiveness using game-based approaches, and a cybersecurity awareness framework for academia [67], amongst others. However, there is a lack of conceptual frameworks focusing specifically on minors.

The National Institute of Standards and Technology (NIST) Cybersecurity Framework [57] is a generic, flexible, and technology neutral model which can serve as a foundation towards formulating a concrete approach for addressing safety, privacy, and security risks that minors may face in the Metaverse. NIST Cybersecurity Framework specifies five functional areas to manage threats: identify, protect, detect, respond, and recover. Taking these areas into consideration, appropriate awareness-raising and educational activities should be designed, developed, and implemented, focusing on Metaverse usage by minors. The objective should be to build knowledge and skills so that minors can:

- Understand the technologies utilised in the Metaverse and the relevant risks.
- Develop critical thinking skills as to how an online predator might try to exploit them in an immersive environment, and be in position to recognise such an intention and successfully escape.

- Realise how someone with a malicious intent can collect information and exploit it to profile minors and lure them into a harmful situation, both physically and mentally.
- Stand up in case of a harmful/offensive situation and have the confidence, resilience, and knowledge to report it to the appropriate authority.

In addition to educating and upskilling minors themselves, other relevant stakeholders and communities, such as parents and educators, should also be trained and informed [51], so they can understand what the Metaverse environment implies, appreciate the associated threats and risks, offer support and guidance, and liaise with appropriate authorities to report incidents and seek further support, when needed. Such knowledge and skills can promote the development of a cyber-resilience culture [58] which will empower Metaverse users to predict, detect, and respond to threats, contributing to a global cyber-resilient society.

4.2 Gamification and Game-Based Learning Approaches to Education

Games have been used as learning tools for ages and playing games constitutes one of the fundamental ways to learn. Therefore, games constitute an avenue towards addressing and responding to prominent educational and training needs. Such efforts can utilise game-based learning (GBL) strategies [59], serious games [60], gamification techniques, and emerging immersive technologies including the Metaverse itself [61], to raise cybersecurity awareness, and increase minors' and adults' familiarity with core safety, privacy, and security concepts pertinent to the Metaverse.

Various serious games and gamification efforts have been employed to address cybersecurity-oriented educational needs, adopting a range of game genres to engage, motivate, and educate learners [59,60,62]. The Cybersecurity & Infrastructure Security Agency (CISA) [71] developed a series of educational cybersecurity games available on mobile devices for adults and children. Each game presents simulated cybersecurity threats, defenses, and response actions. For instance, "Defend the Crown" encourages players to develop and apply a basic understanding of attacks and defense strategies over three challenging stages and 18 levels, while "Hotel Hijinks" is a mobile game which focuses specifically on providing learning materials to high school students related to the Internet of Things (IoT), the cybersecurity challenges posed by it, and cyber safety in a fun and interactive way, and it is available on both iPhone and Android devices. While the intended audience is high school students, this mobile game is available for anyone interested to develop their knowledge on these topics [71].

Other examples of games in the broader field of cybersecurity include: "Operation Digital Ant", a team-based competitive game aiming to familiarise players with different types of insider motives and attacks, and raise their awareness on security countermeasures while advancing through collaborative scenarios and role-play [63]; "AIT Cyber Range", a virtual simulation environment aiming to increase the users' preparedness and dexterity by training them to identify and mitigate various incidents and attacks [64]; and "CyberCEIGE", a video game that teaches professional staff and students computer and network security concepts and the impact of decision making on physical, hardware, software, and user security, using real life scenarios [68], amongst other educational games. The available games feature various levels which must be completed to unlock subsequent levels or scenarios, and adopt dynamic complexities that adjust based on the players' performance, level of expertise, time allocated to complete a task, and other game features [67]. Such GBL approaches can be used for the education of various target groups, such as students, parents, teachers, school leaders, employees at local public authorities, professional and non-professional staff, and others. These target groups can be trained through playing educational games aiming to improve their digital skills and strengthen their own resilience and decision making, in terms of security, privacy, and safety, as well as the overall cyber-resilience of their organisations [66].

Further to GBL, employing gamification techniques and game-like features (such as interactivity, instant feedback, progress indicators, time limits, unveiling of levels, scoreboards, badges and awards) can also be instrumental for achieving the learning objectives, that is to raise security, safety, and privacy awareness. Gamification in the field of cybersecurity typically involves real-life scenarios with a focus on detecting and handling cybersecurity attacks, and incident response procedures that must be followed in the event of a cybersecurity threat [67,69]. Scenario-based learning, problem-based learning, or case-based learning when employed in a gamified or GBL context, support active learning strategies and increase learner engagement by immersing them in learning experiences using interactive scenarios. In such approaches, participants must apply their subject knowledge, critical thinking, and problem solving skills to solve multiple question by working their way through a story line or narrative that is usually based on an ill-structured or complex problem [70]. Another area of employing gamification in cybersecurity education, is through revealing vulnerabilities of the user's own work environment by generating game data based on automated IT-security analysis of installed apps on the user's smartphone [65].

An important consideration for the successful use of novel serious games and game-based pedagogical approaches, is to ensure they are adapted to specific age groups and context of learning. They need to be accessible, inclusive, and properly designed to promote users' upskilling, critical thinking, wellbeing, and ability to respond to Metaverse-related risks and threats. Recent educational efforts adopt an enthralling twofold strategy towards increasing students' cybersecurity awareness while, simultaneously, motivating students to pursue cybersecurity as a career, by employing game-based strategies [59]. While such approaches may be effective for older students, younger users need a more playful approach, so they can learn through play, and test the impact of their decision making process in a safe environment, through trial and error, repetitions, and simulated interactions, before consciously entering a dynamic and complex environment such as the Metaverse.

Undeniably, the Metaverse environment itself can add a new dimension to the field of educational technologies [61] addressing the educational and training needs of both minors and adults. Applications of "Meta-Education" have already shown spectacular results in terms of training speed, performance, and retention [1]. Nevertheless, the underlying technologies, architecture, and infrastructure of the Metaverse have not yet matured. Therefore, it is considered a necessity to determine appropriate strategies for the use of Metaverse in education [61], especially when educating minors. At the same time, it is essential for scientists and educators to continue pursuing an in-depth understanding of the Metaverse's widespread impact on the safety, privacy, health, and security risks it can have on users.

5   Conclusion

This paper discusses the dangers and risks the Metaverse can pose to minors. Undeniably, individuals belonging to such age groups spend a considerable amount of time online. Therefore, it is expected for them to shift to the Metaverse, as soon as it becomes widely accessible. Unfortunately, this unleashes a plethora of threats and risks, with varying degrees of severity and impact on their security, privacy, online and offline safety, mental health and wellbeing. Alongside the immersive features the Metaverse encapsulates for providing an enhanced, rich, holistic experience of a parallel world, it also contributes to the magnification of the psychological impact and negative experiences that may occur in such a multiuser, universally accessible, embodied context. Extremists, terrorists, predators, and criminals are likely to be fully aware of the capabilities the Metaverse can provide them with, and may exploit these to maximise their efforts in radicalising individuals, recruiting new members, spreading their propaganda, effectively planning attacks both in the physical and virtual space and finding new targets more accessibly in the virtual world. Regardless of the legislation, standards, regulations and policies, guidelines and protective countermeasures that shall be developed in the years to come to render the Metaverse an open, accessible space, it is unlikely that it will ever be an absolutely safe, inclusive, and secure space. Therefore, the timely and ongoing education, awareness, and upskilling of minors and all key stakeholders, constitute key priorities.

References

1. Mystakidis, S.: Metaverse. Encyclopedia 2(1), 486–497 (2022). (Basel, 2021). https://doi.org/10.3390/encyclopedia2010031
2. Joshua, J.: Information bodies: computational anxiety in Neal Stephenson's Snow Crash. Interdiscip. Lit. Stud. 19(1), 17–47 (2017)
3. Lacey, C., Caudwell, C.: Cuteness as a 'dark pattern' in home robots. In: 2019 14th ACM/IEEE International Conference on Human-Robot Interaction (HRI), pp. 374–381 (2019). https://doi.org/10.1109/HRI.2019.8673274

4. Lee, L.-H., et al.: All one needs to know about metaverse: a complete survey on technological singularity, virtual ecosystem, and research agenda. arXiv [cs.CY] (2021)
5. Davis, A., et al.: Avatars, people, and virtual worlds: foundations for research in metaverses. J. Assoc. Inf. Syst. **10**(2), 90–117 (2009)
6. Dwivedi, Y.K., et al.: Metaverse beyond the hype: multidisciplinary perspectives on emerging challenges, opportunities, and agenda for research, practice and policy. Int. J. Inf. Manage. **66**(102542), 102542 (2022)
7. Maganis, J.: Top companies building in the metaverse. Crowdcreate, 27 April 2022
8. Dincelli, E., Yayla, A.: Immersive virtual reality in the age of the metaverse: a hybrid-narrative review based on the technology affordance perspective. J. Strat. Inf. Syst. **31**(2), 101717 (2022)
9. Hirsh-Pasek, K., et al.: A whole new world: education meets the metaverse. Report (2002). https://www.brookings.edu/research/a-whole-new-world-education-meets-the-metaverse
10. Kerdvibulvech, C.: Exploring the impacts of COVID-19 on digital and metaverse games. In: Stephanidis, C., Antona, M., Ntoa, S. (eds.) HCI International 2022 Posters, HCII 2022. Communications in Computer and Information Science, vol. 1582, pp. 561–565. Springer, Cham (2022). https://doi.org/10.1007/978-3-031-06391-6_69
11. Petrigna, L., Musumeci, G.: The metaverse: a new challenge for the healthcare system: a scoping review. J. Funct. Morphol. Kinesiol. **7**(3), 63 (2022). https://doi.org/10.3390/jfmk7030063
12. Tsirtsis, A., Tsapatsoulis, N., Stamatelatos, M., Papadamou, K., Sirivianos, M.: Cyber security risks for minors: a taxonomy and a software architecture. In: 2016 11th International Workshop on Semantic and Social Media Adaptation and Personalization (SMAP), Thessaloniki, Greece, pp. 93–99 (2016). https://doi.org/10.1109/SMAP.2016.7753391
13. ITU: Guidelines for children on child online protection (2020). https://www.itu-cop-guidelines.com
14. Nidirect: Social media, online gaming and keeping children safe online (2015). https://www.nidirect.gov.uk/articles/social-media-online-gaming-and-keeping-children-safe-online
15. Cyberbullying Research Center: What is cyberbullying? Cyberbullying Research Center. https://cyberbullying.org/what-is-cyberbullying
16. Slonje, R., Smith, P.K., Frisén, A.: The nature of cyberbullying, and strategies for prevention. Comput. Hum. Behav. **29**(1), 26–32 (2013)
17. Stevens, F., Nurse, J.R.C., Arief, B.: Cyber stalking, cyber harassment, and adult mental health: a systematic review. Cyberpsychol. Behav. Soc. Netw. **24**(6), 367–376 (2021)
18. US Legal, Inc.: Cyber harassment law and legal definition. Uslegal.com. https://definitions.uslegal.com/c/cyber-harassment
19. Cyber harassment: European Institute for Gender Equality. https://eige.europa.eu/thesaurus/terms/1486
20. Pittaro , M.: Cyber stalking: an analysis of online harassment and intimidation. Cybercrimejournal.com (2007). https://www.cybercrimejournal.com/pdf/mpittarojccjuly2007.pdf
21. Ngejane, C.H., Mabuza-Hocquet, G., Eloff, J.H.P., Lefophane, S.: Mitigating online sexual grooming cybercrime on social media using machine learning: a desktop survey. In: 2018 International Conference on Advances in Big Data, Computing and Data Communication Systems (icABCD), pp. 1–6. IEEE (2018)

22. Nguyen, Q.: Don't let your kids try these 9 dangerous TikTok trends 2021. Cyber-Purify. https://cyberpurify.com/knowledge/9-dangerous-tiktok-trends
23. LawInsider. Online gambling definition. https://www.lawinsider.com/dictionary/online-gambling
24. Gómez, P., Feijóo, S., Braña, T., Varela, J., Rial, A.: Minors and online gambling: prevalence and related variables. J. Gambl. Stud. **36**(3), 735–745 (2020)
25. Wall, D.S.: Future identities: changing identities in the UK - the next 10 years DR 19: Identity Related Crime in the UK. Gov.uk (2013). Retrieved 31 December 2022
26. Aldawood, H., Skinner, G.: Educating and raising awareness on cyber security social engineering: a literature review. In: 2018 IEEE International Conference on Teaching, Assessment, and Learning for Engineering (TALE), Wollongong, NSW, Australia, pp. 62–68 (2018). https://doi.org/10.1109/TALE.2018.8615162
27. Aldawood, H., Skinner, G.: A taxonomy for social engineering attacks via personal devices. Int. J. Comput. Appl. **178**(50), 19–26 (2019)
28. Ivaturi, K., Janczewski, L.: A taxonomy for social engineering attacks. In: CONF-IRM 2011 Proceedings, pp. 2–11 (2011)
29. Nicholson, J., Javed, Y., Dixon, M., Coventry, L., Ajayi, O.D., Anderson, P.: Investigating teenagers' ability to detect phishing messages. In: IEEE European Symposium on Security and Privacy Workshops, pp. 140–149 (2020). https://doi.org/10.1109/EuroSPW51379.2020.00027
30. Police.uk: Identity fraud and identity theft. https://www.actionfraud.police.uk/a-z-of-fraud/identity-fraud-and-identity-theft
31. Internet Matters: Learn about privacy and identity theft (2019). https://www.internetmatters.org/issues/privacy-identity/learn-about-privacy-and-identity-theft
32. Ingham, A.: 7 real life cyberbullying horror stories. Family Orbit Blog (2018). https://www.familyorbit.com/blog/real-life-cyberbullying-horror-stories
33. Georgiou, M.: Harassment still exists in the metaverse, even for kids. Newsy (2022). https://www.newsy.com/stories/harassment-still-exists-in-the-metaverse-even-for-kids
34. Florian, M.-C.: Can public space be created in the metaverse? Arch-Daily (2022). https://www.archdaily.com/987613/can-public-space-be-created-in-the-metaverse
35. Marr, B.: How to buy land and real estate in the metaverse. Forbes (2022). https://www.forbes.com/sites/bernardmarr/2022/03/23/how-to-buy-land-real-estate-in-the-metaverse
36. Frenkel, S., Browning, K.: The metaverse's dark side: here come harassment and assaults. The New York Times (2021). https://www.nytimes.com/2021/12/30/technology/metaverse-harassment-assaults.htm
37. Procopiou, A.: Ready player bad: the future rise of extremism and terrorism in the Metaverse. In: 2022 IEEE 2nd International Conference on Intelligent Reality (ICIR), Piscataway, NJ, USA, pp. 31–34 (2022). https://doi.org/10.1109/ICIR55739.2022.00022
38. Sommier, M.: "How ELSE are you supposed to dress up like a Black Guy?": negotiating accusations of Blackface in online newspaper comments. Ethn. Racial Stud. **43**(16), 57–75 (2020)
39. Ozalp, S., Williams, M.L., Burnap, P., Liu, H., Mostafa, M.: Antisemitism on Twitter: collective efficacy and the role of community organisations in challenging online hate speech. Soc. Media Soc. **6**(2), 205630512091685 (2020)
40. Neva: How will the metaverse change online gambling? 800gambler.org (2022). https://800gambler.org/how-will-the-metaverse-change-online-gambling

41. Rial, A., Golpe, S., Isorna, M., Braña, T., Gómez, P.: Minors and problematic Internet use: evidence for better prevention. Comput. Hum. Behav. **87**, 140–145 (2018)
42. Webroot.com: Internet gambling among teens and college students. https://www.webroot.com/us/en/resources/tips-articles/internet-gambling-among-teens-and-college-students
43. Bojic, L.: Metaverse through the prism of power and addiction: what will happen when the virtual world becomes more attractive than reality? Eur. J. Fut. Res. **10**(1), 22 (2022). https://doi.org/10.1186/s40309-022-00208-4
44. Usmani, S.S., Sharath, M., Mehendale, M.: Future of mental health in the metaverse. Gen. Psychiatr. **35**(4), e100825 (2022)
45. Lillibridge, R.: Socializing in the metaverse - science, translated. Science, Translated - Science (2022)
46. Patel, N.J.: Reality or fiction? Kabuni, 21 December 2021. https://medium.com/kabuni/fiction-vs-non-fiction-98aa0098f3b0
47. Singh, K.: There's not much we can legally do about sexual assault in the metaverse. Refinery29, 09 June 2022. https://www.refinery29.com/en-us/2022/06/11004248/is-metaverse-sexual-assault-illegal
48. Eberhart, C.: Metaverse experts reveal if you can murder someone in virtual world - and whether you can be punished if you're violent. The US Sun (2022). Retrieved 31 December 2022. https://www.the-sun.com/tech/5066296/can-you-murder-in-metaverse/
49. Daly, C.: Metaverse murders could be punished just like real crimes under tough new rules. Dailystar.co.uk, 01 June 2022. https://www.dailystar.co.uk/tech/news/murders-metaverse-could-punished-just-27120692
50. Crawford, A., Smith, T.: Metaverse app allows kids into virtual strip clubs. BBC, BBC News, 23 February 2022
51. Hu, R.: Understanding children's vulnerabilities in the metaverse: the role of the online community. Parenting for a Digital Future, 15 June 2022. https://blogs.lse.ac.uk/parenting4digitalfuture/2022/06/15/metaverse-vrchat
52. Falchuk, B., Loeb, S., Neff, R.: The social metaverse: battle for privacy. IEEE Technol. Soc. Mag. **37**(2), 52–61 (2018). https://doi.org/10.1109/MTS.2018.2826060
53. Bosworth, A., Facebook Reality Labs, Clegg, N., Global Affairs: Building the metaverse responsibly. Meta, 27 September 2021. https://about.fb.com/news/2021/09/building-the-metaverse-responsibly
54. Rosenberg, L.B.: The growing need for metaverse regulation. In: Arai, K. (eds.) Intelligent Systems and Applications, IntelliSys 2022. LNNS, vol. 544, pp. 540–547. Springer, Cham (2023). https://doi.org/10.1007/978-3-031-16075-2_39
55. Fernandez, C.B., Hui, P.: Life, the metaverse and everything: an overview of privacy, ethics, and governance in metaverse. In: 2022 IEEE 42nd International Conference on Distributed Computing Systems Workshops (ICDCSW), Bologna, Italy, pp. 272–277 (2022). https://doi.org/10.1109/ICDCSW56584.2022.00058
56. Protecting children in the metaverse: it's easy to blame big tech, but we all have a role to play. Lse.ac.uk. http://eprints.lse.ac.uk/114781/1/parenting4digitalfuture-2022-03-23.pdf. Accessed 19 Jun 2023
57. NIST: National Institute of Standards and Technology (NIST): Cybersecurity Framework. https://www.nist.gov/itl/smallbusinesscyber/planning-guides/nist-cybersecurity-framework
58. Stavrou, E.: Back to basics: towards building societal resilience against a cyber pandemic. J. Syst. Cybern. Inf. **18**(7), 73–80 (2020)

59. Triplett, W.J.: Addressing cybersecurity challenges in education. Int. J. STEM Educ. Sustain. **3**(1), 47–67 (2023)
60. Moumouh, C., Chkouri, M.Y., Fernández-Alemán, J.L.: Cybersecurity awareness through serious games: a systematic literature review. In: Ben Ahmed, M., Abdel-hakim, B.A., Ane, B.K., Rosiyadi, D. (eds.) Emerging Trends in Intelligent Systems & Network Security, NISS 2022. Lecture Notes on Data Engineering and Communications Technologies, vol. 147, pp. 190–199. Springer, Cham (2023). https://doi.org/10.1007/978-3-031-15191-0_18
61. Inceoglu, M.M., Ciloglugil, B.: Use of metaverse in education. In: Gervasi, O., Murgante, B., Misra, S., Rocha, A.M.A.C., Garau, C. (eds.) Computational Science and Its Applications, ICCSA 2022 Workshops, ICCSA 2022. LNCS, vol. 13377, pp. 171–184. Springer, Cham (2022). https://doi.org/10.1007/978-3-031-10536-4_12
62. Globalauthorid: Adaptive serious games to teach cybersecurity concepts using a machine learning approach. http://www.globalauthorid.com/
63. Hofmeier, M., Lechner, U.: Operation digital ant: a serious game approach to collect insider threat scenarios and raise awareness. In: European Interdisciplinary Cybersecurity Conference (2021)
64. Leitner, M., et al.: AIT cyber range: flexible cyber security environment for exercises, training and research. In: Proceedings of the European Interdisciplinary Cybersecurity Conference (2020)
65. Heid, K., Heider, J., Qasempour, K.: Raising security awareness on mobile systems through gamification. In: Proceedings of the European Interdisciplinary Cybersecurity Conference (2020)
66. Povse, D.F.: It's all fun and games, and some legalese: data protection implications for increasing cyber-skills of employees through games. In: 2018 Proceedings of the Central European Cybersecurity Conference (2018)
67. Khader, M., Karam, M., Fares, H.: Cybersecurity awareness framework for academia. Information (Basel) **12**(10), 417 (2021)
68. Center for Cybersecurity and Cyber Operations. https://nps.edu/web/c3o/cyberciege
69. Röpke, R., Schroeder, U.: The problem with teaching defence against the dark arts: a review of game-based learning applications and serious games for cyber security education. In: Proceedings of the 11th International Conference on Computer Supported Education, Heraklion, Greece, 2–4 May 2019 (2019)
70. Mio, C., Ventura-Medina, E., João, E.: Scenario-based eLearning to promote active learning in large cohorts: students' perspective. Comput. Appl. Eng. Educ. **27**(4), 894–909 (2019)
71. CISA: Cybersecurity & Infrastructure Security Agency: Cybersecurity Games (2022). https://www.cisa.gov/cybergames/

The Importance of Cybersecurity Awareness Training in the Aviation Industry for Early Detection of Cyberthreats and Vulnerabilities

Regner Sabillon[(✉)] [iD] and Juan Ramon Bermejo Higuera [iD]

International University of La Rioja (UNIR), Logroño, Spain
regners@athabascau.ca, juanramon.bermejo@unir.net

Abstract. Nowadays, cybercriminals are targeting organizations to launch cyberattacks by exploiting cyberthreats and vulnerabilities. Hackers keep increasing the sophistication of the cyberattacks to orchestrate the different criminal hacking phases from conducting target reconnaissance to successfully achieving the desired objectives that could result in exfiltrating more than one digital asset. Many times, the targets are critical assets that organizations utilize to run their daily operations. The aviation industry is not the exception to this, and it is a matter of time before aviation companies will be dealing with imminent cyberattacks that will impact its financial operations, business reputation, legal and compliance areas, not to mention that its stakeholders can be a victim of a cyberattack at any time. Early prevention, detection and cybersecurity awareness training are key to recognize the initial stages of most common cyberattacks. From airport personnel to aviation crews, it is crucial to professionally delivering comprehensive cyber awareness training that will enforce the main of objectives of cybersecurity to protect aeronautical assets based on the CIA triad – Confidentiality, Integrity, and Availability. This article reviews existing cybersecurity awareness training policies from the industry governance agencies and proposes a customized training program based on the CATRAM. The Cybersecurity Awareness TRAining Model (CATRAM) was developed to deliver cybersecurity training to different organizational audiences, each of these groups with specific content and separate objectives. CATRAM was originally conceived to deliver awareness training for the members of the Board of Directors, Top Executives, Managers, IT (Information Technology) staff and of course, end-users.

Keywords: Cybersecurity Awareness Training · Cybersecurity Awareness Model · Cybersecurity · Security · Education Training and Awareness (SETA)

1 Introduction

Security Education, Training, and Awareness (SETA) must be a part of any comprehensive Information Security Program. In any corporate setting, the Chief Information Security Officer (CISO) is responsible for designing and implementing a successful and measurable SETA. SETA's goal is to make it less likely that members of any organization,

© The Author(s), under exclusive license to Springer Nature Switzerland AG 2023

H. Degen et al. (Eds.): HCII 2023, LNCS 14059, pp. 461–479, 2023.
https://doi.org/10.1007/978-3-031-48057-7_29

including Board of Directors, C-Suite Executives, Managers, Employees, Consultants, Vendors, and Business Partners, who work with its cyber assets, commit accidental cybersecurity breaches.

If people continue to act the same way, cybersecurity awareness training programs may not be effective, preventing a positive corporate impact. If training is provided on a consistent basis with pertinent content that is aligned with the current cyber threat landscape, a cybersecurity awareness program is an organizational long-term investment that will assist in establishing a cybersecurity culture. Directors of cybersecurity might envision a more interactive experience that will enable employees to be more proactive beyond dealing with cyber incidents and threats.

The Cybersecurity Awareness TRAining Model - (CATRAM) [1, 29], in our opinion, has the potential to serve as a substantial foundation for the implementation of any cybersecurity awareness program within an organization. CATRAM is also able to evaluate any persistent and relevant awareness training model in light of the current cyberthreat landscape [37].

According to Whitman and Mattord [41], a SETA program includes security awareness, security education, and security training. It's possible that businesses won't be able to create an internal SETA program, so they might think about outsourcing to companies or educational institutions that specialize in providing security training. SETA programs are put into place to improve security awareness for the protection of information assets, to develop skills for end users so they can carry out their job responsibilities with security in mind, and to build in-depth knowledge for organizational security programs and the protection of information assets.

A SETA program is characterized as (Whitman et al. [41]):

A managerial program designed to improve the security of information assets by providing targeted knowledge, skills, and guidance for organizational employees.

The primary components of any SETA program are security education, security training, and security awareness. Security Awareness is the creation of awareness when dealing with InfoSec or cybersecurity issues. Security Education consists of imparting knowledge of information security issues and operations. Security Training equips participants with the skills, knowledge, and abilities to use their assigned resources wisely.

Users are recognized as the current weakest link in securing systems, regardless of any cybersecurity control or security measure, and as a result, they are unaware that their actions may affect information security (NIST SP 800–12, [22]). Pendergast (2016) also suggests that cybersecurity incidents and data breaches are financially liable to employees [25].

Depending on the maturity level of their digital transformation projects, the NTT Group [13] claims that integrating cybersecurity processes can empower digital transformations of any organization. Companies will be able to identify and control cyber risks, reduce the complexity of their business operations' cybersecurity architecture, add value to their digital business, prioritize areas to deal with business-critical cyber risks, and create a cyber resilience strategy for the digital transformation by doing this.

A study by Fujitsu [9] found that 86% of the participating organizations have a clear digital strategy that includes capabilities to address cybersecurity issues. The study evaluated the digital transformations of 1,625 decision makers in various industries and sectors across fourteen countries. In addition, to strengthen their digital transformations, 52% of these businesses are investing in cybersecurity and 51% are implementing the Internet of Things (IoT).

LeClair et al.'s study [17], focuses on the three major pillars of any cybersecurity program—people, technology, and process—to emphasize the interdisciplinary approach to cybersecurity education. The authors emphasize that in order to acquire the necessary skills for any organization, cybersecurity approaches all industries and requires an interdisciplinary focus. Every employee in any organization will be contributing to the overall business cybersecurity program because cybersecurity awareness programs are designed to train all employees from all departments. Companies must implement various layers of security in all cybersecurity domains to protect their cyber assets from continuous cyberattacks in light of the evolving cyberthreat landscape. In order to safeguard both traditional brick-and-mortar businesses and e-commerce transactions for e-businesses, cybersecurity awareness education programs ought to be coordinated with ongoing innovation [5, 6].

The following is the structure of the paper: The article's Introduction section serves as our foundation. The literature on our research topics is examined in the Literature Review Section. The architecture of our cybersecurity model is discussed in the following section: the Cybersecurity Awareness TRAining Model (CATRAM), that is structured on different types of aviation audiences for planning and delivering cybersecurity awareness training. Section four provides the reasoning for measuring the effectiveness of CATRAM. In Section five, the CSAM 2.0 controls, sub-controls and guidelines are presented to audit the outcomes of the proposed cybersecurity awareness training for different groups of aviation stakeholders [15,16, 24, 27, 28, 30–36]. In the final section, the conclusions are depicted.

2 Literature Review

According to the Gartner Magic Quadrant for Computer-Based Training for Security Awareness [10], which positions leaders, visionaries, challengers, and niche players, SANS Institute, Wombat Security Technologies, PhishMe, MediaPro, Security Innovation, Terranova WW, PhishLine, Global Learning Systems, and The Security Awareness Co. Are the leaders; Popcom Training and Security Mentor are two forward-thinking businesses; BeOne Development, KnowBe4, and Optiv Security are competitors, while niche players such as Junglemap, Digital Defense, Symantec (Blackfn Security), and Secure Mentem round out the list. By including security topics that are in line with the ever-evolving cyberthreat landscape, the new vendors that are positioned as leaders have clearly identified the needs of the market and added new features to their CBT products [18]. By providing gamification, multilingual support, supplemental internal marketing content like newsletters, intranet postings, and security alerts, and integration with partnerships to offer endpoint detection and response, endpoint protection, and data security, vendors continue to differentiate security awareness products and services. According to a separate Gartner [11, 12] study, organizations that have implemented security awareness programs will experience 75% fewer account takeover attacks by 2023. This is because effective security awareness programs require the commitment of upper management and must be compatible with the requirements, practices, and culture of any organization. Choosing, delivering, implementing, and maintaining cybersecurity awareness training that is tailored to a company's particular business environment, strategy, needs, and objectives presents numerous challenges [23]. For instance, deciding which topics to cover in the training, how to train employees, how to check that the training is effective, updating the training program, putting control measures in place to test cyber behaviors in the workplace, and deciding how often stakeholders should be retrained.

Ponemon Institute [26] conducted a survey of 1,021 IT and IT security professionals in the United States as well as Europe, the Middle East, and Africa (EMEA) to learn more about the Domain Name System (DNS) architecture, implementation, and responsibilities for managing organizations' cybersecurity activities. Ponemon Institute and Infoblox created the DNS Risk Index by categorizing five distinct areas based on the study's findings: security operations, threat intelligence, data security, malware mitigation, and DNS attack defense The most important findings of this study are that most businesses do not have dedicated DNS security staff, that most businesses do not track or identify cyber assets, that traffic analysis from firewalls is mostly used to mitigate malware and protect data assets, that using threat intelligence feeds is ineffective, that measures to protect data assets include data encryption, endpoint security, and antivirus, and that the majority of cyberthreat investigations are carried out manually. The findings indicate that advanced malware (63 percent), Advanced Persistent Threats (APTs – 59 percent), DNS-based data exfiltration (54 percent), unauthorized network access (51 percent), ransomware (46 percent), and phishing/social engineering (45 percent) are the top concerns in terms of cyberattacks.

According to the SANS Global Security Awareness Report [38–40], the most important aspects of a successful awareness program are time and communication. The findings pointed to a lack of time and resources allocated to a corporate awareness program, poor communication to engage people, and other issues. The respondents stated that they had a compliance awareness program (27.1%), implemented awareness and behavior change (54.6%), achieved long-term sustainment and culture change (9.8%), defined a program with robust metrics (0.9%), and had no cybersecurity awareness program at all (7.6%).

Employees with inadequate training increase the risk of losing or disclosing sensitive data, such as Intellectual Property (IP) and Personal Identifiable Information (PII). Through the development of a corporate culture and the training of employees, its Security Awareness Program reduces vulnerabilities and safeguards critical assets from exploitation, unauthorized access, cyberattacks, and fraud. Information security, threats, vulnerabilities, countermeasures, securing mobile users, protecting Internet information, and social media mobile device security are some ideal topics to cover during the training [18].

According to a study conducted by Enterprise Management Associates [20], 56% of employees, including IT and security staff, have not received any security awareness training within their organizations. Additionally, 84% of participants acknowledged that awareness training they received at work was also utilized to reduce cyber risks at home.

In addition, the findings of the study confirmed that the current security awareness programs do not provide the appropriate delivery frequency, content, or quality. In addition, the size, market, and budgets of a company all have a significant impact on whether their corporate awareness training is present and mature.

NIST (NIST SP 800–50, 2003) clearly identifies key stages in the IT security awareness and training program [21]:

- Program Design
- Material Development
- Program Implementation
- Post-Implementation

Furthermore, these stages can be mapped using centralized, partially centralized, or fully centralized security awareness and training programs.

To train employees and earn a certification, ESET [8] offers free online cybersecurity awareness training. An overview of threats like malware, phishing, and social engineering is one of the topics. Best practices for managing passwords; best practices for email security and preventative measures that cover home and workplace cyber hygiene best practices. In addition, PhishMe provides access to a free Computer Based Training (CBT) course called PhishMe CBFree, which includes four modules on compliance training and seventeen on security awareness. English, Chinese, French, German, Portuguese, Spanish, and Japanese are the seven languages that can be found in the course. Health Care, Payment Data, Personal Data, and the General Data Protection Regulation (GDPR) are the compliance modules. Cloud computing, advanced spear phishing, business email compromise, ransomware, surfing the Web, data protection, insider threats, malicious links, malware, mobile devices, security outside of the office, passwords, physical security, social engineering, social networking, and spear phishing are all covered in the security awareness modules.

Due to the fact that these organizations rely on Industrial Control Systems (ICS) for their operations, critical infrastructure and industrial organizations can also be the targets of any cyberattack. NotPetya, WannaCry, and Emotet—global malware attacks as well as more focused ICS cyberattacks like Industroyer and TRITON—can have an impact on production outages, cleanups, catastrophic safety and environmental incidents, and more. Data from 850 production ICS networks was analyzed using Network Traffic Analysis (NTA) and deep packet inspections in the Global ICS & Industrial Internet of Things (IIOT) risk report [7]. The most significant findings included the following: 40% of industrial sites have at least one direct connection to the Internet; 53% of industrial sites have out-of-date Windows systems; 69% of industrial sites have plain-text passwords traversing their networks; 57% of industrial sites do not run anti-virus solutions that include automatic signature updates; 16% of industrial sites have at least one Wireless Access Point (WAP) that is incorrectly configured; and 84% of industrial sites have at least one remotely accessible device that does not have multifactor authentication controls.

In our previous multi-case study's initial references [27–37, 42, 43], we used mixed methods (qualitative and quantitative studies) in our literature review approach. The lead researcher searched the Internet and computerized databases for terms like *security training; training in information security; SETA; training in cybersecurity awareness;*

program to raise awareness of cybersecurity; security awareness training program and cybersecurity training framework.

As reported by Axelos [2], cyber-resilience-specific training should be provided on a regular basis, and awareness campaigns should be developed to raise awareness and address specific cyber risks. Additionally, training should be designed and tailored to specific employee roles and responsibilities within the organization. Nevertheless, we must continue to develop novel approaches to the delivery of cybersecurity awareness training and, above all, to maintain participants' participation in cybersecurity awareness activities.

3 The Cybersecurity Awareness TRAining Model (CATRAM)

This paper describes how the Cybersecurity Awareness TRAining Model (CATRAM), as a validated model that can be implemented at any organization working in the aviation industry to consolidate the awareness foundations of a corporate Cybersecurity Awareness Program or to initiate the implementation of an organizational Cybersecurity Awareness Training Program. The model design answers our main research question:

Why it is necessary to increase cyber awareness at the organizational and personal levels?

The outcome of this research was to apply the model for delivering cyber awareness training to support awareness education in any organizational environment operating in the aviation industry. The Cybersecurity Awareness TRAining Model (CATRAM) has been designed to deliver the initial cybersecurity awareness training at the target organization or to re-introduce a better awareness training approach to an existing cybersecurity or information security awareness training program [3, 4]. Table 1 shows a mapping to select, plan and deliver the cyber training organized by different groups of stakeholders.

CATRAM has been validated to provide specific cybersecurity awareness training for personnel:

1. **Board of Directors and Executives**: Members of this group are trained based on the organizational cybersecurity strategy, governance, and program.
2. **Managers**: Department managers are trained to support and lead cybersecurity initiatives in their corporate environment.
3. **End Users**: This group gets awareness training to improve cybersecurity practices in the workplace and their personal lives.
4. **IT and Cybersecurity Personnel**: Information Technology specialists are trained in the use of advanced cybersecurity techniques, methods, procedures, and best practices to support the corporate awareness program and the cybersecurity program.

Table 1. Aviation groups aligned with CATRAM categories.

CATRAM Categories	Aviation Groups
Board of Directors and Executives	Aviation upper management
Managers	Aviation department managers
End Users	Flight deck roles, cabin positions, aviation mechanics, administrative personnel, air traffic controllers and airport personnel
ICT and Cybersecurity Personnel	Technical personnel providing Information and Communications Technology (ICT), Networking and Cybersecurity support and services

3.1 Awareness Course for the Board of Directors and Executives

The course lasts 2 h and can be organized in two different sessions [22]. It is advisable that this course could be delivered in a classroom or board meeting environment.

Objectives

1. Provide a high-level overview of an effective cybersecurity awareness training for your organization.
2. Create cybersecurity awareness for the Board of Directors and C-Suite Executives.

Cybersecurity Awareness Topics

- Initial Survey
- Cybersecurity Introduction
- Cybersecurity and Cybercrime Statistics
- A Corporate Cybersecurity Program
- Cybersecurity Strategy
- Responsibilities of Stakeholders (Board of Directors and C-Suite Executives)
- Cyberthreat Landscape
- Cybersecurity Risk Management
- Cybersecurity Frameworks
- Cybersecurity Awareness and Training
- Cybersecurity Business Continuity
- Incident Response Management
- Conclusions
- Final Survey

3.2 Awareness Course for Managers

The course lasts 2 h and can be organized in two different sessions. The course can be delivered in a classroom setting, online or in a blended environment.

Objectives

1. Provide a high-level overview of an effective cybersecurity awareness training for your organization.

2. Create cybersecurity awareness for Managers.

   Cybersecurity Awareness Topics

- Initial Survey
- Cybersecurity Introduction
- Cybersecurity and Cybercrime Statistics
- A Corporate Cybersecurity Program
- Cybersecurity Strategy
- Responsibilities of Stakeholders (Department Managers)
- Cyberthreat Landscape
- Cybersecurity Risk Management
- Cybersecurity Frameworks
- Cybersecurity Awareness and Training
- Cybersecurity Business Continuity
- Incident Response Management
- Conclusions
- Final Survey

3.3 Awareness Course for End Users

The course lasts 4 hours and can be organized in two or four different sessions. The course can be delivered in a classroom setting, online or in a blended environment. It is recommended to add a short video clip from YouTube as an additional learning resource for your audiences.

   Objectives

1. Educate end users to help protect the confidentiality, availability and integrity of your organization's information and cyber assets.
2. Create awareness of the importance of cybersecurity and cybersecurity controls.

   Cybersecurity Awareness Topics

- Initial Survey
- Cybersecurity Introduction
- Cybersecurity and Cybercrime Statistics
- You are a target for cybercriminals
- Cybercrime
- Hackers
- Cyberthreats
- Social Engineering
- Phishing
- Internet Browsing
- Social Networks
- Mobile device security
- Passwords
- Encryption
- Data security
- Identity Theft

- Wi-Fi Security
- Working remotely
- Physical security
- Protecting your online profile
- Protecting your home network
- Protecting our children online
- Privacy
- Avoiding Scams
- Have you been hacked?
- Conclusions
- Final Survey

3.4 Awareness Course for IT and Cybersecurity Professionals

The course lasts 20 h and can be organized into ten or twenty different sessions. The course can be delivered in a classroom setting, online, self-paced e-doing or in a blended environment.

Objectives

1. Understand cybersecurity concepts.
2. Recognize key cybersecurity objectives for the protection of cyber assets.
3. Understand cybercrime operations.
4. Recognize cybersecurity threat agents that could impact your organization.
5. Understand any cyberattack architecture.
6. Identify the most common cyberattacks.
7. Apply cybersecurity measures to defend against cyberattacks.
8. Understand cybersecurity program architecture and operation.
9. Recognize the importance of developing, enforcing, and maintaining cybersecurity policies.
10. Understand the fundamentals of ethical hacking.
11. Understand the architecture of penetration testing.
12. Get familiar with most cybersecurity frameworks.
13. Understand the basics of cyber threat intelligence.
14. Understand the importance of proper cybersecurity training.
15. Raise cybersecurity awareness in your organization.
16. Apply cybersecurity architecture principles.
17. Recognize the importance of hardening security in data, voice, and video networks.
18. Recognize the importance of security hardening for information, systems, and applications.
19. Identify cybersecurity vulnerabilities.
20. Remediate existing cybersecurity vulnerabilities.
21. Recognize the cybersecurity implications of new and evolving technologies.
22. Understand the principles of Cybersecurity Incident Response and Management.
23. Understand the fundamentals of Digital Forensics.
24. Recognize the importance of the continual evaluation of a corporate cybersecurity program.
25. Recognize the value of corporate cyber wargames to test cybersecurity.

26. Identify the opportunities for cybersecurity education and professional development.

    Cybersecurity Awareness Topics

- Initial Survey
- Cybersecurity Fundamentals
- Cybercrime
- Cyberattacks
- Corporate Cybersecurity Program
- Cybersecurity Policies
- Ethical Hacking
- Penetration Testing
- Cyber Operations
- Cybersecurity Frameworks
- Cyber Threat Intelligence
- Cybersecurity Awareness and Training Program
- Architecture and Networks
- Information, Systems and Applications
- Vulnerability Management
- Evolving Technologies
- Incident Response Management
- Digital Forensics
- Enterprise Cybersecurity Assessment
- Cybersecurity Corporate Wargames
- Cybersecurity Education
- Final Survey

The selected topics for training will certainly create and raise cybersecurity awareness in different aviation groups of stakeholders, one relevant aspect of continuously delivering cyber training will result in recognizing and reporting cyber events and incidents to the proper units or departments for early detection of cyberthreats and vulnerabilities. Furthermore, cybersecurity analysts can stop, reduce, and mitigate the impact caused by any cyberattack before experiencing extensive compromise if it were a full cyberattack [19].

4   Measuring the Model Effectiveness

Once all the training courses have been delivered, the results of CATRAM can be measured. Most of the assessment could be measured at the level of the end user by looking at how security behaviors have changed and how they are aligned with corporate cybersecurity compliance. In any ideal scenario, end users should be informed that the delivery of both announced and unannounced assessment exercises will be used to evaluate the efficacy and effectiveness of the awareness training.

The cybersecurity awareness model's suggested awareness areas and participating groups are presented in Table 2 for the purpose of evaluating compliance and its impact.

A model for evaluating the strength of security culture levels is presented by Hayden [14]. The organization's awareness and training program or a highly regulated industry could contribute to the security culture's strength: a poor security culture, with 80% of bad decisions; a strong security culture with 20% of bad decisions and a moderate security culture with 50% of bad decisions.

We measure compliance with the following criteria to determine cybersecurity awareness:

- Does your company offer a cybersecurity education program?
- Do you give your employees any kind of cybersecurity training?
- Is training provided on a consistent basis?
- Are employees adhering to the organization's security guidelines?
- Are you providing training on how to identify and respond to social engineering?
- Does your workforce understand how to identify and report security incidents?
- Are your employees capable of identifying and responding to any cybersecurity emergency?
- Does your company enforce confidentiality and privacy policies?
- Are your employees adhering to security measures to safeguard data and information?
- Is your awareness training targeted at end users, managers, IT personnel, C-suite executives, and the Board of Directors?
- Does your awareness training cover topics in multiple dimensions?
- Does your training outline cover user behavior, social behavior, and technical topics?

Table 2. CATRAM key identifiers and objectives

Metric Identifiers	Groups	Metric Objectives
Cybersecurity Awareness and Training Effectiveness	Aviation upper management	Identify training gap needs and approve training courses
Cyber policy- making assessment	Aviation upper management	Review, update and approve cybersecurity policies
Cyber monitoring, metric definition, and reporting	Aviation upper management	Approve required cybersecurity metrics
Awareness training completion	Aviation department managers	Verify that all staff completes training for every department
Communication flow	Aviation department managers	Enforce the distribution of awareness communication and proper training documentation
Cybersecurity incidents volume	ICT and Cybersecurity Personnel	Evaluate Help Desk monthly report
Cybersecurity skills	ICT and Cybersecurity Personnel	Evaluate new cybersecurity skills of technical staff that is consistent with the organization growth and operations

(*continued*)

Table 2. (*continued*)

Metric Identifiers	Groups	Metric Objectives
Infected digital devices	ICT and Cybersecurity Personnel	Identify percentage monthly
Phishing awareness and detection	Flight deck roles, cabin positions, aviation mechanics, administrative personnel, air traffic controllers and airport personnel	Identify phishing victims and users that are able to avoid phishing attacks
Social Media risks	Flight deck roles, cabin positions, aviation mechanics, administrative personnel, air traffic controllers and airport personnel	Evaluate percentage of user's time
Password management	Flight deck roles, cabin positions, aviation mechanics, administrative personnel, air traffic controllers and airport personnel	Assess user's behavior for password management

Using the criteria in Table 3, we determine the final cybersecurity maturity rating for the cybersecurity awareness training domain. Mapping the score to a particular maturity level is possible.

According to Gartner [12], leaders in risk management and security must provide employees with awareness training to focus on protecting their online security and the personal aspects of cybersecurity, as well as knowledge transfer of best practices for protecting intellectual property and data in corporate environments. Additionally, Gartner recommends a set of best practices for creating and maintaining a cybersecure workforce:

1. By cultivating a holistic cybersecure personal lifestyle that includes maintaining good hygiene for identity management and being aware of security
2. By committing to corporate training, workshops, and the use of appropriate tools, as well as by engaging in awareness and training behaviors
3. By building believe that confirms workers' internet-based conduct through convenient trial of cybersecure cleanliness

Table 3. Cybersecurity awareness training maturity rating

Rating	Description
Immature (I): 0–30	The organization does not have any plans to manage its cybersecurity. Controls for critical cybersecurity areas are non-existent or very weak. The organization has not implemented a comprehensive cybersecurity program nor an awareness training program
Developing (D): 31–70	The organization is starting to focus on cybersecurity matters. If technologies are in place, the organization needs to focus on key areas to protect cyber assets. Attention must be focused on staff, processes, controls, and regulations The Awareness Education domain is developing. The organization has a foundation model for cybersecurity awareness and additional efforts are required to develop a complete cybersecurity awareness program
Mature (M): 71–90	While the organization has a mature cybersecurity awareness environment. Improvements are required to the key areas that have been identified with weaknesses
Advanced (A): 91–100	The organization has excelled in implementing cybersecurity awareness training best practices. There is always room for improvement. Keep documentation up- to-date and continually review cybersecurity processes through audits

5 Auditing the Cyber Training Outcomes

The outcomes of the proposed cybersecurity awareness training could be audited using the documentation from the CyberSecurity Audit Model (CSAM 2.0). More specifically by referring to Domain 13: Awareness Education, Sub-domain 13.1: Awareness and Cybersecurity audit checklist CSAM 2.0 – Awareness Education (Domain 13). Table 4 provides the main evaluation controls (13.1.1-13.1.5).

Table 4. Control evaluation of the cybersecurity awareness education domain

Reference	Sub Area	Clause	Steps	Control Evaluation		Checklist
				Yes	No	
13.1	Awareness	13.1.1	Organization deploys a cybersecurity awareness program	☐	☐	CSAM 2.0 - Awareness

(continued)

Table 4. (*continued*)

Reference	Sub Area	Clause	Steps	Control Evaluation		Checklist
				Yes	No	
		13.1.2	The awareness training program is delivered on an annual basis	☐	☐	
		13.1.3	Employees are aware of the need of this kind of training program	☐	☐	
		13.1.4	The training program is designed for different staffing levels	☐	☐	
		13.1.5	Training material is constantly updated as new cyber threats emerge	☐	☐	

To verify training compliance, we propose to audit the sub-controls 1–12 that are mapped with the sub-domain clauses in Table 5.

Table 5. Control evaluation of the cybersecurity awareness education

Cybersecurity Audit Checklist: CSAM 2.0 – Awareness Education (Domain 13)					
Clause	No.	Checklist Questions	Findings		
			Compliant	Minor Nonconformity	Major Nonconformity
13.1.1	1	Does your organization have a cybersecurity awareness program?	☐	☐	☐
13.1.1	2	Do you provide some kind of cybersecurity training to your staff?	☐	☐	☐
13.1.2	3	Is training delivered on a regular recurring basis?	☐	☐	☐

(*continued*)

Table 5. (*continued*)

Cybersecurity Audit Checklist: CSAM 2.0 – Awareness Education (Domain 13)

Clause	No.	Checklist Questions	Findings		
			Compliant	Minor Nonconformity	Major Nonconformity
13.1.1	4	Do employees are following security policies of the organization?	☐	☐	☐
13.1.1	5	Are you delivering training to recognize and deal with social engineering?	☐	☐	☐
13.1.1	6	Do your staff know how to recognize and report a security incident?	☐	☐	☐
13.1.1	7	Are your personnel able to detect and respond to any cybersecurity emergency?	☐	☐	☐
13.1.1	8	Do you enforce privacy and confidentiality requirements in your organization?	☐	☐	☐
13.1.1	9	Are your employees following security procedures for data and information protection?	☐	☐	☐
13.1.4	10	Is your awareness training focused and delivered to specific audiences like end users, managers, IT, C-Suite executives, and Board of Directors?	☐	☐	☐
13.1.1	11	Is your awareness training covering multidimensional topics?	☐	☐	☐
13.1.1	12	Does your training outline cover technical, social and user behavior areas?	☐	☐	☐

Table 6 Allows us to calculate the overall maturity rating based on the categories from Table 3.

Table 6. Overall Cybersecurity Awareness Maturity Rating

Cybersecurity Awareness TRAining Model (CATRAM)			
Domain	**13-Awareness Education**		
Control Evaluation	**Ratings**		**Score**
	Immature	☐	
	Developing	☐	
	Mature	☐	
	Advanced	☐	

6   Conclusion

The main objective of this study was to recommend a new validation of two cybersecurity models in the aviation industry; the Cybersecurity Awareness TRAining Model (CATRAM) to address the challenges to deliver cybersecurity awareness training based on staff roles [17] and the CyberSecurity Audit Model (CSAM 2.0) to plan and audit the cybersecurity awareness training outcomes of this domain. These cybersecurity models including all its components were successfully validated by previous case studies performed in Canadian higher education institutions.

CATRAM can aid in the establishment or enhancement of a cybersecurity training program within any organization. The findings of the study demonstrate that offering cybersecurity training tailored to the specific roles and duties of employees can inspire them to not only maintain a high level of awareness in their work environment, but also in their personal lives. The drawbacks of our study include the fact that CATRAM was previously tested but some participants faced challenges such as time constraints, lack of interest in the topics, and low engagement. To improve the results of the model, future testing should involve more organizations. Although the case study results are relevant to future target organizations operating in the aeronautical or aviation industries, they also provide a foundation for future research to evaluate and broaden our cybersecurity models.

As the cyberthreat landscaping keeps constantly changing and evolving, it is crucial to understand the modus operandi of cybercriminals to select targets and launch all types of cyberattacks based on the multiple stages of criminal hacking. Organizations must implement a formal cybersecurity awareness training program as part of their high-level cybersecurity program to continuously deal with cyber events, cyber incidents, cyber threats, vulnerabilities and cyberattacks. Furthermore, cybersecurity awareness and training are in alignment with the latest cyber threats, vulnerabilities, Cyber Threat Intelligence (CTI), Cyber risk management and Incident Response (IR) management that could impact any organization.

References

1. Alotaibi, F., Furnell, S., Stengel, I., Papadaki, M.: A review of using gaming technologies for cyber-security awareness. International Journal of Information Security Res. **6**(2), 660–666 (2016). https://doi.org/10.20533/ijisr.2042.4639.2016.0076
2. Axelos: Cyber Resilience Best Practices. Resilia, Norwich (2017)
3. Beyer, M., et al.: Awareness is Only The First Step: A Framework for Progressive Engagement of Staff in Cyber Security. Hewlett Packard Enterprise (2015)
4. Beyer, R., Brummel, B.: Implementing Effective Cyber Security Training for End Users of Computer Networks. Society for Human Resource Management and Society for Industrial and Organizational Psychology (2015)
5. Cano, J.: La educación en seguridad de la información. Reflexión pedagógicas desde el pensamiento de sistemas. Memorias 3er Simposio Internacional en *"Temas y problemas de Investigación en Educación: Complejidad y Escenarios para la Paz"* (2016)
6. Cano, J.: Modelo de madurez de cultura organizacional de seguridad de la información. Una visión desde el pensamiento sistémico-cibernético. Actas de la XIV Reunión Española sobre Criptología y Seguridad de la Información, pp. 24–29 (2016)
7. Cyber, X.: 2019 Global ICS & IIoT Risk Report. A Data-Driven Analysis of Vulnerabilities in Our Industrial and Critical Infrastructure. CyberX Labs. (2019)
8. ESET.: ESET Cybersecurity Awareness Training. ESET Canada. https://www.eset.com/ca/cybertraining/. Accessed 02 Feb 2023
9. Fujitsu.: The Digital Transformation PACT. https://www.fujitsu.com. Accessed 2 Feb 2023
10. Gartner: Gartner Magic Quadrant for Security Awareness Computer- Based Training Vendors. Gartner, Inc. (2019)
11. Gartner: How to Build an Enterprise Security Awareness Program. Gartner, Inc. (2018)
12. Gartner: How to Secure the Human Link. Gartner, Inc. (2018)
13. Group, N.T.T.: Embedding Cybersecurity into Digital Transformation - A Journey Towards Business Resilience. NTT Security. https://www.nttsecurity.com. Accessed 2 Feb 2023
14. Hayden, L.: People-Centric Security: Transforming your Enterprise Security Culture. Mc Graw Hill, New York (2016)
15. International Organization for Standardization - ISO.: *ISO/IEC 27001:2022 – Information Technology – cybersecurity and privacy protection – Information Security Management Systems – Requirements*. ISO (2022)
16. International Organization for Standardization -ISO.: *ISO/IEC 27032:2012 – Information Technology – Security Techniques – Guidelines for Cybersecurity*. ISO (2012)
17. LeClair, J., Abraham, S., Shih, L.: An interdisciplinary approach to educating an effective cyber security worforce. In: Proceedings of Information Security Curriculum Development Conference, pp. 71–78. Academic Press, Kennesaw, GA (2013)
18. MediaPro: A Best Practices Guide for Comprehensive Employee Awareness Programs. MediaPro. (2017)
19. MITRE.: Cybersecurity Awareness & Training. The MITRE Corporation (2017)

20. Monahan, D.: Security Awareness Training: It's not just for Compliance- Research Report Summary. Enterprise Management Associates. EMA (2014)
21. National Institute of Standards and Technology – NIST.: Building an Information Technology Security Awareness and Training Program. NIST Special Publication 800–50 (2003)
22. National Institute of Standards and Technology – NIST.: An Introduction to Information Security. NIST Special Publication 800–12 Revision 1. (2017)
23. Nguyen, T.N., Sbityakov, L., Scoggins, S.: Intelligence-based Cybersecurity Awareness Training- an Exploratory Project. CoRR, abs/1812.04234 (2018)
24. PCI Security Standards Council - PCI DSS.: Best Practices for Implementing a Security Awareness Program. PCI DSS (2014)
25. Penderdast, T.: How to audit the human element and assess your organization's security risk. ISACA Journal **5**, 1–5 (2016)
26. Ponemon Institute.: Assessing the DNS Security Risk. Research report sponsored by Infoblox. Ponemon Institute LLC. (2018)
27. Sabillon, R., Cano, J.: Auditorías en Ciberseguridad: Un modelo de aplicación general para empresas y naciones. Edición Especial: Ciberseguridad y Ciberdefensa. Revista Ibérica de Sistemas e Tecnologias de Informaçao (RISTI). Portugal. **32**(06), 33–48. https://doi.org/10.17013/risti.32.33-48 (2019)
28. Sabillon, R., Serra-Ruiz, J., Cavaller, V., Cano, J.: A comprehensive cybersecurity audit model to improve cybersecurity assurance: the cybersecurity audit model (CSAM). Proceedings of Second International Conference on Information Systems and Computer Science (INCISCOS) (2017). https://doi.org/10.1109/INCISCOS.2017.20
29. Sabillon, R., Serra-Ruiz, J., Cavaller, V., Jeimy, J., Cano, M.: An effective cybersecurity training model to support an organizational awareness program: the cybersecurity awareness training model (CATRAM). a case study in Canada. Journal of Cases on Information Technology **21**(3), 26–39 (2019). https://doi.org/10.4018/JCIT.2019070102
30. Sabillon, R.: A practical model to perform comprehensive cybersecurity audits. Enfoque UTE **9**(1), 127137 (2018). https://doi.org/10.29019/enfoqueute.v9n1.214
31. Sabillon, R.: Audits in Cybersecurity, In I.Management Association (Eds.), Research Anthology on Business Aspects of Cybersecurity, pp. 1–18. IGI Global. https://doi.org/10.4018/978-1-6684-3698-1.ch001 (2022)
32. Sabillon, R.: Audits in Cybersecurity. Cyber Security Auditing, Assurance, and Awareness Through CSAM and CATRAM, IGI Global, pp.126–148. https://doi.org/10.4018/978-1-7998-4162-3.ch007 (2021)
33. Sabillon, R.: Cybersecurity Auditing, Assurance and Awareness Through CSAM and CATRAM: Emerging Research and Opportunities. IGI Global (2021). https://doi.org/10.4018/978-4162-3
34. Sabillon, R.: Scenario III: Data for a single cybersecurity domain audit (Awareness Education). Mendeley Data (2018). https://doi.org/10.17632/m4dk8n9sx7.2
35. Sabillon, R.: The cybersecurity audit model (CSAM), In I.Management Association (Eds.), Research Anthology on Business Aspects of Cybersecurity, pp.77–139 (2022). IGI Global. https://doi.org/10.4018/978-1-6684-3698-1.ch005
36. Sabillon, R.: The cybersecurity audit model (CSAM). Cyber Security Auditing, Assurance, and Awareness Through CSAM and CATRAM, IGI Global, pp.149–232 (2021). https://doi.org/10.4018/978-1-7998-4162-3.ch008
37. Sabillon, R.: The cybersecurity awareness training model (CATRAM). Cyber Security Auditing, Assurance, and Awareness Through CSAM and CATRAM, IGI Global, pp.233–257 (2021). https://doi.org/10.4018/978-1-7998-4162-3.ch009
38. SANS Institute.: 2017 Security Awareness Report: It's time to communicate.
39. SANS Security Awareness. https://securingthehuman.sans.org/media/resources/STH-SecurityAwarenessReport-2017.pdf. Accessed 2 Feb 2023

40. SANS Security Awareness : 2022 Security Awareness Report. SANS Institute (2022)
41. Ward, M.: Security Awareness and Training: Solving the Unintentional Insider Threat. Cyber Safe Worforce LLC (2016)
42. Whitman, M.E., Mattord, H.J.: Management of Information Security, 6th edn. Cengage Learning, Inc., Boston, MA (2021)
43. Yin, R.K.: Case Study Research and Applications, 6th edn. Sage Publications, Thousand Oaks, CA (2018)

Demystifying the Privacy-Personalization Paradox: The Mediating Role of Online Trust in Websites/Apps with Personalized Ads and Attitude Towards Online Personalized Advertising

Guohua Wu[✉] [iD] and Lei Xu

California State University Fullerton, Fullerton, CA 92831, USA
mwu@fullerton.edu

Abstract. This paper demystifies the privacy-personalization paradox by testing a conceptual model in which the mediating role of online trust in websites/apps with personalized ads and attitude towards online personalized advertising is proposed. Specifically, it is hypothesized that perceived personalization has a direct positive effect on attitude towards online personalized advertising, online trust in websites/apps with personalized ads, and a direct positive effect on privacy concerns. It is also proposed that perceived personalization mitigates its effect on privacy concerns through the mediating influence of online trust in websites/apps with personalized ads and attitude towards online personalized advertising because both attitudes toward online personalized advertising and online trust in website/apps with personalized ads are expected to have a direct negative effect on privacy concerns. A convenience sample of 275 undergraduate students from a large USA southwestern university was collected using Qualtrics. Results from a structural equation model analysis using SPSS AMOS 28 support the hypothesized mediating role of online trust in personalized ads and attitude towards personalized advertising. Theoretical and practical implications of the results are discussed.

Keywords: perceived personalization · privacy concerns · online trust in personalized ads · attitude towards personalized advertising

1   Introduction

The privacy-personalization paradox keeps attracting research attention from across disciplines such as communication, information science, advertising, and marketing [3, 12, 13]. However, empirical research on this research stream has also generated inconsistent findings. Some find that personalization has no effect on privacy concerns. For example, Chellappa and Sin (2005) show that value for personalization and concern for privacy are orthogonal. That is, the two variables are independent from each other in consumers' tradeoff mechanism. Also, in their research on the effects of personalization and privacy assurance on consumers' response to travel web sites, Lee and Cranage

© The Author(s), under exclusive license to Springer Nature Switzerland AG 2023
H. Degen et al. (Eds.): HCII 2023, LNCS 14059, pp. 480–491, 2023.
https://doi.org/10.1007/978-3-031-48057-7_30

(2011) reveal that personalization has no effect on privacy concerns and intention to disclose personal information. Others show that a higher level of personalization tends to worsen privacy concerns, largely confirming an intuitive expectation that a higher level of personalization triggers consumers' privacy concern or anxiety about misuse or abuse of their personal information. Most empirical studies in this line appear to fall within this category [e.g., 3, 13, 29]. Still others find that perceived personalization has an alleviating effect on privacy concerns, which is counterintuitive [e.g., 32].

Given such mixed findings on this research stream, we propose a conceptual model that incorporates the mediating role of two important variables (online trust in websites/apps with personalized ads and attitude toward online personalized advertising) to help demystify the privacy-personalization paradox.

2 Conceptual Background and Hypothesis Development

Drawing on literatures on personalization, attitude toward advertising in general, online trust, and privacy concerns, we develop a conceptual model shown in Fig. 1. It has four variables: (1) perceived personalization; (2) privacy concerns; (3) attitude toward online personalized advertising; and (4) online trust in website/app with personalized ads. We will first introduce each of the four variables and then explain hypothesized relationships among them by providing theoretical or empirical rationales.

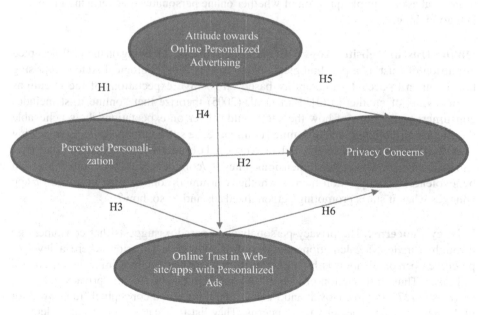

Fig. 1. .

2.1   Four Variables in the Model

Perceived Personalization. Wu (2006) defines perceived personalization as the extent to which a consumer perceives how his or her communicative counterpart's responses are appropriate or personally relevant to his or her communicative behaviors. When a consumer sees a personalized ad on a website/app, he or she evaluate how appropriate or personally relevant it is to her his or her needs, wants, tastes, preferences, or situation based on his or her own demographic, psychographic, geographic or lifestyle profile. Personalization is sometimes referred to as "customization" [e.g., 28], which reflects an advertiser's efforts to tailor its message or offerings in anticipation of a viewer's profile.

Attitude towards Online Personalized Advertising. Attitude toward advertising in general consists of two components: (1) attitude toward advertising as an "institution" and (2) attitude toward an "instrument" (i.e., ads in media) [19, 24]. It is very important to study attitude toward advertising in general in a society [26] because advertising is indispensable to a normal functioning capitalism [22]. When the internet advertising was first born in the late 1990s, advertising scholars began to research public attitudes towards internet advertising [25]. In this age of social media, digital advertising dominance, and relentless pursuit of personalized advertising, it becomes increasingly important to research attitude toward online personalized advertising, especially in the context of consumers' elevated privacy concerns. Attitude towards online personalized advertising in general asks a simple question of whether online personalized advertising in general is a good thing.

Online Trust in Websites/Apps with Personalized Ads. Drawing on the well-accepted definition of trust as a psychological state "Trust is a psychological state comprising the intention to accept vulnerability based on positive expectations of the intentions or behaviors of another" [23], Bart et al. (2005) theorize that "online trust includes consumers perceptions of how the site would deliver on expectations, how believable the site's information is, and how much confidence the site commands." After reviewing over one decade of trust research, Urban, Amyx and Lorenzon (2009) conclude that "trust can be distilled down to three dimensions: integrity/confidence, ability/competence, and benevolence." The question then is whether consumers' online trust in a web or app changes when it starts promoting personalized ads and, if so, how?

Privacy Concerns. The privacy-personalization paradox suggests that consumers go through a trade-off calculation when confronted with a situation where a level of perceived personalization is high enough to trigger their internal information control impulses. Thus, information privacy in this paper fits nicely under "privacy calculus" lable as in [27]. Phelps, Novak and Ferrell (2000) present a conceptual framework for understanding consumer privacy concerns. They list four categories of antecedents to privacy concerns: (1) type of personal information collected; (2) amount of information control offered; (3) potential consequences and benefits; and (4) consumer characteristics. Their two major components of privacy concerns are: (1) beliefs regarding marketers' information practices and (2) ways companies use personal information.

Malhortra, Kim and Agarwal (2004) develop a scale for measuring internet information privacy concerns that consists of three components: (1) information collection; (2) information control; and (3) awareness of privacy practices.

2.2 Hypothesis Development

Perceived Personalization and Attitude towards Online Personalized Advertising. As mentioned earlier in the paper, one of key dimensions of perceived personalization is personal relevance. Online ad avoidance is well documented in research and practice, and personal relevant ads give consumers some tangible benefits of their cognitive energy and time. They may find online personalized ads useful, entertaining, or delightful. Previous research indicates that perceived personalization decreases ad avoidance [4] and that perceived personalization improves responses to Facebook via perceived relevance [8]. This suggests that consumers' responses to specific personalized ads are more favorable than expected. As such, consumers attitudes toward online personalized advertising in general may also more favorable than their attitudes toward offline non-personalized advertising. Thus, it is posited that:

H1: Perceived personalization is positively related to attitude towards online personalized advertising.

Perceived Personalization and Privacy Concerns. The other key dimension of perceived personalization is appropriateness. Although a relatively high level of personal relevance is desirable to consumers, yet consumers' suspicion, doubts, or "feelings of vulnerability" [1] would be aroused when they perceive such a high level of personal relevance as inappropriate. They might second-guess how a marketer knows so much about them. In a real one-to-one conversation, real human beings with normal emotional intelligence are usually capable of sizing up its counterpart's nonverbal cues, facial expressions, body language or voice inflection to detect any inappropriate responses that might exceed the boundary of privacy invasion. Despite advancement in big data analytics and AI, websites/apps equipped with personalization technologies still lack that human touch. Such dynamics might offer insights into mixed findings in the literature because the relationship between perceived personalization and privacy concerns may not be more complex than previously thought. Too high or too low levels of personal relevance will likely trigger privacy concerns, but an optimal level may not do so. However, it's very hard to reach such an optimal level in reality. Thus, it is postulated that:

H2: Overall perceived personalization is positively related to privacy concerns.

Perceived Personalization and Online Trust in websites/apps with Personalized Ads. When consumers encounter personalized ads online, they tend to respond more positively than their offline counterparts because they are usually personally relevant.

Do those positive responses translate into trust in the website or app that feature the ad? Previous research finds a positive relationship between perceived personalization and trust. Wu, Hu, and Wu (2010) find that perceived personalization has a positive effect on initial online trust in an unknown e-vendor. Komiac and Benbasat (2006) and Zhang and Curley (2017) find perceived personalization positively affect trust in recommendation agents. Alimamy and Gnoth (2022) also find perceived personalization has a positive effect on trust in Ikea website and Ikea Augmented Reality Application. Therefore, it is postulated that:

H3: Perceived personalization is positively related to online trust in websites/apps with personalized ads.

Attitude towards Online Personalized Advertising and Online Trust in Websites/apps with Personalized Ads. Although global attitude toward advertising is shaped by consumers' attitude toward advertising as an institution and an instrument [19], it can be reasonably hypothesized that global attitude toward advertising can also influence attitude toward the ad. That is, global attitude exerts a framing or halo effect. For example, someone who likes advertising in general will be more favorably predisposed to ad exposure. Research provides some evidence for it. Mehta (2000) finds that advertising attitude in general influences print advertisement performance, suggesting more favorable attitudes toward advertising in general allows consumers to place more personal confidence in print ads. Extending this line of thinking to online personalized advertising and ads, therefore, it is hypothesized that:

H4: Attitude toward online personalized advertising is positively related to online trust in websites/apps with personalized ads.

Attitude towards Online Personalized Advertising and Privacy Concerns. Someone who holds a more favorable attitude towards online personalized advertising are more likely to cast a positive light upon his or her exposure to personalized ads and are less skeptical or suspicious of a highly targeted ad's underlying motives than someone with a less favorable one. Such framing or haloing effect might loosen consumers' surveillance tendency when privacy concerns become salient. This line of reasoning leads us to hypothesize that:

H5: Attitude towards online personalized advertising is negatively related to privacy concerns.

Online Trust in Websites/apps with Personalized Ads and Privacy Concerns. Experimental results [6] demonstrate that participants perceive personalized ads through a combination of high depth and narrow breadth of personalization more useful without triggering elevated reactance or privacy concerns only when they are on more trusted retailer sites and that participants' privacy concerns are elicited when they are on less trusted retailer sites. These results suggest that trust in a retailer lessens privacy concerns. Thus, it is hypothesized that:

H6: Online trust in websites/apps with personalized ads is negatively correlated with privacy concerns.

3 Method

3.1 Procedures

Undergraduate students from a large US southwestern university participated in this research in exchange for extra credit. A Qualtrics-enabled survey URL was sent to students via email. They were encouraged to forward the URL to their social networks. 275 usable responses were gathered to be included for final data analysis.

3.2 Measurement Scales

Prior research scales were adapted to measure the four variables in the conceptual model were adapted from previous ones. Attitude toward online personalized advertising were derived from Tan and Chia (2007) and Shavitt et al. (1998). Perceived personalization was measured by a four-item scale derived from Srinivasan, Anderson and Ponnavolu (2002). Privacy concerns was measured with a five-item scale used by Dolnicar and Jordaan (2007). Online trust in websites/apps was measured by Lankton and McKnight (2011).

4 Results

4.1 Participants Profile

Among 275 respondents, 256 reported their age, gender, ethnicity, and job status, The age mean is 24.2 and median is 22. Because undergraduate students were encouraged to forward the online survey URl, non-undergraduate student responses were included. For the gender question, 39.1% are males, 59.4% are females, and 1.6% prefer not to say. With regard to ethnicity, 34.4% are Hispanic/Latino, 28.1% White, 27.0% Asian or Pacific Islander, 7.8% other. In terms of job status, 20.7% have a full-time job, 38.3% one part-time job, 8.6% more than one part-time job, and 32.4% don't have a job.

4.2 Measurement Model Assessment

We calculated the composite reliability (CR) and average variance extracted (AVE) for each variable using the formulas proposed by Hair et al. (1998). Table 1 shows that they demonstrate adequate reliability, as their composite reliability scores are higher than .70 (Hair et al., 1998). Meanwhile, they show convergent validity because each variable's AVE (average extracted variance) exceeds the 0.5 benchmark for convergent validity [11]. Furthermore, two of the four constructs have demonstrated discriminant validity, because the square root of the average variance extracted for each variable (perceived personalization .75; privacy concerns .78; attitude towards online personalized advertising .86; and online trust in websites/apps with personalized ads .86) is greater than the correlations between it and other variables [11].

Table 1. Correlations Matrix of Variables

4.1 Constructs	AVE	CR	1	2	3	4
1. Personalization	.56	.83	1			
2. Privacy	.60	.85	.36	1		
3. Attitude	.74	.85	.40	−.29	1	
4. Trust	.78	.85	.37	−.41	.47	1

4.3 Structural Equation Modeling

We used IBM SPSS to calculate the Cronbach's alphas for the four variables in the model
(.82 for perceived personalization; .90 for privacy concerns; .85 for attitude toward
personalized advertising; .86 for online trust in personalized ads). All are above .70
cutoff point [20], indicating the scales are reliable. We used IBM SPSSS AMOS 28 was
to conduct our structural equation modeling. Chi-square = 385, df = 196, p < .001. The
fit indices (CMIN/DF = 2.0; NFI = .91; IFI = .95, TLI = .95, CFI = .95; RMSEA =
.059) are acceptable (Hair et al., 1998). The model fit the data well (Table 2).

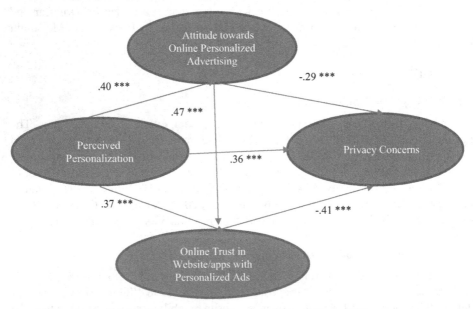

Fig. 2. Results of SEM Analysis. Note: *** p < .001

Figure 2 shows that all path coefficients are significant at p < .001. Thus, all hypotheses are supported. Our results reveal that perceived personalization is positively related
to privacy concerns, attitude toward personalized advertising, online trust in personalized ads, that attitude toward personalized advertising is negatively privacy concerns,
and that online trust in personalized ads is negatively related to privacy concerns. The

Table 2. Measurement Items Used in the SEM Analysis

Construct	Measurement Item	Loading
Attitude toward Online personalized Advertising	1. Overall, I consider online personalized advertising is a good thing	.88
	2. Overall, I like online personalized advertising	.83
Perceived Personalized	1. Online personalized advertising makes purchase recommendations match my needs	.76
	2. Overall, online personalized advertising that I have received is tailored to my situation	.79
	3. Online personalized advertising makes me feel that I am a unique customer	.62
	4. I believe that online personalized advertising is customized to my needs	.79
Competence component for Online Trust	1 I believe websites/apps that promote personalized ads are competent	.72
	2. I believe websites/apps that promote personalized ads perform their role of facilitating online searching/online shopping/social networking very well	.81
	3. I believe websites/apps that promote personalized ads are proficient	.88
Integrity component for Online Trust	1. I believe websites/apps that promote personalized ads keep are truthful in its dealings with me	.81
	2. I believe websites/apps that promote personalized ads are honest	.88
	3. I believe websites/apps that promote personalized ads keep their commitments	.89
	4. I believe websites/apps that promote personalized ads are sincere and genuine	.89
Benevolence component for Online Trust	1. I believe websites/apps that promote personalized ads act in my best interest	.85
	2. Do its best to help me if I need help	.77

(continued)

Table 2. (*continued*)

Construct	Measurement Item	Loading
	3. Are interested in my wellbeing, not just its own	.83
Privacy Concerns	1. When I receive online personalized advertising, I feel uncomfortable when information is shared without my permission	.72
	2. When I receive online personalized advertising, I am concerned about misuse of personal information	.85
	3. When I receive online personalized advertising, it bothers me to receive too much advertising material of interest	.68
	4. When I receive online personalized advertising, I am worried that information may not be safe while stored	.90
	5. When I receive online personalized advertising, I believe personal information is often misused	.83
	6. When I receive online personalized advertising, I think companies share information without permission	.67

Note: All loadings are significant at $p < .001$

partial mediating role of attitude toward personalized advertising and online trust in personalized ads is established.

5   Discussion, Implications, Limitations and Future Research

5.1   Discussion

The privacy-personalization paradox is a fascinating and important topic. It is fascinating because any paradox usually generates a strong interest and its mixed findings have certainly contributed its research attraction. Our research provides us a new perspective through which such inconsistent findings may not be so surprising. It finds empirical evidence to support our notion of the partial mediation of two variables in the underlying dynamics of the paradox of privacy-personalization. Specifically, perceived personalization exerts dual influences on privacy concerns: one is direct and positive; the other is indirect and negative. Perceived personalization triggers privacy concerns directly, but it also mitigates consumers' privacy concerns indirectly via its influence on attitude toward online personalized advertising and online trust in websites/apps with personalized ads.

The mediating variable of attitude toward online personalized advertising demonstrates how global attitude toward advertising is important in the digital advertising domain because offline advertising literature has provided ample evidence for the usefulness of improving attitude toward advertising in general.

Regarding the mediating variable of online trust in websites/apps with personalized ads, it reemphasizes the vast importance of enhancing trust-building efforts by websites/apps. For well-known sites or apps such as Facebook.com, Amazon.com, Twitter.com, reputation management and crisis management would be critical in maintaining consumers' trust. On the other hand, small or medium-sized unknown websites/apps could benefit from enhancing its trust by visitors through displaying web assurance seals to increase security, integrity and privacy [34].

5.2 Implications

Our research has both theoretical and practical implications. Theoretically, the dual influence of perceived personalization on privacy concerns opens a new path of identifying mediating variables in improving our understanding of the paradox. Perhaps there might be other mediating variables waiting to be discovered. Practically, marketers can rest assured that personalization technologies in the age of social media, big data and artificial intelligence will help reap enormous benefits without having to become overly concerned about consumers' privacy concerns because perceived personalization itself has a lessening mechanism to cope with. Nevertheless, more efforts must be made by the digital advertising industry to promote the value of online personalized advertising to consumers and more endeavors should be made by online marketers to keep enhancing consumers' trust in their websites/apps.

5.3 Limitations and Future Research

Like any other research using convenience student samples, our research suffers from its lack of generalization to different populations. In addition, our sample size of 275 is sufficient for a SEM analysis, but a larger sample may warrant in future research. Future research could use non-student representative sample to replicate the research to enhance its generalizability. Perhaps more mediating variables could be identified to further our understanding of the privacy-personalization paradox.

6   Conclusion

We develop a conceptual model to test the hypothesis that both attitude towards online personalized advertising and online trust in websites/apps with personalized ads mediate the effect of perceived personalization on privacy concerns. The four variables in the model are perceived personalization, attitude toward online personalized advertising, online trust in websites/apps with personalized ads, and privacy concerns. Our research finds empirical evidence to support this hypothesis. The mediating role of these two variables helps contribute our understanding of how perceived personalization has a dual influence on privacy concerns with a direct positive effect and an indirect negative effect.

References

1. Aguirre, E., Mahr, D., Grewal, D., de Ruyter, K., Wetzels, M.: Unraveling the personalization paradox: The effect of information collection and trust-building strategies on online advertising effectiveness. J. Retailing **91**(1) (2015)
2. Alimanmy, S., Gnoth, J.: I want it my way! The effect of perceptions of personalization through augmented reality and online shopping on customer intentions to co-create value. Comput. Hum. Behav. **128**, 1–16 (2021)
3. Awad, N.F., Krishnan, M.S.: The personalization privacy paradox: an empirical evaluation of information transparency and the willingness to be profiled online for personalization. MIS Q. **30**(1), 13–28 (2006)
4. Baek, T.H., Morimoto, M.: Stay away from me: examining the determinants of consumer avoidance of personalized advertising. J. Advert. **41**(1), 59–76 (2012)
5. Bart, Y., Shankar, V., Sultan, F., Urban, G.L.: Are the drivers and role of online trust the same for all web sites and consumers? a large-scale exploratory empirical study. J. Mark. **69**(4), 133–152 (2005)
6. Bleier, A., Eisenbeiss, M.: The importance of trust for personalized online advertising. J. Retail. **91**(3), 390–409 (2015)
7. Chellappa, R.K., Sin, R.G.: Personalization versus privacy: an empirical examination of the online consumer's dilemma'. Inf. Technol. Manage. **6**, 81–202 (2005)
8. De Feyzer, F., Dens, N., De Pelsmacker, P.: How and when personalized advertising leads to brand attitude, click and WOM intention. J. Advert. **51**(1), 39–56 (2022)
9. Dolnicar, S., Jordaan, Y.: A market-oriented approach to responsibly managing information privacy concerns in direct marketing. J. Advert. **36**(2), 123–149 (2007)
10. Hair, J.F., Anderson, R.E., Tatham, R.L., Black, W.C.: Multivariate Data Analysis, 4th edn. Prentice Hall, Upper Saddle River, NJ (1998)
11. Fornell, C., Larcker, D.: Evaluating structural equation models with unobservable variable and measurement error. J. Mark. Res. **18**(1), 39–50 (1981)
12. Hayes, J., Brinson, N.H., Bott, G.J., Moeller, C.M.: The influence of consumer-brand relationship on the personalized advertising privacy calculus in social. Media **55**, 16–30 (2021)
13. Kaaniche, N., Laurent, M., Belguith, S.: Privacy enhancing technologies for solving the privacy-personalization paradox: taxonomy and survey. J. Network and Computer Application (2020)
14. Komiak, S.Y.X., Benbasat, I.: The effects of personalization on trust and adoption of recommendation agents. MIS Q. **40**(4), 941–960 (2006)
15. Lankton, N.K., McKnight, D.H.: What does it mean to trust Facebook? Technology and interpersonal trust beliefs. The DATA BASE for Advances in Information Systems **42**(2), 32–54 (2011)
16. Lee, C.H., Cranage, D.A.: Personalization Privacy Paradox: The Effects of Personalization and Privacy Assurance on Customer Responses to Travel Web Sites **32**, 987-994 (2011)
17. Malhotra, N.K., Kim, S.S., Agarwal, J.: Internet users' Information privacy concerns (IUIPC): the construct, the scale and a causal model. Inf. Syst. Res. **15**, 336–355 (2004)
18. Mehta, A.: Advertising attitudes and advertising effectiveness. J. Advert. Res. **40**(3), 67–72 (2000)
19. Muehling, D.D.: An investigation of factors underlying attitude toward advertising in general. J. Advert. **16**(1), 32–40 (1987)
20. Nunnally, J.C.: Psychometric Theory, 2nd edn. McGraw-Hill, New York (1978)
21. Phelps, J., Glen, N., Ferrell, E.: Privacy concerns and consumer willingness to provide personal information'. J. Public Policy Mark. **19**(1), 27–41 (2000)

22. Rotzoll, K.B., Haefner, J.E., Hall. S.R.: Advertising in Contemporary Society: Perspectives Toward Understanding, 3rd ed. University of Illinois Press (1996)
23. Rousseau, D.M., Sitkin, S.B., Burt, R.S., Camerer, C.: Not so different after all: a cross-discipline view of trust. Acad. Manag. Rev. 23(3), 393–404 (1998)
24. Sandage, C.H., Leckenby J.D.: Student attitudes toward advertising: institution vs. instrument. J. Advertising 9(2), 29–44 (1980)
25. Schlosser, A.E., Shavitt, S., Kanfer, A.: Survey of internet users' attitudes toward internet advertising. J. Interact. Mark. 13(3), 34–54 (1999)
26. Shavitt, S., Lowrey, P., Haefner, J.: Public attitudes toward advertising: more favorable than you might think. J. Advertising Research 7–22 (1998)
27. Smith, H.J., Dinev, T., Xu, H.: Information privacy research: an interdisciplinary review. MIS Q. 35(4), 989–1015 (2011)
28. Srinivasana, S.S., Andersona, R., Ponnavolub, K.: Customer loyalty in e-commerce: an exploration of its antecedents and consequences. J. Retail. 78, 41–50 (2002)
29. Sutanto, J., Palme, E., Tan, C., Phang, C.W.: Addressing the personalization-privacy paradox: an empirical assessment from a field experiment on smartphone users. MIS Q. 37(4), 1141–1164 (2013)
30. Urban, G.L., Amyx, C., Lorenzon, A.: Online trust: State of the art, new frontiers, and research potential. J. Interact. Mark. 23(2), 170–190 (2009)
31. Tan, S.J., Chia, L.: Are we measuring the same attitude? understanding media effects on attitude towards advertising. Mark. Theory 7(4), 353–377 (2007)
32. Wang, C., Wu, G.: Chinese Millennials' Attitude Toward Online Personalized Advertising. China International Marketing Conference, Xi'an, China (2015)
33. Wu, G.: Conceptualizing and measuring the perceived interactivity of websites. J. Current Issues and Research in Advertising 28(1), 87–104 (2006)
34. Wu, G., Hu, X., Wu, Y.: Effects of Perceived Interactivity, Perceived Web Assurance and Disposition to Trust on Initial Online Trust 16, 1–26 (2010)
35. Zhang, J., Curley, S.P.: Exploring explanation effects on consumers' trust in online recommendation agents. International J. Human-Computer Interaction 34(5), 421–432 (2018)

Human-Computer Interaction in the Emerging Metaverse: Social Implications and Design Principles for the Sustainable Metaverse

Arisa Yasuda[✉]

School of Computing, Australian National University, Canberra, Australia
arisa.yasuda@anu.edu.au

Abstract. The emergence of the metaverse transforms the way humans interact with computers; the metaverse brings about a new form of human-computer interaction that is more immersive, intuitive, and seamless. In the present paper we thus aim to elucidate the role of human-computer interactions in the age of the metaverse. New forms of human-computer interaction via the metaverse are beneficial for humans in many ways; at the same time, however, there are new types of social issues that are emerging as the metaverse develops and that need to be taken seriously. Specifically, we focus upon issues such as privacy, surveillance capitalism, cyber-syndromes, and amplifications of social problems, and discuss what regulations would be appropriate in order to balance the adequate development of the metaverse with the safety and security of it that is required for social good, in particular for sustainable development goals. We finally propose ethical design principles for the sustainable metaverse in order to address the aforementioned and other social issues.

Keywords: Metaverse · Sustainability · AI Ethics

1 Introduction: Technological Versus Social Facets of the Metaverse

The history of computer innovation shows that the emergence of new technologies affects human lifestyles and fundamentally transforms the way humans interact with computers. One of such technologies in society today (or in the near future) is the metaverse. The concept of the metaverse, from a historical point of view, was introduced in 1992 in Neal Stephenson's science fiction novel *Snow Crash* [1] and attracted attention from some people such as educators; however, it has not attracted so much public attention as it does today [2]. When Facebook changed its name to Meta in 2021 and declared a new era of social interactions through the metaverse, it gained substantial public attention and was popularised broadly [3].

© The Author(s), under exclusive license to Springer Nature Switzerland AG 2023
H. Degen et al. (Eds.): HCII 2023, LNCS 14059, pp. 492–504, 2023.
https://doi.org/10.1007/978-3-031-48057-7_31

There are different ways to define the metaverse from different angles. According to Mystakidis [4], the metaverse is based on the integration of technologies such as Virtual Reality (VR) and Augmented Reality (AR) that enable multi-sensory interactions between virtual environments, digital objects, and humans. In contrast to this technology-focused view, Park [5] presents a more social perspective on the metaverse, arguing that the essence of the metaverse should be understood as service with social meaning and sustainable content rather than as applications of such Extended Reality (XR) technologies as usually conceived. The mataverse has also been recognised as a platform for the next generation of social connection and networking [6]. The metaverse in a mature form is expected to combine a variety of technologies, such as XR, blockchain, AI, and cloud computing, in an integrative manner, thus yielding the new forms of human-computer interactions that are more immersive, intuitive, and seamless [7].

In this paper we thus shed light on human-computer interactions in the emerging age of the metaverse. New forms of human-computer interactions enabled by the metaverse are beneficial for humans in many ways; at the same time, however, there are new types of social issues that are emerging as the metaverse develops and that need to be taken seriously. Specifically we focus upon issues such as privacy, metaverse addiction, and surveillance capitalism, and discuss what regulations would be appropriate in order to balance the adequate development of the metaverse with the safety and security that is required for social good and sustainable development goals. We finally propose ethical design principles for the sustainable metaverse to address the aforementioned and other social issues.

The rest of the paper is organised as follows. In Sect. 2, we analyse human-computer interactions in the metaverse from two points of view (namely, Access/Display and Perception/Input). In Sect. 3, we discuss social issues on the metaverse, such as security and privacy, surveillance capitalism, cyber-syndromes, and amplifications of social problems. In Sect. 4, we propose and discuss ethical design principles for the sustainable metaverse. We conclude the paper in Sect. 5.

2 Analyzing Human-Computer Interaction on the Metaverse from Two Points of View: Access/Display and Perception/Input

We can analyze human-computer interaction on the metaverse through the two points of view of "access and display" and "perception and input" [8] in the following manner.

2.1 Access and Display

The first point of view is concerned with those devices and technologies that enable access and display for a more realistic virtual world [9]. Specifically, access and display on the metaverse are supported by Extended Reality (XR) technologies, and XR encompasses Augmented Reality (AR), Virtual Reality (VR), and Mixed Reality (MR). XR is implemented through those devices, such as smart glasses, that enable access and display for extended realities [7,9]. Each of AR, VR, and MR has its distinct characteristics while all of them share the common goal of improving user experience [10,11].

AR creates interactive experiences via the integration of digital information with the real world [12,13]. For example, AR allows us to interact with virtual objects within the real world and receive augmented information (e.g., visual effects). Put differently, we receive augmented information from the virtual world while the base of communication is in the physical space. In contrast to AR, VR immerses users in a fully simulated digital environment separated from the physical world [10], allowing user experience with increased immersion, realism, and embodiment through specialised devices such as head mount display to the extent that users themselves are elements of the metaverse.

MR integrates digital content into the user's physical environment, thus creating a very realistic augmented world [10,14]; MR may be considered synonymous with AR [15]. MR, from another perspective, merges both AR and VR in that it is primarily based upon the real world but at the same time integrated with the virtual world [16]. MR enhances user experience by providing a more immersive way to interact with virtual content in the real world. Hardware to implement a seamless and natural metaverse is still under development; however, it is predicted by a group of experts [17] that such a metaverse will come to exist by 2040 at the latest.

2.2 Perception and Input

The second point of view is concerned with the metaverse as informationalising both environments and perceptions [8]. Both environments and perceptions are represented as digital information in the metaverse, which is easy to be monitored and recorded on a real-time basis. Data thus collected is subsequently analyzed and utilized to optimize the user experience. New types of data such as on human body movement are already becoming available as wearable devices and tracking technologies develop. Everything in the metaverse can be regarded as information. The richer human-computer interaction becomes, the more data get collected through the interaction.

Information that can be collected in the metaverse includes biometric information on individuals such as fingerprints, facial features, and voice patterns, which can be used to improve user experience, personalise interactions, and provide a more immersive and seamless virtual environment.

In the metaverse, biometric identifiers such as face and fingerprint scans allow users to authenticate their identities and can be used to create personalised metaverse profiles and virtual spaces. Furthermore, biometric identifiers can contribute to creating more immersive interactions in the metaverse. For example, facial expressions and body movements captured by biometric sensors can be translated into the behaviors and emotions of avatars, enabling more realistic and natural communication in virtual environments.

3 Social Implications of the Metaverse

Novel technologies often bring both benefits and concerns. In the metaverse in particular, not only the issues that have been commonly discussed in AI ethics, but also essentially new issues may arise as well as amplifications of existing ones.

3.1 Security and Privacy

The metaverse give rise to data privacy and security risk issues as does the Internet [18]. The collection and use of personal data by companies operating the metaverse may lead to an ever greater impact on personal privacy and security.

The metaverse requires a significant amount of personal information to build a personalised and immersive world for users [19]. In particular, all kinds of information, including human five senses information, can in principle be acquired, and the personal identification and use of the information may accelerate accordingly. Compared with pre-metaverse information technologies, more sensitive and deeper level information can be obtained in the mature metaverese.

While companies have made efforts to build well-maintained platforms and protect users' data, the theft or leakage of users' personal information have continued to occur. Stolen data can be sold to third parties or misused for fraud. For example, voices are increasingly being stolen and used for fraud purposes. AI enables scam groups to simulate people's voices based on a small amount of their voice samples. According to Washington Post [20], impostor scams were the second most popular racket in America in 2022 and 5,100 of those incidents happened over phones. Since the metaverse is a treasure trove of data from which sensitive personal information can be obtained, including the voice information, it is necessary to consider the possibility that it will be used for criminal purposes in the future.

3.2 Surveillance Capitalism

Surveillance capitalism refers to a socioeconomic system that pursues profit by collecting and monitoring personal data [21]. The concept involves tracking individuals' online activities and behaviors, where personal data is treated as a commodity and companies collect it and use it for marketing and advertising purposes [22]. Surveillance capitalism has been discussed in the context of AI ethics; we argue that the metaverse would reinforce and accelerate surveillance capitalism in an unprecedented manner.

It is because of the immersive and addictive nature of the metaverse; users are expected to spend a significant amount of time there, which accordingly will increase the total amount of information collected. Most of our information, from sight, hearing, speech, body movements, and perhaps even the content of our thoughts, can in principle be acquired in the ultimate form of the metaverse (even if there are still limitations on the types of data that the current metaverse can collect).

Since users' digital activities and behaviors are continuously monitored in the metaverse, they can be collected and analyzed to enable targeted advertising, personalised content, and so fourth, and consumers may be affected by commercial manipulation. There are also issues regarding terms of service, especially on how to use data. Taking advantage of the fact that customers do not read the terms and conditions in detail, which may be called a meaningless agreement, data may be obtained under various conditions and used to pursue further profit and power, such as buying and selling to third-party organizations.

Surveillance capitalism may also have implications for the free decision-making of the user. Individual decisions and choices can be influenced by marketing and advertising manipulation as data collection and analysis enable prediction of individual behavior and preference (and individually tailored information and content are presented). For instance, filter bubbles and other forms of selection may be formed, narrowing users' choices or minds themselves.

Gina Neff interviewed in [17] warns that the trend of surveillance capitalism would limit the ability of regulators and the state to protect individuals and concentrate power in the hands of corporations. The manipulation of customer behavior has been discussed in the AI ethics context as well. According to Zuboff [23], companies seek to maximise profits and achieve market dominance by predicting and manipulating customer behavior.

Why is the trend of organizations collecting and retaining excessive amounts of personal data accelerating? According to Doctorow [24], there are three reasons for this. Firstly, companies must use a variety of methods to increase sales because of consumers' growing ability to resist. Competitors are also using data to compete, so companies need to understand and manipulate customer behavior. Secondly, since data collection and storage are relatively inexpensive and become an asset in the future, organizations find it beneficial to continue to aggregate and retain data. Thirdly, organizations can take the risk of continuing to retain data since the penalties for data breaches are currently not really fatal [25].

Put simply, the current digital environment demands that companies and organizations collect as much data as possible. Data is seen as an important resource for increasing a company's competitiveness and profits, and this tends to drive the collection of data. Weak penalties for data leaks and compromises also drive the trend toward data collection. When penalties are minor, companies and organizations can take the risk of continuing to collect data, and thus data collection is becoming increasingly widespread and pervasive in society.

Overall, the metaverse accelerates surveillance capitalism by increasing the type and amount of information collected and the scale of the surveillance problem (which, of course, raises ethical concerns about data collection and use; to address them, appropriate legal frameworks and regulations need to be put in place in order to protect the privacy of individuals).

3.3   Cyber-Syndromes in the Metaverse

The immersive nature of the metaverse can make people addicted to it, and may lead to what are generally called cyber-syndromes. A cyber-syndrome is a physical, social, and/or mental disorder that affects humans due to the misuse of technology and excessive interaction with cyberspace [27]. Cyber-syndromes in the metaverse can be even more dangerous than cyber-syndromes observed through the traditional use of the Internet. The overview of cyber-syndromes is given in the following figure (and the details are explained below) (Fig. 1).

Fig. 1. Three Types of Symptoms of Cyber-syndromes

3.3.1   Physical Disorder
Physical Fatigue. With regard to physical issues, the highly addictive nature of the metaverse can cause health problems for users. For example, smartphone-based metaverses require users to stay in the same position for long periods of time. This can lead to the text neck syndrome (a postural problem that causes neck pain and tension) [26,27]. By keeping the head and neck down and looking at the screen, the muscles in the neck and shoulders become tense, causing pain and discomfort. Other symptoms such as eye strain and headaches may also be suffered [28,29]. (It should be noted that these and the following physical issues are not necessarily problems specific to the metaverse; just for completeness we still mention them briefly.)

Sleeping Disorder. It is also possible that over-dependence on the metaverse can lead to sleep deprivation. Spending extended periods of time in the metaverse leads to increased screen time and blue light screens may suppress the production of melatonin, a sleep-regulating hormone, which can disrupt the body's natural sleep-wake cycle and make it difficult to fall asleep [30]. The metaverse also offers immersive and interactive experiences that are mentally and emotionally stimulating, such as combat game worlds. Intense or stimulating activities before bedtime can make it difficult to relax and unwind, making it difficult to fall asleep.

Metabolic Problem. Engaging in virtual activities in the metaverse often involves prolonged periods of sitting and limited physical movement. It does not provide users with the same opportunities for exercise and movement, at least not in the same way as in the real world. This sedentary and inactive behavior can lead to reduced physical activity levels and metabolic problems such as weight gain [31]. Additionally, they may neglect proper nutrition and rely on convenience foods that are high in calories, sugar, and unhealthy fats.

3.3.2   Social Disorder

Interpersonal Ability. The virtual and digitally mediated nature of the metaverse can affect interpersonal skills. In the metaverse, people interact with each other through avatars and digital representations, and then they may not fully grasp the nuances and complexities of face-to-face communication in the real world. As a result, they may lack the practice and development of nonverbal cues, body language, emotional intelligence, and other interpersonal skills essential for effective communication and relationship-building in the real world. Furthermore, spending excessive time in the metaverse may reduce opportunities for social interaction in the real world. People may become immersed in virtual relationships and communities, neglecting offline connections and social responsibilities. In addition, the metaverse can limit the depth and quality of interpersonal relationships. Communication in virtual environments, with current technology, often relies on text-based or limited audiovisual communication, which may not have the richness and nuance of face-to-face conversations. As a result, it may not be possible to sufficiently develop the ability to communicate with others.

Isolation. People in the metaverse can feel socially isolated. First, the metaverse is a virtual environment, and while it is possible to interact with others, there is no physical connection as experienced in the real world. Second, the metaverse is often disconnected from real-world identities, and people using avatars or pseudonyms should feel a lack of meaningful tangible connection, feeling as if the individual is interacting with an unrealistic facade rather than a real personality. In addition, the metaverse may limit the depth and quality of interpersonal relationships, resulting in shallow or superficial interactions that may not satisfy the individual's desire for deep emotional connection and meaningful relationships. Besides, those who spend excessive time in the metaverse may experience a diminished sense of community and belonging in the physical environment. This can contribute to a sense of isolation and detachment from the real world.

3.3.3 Psychological Disorder

Delusional Disorder. Metaverse experience may trigger delusional disorder. For example, users who engage in a virtual war in the metaverse may have psychological or physical damage even in the real world, since the metaverse provides a more realistic experience than playing in a traditional screen-based medium. It can even lead to a lack of distinction between reality and the real world after returning from the metaverse, which can cause trauma and anxiety. Overuse of computer technology is thought to be associated with mood disorders such as depression and anxiety among adolescents [32–34], and the immersive nature of the metaverse can exacerbate these problems.

FOMO. The metaverse may cause FOMO (Fear Of Missing Out) [35]. The metaverse often operates literally always, with a continuous flow of information, making it hard to miss out on relevant information such as social trends and technical skills. Also, when users see others building connections and engaging in exciting activities in the metaverse, they may fear that they will be excluded or isolated if they do not actively participate.

3.4 Amplification of Social Problems

Inequality and Digital Divide. The metaverse widens the gap between those who have access to advanced technology and resources and those who do not. Socioeconomic disparities in the real world are reflected, perpetuated and reinforced in the metaverse, and those individuals who have better access to it will have more opportunities, privileges, and advantages. This can exacerbate existing inequalities and create additional digital divides.

Online Harassment and Bullying. The anonymity and distance provided by the metaverse may encourage individuals to engage in harmful behaviors such as cyber-bullying, harassment, and trolling. The lack of face-to-face interaction and physical impact can lead to a toxic online environment where social issues such as discrimination, hate speech, and prejudice are prevalent and can negatively impact an individual's mental well-being.

Prejudice and Discrimination. Another issue is the amplification of social prejudice and discrimination in the metaverse. Data used to create virtual environments and interactions in the metaverse are often derived from real-world data that contain various biases and harmful social conventions. It is essential to ensure that the data used to create metaverse technologies is diverse, representative, and unbiased. Just as the metaverse reinforces the surveillance problem described above, it may perpetuate and reinforce existing social prejudice and discrimination in the virtual world, and even create new forms of prejudice and discrimination that are only possible in the virtual world.

4   Ethical Design Principles for the Sustainable Metaverse

In this section we propose ethical design principles for the sustainable metaverse from environmental, economical, and social perspectives. The current metaverse is facing a variety of problems, including the aforementioned issues. By the sustainable metaverse we refer to the vision of a virtual universe or digital ecosystem that is developed and operated in a manner that prioritises long-term environmental, social, and economical sustainability, as illustrated in the figure below. Our goal is to create and maintain a virtual space that balances technological advances and immersive experiences with responsible and ethical practices (Fig. 2).

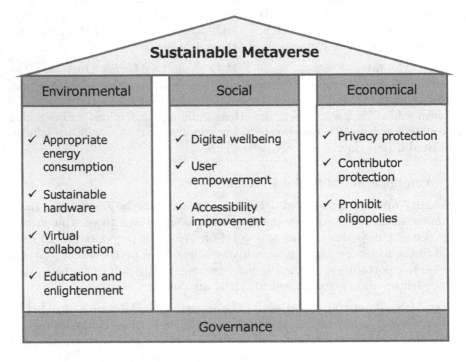

Fig. 2. Sustainable Metaverse

4.1   Environmental Perspective

From an environmental perspective, we have to consider how to approach e-waste and resource issues. In the following we will also consider ways in which human-computer interactions in the metaverse can contribute to resource efficiency and conservation in the right way. We argue that it is possible to create a rich virtual experience and collaboration while minimizing environmental impact.

Energy consumption can be significantly reduced by designing and optimizing metaverse platforms and applications to be more energy efficient. This includes using efficient algorithms, optimizing server infrastructure, and promoting best practices in software development. In addition, renewable energy sources should be prioritised as a source of power for data centers and server farms. Overcoming the e-waste problem requires sustainable hardware; manufacturers of XR equipment must prioritise sustainability in their production processes, which includes using environmentally friendly materials, promoting recyclability, and minimizing the use of hazardous substances. An extended producer responsibility program can also be implemented to ensure responsible disposal and recycling of devices.

In order to contribute to sustainability in the real world, we can take advantage of certain characteristics of the metaverse in the following manner. Virtual collaboration through the metaverse can reduce the amount of physical transportation. It should be used proactively since it can mitigate the burden on the environment by reducing greenhouse gas emissions and the risk of traffic accidents. Environmental data can also be collected and analyzed through artificial agents and entities on the metaverse. This can provide useful information for monitoring ecosystems, identifying environmental problems, and developing sustainable practices and policies. In addition, educational content and experiences on environmental issues can be provided in the metaverse to increase users' environmental awareness. It serves to promote knowledge and behavior change about sustainability and spread environmental awareness. In such a way, the metaverse can contribute to solving environmental problems and achieving sustainability.

4.2 Social Perspective

Here we consider design principles from a social perspective.

Various aspects of a person's digital well-being need to be controlled by suitable AI systems. For example, screen time needs to be regulated to prevent the aforementioned metaverse addiction. It is also important to take preventive measures to enhance safety. Harassment and cyberbullying can be amplified in the metaverse, as discussed above. User safety and well-being should be prioritised by implementing measures to prevent and address other harmful behaviors. This would include moderation systems, reporting mechanisms, and community guidelines that promote respectful interactions and discourage abusive behavior.

Moreover, users need to be empowered. Providing resources and educational materials to help users safely navigate the metaverse, make informed decisions, and protect themselves from potential risks will promote digital literacy and empowerment. The future metaverse will be populated by digital natives, who may become more familiar with how to manipulate digital systems. However, digital literacy and critical thinking skills to select and discard correct information are different matters and require suitable training even for them. Therefore, we have to work on promoting digital citizenship, critical thinking skills, and responsible online behavior.

In addition, accessibility needs to be improved. It is necessary to ensure that the metaverse is accessible and welcoming to people of diverse backgrounds, abilities, and identities. This requires designing interfaces and interactions that address the needs of diverse users, supporting multiple languages, and providing options for customisation and personalisation.

4.3 Economical Perspective

We finally discuss design principles from an economical perspective.

Privacy protection is relevant here. Robust data protection and privacy measures need to be implemented to protect user data and prevent unauthorised use and exploitation. To ensure economical sustainability, it is necessary to respect users' privacy rights, obtain clear consent for data collection and use, and provide transparency on how user data is handled. And it is necessary to adequately penalise companies that cause problems.

Protection of contributors is also required to address the surveillance capitalism issue discussed above. Rather than monopolizing profits for a company or a collection of companies, it is necessary to ensure that content creators, artists, developers, and other contributors receive fair evaluation and compensation for their work within the metaverse. For example, companies need to consider how to trade items across platforms and how to contribute to copyright protection for the content they create. This also includes establishing transparent data protection and revenue sharing models and fair payment structures that recognise and reward the value that contributors bring to the virtual environment. To avoid exploitative and predatory monetisation, exploitative practices such as pay-to-win mechanisms and manipulative tactics that prioritise short-term profits over the welfare of users need to be avoided, and the development of such legislation needs to be considered.

We would also have to address the issue of oligopolies on the metaverse. Healthy competition is crucial to stimulate innovation within the metaverse. We therefore have to avoid oligopolistic practices, promoting open standards, and providing opportunities for new entrants and small businesses to prosper, and thus promoting innovation, choice, and quality in the virtual economy.

Overall, the sustainable metaverse envisions a digital ecosystem that not only provides an immersive experience, but is also aligned with principles of sustainability, social responsibility, and ethical behavior. We must create virtual worlds that can thrive and evolve in ways that are beneficial to individuals, society, and the environment in the long term.

5 Concluding Remarks

In this paper we have investigated and analyzed human-computer interactions in the metaverse, where new forms of interaction are emerging due to the development of XR technology and the technologically enabled enhancement of human perception. We have discussed the ethical issues that would arise on the metaverse, including privacy and security, surveillance capitalism, cyber-syndromes, and amplifications of social problems. These issues on the metaverse are fundamentally different in their characteristics from those on the real world and the traditional Internet, and may lead to potential threats to the sustainable development and social health of the metaverse. We have finally proposed ethical design principles for the sustainable metaverse from three perspectives (i.e., environmental, social, and economical), including energy efficiency and e-waste management, promotion of social inclusion and diversity, and protection of privacy and security. The proposals provide guidelines to ensure that the development of the metaverse is environmentally sustainable and socially sound. How to implement the ethical design principles in a realistic manner through the coordination of various stakeholders and relevant policies would need to be explored further and thus be our future work.

Acknowledgements. This work was supported by JST (JPMJMS2033-02).

References

1. Stephenson, N.: Snow crash: A novel. Spectra (2003)
2. Tlili, A., et al.: Is Metaverse in education a blessing or a curse: a combined content and bibliometric analysis. Smart Learn. Environ. **9**(1), 1–31 (2022)
3. Kraus, S., Kanbach, D.K., Krysta, P.M., Steinhoff, M.M., Tomini, N.: Facebook and the creation of the metaverse: radical business model innovation or incremental transformation?. Inter. J. Entrepreneurial Behav. Res. (2022)
4. Mystakidis, S.: Metaverse. Encyclopedia **2**(1), 486–497 (2022)
5. Park, S.M., Kim, Y.G.: A metaverse: taxonomy, components, applications, and open challenges. IEEE Access **10**, 4209–4251 (2022)
6. Hwang, G.J., Chien, S.Y.: Definition, roles, and potential research issues of the metaverse in education: an artificial intelligence perspective. Comput. Educ. Artifi. Intell. **3**, 100082 (2022)
7. Dwivedi, Y.K., et al.: Metaverse beyond the hype: Multidisciplinary perspectives on emerging challenges, opportunities, and agenda for research, practice and policy. Int. J. Inf. Manage. **66**, 102542 (2022)
8. Wang, Y., Siau, K.L., Wang, L.: Metaverse and human-computer interaction: a technology framework for 3D virtual worlds. In: HCI International 2022-Late Breaking Papers: Interacting with Extended Reality and Artificial Intelligence: 24th International Conference on Human-Computer Interaction, HCII 2022, Virtual Event, 26 June -1 July 2022, Proceedings, pp. 213–221. Springer Nature Switzerland, Cham (November 2022). https://doi.org/10.1007/978-3-031-21707-4_16
9. Lee, L.H., et al.: All one needs to know about metaverse: a complete survey on technological singularity, virtual ecosystem, and research agenda (2021). arXiv preprint arXiv:2110.05352
10. Zhang, X., Yang, D., Yow, C.H., Huang, L., Wu, X., Huang, X., Cai, Y.: Metaverse for Cultural Heritages. Electronics **11**(22), 3730 (2022)
11. Rauschnabel, P.A., Felix, R., Hinsch, C., Shahab, H., Alt, F.: What is XR? towards a framework for augmented and virtual reality. Comput. Hum. Behav. **133**, 107289 (2022)
12. Ardiny, H., Khanmirza, E.: The role of AR and VR technologies in education developments: opportunities and challenges. In: 2018 6th rsi international conference on robotics and mechatronics (icrom), pp. 482–487. IEEE (October 2018)

13. Farshid, M., Paschen, J., Eriksson, T., Kietzmann, J.: Go boldly!: Explore augmented reality (AR), virtual reality (VR), and mixed reality (MR) for business. Bus. Horiz. **61**(5), 657–663 (2018)
14. Rauschnabel, P.A.: Augmented reality is eating the real-world! the substitution of physical products by holograms. Int. J. Inf. Manage. **57**, 102279 (2021)
15. Speicher, M., Hall, B.D., Nebeling, M.: What is mixed reality?. In: Proceedings of the 2019 CHI Conference on Human Factors in Computing Systems, pp. 1–15 (May 2019)
16. Wedel, M., Bigné, E., Zhang, J.: Virtual and augmented reality: advancing research in consumer marketing. Int. J. Res. Mark. **37**(3), 443–465 (2020)
17. Anderson, J., Rainie, L.: The metaverse in 2040. Pew Research Centre (2022)
18. Di Pietro, R., Cresci, S.: Metaverse: security and privacy issues. In: 2021 Third IEEE International Conference on Trust, Privacy and Security in Intelligent Systems and Applications (TPS-ISA), pp. 281–288. IEEE (December 2021)
19. Huang, Y., Li, Y.J., Cai, Z.: Security and privacy in metaverse: a comprehensive survey. Big Data Mining Analy. **6**(2), 234–247 (2023)
20. Verma, P.: They thought loved ones were calling for help. It was an AI scam. The Washington Post (March 5 2023). https://www.washingtonpost.com/technology/2023/03/05/ai-voice-scam/
21. Bibri, S.E., Allam, Z.: The Metaverse as a virtual form of data-driven smart urbanism: on post-pandemic governance through the prism of the logic of surveillance capitalism. Smart Cities **5**(2) (2022)
22. Zuboff, S.: The age of surveillance capitalism: the fight for a human future at the new frontier of power: Barack Obama's books of 2019. Profile books (2019)
23. Zuboff, S.: Big other: surveillance capitalism and the prospects of an information civilization. J. Inf. Technol. **30**(1), 75–89 (2015)
24. Doctorow, C.: How to destroy surveillance capitalism. Medium Editions (2020)
25. Wolff, J., Atallah, N.: Early GDPR penalties: analysis of implementation and fines through May 2020. J. Inf. Policy **11**, 63–103 (2021)
26. Neupane, S., Ali, U., Mathew, A.: Text neck syndrome-systematic review. Imp. J. Interdiscip. Res. **3**(7), 141–148 (2017)
27. Ning, H., Dhelim, S., Bouras, M.A., Khelloufi, A., Ullah, A.: Cyber-syndrome and its formation, classification, recovery and prevention. IEEE Access **6**, 35501–35511 (2018)
28. Coles-Brennan, C., Sulley, A., Young, G.: Management of digital eye strain. Clin. Exp. Optom. **102**(1), 18–29 (2019)
29. Rosenfield, M.: Computer vision syndrome: a review of ocular causes and potential treatments. Ophthalmic Physiol. Opt. **31**(5), 502–515 (2011)
30. West, K.E., et al.: Blue light from light-emitting diodes elicits a dose-dependent suppression of melatonin in humans. J. Appli. Physiol. (2011)
31. Ford, E.S., Kohl, H.W., III., Mokdad, A.H., Ajani, U.A.: Sedentary behavior, physical activity, and the metabolic syndrome among US adults. Obes. Res. **13**(3), 608–614 (2005)
32. Jang, K.S., Hwang, S.Y., Choi, J.Y.: Internet addiction and psychiatric symptoms among Korean adolescents. J. Sch. Health **78**(3), 165–171 (2008)
33. Young, K.S., Rogers, R.C.: The relationship between depression and Internet addiction. Cyberpsychol. Behav. **1**(1), 25–28 (1998)
34. Ha, J.H., et al.: Depression and Internet addiction in adolescents. Psychopathology **40**(6), 424–430 (2007)
35. Usmani, S.S., Sharath, M., Mehendale, M.: Future of mental health in the metaverse. General Psychiat. **35**(4), e100825 (2022)

COVID-19 Contact Tracing Mobile Applications in New York State (NYS): an Empirical Study

Xiaojun Yuan(✉), DeeDee Bennett Gayle, Ellie Seoe Jung,
and Yvonne Appiah Dadson

College of Emergency Preparedness, Homeland Security and Cybersecurity, University at
Albany, State University of New York, Albany, USA
{xyuan,dmbennett,sjung,ydadson}@albany.edu

Abstract. In this paper, we surveyed to examine individual use of mobile apps for
COVID-19 contact tracing in New York State (NYS). Additionally, we investigated
the impact of privacy and security concerns on adopting these apps and whether
there are differences in adoption rates among different racial and age groups. We
adopted the Antecedent-Privacy Concerns-Outcomes (APCO) framework to identify factors affecting the individual-level adoption of these apps. Results indicate
no significant correlation between race and the perceived usefulness of the NYS
COVID-Alert app. Only certain demographic variables affected privacy concerns,
trust, or behavioral intentions related to contact tracing apps. Specifically, the
more influential factors were pandemic experiences, political affiliation, education, and income. Political affiliation and education were more influential demographic factors regarding the adoption and perceived usefulness of contact tracing
applications.

Interestingly, respondents with the highest and lowest income were less likely
to be concerned about the privacy and security concerns of the COVID-19 mobile
apps. However, middle-income respondents were more likely to be concerned
about privacy and security. Our findings shed light on the challenges and opportunities associated with contact-tracing mobile apps in the context of the COVID-19
pandemic and provide insights into how these apps can be optimized to improve
their effectiveness and reach.

Keywords: Contact tracing apps · Antecedent-Privacy Concerns-Outcomes
(APCO) model · Amazon Turk · Privacy · Security

1 Introduction

The COVID-19 pandemic has had a profound impact on global health, and as a result,
contact tracing has emerged as a crucial tool in mitigating the spread of the virus.
Throughout the pandemic, contact tracing emerged as a fundamental mitigation strategy by breaking the chain of human-to-human transmission, locating those exposed
to confirmed cases, isolating them immediately, monitoring them to guarantee prompt
isolation, and providing testing and treatment if they exhibit symptoms [1, 2]. In addition, it has been integrated into the national public health plans of several nations that

© The Author(s), under exclusive license to Springer Nature Switzerland AG 2023
H. Degen et al. (Eds.): HCII 2023, LNCS 14059, pp. 505–524, 2023.
https://doi.org/10.1007/978-3-031-48057-7_32

have successfully controlled the SARS-CoV-2 outbreak, notably Singapore, Taiwan, and Vietnam [3–5].

Smartphone-based COVID-19 applications became one of the most frequently used technologies among all the mitigation and control measures, such as mandated lock-downs, home isolations, and social distance requirements to "flatten the curve." As a result, contact-tracing mobile applications (CTAs) have been developed and imple-mented worldwide. Still, their success depends on several factors, including their perceived usefulness and adoption rates among different demographic groups.

To guarantee that contact tracing apps will genuinely improve public health, users must feel confident that their data is secure and safeguarded, as collecting sensitive personal data could threaten privacy, equality, and fairness [6]. For instance, contact-tracing apps should be available and accessible to everyone, independent of the required technology or their level of digital literacy. Nevertheless, many such apps are only compatible with specific phones. Existing literature revealed several personal privacy, adoption, and use issues tied to individual demographics, especially in countries where use was not compulsory. For example, in the U.S., CTA was voluntary and introduced primarily at the state level, not nationally.

Furthermore, there is evidence partisan politics influenced the states' introduction of such apps and potential use [6–9]. Hence, the adoption, use, and privacy issues surround-ing app-based contact tracing in the U.S. were probably influenced by this dynamic. In this paper, we investigate the perception of the mobile apps for COVID-19 contact trac-ing in New York State (NYS) and how this differs by race and age. We also explore the impact of privacy and security concerns regarding the adoption of these apps and whether there are differences in adoption rates among different racial and age groups. We conducted a survey of individuals across a diverse range of demographic groups in New York state.

2   Background

Contact tracing has been used in distinctive ways to curb the transmission of infectious illnesses [1, 10]. During the outbreak of SARS in 2003 and Ebola in 2014, contact trac-ing was extensively and successfully employed [11, 12]. The effectiveness of extensive contact tracing in response to SARS in 2003 spurred its adoption in the management of SARS-CoV-2, also known as COVID-19 [13, 14]. The epidemiological evaluation of contact tracing is dependent on five factors: integration with local health policy, increased user adoption and adherence, proper quarantine of infectious individuals, prompt notifi-cation, and the ability to evaluate effectiveness objectively [15]. For all its capabilities, contact tracing has a varied level of success. One rationale is that the effectiveness of con-tact tracing to break the transmission chain is only as successful as the proportion of traced contacts. This proportion is partly influenced by the quality of the information infected people provide, making human memory a vital component of contact tracing efficacy [16]. The National Academies of Sciences, Engineering, and Medicine recognized three major behavioral obstacles throughout the contact tracing process: unresponsiveness to phone calls from local public health officials, reluctance to share information because of mistrust in government, and hesitation to disclose the names of potentially exposed persons due to fear of stigmatization or unwillingness to expose others to quarantine restrictions [16, 17].

2.1 Contact Tracing Apps

Contact tracing apps were mandatory and more centralized in East Asian countries such as China, Taiwan, South Korea, and Singapore [18, 19]. On the contrary, most European nations, including the United Kingdom, Austria, France, and Germany, introduced voluntary and decentralized apps. Additionally, European countries chose higher privacy-preserving Bluetooth-based Contact Tracing Apps (CTAs) [20–22] as part of a collaborative effort to empower public health authorities worldwide in creating digital contact tracing apps. Whereas other CTAs used GPS-based notifications, which led to less individual privacy.

After the end of the lockdown in East Asian countries such as China and particularly Taiwan, contact tracing apps were mandated and have proven efficient alongside human contact tracing methods in finding new cases [4, 23, 24]. These countries have a slightly higher acceptance rate. However, while existing CTAs in these nations have a more privacy-protective design, privacy and security concerns are more prevalent in countries such as Europe and the United States [22].

One significant barrier to the efficient usage of such apps was the social policies that govern an individual's willingness to participate. Previous research indicates that the efficacy of CTAs has been focused on population adoption, privacy and security concerns, and sociodemographic backgrounds [15, 25–29]. Contact tracing apps have not been fully implemented because of public concerns about data privacy and security [25]. Authorities must provide convincing proof that contact tracing- apps are valuable and trustworthy to increase the number of users [20, 30]. The app must establish trust and usefulness in its users to reach a substantial number of people. However, there are no standard criteria for trust [26, 28]. Cultural differences and social norms frequently influence citizens' willingness to adopt and use these apps. Numerous cultural contexts and individual traits, such as sociodemographic background and personality factors, affect one's level of acceptance [26, 28]. Existing studies also revealed that racial groups are more vulnerable to examination and have more significant implications when adopting digital technologies [29].

In the United States, no such national app was developed. Instead, many state and local governments created CTAs to assist with contact tracing efforts. More than 19 states developed and implemented CTAs before the end of 2020 [31, 32]. The state-developed apps were not all linked to one another or operated similarly. For example, North and South Dakota were the first states to launch their Care19 contact tracing apps [33]. The app is based on GPS location data that has been anonymized. Utah was the third state to build a contact tracing app. The Health Together app uses GPS tracking and Bluetooth data [34]. Unlike Care19, this app does not provide anonymity, as public health officials can access user information.

CTAs were not limited to country or government development and dissemination. Business organizations like Apple and Google partnered to introduce the Exposure Notification app for iOS and Android smartphones. The Exposure Notification App uses Bluetooth low-energy (BLE) technology to identify when phones are in proximity, using the app to track and trace COVID-19. In the U.S., some State and local governments also partnered with Apple and Google to create CTAs for local use [32, 35].

2.2 Antecedent-Privacy Concerns-Outcomes (APCO) Framework

Given the prominent concerns about privacy, trust, and demographic impacts on the use and adoption of CTAs during COVID-19, this study employed the Antecedent-Privacy Concerns-Outcomes (APCO) framework (Fig. 1). This framework has been previously used to model use, adoption, and privacy concerns regarding technology in various settings [36–38]. The APCO was used to identify factors affecting the individual-level adoption of these apps. This model is composed of antecedent factors that impact privacy concerns and lead to different outcomes. Demographics, including race/ethnicity, income, age, education, and political affiliations, were included in this study to account for demographic differences. Additionally, questions about privacy experiences and awareness regarding the pandemic and contact tracing were involved. Finally, the behavioral reaction (or intention to use CTAs) and the privacy calculus were considered in this study.

Smith, Dinev, & Xu (2011) developed the APCO macro model, combining empirical privacy studies within the interdisciplinary information systems domain [38]. The model displays relationships between privacy issues at various levels, classified as antecedents, privacy concerns, and outcomes. Personal qualities or elements that develop from situations involving the exposure of personal information are antecedents. Privacy experiences, privacy awareness, personality, and demographic characteristics are individual-level APCO antecedents [39]. Privacy concerns, a core notion in information science literature, assess individuals' attitudes and beliefs about exposing personal information. Bansal et al. (2016) highlighted that the APCO framework represents individual-level outcomes through behavioral reactions, such as readiness to divulge personal information [40]. Also, trust and the privacy calculus theory, which investigates individual decision-making processes involving personal information disclosure, are the individual-level outcomes [41, 42]. Knight, Yuan & Bennett-Gayle (2022) introduced the Technology-Specific Privacy/Security Concerns framework modeled on the APCO model [36].

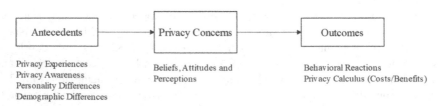

Fig. 1. The Antecedent-Privacy Concerns-Outcomes (APCO) framework [38]

In Yuan, Bennett Gayle, Dadson, and Jung (2022), it was reported that race and gender were critical factors to consider in expanding the Antecedent-Privacy Concerns-Outcomes (APCO) framework. In particular, race influenced the perception of the seriousness of the pandemic, with Asians and Black being serious about the pandemic.

Additionally, there were age-affected privacy and security concerns. The youngest group of respondents did not have many privacy or security concerns about mobile apps.

This paper examines the use of COVID-19 contact tracing apps in New York State (NYS). It aims at investigating the differences in perception, adoption, or privacy concerns among racial and ethnic populations and across age groups.

The following research questions (RQs) were addressed.

RQ1: Are there statistically significant demographic differences among respondents that perceive the usefulness of COVID-19 contact tracing mobile apps?
RQ2: Are there statistically significant demographic differences among respondents that identify privacy and security concerns with COVID-19 contact-tracing mobile apps?
RQ3: Is there a correlation between trust in the organization that produces the contact tracing mobile app and privacy/security concerns?

3 Methods

We disseminated a Qualtrics survey via Amazon Mechanical Turk to explore the perceived usefulness of NYS mobile apps for COVID-19 and the privacy and security concerns of the technologies used. During the initial phase in March 2022, we recruited 120 Turkers, who identified as New York State residents [37]. During the second phase in May 2022, we recruited 129 Turkers in New York State. This paper will report the analysis of the data collected from 249 total Turkers.

The study variables used to develop the survey were based on the APCO framework. The survey tool was adopted based on previous research studies [43–45]; see Table 1. In previous studies, experiences were focused on the user experience with a particular device or with data privacy. However, in this study, we have expanded privacy experiences to include user experience with CTAs, other mobile applications, and during the pandemic in general. Similarly, previous research has focused primarily on gender and age as demographic considerations that influence use differences. In this study, we also include race/ethnicity, education, income level, and political affiliation as potential influential factors in CTAs use. This expansion was necessary given the social climate regarding the pandemic and contact tracing in the U.S. at the time [37, 46–48].

The survey aimed to assess the perception of the use of mobile apps for COVID-19 contact tracing among New Yorkers and to capture participants' attitudes toward different strategies and entities that could potentially help minimize the spread of COVID-19. In the survey, Turkers were shown images of the mobile apps (COVID Alert NY and Exposure Notification) and then asked a series of questions regarding the apps.

The survey consisted of multiple sections to collect demographic information and to understand the perception of the COVID-19 pandemic and contact tracing mobile apps, such as "How serious do you perceive the COVID-19 pandemic?" The demographic information includes age group, gender, race, education, and income. The survey encompassed questions related to political orientation, including political affiliation, to better comprehend the impact of political ideology on attitudes and behaviors toward COVID-19. It was important for us to ask a two-pronged question regarding political affiliation to capture which party respondents felt handled the pandemic better and which political party they most aligned with. In some cases, the answers to these questions might differ.

Table 1. Study variables based on the APCO framework [adapted and modified from ([43–45])]

Variable (This Study)	APCO variable	Survey Question
Pandemic Experience	Privacy Experiences	How seriously do you perceive the COVID-19 pandemic?
Mobile App		How often have you previously used mobile applications on your phone?
Contact Tracing App		How often have you previously used COVID Alert NY, a contact tracing application, on your mobile phone?
Gender	Demographic Differences	What is your gender?
Age		What is your age?
Race		What is your race?
Education		What is your highest level of education?
Income		What was your total household income before taxes during the past 12 months?
Political Affiliation		Which party do you support to handle national problems such as COVID-19? How do you describe yourself politically?
Privacy Awareness	Privacy Awareness	To what extent are you familiar with the privacy policies for mobile applications?
Perceived Privacy Risk	Privacy Security	How often has a concern about your privacy and security prevented you from using mobile applications on your phone?
Activity Engagement	Benefits	To what extent has the use of contact tracing applications allowed you to engage in the following activities: Work, Education, Recreation
Health Interest in App		In your opinion, to what extent do contact tracing applications provide a health benefit to the community?
Trust in App	Trust	Please indicate your comfort level with trusting each of the following applications with your information.: COVID Alert NY, Exposure Notification

(*continued*)

Table 1. (*continued*)

Variable (This Study)	APCO variable	Survey Question
Trust in Organization		Please indicate how helpful or not you perceive each of the following to minimize the spread of the virus.: N.Y. State Government, NY State Department of Health, Centers for Disease Control and Prevention, World Health Organization
Risks/Costs	Behavioral Reactions	Please indicate how helpful or not you perceive each of the following to minimize the spread of the virus.: Contact tracing, Contract tracing mobile applications
Change Privacy Settings		How often have you opted out or changed any permissions for mobile applications?
Continuance Intention		How likely are you to use the contact tracing application, if mandatory?

The perceived helpfulness of different strategies and entities captured the attitudes toward mitigation efforts, contact tracing, contact tracing mobile applications, New York state government, New York State Department of Health, Centers for Disease Control and Prevention (CDC), and World Health Organization (WHO). The questions were measured on a 7-point Likert scale, which ranged from extremely unhelpful to extremely helpful. The survey also included the usage and familiarity of mobile apps and contact tracing apps to evaluate the privacy and security concerns as potential barriers to adoption. The survey was anonymous, and the participants were informed about the purpose of the study and their rights as research participants.

3.1 Data

The data collected from the survey was analyzed using statistical libraries in Python. Correlation and regression analyses were used to examine the relationships among the variables of interest. Participant demographics are shown in Table 2.

As shown, most respondents were between 25 and 44 years old, and over 70% were White. It should be noted that in New York State, White residents represent 64% of the state, while Black residents are 17.6% and Asian 9.9% [49]. Most respondents were men (54%); however, 44% were women. Respondents with bachelor's degrees represented more than half of the sample (56.22%), although all educational levels appeared among respondents. Regarding political affiliation, it is clear that for some respondents, their political affiliation did not correspond with which party they felt handled the pandemic better.

Table 2. Participant Demographics

Demographics			No	Percentage
Age		18 to 24 years	13	5.22%
		25 to 34 years	100	40.16%
		35 to 44 years	77	30.92%
		45 to 54 years	31	12.45%
		55 to 64 years	24	9.64%
Race		American Indian or Alaska Native	2	0.80%
		Asian	33	13.25%
		Black or African American	30	12.05%
		Other	8	3.21%
		White	176	70.68%
Ethnicity		Latino	37	15.29%
Gender		Female	110	44.18%
		Male	135	54.22%
		Other	4	1.61%
Political	Party Affiliation	Democrat	140	56.22%
		Independent	56	22.49%
		Republican	41	16.47%
		Other	12	4.82%
	Party Support	Democrats	147	59.04%
		Republicans	49	19.68%
		I don't support any party	36	14.46%
		Other	17	6.83%
Education		Associate's degree	14	5.62%
		Bachelor's degree	140	56.22%
		Completed some college	26	10.44%
		Completed some high school	2	0.80%
		Completed some postgraduate	5	2.01%
		Doctorate degree	2	0.80%
		High school diploma or GED	13	5.22%
		Master's degree	41	16.47%
		Professional degree beyond bachelor's (for example, Ph.D., MD., J.D., etc.)	6	2.41%

(*continued*)

Table 2. (*continued*)

Demographics		No	Percentage
Income	Less than $25,000	30	12.05%
	$25,000 to $34,999	23	9.24%
	$35,000 to $49,999	41	16.47%
	$50,000 to $74,999	65	26.1%
	$75,000 to $99,999	39	15.66%
	$100,000 to $149,999	35	14.06%
	$150,000 or more	15	6.02%

4 Results

The study used survey questions to assess the variables of seriousness, perceived usefulness, perceived helpfulness, comfort, familiarity, and privacy security concerns. Seriousness measured the participants' perception of the COVID-19 pandemic's severity. Perceived usefulness refers to the degree to which participants perceived a CTA as useful in achieving their goals. Perceived helpfulness measured the degree to which participants perceived the CTAs to be helpful in engaging in daily activities. Comfort refers to the level of comfort or trust in CTAs reported by participants when using the CTAs. Familiarity measures the extent to which participants were familiar with the CTA and other mobile apps prior to the study. Privacy security concerns assess the level of concern participants had regarding the privacy and security of their information when using CTAs or other mobile apps. These variables were measured using Likert-type scales with higher scores indicating higher levels of seriousness, perceived usefulness, perceived helpfulness, comfort, familiarity, or privacy security concerns. Descriptive statistics such as means, standard deviations, and variances were calculated to provide an overview of the distribution of responses for each variable, see Table 3.

Table 3. Means, standard deviation, and variances for key variables.

	No	Mean	Standard Deviation	Variance
Serious	249	5.95	1.44	2.06
Perceived Helpfulness	244	5.08	1.54	2.37
Perceived Usefulness	249	3.95	1.75	3.05
Comfort	249	4.80	1.73	2.99
Familiarity	249	5.51	0.99	0.99
Privacy Security Concern	249	4.25	1.44	2.06

The mean seriousness of COVID-19 was 5.95, indicating that, on average, the respondents perceived the pandemic as moderately serious. The standard deviation of 1.44 suggests that the scores were relatively dispersed, with some respondents perceiving them as much more or much less serious than the average. The variance of 2.06 indicates that the distribution of seriousness was somewhat spread out, with a moderate amount of variability. The mean perceived helpfulness was found to be 5.08, with a standard deviation of 1.54 and variance of 2.37. This indicated that on average, respondents neither found the apps to be useful nor not useful. Additionally, respondents reported a greater level of comfort in trusting and using mobile apps. This also revealed that respondents were more familiar with mobile apps in general. However, for privacy and security concerns, most respondents expressed apprehension towards these aspects.

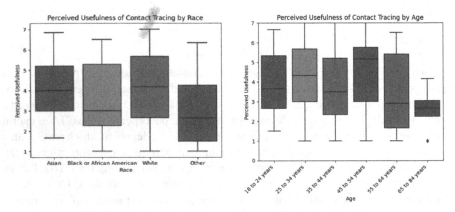

Fig. 2. Perceived Usefulness of Contact Tracing by Race/Age

As for the perceived usefulness of contact tracing by different racial groups (See Fig. 2), Asian and White respondents perceived contact tracing to be slightly more useful than other racial groups. The perceived usefulness of contact tracing did not show a clear association with age groups.

4.1 Perceived Usefulness

In Table 4, demographics, privacy experiences, privacy concerns, and benefits are correlated to perceived usefulness among respondents. Several variables were statistically significant. As shown, perceived usefulness was positively correlated with how serious the respondent indicated the pandemic was to them (.43, p < .001). Demographics played a role, as well, where political affiliation and education produced statistically significant results. There was a moderate positive correlation for those who supported the democratic party in handling the pandemic (0.29, p < .001) and for those who described themselves as democrats (.22, p = .003). Conversely, there was a weak negative correlation for those who did not support any party (-.30, p < .001), who supported an 'other' party (-.13, p = .04), who described themselves as independent (-.15, p = .01), and who described themselves as 'other' (-.14, p = .03). Educationally, respondents with at least some high school education were less likely to perceive the CTA as useful (-.17, p = .008). In comparison, respondents who had at least some college were more likely to perceive the CTA as useful (.13, p = .04).

The perceived helpfulness of the CTA was also correlated with usefulness, a strong statistically significant correlation (0.67, p < .001). Comfort with CTA also had a strong positive correlation (0.68, p < .001). Individuals that had familiarity with general mobile apps and those with privacy security concerns were found to have a moderate positive correlation with the perceived usefulness of CTA (0.32, p < .001) and (0.28, p < .001), respectively.

4.2 Privacy and Security Concerns

Also shown in Table 4, Privacy and security concerns were correlated with income, education, and political affiliation. Note that political affiliation was captured in terms of party support by the respondent and by who they felt handled the pandemic better. Specifically, Educationally, respondents who had at least some college education were more likely to have privacy and security concerns the CTAs (.13, p = .04). In contrast, respondents who had graduate education were less likely to have privacy and security concerns about the CTAs (−.16, p = .01).

The respondents who had an income of $25,000 or less were less likely to have privacy and security concerns to the CTAs (−.15, p < 0.05). Respondents who earned between $100,000 and $149,999 were another income category that demonstrated statistical significance (−.14, p < .05).

Privacy and security concerns were negatively correlated with comfort. The respondents who were less comfortable using or trusting CTAs were more likely to have privacy and security concerns (−.21, p = .001). The respondents who perceived the CTAs to be useful also had privacy and security concerns (.28, p < .001).

4.3 Comfort

Comfort with the CTAs (as a proxy for trust) was found to have interesting correlations with age, race, and political affiliation, also shown in Table 4. Respondents between the ages of 45 and 54 exhibited greater comfort with CTAs (.13, p < .05). Democratic supporters were also more comfortable with CTAs (.38, p < .001), while those who did not support any political party (−.28, p < .001) or supported Republicans (−.18, p = .005) were less comfortable with CTAs. Additionally, politically identifying as a Democrat was associated with greater comfort with CTAs (.29, p < .001) while identifying as an Independent was linked to less comfort with CTAs (−.18, p = .005). Respondents who identified as Republican were also less comfortable with CTAs (−.15, p = .02). Among the education levels, those who have completed some high school education, as well as those who possess a high school diploma (or the equivalent) were less comfortable with CTAs (−.2, p = .001).

Comfort was positively correlated with perceived helpfulness (.78, p < .001), familiarity (.23, p = .02), and perceived usefulness (.68, p < .001).

Table 4. Correlations related to demographics and perceived usefulness, privacy and security concern, and comfort.

Variables		Perceived Usefulness (r, p-value)	Privacy and Security Concerns (r, p-value)	Trust (r, p-value)
Pandemic Experience		(0.44, p < .001)**	(-0.009, p = .89)	(0.54, p < .001)**
Gender	Female	(-0.08, p = .21)	(-0.10, p = .11)	(0.03, p = .65)
	Male	(0.08, p = .21)	(0.12, p = .06)	(-0.04, p = .56)
	Other	(0.005, p = .94)	(-0.082, p = .19)	(0.03, p = .60)
Race	Asian	(0.04, p = .56)	(-0.08, p = .21)	(0.09, p = .15)
	Black/African American	(-0.09, p = .17)	(-0.08, p = .22)	(0.007, p = .91)
	Other	(-0.11, p = .08)	(0.04, p = .53)	(-0.18, p = .005)*
	White	(0.08, p = .20)	(0.10, p = .13)	(0.004, p = .95)
Ethnicity	Latino	(0.18, p = .004)*	(0.18, p = .003)*	(0.08, p = .19)
Age	18 to 24 years	(-0.03, p = .69)	(0.04, p = .54)	(-0.04, p = .57)
	25 to 34 years	(0.09, p = .14)	(-0.014, p = .83)	(0.04, p = .52)
	35 to 44 years	(-0.08, p = .20)	(-0.03, p = .65)	(-0.04, p = .51)
	45 to 54 years	(0.12, p = .05)	(0.07, p = .27)	(0.13, p = .04)*
	55 to 64 years	(-0.10, p = .11)	(-0.05, p = .42)	(-0.09, p = .16)
	65 to 84 years	(-0.10, p = .13)	(0.03, p = .64)	(-0.07, p = .26)
Party Support	Democrats	(0.29, p < .001)**	(-0.05, p = .42)	(0.38, p < .001)**
	I don't support any party	(-0.30, p < .001)**	(-0.02, p = .77)	(-0.28, p < .001)*
	Other	(-0.13, p = .04)*	(-0.10, p = .13)	(-0.046, p = .47)
	Republicans	(-0.02, p = .80)	(0.14, p = .03)*	(-0.18, p = .005)*
Political Affiliation	Democrat	(0.22, p = .003)*	(-0.07, p = .29)	(0.29, p < .001)**
	Independent	(-0.15, p = .01)*	(0.10, p = .11)	(-0.18, p = .005)*
	Other	(-0.14, p = .03)*	(-0.08, p = .19)	(-0.07, p = .28)
	Republican	(-0.046, p = .47)	(0.02, p = .72)	(-0.15, p = .02)*

(continued)

Table 4. (*continued*)

Variables		Perceived Usefulness (r, p-value)	Privacy and Security Concerns (r, p-value)	Trust (r, p-value)
Education	High School	(-0.17, p = .008)*	(0.03, p = .59)	(-0.20, p = .001)**
	College	(0.13, p = .04)*	(0.13, p = .04)*	(0.12, p = .07)
	Graduate	(-0.05, p = .45)	(-0.16, p = .01)*	(-0.009, p = .88)
Income	Less than $25,000	(-0.11, p = .10)	(-0.15, p = .02)*	(0.01, p = .85)
	$25,000 to $34,999	(-0.02, p = .80)	(-0.004, p = .95)	(-0.09, p = .18)
	$35,000 to $49,999	(0.082, p = .20)	(0.13, p = .05)*	(0.005, p = .94)
	$50,000 to $74,999	(0.05, p = .39)	(0.07, p = .30)	(-0.009, p = .88)
	$75,000 to $99,999	(0.043, p = .49)	(0.07, p = .25)	(0.05, p = .48)
	$100,000 to $149,999	(-0.018, p = .77)	(-0.14, p = .03)*	(0.04, p = .49)
	$150,000 or more	(-0.12, p = .06)	(-0.04, p = .51)	(-0.05, p = .47)
Perceived Helpfulness		(0.67, p < .001)**	(-0.029, p = .65)	(0.78, p < .001)**
Comfort		(0.68, p < .001)**	(-0.21, p = .001)**	--
Familiarity		(0.32, p < .001)**	(0.29, p < .001)**	(0.23, p = .002)*
Privacy Security Concern		(0.28, p < .001)**	--	(-0.21, p = .001)**
Perceived Usefulness		--	(0.28, p < .001)**	(0.68, p < .001)**

5 Discussion

Contact tracing applications were used globally during the COVID-19 pandemic. In some countries, use was compulsory and nationwide; however, in the U.S., the use was voluntary and initiated at the state and local levels. Previous research identified that demographics and privacy experiences might influence the app's adoption in nations where use was not mandated. Given that the U.S. did not have a nationwide rollout of CTA, research regarding the use and adoption of the apps has been limited. In this study, the use and adoption of the New York State COVID-Alert NY (and, to some extent, the Exposure Notification App) was investigated to understand the influence of demographic factors on perceived usefulness and privacy security concerns.

5.1   Perceived Usefulness

Results indicate no significant correlation between race and the perceived usefulness of the NYS COVID-Alert app. On average, Asian and White race groups perceived the contact tracing apps more useful than Black and Other race groups. These findings differ from at least one previous study [29]. Similarly, the correlation between age and the app's perceived usefulness was insignificant. On average, the 45–54 years old group perceived it to be more useful than any other age group. Those in the 65–84 age group perceived it to be not useful.

While age and race were not significant factors, other demographic variables were. Survey respondents with at least some high school education were less likely to perceive the CTA as useful. This finding was a weak correlation but was found to be statistically significant. Conversely, respondents with at least some college were more likely to perceive the CTA as useful. This correlation was also weak and statistically significant to the 95th percentile.

Given the political climate of the U.S. amid COVID, political affiliation was included in the demographic factors to identify instances where politics potentially played a role in how the CTA was perceived. Political affiliation proved statistically significant among respondents, where democrats were more likely to perceive the app as useful. There was a moderate positive correlation for those who supported the democratic party in handling the pandemic and for those who described themselves as democrats. Respondents who identified as independent or had another political affiliation were less likely to perceive the CTA as useful. The correlations were weak for those who did not support any party, who supported an 'other' party, who described themselves as independent, and who described themselves as 'other'.

Demographic factors likely played a role in the use of CTA, similar to previous findings [26, 28]. However, it was not based on race and age. The evidence suggests the political climate and education were more important factors.

The use of the APCO framework introduced the idea of other antecedents potentially impacting the use of CTA. Beyond demographic factors, pandemic experiences, comfort, and familiarity were also considered. How serious the respondent perceived the pandemic positively correlated to their perceived usefulness of the CTA. Perceived helpfulness, comfort, and familiarity with the app were also all positively correlated to perceived usefulness.

Previous studies have indicated that privacy and security concerns influence perceived usefulness [15, 25–29]. Our findings provide some proof of a statistically significant, moderate to weak positive correlation between privacy and security concerns and perceived usefulness.

5.2   Privacy and Security Concerns

The APCO framework used in this study is based on the understanding that privacy and security concerns can influence the use and adoption of certain technologies. Significantly few demographic factors were correlated to privacy and security concerns among respondents. Political affiliation, education, and income were weakly correlated to privacy and security concerns. Respondents who indicated they preferred the republican party to handle COVID-19-related matters were more likely to have privacy and security concerns.

Respondents with at least some college (but not a bachelor's degree) were also more likely to have privacy and security concerns; *however*, where individuals had graduate degrees or more, the polarity of the correlation switched. This indicates that individuals with graduate and terminal degrees were less concerned about privacy and security using the CTA.

The findings related to income were interesting. Respondents with the highest income and the lowest income were both less likely to be concerned about the privacy and security concerns of the COVID-19 mobile apps. However, middle-income respondents were more likely to be concerned about privacy and security. These statically significant findings were where respondents making less than $25,000, respondents earning between $35,000 and $49,999, and respondents making between $100,000 and $149,999.

Comfort and familiarity were also found to be statistically significant. Comfort was negatively correlated, and familiarity was positively associated with privacy and security concerns. This indicates that familiarity with the app may not be enough to alleviate data privacy issues.

5.3 Comfort

We used a question around comfort to understand trust in the app or the organizations that developed the app. We ran an additional analysis to determine if there were any demographic differences in who was more (or less) likely to be comfortable with the app. Among our demographic factors, race, age, education, and political affiliation were significantly correlated with comfort/trust.

All race/ethnicity groups were positively correlated with comfort except one, where we found statistical significance. Individuals who self-identified as Native American, Pacific Islander, or having multiple race ancestry were classified in one category named 'other.' This group only represented approximately 3% of our study sample. For this group, there was a negative association with the comfort of the CTA, albeit weak.

Nearly all age groups were negatively correlated with comfort; however, respondents aged 45–54 were positively correlated with comfort. This group represented approximately 12% of our sample. The other age group that was positively associated with comfort was 25–34; however, this was a very weak correlation and not statistically significant. However, the 25–34 group represented over 40% of the study sample.

Only one education group was significantly correlated with comfort. Respondents with at least a high school diploma were less likely to feel comfortable with the CTA. This moderate correlation was statistically significant to the 99th percentile.

Again, political affiliation was correlated with some aspect of use regarding the CTA. Respondents who indicated they preferred the democrats to handle the pandemic were more likely to find comfort with CTA. This moderate correlation was statistically significant to the 99th percentile. Conversely, respondents who indicated they preferred the republicans to handle the pandemic were less likely to find comfort with CTA. This weak correlation was statistically significant to the 95th percentile. Furthermore, respondents who self-identified as democrats were more likely to find comfort in the

app, and respondents that self-identified as independent or republican were less likely
to find comfort in the app.

5.4 APCO

Our findings indicate that only certain demographic variables influenced privacy concerns, trust, or behavioral intentions. For example, gender was not a statistically significant variable related to perceived usefulness, comfort, or privacy concerns for the CTA.
Similarly, Alashoor et al. [45] revealed that older users are more inclined than younger
users to disclose correct personal information. However, there were no differences based
on gender, education level, or ethnicity. Five variables were statistically associated with
privacy and security concerns; 1) mobile app experiences, 2) CTA experiences, 3) political affiliation, 4) education, and 5) income. Similarly, five variables were statistically
associated with comfort (as a proxy for trust); 1) pandemic experiences, 2) race, 3) age,
4) education, and 5) political affiliation. Finally, five different variables were statistically
correlated to perceived usefulness; 1) comfort, 2) pandemic experiences, 3) privacy and
security concerns, 4) political affiliation, and 5) education.

Political affiliation and education proved to be more influential demographic factors
possibly influencing the adoption of CTA and its perceived usefulness. Previous studies
have included cultural factors as antecedents in the APCO framework but not political
affiliation [50]. The unique variable related to the disaster event, pandemic experiences,
seemingly influenced respondent comfort with and their perceived usefulness of CTA.
Given our findings, we note a framework for APCO for the use of CTA in NYS in Fig. 3
[45].

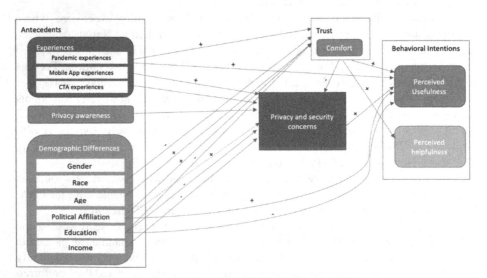

Fig. 3. APCO model of CTA adoption in NYS.

6 Conclusion

This paper examined the use of the COVID-19 contact tracing app, COVID Alert NY, by New York State (NYS) residents. The research questions focused on identifying differences in perception, adoption, or privacy concerns among racial and ethnic populations and across age groups. However, the findings indicate only certain demographic variables influenced privacy concerns, trust, or behavioral intentions related to the contact tracing app. In particular, the more influential factors were pandemic experiences, political affiliation, education, and income. The findings of this study point to the potential for expanding the antecedents in the APCO framework to account for the use of disaster technology to be influenced by disaster experiences and partisan politics. The findings could provide important guidance to public health officials regarding potential personal influences on adopting mobile applications for infectious disease outbreaks. Future studies could investigate the use of other contact tracing applications in other states to compare findings with a representative sample. Additionally, qualitative studies could focus on understanding why these differences exist.

Our sample was limited to individuals who completed an online survey through Amazon Mechanical Turk, which may not be representative of the general population. Second, our study did not explore other factors, such as personality differences, that may be associated with perception. Finally, our study did not dive into the beliefs or attitudes of the respondents to identify perceived usefulness or privacy concerns.

Furthermore, contact tracing mobile applications were not the only mobile application used during the pandemic. Future studies could investigate digital vaccine certificates or proof of vaccine applications used in the states.

References

1. Wacksman, J.: Digitalization of contact tracing: balancing data privacy with public health benefit. Ethics Inf. Technol. **23**(4), 855–861 (2021). https://doi.org/10.1007/s10676-021-09601-2
2. World Health Organization [WHO]. Coronavirus disease (COVID-19): Contact tracing 2021. https://www.who.int/news-room/questions-and-answers/item/coronavirus-disease-covid-19-contact-tracing. Accessed 5 March 2023
3. Pung, R., Chiew, C.J., Young, B.E., Chin, S., Chen, M.I.-C., Clapham, H.E., et al.: Investigation of three clusters of COVID-19 in Singapore: implications for surveillance and response measures. Lancet **395**, 1039–46 (2020). https://doi.org/10.1016/S0140-6736(20)30528-6
4. Cheng, H.-Y., Jian, S.-W., Liu, D.-P., Ng, T.-C., Huang, W.-T., Lin, H.-H., et al.: Contact tracing assessment of COVID-19 transmission dynamics in taiwan and risk at different exposure periods before and after symptom onset. JAMA Intern. Med. **180**, 1156–1163 (2020). https://doi.org/10.1001/jamainternmed.2020.2020
5. Thai, P.Q., Rabaa, M.A., Luong, D.H., Tan, D.Q., Quang, T.D., Quach, H.-L., et al.: The first 100 days of SARS-CoV-2 control in Vietnam. Epidemiology (2020). https://doi.org/10.1101/2020.05.12.20099242
6. Morley, J., Cowls, J., Taddeo, M., Floridi, L.: Ethical guidelines for COVID-19 tracing apps. Nature **582**, 29–31 (2020). https://doi.org/10.1038/d41586-020-01578-0

7. Ahmed, S.A.K.S., Ajisola, M., Azeem, K., Bakibinga, P., Chen, Y.-F., Choudhury, N.N., et al.: Impact of the societal response to COVID-19 on access to healthcare for non-COVID-19 health issues in slum communities of Bangladesh, Kenya, Nigeria and Pakistan: results of pre-COVID and COVID-19 lockdown stakeholder engagements. BMJ Global Health **5**, e003042 (2020). https://doi.org/10.1136/bmjgh-2020-003042

8. Unruh, L., Allin, S., Marchildon, G., Burke, S., Barry, S., Siersbaek, R., et al.: A comparison of 2020 health policy responses to the COVID-19 pandemic in Canada, Ireland, the United Kingdom and the United States of America. Health Policy **126**, 427–437 (2022). https://doi.org/10.1016/j.healthpol.2021.06.012

9. Wang, X., Du, Z., James, E., Fox, S.J., Lachmann, M., Meyers, L.A., et al.: The effectiveness of COVID-19 testing and contact tracing in a US city. Proc. Natl. Acad. Sci. U.S.A. **119**, e2200652119 (2022). https://doi.org/10.1073/pnas.2200652119

10. Fairchild A. Contact tracing's long, turbulent history holds lessons for COVID-19. Contact Tracing's Long, Turbulent History Holds Lessons for COVID-19 2020. https://news.osu.edu/contact-tracings-long-turbulent-history-holds-lessons-for-covid-19/. Accessed 5 March 2023

11. Sacks, J.A., Zehe, E., Redick, C., Bah, A., Cowger, K., Camara, M., et al.: Introduction of Mobile Health Tools to Support Ebola Surveillance and Contact Tracing in Guinea. Glob Health Sci Pract **3**, 646–659 (2015). https://doi.org/10.9745/GHSP-D-15-00207

12. Sun, K., Viboud, C.: Impact of contact tracing on SARS-CoV-2 transmission. Lancet Infect. Dis. **20**, 876–877 (2020). https://doi.org/10.1016/S1473-3099(20)30357-1

13. Brown, J., Ring, K., White, J., Mackie, N.E., Abubakar, I., Lipman, M.: Contact tracing for SARS-CoV-2: what can be learned from other conditions? Clin. Med. (Lond.) **21**, e132–e136 (2021). https://doi.org/10.7861/clinmed.2020-0643

14. Riley, S., Fraser, C., Donnelly, C.A., Ghani, A.C., Abu-Raddad, L.J., Hedley, A.J., et al.: Transmission dynamics of the etiological agent of SARS in Hong Kong: impact of public health interventions. Science **300**, 1961–1966 (2003). https://doi.org/10.1126/science.1086478

15. Colizza, V., Grill, E., Mikolajczyk, R., Cattuto, C., Kucharski, A., Riley, S., et al.: Time to evaluate COVID-19 contact-tracing apps. Nat. Med. **27**, 361–362 (2021). https://doi.org/10.1038/s41591-021-01236-6

16. Garry, M., Hope, L., Zajac, R., Verrall, A.J., Robertson, J.M.: Contact tracing: a memory task with consequences for public health. Perspect. Psychol. Sci. **16**, 175–187 (2021). https://doi.org/10.1177/1745691620978205

17. Groves, R., Travis Bassett, M., Hout, M.: Encouraging Participation and Cooperation in Contact Tracing: Lessons from Survey Research. National Academies Press, Washington, D.C. (2020). https://doi.org/10.17226/25916

18. Akinbi, A., Forshaw, M., Blinkhorn, V.: Contact tracing apps for the COVID-19 pandemic: a systematic literature review of challenges and future directions for neo-liberal societies. Health Inf Sci Syst **9**, 18 (2021). https://doi.org/10.1007/s13755-021-00147-7

19. Zastrow, M.: Coronavirus contact-tracing apps: can they slow the spread of COVID-19? Nature (2020). https://doi.org/10.1038/d41586-020-01514-2

20. Kolasa, K., Mazzi, F., Leszczuk-Czubkowska, E., Zrubka, Z., Péntek, M.: State of the art in adoption of contact tracing apps and recommendations regarding privacy protection and public health: systematic review. JMIR Mhealth Uhealth **9**, e23250 (2021). https://doi.org/10.2196/23250

21. O'Neill, P., Ryan-Mosley, T., Johnson, B.: A flood of coronavirus apps are tracking us. Now it's time to keep track of them. MIT Technology Review (2020). https://www.technologyreview.com/2020/05/07/1000961/launching-mittr-covid-tracing-tracker/. Accessed 5 March 2023

22. Kostka, G., Habich-Sobiegalla, S.: In Times of Crisis: Public Perceptions Towards COVID-19 Contact Tracing Apps in China, Germany and the US (2020). https://doi.org/10.2139/ssrn.3693783

23. Wang, X., Hegde, S., Son, C., Keller, B., Smith, A., Sasangohar, F.: Investigating mental health of US college students during the COVID-19 pandemic: cross-sectional survey study. J. Med. Internet Res. **22**, e22817 (2020). https://doi.org/10.2196/22817

24. Xu, W., Wu, J., Cao, L.: COVID-19 pandemic in China: context, experience and lessons. Health Policy Technol **9**, 639–648 (2020). https://doi.org/10.1016/j.hlpt.2020.08.006

25. Russo, M.: A cross-country comparison of contact-tracing apps during COVID-19. CEPR 2021. https://cepr.org/voxeu/columns/cross-country-comparison-contact-tracing-apps-during-covid-19. Accessed 31 Oct 2022

26. Kaya, E.K.: Safety and Privacy in the Time of Covid-19: Contact Tracing Applications. Centre for Economics and Foreign Policy Studies (2020)

27. Cho, H., Ippolito, D., Yu, Y.W.: Contact Tracing Mobile Apps for COVID-19: Privacy Considerations and Related Trade-offs (2020). https://doi.org/10.48550/arXiv.2003.11511

28. Villius Zetterholm, M., Lin, Y., Jokela, P.: Digital contact tracing applications during COVID-19: a scoping review about public acceptance. Informatics **8**, 48 (2021). https://doi.org/10.3390/informatics8030048

29. Hendl, T., Chung, R., Wild, V.: Pandemic surveillance and racialized subpopulations: mitigating vulnerabilities in COVID-19 apps. Bioethical Inquiry **17**, 829–834 (2020). https://doi.org/10.1007/s11673-020-10034-7

30. Vandamme, A.M., Nguyen, T.: Show evidence that apps for COVID-19 contact-tracing are secure and effective. Nature **580**, 563–563 (2020). https://doi.org/10.1038/d41586-020-01264-1

31. Sato, M.: Contact Tracing Apps Now Cover Nearly Half of America. It's not Too Late to Use One. MIT Technology Review (2020)

32. Johnson B. The US's draft law on contact tracing apps is a step behind Apple and Google | MIT Technology Review (2020). https://www.technologyreview.com/2020/06/02/1002491/us-covid-19-contact-tracing-privacy-law-apple-google/. Accessed 5 March 2023

33. Setzer, E.: Contact-Tracing Apps in the United States - Lawfare 2020. https://www.lawfareblog.com/contact-tracing-apps-united-states. Accessed 23 Feb 2023

34. Healthy Together App | Division of Technology Services (n.d.). https://dts.utah.gov/news/healthy-together-app. Accessed 23 Feb 2023

35. Barber, G.: Google and Apple Change Tactics on Contact Tracing Tech. Wired (2020)

36. Knight, T., Yuan, X., Bennett Gayle, D.: Illuminating Privacy and Security Concerns in Older Adults' Technology Adoption. Work, Aging and Retirement (2022)

37. Yuan, X., Bennett Gayle, D., Dadson, Y., Jung, E.: Perception and use of COVID contact tracing mobile applications in New York State (NYS). Proc Assoc Inf Sci Technol **59**, 845–847 (2022). https://doi.org/10.1002/pra2.746

38. Smith, H.J., Dinev, T., Xu, H.: Information Privacy Research: An Interdisciplinary Review. MIS Quarterly, pp. 989–1015 (2011)

39. Xu, H., Dinev, T., Smith, H., Hart, P.: Examining the Formation of Individual's Privacy Concerns: Toward an Integrative View. ICIS 2008 Proceedings (2008)

40. Bansal, G., Zahedi, F.M., Gefen, D.: Do context and personality matter? trust and privacy concerns in disclosing private information online. Information & Management **53**, 1–21 (2016). https://doi.org/10.1016/j.im.2015.08.001

41. Li, Y.: Theories in online information privacy research: a critical review and an integrated framework. Decis. Support. Syst. **54**, 471–481 (2012)

42. Xu, H., Teo, H.-H., Tan, B.C., Agarwal, R.: The role of push-pull technology in privacy calculus: the case of location-based services. J. Manag. Inf. Syst. **26**, 135–174 (2009)

43. Dinev, T., Hart, P.: An extended privacy calculus model for e-commerce transactions. Inf. Syst. Res. **17**, 61–80 (2006)

44. Lankton, N., Tripp, J.: A Quantitative and Qualitative Study of Facebook Privacy Using the Antecedent-Privacy Concern-Outcome Macro Model. Accounting Faculty Research (2013)

45. Alashoor, T., Han, S., Joseph, R.: Familiarity with big data, privacy concerns, and self-disclosure accuracy in social networking websites: An APCO model. Communications of the Association for Information Systems **41** (2017). https://doi.org/10.17705/1CAIS.04104

46. Ruprecht, M.M., Wang, X., Johnson, A.K., Xu, J., Felt, D., Ihenacho, S., et al.: Evidence of social and structural COVID-19 disparities by sexual orientation, gender identity, and race/ethnicity in an urban environment. J. Urban Health **98**, 27–40 (2021). https://doi.org/10.1007/s11524-020-00497-9

47. Papadimos, T.J., Soghoian, S.E., Nanayakkara, P., Singh, S., Miller, A.C., Saddikuti, V., et al.: COVID-19 blind spots: a consensus statement on the importance of competent political leadership and the need for public health cognizance. J Glob Infect Dis **12**, 167–190 (2020). https://doi.org/10.4103/jgid.jgid_397_20

48. Kopel, J., Perisetti, A., Roghani, A., Aziz, M., Gajendran, M., Goyal, H.: Racial and gender-based differences in COVID-19. Frontiers in Public Health **8** (2020)

49. US Census Bureau. DEMOGRAPHICS NEW YORK STATE. American Community Survey (ACS 1-Year Estimates) (2021). https://data.census.gov/table?q=DEMOGRAPHICS+NEW+YORK+STATE+ . Accessed 6 March 2023

50. Altmann, S., et al.: Acceptability of app-based contact tracing for COVID-19: cross-country survey study. JMIR Mhealth UhealthUhealth **8**(8), e19857 (2020). https://doi.org/10.2196/19857

Author Index

© The Editor(s) (if applicable) and The Author(s), under exclusive license
to Springer Nature Switzerland AG 2023
H. Degen et al. (Eds.): HCII 2023, LNCS 14059, pp. 525–526, 2023.
https://doi.org/10.1007/978-3-031-48057-7

Printed in the United States
by Baker & Taylor Publisher Services

Printed in the United States
by Baker & Taylor Publisher Services